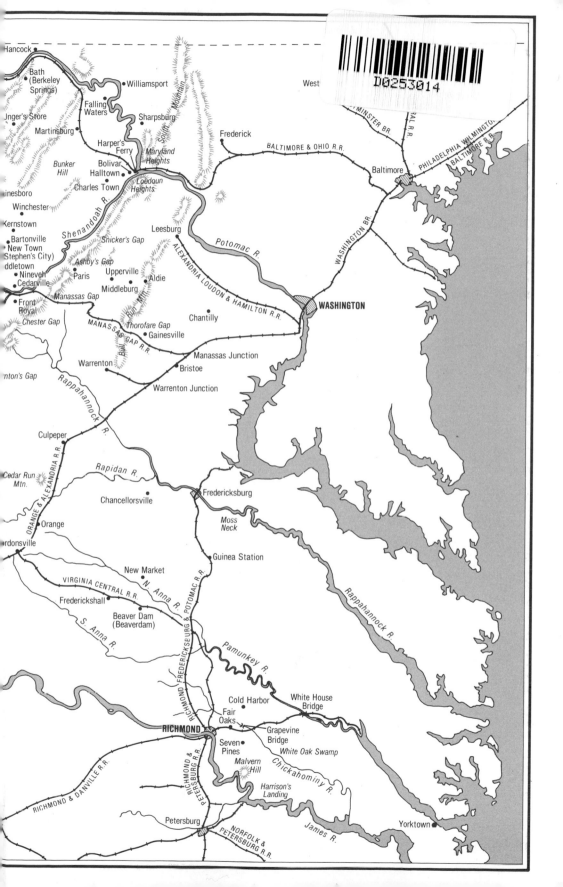

STONEWALL

By the same author:

THE MAN WHO PRESUMED:
A BIOGRAPHY OF HENRY MORTON STANLEY

BURTON: A BIOGRAPHY OF SIR RICHARD FRANCIS BURTON

PRISONERS OF THE MAHDI

QUEEN VICTORIA'S LITTLE WARS

THE GREAT ANGLO-BOER WAR

MR. KIPLING'S ARMY

THE GURKHAS

EMINENT VICTORIAN SOLDIERS: SEEKERS OF GLORY

THE GREAT WAR IN AFRICA, 1914–1918

ARMIES OF THE RAJ:
FROM THE MUTINY TO INDEPENDENCE, 1858–1947

BALLS BLUFF: A SMALL BATTLE AND ITS LONG SHADOW

STONEWALL

A BIOGRAPHY OF

GENERAL

THOMAS J. JACKSON

BY

BYRON FARWELL

W · W · NORTON & COMPANY

New York London

The text of this book is composed in Baskerville 169
with the display set in Bulmer
Composition and Manufacturing by the Haddon Craftsmen, Inc.
Book design and cartography by Jacques Chazaud

Library of Congress Cataloging-in-Publication Data

Farwell, Byron.
   Stonewall: a biography of General Thomas J. Jackson / by Byron
Farwell.
      p.   cm.
Includes index.
1. Jackson, Stonewall, 1824–1863.   2. Generals—Confederate States
of America—Biography.   3. Confederate States of America. Army—
Biography.   I. Title.
E467.1.J15F37   1992
973.7'3'092—dc20
   [B]   91-44988

ISBN 0-393-03389-9

W.W. Norton & Company, Inc., 500 Fifth Avenue, New York, N.Y. 10110
W.W. Norton & Company Ltd., 10 Coptic Street, London WC1A 1PU

2 3 4 5 6 7 8 9 0

For my wife

Ruth

Contents

☆ ☆ ☆ ☆ ☆ ☆ ☆ ☆ ☆ ☆ ☆ ☆ ☆ ☆

Foreword

Few men have been so admired in their lifetime and fewer still have found such durable reputations as Thomas Jackson, an orphan boy who through tenacity, willpower, military skills, and great luck became one of the most acclaimed generals of his era. The reputation he gained at the First Battle of Bull Run grew enormously during his famous and marvelously successful Valley campaign, which came just as Southern forces everywhere else were in retreat and Southern hopes were at their nadir. By the end of that campaign he had become the most famous general, North or South, and his fame was not confined to North America. There could not have been a literate European who did not know the name of "Stonewall" Jackson. During the war visiting European officers, among them the future Field Marshal Viscount Wolseley, made a special effort to meet the renowned Confederate general. Since his death countless statues have been raised to him, highways have been named after him, his house has become a museum, the little wooden building in which he died is now a shrine, and his battles have been studied at war colleges and by serious soldiers everywhere. His reputation has proved remarkably durable. It is said that Field Marshal Erwin Rommel as a young officer made a special study of Jackson's Valley campaign.

In addition to his fame as a military commander, his piety has been praised, and from lectern and altar he has been hailed as a faultless Christian hero. His virtues have been celebrated in hundreds of poems, songs, and stories, and, of course, in many biographies. The "classic" biography of Jackson, first published in 1898 and still in print, is *Stonewall Jackson and the American Civil War*, published in two volumes, written by Colonel G. F. R. Henderson, an English officer. Henderson, like all the biographers who preceded him and those who have since written of Jackson's life, was an ardent partisan. He believed Jackson's was a "name without spot or blemish." He was so lost in admiration that B. H. Liddell Hart, the famous British military historian, rightly called Henderson's biography "more epic than history." The Reverend Robert Dabney, who wrote one of the first popular biographies, admitted that his "prime object" was "to portray and vindicate his Christian character." The best by far of the later biographies is the two-volume *Stonewall Jackson*, published in 1959 by Lenoir Chambers, a Virginia journalist who was also a votary.

The polishing of Jackson's reputation has sometimes been carried to extraordinary lengths. Even Henderson's work, as it has been printed since 1910, was altered so that not only the character of Jackson himself but those of his relatives were tidied up. Nowhere is this more evident than in the depiction of Jackson's uncle Cummins, who was, said the mature Jackson, "like a father to me." In the current edition of Henderson's biography, Cummins is presented as a diamond in the rough, a strong man of the frontier, a leader, an energetic and generous man who built a mill and cleared land, a hearty, well-liked man of affairs. This picture has been reproduced by other biographers. That he was an indulgent and loving uncle seems clear, but as a model for a young boy he seems to have lacked some desirable qualities.

In the first edition of Henderson's work Cummins was described as being "as unscrupulous as he was violent. His associates were by no means the most respectable." This seems a fair assessment, but in 1910, after Colonel Henderson's death, at the request of Jackson's widow and Thomas L. Arnold (Jackson's nephew), Mrs. Henderson kindly altered the text, deleting this description and substituting one supplied by Arnold declaring that Cummins "was scrupulously exacting in the matter of integrity and veracity. His associates included the most respectable. . . ."

Thus was altered the character of Cummins, a man of sharp practices who regularly quarreled with, sued, and was sued by his neighbors and relatives. Even his own mother took him to court, claiming that he was cheating her. A scofflaw who ignored the rights and wishes of his neighbors, he may also have been a felon, for court records reveal that he was once hauled into court accused of counterfeiting. (A local history referred to him as "the well known counterfeiter.")

That Jackson's beloved sister detested the cause for which her brother fought and died and that she divorced her husband because he was a Southern sympathizer are omitted from almost all biographies, although court documents relating to the divorce have long been extant and available.

One might think that Jackson's vindictive behavior toward his commanding officer in Florida could hardly be ignored, but biographers have done so, some not even mentioning his presence there, while others have passed quickly over this period and have tried to explain away his behavior. One modern biographer, searching for excuses, blamed the "clammy" climate in Florida, forgetting, perhaps, that the period in question was in winter, and Florida's climate has changed little in the past 150 years.

Most earlier biographers have accepted the many myths that were woven about Jackson. Some are so patently absurd that it seems extraordinary that scholars have swallowed them. That Jackson continually sucked a lemon is the most durable of the myths—and the most easily disproved. The most risible is that Jackson, who could never stay awake when tired, once stood as a lonely guard over his tired, sleeping brigade. (There was even a popular poem about this.) Among other myths were those of Barbara Frietchie defying him in Frederick, Maryland, and of his reliance upon information supplied by Belle Boyd, to whom he seems never to have spoken.

I have been unable to find the source for the belief that Jackson's middle name was Jonathan and that he was named after his embezzling father. Jackson gave himself a middle initial but was never known to call himself Jonathan. He signed his name simply "T. J. Jackson."

The name "Stonewall," Jackson always maintained, was applicable only to his brigade. It was, in fact, a singularly inappropriate sobriquet for him, implying as it does someone adept at defensive operations, while Jackson was a most aggressive and daring fighter who earned his towering reputation by offensive operations. "Lucky" would certainly have been more appropriate, for as journalist and biographer Holmes Alexander said of him, "He was fortune's favorite." It is not to take away from him his many skills as a leader to say that time after time luck smiled on him, and time after time he escaped the consequences of his rash maneuvers.

I have eschewed the use of "rebels," "secesh," "Yankee," and "Yank." Incidentally the terms "Johnny Reb" and "Billy Yank" came into use only after the war, as did "War between the States." Generals' nicknames have not been used except in passing. That young Confederate soldiers, many in their teens, referred to Jackson as "Old Jack" is understandable. Most generals, North and South, had nicknames that began with old: "Old Jube" (Jubal A. Early), "Old Baldy" (Richard Ewell), "Old Slow Trot" (George H. Thomas), "Old Pete" (James Longstreet), and so forth. Such nicknames can give false impressions. Jackson at thirty-eight was a very young lieutenant general—and would be in any army.

Casualty figures are always open to dispute, and those of the Confederates are less likely to be accurate than those of the Federals. The records of the Army of Northern Virginia are among those that have suffered the most from neglect and the ravages of time. To add to the confusion of numbers, the strength of Civil War forces could be reckoned in several ways: effective strength (all enlisted men present for duty), total strength (effective strength plus those who were sick, under arrest, or on extra duty), aggregate strength (all officers and enlisted men present), or combat strength (effective strength plus the officers present for duty). In the records and memoirs it is not always possible to determine which figures are being used.

Most Civil War battles bore two names, one Confederate and one Union. The South tended to name battles after towns, and the North after physical features. I have sometimes used Northern names and sometimes Southern, depending only on the name which seemed to me currently most common.

As many people today still choose sides when the American Civil War is discussed, it is perhaps reasonable to ask a biographer of a Confederate general where he stands. Although born in Iowa, I have lived happily for more than twenty years in various parts of Virginia and a year in Mississippi; fourteen years of my adult life have been spent in Europe and Africa, three of them in a war. I believe it was for the best that the Union was not divided, but I find it impossible not to admire equally those men and women, both North and South, who gallantly endured the war's hardships and sufferings for causes they believed in so fervently. I have aimed here to present a balanced picture of an interesting man and a justly famous general.

Several people have been helpful to me in writing this book, among them, Professor Terry Alford, Dr. Ross N. Brudenell, Miss Jane St. C. Crane, Ambassador and Mrs. Fred Hadsel, Colonel Milton Hamilton, Dr. Robert J. T. Joy, Mrs. C. J. ("Liz") Moore, Brigadier General Edwin Simmons, Professor Charles W. Turner, Judge Paul R.

Teeter, and Dr. James Wengert. I owe a special debt of gratitude to William B. Carey, attorney, of Berkeley Springs, West Virginia, who gave most generously of his time and talents to provide valuable assistance in my research. As always, I am most grateful to my wife, Ruth, whose keen eye and sound judgment have improved each page. If errors there be, they are mine alone.

STONEWALL

1

Birth and Boyhood

In the small town of Clarksburg, [West] Virginia, sometime around midnight on 20–21 January 1824 Judith Beckworth Jackson, née Neale, gave birth to her third child and second son,[1] The baby was born in a three-room brick house with an inset porch and a half attic standing on two lots on Main Street, nearly opposite the courthouse. Named Thomas after Judith Jackson's father, Thomas Neale, the newborn was not given the dignity of a middle name or initial; these became attached much later.

Clarksburg, the seat of Harrison County, lay in a sparsely settled area. The town had a population of only about five hundred. There were probably not twelve thousand inhabitants in the entire county. Still, it boasted such evidence of government as a two-story courthouse with a cupola, a jail, and a whipping post.

The infant's father, Jonathan Jackson, was a popular young lawyer, but he was also, unfortunately, a gambler and hopelessly irresponsible, if not to say dishonest, in money matters. In 1810, after reading the law, twenty-year-old Jonathan had become a squire for his cousin John George Jackson (1777–1825) and soon after became his law part-

---

1. Although 21 January is the date usually accepted as Thomas Jackson's birthday, Dr. James McCally, who delivered him, thought the baby was born somewhat before midnight on the twentieth. No record of his birth exists.

ner. At this time he was described as having average intelligence and an amiable disposition. Probably through his cousin's influence, he was appointed excise master (collector of United States revenue) for Harrison County, but perhaps because of his passion for gambling, he was plagued with money problems, and John George Jackson wrote his wife on 20 January 1814 to say: "I refuse being his surety and wrote him of this by mail that if he did not behave himself, I would have him removed from office."

In the following year, when Jonathan's accounts as excise master came up short by the healthy sum of $3,500.76, John George Jackson, now a congressman, moved quickly to replace him with his brother-in-law Daniel Kincheloe. Jonathan, with the audacity peculiar to amiable transgressors, wrote to advise him that should Kincheloe or anyone else be appointed he would still like to "continue to perform the duties and act as clerk."

On 12 February 1817 Congressman Jackson wrote to his wife to deplore the "friendship and confidence" he had shown to Jonathan, who was said to be "a large defaulter and suit has been ordered against him." Five days later he again wrote his wife: "Jonathan Jackson called to see me yesterday. I gave him such a lecture as will perhaps prevent my seeing him again while he stays here."

Jonathan's considerable landholdings, were sold by a United States marshal "at the tavern of N. W. Meek in the town of Clarksburg." John (presumably John George) Jackson, Edward Jackson (Jonathan's father), and a James McCally had been Jonathan's sureties, and it would appear that they, too, suffered. Jonathan was left with not much more than his slaves, one of whom later successfully escaped.[2]

When Jonathan proposed to marry, the notion understandably roused among some of the senior Jacksons a few misgivings—not about his bride-to-be but about their own kinsman. On 29 January 1817 John George Jackson wrote to his wife: "I shall not interfere. If the disposition to gaming were suppressed, and perhaps that connection will destroy it, I would say it was not objectionable."

Undaunted by his financial problems, on 28 September 1817, at

2. Pursuit of Jonathan's slave and another belonging to E. B. Jackson was made, and both were apprehended in Canada, but recovery was thwarted by a magistrate. Their successful escape encouraged two slaves of John George Jackson, for which he had paid six hundred dollars each, to flee, and he complained directly to President James Monroe: "The sentiments of hostility which this conduct of our British neighbors excites are increasing daily and that it will ultimately produce collision cannot be doubted by those who know human character."

age twenty-eight, he married nineteen-year-old Judith (always called Julia) Neale near Parkersburg, [West] Virginia, where the Neales had settled after moving from Loudoun County, Virginia. Julia has been described as "a brunette with dark brown hair and dark gray eyes, of medium height, handsome face; a close student and well educated."

Marriage did not reform Jonathan. Court records show evidence of numerous borrowings secured by the young couple's livestock and even by Julia's household furnishings. In April 1823 Jonathan borrowed $150, offering as collateral "one black horse, one gray horse, two milk cows and calves, one large looking glass, one set castors, one dozen knives and forks, one lot stoneware including four milk pans, one churn, and two jars, one cutting box and appendages (except the knife), one whet stone, three hundred pounds of bacon, one half barrel of wine, one breakfast table, half round." In November of the same year he borrowed $60, using as collateral "one large cooking stove with all its appendages and apparatus." The following year he put up, among other items, the family bed and bedding.

The marriage lasted less than ten years. Julia Jackson was twenty-eight, when on 6 March 1826 her eldest child, six-year-old Elizabeth, died of typhoid fever. Twenty days later Jonathan succumbed to the same disease. The day after his death Julia gave birth to a daughter, whom she named Laura Ann. The young widow was thus left with three small children, the oldest, Warren, only five. Although it has been widely believed that Julia was left so impoverished that she was forced to give up her home, court records show her to have continued to live in it,[3] and the 1830 census shows her to have been the owner of twelve slaves.

Julia had other, less tangible assets as well. Jacksons, clannish and protective, were thick on the ground in western Virginia, and many were prominent in adjoining Lewis County. The family tree was liberally sprinkled with judges, politicians, lawyers, landowners, and prosperous merchants. Perhaps also of help to the young widow were the Freemasons, for Jonathan had been one of the founders of Herman

3. The house was conveyed by John Wilson, Jr., to Julia on 1 October 1828, and she, on 3 November 1830, conveyed the house and its two lots in trust to Augustine Smith for one hundred dollars. The trust deed provided that she would have the use of the property and household articles until her death, when the title would be vested in her daughter, Laura. The trust deed was a method of borrowing money. Although not indicated, Julia Jackson was probably required only to pay the interest on the hundred dollars. Presumably her daughter, Laura, paid off the debt, for she sold the house on 4 June 1859 and subsequently a hotel was built on the lots.

Lodge in Clarksburg (20 June 1814) and had served as an officer, though no records support this.

Early biographers report that for four years Julia taught school and sewed. She was still an attractive young woman, and on 4 November 1830, over the objections of some of the Jackson clan, she married Blake B. Woodson, a lawyer fifteen years older than she and a widower with eight children, none of whom lived under his roof.[4] Less than a year later, on 17 May 1831, Julia became a member of the Clarksburg Presbyterian Church.[5] Soon after Woodson was appointed clerk of the superior court in newly formed (28 February 1831) Fayette County, a mountainous area of 659 square miles about 90 miles south-southwest of Clarksburg. This was a salaried position of some importance, and the couple moved to a house at New Haven, near the present town of Ansted and Hawk's Nest State Park.

It is not certain whether the three Jackson children accompanied their mother and stepfather, but it was about this time that for unknown reasons, perhaps Julia's health (she was pregnant again) or perhaps because Woodson was unwilling or felt unable to support them, the three Jackson children were parceled out to relatives. Warren, nearly ten years old, was sent to an uncle, Alfred Neale, who lived in Wood County, Ohio. Other members of the Neale family, approached by Woodson's half brother, agreed to take in seven-year-old Thomas and five-year-old Laura, but before their move could be arranged, they were scooped up by a paternal uncle, either John or Cummins Jackson, who carried them off to Jackson's Mill near Weston, [West] Virginia.[6]

A few weeks later, on 7 October 1831, their mother gave birth to another son, Wirt Woodson. It was a difficult birth from which Julia never recovered. When she understood that her death was near, she sent for her children, and they were brought to her bedside in time for

4. The whereabouts at this time of Woodson's children by his first marriage is unknown, and the mystery remains. Woodson came from Cumberland and began practicing law in Clarksburg in 1824. Some of his children were fully grown; presumably the others had been parceled out to his own or his first wife's relatives.

5. The Reverend R. L. Dabney errs when he says (*Life and Campaigns of Lieut. Gen. Thomas J. Jackson,* p. 10) that Julia "became a member of the Wesleyan or Methodist communion."

6. In 1924 Jackson's Mill became the Pioneer State 4-H Camp. Today it is the Jackson's Mill 4-H Conference Center, a 523-acre facility operated by the West Virginia University Extension Service. The land around the site is more heavily wooded than in Jackson's day. On Labor Day each year a Stonewall Jackson Jubilee is held here, and arts and crafts are exhibited.

her to say a farewell and to give them her blessings, a solemn scene Thomas was to remember vividly all his life. On 3 December 1831 she died. Three days later Woodson wrote to his brother, William: "I am still pursued by cruel adverse fortune." Describing Julia's death, he wrote piously: "No Christian . . . could have died with more fortitude. Perfectly in her senses, calm and deliberate, she met her fate without a murmur or a struggle. . . . I have known few women of equal, none of superior merit. . . . She has left as a pledge of her affection, one of the most interesting infants I ever saw. His name is Wirt." The bereaved husband did not erect a stone over her grave. Fourteen months later he remarried, and in another five months he was dead.

It was well for Laura and Thomas that they were so whole-heartedly welcome at Jackson's Mill. Edward Jackson (1759–1828), Thomas's paternal grandfather, had been a man of substance who in 1801 built a two-story log house and a sawmill on the swift-flowing West Branch River in the Monongahela Valley, near Weston, a town of about thirty-odd houses, the seat of Lewis County, some twenty miles from Clarksburg. There he sired three sons (including Thomas's father) and three daughters by his first wife, Mary Hadden, and six sons and three daughters by his second wife. Still living at Jackson's Mill when the children arrived in 1831 were his widow, Elizabeth Brake, age fifty-nine; at least one daughter, Margaret, called Peggy, then age nineteen and soon to be married; and assorted bachelor sons, including Cummins, twenty-nine; James, twenty-six; Edward, fourteen; Andrew, ten; probably Return Meigs Jackson, seventeen; and perhaps John E. Jackson, twenty-one. In 1820 Edward Jackson had owned nine slaves, but by 1835 the family owned only four: Aaron, Cecelia (always called Seely and in charge of household affairs), Malinda, and Marg.

Other Jacksons were settled nearby, including the family of George Jackson, an older brother of Edward's who had established a mill on nearby Simpson's Creek and whose first wife had the same name as Edward's second wife. George Jackson sired fourteen of Thomas Jackson's legitimate cousins.

The Jackson clan of Edward Jackson, who died in 1828, was now headed, through force of personality rather than legal right, by tall, muscular Cummins Jackson (1802–1849), and under his energetic direction the family continued to prosper, holding titles (though some were dubious) to about fifteen hundred acres of land in the area.

Cummins was a builder. In the early 1840s he erected near the mill a fine two-story house; L-shaped, its sides equal in length, it boasted five windows in each. Under his management, Jackson's Mill came to include, among other structures, a gristmill, a sawmill, two bolting machines, and a blacksmith shop.

Tom, as he was called as a boy, always looked back fondly on this foster home and his eleven years at Jackson's Mill, remembering it as a place where there were "none to give mandates; none for me to obey but as I chose; surrounded by my playmates and relatives, all apparently eager to promote my happiness." His uncle Cummins was undoubtedly the greatest influence upon his boyhood. An affectionate and indulgent father figure, he won Tom's lifelong loyalty, but his faults were many and his scruples few.

Standing more than six feet tall and weighing over two hundred pounds, he was noted for his strength. It was said that he could carry a barrel of flour under each arm or lift up a keg of cider and drink from the bunghole. A man who enjoyed a good time, he relished the company of other men and loved to race horses; he had no interest in religion and was a member of no church. He was able, ambitious, energetic, and, some said, genial and generous; certainly he was good to the orphan nephew he took in. But he was also a scofflaw.

Earlier, in 1833, shortly after the arrival of Tom and Laura at Jackson's Mill, Cummins, without bothering about official permission, threw a dam 6 feet high and 150 feet long across the West Branch. He did not, apparently, trouble himself about the impact upon his neighbors, many of whom balked at this "great obstruction of the trade and navigation of, and upon [,] the said river." The dam quickly provoked a six-year lawsuit.

Cummins was, it seems, a fine friend but a bitter enemy, unscrupulous in bringing down his prey. He had a quick temper and, as people said, a passion for "goin' a-lawin'," suing others and provoking others to sue him. In the course of his short life he was frequently accused of dishonesty, and he sued or was sued in every session of the circuit court. The surviving court records of Lewis County are replete with cases in which Jacksons sued their neighbors and each other. Lawsuits were part of the entertainment in backwoods communities, but no man in the county was more litigious than Cummins E. Jackson. Between 1831 and 1844 he instituted eleven suits in chancery alone. The sums involved were often small, $3.94 in one case. Between 1841 and 1843 he instituted at least five suits in other courts as well. Justice was not always swift. One case dragged on for sixteen years. Following in his uncle's footsteps, Thomas Jackson carried into manhood an alacrity to resort to the law and the courts.

Cummins's most serious difficulty arose when he was accused of counterfeiting. In 1844 the fall term of the United States Court, Western District of Virginia, indicted him on 29 August "for passing counterfeit coin purporting to be silver of the value of fifty cents. . . ." Bail was posted—one thousand dollars from Cummins and an additional thousand dollars from Edward and Edward J. Jackson. One year later, when he was due in court, he failed to show up, and the bail money was forfeited. For whatever reason (probably because a witness did not appear) Cummins was never tried for this offense.

He was involved in other outrageous schemes. In 1834 he persuaded an old man, James Burchnell, probably by paying him, to apply for a pension, fraudulently claiming to be a veteran of the Revolutionary War. The pension, once granted, was to be assigned for "the sole use and benefit of . . . Cummins E. Jackson." (The scheme failed, but Cummins was not tried.)

In 1835, just before her death, his own mother, Elizabeth Brake Jackson, sued him for fraud in the Eighteenth Judicial District of Virginia, claiming that he conspired with others "to cheat and defraud" her and that he, "by fraud, force, management and the use of money and papers of said Edward Jackson, deceased, got into possession of the slaves and personal property of which said Edward Jackson died in possession of, and the said Cummins E. Jackson now fraudulently claims and holds as his own. . . ."[7]

Another family disorder, the nature of which is not clear, appears to have erupted in 1834 and 1835. On 21 April 1834 a Richard Fowkes was appointed as Laura's guardian, but records show that this appointment was "rescinded the same day."

That same year Margaret Jackson married and left Jackson's Mill, and the following year the children's stepgrandmother died, leaving nine-year-old Laura in a house full of young men and boys. A few months later she was taken to live with her aunt Rebecca Jackson White and her husband, George, in Parkersburg. Two years later it was decided for unknown reasons to send Tom to live with his uncle Isaac Brake and aunt Rachel Brake (a sister of his grandfather) in Harrison County, but young Tom took a dislike to this uncle, refused to stay, and trudged back to Jackson's Mill and his indulgent uncle Cummins.

A year after his return his brother, Warren, now a sixteen-year-old schoolteacher, stopped by Jackson's Mill on his way to visit his foster

7. Elizabeth Jackson died the following year, and the case against her son was taken up by her third child, James Madison Jackson (1805–1872), but when Cummins died in 1849, the suit disappeared in Cummins Jackson's tangled financial affairs.

parents, the Neales. He invited twelve-year-old Tom to come along with him. Cummins appears to have given his permission, and the two boys buoyantly set out on an eighty-mile journey, without maps, through largely undeveloped country.

Alfred and William Neale had bought James Island in the Ohio River, about one mile above Parkersburg, where they were simultaneously clearing land for farming and selling the wood to fuel the steamships that plied the river. To the admiring Jackson boys this seemed like a fine way to make money, and they determined to find land for themselves. Drifting down the river, probably by raft, they halted long enough at Belleville (now in West Virginia), to pay a visit to their aunt and uncle White (Rebecca Jackson and George). Growing ever more venturesome, they drifted farther down the Ohio, hundreds of miles, to the Mississippi. It has been conjectured that they were somewhere near the southwestern corner of Kentucky when they at last found a suitable island and set about the business of cutting wood.

Little is known of their venture. When they eventually worked their way back to the Neales in February 1837, they were in wretched condition, threadbare and ailing, with nothing to show for their enterprise except two new trunks.[8] Neither ever volunteered many details of their ordeal. They separated quietly, Warren going back to his school in Buckhannon (in present-day Upshur County), where four years later, in November 1841, he died. Cummins and his brothers appear to have welcomed Tom back to Jackson's Mill with open arms, and he slipped easily into his old life, an ordinary boy in a thriving nineteenth-century backwoods community. None of those around him found him in any way extraordinary—at least at the time, although stories of childhood virtue and sagacity blossomed after his death. Most are of doubtful veracity; some are certifiably false; all attest to his "strict adherence to truth, his unfailing honesty and his courage."[9]

Undoubtedly true are the stories that like the boys around him, he learned to trap and hunt and fish. He learned to ride well enough,

8. Thomas eventually gave his trunk to Laura, who still had it in 1911 when she died at the age of eighty-five; Warren gave his to his half brother, Wirt Woodson.

9. *The Family and Early Life of Stonewall Jackson* by Roy Bird Cook, p. 49. Mr. Cook, a local pharmacist, devoted much time to the study of Jackson's boyhood, and all biographers have relied upon his findings, but a review of the available records, including Cook's own notes and papers, now at West Virginia University, reveal that he did not tell all that he knew or suspected.

although ungracefully, to serve as a jockey on Uncle Cummins's horses in local races. Like other country boys, he made cornstalk fiddles. When he once came into possession of a real but dilapidated violin, he succeeded in making it serviceable with the help of a gunsmith in Weston and optimistically set about to teach himself to play. He struggled manfully and failed miserably. Throughout his life he was drawn to music, but he suffered from an unconquerable handicap: He was almost completely tone-deaf.

As he grew older, he helped with millwork, learned to handle oxen, and acquired those skills country boys learned in mid-nineteenth-century America. For companions he had relatives and neighbors. His uncle Andrew was only three years older than he, and a cousin, Sylvanus White, was only three years younger. A neighbor, Joseph Andrew Jackson Lightburn, exactly Tom's age, one of the eleven children of a nearby prosperous farmer and miller, became a close friend.

At the various schools he attended for brief periods he found more comrades, among them Peregrine Hays, son of Congressman Samuel L. Hays, a family friend. But schooling was erratic, and school terms were brief, rarely lasting more than three months. Records show that for thirty-nine days in 1837 Tom Jackson attended a school operated by Phillip Cox, Jr., and that there he studied arithmetic. He seemed to have a good head for figures, though no one thought him a bright student. Peregrine Hays in later years recalled that he was considered the dullest of Jonathan Jackson's three children.

Later he attended a school at McCann's Run, and in 1859, when he was fifteen, he spent two months in school at Weston, the county seat, where the nearest post office and general store were located. Colonel Alexander Scott Withers was the schoolmaster. A colorful frontier figure, who had been educated at William and Mary College, he affected a tall silk hat, knew Greek and Latin, took an active part in public affairs, and had published in 1831 and 1832 a widely read book called *Chronicles of Border Warfare*, said to be the first book printed west of the Alleghenies. He had scant interest in routine teaching, but in his own fashion he did his best to instruct rural youths in his version of the proprieties and he served as an exemplar of a gentleman in backwoods western Virginia.

It was said that one day when he bought a sack of meal at Jackson's Mill, Tom and his friend Joe Lightburn, not averse to an outing, obligingly offered to deliver it, an offer he declined, explaining that his slaves would fetch it later. In Fauquier County, where he came from, he told the boys, gentlemen did not perform such menial chores. "They have servants for such tasks and work their heads instead of their hands," he added loftily.

Tom was heard to mutter that if he had the money to go to William and Mary College, he supposed he might very well know how to work his head.

Not long after his return from the Mississippi, Tom found work assisting Major Minter Bailey of Weston, the commissioner in charge of letting contracts for the Staunton–Parkersburg turnpike in Lewis County. He liked the work, and he made a good impression. When a constable was needed for District 2 (the northern portion) of Lewis County, Major Bailey and Colonel Withers, both justices of the peace, recommended him. On 11 June 1841, at a session of the county court, he was deemed to be "a man of honesty, probity and good demeanor" and was duly appointed. He was then seventeen years old.

The title was something of a misnomer. The position was perhaps best explained by the Reverend Robert L. Dabney, who later served for a time as Jackson's chief of staff during the Civil War:

> The Justices of the Peace, besides the County Courts which they hold jointly, are authorized to decide singly, in their own neighborhood, upon controversies for property or money, where the dispute does not exceed twenty dollars. Of this little court, the Constable is the executive officer, serving its warrants, summoning its witnesses, and carrying into effect its decisions. The Justice, as conservator of the peace, may also issue his warrant for the arrest and examination of any person suspected of crime, however grave; and in this preliminary stage of proceedings, the Constable is his agent. This officer is also charged with the regulating of certain misdemeanors, and with the enforcement on slaves and free Negroes of the police regulations peculiar to their condition. He is, in a word, a sort of minor sheriff.[10]

The minimum age for holding the office was eighteen, but this was not known or it was waived or Tom lied about his age. Uncle Cummins and Major Minter Bailey signed a two-thousand-dollar bond, and for the next ten months Constable Jackson performed his official duties.

The job was not an onerous one. There was still time to help out at the mill. In August 1841 Cummins dispatched Tom to Parkersburg,

10. *Life and Campaigns of Lieut. Gen. T. J. Jackson* by Prof. R. L. Dabney, p. 21.

about eighty-five miles away, to pick up a piece of mill machinery due to arrive by boat from Pittsburgh. Tom took with him another young man, believed to be Thaddeus Moore of Weston, who recorded their trip in some detail.[11]

Early on Sunday, 1 August, Tom rode into Weston, leading a horse for his companion. That day the two boys went together to hear a sermon delivered by a Presbyterian minister and enjoyed it so thoroughly that they returned at "early candlelight" to hear him preach again.

The two set off the next morning for Clarksburg, where they spent the night with relatives. They had to repair one of the horse's girths before leaving, and while it was being prepared, Tom walked to the house where he had been born. His friend recorded that he felt "genuine sorrow" for him as he stood wordlessly looking at it.

Riding out of town, the two halted to say hello to Luther Haywood, a man they knew, who was standing at his office door. He plied them with so many questions that they lost time. "We whipped up and went on in haste," the diarist wrote, "Thom. saying we must reach the Ohio by the next day."

By midday they had come to Matthew Neely's house, where Tom was known. Young Mary, Matthew's daughter, "handsome and modest . . . with the most beautiful black sparkling eyes," served them fried chicken and biscuits. Tom's companion was willing to linger and suggested hopefully that the horses might need a longer rest, but Tom insisted that they press on.

That night they put up at the Stone House at Pennsboro, where they encountered Sam Houston, then president of Texas. He remembered the Jacksons and inquired about Joseph Jackson (a future governor of Virginia) and sent his special greetings to John Jackson (presumably Tom's great-uncle). "He was a severe looking man," thought the diarist, "but was of a kindly disposition. We hardly appreciated him until after the meeting."

They reached the Ohio the next day in good time, and on 4 August they were again in the midst of friends and relations. That evening they swam in the Little Kanawha "to wash off the sweat before supper."

The following day they picked up the part for the mill and set off

---

11. This remarkable account was found among the papers of the Haymond family of Clarksburg and was first published in newspapers in 1924. Thaddeus Moore died in 1857.

for home. At the farm of a "Mr. Adams" they found him "out there burying one of his Negroes," and they stopped to watch, noting with approval that he had provided "a nice black coffin and the grave was deep." Riding on, the two fell into a discussion about slavery: "Thom. seemed to be very sorry for the race and thought they should be free and have a chance, and said that Joe Lightburn said they should be taught to read so they could read the Bible and he thought so too. I told him it would be better not to make known such views and if they were carried out we would have to black our own boots. He said with him that would be only on Sunday and not even [then] in winter." Home again in Weston, the diarist ended his account. Tom Jackson, he concluded, was "a first rate boy and I am just getting to know him." But young Jackson was not destined to remain much longer in rural western Virginia.

2

☆ ☆ ☆ ☆ ☆ ☆ ☆ ☆ ☆ ☆ ☆ ☆ ☆ ☆

West Point: Plebe Year

In the spring of 1842 Congressman Samuel Lewis Hays had in his gift a vacancy at the United States Military Academy at West Point, New York, and four young men in his district, which included Lewis County, applied for the appointment. Tom Jackson, in spite of his meager education, was one of the four. It was not through any compelling desire to become a soldier that he applied; he had noted that educated men fared better in the world than uneducated men, and he had a hunger to improve himself and his prospects. An appointment would be an opportunity to obtain a first-class education at no cost. Actually, it was better than that, for the government paid cadets sixteen dollars per month.

Of the others who applied, one, Johnson N. Camden, a bright boy of good family, was too young. Although exceptions were sometimes made, as was the case with George B. McClellan, who entered at age fifteen, the rule was that a young man must be at least sixteen. (Camden, who was later admitted to the Military Academy, resigned in his second year to study law and eventually became president of an oil company and a United States senator.) Tom's friend Joe Lightburn also applied, as did Gibson J. Butcher, an orphan described as "a poor, sprightly young man, then writing in the Clerk's office of Lewis County."

Captain George Washington Jackson, one of Thomas's many

cousins, helped Congressman Hays make the selection, conducting tests for the applicants at Weston. The United States Military Academy, patterned after L'École Polytechnique in France, was then strictly an engineering school, which aimed to produce good engineers who were also officers, rather than good officers who were also engineers. Heavy emphasis was therefore placed upon mathematics, and as Butcher scored the highest in that subject, he received, on Congressman Hays's recommendation, a conditional appointment from the secretary of war on 19 April 1842. Two or three weeks later he set off for West Point.

Like many young men before and since, Butcher had little conception of the rigors of the first ("plebe") year at the Military Academy. Within a few days of his arrival, "after seeing the movements and learning the duties which I had to perform I came to the conclusion that I never would consent to live the life," he said. On 2 June, without bothering to explain his reasons or even to notify the authorities that he had arrived, Gibson Butcher left West Point. (He later became director of a bank and after the Civil War served a term in the West Virginia legislature.)

On his way home young Butcher stopped off at Jackson's Mill, where Thomas and his uncles learned that he had thrown up the appointment. A second chance had come their way. There were hurried consultations with Captain George Jackson and family friends, and young Jackson earnestly declared that although he knew he was ignorant, he would study hard. "I know I have the energy and I think I have the intellect," he said.

The decision was made to pack him off to Washington to plead his case in person to Congressman Hays, as yet unaware that his appointee had bolted. Recommendations were urgently solicited, clothes were hastily packed, two horses were saddled, and young Jackson, accompanied by a black boy to bring the horses home, set off for Clarksburg to catch the stagecoach of the Pioneer Stage Line (ten dollars for 210 miles). The two rode into the town in what they thought was good time, only to discover that they had narrowly missed the stage. Nothing daunted, they dug their heels into their horses' flanks and by hard riding caught up with it near Grafton, about fifteen miles east of Clarksburg.

The stage carried Jackson to Green Spring, 16 miles east-south-east of Cumberland, Maryland; there he boarded a Baltimore & Ohio train for Washington, D.C.—his first train ride. He arrived in Washington on 17 June, only fifteen days after Butcher's departure from the

Military Academy, and hastened at once to the office of Congressman Hays.

Jackson handed the astonished congressman Butcher's letter of resignation:

> It is with deep regret that I have now to send you my resignation as "Cadet" in the West Point Military Academy. . . . I did not know as much about the institution when I applied for the appointment as I know now. . . . I have only to regret the disappointment which I have made, and especially having disappointed you. . . . Mr. Jackson will deliver this letter to you, who is an applicant for the appointment.

Young Jackson had four other letters for Hays, all recommending "Thomas J. Jackson,"[1] lauding his abilities and character. Smith Gibson wrote that he had known Jackson all his life, and "he is in my opinion well skilled in mathematics and is quite a smart youth for his age and opportunity." Evan Carmack, presented his "verey [*sic*] best respects" and recommended young Jackson be appointed a "cadebt [*sic*] at West Point," as "taking everything into consideration that a better selection could not well be made, west of the mountains. . . ." A third letter bore thirteen signatures, including that of Peregrine Hays, the congressman's son, and Colonel Alexander Scott Withers; a fourth carried eighteen signatures. Uncle Cummins had worked well.

Congressman Hays was impressed. Probably all who had written or signed the letters were known to him. He at once forwarded the letters to the secretary of war with a covering letter apologizing for Butcher's defection and recommending Thomas J. Jackson, stating: "I am personally and intimately acquainted with young Jackson he is about 19 years of age [18½ actually]—fine athletic form and of manly appearance. He was left an orphan at an early age [so] . . . he had to rely entirely on his own exertions [in] sustaining as he does a good moral character—and an improvable mind. . . ."

The next day Jackson was offered a conditional appointment, which he immediately accepted. Congressman Hays hospitably invited him to stay in town for a few days, as enrollment date at the academy was not until 1 July, but Jackson was too eager to begin his cadetship to

---

1. This is Jackson's first known use of a middle initial. The "J." was (and, by most, is still) thought to stand for "Jonathan," the name of Jackson's father, although Jackson himself never said so, nor did he ever use other than the initial. He also never expressed any affection or regard for the father he never knew.

tarry. He took time only to climb to the top of the unfinished Capitol for a look at the inchoate District of Columbia before taking the next train to West Point, New York.

Jackson doubtless felt much as did many another young man journeying east from a rural western home in the mid-nineteenth century. John C. Tidball, coming from Ohio in 1844, wrote: "This was the first time I had ever been east of the Alleghenies or had seen cities like those of the Atlantic seaboard, and all was astonishing newness to me."

At the West Point station Jackson, like most other provisional cadets, must have loaded his baggage onto a horse-drawn cart and followed it up to the impressive gray buildings of the Military Academy, sitting high on a bluff overlooking the Hudson River. Crossing the parade ground (called The Plain), he could see looming in the northwest two spectacular mountains: Crow's Nest and Butter Mountain (now called Storm King).

The United States Military Academy, which had been founded forty years earlier (16 March 1802), consisted at this time of two stone barracks, one of three stories and one of four; an academic building with a riding hall on the ground floor; a long mess hall; a chapel built in 1836; a cadet hospital built of native stone in 1839; and a spanking new library. There were also quarters for the officers, enlisted men, and other staff. Since there was no physical training and no organized sports, there was no gymnasium.

At the adjutant's office Jackson turned over all his money (cadets were forbidden to have cash; needed items were purchased with chits). At the quartermaster's he was issued the minimum equipment he would need before taking his entrance examinations, such necessities as a chair, two blankets, a "comfortable" (comforter), an arithmetic text, a slate, a bucket, a tin cup, a washbasin, soap, stationery, a candle, and a candlestick.

When Jackson, escorted by a cadet sergeant, arrived at his barracks, four plebes from Virginia—Ambrose Powell Hill, Dabney H. Maury, George E. Pickett, and Birkett Davenport Fry, all destined to become Confederate generals—were idling nearby. Except for Fry,[2] they came from affluent and cultured families east of the Blue Ridge Mountains. Indeed, in the highly stratified society of the antebellum South, Maury and Hill were true Virginia blue bloods—and great snobs. Young Maury, the son of a navy captain, held an A.B. degree

2. Fry came from a well-to-do family in Kanawha County in what is today West Virginia.

from the University of Virginia and had studied law before coming to West Point. A. P. Hill came from the landed gentry of north-central Virginia. His family had long been settled in the commonwealth; his father was a prosperous farmer, merchant, and politician.

"The personal appearance of the stranger was so remarkable as to attract the attention of several of us who were standing near and chatting together," wrote Maury later. They saw a lean young man, standing about five feet ten,[3] with large hands and feet (said to be nearly a size fourteen), and ill-cut brown hair on a head that seemed a bit too large for his body. He wore a homespun shirt, large heavy brogans, and a broad-brimmed wagoner's hat; over his shoulder he carried well-worn saddlebags. He was hardly the picture of a Virginia gentleman, but his clothes were no more rustic than those of most of the provisional cadets. However, he must have had a determined glint in his blue-gray eyes,[4] for Maury drawled: "That fellow looks as if he had come to stay." As most of the badly educated young men from the backwoods did not last long at West Point, he probably considered the thought amusing.

Learning that the new plebe was from Virginia, Maury climbed the stairs to his room "to show my interest in a fellow countryman in a strange land." It requires little reading between the lines to infer the degree of condescension in the cosmopolitan Maury's voice and manner as he introduced himself to the awkward newcomer. Jackson was certainly out of his accustomed element and probably feared being mocked or snubbed; he was for the first time in his life among strangers, parted from all relatives, but he would not be patronized. As Maury later recorded, he "received my courteous advances in a manner so chilling that it caused me to regret having made them, and I rejoined my companions with criticism brief and emphatic as to his intellectual endowments."

On 1 July, together with the other provisional cadets, Jackson took the preliminary examinations that included a physical examination which thirty failed to pass. On leaping this first hurdle, he was formally

3. In descriptions of Jackson, his height seems to have increased with his reputation, and in later accounts he is sometimes spoken of as being six feet tall. However, Mr. Keith Gibson, curator of the Virginia Military Institute's museums, and the author measured the uniform worn by Jackson at First Manassas, when he had certainly attained his full height, and quite obviously he could not have exceeded five feet ten inches. His passport application in 1856 lists his height as five feet nine and three-quarters inches.

4. The exact color of Jackson's eyes has been variously described as bright blue, gray, and blue-gray.

enrolled for the standard six months' probation. One technicality, not at first apparent, remained to be overcome. As an orphan and still a minor, he was required to have a legal guardian, but none had ever been appointed. It was arranged for his uncle Edward Jackson, only seven years his senior, to be so designated. On 12 July at the County Court of Lewis he and Colonel Alexander Scott Withers signed the hundred-dollar bond, and Edward "assented to the above acceptance by my ward of his conditional appointment as Cadet . . . to serve the United States eight years unless sooner discharged." As soon as these papers were received by Secretary of War John C. Spencer on 22 July, Jackson's appointment was authorized, and Congressman Hays dispatched a letter to the superintendent of the Military Academy lauding the young man's virtues and pleading for generous treatment.

There were 112 provisional cadets at the United States Military Academy that year, and they came from every congressional district and several territories. Although a decade earlier Davy Crockett had damned West Point to his fellow congressmen as drawing "a line of demarcation between the two classes of society—it separated the children of the rich from the children of the poor," the academy was, in fact, remarkably democratic in its selection of candidates, although, of course, those from affluent families had been better educated and thus had a decided edge, particularly in a cadet's first year.

A study of the backgrounds of the cadets in the classes of 1842 through 1854 reveals that nearly 30 percent were the sons of farmers and planters, just over 12 percent were merchant's sons, and about the same percentage were the sons of lawyers. Only 20 fathers were classified as indigent, and only 41 as affluent. By far the greatest number (861) were from the middle classes and of moderate means, and of these, 329 were, like Jackson, from rural areas. Many of these were ill educated, and indeed, more than fifty, lacking skills, knowledge, and "improvable minds," were soon sent home for academic failures.[5]

In July summer camp began, and the cadets went under canvas. Dabney Maury, sprawling one day on his "comfortable" (there were no cots in the tents), was reading a yellow-backed novel when he spied Jackson among a detail policing the area. "Desirous again to be affable and playful with our countryman," said Maury, he lifted the tent wall

5. In 1842, when Jackson entered the academy, no cadet from Iowa or Wisconsin had ever succeeded in graduating, and only one from Arkansas, and three from Florida. Virginia had produced 122 graduates, third in number after New York with 248 and Pennsylvania with 137.

and called out "with an air of authority and mock sternness, ordering him to be more attentive to his duty, to remove those cigar stumps, and otherwise mind his business."

Jackson flashed the grinning Maury a "stern and angry" look and turned away.

Maury returned to his novel, but perhaps his playfulness no longer seemed quite so amusing to him, for when the police detail had finished, he confessed to his friend Fry: "I have made Cadet Jackson of Virginia angry and must at once humble myself and explain that I was not really in charge of that police detail."

He found Jackson near the guard tent. Walking up to him, he said suavely: "Mr. Jackson, I find that I made a mistake just now in speaking to you in a playful manner—not justified by our short acquaintance. I regret that I did so."

Jackson regarded Maury stonily as he considered the apology and then replied solemnly: "That is perfectly satisfactory, sir."

Maury stumped back to his friends and announced: "In my opinion, Cadet Jackson of Virginia is a jackass." It was an opinion, he said, "unanimously concurred in." Henceforth Maury and his snobbish Virginia coterie had nothing to do with their "countryman."

Cadets from aristocratic families were prone to form cliques. Thomas Neill, the son of a prominent Philadelphia doctor and a year behind Jackson at West Point, wrote home in 1843: "In almost every class those who are gentlemen associate together, and have nothing to do with those forward, impudent fellows who can never be gentlemen." Such cliques were often regional, as was that formed by Maury and his friends, but sectional quarrels, as between North and South, rarely occurred in Jackson's day. Truman Seymour of Vermont, a classmate, declared that cadets seldom argued sectional issues and that the academy staff tried to stimulate national feelings. Even eight years later, when J. E. B. Stuart was a cadet, he wrote to a friend that "there seems to be a sentiment of mutual forebearance . . . [and] as a general thing we know no North or South."

Even so, there must have been an undercurrent of sectionalism and a sensitivity to it on the part of the staff. The Dialectical Society at West Point met on Saturday afternoons to debate topics members had selected and the superintendent had approved. Plebes were not eligible, and upperclassmen joined only when invited. Jackson was never asked to join, but it was during his second year at the academy (1843) that the superintendent, for the first and only time, vetoed a topic. It was "Has a State under any circumstances the right to nullify an Act of Congress?"

Jackson had no time during his plebe year to resent the aloofness of the Virginia gentlemen of Maury's clique. He had all that he could do to prove that he had "an improvable mind," to endure the hazing (called devilment) by upperclassmen during "beast barracks,"[6] and to sustain the endless drilling, in which he was taught to stand straight and in which his loose mountain lope was changed forever to a stiff military gait.

The provisional cadets wore their civilian clothes through the summer, and John Tidball described them: "Some were arrayed in straw hats while others sweltered in fur caps; some sported long-tailed coats . . . the great majority were fully rustic in homemade clothes, while a few were foppish with city fashions." By the end of the summer the obvious misfits in the class had been weeded out and sent packing; only then were full-dress cadet uniforms issued to those remaining. (The gray blouse with the black braid that is now the daily wear did not come into use until 1889.) Jackson's homespun was then packed away forever. In the early autumn the upperclassmen returned from furlough, and West Point took on a new life.

Although most of the details of Jackson's boyhood remain murky, his years at West Point are well documented. We have quite a clear picture of the kind of life he led and of the problems he faced—with one exception. Curiously there is no record of, nor, curiously, did Jackson ever mention, the names of any of his roommates.

For most of the year the cadets lived in small, drafty barracks rooms, twelve by twelve feet, each housing four or five cadets, who slept on iron beds. Floors were bare; each room had a coal grate, and prominently posted in every room were instructions for the placement of each piece of clothing and equipment. Cadets were ordered to bathe once a week and forbidden to bathe more often without the express approval of the superintendent. Water was carried in buckets from a well with a wooden pump.

When Jackson entered, the superintendent was Major Richard Delafield, an 1818 graduate (number one in his class) who had been posted to the academy four years earlier. A strict enforcer of every rule, he was generally unpopular with the staff and with the cadets, some of whom considered him a tyrant. Cadet John Pelham (class of 1856) called him "arbitrary" and "a hypocritical and deceitful man." He was

6. When cadets first arrived at West Point, they were put into tents and taught some of the basics of military life and their lowly position as plebes at the academy by upper classmen. This period and place were (and are) called beast barracks.

replaced on 15 August 1845 by Captain Henry Brewerton (who was, like all superintendents before him, a West Point graduate in the Corps of Engineers). When Delafield departed by riverboat, an Irish janitor was heard to remark that "there was many a dry eye at the dock."[7]

Although the commandant of cadets was an artillery first lieutenant, the engineers were kings at the academy. Cadet Tidball always remembered the "utter reverence" with which officers in the Corps of Engineers were regarded:

> It become [*sic*] a kind of fixture in our minds that the engineers were a species of gods, next to which came the "topogs" [topographical engineers, then a separate corps] . . . only a grade below the first, but still a grade—they were demi-gods. . . . The line was simply the line, whether horse, foot or dragoons. . . . For the latter a good square seat in the saddle was deemed more important than brains. These ideas were ground into our heads with such Jesuitical persistency, I do not believe anyone in the old [1840s] regime entirely overcame the influence of it.[8]

The cadets' twelve-hour days were divided into two or three hours of drill and nine or ten hours of classes and study. Classes, called sections, consisted of about fifteen cadets with the brightest in the first section. There were no elective subjects. Then as now, every cadet recited every day in every class and was graded every day in every subject.[9] Christmas Day and New Year's Day were the only holidays observed. Plebes spent three hours on algebra, geometry, or trigonometry each morning. Back in western Virginia young Jackson was thought to be clever with figures, but at West Point, according to a fellow cadet,

---

7. The appointment as superintendent of the Military Academy did not carry the prestige it later acquired, nor did it usually lead to promotion, but Delafield, who served two tours (1838–45 and 1856–61), eventually became a brevet major general and chief of engineers.

8. Quoted in the excellent scholarly study of the antebellum years at the Military Academy by Professor James L. Morrison, *"The Best School in the World"* (Kent, Ohio: Kent State University Press, 1986). Even today top-ranking graduates (who have the pick of the assignments) usually select the Corps of Engineers, whose officers wear brass buttons with a distinctive design that differ from the standard buttons worn by all other American officers.

9. The system of daily recitation was not unique to West Point. Samuel Eliot Morison, speaking of Harvard at this period, wrote: "The faculty were not there to teach, but to see that the boys got their lessons: to explain difficulties or elucidate a text would have seemed improper." Even when professors lectured, recitations followed.

he "could add up a column of figures, but as to vulgar or decimal fractions, it is doubtful if he had ever heard of them."

Although Spanish would have been more useful to the future officers, only French was taught, and a professorship in the language was not created until 1846. Jackson studied under "First Teacher" Mr. Claudius Berard and "Second Teacher" Mr. H. R. Agney. Not much effort was made to teach cadets to speak the language, but they were expected to master the grammar and the vocabulary.

For cadets such as Maury, with a bachelor's degree, or classmate George B. McClellan, who, although only fifteen and the youngest in his class, had attended the University of Pennsylvania for two years, the academic requirements at West Point presented few problems. Young McClellan wrote home to his brother, John: "I do study a little (not much I must confess)." But for cadets such as Thomas Jackson the going was rough indeed, a struggle for survival. In the early months of his plebe year Jackson found himself near the bottom of his class— among the "immortals," as those on the verge of failure were then called—but he was a most determined young man. He redoubled his efforts.

William Edmonson Jones (later a Confederate major general known as Grumble Jones), who was graduated two years behind Jackson, remembered that "he was always at his books and many times when others were asleep he was still at work." Cadet Parmenus Taylor Turnley, who died in 1911 as the oldest living classmate in Jackson's class, remembered how just before lights out Jackson would "pile up his grate with anthracite coal, and lying prone before it on the floor would work away at his lessons by the glare of the fire, which scorched his very brain, till a late hour of the night." Poring over each page of each assignment, by diligence and sweat Jackson set out to prove that he did indeed have an improvable mind.

His dogged determination evoked the admiration of some cadets, including a third classman from Mississippi, William Henry Chase Whiting, at this time the most academically brilliant cadet ever to attend the academy. (His record was not exceeded until the arrival of Douglas MacArthur of the class of 1903.) He generously gave Jackson so much help during that difficult first year that Jackson became known as "Whiting's plebe." Neither could have imagined that twenty years hence Whiting would be serving under his protégé in the Army of Northern Virginia.

General examinations were held twice a year, and every cadet was graded and ranked. Of those who entered the academy with Jackson and passed the preliminary examinations, twenty-nine failed or dropped out in the first nine months. Most failures in the antebellum years (about 85 percent) were due to deficiencies in mathematics, which counted in the weighted order of merit for three times as much as French, chemistry, or drawing. More than 70 percent of a cadet's time was spent on mathematical, scientific, or engineering studies, and four out of five of the books in the fifteen-thousand-volume library were devoted to them.

Although the library was intended primarily for the use of the professors, cadets were permitted to use it, but only in full uniform with coat buttoned to the neck. No lounging on their part was tolerated. They were required to sit bolt upright. Withdrawals were permitted, but fiction could be taken out only on Saturday afternoons and had to be returned the following Monday morning. Jackson never withdrew a work of fiction. In his four years at West Point he took out only three books: Sir Walter Scott's *Napoleon Buonaparte,* Edward Turner's *Elements of Chemistry,* and a military dictionary. (By contrast, Robert E. Lee, who had been graduated second in his class in 1829, made forty-seven withdrawals.)

At the end of his plebe year Jackson was among the eighty-three cadets remaining; his class standing was:

Order of general merit—51
Order of merit in mathematics—45
Order of merit in French—70
Order on conduct roll   38 (out of the entire cadet corps of 223)
Demerits—15 (well short of the 200 that spelled dismissal)

From a position near the bottom of his class he had, with Whiting's help, clawed his way up, an achievement of which he was justly proud. Later, when asked by his aunt Clementine (Mrs. Alfred Neale of Parkersburg) how he had succeeded, he told her, "Aunt, I *studied* and *cried* and *prayed,*" to which she responded: "Poor desolate boy!"

He had beaten the odds through sheer grit, but he was still in the bottom half, close to the bottom third, of his class.

3

☆ ☆ ☆ ☆ ☆ ☆ ☆ ☆ ☆ ☆ ☆ ☆ ☆ ☆

West Point: Climbing Upward

Although by the end of the first year the worst was over, Jackson did not relax his efforts. He determined to improve not only his grades and his class standing but his manners and character as well. He began to keep a notebook and earnestly filled it with improving maxims:

> You may be whatever you resolve to be.[1]
> Endeavor to do well everything you undertake.
> Sacrifice your life rather than your word.
> It is not desirable to have a large number of intimate friends; you may have many acquaintances, but few intimate friends.
> Resolve to perform what you ought; perform without fail what you resolve.
> Silence: Speak but what may benefit others or yourself; avoid trifling conversation.
> Industry: Lose no time; be always employed in something useful; cut off unnecessary actions.

1. Although it is now widely believed that Jackson was the author of this maxim, which, attributed to him, is cut in stone over the barracks door at the Virginia Military Institute, he never claimed to have originated it, and he probably copied it from a book of maxims.

Frugality: Make no expense but to do good to others or yourself;
   waste nothing.
Tranquility: Be not disturbed at trifles, nor at accidents, common
   or unavoidable.

Such adages have been written down and admired by many
young men. What is remarkable is that Jackson all his life strove, with
considerable success, to follow them. He had come to the Military
Academy determined to do well, and he wholeheartedly embraced the
West Point ethic. He was convinced by his first year's experience that if
he tried hard enough, he could succeed in whatever he undertook. It
was a self-confidence he ever after sustained. The rigid and obsessive-
compulsive features of his personality, which became so striking in the
adult Jackson—the listing of things he *should* do and ways he *should*
behave, the stiff postures, the narrow focus upon technicalities, the
strong sense of duty, the absence of humor, the rare enjoyment of
fun—were not disadvantageous to a hardworking cadet; they were
traits for the most part fostered and encouraged at the Military Academy.

Like most cadets from rural areas, Jackson had arrived almost
devoid of social skills. It was here that he learned how to bow to ladies,
to use a handkerchief, to keep his fingernails clean, to employ proper
table manners, and to wend his way through mazes of etiquette not
always observed in western Virginia. Beyond his fierce desire to succeed academically, he worked hard to improve his standing on the
social scale and to acquire the graces of what was considered "polite
society." It was an age when civility was prized and manners were
important. The distinction between those who were gentlemen and
those who were not was marked. Jackson well knew the difference, and
he knew that a West Point degree conferred on its possessor, particularly in the South, the title of gentleman.

From a book of etiquette he carefully copied in his notebook rules
of behavior:

Good-breeding is opposed to selfishness, vanity or pride.
Never weary your company by talking too long or too frequently.
Always look people in the face when addressing them, and gener-
   ally when they address you. . . .
Good breeding, or true politeness is the art of showing men by
   external signs the internal regard we have for them. It arises

from good sense, improved by good company. It must be acquired by practice and not from books.

Although he never acquired the social ease of his aristocratic class-mates and his stiff West Point manners were later sometimes mocked, they were always correct. The loose-limbed country boy who arrived at the Military Academy in 1842 emerged in 1846 ramrod straight, an officer and a gentleman.

Instruction in dancing had been compulsory at West Point since 1823, and dancing masters took the cadets in hand during summer camps, where they decorously danced with one another. Presumably young Jackson mastered ballroom dancing, but neither he nor any of his classmates ever made mention of it.

Riding was taught as well, and snobbish Dabney Maury later spoke of Jackson's horsemanship. "He was singularly awkward and uncomfortable to look at upon a horse," he said. "At the riding school at West Point we used to watch him with anxiety when his turn came to cut at the head or leap the bars." It was likely to have been amusement rather than anxiety with which the graceful riders from eastern Virginia watched the inelegant Jackson.[2] With some satisfaction Maury concluded: "He had a rough hand with the bridle, an ungainly seat, and when he would cut at a head upon the ground, he seemed in danger of falling from his horse."

Although Jackson's situation at the academy steadily improved, home problems haunted him. The most curious of these was a lawsuit instituted by Jackson himself, who sued "for the use and benefit of Cummins E. Jackson vs John Wurst." Even though he could not be present, he won the case and was awarded fifty dollars plus interest. Why Uncle Cummins did not sue in his own name is a mystery.

A more serious problem stemmed from the accounts he had kept, or had failed to keep, as a constable in Lewis County. In May 1843, as he was finishing his plebe year, a Mr. John Hay entered a lawsuit against him, claiming that he had given Jackson more than $300 in notes for collection and that he had received no accounting for them. The case inched along for nearly two years before it was discovered that Hay had actually been overpaid $4.67.

2. Although instruction was given in horsemanship, cavalry tactics were not taught, and although most cadets could expect to be sent to fight Indians in the Far West, nothing was taught about the Indians or their style of warfare.

Most serious of all was a case entered in the circuit superior court of law and chancery for "the use and proper costs" of Stephen P. Jackson (no relation), who sued Cummins Jackson and Minter Bailey (Jackson's sureties as constable) as well as Cadet Jackson for $2,000, charging that "Thomas Jackson did not truely [*sic*] execute and discharge the duties of the said office of constable during his continuance in office." As proof, receipts signed "Thos. Jackson const" were presented to show that bills amounting to $350.51 ¾ for which he had given no accounting had been given to the young constable for collection.

On 28 June 1844 and again on 3 July 1844 warrants were issued for the arrest of the sureties, and the sheriff of Lewis County was ordered to find and "safely keep" them so that he could "have their bodies before . . . the court." Cadet Jackson, of course, was safe from arrest in his barracks at West Point. Although they were readily available, there is no evidence that either Minter Bailey or Cummins Jackson was in this case ever safely kept by the sheriff. The outcome of the case is unknown, but more than five years later, when Lieutenant Jackson was fighting in Mexico, it was still pending, and Bailey had filed an affidavit saying he thought the bills were simply uncollectible as the debtors were too poor.

Still another suit, the details of which are blurred, was brought forward by two well-known lawyers in Lewis County, G. D. Camden and J. M. Bennett. Papers served on Cummins Jackson and Major Minter Bailey noted: "Thos. Jackson, not inhabitant of county." Later the action was "abated as to Thomas Jackson." In 1844 there was "confessed judgment," and the case was settled for $255.33. In what way Thomas was involved is not clear, but the charges doubtless sprang from his troubled accounts as constable. Cadet Jackson's reactions to these suits are not recorded, but they must have added to the strain of his first West Point years.

It was at this time that health problems began; Dabney Maury said that Jackson became "hypochrondriacal." In his letters to his sister he now always spoke of the state of his health, and some of his fellow cadets began to observe behavior they thought eccentric. William Jones said that Jackson believed "insidious diseases were at his vitals" so that "he always sat bolt upright without touching the back of his chair lest a bending posture might further injure his health." Dabney Maury wrote that Jackson "was convinced that one of his legs was larger than the other and that one of his arms was likewise unduly heavy. He had acquired the habit of raising that arm straight up so that, as he said, the blood could run back into his body."[3]

As it became increasingly apparent that in all probability he would be graduated, Jackson began to consider seriously whether or not he wanted to make a career in the army. On 28 January 1844, midway through his second year, he wrote to Laura:

> If no change takes place in the army and I continue to progress as well as I have so far, my pay when I leave this institution will be about one thousand dollars; though fate may decree in the lower part of my class, in which case I shall have to go into the infantry and will receive only seven hundred and fifty dollars a year. But I feel confident that unless fortune frowns on me more than it has yet I will graduate in the upper half of my class and high enough in it to enter the Dragoons. But be that as it may, I intend to remain in the army no longer than I can get rid of it with honor, and mean to commence some professional business at home.

By the end of his second year his class had been whittled down to seventy-eight, and his standing in it was much improved:

Order of general merit—30
Order of merit in mathematics—18
Order of merit in French—52
Order of merit in drawing—68
Order of merit in English grammar—55
Demerits—26

In January 1844 he began to look forward longingly to the furlough to which he would be entitled at the end of his second year. In a

3. Many of his contemporaries and some of his biographers regarded Jackson's ailments as largely psychosomatic, but Jackson may well have developed a circulatory deficiency. According to Dr. John H. Cook III, unilateral lymphedema, although unusual in so young a man, is a possibility. This would cause his arm to feel heavy, and holding his arm upright would decrease the discomfort if he suffered from the arterial insufficiency usually associated with this disease.

In 1964 Dr. James L. Mathis, a psychiatrist, made a study of Jackson's illnesses, both at West Point and later, and concluded that Jackson probably would not have passed the present-day psychiatric tests for military service and "it is almost certain that he would not be admitted to West Point." This is disputed, however, by Dr. James Wengert, a leading psychologist at the Veterans Administration Medical Center in Omaha, Nebraska, who in 1989, on the author's behalf, studied Jackson's illnesses.

letter to Laura he charged her to "tell Uncle Cummins if you should see him shortly that I want him to write to me, giving me permission to come home; for without his consent the superintendent will not give me a furlough."[4] In the same letter he asked her to tell "Seely" (Cecelia), his uncle's slave housekeeper, "that there is not a day that passes by without my thinking of her, and that I expect to see her in less than five months."

In the summer of 1844 Jackson was given his long-awaited and only furlough, from mid-June to mid-August. He made all haste back to Jackson's Mill, where his newly acquired manners amazed his friends and relations. "He was the most precise man I ever met to everybody," marveled his cousin Sylvanus White.

Temporarily freed from the monastic life of West Point, young Jackson was not averse to cutting a figure with the local belles. One long-remembered Sunday morning found him resplendent in his dress gray uniform[5] riding beside Miss Caroline Norris, escorting her to the Broad Run Baptist Church. At the ford over the West Branch, Miss Norris neatly guided her horse across, but Jackson's unfortunate mount slipped on a stone, and horse and rider pitched into the stream. Cascading water, the mortified Jackson struggled to his feet without a word and grimly remounted. It was noted later in church that Miss Norris seemed somewhat disconcerted during the service, as well she might have been with a morose, stiff-backed, sodden cadet dripping on the pew beside her.

During this furlough Jackson paid a long visit to Laura, now living with relatives in Beverly, [West] Virginia, then the seat of Randolph County. In spite of their early separation, the orphaned brother and sister were warmly attached. The correspondence they had begun flourished, with only one known interruption, until the outbreak of the Civil War.

Rumors, not given credence by the Jackson family but repeated by more than one source, claim that Jackson fathered a child by a girl at Beverly. If the rumor was true, Thomas was not the first of his kin to

---

4. This letter of 28 January 1844 is puzzling. Why did Jackson not write directly to Uncle Cummins? Why did he ask Laura to make such an inquiry when she was not even in the same part of the country? And why was Cummins's permission necessary when Edward Jackson was his legal guardian?

5. Special furlough uniforms were not authorized during Jackson's tenure at the academy. Only in 1848 were special blue frock coats without insignia and blue "furlough caps" authorized.

sire an illegitimate child. There is evidence, persuasive, if not conclusive, that Congressman Hays, who gave Jackson his appointment to West Point, was the illegitimate child of Great-Uncle George, thus making Hays one of Thomas Jackson's many cousins.[6] Court records also reveal that in the early 1800s a Miss Frances Emelia Triplett won a paternity suit against Great-Uncle George Jackson's son John George Jackson and that she named her son after him. This did not prevent John George from marrying that same year nineteen-year-old Miss Mary Payne, Dolley Madison's sister, with President James Madison giving the bride away at his home, Montpelier.

Thomas Jackson's uncle Edward J. Jackson (1817–1848) never married, but he acknowledged two illegitimate children—Sarah Brown Waggoner and Van Flesher—to whom he left his property. Another uncle, David E. Jackson (1788–1837), married Juliet Norris, although he was in love with her sister Polly and had, in addition to four legitimate children, two others by Polly. One of David's children by Juliet, William Pitt Jackson (1812–1837), had an illegitimate son also named Thomas Jackson.

If Jackson did discover the pleasures of feminine flesh, he was not the only cadet to do so. Cadet A. P. Hill came back to the academy "with Gonorrhea contracted on furlough," thought to have been acquired in the "harems of pleasure" then to be found on Church and Mercer streets in New York City.[7]

It was probably not until he returned to West Point that Jackson learned that he had been appointed cadet sergeant. Cadet officers and noncommissioned officers were selected for "soldier-like performance of duties," and "exemplary . . . good conduct." Describing his position to Laura not quite accurately as that of a "cadet officer," he explained jubilantly that now his "duties are lighter than usual."

He had survived the courses in French, English grammar, and mathematics, but there were still academic hurdles to clear in his third year. The most frustrating of these was drawing, taught by Mr. Robert

6. Michael I. Shoop, of the Garland Gray Memorial Research Center, who in 1981 published the genealogies of the Jackson, Junkin, and Morrison families, considered Hays an illegitimate son of the prolific George Jackson (1757–1831).

7. Mercer Street, which runs north from Canal to Eighth Street, is now largely commercial and industrial with art galleries and space in lofts rented to artists; much of it is in the SoHo district. Church Street, running north from lower Manhattan to just below Canal Street, houses business and industrial buildings. Prostitution has moved elsewhere.

W. Weir. Classes included lettering, topographical drawing, signs and symbols, drawing of the human figure, and painting in oils and water-colors. Years later (30 May 1862) Jackson told Confederate Congress-man Alexander R. Boteler: "My hardest tasks at West Point were the drawing lessons, and I could never do anything in that line to satisfy myself or anyone else."

Weir was a distinguished man, a well-known artist in his own right. His painting *Embarkation of the Pilgrims* hangs in the Rotunda of the Capitol in Washington, D.C. A few years after Jackson was graduated, when Cadet James Abbott McNeill Whistler became one of his pupils, Weir was, for the first and only time, faced with a student whose talents outshone his own.[8] Never forgotten was the day Weir picked up a brush to touch up a painting of young Whistler's and was stopped with the anguished cry "Don't, sir, you'll spoil it."

Another teacher of renown was Professor William H. C. Bartlett, who taught natural and experimental philosophy; this was the science course (established in 1812) and included electromagnetism, electrody-namics, physics, mechanics, astronomy, acoustics, magnetism, and op-tics. One-hour classes in the subject met every weekday morning dur-ing the academic year. Cadets did not conduct experiments, but they were expected to learn to use the sextant, barometer, and zenith tele-scope as well as other scientific instruments.

Although it was considered by most cadets to be a difficult course, Jackson seems to have hit his stride there. Under Bartlett he did some of his best work. Much like Jackson, Bartlett as a plebe had arrived at West Point from Missouri with only a backwoods education. Neverthe-less, he was graduated at the head of his class in 1826 and was now considered one of the academy's leading scholars. He wrote several textbooks which Jackson was later to use when he became a professor.

Chemistry, a course which embraced geology and mineralogy, was not included in Bartlett's course. Taught by First Lieutenant Jacob W. Bailey, an artillery officer who had been graduated in 1832, it was taken up in the third year, but grades in this subject did not count as high in the order of merit as did mathematics or natural and experi-mental philosophy.

At the end of his third year, in a class now down to sixty-two, Jackson had a respectable standing in all subjects except drawing:

8. Whistler, son of a military engineer, was a cadet from 1851 to 1853 but was dismissed for failing the course in chemistry. In later years he would remark that if silicon had been a gas, he would have been a major general.

Order of general merit—20
Order of merit in chemistry—25
Order of merit in natural and experimental philosophy—11
Order of merit in drawing—59
Order of merit on conduct roll—1 (out of a cadet corps of 204)
Demerits—0

The absence of demerits—a remarkable achievement—indicated that Jackson was impeccably neat, clean, precise, an observer of every rule and regulation. Contrary to popular belief, West Point did not, and still does not, train cadets to become generals. In the 1840s few classes were devoted to the study of war, and not until 1860 was a West Point graduate promoted to general. What cadets were taught with great thoroughness was discipline. It is discipline which constitutes the warp and woof of an army; it is that which distinguishes it from a mob. As Jackson's record at West Point clearly shows and as his later career demonstrated, he accepted as his own the army's belief in its primacy. He learned to value it, to endure it, and to impose it upon others.

The present strict honor code enforced at West Point—"A cadet will not lie, cheat or steal or associate with those who do"—was unknown in the antebellum years. Although a high degree of trust was placed in a cadet's word, cheating was not considered a grievous crime involving moral turpitude. A cadet caught in the act received only a zero mark and a few demerits.

Only three cases of theft were reported between 1833 and 1861, although perhaps there were others that were unreported. Jackson was the victim of one unscrupulous cadet. The Model 1841 muskets issued to cadets did not carry serial numbers, but Jackson had made or had inherited an identifiable mark on his, so that one day when he found his own immaculately clean weapon replaced by a dirty musket, he stormed out to locate the culprit, whom he discovered in the person of a plebe from Missouri: Thomas Frelinglyson McKinney McLean. Jackson's Old Testament sense of justice did not readily admit of mercy. He demanded a court-martial, and it was only with difficulty that he was calmed and persuaded to refrain from pressing charges. This was the only time he was ever known to temper justice with mercy. McLean was dismissed from the academy for other reasons just before graduation and, as Jackson might have predicted, came to a bad end.[9]

9. According to his classmate William Edmonson ("Grumble") Jones, later a Confederate major general, McLean lost ground academically, told lies to avoid de-

It was during his third year, on 1 September 1844, that Laura married Jonathan Arnold of Beverly. Thomas was pleased and wrote (10 February 1845): "I think that if happiness exists in this world, matrimony is one of its principal factors. I conclude that you ought to possess it, inasmuch as you are married, surrounded by your friends and relatives, living near the place of your birth, superior to the wants of life and above all possessing a religion." In this same letter he instructed her to address letters to him as "Thos. J. Jackson . . . on account of another cadet's name being Thos. K. Jackson."[10]

It was about this time that he learned of the counterfeiting charges brought against his uncle Cummins.[11] A year later, in 1845, when he heard that Cummins had forfeited his bail by failing to appear in court, he wrote to Laura, speaking of his "remorse for the misfortunes of an uncle who has been to me a true friend," and on New Year's Day 1846 he returned to the subject: "The misfortune of Uncle Cummins brought to my heart feelings of regret & sympathy which time will never be able to erase. But I sincerely trust that he will ride clear from all harm, which should be the case if as I have been informed there was false evidence against him. I have not written home since my return from furlough neither have I received one from there."

On 2 August 1845, as he was about to begin his final year at the Military Academy, he wrote to Laura about his future career:

> I have before me two courses, either of which I may choose. The first would be to follow the profession of arms; the second, that of a civil pursuit, as law. If I should adopt the first I could live indepen-

merits, and lost his furlough for assaulting his cadet captain. He seduced a young woman in a neighboring village and was finally dismissed on the eve of graduation. During the gold rush he went to California. There he, with others, robbed and murdered a ferryman and then took refuge with the local Indians, among whom he was said to have become a minor chief.

10. Thomas Klugh Jackson was graduated in the class of 1848 and served throughout the Civil War as a Confederate major; later he was a farmer and merchant in Alabama.

11. Cummins E. Jackson was indicted on 28 August 1844. There were only rumors of his counterfeiting until William B. Carey, of Berkeley Springs, West Virginia, researching for the author located the proof. A record of the indictment and subsequent proceedings is contained in Federal Order Books Nos. 1 and 2 of the District Court of the United States for the Northern District of Virginia, at Clarksburg (West Virginia). These books are now with the National Archives Mid-Atlantic Regional Office in Philadelphia.

dently and surrounded by friends whom I have already made, have no fear of want. My pay would be fixed [and] the principal thing I would have to attend to would be futurity. If I adopt the latter I presume that I would still find plenty of friends, but my exertions would have to be great in order to acquire a name. This course is most congenial to my taste, and consequently I intend to adopt it, after spending a few years in pursuing the former.

Jackson was never awarded cadet officer status. Indeed, he lost his cadet sergeant's stripes at the end of the school year and served his final year as a cadet private. The reasons for his demotion are unknown, but it is clear that the commandant and the tactical officers failed to detect signs of extraordinary military promise in this stiff, correct, and punctilious cadet.[12]

In his last year Jackson and his classmates studied engineering under Dennis H. Mahan, an aloof and demanding, often sarcastic, professor who taught the "Art of Engineering in all its branches." He was respected and feared by generations of cadets, for he taught at West Point for forty-one years. His course included civil engineering, architecture, and military engineering, which covered, among other things, field fortifications and mines.

Artillery and infantry tactics were taught by Captain Erasmus Darwin Keyes, 3rd Artillery.[13] Geography, history, and ethics were taught by the academy's chaplain, the Reverend Martin P. Parks from North Carolina, a West Point graduate who in 1846 resigned to become assistant pastor of Trinity Episcopal Church in New York City. One of the texts in Parks's history class appears to have been William Rawle's *View of the Constitution of the United States* (Philadelphia, 1825). Later quoted by Southern graduates, Rawle argued that the United States was a dissoluble union and that when it was dissolved, the individual states could claim the allegiance of their citizens.

It was in Parks's ethics class, which sat for an hour three times a week, that Jackson starred, rising to the first section and achieving the highest order of merit he ever reached in any subject. To Laura he described "this science, which I consider as preferable to any other in

12. Although J. E. B. Stuart, Halleck, Beauregard, and Burnside all were first captains at West Point, Grant, Sherman, Sheridan, Pemberton, and several other Civil War generals were, like Jackson, graduated as cadet privates.

13. Keyes, who had been graduated from the Military Academy in 1832, rose to the rank of major general in the Union army and commanded a corps opposite Jackson at the battles of Seven Days.

the course." The subject was, of course, very close to the theology that absorbed him in later years.

Fifty-nine cadets were graduated in 1846, making it the largest class in the Military Academy's history, and Jackson, the young man whose mind had indeed proved improvable, stood in the top third:

Order of general merit—17
Order of merit in engineering—12
Order of merit in ethics—5
Order of merit in chemistry, mineralogy and geology—11
Order of merit in artillery—11
Order of merit in infantry tactics—21
Order on conduct roll—24 (out of a cadet corps of 213)
Demerits—7

In four years he had acquired only forty-eight demerits, a remarkable record.[14] Unlike many of his classmates and generations of cadets, he appears never to have slipped out of barracks for a drink or a meal at the establishment of the famous Benny Havens.[15] Years later when asked by his sister-in-law Miss Margaret Junkin if he had ever deliberately broken the rules at West Point, he paused to think and then replied seriously: "Yes. I remember one overt act; but it was the only one on which I consciously did what I knew to be wrong: I stepped behind a tree to conceal myself because I was beyond bounds without a permit."

Each year Jackson had improved his class standing, and First

14. Jackson's record was not, however, as spectacular as that of Robert E. Lee, who was graduated second in his class and in four years received not a single demerit.

15. Benny Havens's tavern, located on the west bank of the Hudson a little more than a mile from the south gate of the academy, offered hot rum "flips," roast turkey, flapjacks, and other culinary delights absent from the meat-and-potatoes diet at the cadet mess. The academy authorities made occasional raids on Benny Havens to catch cadets out of bounds, and it is said that Jefferson Davis fell off a cliff and almost killed himself attempting to escape from such a raid.

Benny Havens's establishment has been immortalized in a famous ditty, "Benny Havens, Oh!," which is still sung to the tune of "The Wearing of the Green." Many verses have been added over the years, but the first were composed by Ripley Arnold (class of 1838), who was murdered in Texas in 1853. One of the oldest and most popular of the verses was:

Come fill your glasses, fellows, and stand up in a row
To singing sentimentally we're going for to go;
In the army there's sobriety, promotions very slow,
So we'll sing our reminiscences of Benny Havens Oh!

Lieutenant George Taylor, one of his tactical officers, thought that had the course lasted longer, he would have been graduated number one, although this seems doubtful. Significantly he was well ahead of those who had scoffed at him on his arrival. Dabney Maury stood only thirty-seventh in his class and was assigned to the mounted rifles; A. P. Hill had escaped dismissal but had been set back a year because his gonorrhea resisted treatment; and Fry, although he became a Confederate brigadier general, was a nongraduate. George Pickett, destined to become a Confederate major general and to send his men on the disastrous charge at Gettysburg seventeen years hence, was the class goat. Graduating at the bottom of his class, he was, of course, assigned to the infantry.

The star of the class, who beat George B. McClellan for first place was Charles S. Stewart, who, like almost all those who have placed number one at the Military Academy (Douglas MacArthur was an exception), was not an outstandingly successful soldier and, unlike nearly half of his classmates, did not rise above the rank of colonel. The top four ranking cadets went to the Corps of Engineers; the next two went into the Topographical Engineers; numbers seven and eight became ordnance officers; Jackson was among the fifteen who entered the artillery; the rest went into the infantry, mounted rifles, or dragoons.[16]

Jackson's class was graduated on 1 July. As was then customary, there were no commencement exercises, and diplomas were not distributed; Chaplain Parks simply delivered a sermon addressed to the graduating class, and the graduates' names were published in orders. The fledgling officers were not directly commissioned second lieutenants but only brevet second lieutenants, their commissions dated 30 June 1846. They would serve as officers, but each would have to wait for an opening in his regiment or corps before he could become a full second lieutenant.[17] Jackson was assigned to the 1st Artillery and ordered to report to Captain Francis Taylor at Fort Columbus on Governors Island, New York.

Fewer than three months earlier Jackson had warned Laura that "rumor appears to indicate a rupture between our government and the Mexican." By the time of his graduation the United States had de-

16. The fifty-nine members of the United States Military Academy class of 1846 supplied the Union army with fifteen generals, including McClellan, and the Confederate army with nine.

17. The regular army of the United States then consisted of fewer than nine thousand men of all ranks.

clared war on Mexico, and the newly minted officers knew that most would soon find themselves in battle. But first there was a postgraduation leave, marking an end to West Point's rigorous discipline and an end to the threat of demerits.

Before scattering to their homes and on to their new posts, Jackson and a group of friends went off to New York City to celebrate. Included were Cadmus M. Wilcox from Tennessee, who was graduated fifty-fourth in his class but was soon to distinguish himself at Chapultepec and later to become a Confederate major general; Archibald Blair Botts, a Virginian who in fewer than six months would be among the thousands to die of disease at Camargo, Mexico; and Clarendon ("Dominie") J. L. Wilson, another Virginian, who was destined to find fame and death in New Mexico.

It was a sweltering night in the city when the group descended on Brown's Hotel and thriftily rented a room on the top floor just under the roof. Wilcox, who had been invited out to dinner by the secretary of war, William L. Marcy, left the others and did not return until one o'clock in the morning. As he climbed the last flight of stairs and walked down the corridor to their room, he heard shouting, the stamping of feet, and a cacophony of song. The door to the room was locked, and the uproar was so great that he hammered on it for some time before he was heard and the door flung open. Slumbering peacefully on the bed, still in his new uniform, was Archibald Botts; Wilson and Jackson, in their underclothes, were the principal source of the racket, and the most raucous of all was Brevet Second Lieutenant Jackson, who was bawling out what might have been an attempt at a cadet song. This is the first and last recorded instance of Jackson's being drunk—or attempting to sing anything other than a hymn.

4

The War in Mexico

Probably no war undertaken by the United States ever had less justice on its side than did the war with Mexico from 1846 to 1848. Ulysses S. ("Sam") Grant, who first tasted fame in that war, later pronounced it "one of the most unjust ever waged by a stronger against a weaker nation." It was a war which disturbed the consciences of many Americans, but after a year and a half of fighting and infighting, President James K. Polk got what he wanted: a southern border on the Rio Grande, with New Mexico, California, and what are today the states of Nevada and Utah, plus parts of Colorado and Wyoming, added to the Union. The United States was thus enlarged by nearly one-quarter.

Trouble began in 1845, when, after much discussion and prolonged negotiations, Texas, which had won its independence from Mexico in 1836 after a brief war, was, at the Texans' request, annexed to the United States. Mexico had already announced its intention to declare war if this was done, but Americans, serene in their belief in their "manifest destiny," which gave them "the whole boundless continent," ignored the threat and added Texas to the Union as its twenty-eighth and largest state.

The chief source of contention was Mexico's claim that its northern border lay at the Nueces River and the American claim that the border was the Rio Grande. In March 1846 General Zachary Taylor moved thirty-five hundred men—constituting more than two-thirds of the regular army—to Camp Texas (present-day Brownsville), opposite Matamoros, and called upon the governors of Texas and Louisiana to provide volunteers. On 1 May Camp Texas was besieged by six thousand men under General Mariano Arista, but the Mexicans were driven off, and Taylor quickly won two other victories: Palo Alto on 8 May and Resaca de la Palma the following day. On 13 May the United States formally declared war upon Mexico.

Five days later Taylor invaded Mexico, but his advance south was held up because the transportation which Washington had promised did not arrive until three months later. This was but the first of the many contretemps between the American generals in Mexico and the politicians in Washington that were to be a marked feature of a conflict many called "Mr. Polk's war," the part played by the president being particularly discreditable. But the delay seemed a happy event to young Jackson, for it enabled him to reach Mexico in time to win his first military laurels.

Jackson's leave following his graduation was brief. After a short visit with Laura, her husband (whom he always called Mr. Arnold), and their infant son, his namesake, Thomas Jackson Arnold, Brevet Second Lieutenant Jackson returned to Lewis County, arriving at Weston on Monday, 20 July 1846. Two days later he received orders to report to Captain Francis Taylor, commanding Company K, 1st Artillery, at Fort Columbus on Governors Island, New York; he left the following day, 23 July.

He found Captain Taylor, not at Fort Columbus but at Fort Hamilton, New York. Taylor, who had graduated ninth in the U.S. Military Academy class of 1825, was a veteran of more than twenty years' service. Jackson described him to Laura as "a Virginian and a very fine man."[1] His battery was already under orders for Mexico, and about mid-August he and Jackson, with thirty men and forty horses, set off to join the army of General Zachary Taylor ("Old Rough and Ready"), then advancing on Monterrey. Marching overland for about four hundred miles to Pittsburgh, they boarded a riverboat and steamed down the Ohio and Mississippi to New Orleans. There they boarded the *James L. Long* for Point Isabel, Texas, General Taylor's

1. Taylor, who won two brevets for his bravery at Cerro Gordo and Churubusco, died on 12 October 1858 at Fort Brown, Texas.

base of operations. Thirty-six days after leaving Fort Hamilton they landed: 24 September 1846, the day Mexican forces surrendered to General Taylor at Monterrey.

From shipboard Jackson wrote to Laura: "I have arrived in sight of Point Isabel Texas and we are now at anchor in a strong gale." Although there was no regular mail service, letters could be sent "through the kindness of a third person or the quartermaster." Jackson was hopeful that his letter would arrive, for he had been told that there were "about one hundred vessels in port, some of which I presume will soon sail for New Orleans."

Captain Taylor's detachment landed when the gale subsided, but Jackson found to his disappointment that they had arrived during a lull in the fighting. As part of the Mexican surrender agreement at Monterrey, General Taylor had granted a Mexican request for an eight-week armistice. Although this was later revoked by President Polk, Captain Taylor's battery at Point Isabel found little to do. Brevet Second Lieutenant Jackson, however, settled into fine quarters on the outskirts of the city: a house set in an orange grove with "a fine bathing establishment, the pool being about twenty-five to thirty feet."

Jackson may have taken part in installing some guns for the defense of Point Isabel, but his principal assignment was in acting as company commissary, an appointment he enjoyed, even though in spite of repeated requests, he seems never to have been granted the extra compensation due him.

It was not until mid-October that Captain Taylor's detachment boarded riverboats and started up the Rio Grande. On the thirty-first they landed at Camargo, an unhealthy city in Chihuahua State noted for its mosquitoes, tarantulas, scorpions, and a host of other vermin. That same day they began their way overland toward Saltillo, their guns, limbers, wagons, and caissons pulled by horses and mules. Brevet Lieutenant Dabney Maury, with a troop of mounted rifles assigned to escort the artillery, saw his "countryman" struggling through the mud with his battery's guns and their horses and mule teams. "He worked at them in the muddy roads as he used to do at West Point, and they had to move along," he remarked.

To the chagrin of young soldiers eager for action, Saltillo, capital of the state of Coahuila, was occupied without a fight on 16 November. There General Taylor's army was augmented by a force three thousand strong under Brigadier General John E. Wool, which had marched overland for six hundred miles from San Antonio. At Saltillo the invasion came to a halt while generals and politicians argued over the army's next steps.

The sights of his first foreign country fascinated Jackson. He found the countryside "mostly a barren waste," so sterile he "would not suppose the inhabitants would be able to pay their taxes," but he was awed by the enormous wealth in the cities. In Saltillo he was told of a man who owned more land than existed in the whole state of New York. The magnificence of many of the churches dazzled him, especially one in Saltillo, "the most highly ornamented in the interior of any edifice which has ever come under my observation." He was struck by a "magnificent silver altar" and "statues which cannot fail to attract the attention of the astonished beholder," by the "most gorgeous apparel" of the priest, and by the sacred music "of the highest character." He was deeply moved by the sight of a "female looking at a statue and weeping like a child." In the streets, he noticed, "the inhabitants take off their hats on approaching the church and do not replace them until they have passed it."

Meanwhile, back in Washington, General Winfield Scott, the vain, imperious, and gifted commander of the United States Army, laid plans for an amphibious assault on Veracruz. President Polk did not approve of the plan primarily, it seems, because Scott was a Whig, and Polk, a Democrat, feared the fame that would accrue to a general successful in Mexico. Instead, Polk suggested to Taylor that he march his army three hundred miles across the desert to San Luis Potosí and from there go on to capture Mexico City. Taylor thought this plan unsound and said so, suggesting instead an attack on Veracruz much as Scott had planned. With his two principal generals in agreement, Polk was forced to yield, and on 24 November 1846 Scott was ordered to undertake the campaign. He left Washington at once.

Initially it appeared that Wool's force, to which Jackson was attached, would be left behind to garrison Saltillo, but Scott decided to use most of Taylor's best troops, and on 7 January 1847 Company K, 1st Artillery, left Saltillo and marched back to Point Isabel. It was here that Jackson met a fellow officer who was to have a profound effect upon his life: Second Lieutenant Daniel Harvey Hill, three years older than Jackson and a West Pointer of the class of 1842. In the course of a long walk the two young officers took along the beach, Jackson plied him with questions about the war, for Hill had taken part in some of the early fighting. Hill was impressed and remembered Jackson's saying: "I really envy you men who have been in action. . . . I should like to be in one battle." According to Hill, "His face lighted up and his eyes sparkled as he spoke, and the shy, hesitating manner gave way to the frank enthusiasm of the soldier."

From Point Isabel Jackson's company moved on to join Scott's invasion force then assembling on Lobos Island near Tampico. An amphibious operation such as Scott planned always presents difficult problems, most of which in the middle of the nineteenth century had been little studied. From 21 February until 2 March Scott wrestled with the countless frustrations involved in loading some ten thousand men, mostly volunteers, with their supplies, ordnance, gear, and impedimenta on board transports, but at last all was ready, and after picking up some additional troops from Lobos Island, the invasion force, now numbering thirteen thousand, moved on 2 March to a roadstead known as Antón Lizardo, about twelve miles south of Veracruz. Jackson's company was in the *Arkansas,* a small transport. The troops were eager to land and begin the assault on the formidable defenses of the town, but a landing site had to be selected, a process which consumed four days.

On 9 March a beach opposite the island of Sacrificios, some two and a half miles from the city, was decided upon, and the largest amphibious operation ever undertaken by American military and naval forces up to that time was begun. While bands on board the ships played and townsmen, mostly foreign residents from Veracruz, sailed out to watch the show, the troops were put ashore in sixty-seven specially constructed surfboats.

Although they had expected an opposed landing, the Mexicans made no attempt to challenge them, and the difficult operation went off smoothly. Jackson went ashore with the third wave, which contained Brigadier General and Brevet Major General David E. Twiggs's brigade, a small unit made up of odds and ends of regulars, including Colonel Persifor F. Smith's mounted infantry (dismounted); the 1st, 2nd, 3rd, and 7th Infantry; and the 1st and 4th Artillery. By midnight ten thousand American troops were on the shore. The landing had been accomplished without a single serious accident, a remarkable feat. Jackson later spoke of the operation as the most thrilling spectacle he had ever seen.

The siege of Veracruz now began. Thanks to the cooperation of Commodore David Conner, large naval guns, some weighing sixty-three hundred pounds, were landed, and in the heat, amid dust, sand, and swarms of flies, they were manhandled by sweating soldiers and sailors into emplacements skillfully selected by Captain Robert E. Lee of the Corps of Engineers. Racing to complete their investment of the town, the soldiers skirmished with small detachments of Mexicans, but there were no major battles. Inside Veracruz there were thirty-five hundred Mexican troops, and another thousand were posted on an offshore island in the great fort of San Juan d'Ulúa. Although both were well protected, they had no hope of relief, and on 26 March Mexican officers opened negotiations for surrender, which was effected two days later with great ceremony. American losses were nineteen killed and sixty-three wounded.

Jackson had taken part in his first active military operation and had come under fire for the first time when a cannonball had passed within five steps of him. The reduction of Veracruz, he wrote exuberantly, excelled "any military operations known in the history of our country."

Jackson was pleased to be with Scott's army. In a letter home he wrote that "although it would have afforded me much pleasure to have been with the gallant General Taylor at the battle of Buena Vista" (22–23 February), still, "I am now with the most important portion of the army and on the most important line of operations."

To Laura, he explained what he saw as the realities of military fame:

> I presume you think my name ought to appear in the papers, but when you consider the composition of the army, you will entertain a different view; it is such that only those who have independent commands are as a general rule spoken of. . . . If an officer wishes to distinguish himself, he must remain long in the service until he obtains rank; then he receives praise not only for his efforts, but for the efforts of the officers and men under him. That portion of the praise which may be due to me must of course go to those above me, or be included in the praise of the army.

Promotion in the peacetime army was glacially slow, but it accelerated remarkably in time of war. Jackson must have known that he would soon be promoted, and he worried a bit that this would take him out of Company K, "but it will give me more rank, which is of the greatest importance in the army." Indeed, on the day after the surrender of Veracruz he learned of his promotion as of 3 March to second lieutenant.

The newly fledged second lieutenant felt free to criticize his superiors—at least in letters home. When Scott granted parole to Mexican troops, allowing prisoners to go free on their promise not to fight again, Jackson was severe: "That I cannot approve of, in as much as we had them secure, and could have taken them prisoners of war unconditionally." Aware that such sentiments might get him into trouble, he warned both Laura and Uncle Isaac Brake not to send any of his letters to the newspapers.

On 8 April General Twiggs with twenty-six hundred men and two field batteries, one of which was Company K, set off for Mexico City, about two hundred miles as the crow flies but nearly twice as far by the twisting "national road" that followed the route taken by Hernando Cortez in 1519 upward to the highlands. Four days later Twiggs's little army came to a halt when it encountered twelve thousand Mexicans commanded by the flamboyant one-legged General Antonio López de Santa Anna, the Alamo victor, in a strongly fortified position at a defile known as Cerro Gordo.

Santa Anna's right was anchored at the top of an unscalable cliff; the left of his line lay in rugged terrain cut by deep ravines and covered with heavy growth. Scott hurried up with heavy reinforcements from Veracruz to form an army of 8,500 men to face him. After Brigadier General Gideon Johnson Pillow, a political general who had been President Polk's law partner, twice attacked and twice failed to break the Mexican right, Scott sent forward his engineers to see what could be done. Captain Robert E. Lee, Captain Joseph E. Johnston, First Lieutenant Pierre G. T. Beauregard, Second Lieutenant Gustavus Woodson Smith, and Second Lieutenant George B. McClellan were assigned the task, and it was Captain Lee who, after a narrow escape during a bold reconnaissance, brought back a plan of attack which Scott accepted. Twiggs was sent into the rough country on his right, and in spite of the rugged terrain and stubborn resistance, he succeeded in turning the Mexican left and routing the remainder. Santa Anna himself barely escaped, leaving behind 3,000 prisoners and an estimated 1,000 dead and wounded on the ground. American losses were 64 killed and 353 wounded. Among the wounded was Brevet Captain Joseph E. Johnston.

Cerro Gordo was primarily an infantryman's fight, but the artillery played a part, and Jackson participated for the first time in a real battle. Many years later, when Dr. Hunter McGuire asked him what his feelings had been that first time, he was answered shortly: "Afraid the fire would not be hot enough for me to distinguish myself." Captain Taylor in his after-action report noted that "through the great exertions of Lt. Jackson, the caissons were brought up early in the night."

Jackson proudly relayed to Laura that his captain had "spoken of me in very flattering terms." However, the hero of Cerro Gordo was another artilleryman, the colorful Captain John Bankhead Magruder, who in the heat of battle found some abandoned Mexican guns, quickly turned them about, and fired them into their former owners. As no medals to acknowledge gallantry in action existed at this time, officers who so distinguished themselves were given brevet rank.[2] For his "gallant and meritorious conduct" Magruder was breveted major.

Breveted a major general was Brigadier General James Shields, commanding a brigade of one New York and two Illinois regiments of ill-trained volunteers. His brigade had been badly cut up by Mexican cavalry, and he himself was seriously wounded in the head. His next serious wound, fifteen years later, was from one of Jackson's guns.

Scott was well pleased by his victory. In a letter to General Taylor he boasted that "Mexico no longer has an army." Once again he granted his prisoners of war parole, although few of them could have had any notion of the meaning of the word and Santa Anna's forte was restoring broken armies. In any case, the Mexican government made no move to surrender. Therefore, Twiggs's men pressed forward on the road inland and reached Jalapa Enríquez, twenty miles from Cerro Gordo, on 19 April. The rest of Scott's army soon followed.

Jalapa, a city of about ten thousand inhabitants, lay forty-five hundred feet above sea level, and its climate was delightful. "Lovely Jalapa," Jackson called it when he arrived in mid-April, and Second Lieutenant Sam Grant thought it "the most beautiful place I ever saw." Captain Edmund Kirby-Smith of the 3rd Infantry, even more ecstatic, found it "the prettiest town I have ever seen, surrounded by the finest country with the most delicious climate in the world, the thermometer never rising above eighty degrees or falling below sixty."

From Jalapa Jackson wrote to his sister (22 April): "I am in better health than usual." Although he seems never to have realized it, he was always in better health when he was active, and particularly were aches and pains forgotten when he was on active service before the enemy.

But Jackson was left behind when Scott sent a division forty miles

2. No medals for bravery existed in the American army at this time. Commissioned officers who distinguished themselves in battle were awarded brevet ranks that were higher than their substantive ranks. Although they might at times serve in their brevet ranks when outside their regiment or corps, as on court-martial duty, a brevet was mostly a courtesy title by which officers were addressed socially. Regulations applying to brevets were so vague that there was much confusion over their proper use and the authority they carried.

beyond Jalapa to take the castle at Perote, where it captured some fifty cannon, twenty-five thousand rounds of artillery ammunition, and more than five hundred muskets. On 15 May Scott's advance forces entered Puebla de Zaragoza, 7,150 feet high and one of the oldest cities in Mexico. In the central plaza in front of the famous cathedral, boasting paintings attributed to Murillo and Velázquez, the ragged and travel-worn troops, many now shoeless, formed up to take formal possession of the town.

Scott was only seventy-five miles from Mexico City, but he was unable to press on. Not only was he short of supplies of all kinds, but the enlistment periods of his volunteers were running out, and only about a hundred out of thirty-seven hundred had agreed to reengage, leaving him in the heart of enemy territory with only seventy-one hundred effectives.

Scott now took the extraordinary step of drawing in his army and severing his line of communication. Forces large enough to cut through the guerrilla bands that roamed the land between his army and the sea could get through, but a regular supply line no longer existed. "Scott is lost," said the Duke of Wellington when he heard of this bold decision. "He has been carried away by his successes. He can't take the city and he can't fall back upon his base." Jackson, however, thought otherwise, and he wrote that the American army could live "as a flock of locusts would moving from point to point wherever supplies is [*sic*] to be had."

Second Lieutenant Jackson was right, and the Iron Duke was wrong.[3] Scott managed to bring forward reinforcements that raised his army to fourteen thousand (although twenty-five hundred were too sick to fight). Jackson feared that he was to have no active part in the glorious battles that lay ahead, for his promotion moved him from Captain Taylor's Company K with its light and mobile field guns to Company G, which was equipped with heavier, less maneuverable guns. Worse still, as he groaned in a letter to Laura, "I have the mortification of being left to garrison the town of Jalapa."

Jackson had entertained some hope of being allowed "to go forward as a dragoon officer or in some other capacity," but this was not to be. He confided to Laura: "I throw myself into the hands of an all wise God, and hope that it may yet be for the better. It may have been one of His means of diminishing my excessive ambition; and after

---

3. Wellington was later to eat his crow with sauce and to pronounce Scott's campaign in Mexico "the most brilliant in modern warfare."

having accomplished His purpose, whatever it may be, He then in his [*sic*] infinite wisdom may gratify my heart."

Still, there were pleasures to be found in Jalapa. The markets abounded in fruits and vegetables, the views of towering, snow-covered Citlaltépetl (called "Orezava" by Jackson) were unrivaled, and the town had its share of charming senoritas. On 25 May he wrote Laura: "I am in fine quarters and making rapid progress in the Spanish language and have an idea of making some lady acquaintances shortly." There was nothing serious, he assured her. "There are many pretty ladies here but you must not infer from this that you will have one of them for your sister-in-law for such is not my intention at present and not theirs I hope."

The twenty-three-year-old lieutenant was a close observer of his superiors. He thought General Scott "most vain and conceited," but also "by far the most talented and scientific." General Taylor, he opined, "is a plain, honest, sound minded straight-forwarded & un-desiring man (the noblest work of God)." He admired Taylor but con-sidered Scott the better general, a conclusion with which most histori-ans would agree.

That he was able to escape from delightful Jalapa to the, for him, greater delights of war was due to Scott's determination to improve his field artillery. This arm was the pride of the United States Army. Fif-teen years before the war, then Secretary of War Joel Poinsett had sent a board of officers to study European artillery and to bring back sam-ples of weapons for the Ordnance Department to test. The result was the creation of a family of artillery pieces that by the time the war with Mexico began had made American artillery probably the finest in the world. The basic fieldpiece was a bronze 6-pounder gun weighing 880 pounds with a range of 1,500 yards. A second bronze fieldpiece was the 12-pounder howitzer, weighing 1,757 pounds. A series of heavy siege guns had also been developed, but in Mexico it was the field artillery, and particularly the mobile 6-pounders, which were of the greatest value.

There were ten "companies" of artillery in each of the U.S. Army's four artillery regiments, but only one company in each was designated as light or "flying" artillery, highly mobile batteries similar to British horse artillery. Scott had been so impressed by Captain Ma-gruder's performance at Cerro Gordo that on 16 July he ordered four companies to be equipped and trained as "light (field) artillery." Natu-rally, one of these was Captain Magruder's Company I, 1st Artillery.

Magruder, called behind his back "Prince John," was a forty-year-old Virginian who had been graduated from the Military Academy fifteenth out of a class of forty-two in 1830. A bon vivant, a flamboyant character who did everything in the grand style, he was known for his elaborate courtesy, his extravagant hospitality, and his love of life's amenities. He was an exceptionally brave man as well, and a strict disciplinarian. Jackson resolved to join him. "I wanted to see active service," he wrote, "to be near the enemy in the fight; and when I heard that John Magruder had got his battery I bent all my energies to be with him, for I knew that if any fighting was to be done, Magruder would be 'on hand.' "

Jackson carried the day, and in the last week of July he jubilantly set out at once with a detachment of soldiers to join Company I. In a mountain pass near Puebla they were fallen upon by guerrillas and in a short, bloody fire fight killed four and captured three of their attackers. Jackson reported to Laura that he was happy to acquire "a beautiful sabre and some other equipment."

With reinforcements at hand, including a battalion of marines, Scott organized his army of ten to eleven thousand effectives into four divisions, and leaving behind his sick and wounded with a small garrison at Puebla, he lunged toward Mexico City. Magruder's battery was attached to the division commanded by Major General Gideon Johnson Pillow. The first division left Puebla on 7 August 1847, and Pillow's division left last on 10 August.

The route taken by the army wound through vast haciendas, past orchards and rich farmland, and up the Continental Divide. The uphill marching was rewarded by spectacular vistas. On their left loomed Popocatépetl, at 17,887 feet the second-highest mountain in Mexico, only 45 miles from their goal: Mexico City. After a three-day march the first troops reached the high ridge at the base of Popocatépetl, and the capital itself came into view, shimmering like a magical city in the distance. General Scott described it later as "the object of all our dreams and hopes—toils and dangers;—once the gorgeous seat of the Montezumas," and averred that "recovering from the trance into which the magnificent spectacle had thrown them, probably not a man in the column failed to say to his neighbor or himself, 'That splendid city will soon be ours!' " But as everyone knew, the task of reducing the city would not be easy; Santa Anna had amassed a force three times larger than Scott's, and there were many easily defended strongpoints.

Geography certainly favored the defenders. In the path of the invaders were lakes, marshes, and the huge Pedregal—an old lava bed, five miles across, filled with sharp lava rocks and laced with ravines—through which ran, unknown to Scott, no more than a few paths. Causeways crossed the marshes, but offering no room to maneuver, they were shooting galleries for the defenders.

Scott decided to swing his force on a wide arc south of Lake Chalco, moving northwest, keeping Lake Xochimilco on the army's right and the Pedregal on its left, and attack Mexico City from the south. In his path, near the villages of Contreras and Churubusco, lay two heavy concentrations of the enemy that effectively commanded the roads into the city. With only four days' rations left for his troops, Scott could not afford delay. Again he sent his engineers to reconnoiter, and Captain Lee and Lieutenant Beauregard discovered unmapped trails leading into the Mexican positions, including one through a corner of the Pedregal that could be widened sufficiently, though with great difficulty, for men and guns to be passed over it. Using these, Scott decided to attack both positions simultaneously. Although they were only seven miles apart, the distance was too great for them to provide mutual support.

The widened path through the Pedregal led past the main Mexican strongpoint, called the Padierna, just north of Contreras, and onto a main road to Mexico City. Once astride the road, the Americans would be behind the enemy's positions and between Contreras and the city. Pillow's division was ordered to take this route, and on 19 August it came upon a low ridge that overlooked the Padierna. Magruder's battery and a battery of howitzers under Captain Franklin D. Callender were ordered forward; Captain Lee and Second Lieutenant McClellan were waiting to guide them to their positions.

The last mile to the ridge was a difficult one for the guns: The lava road was execrable, and the cannoneers came under enemy fire. When Magruder's first section (two guns), commanded by First Lieutenant John Preston Johnstone (a nephew of Joseph E. Johnston's who spelled his name differently), came up, it was positioned on the reverse slope about nine hundred yards from the enemy. Although it was partially protected by a ledge of rocks, its position was precarious. When Callender's howitzers were in place, about two o'clock in the afternoon, the Americans opened fire. The Mexican response was a barrage from twenty-nine guns, some of which were heavy 18-pounders and 8-inch howitzers. Men and horses seemed to dissolve into bloody tangles. A ball from an 18-pounder tore off Lieutenant Johnstone's leg. He died in great agony that night.

In the midst of this bloody, unequal artillery duel, Magruder looked around for Jackson. He was nowhere in sight, and Magruder concluded that he was either wounded or dead. But Jackson was fighting his guns on Magruder's right, out of his line of sight. In his after-action report Magruder wrote: "In a few moments Lieutenant Jackson, commanding the second section of the battery, who had opened fire upon the enemy's works from a position on the right, hearing our fire still further in front, advanced in handsome style, and, being assigned by me to the post so gallantly filled by Lieutenant Johnstone, kept up the fire with great briskness and effect. His conduct was equally conspicuous during the whole day and I cannot too highly commend him. . . ." But no matter how briskly fired, Magruder's four little 6-inch guns could have little effect on the Mexican earthworks, and two engineer officers advised him to retire.

Magruder ordered a cease-fire and put his men under cover but held his position, for he knew that a brigade under Colonel Bennet Riley was moving across the Pedregal toward the highway, and he saw that he might be able to give some protection to its left flank. Brigadier General Persifor F. Smith, a Princeton lawyer from New Orleans who had recently distinguished himself at Monterrey, came up with his brigade under fire to protect the batteries. A second infantry brigade followed Riley's, and Smith, on his own initiative, decided to follow after, asking Magruder to recommence firing to cover his movements, an action that once again called down upon his guns the heavy metal of the Mexican batteries with further losses of horses and men.

General Pillow sent word to Magruder that he could retire if he thought his fire not very effective, but Brigadier General Franklin Pierce (the future president of the United States) arrived on the scene with the news that Riley's brigade was in trouble, so Magruder decided that he must stay where he was. He hoped he could hang on until nightfall. A rifle company came to his aid, and then, about ten o'clock that night, two regiments sent up by General Pierce arrived. Only then did Magruder retire his crippled battery "to a safe position for repairs."

During a rainy night Captain Lee led troops across the Pedregal and into positions from which they attacked at dawn. Led by Riley's brigade, the Americans drove the enemy from their positions and put them to flight.

The gallantry of Magruder and his men did not go unnoticed. General Twiggs spoke of "the coolness and determination evinced by the officers and men whilst under this hot fire." General Pillow wrote of "their great gallantry and daring, the proof of which is found in their losses, and in the fact that both of their batteries were much cut up by the terrible fire of the enemy's heavy guns."

In his after-action report Magruder wrote: "From 2 o'clock, P.M., until 11 at night, this battery of 6-pounders held a position within grapeshot of the enemy's entrenchments . . . and I can attribute my comparatively small loss in men and horses only to the extraordinary precautions taken by the officers to afford them cover, for which the ground was favorable, although it was otherwise for the battery." He lauded the mortally wounded Johnstone, and of Jackson he wrote: "[H]is conduct was equally conspicuous throughout the whole day, and I cannot too highly commend him to the major general's favorable consideration."

On the same day the Mexican position in a fortified convent at Churubusco was successfully assaulted. Among its defenders was a unit of the San Patricio Battalion, made up of about eighty Irishmen, deserters from the American army whose desperation was enhanced by the thought that a noose around the neck rather than a parole was likely to be their fate if captured. The Churubusco survivors retreated into the inner defenses of Mexico City. Some were pursued almost to the city gates by two bold dragoons who failed to hear the order to halt: First Lieutenant Richard Stoddert Ewell, an 1840 graduate of the Military Academy, and Captain Philip Kearny, whose left arm was so mangled by grapeshot in this affair that it had to be amputated. Ewell burned with a special fury: His younger brother had been mortally wounded at Cerro Gordo.

The Mexicans lost 4,297 in killed and wounded (Scott's estimate), 2,637 were taken prisoner, including 69 of the San Patricio deserters; perhaps 3,000 were missing. American losses were 137 killed, 877 wounded, and 38 missing. Santa Anna had lost about a third of his army; Scott about one-seventh of his.

Scott now put forward peace proposals. His men were close to exhaustion; his food supply was low; he had a large number of sick and wounded to be cared for as well as a great number of prisoners of war. Santa Anna was happy to negotiate, for it gave him time to rally his dispirited men, bring in fresh troops from the north, and renew the confidence of the public in his efforts.

On 8 September, hearing that the enemy was making bronze cannon at a place called Molino del Rey, a former gun foundry and old fort west of the Churubusco battlefield, and realizing that although willing enough to parley, the Mexicans had no intention of ending the war, Scott sent Major General William J. Worth, an old Indian fighter, with some three thousand troops to capture the place. Worth's plan was respectable and deserved to succeed, but it failed in its execution. His five-hundred-man forlorn hope (storming party) was badly shot up and fell back to watch helplessly as the Mexicans came out of their defenses to murder the American wounded left on the ground.

When cavalry threatened Worth's left flank, Magruder's battery was whistled up. It came into position at a gallop, swung into action, and Jackson, acting now as the company's first lieutenant, directed the guns on the horses. Unable to stomach the artillery fire, the Mexican cavalry fell back.

The Battle of Molino del Rey lasted only two hours. Worth's force eventually prevailed, but Scott had blundered. The attack was an expensive effort, too expensive: It left 116 dead and 671 wounded, many severely. Even worse, it was a useless effort, for no gun-making operations were taking place. Scott's force was now reduced to fewer than 7,500 effectives.

The huge castle of Chapultepec, rising two hundred feet above a marsh, was now the only major strongpoint outside the city, but with walls about three-quarters of a mile long and a quarter mile wide, it was a formidable obstacle. Enclosed within it was the Mexican Military Academy.

On the evening of 11 September Scott called a meeting of his senior officers and his engineers to discuss a plan for an attack on the castle. It was a gloomy meeting. Captain Lee argued strongly for an attack from the south; Lieutenant Beauregard argued to even greater effect for an attack from the west, to which Scott finally agreed. Worth declared privately, "We shall be defeated," and even Scott was heard to mumble, "I have my misgivings." Still, plans for the assault were laid, forlorn hopes selected, and a dawn bombardment was planned. Scott entertained hopes that he could reduce Chapultepec by artillery fire alone, and at five o'clock on the morning of 12 September the Americans began a day-long bombardment. Holes were breached in the castle's walls, and the roof was partly destroyed, but the Mexican troops, including young cadets from the military college, stoutly refused to surrender. Even so, unknown to Scott, Mexican morale had been badly shaken by the long bombardment.

On this day Magruder's battery drove off threatening Mexican cavalry hovering on the American flank. Scott's attack was scheduled for the next day, the thirteenth. It was a beautiful day, and under a clear blue sky the cannon thundered and the Americans launched their attack. The 11th and 14th Infantry and Jackson's section of 6-pounders, all under the command of Colonel William Trousdale, were sent along a causeway on the northern flank of the castle. Jackson, eager for action and delighted to have an independent command, rashly dashed ahead and outdistanced the supporting infantry. Although he soon found himself under fire both from musketry on the walls and from an entrenched battery in his front, he pressed on until he found his way blocked by a ditch. He and his men, working desperately, manhandled one gun across and put it into battery, but men and horses were falling fast, and some cannoneers dropped their work to seek shelter behind rocks and an embankment. In a futile effort to rally them, Jackson paced back and forth through the fire, calling, "See, there is no danger. I am not hit!"[4]

For a time he and a sergeant manned the only gun that had been put in action across the ditch. Then Magruder came up, losing his horse to musketry on the way; the second gun was manhandled across the ditch and put into action; and the Mexican artillery was at last silenced.

In spite of the fears of the senior officers and the stout resistance of the Mexicans, the attack went much as planned. The infantry was briefly delayed while waiting for the scaling ladders to come up, but the castle was carried with great élan. The Americans, remembering the slaughter of their wounded at Molino del Rey, showed their foe little mercy. Six young Mexican cadets chose to die rather than surrender, and one, clutching the Mexican flag, threw himself from the wall.[5]

On a small hillock below Chapultepec twenty-nine of the sixty-nine members of the San Patricio Battalion who had been captured at Churubusco stood on mule carts with nooses around their necks. A thirtieth, who could not stand because he had lost his legs in that battle, sat. At the unfurling of the Stars and Stripes from the castle walls, the

4. Jackson was later to aver that this was the only falsehood he ever willfully told.

5. The legend of the young cadets—Los Niños Heroicos or Los Niños Perdidos—has been much embellished in Mexican history, and the heroic children have been memorialized in song, story, paintings, and an impressive monument which can be seen today at the foot of Chapultepec. In March 1947 Harry S. Truman, against the advice of all his advisers, placed a wreath on the monument, creating more goodwill among Mexicans than any other American president before or since.

mules were whipped forward, and the thirty were left swinging from their gibbets.[6]

With Chapultepec taken, swarms of Mexicans fled toward the capital itself, clogging the causeway. Jackson's guns fired again and again into their massed, demoralized ranks. Some of his shots, he knew, must have penetrated the city. Seven years later, when asked by his sister-in-law if he felt any qualms about this slaughter of fleeing soldiers and perhaps civilians, Jackson seemed surprised. "None whatever," he replied. "What business had I with results? My duty was to obey orders."

The victorious Americans closely pursued the fleeing Mexican soldiery, dashing down the causeway and tumbling into Mexico City. By the end of the day they occupied both its northwest and the southwest corners. During the night Santa Anna, who had lost fourteen hundred men, quickly evacuated the capital. The following morning saw some sporadic fighting, but by noon Scott was able to ride triumphantly into the Plaza de Armas to be greeted by the cheers of what was left of his army.

In his after-action report Captain Magruder was again full of praise for Jackson: "If devotion, industry, talent and gallantry are the highest qualities of a soldier, then he is entitled to the distinction which their possession confers. I have been ably seconded in all the operations of the battery by him; and upon this occasion, when circumstances placed him in command, for a short time, of an independent section, he proved himself eminently worthy of it."[7] Generals Worth, Pillow, and even Scott himself mentioned Jackson in the most flattering terms in their dispatches. Worth spoke of "the gallant Lt. Jackson, who, although he lost most of his horses and many of his men, continued chivalrously at his post, combatting with noble courage." Pillow twice referred to the "brave Lieutenant Jackson" in his report. Scott mentioned him twice. Jackson happily reported to Laura that he was "proud of the source from which such praise comes."

6. Scott was reluctant to hang all of the captured San Patricio deserters, but he believed that he could not show leniency to those who had deserted and then taken up arms against their fellow countrymen, so he decided to hang only those who had deserted during the war. The fate of the remaining St. Patrick's warriors, however, was not enviable. They were whipped and imprisoned; some were branded. There was a need to set an example, for the desertion rate was exceptionally high: 9,207 deserted.

7. This report was addressed to Captain (later Major General) Joseph Hooker, then serving as General Pillow's assistant adjutant general.

Jackson had every right to feel proud of himself. Six weeks after Chapultepec he wrote Laura:

> I have been exposed to many dangers in the battles of this valley but have escaped unhurt. I was once reported killed and nothing but the strong and powerful hand of Almighty God could have brought me through unhurt. Imagine, for instance, my situation at Chapultepec, within full range, and in a road which was swept with grape and canister, and at the same time thousands of muskets from the castle itself above pouring down like hail upon you.

He had indeed been both valiant and fortunate.

5

☆ ☆ ☆ ☆ ☆ ☆ ☆ ☆ ☆ ☆ ☆ ☆ ☆ ☆

At Peace
in Mexico

With the fall of Mexico City serious fighting came to an end. Although there was still some guerrilla activity in the countryside and some sniping and considerable disorder in Mexico City—Santa Anna had turned loose some two thousand convicts before leaving—Scott quickly established law and order. So successful was he that a number of prominent Mexicans who favored the annexation of Mexico by the United States begged him to resign from the American army and issue a pronunciamento that he was assuming the dictatorship of the country for six years. As about 70 percent of his troops were volunteers who could be discharged in Mexico, it was believed that he could, by offering a pay raise, retain a sizable American force. Scott toyed with the idea and was flattered to be asked, but he never seriously considered it.

On 20 September the wounded were brought into the city's hospitals, and Jackson dutifully visited those from his company. Writing to Laura, he confessed: "I can hardly open my eyes after entering a hospital, the atmosphere of which is generally so vitiated as to make the healthy sick. I would not live in one a week, under the circumstances in which I have seen them, for the whole of Mexico. . . . To die on the battlefield is relief when compared to the death of a contaminated hospital."[1]

1. Ether was used by the army as an anesthetic for the first time in this war, although it appears not to have been widely used.

But such horrors were soon put behind by the survivors. General Scott, ensconced in the National Palace, well knew how to play the role of the conqueror in the halls of Montezuma. Officers unpacked their best uniforms to attend his military-social levees. At the first of these he stood at the door, affably shaking each officer's hand, but when Jackson's turn came, he drew himself up to his full six feet five inches, thrust his hands behind his back, and sternly declared: "I don't know that I shall shake hands with Mr. Jackson."

The room went silent, and Jackson stood abashed. But a broad smile creased the general's face. "If you can forgive yourself for the way you slaughtered all those Mexicans, I'm not sure that I can," he boomed as he clasped the hand of the vastly relieved young officer.

Jackson was now an acknowledged hero; from the commander-in-chief down, everyone was well acquainted with his deeds. For gallantry and meritorious conduct at Contreras Jackson was given the brevet of captain and a substantive promotion to first lieutenant, both to date from 20 August. For his gallantry and meritorious service at Chapultepec he was breveted major as of 13 September. It was a spectacular rise, from brevet second lieutenant to substantive first lieutenant and brevet major within six months. It was, however, some months before he was notified of his brevets.

In his new substantive rank he was transferred back to Captain Taylor's Company K, then part of Persifor F. Smith's brigade. Smith, now a major general, having been promoted for his services at Contreras and Churubusco, had been appointed by Scott to be governor of Mexico City. In the newfound leisure of peace Jackson discovered that he had ample time to enjoy the many diversions which this city of 180,000 inhabitants offered and to frequent places "of fashionable resort." The country boy from rural western Virginia had proved himself in battle and won praise, honor, and promotion. The twenty-three-year-old hero now wished to cut a figure in society. Like many another young man, he began by buying an expensive horse. Laura chided him, but he was unrepentant and replied (28 February 1848): "You speak of my fine horse as being in your opinion rather extravagant, but if an officer wishes to appear best he should appear well in everything. I bought the horse, having plenty of money and need of him, and I have since been offered three hundred and fifty dollars for him; that is one hundred and seventy more than I gave, and I can at any time get more than I gave."

There existed a complex pay structure for army officers, the amount depending not only on rank but also on the particular duties they performed. Jackson's pay while with Magruder had been $104 a month. Although with Taylor's battery he was only earning "about ninety," he expected soon to make more. He assured Laura, "I have plenty of money, and am in the long run economical, although it would not appear so to you, as here everything is dear and with you cheap. I dress as a gentleman should who wishes to be received as such. I do not gamble, nor spend my money, as I think, foolishly."

In a letter to Laura on 23 March 1848 he wrote: "The morning hours I occupy in studies and business, and the evenings in a similar manner, but generally taking a walk after dinner, and sometimes a ride on the Paseo or elsewhere in the evening." The Paseo, he informed her, was "a wide road in the southwest of the city about a half mile in length, with a beautiful fountain in the center, and is a place of fashionable resort. Families of wealth appear there in their carriages at sunset, partly if not entirely for show. There is also a place of morning resort between the city and the Paseo called the Almeda [*sic*], which is a beautiful grove of about four hundred by six hundred yards and containing, I think [,] eight fountains. . . . I propose on riding to both of these places this evening hoping to see something more attractive than at home."

He resumed his Spanish studies, but there were difficulties. For some time the only Spanish grammar he could find was in Latin, of which he knew little, but even the acquisition of one in English failed to smooth his way.[2] A "Spanish gentleman" coached him a bit, and he boasted to Laura that he was reading in Spanish Lord Chesterfield's letters to his son. But he never mastered the language. A short letter in Spanish that he wrote to Laura a few years later was a schoolboyish effort. Still, it always seemed a romantic language to him, a language for lovers.

There is no doubt that he was dazzled by the young Mexican women he met. In Mexico City, he rhapsodized, are "to be found mirth, beauty, fine manners, variety, and in fine all that man can reasonably want." He had not been there six weeks before he was writing Laura: "As I believe that this country is destined to be reformed by ours, I think that probably I shall spend many years here and (though I have not yet) to make my life more natural by sharing it with some amiable Senorita. . . ." Whether he wrote with someone specifically in

2. In the remains of Jackson's library there are two Spanish grammars: one in Latin, published in 1838, and a dog-eared one in English by Mariano Cubi I Solar, published in 1840. On the flyleaf of the latter is the notation "Thomas J. Jackson, $3.50."

mind "to make his life more natural," or whether he was simply in love with love, or whether he boyishly wanted to tease his sister will probably never be known. It seems probable that a mixture of all three prompted his remarks, although his second wife was later to say that "he came very near losing his heart in Mexico."

Laura fretted over his letter until he wrote: "Do not allow my words about marrying in Mexico to disturb you. I have sometimes thought of staying here, and again of going home. I have no tie in the country equal to you."

Jackson was not alone in his admiration of Mexican women. Lieutenant A. P. Hill, also in Mexico with the 1st Artillery, playfully warned his father that he might return with a Mexican bride. "The ladies of Mexico *are* so beautiful," he declared.

The young officer with "plenty of money" and the $180 horse made a number of Mexican male friends, and they appear to have introduced him to a life of ease such as he had never known. For a time he seems to have shared the quarters of theological students, where, to his delight, servants woke him each morning with spiced cakes and chocolate. He described his day in a letter to Laura: After dressing and briefly attending to military affairs, he rode back to his quarters for a breakfast of meat, fruit, and coffee. He seems to have spent little time on military duties and much time larking with his new friends or wandering around the city. Evenings he was sometimes invited to balls, where he learned to polka and to waltz.

On 23 March he proudly wrote to Laura:

> Among the families which I visit are some of the first in the republic, as Don Lucas Alleman, Martinez del Rio and I also have the acquaintance of others of some distinction.[3] My studies are now principally directed to the formation of my manners and the rules of society and the more thorough knowledge of human nature. . . . [T]his country offers me greater advantages for acquiring graces than I will probably ever meet with again unless I should

3. Don Lucas Alamán (the correct spelling) was indeed a man of great culture and learning. He had lived in Europe, had served in the Spanish Cortes, and had been Mexico's minister of foreign relations under Santa Anna. He was the author of two noted books on Mexican history, the organizer of the government archives, and the founder of the National Museum. He was, however, an odd acquaintance for an American officer, for he was opposed to democracy, and he is generally credited as being the man most responsible for the hostility of Mexicans toward Americans in this era. Dr. Martínez del Rio was another distinguished Mexican, a physician educated in France and England with broad interests outside Mexico.

visit Europe. . . . Owing to my knowledge of the language of the country, and the acquaintances I have made, I think I pass my time more agreeably than the greater portion of the officers of the army. . . .

Although he wrote faithfully to Laura and at times to aunts, uncles, and cousins, he could not keep a journal. "I can not find the time," he told Laura, who had urged him to do so, "as although I am usually up at six o'clock and retire to bed at ten and eleven, still the day is not long enough. . . ."

A number of officers founded, on 13 October 1847, the Aztec Club, which met in the home of Senor Boca Negro, onetime Mexican minister to the United States, but Jackson chose not to become a member, preferring to find his social life in the civilian community.

A group of young officers that included Ulysses S. Grant and other future Civil War generals clubbed together to climb Popocatépetl, but Jackson, ever conscious of threats to his health, declined to join them. In his letters to Laura he made frequent mention of the climate and its dangers. The thin air of the capital, he told her, "seems to penetrate the pores in a moment, and a cold may be the consequence and a speedy death the final result. . . ." In spite of such alarms, however, he seems to have enjoyed splendid health.

These months in Mexico after the fighting stopped were always numbered as among the happiest in his life, truly halcyon days. He was kept informed of events back in western Virginia, where Uncle Cummins and Minter Bailey were in the courts still filing affidavits and wrangling over his accounts as constable. Although Jackson was still interested in the events in western Virginia, they seemed far away, and nothing was able to diminish his delight in Mexico City.

With time on their hands, the generals turned to quarreling over who had performed what services and who deserved the greater credit for the victories. General Worth preferred charges against General Scott; Scott had Worth arrested and prepared court-martial papers against him and the chief troublemaker, General Gideon J. Pillow. It was all most unseemly. Five months after Scott had entered Mexico City in triumph, President Polk relieved him of his command and ordered him home. "Turned out as an old horse to die," noted Robert E. Lee sadly.[4] In his letters, Jackson briefly mentioned the quarrels

4. Scott did not die, however, and he did not long remain out to pasture. He was greeted as a hero on his return, and Congress authorized a special gold medal for him.

among his superiors, but they seem to have been of little interest to him.

Although at odds with the president and with his generals, Scott was still a hero to most of the younger officers and to many of the troops. First Lieutenant William Wilkins described his departure from Mexico City: "Gray haired officers and rugged soldiers wept when they parted from their General, and a host of officers followed him to the Penon to obtain word from, or to exchange one look with their hero and their idol."

Not only generals bickered. Less exalted officers began to get on each other's nerves. Some, less enchanted than Jackson with Mexico City, found reasons to grumble. "There is nothing more demoralizing to a large body of men than the idle occupation of a large and luxurious capital," wrote one. The most common vice, indulged in by Americans and Mexicans alike, was gambling. Sam Grant, in a letter to his fiancée, blamed the Mexicans: "All gamble, priests and civilians, male and female, and particularly on Sundays."

The gallant Magruder, who had won two brevets in the war, lashed out at General Franklin Pierce one night over a card table and threatened a duel. D. H. Hill later claimed that Jackson had carried Magruder's challenge to Pierce, but this seems unlikely; in any case no duel was ever fought.

For reasons unknown but sufficient to them, First Lieutenant Daniel Smith Lee, adjutant of the 11th Infantry,[5] and First Lieutenant and Brevet Captain Benjamin Franklin Harley from Philadelphia, also in the 11th Infantry, quarreled so bitterly that Lee challenged Harley to a duel and asked Jackson and Second Lieutenant Birkett Fry, Jackson's former classmate—both from Virginia west of the Blue Ridge, as was Lee—to act as his seconds. Since Lee was the challenger, Harley had his choice of weapons. An expert rifle shot and, it was said, an experienced duelist, he chose "Mississippi rifles" at forty paces.[6]

Ironically President Polk, his would-be nemesis, had to make the presentation. When the Civil War began, Scott, seventy-five years old and grown obese, was still at the helm of the American army.

5. Daniel Smith Lee, a graduate of the Virginia Military Institute (class of 1845), wrote a series of letters during the war to a Lexington, Virginia, newspaper extolling his own exploits. He was wounded six times, though never seriously. He later became adjutant general of Iowa and the U.S. consul in Basle, Switzerland.

6. "Mississippi rifle" was the name given to the standard United States rifle, Model 1841, caliber .54. The original models, used in the duel, fired a half-ounce ball wrapped in leather or in tallow-soaked cloth. In the 1850s many of these rifles were

Fry is the only participant to have left a full account of the affair, but according to Captain James Jay Archer, who witnessed the scene, Jackson, intent upon seeing everything done properly, "instructed the principals as if he were drilling an awkward squad." At the command to fire, rifles cracked, but both men were left standing. Jackson turned to Fry and asked, "What shall we do now? They will demand another shot."

"We will grant it with pistols at ten paces," Fry replied.

Harley's seconds did indeed demand a second shot, but as this made Harley the challenger, Lee had the choice of weapons. When Jackson announced the new choice, Harley wisely withdrew, and the affair ended.

It was while he was in Mexico, and probably before the capture of Mexico City, that Jackson began the serious study of what was to be a growing preoccupation. Although he had always considered himself a Christian, he had never been baptized and was still a member of no church. Captain Taylor, the commander of Company K, 1st Artillery, and a devout Episcopalian, urged him to study the Bible and to think more about his soul. Impressed with his fervor, Jackson took his injunctions to heart and began to read the Bible in the same thorough manner he had studied Professor Bartlett's textbook on optics.

In February 1848 Laura wrote pathetically of being so ill that "I may not live to receive your answer." Jackson replied immediately:

> I hope that these words imply nothing beyond what they literally state. This is the earnest prayer to God of your brother. But if He in His great wisdom has afflicted you with disease incurable, then may He in His infinite goodness receive you into His heavenly abode, where though I should be deprived of you here in this world of cares, yet I should hope to meet with you in a land where care and sorrow are unknown: there with a mother, a brother, a sister and yourself, and I hope, a father, to live in a state of felicity, uncontaminated by mortality. . . .[7]

---

rebored to take the .58 caliber "Minie [*sic*] ball," which, in spite of its name (universally mispronounced *minnie*), was not a ball but a hollow conical bullet which expanded when fired to take the rifling. Designed by Claude Étienne Minié, a French army captain, it first appeared in the United States in 1849 and was readily adopted, for its use greatly improved the rifle's accuracy, range, and rate of fire.

7. Jackson's uncertainty as to his father's presence in heaven clearly indicates that he was well aware of his father's ethical shortcomings.

Full of religious zeal, he investigated Catholicism. He requested and was granted an interview with sixty-three-year-old Cuban-born Archbishop Juan Manuel Irisarri y Peralta, the interim head of the diocese and one of the leading men of the city. When the Americans were at the city gates, it was he who had issued a pastoral urging resistance to the invaders, and he had personally protested to Scott the use of church property by the occupying troops. He must have been perplexed, perhaps interested and amused, by this earnest young American officer who came asking him to explain his religion, for the two apparently had more than one conversation. Unfortunately neither left a record of their talks, but Jackson was never—unlike many Protestants in this era—anti-Catholic.

On 2 February 1848 the Treaty of Guadalupe Hidalgo was signed, establishing a boundary between the two countries running westward along the Rio Grande to the southern boundary of New Mexico, then along the Gila River to the Gulf of California and west to the Pacific just south of San Diego. The United States agreed to assume the debts the Mexican government owed its citizens and to pay fifteen million dollars for the ceded territory—in all, about twenty-five million dollars. Thus were acquired 529,017 square miles of land for a cost of forty-nine cents per acre. The treaty was not ratified until 4 July, but by mid-June the American troops had evacuated Mexico City; by 2 August all had embarked at Veracruz and sailed for home.

It had been a costly war. Of the 104,556 American soldiers and marines, regulars and volunteers, who had served in Mexico, only 1,721 had been killed in action or had died of wounds, but 4,102 had been wounded, some grievously, and 11,155 had died of diseases, of accidents, of unknown causes or had been executed.

Although most of the officers and men were volunteers with little or no training as soldiers, and none of the generals was a graduate of the Military Academy, West Point graduates, particularly company-grade officers, some of whom had spent more than twenty years in the service, had played significant roles. Scott said: "I give it as my fixed opinion that but for our graduated cadets, the war between the United States and Mexico might, and probably would, have lasted some four or five years, within its first half, more defeats than victories falling to our share." Many of these junior officers were to achieve high rank and find fame on one side or the other in the Civil War.

Of the combatants in Jackson's class, only two died in battle, Colville J. Minor at Monterey, California, and Alexander P. Rogers, who fell while with a forlorn hope at Chapultepec. One classmate, Archibald Botts, who had slumbered so peacefully through the gradua- tion celebration in New York, died of disease, and two others were wounded. The class of 1844 was to suffer proportionately more battle deaths than any West Point Class in history.[8] Many West Pointers won brevets for their bravery in Mexico, and none deserted, although, in spite of the dreadful punishments awaiting them if caught, 9,207 other soldiers did desert, an astonishingly high incidence.

Jackson left Mexico City, probably on or about 12 June, and arrived on the coast on 8 July. Two days later he boarded the *Mary Kingsland* along with 11 other officers and 102 men of the 1st Artillery, 73 men of the 9th Infantry, and 73 horses. They sailed that same day and docked on 17 July in New Orleans, where they discovered the *Arkansas,* which had carried them to Veracruz, waiting to embark the artillerymen and sail to Governors Island in New York Harbor. There was little time to sample the pleasures of the city, but like many an- other, Jackson found time to pose for a daguerreotype.

Many soldiers return from war adorned with mustaches or beards, visual evidence that they have changed, demonstrating that after all they have seen and experienced, they are no longer the same youths who left for the war. So it was with Jackson. He had grown a beard. The good living of Mexico City had added a bit more flesh to face and form, and he was particularly pleased with the likeness. He sent it to Laura, asking her to "keep safely as I prize it highly."

On 16 August 1848 the *Arkansas* docked in New York, and Jackson immediately reported for duty at Fort Columbus. Curiously, he waited ten days before writing to Laura to announce his arrival. Perhaps he was waiting to see where he would be stationed. On 26 August, when he finally wrote, he had still not been notified, but he was aware that wherever he went, there would be no more rapid promotions or new brevet ranks. On 6 July 1848 the adjutant general had reported that the regular army consisted of 8,866 regulars, of whom 7,500 were effective. That same day President Polk concluded that no permanent increase in the size of the army was necessary, and the Congress agreed.

---

8. By the end of the Civil War 13.6 percent of Jackson's class had died on the battlefield. (Two were killed fighting Indians in the Far West.) Of the unfortunate class of 1844, 28 percent died in battle, the highest percentage of battle deaths suffered by any class before or since. For comparison, in this century the class of 1942 suffered 46 battle deaths (all in World War II) out of 374, or 12.3 percent deaths in battle.

The war was indeed over. There would be no more amiable senoritas, no more riding his $180 horse at sunset on the Paseo, or waltzing in the halls of Montezuma. No more honor to be won and, in the foreseeable future, no prospect of promotion.

6

☆ ☆ ☆ ☆ ☆ ☆ ☆ ☆ ☆ ☆ ☆ ☆ ☆ ☆

Garrison Duty

Jackson had been put in temporary command of Company K in New Orleans, but this assignment ended five days after landing, when Captain Taylor resumed command. On 13 August 1848, thirteen days after his return to New York, he was ordered to report to Carlisle Barracks, Pennsylvania, to serve on a general court-martial. This duty lasted about a month. He found the work congenial and the social life agreeable. Carlisle may have lacked the romantic air of Mexico City, but as he wrote to Laura on 5 September, "there has been a soirée almost every day since my arrival, and at which I have enjoyed myself well."

When his court-martial duty ended, he requested three months' leave. As soon as it was granted, he made all haste to western Virginia, first to Beverly to see Laura and her family, enlarged now by a second child. His valorous conduct in Mexico was common knowledge, and he must have had the agreeable experience of being greeted as a returning hero. December found him at Jackson's Mill. It was a sad time, for his uncle Edward had died only a month earlier. Although he could not know it, this was to be the last time he would see his uncle Cummins.

The discovery of gold in California had been first reported in the *New York Herald* on 19 August 1848. By the following year Uncle Cummins, like thousands of others, had caught the gold fever. Bold men were making fortunes in California, and thirty-six-year-old Cummins

Jackson, not a man to be left behind, led a group of his friends and neighbors to the goldfields. It was a fatal venture, for shortly after the party reached Shasta County, he was struck down by typhoid fever. He died on 4 December 1849. Seven months later, when his death was confirmed, Jackson wrote to Laura (6 July 1850): "I have recently received a letter from Uncle John White and Aunt Catherine. . . . Uncle had recently received a letter from our cousin in California saying that Uncle Cummins is undoubtedly dead. This is news that goes to my heart. Uncle was like a father to me."

It was probably at the end of his leave that Jackson stopped off for a day or two in Richmond and called on his friend John Carlile, then a thirty-one-year-old state senator. Jackson told Laura that he regarded him as "one of the promising sons of Virginia." Carlile, who had been born in Winchester and had practiced law in Beverly and Clarksburg, was more than once to extend a hand to Jackson. On this occasion Jackson noted with satisfaction that Carlile "allowed no opportunity to pass unimproved in which he could manifest his kindness." Three years later Carlile befriended him by enabling him to take one of the most important steps in his career; ten years later the two found themselves enemies, their loyalties given to opposite sides in the war.[1]

His leave over, Jackson reported to Fort Hamilton, his home for the next two years. The fort, he wrote, "is on Long Island, about ten miles below the city of New York, and on the east bank of the Hudson river." Its construction had began in 1814, and in the succeeding forty-five years it had been added to and improved. In the five years preceding the Mexican War Captain Robert E. Lee had been in charge of repairing and developing both Fort Hamilton and nearby Fort Diamond (later renamed Fort Lafayette), duty he had found dull and uninteresting. In 1848, when Jackson arrived, Fort Hamilton was a massive quadrangular structure of gray granite with fourteen casemates and twenty-six barbettes. Mounting heavy 32-pounders and even some guns of larger caliber, it was prepared to defend itself from attack by land or from the channel.

Just outside the fort's walls lay a pleasant community known as the Narrows, a part of New Utrecht (since absorbed by Brooklyn). It boasted a large hotel popular with New Yorkers, who repaired to it in

---

1. John Snyder Carlile was a strong Unionist who faithfully represented the pro-Union sentiments of his constituents in western Virginia at the secession convention of 1861. He was then instrumental in the formation of the new state of West Virginia and was one of the new state's first senators.

summer to escape the heat of the city. As an eligible young bachelor Jackson found himself much in demand. "I have a delightful station and hope to pass a pleasant summer," he wrote in the spring of 1850. Basking in the company of a flock of pretty young women, he thoroughly enjoyed himself, hampered only by what he considered the precarious state of his health.

Routine garrison duties filled his days. For brief periods he served as company commander and often as company quartermaster and commissary, duties he seemed to enjoy, for he had developed a taste for business. He was called frequently to serve on courts-martial, and although he served at Plattsburg Barracks, West Point, and Fort Ontario (near Oswego), Carlisle Barracks remained his favorite post. On 3 December 1849 he wrote to Laura: "I returned a few days since from Carlisle, where I had a pleasant week among its amiable and I might say lovely ladies. This is my third trip there on courts martial." At West Point he waxed nostalgic over the "many pleasant and agreeable associations of my youth." Unlike most officers, he did not find courts-martial assignments onerous, for like his Uncle Cummins, he had a taste for litigation.

After he obtained his brevets, courts-martial were also profitable, for he received the pay and allowances of his brevet rank. He needed the extra money, for his financial position at this time was not entirely satisfactory. On 24 April 1850 he wrote to an uncle that "my pecuniary affairs are so [*embarrassed* was written and then crossed out] arranged that I have not ten dollars which I can call my own."

In December 1848 he had received word of his promotion to first lieutenant and brevet captain. The latter was a disappointment; he felt he deserved more. On 2 February 1849 he wrote to former Congressman Samuel L. Hays—"my best friend," he called him—to remind him that "the list of brevets is now being made out, and from what you intimated to me, and from the information received since, and the strong grounds on which I have been presented, I have but little or no doubt but that I shall be advanced; provided my claims should be presented to the Secretary of War. . . ." He feared, though, that "the case may [,] from forgetfulness, not be brought to his consideration at this time." He need not have worried. The following June he was informed of his brevet majority.

It was during this period that Jackson became engrossed in the two absorbing interests which were to engage his attention for the remainder of his life: religion and his health. The trip back to New York from his first leave after the war had been arduous. The winter had been a cold one, and the roads in the mountains of western Virginia were execrable. He arrived at Fort Hamilton suffering from rheumatism, which, he complained to Laura, he had acquired in her "salubrious mountain air." In March he was complaining of pain in his right side, but he assured Laura that he was being cared for by "one of the first medical men of New York City." By April he had improved and "commenced visiting more frequently, and every few evenings received an invitation to some social party," although he had frequently to make his regrets, he told Laura, for his lack of strength limited his activities.

Absorption in his ailments did not prevent him from determining to improve his mind. He intended, he declared, to be a "hard student." To Congressman Hays he wrote that he proposed "to make myself not only acquainted with Military art and science; but with politics, and of course, I must be well versed in history. My historical studies I have arranged in the following order: first a general history, ancient and modern, and then, special histories of important events, countries, etc. I have commenced with Rollins Ancient History, and I have read about one-fourth of it; reading from forty to fifty pages per day." This was before he developed problems with his eyes.

In June he complained that he "could not look long at objects through the window" and that opening his eyes out of doors was painful. The flame of a candle he found so unbearable that he was "reduced to the necessity of masking my looking glass on account of its reflection." Physicians he consulted told him to use his eyes as little as possible and advised against the use of spectacles.

When Laura informed him that she, too, was having eye troubles, he undertook to advise her:

> I feel much concern about your eyes, for fear that you will strain them. Remember that the best physicians are opposed to straining that important organ; and when it fails, or begins to fail, naturally, they recommend spectacles. But this should be the last resort, and should only be used when necessary. For instance, some persons can walk about out-of-doors and indoors without the light hurting their eyes, but must use the auxiliary in reading.
>
> The great objection to spectacles is that when their use is once commenced, it must be generally continued through life. A person in purchasing a pair should select the lowest number which will answer the proposed end; and then, as circumstances require, increase it. But I would advise you not to use them as long as you can do without them at the same time avoiding pain.

Cholera swept through New York City that summer, but Jackson professed himself unconcerned. "Those who keep their systems in healthy state have little to fear," he wrote. Dyspepsia tormented him, and he resorted to a variety of diets and exercises. He described his regimen in some detail to Laura:

> I have so strictly adhered to my wholesome diet of stale bread and plainly dressed meat (having nothing on it but salt) that I prefer it now to almost anything else. The other evening I tasted a piece of bread with butter on it, and then bread without it, and rather give my preference to the unbuttered bread; and hence I may never taste any more of this once much relished seasoning. And I think if you would adopt for your breakfast a cup of moderately strong black tea, stale wheat bread (wheat bread raised, and not less than twenty-four hours old), fresh meat—broiled or roasted is best—the yolk of one or two eggs—the white is hardly worth eating as it requires digestion and affords but little nutrition. For dinner the same kind of bread and meat, one vegetable only, say peas, beans or this year's potatoes, and for drink, plain water. For tea, the same kind of bread and drink as for breakfast, and nothing else, unless you choose a little butter. The great beauty of the foregoing is that it furnishes all the nutrition which food can give, and at the same time does not interfere in the digestive process like other substances, salt meats, cabbage, lettuce, desserts such as pies, preserves, nuts and all kinds of sweetmeats. Of what I have recommended, you can eat as much as your appetite craves, provided that you take regular meals and plenty of exercise, say, not less than three hours per day.

He became obsessed with his diets. He did not refuse invitations, but as a friend once said, "Fancy suppers disagreed with him," so regardless of the formality of the occasion, he carried his own food to balls and banquets and munched his stale bread and washed it down with water, undeterred by the splendid dishes and fine wines surrounding him.

He poured forth advice to Laura, instructing her that green tea and coffee were injurious to her health, that fruit should be eaten only when fully ripe and then only in the forenoon, and that she ought to be in her bed by eleven at night. Jackson himself went to bed early, leaving every social engagement when tattoo sounded. When the playful daughters of Judge Charles W. Church once tried to trick him into overstaying by deliberately prolonging a card game, they were nonplussed when he laid down his cards on the hour and firmly said his farewells.

In every letter to Laura—and he wrote almost every month—he now discussed his health. In December he referred to nervous dyspepsia as his "disease." In January 1850 he complained of a sore foot, which interfered with his exercises: "running, leaping, swinging, etc." He began chopping wood every day, having been told it was excellent exercise. In March he again complained of his eyes. In April he wrote that his exercises were "of a violent character, when the chilblains on my feet do not prevent." But in spite of his diets, his ailments, and his exercise, he put on weight. In December 1848 he had weighed 133 pounds; by the spring of 1850 he weighed a robust 166 pounds, more than he had ever before weighed.

In August, while serving on a court-martial at Fort Ontario, he stayed at a "water cure establishment" and found the treatments of great help "for such infirmities as mine." He became a convert. This was to be the first of many hydropathic treatments. The following month he was at West Point and reported to Laura that he had been "quite unwell, and had it not been for my judicious application of water, I cannot say what would have been the result."

Jackson had been six months at Fort Hamilton before he revisited Manhattan. The city's "beauties and wonders" captivated him. It was a place where "everything is in motion, everything alive with animation," he told Laura, a place where everything could be found except "peaceful quiet." Laura asked him to describe the latest New York fashions, but he protested that he did "not even know the names of the different parts of a lady's apparel." He sent her instead copies of *Graham's Magazine* and *Godey's Lady's Book*. Laura's husband asked him for book catalogs, and he sent those of Harper and Brothers' and Appleton's, "the two most celebrated book firms in the United States." He offered to bring Laura seeds and plants from the city when next he came, and he advised her to cultivate flowers: "It shows a refined taste to abound in admiration for the beautiful, and it has the added advantage of endearing children to their homes." He wanted to buy a violin for young Thomas Arnold but prudently asked first if there would be any objection.[2]

Among the residents of the Narrows Jackson was known as stiffly

2. There were objections to violins in many Christian families, the fiddle being regarded as an instrument of the devil and quite likely to lead a young person into sinful ways.

courteous, serious, and slightly eccentric, "a pious man" who possessed a "serious religious mind," one who "never allowed any pleasure or even duty to interfere with church attendance." He had begun praying three times a day, yet he had been at Fort Hamilton almost six months before, at the age of twenty-five, he determined to be baptized.

The records of the small St. John's Episcopal Church, just outside the fort, where in 1842 Robert E. Lee had been a vestryman, contain the entry: "On Sunday, 29th day of April, 1849, I baptized Thomas Jefferson Jackson, major in the U.S. Army. Sponsors, Colonels Dimick and Taylor. M. Schofield, Rector."[3]

The ranks the rector gave the sponsors were not entirely accurate. Brevet Lieutenant Colonel Francis Taylor, the battery commander who had so zealously proselytized Jackson in Mexico, still held the substantive rank of captain. Brevet Colonel Justin Dimick, a West Pointer, had served fifteen years as a lieutenant before being made a brevet captain in 1834; he had won a brevet of major fighting Indians in Florida and brevets of lieutenant colonel and colonel in Mexico, where he had been wounded at Chapultepec, but after thirty years' service his substantive rank was also only captain.

The Reverend Michael Schofield not only failed to get the titles of the sponsors right but carelessly conferred on Jackson a middle name. It scarcely mattered, for Jackson, although he often signed his name "T. J. Jackson," never used more than a middle initial at any time.

The baptism of an adult usually presages membership in a church, but Jackson held aloof. For the time being it seemed to be enough that he was officially a Christian and a Protestant.

As always, he struggled to pass on his enthusiasms to his sister. He wrote glowingly of his new religious fervor, of his endeavor "to live more nearly unto God," and of his vow to forfeit his life "rather than violate the known will of God." His many aches and pains, he was now confident, were "decreed by Heaven's Sovereign, as a punishment for my offenses against His holy laws." When Laura's daughter, Grace, fell sick, he wrote earnestly: "Do you not think, my dear sister, that her illness has been the result of a divine decree?"

Jackson, who had always indulged in an older brother's penchant for lecturing his sister, now began to evangelize:

> You remember that you were once a professed follower of Christ, and that subsequently you disavowed his cause. This, my Dear

---

3. The baptismal font, made of Italian marble on a pedestal of limestone, can still be seen. It underwent some restoration in 1934.

Sister, I do not believe will go unpunished, unless you return to him. Will you not do it? You professed religion when quite young, and possibly could not at that tender age appreciate its blessings. . . . I fear that unless you again acknowledge obedience to his Divine Laws, that some great affliction will be your lot. . . . Oh! Sister, do drop your Infidel Books. Come lead a happy life and die a happy death. . . .

My daily prayers are for your salvation. . . .

A few months after writing this letter, in the fall of 1850, he again took leave, visited Laura and her family in Beverly, and went on to Weston and Jackson's Mill to see other relations and friends. His nephew, Tom Arnold, then five years old, vividly remembered his uncle's visit mainly because of the fascinating presents he brought, most acquired in Mexico: There was a small block of a substance reputed to turn color in the presence of poison, an inkstand surmounted by a pair of doves, an artillery sword, a pair of large Mexican spurs, a small brass cannon on wheels, a tin sword and scabbard, and other delightful military accoutrements. It was probably at this time that Jackson was presented with a sword of honor at Weston. This leave, which seems to have been passed agreeably, was a watershed in his postwar military career.

The routine garrison duty at Fort Hamilton and the pleasant trips to Carlisle Barracks and West Point now came to an end. In October 1850 he was transferred from Company K to Company E in the 1st Artillery. It was a move that had serious consequences. His new company commander was thirty-three-year-old Captain and Brevet Major William Henry French, who had graduated from West Point nine years before Jackson. He had fought in some of the many little wars against the Creeks and the Seminoles in Florida and, like Jackson, had won two brevets in the Mexican War. He was a tall, robust man of wit and intelligence with a good reputation as a light artilleryman. He was also happily married, a fact of some importance.

Within a few months Jackson and Captain French's company found themselves in the wilderness of central Florida, an area that had not long before been the scene of the bloody Seminole War of 1835–42. The entire state boasted of fewer than eighty-eight thousand people, nearly half of whom were slaves; more than a quarter of the population lived in the northern tier of cotton counties that bordered Georgia and Alabama. A third of the state's thirty-eight million acres had not even been surveyed.

Company E, 1st Artillery, ordered to Fort Meade, Florida, arrived there seven days before Christmas, 1850. Their new home was a crude stockade standing in sandy soil surrounded by pine and palmetto some twenty-three miles south of present-day Lakeland and about forty miles east of Tampa, then a village of about two hundred souls still struggling to recover from the savage hurricane of 1848. An important military post, it had recently been the embarkation point for the thirty-eight hundred Seminoles who were sent into exile in Indian Territory. Nearby was Fort Brooke, a camp at the head of Tampa Bay which could accommodate three thousand troops, the headquarters for Brevet Brigadier General Thomas Childs, commander of troops in Florida.

Fort Meade was in stark contrast to the manicured, well-ordered military posts in the Northeast. It held a commissary, a small hospital, a beef contractor's establishment, a sutler's store, and little else. Gone now was the cultivated social life Jackson had come to enjoy, and there were no other compensations for the stultifying routine of a frontier post. Even patrols were routine with little of the spice of danger, for only about three hundred Indians were left in the state; most had been killed, exiled, or herded onto reservations. Company E settled itself into the tedious work of building barracks and camp offices.

The only officers on the post, except for Captain (Brevet Major) French and First Lieutenant (Brevet Major) Jackson, were Second Lieutenant Absalom Baird and Assistant Surgeon Jonathan Letterman. Baird was destined to have a distinguished career, winning the Medal of Honor and becoming a brevet major general, but in 1850 he was a recent West Point graduate and had just been made a substantive second lieutenant in April. Dr. Letterman's career was to be even more notable. An organizational genius, he was to be known as the father of modern battlefield care of the wounded,[4] but in 1850 he, too, was a young man. Fresh out of Philadelphia's Jefferson Medical College, he had been appointed assistant surgeon only in June 1849.

On 27 January 1851, five weeks after arriving at Fort Meade, Jackson led twelve privates and two noncommissioned officers on a six-day patrol "for the purpose of scouting as far as Lake Tohopekiloga [Tohopekaliga]." Although he inspected the shores of three lakes, he

---

4. Letterman established an ambulance corps and a system of field hospitals during the Civil War. His methods proved so effective that after the bloodiest day of the war the battlefield of Antietam was cleared of wounded within twenty-four hours. Letterman Army Medical Center in San Francisco, California, is named after him.

reported that "I am of the opinion that neither [*sic*] was the one sought for," and he found no Indians, only some poles, "cut about three months since," that might have supported an Indian cooking pot. The patrol was introduced to the hard marching for which Jackson later became famous. Thirty-three miles in one day was his easiest march.

Three weeks later he was sent out again, and again he encountered no Indians, but this time he managed to find Lake Tohopekaliga. Jackson enjoyed patrolling. On 1 March 1851 he wrote to Laura: "I like scouting very much, as it gives me a relish for everything; but it would be more desirable if I could have an occasional encounter with Indian parties."

Jackson had apparently written to his sister that he had entertained the thought of leaving the army, for in this letter he thanked her and "Mr. Arnold" for their offer to help him financially should he leave, "[b]ut it is doubtful whether I shall relinquish the military profession, as I am very partial to it. Should I do so, however, I hope that I will never stand in need of pecuniary assistance. All the aid which will be desired will be in attaining fame."

He did not mention that only three days before, on 25 February, he had written to Colonel Francis H. Smith, superintendent of the Virginia Military Institute in Lexington, Virginia, to accept an offer he had made to place his name before the Board of Visitors of the institute and propose that he be appointed professor of natural and experimental philosophy.[5]

If French could have kept his energetic lieutenant constantly on patrol, all might have been well at Fort Meade, but trouble flared over the company's construction work. Keen for responsibility, Jackson argued that because he was performing the work of the post quartermaster, he ought to be in charge of all construction. French rightly disagreed. Deprived of what he regarded as his prerogative, Jackson seethed. He found the situation so intolerable that he began casting about wildly for ways to free himself. He requested a transfer to another regiment; he asked for nine months' leave with permission to leave the country in order to visit Europe. French, perhaps eager to rid himself of his troublesome subordinate, wrote the letter of application for a transfer for him, in order, he said, "that it might be properly worded and most strongly expressed." Nothing served to smooth Jackson's ruffled feathers. A month's sick leave to relieve his "weak eyes" only provided more time for his resentment to reach the boiling point.

5. Possibly the letter was misdated.

By early March Company E had almost completed the construction of its barracks and other structures, and French moved his wife into his new quarters. By the end of the month the enlisted men were ensconced in their barracks, but Jackson's quarrel with his commanding officer lived on. Back from his sick leave, he stopped speaking to French except in the line of duty. He had, as French wrote in a report, "adopted the system of non-intercourse vulgarly styled 'cutting.' " It did no good to summon Jackson and read him the army regulations forbidding such behavior. It did no good to reason with him or to assure him that he, French, was "not unfriendly to him" but was doing what he considered the correct thing. If he wished to complain, French assured him that "a respectful communication to a common superior would be cheerfully forwarded."

On 23 March a smoldering Jackson set about writing a report of his grievances, charging that French had denied him his rightful authority over the company artificers, that he had given him "no controll [*sic*] whatever over the construction of the buildings," and requesting that he be restored to his "proper position." When he finished his report, he handed it to French to be forwarded.

French forwarded it with his own endorsement on the back: "Respectfully transmitted, and I would briefly remark that my entire Command has been employed erecting cantonments on the new site at the Ridge . . . that personally I have given superintendence to the entire work. Under these circumstances it can hardly be considered that a Subaltern or Company Officer is to assume to himself more importance than the commandant of the post."

On 26 March French followed this up with a letter addressed to Second Lieutenant Thornley S. Everett, acting assistant adjutant general[6] for General Childs at Tampa:

> The pretensions of Brev Maj Jackson, Actg Asst Qr Master at this post to exercise an independent station as far as his duties as Quarter Master are involved, are of long standing and he has continued to urge them with a pertinacity so constantly increasing that any communication he might desire to forward upon the subject of

6. There was only one adjutant general in the army; the adjutants of all lesser commands were styled assistant adjutant general (AAG). There were no executive officers, so the AAGs served those functions as would a chief of staff. The same system was later employed in the Confederate army, where Samuel Cooper, the adjutant general, was the ranking Confederate general officer.

what he styles his "Rights" would be transmitted by me to higher authority.

Hence this letter.—On account of this Official Misunderstanding Bevt. Major Jackson has for some time back carried it into his private relations with me to such an extent that I am obliged to call his attention to Paragraph no. 418 Gen. re. 1847.

This unpleasant state of things has grown out of a mistaken view which Bvt Major Jackson has taken in reference to his relation to his Commanding Officer, and as this anxiety manifested in his Communication, to be relieved from subordination has manifested itself in minor ways with Officers junior to him, I am impressed with the belief that the opinion and decision of the General Commanding will do much to create a better feeling at this post.

On 29 March General Childs replied through Second Lieutenant Everett with commendable promptness to Jackson's charges. He dismissed them out of hand and in a final paragraph deplored his conduct: "The difference of opinion amongst Officers, may honestly occur, on points of duty.—It ought never to degenerate into personalities, or be considered a just cause for withholding the common courtesies of Life so essential in an Officer and to the happiness and quiet of garrison Life."

This was certainly good advice to men confined to a one-company post in the Florida wilderness. Unfortunately Jackson did not heed it. A dark side of his character revealed itself, an obsessive vindictiveness possessed him, and he set about blotting his own reputation while doing his best to ruin the career and moral repute of Captain French. Like Uncle Cummins, Jackson was a bad enemy.

On the morning of 12 April Jackson appears to have lost his head completely. He summoned two sergeants (Henry Newman and George Lytle), the company clerk (Corporal Henry R. Bruning), and four privates (William Hendricks, Joseph Brown, Edward Cooney, and Henry Barrows). To each he addressed a series of questions. Had any seen Captain French and his servant girl Julie together? Under what circumstances? Had they noticed anything improper about his conduct? Had they heard any rumors in the company about Captain French and the servant girl?

This extraordinary procedure set the entire post buzzing. The first sergeant, hearing of it, promptly reported the matter to Captain French. So, too, did some of those Jackson had questioned. French hastily called in all the men involved, except for Private Hendricks, who could not be located, and Private Cooney, whose part was apparently as yet unknown. Also summoned were eight soldiers selected at random and Second Lieutenant Baird, acting as post adjutant, who was instructed to record the proceedings. Each man Jackson had questioned was then ordered to relate the questions he had been asked and his answers to them.

Sergeant Newman stated that when Jackson questioned him, he did not at first understand him and then had said that he once saw French walking with his servant girl toward the commissary's store about sundown but had seen no improprieties and knew of no talk which would lower him "in the estimation of a gentleman."

Sergeant Lytle reported that he had said he knew of nothing improper but that he did recall seeing French and the servant girl going to the store to buy candles. He said he had told Jackson, "I thought I had heard some of the men say that Julia's beaux had better not go about Major French's as the major had taken her himself. I said the remark was made jokingly and that I paid little attention to it."

Private Wilson, who had been interviewed later, confessed that he had told Jackson that he had heard "about a month ago" that French had been seen walking with Julia but that "it was said jokingly and I paid no attention to it." Finally, each of the eight soldiers French had summoned was instructed to testify if he had ever heard any comments damaging to his commanding officer's character; all denied having heard anything.

Private Cooney, testifying later, reported that he had told Jackson that "a woman of the camp had spoken to me in the presence of her husband and asked me if I did not see something curious or strange occur at Major French's the other evening when myself and Hendricks passed by. I told her I did not. . . ."

Jackson had questioned Cooney closely. Had he seen anything inside French's quarters? Cooney replied that he had seen a foot. Were they "men's or women's legs"? Were they "bare or uncovered"?

In spite of his zeal, Jackson had turned up nothing substantial. It appears from the record that he had acted on the basis of the least substantial of camp rumors, which seem to have been started by camp servants. His own investigation completed, French lost no time. He ordered Jackson placed under arrest for conduct unbecoming an officer and a gentleman.

The following day at noon Lieutenant Baird left on leave, but French was becoming paranoid, and because Baird's servant seemed to have been one of the worst gossips, he suspected what he called a "conspiracy." Baird was recalled, and he, too, was placed under arrest.

On the same day, 13 April, Jackson formally charged French with conduct unbecoming an officer and a gentleman. He listed four specifications. First, French, while his wife and children were in their new quarters, had stayed several nights at his old quarters with his female servant, and "during said time, he was so intimate with her, as to have sat with her on the same bed, in one of his apartments alone, talking familiarly with her." Second, French had been seen walking with Julia "in the direction of the woods." The last two specifications were little more than vague charges that enlisted men had seen French and Julie together. Jackson listed the names of the two sergeants and Privates Barrows and Brown as witnesses and forwarded the charges, as he was required to do, through Captain French.[7] He included a defense of his own conduct:

> I considered that it was my duty as the next officer in rank to him, to investigate the subject, and for such investigation he has placed me in arrest. I respectfully request that I be released from arrest as I was actuated by a sense of duty. . . . I am of the opinion that the interest of the service loudly calls for a Court of Inquiry, on the conduct of the Commanding Officer of this Post as I believe that it would elicit facts which can not otherwise be elicited.

French endorsed Jackson's document and added a personal letter, both of which were sent to the headquarters of the Fifth Military Department in New Orleans, commanded by Brevet Major General David Emanuel Twiggs of Mexican War fame:

> After Bvt Major Jackson had been placed under arrest by me on the 12th instant, he preferred the accompanying charges and specifications. Although the statements of Bvt Major Jackson's witnesses . . . plead ignorance of any act of impropriety as having been committed by me, yet in order that truth may keep an even pace with so malicious a slander and falsehood as is borne on the face of these charges, I will give an account of my family at the period of these alledged [*sic*] occurrences, which can be corroborated by every officer and soldier at this post, except the malevolent Bt. Major Jackson.

7. Jackson's charges, written in his own hand and now at the National Archives, are dated "March 13," but this date is surely wrong; they were perhaps written a month later.

His wife was pregnant, French explained, so he had moved her as soon as possible into the new quarters, a half mile away on the road to Tampa. This was on 6 March. He, his children, and his servants remained behind. His wife's meals were sent to her by a "little colored girl." Four days later the entire family moved to the new quarters, living alone there until the last of March, when the rest of the troops were moved into the nearby newly built barracks. On two or three occasions, when servants had forgotten something, he had accompanied his servant to the store when it would have been necessary for her to return after dark:

> Finally the person called a servant girl by Brevet Major Jackson, is a respectable white woman who has lived in my family for nearly nine years. Has faithfully attended my wife and children in health and devotedly nursed them in sickness.
> The family is attached to her, and I know of nothing which should or shall prevent me from appearing in public as in private I am, and ought to be, her friend and protector.

French now drew up his own charges of conduct unbecoming an officer and a gentleman with eight specifications against Jackson, who, he said, had attempted "to injure the private reputation of his superior commanding officer," had questioned enlisted men about the "private affairs of his superior commanding officer," and in his conversation with Private Cooney had behaved in a manner "beneath the dignity of an officer and the honor of a gentleman."

A curious sort of stiff, formally correct pas de deux was now performed. The opening movement was Jackson's. On 15 April he wrote to French, stating that although his eyes had become so troublesome that he thought it "unsafe to use them either for forwarding or writing," he was desirous that "additional accusations against you shall be forwarded by the Steamer which leaves Tampa Bay for N. Orleans on Tuesday next. . . ." He had in hand "about twenty specifications which are for conduct unbecoming an officer and a Gentleman" which had been "made out for some time, but owing to ill health have not been copied." He had tried to persuade Dr. Letterman to do this for him, but as the doctor had refused, he now formally requested the services of Corporal Bruning.

"Every facility consistent with military propriety will be granted to you in making out your charges against me," French replied, and Corporal Bruning, French's own company clerk, was detailed to copy Jackson's charges.

With the corporal's help, Jackson filed eighteen new specifications to his original charge plus another charge with four specifications. In the new charges he accused French of a number of lies. French had reported that the new barracks were being constructed from local materials. Not true, said Jackson, for nails, ironwork, windows, and some boards were supplied by the quartermaster. French had falsely stated that Artificer Richard E. Hayes ranked as high as or higher than Sergeant Lytle. There were charges as to what was said or not said to the postman, something about a private's musket, another about guard duty. Piling Pelion upon Ossa, he added still another charge that French was guilty of conduct to the prejudice of good order and military discipline in that he had opened mail addressed to the acting assistant quartermaster—i.e., Jackson—and that he had ordered a sick private to go on a scouting trip. Three specifications charged that French spoke falsely when he said Jackson seemed anxious to be relieved of subordination, although this was surely true, for not only had Jackson applied for a transfer to another unit, but he had, in fact, by this date been offered and had accepted the position he had sought at the Virginia Military Institute.[8]

French, understandably enraged, filed new charges of his own, accusing Jackson of submitting "grave and malicious charges . . . with malicious intent," adding bitterly: "When Jackson is brought to trial for his outrageous conduct the evidence which I will bring before the court will cover him with the infamy he deserves."

Thirty days passed before a reply came from headquarters in New Orleans, days in which life at Fort Meade must have been far from pleasant. Of the four officers at the post, only Dr. Letterman remained unscathed. The commandant was charged with moral lapses, and two subalterns were under arrest. There can be little doubt that the gossip and rumors flew thick among the soldiers, servants, and sutlers.

On or about 21 May the long-awaited verdict arrived. General Twiggs returned all papers to French, ordered Jackson and Baird re-

---

8. On 27 March 1851 the Board of Visitors of the Virginia Military Institute, at the strong urging of John Carlile, agreed to hire Jackson as professor of natural and experimental philosophy and instructor in artillery at a salary of twelve hundred dollars per annum plus quarters. Exactly when Jackson learned of his appointment is uncertain, but it is certain that he knew of it by 22 April and perhaps earlier.

leased from arrest, and stated flatly that there would be no further inquiry. There were more important things for the officers to do, and it was strongly suggested that they be at it.

French, fearing for his reputation, sent off a letter to the adjutant general in Washington, appealing Twiggs's decision and asking that the matter be put before Lieutenant General Winfield Scott, the general in chief of the army. Once again he took up all of Jackson's charges and specifications one by one and answered them in detail, ending with the request that Jackson—who, as soon as he had been released from arrest, had lost no time in departing on the nine months' leave which had been granted him—"may be sent back to this post for trial and if he endeavors to resign that he be not permitted to do so." Twiggs endorsed the appeal by stating the action he had taken and expressing the hope that Scott would not sustain French's application.

Not until 27 August did Scott, through the adjutant general, return a scathing reply:

> He directs me to express his regret, that there is exhibited by these papers, conduct on the part of both Maj. French and Maj. Jackson which require to be noticed.
>
> It was certainly a mistaken sense of duty, which led Lieutenant Jackson to examine privately, the soldiers of the company as to alleged moral conduct, on the part of their captain. Even if such ill-conduct by becoming a matter of public scandal, is a proper subject for investigation by a Military Tribunal, this mode of seeking, or collecting testimony is highly objectionable. It is well calculated to originate scandal where none already existed, to bring into contempt the officer who is made the subject of it, and is highly prejudicial to good order and discipline. Nor, after an attentive examination, is it perceived, that the circumstances set forth in the additional specifications presented by Lieut. Jackson against Captain French, (whenever they are not so vaguely expressed as to make it impossible to investigate them,) contain anything which would support the grave charges they are intended to establish.

A short paragraph reprimanded French for having forgotten "his proper official dignity." Twiggs's decision to dismiss all charges without a trial was confirmed.[9]

9. Some apologists have blamed Jackson's conduct on the weather, but Florida temperatures from January to March are not disagreeable, and Jackson himself never complained of the weather. Others have regarded Jackson's behavior at Fort Meade

While French was left to live with his grievances in the midst of Fort Meade and its gossips, Jackson, having shaken the sands of Fort Meade from his boots, was, at his leisure, free to send in his resignation, effective at the end of his leave. The stinging reprimand from the general in chief of the United States Army appears to have affected him not at all. By the time it was issued, he had resigned his commission and probably did not even see it. He would serve no more as a lieutenant. For the next ten years he was to be Major Jackson, a professor at the Virginia Military Institute in Lexington, Virginia.

---

as reflecting his high "moral structure," his "Puritan righteousness," and his strong sense of duty, or as pointing to his immaturity and his ill health, but the papers themselves depict a vindictive, rancorous soldier obsessed with a determination to destroy the character of his commanding officer.

Lexington Years:
The VMI Professor

The Virginia Military Institute (VMI) in Lexington, Virginia, was not quite twelve years old when its governing body, the Board of Visitors, selected Jackson to be its professor of natural and experimental science and instructor in artillery. He was not the board's first choice.

The state military school began its existence as a mere arsenal, a place to house the state's thirty thousand muskets left over from the War of 1812. Standing on a promontory overlooking what was then called the North Branch of the James River (now the Maury River, named after oceanographer and naval officer Matthew Fontaine Maury), it lay on the northern edge of the village of Lexington and adjacent to the all-male Washington College (now the coeducational Washington and Lee University), founded in 1749.

In 1820 the arsenal was guarded by a captain, a sergeant, and eighteen privates, all state troops. Three musicians—one a soldier and two civilians—completed the roster. The post occupied about eight acres and, in addition to the arsenal, held a barracks, quarters for the officer, repair shops, and various minor structures.

The originator of the idea to convert the arsenal into a military academy is unknown, but John Thomas Lewis Preston, a Lexington lawyer, was its most energetic promoter. He had serious opposition. One newspaper opined that women and children would not be safe if the muskets were to be guarded by a mere boy, "especially a Virginia boy . . . proverbially indiscreet as our youths are." Nevertheless, the 1835–36 session of the Virginia General Assembly approved a measure to disband the guard and establish a military school where the cadets could guard the muskets as well as acquire an education based upon the system used at the United States Military Academy in New York.

Thus was established the Virginia Military Institute: "The healthful and pleasant abode of a crowd of honorable youths pressing up the hill of science, with noble emulation, a gratifying spectacle, an honor to our country and our state, objects of honest pride to their instructors, and fair specimens of citizen-soldiers, attached to their native state, proud of her fame, and ready in every time of deepest peril to vindicate her honor or defend her rights."[1]

A five-man Board of Visitors, which included the commonwealth's adjutant general, ex officio, was appointed by the governor. As its first president the board chose Claudius (Claude) Crozet, a 1807 graduate of France's École Polytechnique, a former artillery officer under Napoleon, and an engineer of distinction who had constructed the first tunnel through the Blue Ridge Mountains. For the institute's "principal professor and commandant" (later styled superintendent), salary fifteen hundred dollars per annum, payable quarterly, it chose twenty-eight-year-old Francis Henny Smith (1812–1890), a Virginian and a West Pointer who had been graduated fifth in a class of forty-one in 1833. His military career had been brief: He had served a year as an instructor at West Point, resigned as a second lieutenant only three years after graduation, and for the next three years taught mathematics at Hampden-Sydney College. He was to remain at VMI for a half century.

On 11 November 1839, in the midst of a snowstorm, Cadet John Bowie Strange (later colonel of the 19th Virginia) relieved the last of the arsenal's enlisted men, and the Virginia Military Institute was open for business. The corps of cadets included 20 "state cadets," representing senatorial districts, who received their education free, and 13 "irregular cadets," who paid their own fees and expenses. Twice as many cadets were admitted the second year, and by the time Jackson arrived there were 117 young men enrolled. The school had no difficulty obtaining students, for as Crozet said, a "wise and prudent parent" would realize

---

1. These words were the climax of an article signed "KNOX" that appeared in the *Lexington Gazette* on 20 May 1841. Today they are on a bronze plaque in the VMI Memorial Garden.

that "at an age when passions are yet unmitigated by the lessons of experience, it is generally imprudent to trust to the self-government of a young man."

Although Smith was an admirer of Sylvanus Thayer, the Father of West Point, who had been stamping his imprint upon the Military Academy while Smith was there, he did not regard the military aspect of VMI as its essential feature. The principal mission of the institute, as he saw it, was to train teachers, primarily teachers of science and mathematics, who could instruct Virginia youths in every part of the state. In step with educational reformers of his day, Smith believed that a college should teach students to be efficient and useful, and he questioned the utility of classical and metaphysical subjects. In 1851 he published a pamphlet, *College Reform*, in which he set forth his educational ideas. "This is a practical age," he asserted. "The American people are emphatically a practical people." He took pride in the absence of courses in Greek at VMI.

Practicality and utility did not exclude a dedication to Christianity and character building. As at West Point, church attendance was compulsory, and prayer meetings and Bible readings were held in Smith's office for many years. At commencement exercises Bibles were given to graduates.

By 1850 the Board of Visitors had decided that the work of an overburdened Major William Gilham, who was commandant of cadets and instructor in tactics and taught all the science courses, should be divided and that a professor should be hired to teach natural and experimental philosophy. Smith was instructed to prepare a list of candidates with the dictum that the new professor must be a West Point graduate and a Southerner, preferably a Virginian. General Corbin Braxton, then chairman of the Board of Visitors, had made this second point quite clear. "It matters not the qualifications of a Northern man at this time," he said; "the state of public feeling is such in this state that none could be acceptable."

Smith developed an impressive list that included George B. McClellan, William Rosecrans, Gustavus W. Smith, Charles Pomeroy Stone, and John James Peck. Jackson's name was not included. In spite of General Braxton's injunction, Smith's personal choice was a New Yorker: Brevet Major Peck, an artilleryman who had graduated eighth in a class of thirty-nine in 1843 and who had won two brevets for service in the Mexican War. On 23 September 1850, the very day the board met, an application arrived from Captain Robert Emmett

Rodes, who had graduated from VMI in 1848. So few members favored Peck that Rodes, whom Smith considered too young, was elected. Smith, however, persuaded the board that it should rescind its vote, assuring the members that he would find someone more qualified, although many of the remaining candidates on his list had already indicated that they were uninterested in the appointment.

The following day the board voted to offer the appointment to Alexander P. Stewart, a teacher at Cumberland University and a West Pointer (class of 1843). Stewart replied that he could not give an answer until March 1851, and the appointment then hung fire, waiting for his decision. When he declined, the search began anew. Discouraged, Smith one day took his problem to Major Daniel Harvey Hill, then a professor of mathematics at Washington College. Hill, a West Pointer from the class of 1842, had won two brevets in the Mexican War and had been presented with a sword of honor by his native state of South Carolina. When he married Isabella Morrison, daughter of the Reverend Dr. Robert Hall Morrison, president of Davidson College in North Carolina, he resigned his commission because, as he said, he could not "contemplate without horror her entrance into one of our wretched garrisons." Smith handed Hill a copy of the *Army Register* and asked him to suggest someone suitable.

Hill glanced down the lists until his eye came upon the name of Jackson. He remembered the day they had walked on the beach at Point Isabel, and doubtless he remembered, too, his distinguished war record. He handed the *Army Register* back to Smith and pointed to Jackson's name. On 4 February 1851 Smith wrote to Jackson at Fort Meade:

> The Board of Visitors of this Institution will elect a professor of Natural & Experimental Philosophy in June next and your name has been mentioned among others for the appointment. Would such a situation be agreeable to you? You are perhaps aware that the Virginia Military Institute is an institution of the State organized upon the model of the U.S. Military Academy. It has always enjoyed a large share of the favor of the State, and as an evidence of its popularity, we are now reconstructing our Barracks at an expense to the State of $46,000. The salary allotted is $1,200 and quarters. Should you desire such a position I would be pleased to present your name to the Board.
>
> I have no authority to pledge the Board in support of any

candidate, and am only authorized to make inquiries which will enable them to act understandably.

Jackson immediately replied: "I cannot consent to decline so flattering an offer. Please present my name to the Board." He immediately set about ensuring his appointment. Relations, friends, friends of friends, and friends of relatives—all were applied to for help. When he heard that John Stringer of Lewis County was to be appointed to the board, he asked Laura to send his address. John S. Carlile, who had been so kind to him when he was on leave, was a new board member of whose support he was certain. Gleefully he reported to Laura: "Indeed I have found that all to whom I have applied for assistance are ready to give me a helping hand." He happily discovered that "Philosophy, is my favorite subject," or so he told Laura. He had strong hopes, he said, that "through the blessings of Providence" he would obtain the appointment.

Once again he was in luck. His friend Carlile on 27 March 1851, attending his first board meeting, nominated him in the strongest terms. A persuasive speaker, Carlile sketched Jackson's family background, lauded his high character, cited his brilliant war record, and even unblushingly called him "the idol of the people." Impressed, the board unanimously elected him, sight unseen. It is safe to say that no member of the board knew that he was at that moment under arrest for conduct unbecoming an officer and a gentleman.

Deeply engrossed in his quarrel with French, Jackson delayed his final acceptance until 22 April. To Smith he explained: "I regret that recent illness has prevented my giving you an earlier answer." Without mentioning his actual predicament he added that he might not be able to meet the board on 25 June as requested because of "circumstances over which I have no control." He was still under arrest. But "circumstances" were resolved so opportunely that no delay was necessary. "All things work together for good to them that love God," Jackson noted piously.

Released from arrest, he embarked on his nine months' leave. Taking ship from Tampa, he sailed around the Keys to New York and then set off overland for western Virginia to see once again Laura and her family and to visit friends and relations. At Jackson's Mill he found his cousin and boyhood chum Sylvanus White, just back from California, where he had gone with the ill-fated Cummins. The two spent a night together exchanging stories of their experiences, and Jackson heard the sorry details of Cummins's death. Although he seems not to have mentioned his trouble in Florida, he confided to his cousin that he had begun the practice of giving a tenth of his income to charitable causes or institutions.

Relinquishing, for the time being, his plan to visit Europe, in June Jackson was in Lexington, where, presumably, he met Colonel Smith,[2] some of the board members, and his future colleagues. He then hurried off to New York, where he made, or most probably renewed, his acquaintance with Dr. Roland S. Houghton, whose wife was the author of *Water-Cure for Ladies* (1844). The Houghtons had been friends of Edgar Allan Poe, who had dedicated two poems to Mrs. Houghton. It was in her home at 47 Bond Street, New York, that Poe wrote "The Bells." And it was in this house that Jackson met Dr. Lowry Barney, who was visiting the city.

He appears to have been greatly impressed with Dr. Barney, for when the doctor returned to his home, about a mile from Henderson Harbor, New York (a resort village on an inlet of Lake Ontario sixteen miles southwest of Watertown), Jackson went with him, convinced that he could cure his dyspepsia. He spent six weeks in the Barney home, and the doctor's daughter, Elva, has left a description of his visit. However, as she was only three years old at the time, her "recollection" was probably more a remembrance of what she later heard:

> On his walks he often carried an umbrella, and, curiously, kept a cup at the store so that he could drink of the waters of Lake Ontario. He also ate a great deal of fruit, and we still have a silver paring knife he used. . . . He was tall, slender, and very courtly, and often talked of his Mexican War campaigns, in which my father and oldest members of the family were much interested. To me he had a cheerful "howdy."

Dr. Barney put Jackson on still another diet, one in which freshly baked corn bread, fresh buttermilk, and fresh fruit figured prominently. The regimen seemed to help, or at least Jackson thought it did. Two years later, while on his first honeymoon (18 August 1853), he wrote to the doctor: "I have derived so much benefit from your wholesome and wise instructions that gratitude to you will accompany me to my grave."

2. The rank of colonel for the superintendent, major for the full professors, and other ranks for junior officers, were those conferred by the state; they carried no authority outside the institute and did not even confer rank in the active militia. Jackson, of course had earned the brevet rank of major, and he was still, until February 1852, on leave from the American army.

In August Jackson returned to Lexington, and on the thirteenth orders announcing his appointment were published.[3] Because Major William Gilham, the commandant of cadets, was away, he was immediately designated acting commandant. On his first day he appeared on the parade ground impressively dressed in a blue military coat, white trousers, white gloves, shining black boots, and a kepi; those who saw him observed that both coat and boots seemed too large. The cadets were being drilled by Cadet Adjutant Thomas T. Mumford, and Jackson stood with a group of spectators on the edge of the parade ground to watch.

One of the marchers caught sight of him and impudently called out what passed for a witticism: "Come out of those boots. They are not allowed in this camp." Horrified, Mumford turned the command over to another cadet officer and ran to apologize. But Jackson, his hearing probably already damaged by his service in the artillery, had perhaps not heard or understood. Undisturbed, he simply ordered Mumford to carry on.

When morning drill was over, a vastly relieved Mumford escorted Jackson to headquarters to explain the procedures. Jackson asked for the order book, which he pored over, and next the cadet regulations, which he read and kept. Then, according to Mumford, he turned to him and said: "Adjutant, I am here amid new men, strange faces, other minds, companionless. I shall have to rely upon you for much assistance until I can familiarize myself with the routine duties, and the facilities for executing them. There is a great similarity, I see, to West Point, where I was educated. I trust ere long to master all difficulties."

The institute at this time had, in addition to Superintendent Smith, who taught mathematics, three other full professors. John T. L. Preston, who had done so much to bring the school into being, taught modern languages and English literature. William Gilham, who had graduated from West Point in 1840 just above William Tecumseh Sherman, had served for a time as acting assistant professor of natural and experimental philosophy at West Point but resigned his commission in 1846 to become professor of physical sciences, chemistry, instructor of tactics, and commandant of cadets at VMI (he became a leader in the application of chemistry to agriculture); he was known for his ready wit, his high-pitched voice, and his hot temper. He had taught

3. Jackson's appointment caused no stir in Lexington. There was no mention of it in the *Lexington Gazette*. In fact, his name does not appear at all in local newspapers of 1851 or 1852.

natural and experimental philosophy as well until Jackson's arrival. Thomas H. Williamson had entered West Point in 1829 but had not been graduated; he had been hired as an instructor of tactics and drawing; by 1851 he had become professor of engineering as well. All were Virginians, and Smith and Gilham, like Jackson, had served in the artillery. With the arrival of Jackson, Gilham became, in addition to his other duties, instructor in infantry.

There were also several young instructors. Daniel Trueheart, who, like Jackson, was devoted to hydropathic practices, taught tactics and engineering; Raleigh Edward Colston, a Frenchman by birth, taught French; Robert Emmett Rodes, who had applied for Jackson's position but had been passed over, was an assistant in chemistry; and James W. Massie, was an instructor in mathematics. All were VMI graduates.

Professors and instructors wore blue uniforms similar to those worn by officers in the Corps of Engineers with the exception of their buttons, which, like those of the cadets, bore the seal of the Commonwealth of Virginia. The cadets wore uniforms much like those still worn for dress parades at VMI and at West Point. Gray jackets were worn all year; trousers were changed in summer from gray to white. Their hats were tall, cylindrical affairs each bearing a pompon and a plate of the Corps of Engineers. They carried newly issued bronze-barrel percussion muskets, which replaced outmoded flintlocks previously issued.

Classes had not yet begun when Jackson arrived, so he had ample time to learn his new administrative and military duties. Cadet Adjutant Mumford (who was to serve as a cavalry commander under Jackson) later wrote that at VMI Jackson was "painfully exacting in details. Yet there was an earnestness in his manner and precision in his commands that indicated unmistakably what was meant."

By the end of summer, when classes resumed, the castellated new barracks were not yet complete. To keep the cadets occupied and out of the way, they were sent off on 9 September under the command of Major Jackson to tour the countryside. Jackson's only orders were to bring them back by 27 September. He marched them to the local spas—Rockbridge Alum, Bath Alum, and Warm Springs—then back to Lexington, in all about one hundred miles. The Virginia springs were enjoying increasingly popular reputations, not only as health spas but as social centers, places to see and be seen. The cadets were a welcome diversion, their parades and guard mountings popular attractions. In spite of the lateness of the season, they found no lack of entertainments or of young women to grace them.

Jackson enjoyed the springs, and in the years ahead he was to visit them often. Medical authorities recommended them for a wide variety of ailments, including "scrofulous, eruptive and dyspeptic affections . . . hepatic derangements, nervous debility and uterine diseases."

From Warm Springs he wrote to his uncle Alfred Neale: "I have reported at Lexington and am delighted with my duties, the place and the people. . . . I am anxious to devote myself to study until I shall become master of my profession."

Apparently notified that the barracks were finished, Jackson marched back on 24 September, and at four o'clock that afternoon the corps of cadets moved into their new quarters, an architectural and engineering marvel, containing such wonders as gas lights and central heating. Jackson, too, moved in, sharing a room on the third floor (or stoop, as floors have always been called at VMI and at West Point) of the east tower with Major Gilham; his second year, after Gilham moved into a newly completed Gothic Revival residence on the institute's grounds, he moved to the fourth stoop and shared a room with a young instructor, Lieutenant Thomas A. Harris, who had been graduated from VMI only one year before. (Harris later became a surgeon in the Confederate army.)

On 26 September Colonel Smith assigned classes, and Jackson found he was to teach two hour-and-a-half periods each morning plus artillery drill in the afternoon. The regime at the institute was much like that at West Point. Reveille was sounded by a fife and drum at dawn; breakfast was at seven o'clock, winter and summer; guard mount was at eight; classes met from eight-thirty until dinner at one. In the afternoon there were classes from two to three-thirty, followed after a brief recreation period by drill and a dress parade before supper. In the summer cadets were marched on Tuesdays, Thursdays, and Saturdays to the North River, where they were required to bathe and at least once had to be admonished that they "must not further annoy the ladies near Jordon's Point by bathing too close to the bridge."

Discipline was not always easy to maintain among the free-spirited young Virginians who attended the institute. On 21 April 1851, just before Jackson's arrival, VMI had experienced its first mutiny. Smith was absent and Major Preston was temporarily in command when a sensational murder trial was held in Lexington. The senior cadets (first classmen) were given permission to attend for three or four days, but when the trial lasted longer than expected, further permission was refused. Indignant, they decided to ignore Preston's orders.

When Smith returned, he expelled the entire first class. Its members were reinstated after a respectful appeal had been addressed to the Board of Visitors, but they were confined to the institute's grounds until graduation on 4 July.

At the beginning of 1852, during Jackson's first year as a teacher, there was again a revolt of the first classmen. The grievance, even more puerile than that of the previous April, sprang from a cadet captain ordering a private to keep his eyes to the front. The class predictably sided with the private. Feeling ran so high that the captain's life was threatened, and he was relieved of his command. After an investigation of some months, his action was declared proper, and to the chagrin of his classmates, he was reinstated. (The private who was the cause of it all was murdered fifteen years later in Texas.)

When Jackson arrived at VMI, Winfield Scott's *Infantry Tactics* was still in use, and the battalion formation was the single rank, but Scott's manual was superseded in 1855 by *Rifle and Light Infantry Tactics*, a two-volume work written by Colonel William Joseph Hardee, who had been commandant of cadets at West Point.[4] Jackson supplemented his drills with recitations by first classmen using as texts Charles Kingsbury's *Artillery* and a book called *Artillery Tactics* written by a board of officers.

For artillery drill Jackson had at his disposal four brass 6-pounders and two 12-pounder howitzers designed and manufactured specifically for the institute by the Watervliet Arsenal in New York. Each was about 200 pounds lighter than its service counterparts, the 6-pounders weighing 564 pounds and the howitzers 578 pounds. Powder charges were also reduced, and shot was recommended "for only occasional use."[5]

The six-gun battery was splendid, but the school provided no horses. Jackson proposed a scheme for utilizing those kept to haul wood, some of the officers' mounts, and a horse assigned to the mess hall. When the proposal was rejected out of hand, he was driven to substituting cadets and harnessing them to pull the guns, caissons, and limbers. When a cadet once failed to trot at the order "Limbers and

4. Chambers and others, following Colonel William Couper's history of VMI, mistakenly give the date of change as 1851, but Hardee's book was not published until 1853.

5. Although these guns were to see active service during the Civil War, the howitzers were not the famous 12-pounder Napoleons which were the standard field-pieces of the Civil War. The Napoleons, developed under the auspices of Napoleon III, did not appear until 1856.

caissons, pass your pieces, trot, march!" Jackson duly reported him: "Cadet Hambrick, not trotting at artillery drill." Required to excuse his failure in writing, Cadet Hambrick replied: "I am a natural pacer."

In later years Major William N. M. Otey (name later changed to William N. Merser) remembered the artillery drills during his cadet days: "Frequently in artillery drill I saw the cadets who were acting as horses to limber chest and caisson run away in mimic fright and often scatter the watching crowds of gentlemen and ladies, while the Major was yelling himself hoarse in vain endeavor to check them."

Unless he was harassed by playful cadets, artillery instruction was easy enough for Jackson, but the classroom teaching of optics, acoustics, astronomy, analytical mechanics, and the myriad other subjects that came under the heading of natural and experimental philosophy was a different story. All the texts he used for this course were those written by his old West Point professor William H. C. Bartlett: *Analytical Mechanics, Optics and Acoustics,* and *Astronomy.* Throughout the summer he prepared for the coming classes, even sometimes using his weak eyes at night.

In classrooms (known at VMI, as at West Point, as section rooms) Jackson revealed himself a disaster as a teacher. He lectured in a "high pitched drawl" and in a concise, didactic manner unrelieved by digressions or allusions. It was said that he "never descended to the level of his pupil's understanding." If an unlucky cadet asked for an explanation of a point not clear to him, Jackson merely repeated what he had said in the same words in the same way. He was never known to rephrase an explanation, to approach a problem from a different angle or to try to make a formula or a theory more clear. When he conducted experiments, they often failed, for he was clumsy with his hands. One cadet, writing home, confided that he was studying optics, which was not only "very difficult" but it was "taught by such a *hell of a fool,* whose name is Jackson."

Although at the end of his first year Superintendent Smith wrote, "The more I see of him the more pleased I am with the selection the Board has made," he was aware that the sentiment was not shared by everyone. On 16 June 1852 a Mr. Charles Mason had written to register a complaint made by his son that Major Jackson had a "rigid aversion towards him in his recitations." Although the letter was mild and friendly in nature, it was the first complaint ever made against a VMI professor. No action was taken, and it is not clear that Jackson was even aware of its existence. However, in 1857 the VMI Board of Visitors heard more serious complaints about the quality of Jackson's teaching forwarded by the Society of Alumni, which delegated its president, Professor John B. Strange (class of 1842 and the first cadet to stand guard over the arsenal), to summarize them. On the motion of old General William Richardson, the adjutant general, the matter was tabled. The same action was taken when, a year later, Jackson learned of the complaint and demanded an investigation.

Sometime after Jackson had left the institute and had joined the Confederate army, Smith confessed: "As a professor of Natural and Experimental Philosophy, Major Jackson was not a success. He had not the qualifications for so important a chair. He was no *teacher*, and he lacked the tact required in getting along with his classes. Every officer and every cadet respected him for his many sterling qualities. He was a brave man, a conscientious man, and a good man, but he was no professor."

Jackson himself never considered that he had failed. A friend once ventured to suggest that with his precarious health and his weak eyes it seemed unwise to have accepted a teaching position. "Not in the least," he shot back. "The appointment came unsought, and was therefore providential; and I knew that if Providence set me a task, he would give me the power to perform it. So I resolved to get well, and you see I have. As to the rest, I knew that what I willed to do, I could do."[6]

Not only was he a poor teacher, but—and this seems curious when compared with his later Civil War experience—he was unable to maintain discipline in his section room. While he listened to one cadet recite, others would throw "paper pellets" and "create wanton disrespect in his section room." Cadet Giles B. Cooke (later a major on the staff of General Robert E. Lee) recalled how "we used to annoy Major Jackson a great deal by cat-calls, dog barks, etc. One day I was imitating a puppy. He tried in vain to find the cause, much worried. Finally he said, 'There seems to be a puppy in the room.' "

"He was imperturbable," one cadet remembered, "never losing his dignity nor seeming in the least annoyed." Major Otey wrote: "I often look back and wonder at the calm patience of Maj. Jackson under the fire of some mischievous cadet, seeking to irritate and annoy him during lecture hours."

Jackson's imperturbability may have sprung in part from his poor hearing, but he did not hesitate to court-martial those who were blatantly undisciplined and those who were brazenly disrespectful. Cadet

6. The friend's name is unknown. Jackson's response is as reported by his second wife, Mary Anna Jackson, née Morrison.

W. H. Cox was court-martialed for telling Jackson to his face that he would "dictate his own course of conduct" and that Jackson was "incapable of judging" his recitations. More than one cadet tried to harm him. On at least two occasions brickbats were thrown at him.

Along with other professors, Jackson acquired nicknames, such as Hickory or Old Hickory, Old Jack, Tom Fool Jackson, or Square Box, a reference to the size of his feet. Drawings of enormous feet frequently appeared on the blackboard of his section room. Cadets dusted off old tricks. One "rat" (all plebes were so called at VMI, and still are)[7] was tied in a chair and tilted against the door to Jackson's room so that when he opened it, plebe and chair fell in on him. Jackson court-martialed the perpetrators.

Courts-martial were quite common, and Jackson served on many during his tenure at VMI. He sat on one only five days after his arrival. One can assume that, given his experience on military courts, he performed competently. Often enough he was the accuser, and one of the most serious cases involved Cadet James A. Walker, a top student and a first classman due to graduate in less than two months. The affair started, as serious matters often do, with a small incident. Cadet Walker attempted to argue with Major Jackson, who ordered him to desist. Not only did he refuse to stop, but the written excuse he submitted was purposely insolent. The record of the court-martial that followed covers sixty-two pages and reveals a truculent and headstrong cadet and a professor who, quite understandably, lost his patience. Walker was dismissed. Two days later, on 17 May 1852, Superintendent Smith wrote urgently to the young man's father: "I would advise you to come up at once and take him home as I have reason to believe that he may involve himself in serious difficulty." Walker was threatening to kill Jackson.

An armed, angry young hothead roaming the town with the avowed intention of waylaying and killing him was not a threat to be taken lightly. Jackson faced it as Jacksons were wont: He resolved to go to law. A warrant requiring Walker to keep the peace might dampen his ardor for vengeance.

Prudently Jackson first consulted his friend D. H. Hill, who was aghast. He knew Lexington and VMI well, and he warned that such an

7. The origin of the custom of calling plebes rats is unknown. Plebes called each other brother rats. A play called *Brother Rat*, depicting life at VMI, was written by two VMI graduates and opened in Baltimore on 7 December 1936; it later enjoyed a long run in New York. In 1938 it was made into a motion picture which featured Ronald Reagan as a rat.

action would be construed as cowardly and that he would lose the respect of the cadets and the town. Jackson listened attentively, thanked Hill sincerely, and, undeterred, went straight to a magistrate, an errand that proved futile, for the officer of the court could not screw up his courage to serve the warrant.

Having done what he considered the right and responsible thing, Jackson declined to take any further steps to protect himself. The courage that had won him brevets was not a trait whistled up in the heat of battle; it was a basic part of his character. In spite of the urging of friends, he refused to alter his daily routine. Until Walker's father was able to reach Lexington, Jackson steadfastly walked his familiar route to and from the institute at his usual times. It was perhaps this steadiness that held the cadet at bay until his father collected him.[8]

Jackson's habitual austerity did not betoken a cold nature, for he was a warmhearted man, a fact attested to not only by the women who came to know him but by more than one cadet. Cadet Thomas M. Boyd when a plebe saw a gentle side to stern Major Jackson's nature. He was one day ordered by a cadet masquerading as an officer to take a "requisition" to him for signature. Hesitantly Boyd approached Jackson during a class in the section room, doffed his cap, and presented his paper. Jackson glanced at it briefly and told him to sit down. As he waited, he became uncomfortably aware of smirks on the faces of the older cadets, and he expected the worst. When the class was at last dismissed, Jackson turned to him and asked mildly, "Do you know what this paper contains?" Boyd confessed that he did not:

> I had risen from the seat I occupied, and stood before him, cap in hand; in reply to his question I told him how it came into my possession, and what I was ordered to do with it. That I did not know one half of the officers, and as the gentleman who gave me the order wore a blue coat, sash and sword, I supposed he had authority. He said he did not censure me at all, that all of the cadets were in the habit of quizzing the newcomers, and someone was

8. James Alexander Walker was eventually graduated from the University of Virginia and practiced law in Pulaski County, Virginia. When the Civil War began, he was elected captain of the local company and went to Harper's Ferry, then commanded by Jackson. He became colonel of the 13th Virginia and then a brigadier general commanding the Stonewall Brigade. After the war he was successively lieutenant governor and congressman. Thirty-nine years after his ignominious departure from VMI, Walker was chief marshal for the ceremonies surrounding the unveiling of Jackson's monument in Lexington.

playing a joke on me. The order I brought was a bogus requisition for high heeled socks, pickled crowbars, and a box of Specs best cigars. [The cadets' nickname for Superintendent Smith was Old Specs or Specks.[9]] I had not dared to open the order, and when advised of its absurd nature my embarrassment was painful. He observed this and to remove my feelings, asked me how long I had been at the institute, from what part of the state I hailed, etc. His manner before the class was stern, he sat erect with his coat buttoned to the chin, but now he was kind and pleasant, and I shall never forget my encounter with Stonewall Jackson.[10]

Cadet M. D. Ellzey, then a plebe who had no idea that Major Jackson was even aware of his existence, was unnerved one evening when Jackson appeared at the door of his barracks room. "I hear you are going down to Lynchburg to have Dr. Owens cut out your tonsils," he said. "I came down to advise you not to do it, at least not without consulting your parents. I had mine cut out, and I have great difficulty in hearing ever since, and I am afraid it is increasing."

Ellzey admitted that he had been having trouble with a sore throat but promised that he had no intention of having his tonsils removed.

"I am glad to hear it," Jackson said. "I'm satisfied it has done me a great deal of harm. I must be going, sir. Good day." Turning on his heel, he left Ellzey to stare at his astonished roommates.

The end of his first academic year found Jackson well pleased with himself and proud of the school. Neither his deficiencies as a professor nor his difficulties with cadets diminished his pleasure at being in Lexington. On 5 June 1852 he wrote happily to Laura: "I wish that you could see our Institute, for I consider it the most tasty edifice in the state." He was delighted as well with the town of Lexington and its people.

Graduation exercises were usually held on 4 July, but in 1852 the fourth fell on a Sunday, so they took place on the following day. The graduating class was addressed by General William Booth Taliaferro

9. Most of the professors' nicknames, like those given to Civil War generals later, began with "Old," even when the person to whom it was given was sometimes quite young. At VMI William Gilham was Old Gil, John Preston was Old Ball, Thomas Williamson was Old Tom, and Raleigh Colston, who taught French, was Old Parlez or Old Polly. For reasons now obscure, William H. Richardson, a member of the Board of Visitors, was called Old Frederick.

10. Boyd's manuscript, now in the library of West Virginia University, is dated 1887.

(pronounced Tah-liver). Although at twenty-nine he was not two years older than Jackson, he was already a man of some importance in the state. Standing six feet tall, scion of a prosperous family, he looked, as indeed he was by tradition and character, a Virginia gentleman. He was a graduate of William and Mary College and had studied law at Harvard. In 1847 he had been commissioned a captain in the army, and the following year, at the conclusion of the Mexican War, he was mustered out as a major of the 9th Infantry. In 1852 he was a member of the Virginia House of Delegates (the lower legislative house in Virginia's General Assembly), a brigadier general in the state militia, and a member of VMI's Board of Visitors. He was to play a significant role in the career of the new VMI professor who listened to his speech that day.

The *Lexington Gazette* described the sumptuous dinner, washed down with "a little wine for their stomach's sake," held at the Lexington Hotel that evening for the graduates and alumni. It was followed by a fireworks display and then "a splendid ball at the mess hall of the Institute . . . to the enlivening strains of Scott's music band." Undoubtedly Jackson was present. If he brought his bag of corn bread, eschewed wine, or, as a newly minted Presbyterian, declined to dance, no one seemed to notice or care.

CHAPTER

8

Lexington: Religion and Marriage

"**I** have for months back admired Lexington; but now, for the first time, have I truly and fully appreciated it. Of all the places which have come under my observation in the United States, this little village is the most beautiful." So wrote Jackson in a letter to Laura (7 September 1852) at the end of his first year at VMI.

According to the census of 1850, Lexington, the seat of Rockbridge County,[1] had a population of 1,743, of whom 638 were blacks; ten years later it had increased by only 392. The population of the entire county numbered only 11,484 whites and 4,561 blacks, of whom 364 were free. Only 348 people, black or white, had been born outside Virginia, and of these 345 were foreign-born. Most of the churchgoers were Presbyterians (reformed and unreformed) with Methodists running a poor second. Among the whites, at least two-thirds were of Scotch-Irish descent, the highest percentage of Scotch-Irish in the Shenandoah Valley.

There were no great plantations in the county, but much tobacco was grown—four hundred thousand pounds in 1860—and Samuel McDowell Reid, a large land owner, employed sixty-one slaves in his

---

1. So named for the natural rock bridge, 215 feet high and 50 to 100 feet wide with a 90-foot span that arches over Cedar Creek 16 miles from Lexington.

tobacco fields. Few counties in Virginia had a more vigorous or expansive slave economy. (Among the counties west of the Blue Ridge, only Kanawha County in what is today West Virginia had a faster-growing slave population.)

The principal business of Lexington was education. Indeed, Washington College was founded in 1749, just a year before the town was planned.[2] It held, in addition to Washington College and VMI, a variety of private schools, including two girls' academies and a respected law school operated by Judge John W. Brockenbrough, which developed into the law school of Washington & Lee University.

Not everyone shared Jackson's delight in the town and its people. A visitor who arrived in 1856 described it as "an indifferent town and rather small, with muddy streets." Still later Cadet John S. Wise, coming from the prosperous and sophisticated tidewater area of Virginia, found it grim, the "portals of the Presbyterian church looked cold as a dog's nose . . . and the hair of those pretty Presbyterian girls was among the smoothest and flattest things I ever saw."

In spite of its undeniably muddy streets, Lexington was a town so proud of its culture that its citizens sometimes grandly referred to it as the "Athens of the Valley." Many of its houses held books, and families subscribed to such magazines such as *Knickerbocker,* the *Eclectic,* and *Harper's.* Other magazines, including the leading British periodicals, such as *Blackwood's, Punch,* and the *Illustrated London News,* could be regularly purchased. Two bookstores flourished. One was owned by Dr. J. W. Paine, who for a time also conducted a private classical school; the other was owned by John B. Lyle, who became a good friend of Jackson's. He has been described as a "courteous, jolly and lovable old bachelor" and an exceptionally devout Christian. His bookstore on Main Street was a favorite meeting place, almost a clubhouse for men with religious, musical, or literary interests.

The intellectual and cultural center of the town was not the colleges or the bookstores but the handsome headquarters and library of the Franklin Society (officially the Franklin Society and Literary Company), a debating group composed of about forty of the county's leading citizens who met weekly to discuss local, national, and international affairs. It was at one such meeting that John Thomas Lewis Preston had put forth the notion of converting the arsenal to a military school.

Jackson felt at home in Lexington from the beginning, and he

2. Lexington was laid out as an entirely new town to be the county seat in 1778, but it was not incorporated until 1841.

soon made friends and acquaintances in the town. Before his quarters at the barracks were ready, he roomed at the Lexington Hotel, where he met instructors from Washington College, young lawyers, and other young professionals. He attended concerts and lectures; he was invited to social events and to parties. He told Laura: "I am enjoying myself more than I have done for years."

Even so, his quarrel with French was not forgotten. On 22 February 1852, when he sent in his resignation from the army, he added a request that his application for a court of inquiry also be filed so that "in leaving the service I may do so with an unblemished character." As far as is known, no one in Lexington ever learned of the unsavory Florida affair.[3]

Included in unfinished business were the lawsuits in western Virginia and the settling of the complicated affairs of Cummins Jackson, which involved more litigation in the circuit court of Lewis County. Cummins had died intestate, and such of his property as remained was divided among nearly a hundred nieces, nephews, and other relatives. On 11 May 1854 Jackson and his wife granted to his uncle John White all their interest in "the estate of the late Cummins E. Jackson and the late Edward Jackson."

Jackson was twenty-seven years old when he arrived in Lexington, a handsome man with striking eyes, wearing sideburns from ears almost to his clean-shaven chin; only later did he grow a full beard. He usually bore a serious mien and, except among his intimate friends, was seldom seen to smile. Cadets swore that he never smiled. Some who knew him declared that he had no sense of humor, but Dr. Hunter McGuire, who became intimate with him during the Civil War, maintained that he had "a keen sense of humor," and he described his laugh: "He would catch one knee with both hands, lift it up, throw his body back, open wide his mouth, and his whole face and form be convulsed with mirth—but there was no sound." Jokes, witticisms, or banter did not attract him. He neither drank nor smoked; he enjoyed serious conversation, took statements literally, and was, some thought, rather dull. Not surprisingly, clergymen enjoyed his society, and he theirs. He relished the company of young women although he was somewhat shy and lacked the easy grace of most of his contemporaries in Lexington society.

3. In the memoirs of Jackson's second wife, his experience in Florida is passed over in two sentences, only noting that he was ordered to Fort Meade, remained there "about six months," and found the climate "enervating and injurious to his health."

Clement D. Fishburne was a sophomore at Washington College when he first met Jackson at Lyle's bookstore. "His manners were not what might not be called captivating but they were pleasant and courteous," he said. Fishburne later saw Jackson often on social occasions and in later life he recalled his impressions: "While his courtesy was unfailing, there were some peculiarities about him. He never assumed a lounging and (so-called) 'easy' position. He never crossed his legs in company and rarely touched the back of his chair. He seemed to take a lively interest in every general conversation and was, to this extent, responsive, though he never gave the impression that he was a great talker."

Some noticed that he avoided sitting whenever possible. A doctor in town declared: "The Major stood up habitually, thinking it best for his health to keep his alimentary canal straight." He walked, said another acquaintance, with "a stilted motion, whose every step seemed to be a distinct act of volition." The Reverend Robert Dabney, on the other hand, thought his step "at once suggested the idea of the dismounted horseman."

Jackson's compulsive punctiliousness soon became legendary. He once roused an astonished cadet from his cot to apologize for having marked his answer in the section room wrong when, as he had just discovered, it had been correct. He was known to venture into a rainy night to confess that although he had earlier in the day declared that an event had taken place on one day of the week, it had actually occurred on another.

It had been more than two years since his baptism in the Episcopal Church in New York City. Now, after only three months in Lexington, he was examined and on 22 November 1851 confirmed in the Presbyterian Church (No. 974 in the church register). It was said by some that Colonel Smith, an Episcopalian, hired only those of his own faith at VMI, a charge he hotly denied, and certainly Jackson felt no need to conform. However, most of the professors at VMI were Episcopalian, and all of those at Washington College were Presbyterians.

The handsome new Presbyterian church (still extant) was the spiritual home for the largest and most influential congregation in the county. Its pastor was the Reverend Dr. William S. White (1800–1873), an elderly man with a limp, who had come from Charlottesville only three years before Jackson's arrival. He was a man of considerable education, having attended Hampden-Sydney College, Union Seminary, and Princeton, where he had earned his Doctor of Divinity degree. He was a member of the board of Washington College, and he was to serve as a minister in Lexington for nearly twenty years.

Predictably, joining a church fired Jackson's zeal to lead his sister into more Christian ways. In a letter he wrote on 10 January 1852 he made manifest his concern over an illness she had reported, but it was her indifference toward religion that most deeply troubled him, launching him into a dissertation on the wisdom of leading a Christian life[4] and ending with the impassioned plea "Oh sister! do pray to God for his mercy, and eternal life through our Redeemer Jesus Christ." Descending to the mundane, he added: "I have not yet been able to procure the peaches of which I spoke. . . ."

Ten days later, having learned that she was still not well, he wrote again, advising her: "[L]ook back through your past life, and see if you can find some cause for your affliction." The state of her soul dominated his letters. In one (6 June 1853) he wrote:

> My dearest sister, with tears in my eyes, and a heart devoted to my God, I look into the future beyond the limits of this transient life of care; and see the dark gloom which is to exist throughout infinite duration. That whilst I am to shine like a star in the firmament forever, you are to be assigned to unending misery. . . . My Sister, do reflect upon my course of life, think and see, if I could have ever erred since arriving at mature age, and then consider how I could ever have been satisfied of the truth of the Gospel; unless it is true. Have I ever erred in the affairs of this life? Remember too, what strong influences have been brought to bear on me and yet in spite of all opposing obstacles, I am one of the most devoted of Christians. . . .

On 6 November 1852 the Rockbridge Bible Society, an affiliate of the American Bible Society, was founded with Jackson as a member of the twelve-member board. He contributed ten dollars, which entitled him to life membership, and attended ten of the subsequent twelve monthly meetings before a disagreement with other board members, particularly Colonel Francis Smith, prompted his resignation.

It was not their only difference. In March 1854 Smith appointed Jackson president of a court-martial to try two cadets accused of stealing sugar from the mess hall. When the court found the defendants not

---

4. The gravamen of Jackson's argument was what is sometimes called "Pascal's Wager," which is that even if one is not sure God exists, why take a chance? To follow Christian precepts costs nothing and might gain one admittance to paradise; thus a wager impossible to lose.

guilty, Smith was so outraged that he ordered it reconvened. Jackson refused to comply.

Religious activities increasingly occupied his time. In February 1852 he taught his first Sunday school class to a group of elementary school-age boys, and he began to attend weekly prayer meetings. When Dr. White admonished his flock for their failure to lead in prayer, Jackson, conscientious as always, consulted him privately. He was naturally diffident, he said, and found public speaking difficult, but if White thought it was his duty, he would volunteer. White, with the easy assurance of those to whom public speaking is second nature, encouraged him, but when Jackson was called upon, his embarrassment was so great and so painful to witness that White sympathetically refrained from calling on him again, until Jackson assured him that he wanted to try once more to lead in prayer and he wanted to learn to do it well.

It was probably to improve his speaking abilities that he joined the Franklin Society. On 12 March 1853 he was proposed for membership by William McLaughlin, a twenty-six-year-old lawyer,[5] and he was formally elected a debating member of the society at the next meeting on the twenty-sixth. (Two-thirds of the members had to approve a new member.) The society was already fifty-six years old. In 1816 it had been given a charter by the commonwealth (renewed in 1849, as it was again in 1870). By Jackson's time its library housed the largest collection of books west of the Blue Ridge. Shareholding members—those who purchased a share from the society—were entitled to borrow books. Debating members, who simply paid yearly dues, had the use of the library without borrowing privileges. Had Jackson wished to become a shareholder, a share would have cost him one hundred dollars—a month's salary.

The subjects debated by the society were political topics of the day, American foreign policy, moral and ethical questions, and local problems. From time to time lecturers were booked and tickets were available to the public. Regular meetings were held on Saturday nights. The president assigned a committee, usually of two members, to propose three or four questions for debate, and the membership voted on those they wished to discuss. Jackson was appointed to such a committee at his first meeting. The speakers, one for the affirmative and one for the negative, were assigned to each topic. After their formal argu-

---

5. William McLaughlin later became a judge. He rose to be a colonel of artillery in the Confederate army and commanded the VMI artillery at the Battle of New Market in 1864.

ments the debate was thrown open to the members, and when they had exhausted all comments, a vote was taken.

Unless a debating member bought a share in the society within five years, his membership expired. Jackson was an active member, but at the end of his first year he resigned, his letter of resignation being read at the meeting of 11 March 1854. Whether this was because he did not understand the terms of membership or whether he had a quarrel with another member is unknown, but he was persuaded to withdraw his resignation, and he remained a member for five years until his membership lapsed because he had not bought a share.

In the first debate he attended he chose the negative side on a current local topic: "Would capitalists be safe in loaning their money to the North River Navigation Company to enable it to complete its improvement in case the James River Company guaranteed a portion of its tolls for the payment of the principal and interest thereof as contemplated?"

The Reverend Robert Dabney, who corresponded with those who had known Jackson at this period, described his early attempts to speak extemporaneously:

> His first essays were as painful to his audience as they probably were to himself; confusing, halting, and frequently ending in an abrupt silence, when the power of controlling his thoughts for the time deserted him. Thus arrested by his own embarrassment, he would sit down. . . . At a suitable moment he would rise again, and renew his effort, perhaps to end it with a similar painful halt. . . . His manner was rapid and emphatic, his thoughts marked by great directness. . . .

During the fall and winter of 1855–56 the society held a series of public lectures every third Friday, and a number of Washington College and VMI professors spoke. Records of the society show that on 20 December 1855 "Major Jackson . . . delivered an interesting and instructive lecture on the subject of Motion and sound." VMI cadets were permitted to attend, and according to Cadet John G. Gittings, Jackson spoke of acoustics as an "undeveloped science" but predicted future discoveries, particularly in the "transmission of sound," a prediction verified twenty-one years later by Alexander Graham Bell's patent of the telephone in 1876.

Some of his thoughts on current ideas and events are reflected in the records of the debates in which he participated, and they indicate that he kept abreast of the news. He opposed any expansion of the powers of the federal government and did not think it should have anything to do with the Union Pacific Railroad. He was on the side of Britain, France, Turkey, and Sardinia in the Crimean War. In spite of his own part in the duel in Mexico, he now opposed dueling, and he was in favor of prohibiting the sale of alcoholic beverages.

In educational matters, as became a VMI professor, he was against the traditional classical education. He was the only extemporaneous speaker for the affirmative side in the debate as to whether "the cause of female education requires the establishment of a system of colleges similar to that in existence for young men." (The vote was 10 negative and 8 affirmative.)

He argued in one debate that ministers should be trained in seminaries, that the Bible supported the concept of predestination, and that the Bible did not authorize fairs and festivals to raise money for churches. Jackson, who was himself later to be often compared with Cromwell, led the affirmative in a debate on 19 November 1853: "Is the character of Oliver Cromwell such as to recommend him to the favorable notice of the historian?" (Jackson's side lost by a vote of nine to eight.)

Most members of the Franklin Society were, as was Jackson at this time, staunch Unionists who disapproved of secessionist ideas. However, Jackson and most other members approved of slavery. In March 1856 the society debated whether "the system of slavery as it exists in the Southern states is conducive to the perfect division of society"; the vote was 16–2 for the affirmative.

In the entire decade that Jackson spent in Lexington, the most heated debate was that introduced in February 1854. Jackson's good friend D. H. Hill resigned from Washington College to accept a position at Davidson College in North Carolina, where his father-in-law was president, and Dr. George Junkin insisted that his replacement be a Presbyterian. It was Colonel Smith's view that college professorships should be open to qualified men of any denomination. The question before the Franklin Society was: "Is it good policy in Washington College to confine itself to the Presbyterian denomination in the selection of professors?" Feeling ran high, and both Smith and Junkin had their supporters. The debates, which continued weekly into June and included several extra meetings, drew record crowds of seventy or more, about triple the usual number of spectators and participants.

In this emotionally charged battle between Smith (his superintendent) and Junkin (by this time his father-in-law), Jackson apparently decided that discretion was the best course. It was one of the few debates of any consequence in which he did not participate. He did not even attend most meetings during this period.

Still preoccupied with his health, Jackson often went in summer to visit the nearby spas, for he was by this time a firm believer in hydropathic treatments. In July 1852 he stayed for three weeks at Rockbridge Alum Springs. Board was only ten dollars per week, and the place was so crowded with four hundred guests that he had to be satisfied with half a bed.

Although often ill himself, he was not always sympathetic to those who suffered from ailments different from his own. He was known to inform headache sufferers: "If you follow my rule, which is to govern yourself absolutely, I do not think you would have these sufferings. My head never aches. If anything disagrees with me, I never eat it." When others suffered from complaints similar to his own, he invariably recommended that they follow his regimen. When Laura reported trouble with her eyes, he advised her to do as he did and bathe her eyes in cold water six times each day.

Pious works, public debates, artillery drill, natural philosophy, and his health did not totally occupy the thoughts of young Major Jackson, for D. H. Hill described a conversation with him one day in which the name of Elinor Junkin, a daughter of the Reverend Dr. George Junkin, he who was president of Washington College, figured prominently. "I don't know what has changed me," Jackson mused. "I used to think her plain, but her face now seems to me all sweetness."

Hill, roaring with laughter, exclaimed: "You are in love!"

When and how Jackson proposed to Elinor is unknown, but the serious-minded major found favor with her austere, unbending, outspoken Presbyterian father. Now seventy-three years old, Dr. Junkin was a descendant of Scottish Covenanters who had fled to Ireland to escape the persecution of the Stuarts and in the previous century had emigrated to America. He was ordained in the Associate Reformed Presbytery of Philadelphia in 1818 and eighteen months later married Julia Rush Miller, by whom he eventually had eight children. He was a pastor for eleven years in Milton, Pennsylvania, where he helped found the Milton Academy and began a fortnightly newspaper called the *Religious Farmer*. He served in various church offices and was twice named president of Lafayette College in Pennsylvania, first in 1826 and again in 1848. In between he was appointed the first president of Miami University in Ohio in 1841. Known as Old Doc by the students, he spoke in a falsetto voice that, it was claimed, "often runs up to high G."

In 1853 the Junkins had three daughters at home: Margaret, thirty-three, Elinor, twenty-eight, and Julia, eighteen. The two older daughters were inseparable. They dressed alike, shared a room, walked, rode, and read together. Margaret (Maggie to intimates), the older and the more intellectual of the two, wrote poetry as well as articles for magazines and later in life wrote several books. At thirty-seven she married John Thomas Lewis Preston, then a widower of forty-six with seven children. Elinor (so spelled), called Ellie, born less than a year after Jackson (6 March 1825), was prettier, more vivacious, less introspective than her sister.

The courtship did not run smoothly. For unknown reasons the couple parted for three months, and Jackson, according to Hill, talked wildly of becoming a missionary and dying in a foreign land. He once woke the Hills in the middle of the night to beg Isabella Hill to intercede for him. Eventually love triumphed, and a date for the wedding was set. As did many young women at that time, Ellie extracted a promise that no one be told of their plans. The literal-minded Jackson, therefore, did not tell his sister, not even when he paid her a short visit in July. Laura found it hard to forgive him, and the wedding caused a temporary break in their relationship. She ought to have become suspicious when he asked her to send one of the pictures of him she possessed: not the one with the beard taken in New Orleans when he returned from Mexico, but a smiling picture—"and don't fail to send it well wrapped by the first mail." His letters that spring smack of his high spirits. There was less talk of his health and more about his social life. In April he informed her that he was invited to a large party that night and that "among the scramble" he expected "to come in for my share of fun."

It was during the spring and summer of 1853 that Mrs. Hill's attractive young sisters—Eugenia, twenty, and Mary Anna Morrison (always called Anna), twenty-two—came from North Carolina for a visit. Jackson met them when he called on the Hills soon after their arrival. Anna was to remember that he was their "first gentleman caller" and that he offered them his services as their escort whenever Major Hill might be occupied, gravely telling them to call upon him as they would a brother. In private the young women laughed over his playing such a role. With four brothers at home they felt they had a sufficiency, but they liked the handsome young major, even though they thought his manners "rather stiff."

The spirited and good-humored Morrison girls were such pleasant company that Jackson soon fell into the habit of calling every Sunday to see if they had escorts to church, and he frequently accompanied them on long country rambles. "We teased him a great deal," Anna said, but none of their wiles could ever trap him into admitting the fact of his engagement, made known to them in confidence by their sister.

On the morning of Thursday, 4 August, Jackson, who had left Lexington at the beginning of the summer vacation, surprised the Hills by calling on them when they thought he was out of town. He was in high good spirits and spent an hour listening to the Morrison girls sing and calling for his favorite songs, but no amount of teasing on their part could extract from him the reason for his return.

That afternoon in the parlor of the Junkin home on the grounds of Washington College, in a private ceremony performed by Dr. Junkin, Thomas Jackson married Elinor Junkin. The honeymoon took the couple to Philadelphia, West Point, Niagara Falls, down the St. Lawrence to Montreal and Quebec, and then back through Boston and New York.

Dr. Junkin appeared pleased to see his daughter married to the devout Major Jackson, but Ellie's sister Maggie had a struggle with her emotions. She wrote and presented to Ellie a long poem on the marriage, remarkable in its resemblance to a graveside elegy rather than an epithalamium. The third of the ten stanzas gives the tone of the whole:

> *You do not know how fond Ellie*
> *Are all the thoughts you share*
> *You cannot think how sobbingly*
> *I breathe your name in prayer*
> *And plead that God will teach me how*
> *I sweetly may resign*
> *That deepest sympathy of soul*
> *So long I've claimed as mine.*[6]

Perhaps the sisters found it unbearable to be separated even for a few days, for Maggie went along on the honeymoon. Although it is not

6. This poem was never published as far as is known. It exists in manuscript at the Virginia Historical Society in Richmond, Virginia.

certain that she left Lexington with the bridal couple, she was with them by the time they reached West Point and accompanied them until they returned to Lexington.

Jackson was perhaps not always happy to have his new sister-in-law with him. When they ventured out in a small boat to the foot of the falls, Maggie, terror-stricken, tried to struggle from her seat. Jackson held her—"pinioned me down with his strong arms," as she put it— while he questioned one of the rowers: "How often have you crossed here?"

"I have been rowing people across, sir, for twelve years."

"Did you ever meet with an accident?"

"Never, sir."

"Never were capsized, never lost a life?"

"Nothing of the kind, sir."

Turning to Maggie, in "a somewhat peremptory voice," he said: "You hear what the boatman says, and unless you think you can take oars and row better than he does, sit still and trust him as I do."

In Montreal the newly married couple had their first quarrel. A Highland battalion[7] was scheduled to give an exhibition drill on a Sunday, and Jackson, his martial interest aroused, proposed to attend it. When Ellie objected strenuously to such a desecration of the Sabbath, he argued that if an event was worthwhile and not available at any other time except on a Sunday, even though it might be considered worldly, attending it could not be wrong. Maggie, who appears to have been present and may have added her weight to her sister's argument, wrote that Ellie regarded this as "a very sophistical way of secularizing sacred time."

"It is possible that my premises are wrong," Jackson finally conceded as he prepared to go. "When I get home, I will go carefully over all this ground and decide the matter for myself." But before that time he offended once again by spending a Sunday in a convivial conversation with some old army friends he encountered.

At Quebec, on the Plains of Abraham, Jackson doffed his cap to approach the monument to Wolfe. His eyes bright with tears, he read Wolfe's dying words: "I die content." Casting his arm in a wide sweep that took in the surrounding plain, he exclaimed to the admiring young women beside him: "To die as *he* died, who would not die content?"

---

7. This was probably the 1st Battalion of the Highland Light Infantry, which was in Canada at this time, although it could have been a unit of Canadian Highlanders.

It was late in August when the Jacksons and Maggie returned to Lexington. The young couple took up residence in the Junkin house, occupying two rooms and a back porch. Jackson now set himself to smooth Laura's ruffled feathers. He wrote affectionate letters and sent her "the little purchases" he had made on his honeymoon for her and her children. "I am enjoying life," he confided. "To me my wife is a great source of happiness. She has those requisites of which I used to speak to you, and sends her love to you." But Laura did not soften easily. Brother and sister had been close and trusting; it seemed unforgivable to her that he would keep secret his engagement. It was not until 14 February of the following year that she finally wrote to him. He responded by sending her a lock of Ellie's hair and requesting that she send in return a lock of her daughter's and one of her own.

There was now time to keep his promise to examine the question of what might with propriety be done on a Sunday. The book that appears to to have decided the question for him was was *The Principles of Courtesy* by George Winfred Hervey.[8] "Designed to illustrate and enforce the duty of Christian courtesy," it supplied homilies to guide a conscientious Christian in every aspect of life. The courteous virtues—gentleness, cheerfulness, humility, et al.—were examined, and specific instructions were offered for the proper observance of the Sabbath, the correct posture at prayer, the seemly manner of singing hymns. Rules were set forth governing the proper deportment when attending weddings and funerals, when making visits to the poor, and when smoking: in the city only "in the company of chimneys, on a fire-proof roof"; in the country only "far from all human haunts."

Jackson took to heart Hervey's strictures on Sabbath behavior:

> Were this day intended to be observed as a season of bodily renovation and repose, then whatever could contribute to this object would be allowed. But it is especially for the weary enslaved soul that this day is ordained to be hallowed. If we examine Isaiah's exposition of this command, we will find it requires us to abstain from every thought, word and action which affords gratification to a worldly mind.

In future he would refrain from writing, sending, or reading a letter on a Sunday. He even tried to time the mailing of letters so that

---

8. Jackson's heavily underlined copy of this book is still extant in what remains of his library at the Confederate Memorial Institute in Richmond, Virginia.

none of his, even important business letters, would travel then. Except for the exigencies of war, he struggled successfully most Sundays to keep "every thought, word and action" away from worldly affairs.

The biblical command to "pray without ceasing" he followed by a method of his own. He explained it to a friend:

> I have so fixed the habit in my own mind that I never raise a glass of water to my lips without lifting my heart to God in thanks and prayer for the water of life. Then, when we take our meals there is grace. Whenever I drop a letter in the post office, I send a petition along with it for God's blessing upon its mission and the person to whom it is sent. When I break the seal of a letter I have just received, I stop to ask God to prepare me for its contents, and make it a messenger of good. When I go to my classroom and await the arrangement of the cadets in their places that is my time to intercede with God for them. And so in every act of the day I have made the practice habitual.

When asked if he did not sometimes forget, he replied: "I can hardly say that I do; the habit has become almost as fixed as to breathe."

In the autumn of 1853 Jackson thought he saw a possibility to better his status. Edward Hill Courtenay, professor of mathematics at the University of Virginia, had died, and the university was seeking a replacement. Courtenay had been graduated at the head of his 1821 class at West Point, and he had had a distinguished career as an engineer and mathematician. In January 1854 Jackson formally applied to the Board of Visitors for the position, pulling all the strings he could find. Colonel Smith, fellow professors, Francis Taylor, his former commanding officer, a former naval surgeon who lived in Rockbridge County, and even Brevet Colonel Robert E. Lee, then superintendent of the United States Military Academy, bore testimony to his "character and merit."

A friend asked if he had not changed his ideals considerably, for he was unlikely to find military fame as a professor at the University of Virginia, and Jackson conceded that he had and that he now questioned the morality of war. He would never seek a commission in the army, he declared, unless the United States engaged in a defensive war.

There were several reasons why Jackson tried for the vacant post at Charlottesville. Although he enjoyed Lexington, his relations with Smith had not been smooth. Junkin and Smith were at odds, and it could not have improved his relations with the superintendent when he married a Junkin daughter and moved into the Junkin house. The university's three-thousand-dollar salary—more than double his VMI pay—was doubtless attractive. He wanted to set up a home of his own; Ellie was pregnant, and he could expect to begin a family.

Not until June did the board meet to select Courtenay's replacement; then it appointed Albert Taylor Bledsoe, an 1830 graduate of the Military Academy who had taught at Kenyon College and at Miami University in Ohio and had for the previous six years taught mathematics at the University of Mississippi. He was a contributor to literary, scientific, and theological journals, and he possessed a law degree. Clearly, the older, more experienced, and better-known Bledsoe was the better choice. Jackson seemed to bear his disappointment without distress, regarding it as "God's will," and until war took him away from Lexington, he never again attempted to leave the Virginia Military Institute.

On 23 February 1854, while he was still soliciting testimonials from friends and acquaintances, Ellie's mother died. Jackson described her deathbed in considerable detail to Laura. She "asked us to kiss her," he wrote, "and told her children to live near to Jesus and to be kind to one another." Her death, he said, "was no leaping into the dark. She died in the bright hope of an unending immortality of happiness."

In June of that year Laura lost a child, and Jackson determined to pay her a visit, taking Ellie with him. It was not a wise or a considerate decision, for by this time Ellie was six months pregnant, and the mountain roads to Beverly were rough. She dreaded the jolting, swaying trip in a stagecoach, as well she might. Although, as she had anticipated, the journey was a trial, the visit was a success. In Beverly she met Laura for the first and last time, and any lingering ill feeling on Laura's part appeared to vanish. She was glad she had gone, Ellie said.

On 24 July 1854 the Jacksons were at Healing Springs, then being developed as a resort, the springs reputedly effective, according to Dr. J. R. Moorman's 1854 edition of *The Virginia Springs,* for a "wide range of morbid conditions," particularly rheumatism, neuralgia, skin problems, as well as "extreme cases that had failed to be relieved elsewhere." From here Ellie wrote a detailed letter to Laura describing their trip back from Beverly:

> The journey over the mountains was extremely tiresome to me, as the road over Cheat Mt. had been newly McAdamized[9] & the load was heavy for two horses.

9. A macadamized road was not a tarred, smooth-surfaced road, but one made of crushed rock.

We had a very agreeable companion with us whose vivacity and intelligence beguiled our way very much, his name was Henry O. Middleton & he is a great land owner and speculator.[10] Much of his talk was about land. It was nine o'clock when we reached Monterey and we left at two in the morning, so we did not have very much rest, but by lying down on the seat with my head on the Major's knees & Mr. Middleton's overcoat for a pillow I rested somewhat & did not feel the jolting so terribly as I did sometimes. . . .

Turning to the present, she wrote:

We reached these springs about noon on Tuesday. A good many people have come since we did and now I suppose there are 50 or 60 here. The water is disagreeably warm to drink, but is very pleasant to bathe in—I drink about 5 glasses a day—and the Major drinks more. They keep an excellent table and we get the very nicest brown bread—plenty of venison & other meat and twice they had tomatoes, but they were brought from Richmond. They have been examining my face this morning & think it a little improved. [She had recently suffered a partial paralysis of her face.] I let the water run over it when in the bath. The Major thinks the water is doing him good. . . .

The long, hard trip had been trying indeed for the suffering young woman.

Three months later, on 22 October, Ellie was delivered of a stillborn baby girl. That evening she herself died.

Two days later snow was falling as the VMI cadets carried the body of Elinor Jackson to the Lexington Presbyterian Cemetery.[11] Dr. White officiated. Cadet Thomas M. Boyd always remembered how Jackson looked:

With cap in his hand he stood beside the open grave. He was extremely pale but calm and resigned. He did not shed a tear, yet everyone who saw him was impressed with the intense agony he was enduring. . . . In a day or two after the interment of the body he

10. Henry Middleton (1797–1876), son of a former governor of South Carolina, had been graduated number one from West Point in 1815 but resigned his commission only sixteen months later. He became an attorney and land speculator. He was the author of several books on economics and politics in which he advocated free trade and denied the right of the federal government to issue paper currency.

11. Now the Stonewall Jackson Memorial Cemetery.

was back at his post, and pursued his even, quiet, regular life. He had grown paler, but beyond this, and the bit of crepe on his cap and the handle of his sword, no one would have known the severe ordeal through which he had passed, nor the bitterness of that intensely passionate soul.

Jackson blamed himself for the folly of the journey to Beverly. Several months later he confided to a friend: "I do not see the purpose of God in this, the most bitter, trying affliction of my life, but I will try to be submissive though it break my heart." His letters speak eloquently of his sorrow and of his misery. In a notebook he wrote: "Objects to be effected by Ellie's death: To eradicate ambition; to eradicate resentment; to produce humility."

9

Europe and Remarriage

J
ackson, a warm and affectionate man behind his austere exterior, had always held strong family affections, and the death of Ellie drove him to seek solace in such family ties as remained. In the summer of 1855 he again visited Laura and her family in Beverly and then journeyed on to other still-living relations elsewhere. He saw—for the last time—Jackson's Mill, Weston, and Clarksburg. Traveling farther west, he visited the Whites, the Alfred Neales, and his half brother Wirt Woodson, now twenty-four, who had been raised by the Neales. He traveled to Fayette County, where he had bidden a last good-bye to his mother, and he tried unsuccessfully to find her grave at Hawk's Nest, near Ansted.[1] Someone remembered that there had once been a wooden marker, but it was long gone. He located the graves of his sister Elizabeth, his brother Warren, and his father. He made arrangements with his aunt Catherine Williams to have the graves attended to, and he wrote to Laura about erecting stones.

Seeing Wirt fired in him a brotherly zeal for his welfare. Wirt was badly educated, and Jackson during his short visit strove to correct his

---

1. It is most doubtful if the marker now in place actually marks the grave of Jackson's mother, but she was buried somewhere nearby. The stone was erected by a Jackson admirer after the Civil War.

speech and to teach him some grammar. Wirt had little love for learning, and his newfound brother's exhortations to study and improve himself failed to galvanize him, but Jackson was not to be deterred. For the next two years Wirt and the Neales were buffeted with advice.

Wirt thought he would like to be a farmer, and Jackson was willing to help him. He offered to lend him the considerable sum of a thousand dollars to buy a farm in Missouri, although three conditions were attached: Wirt was to pay not more than seven dollars an acre, the land was to be approved by Alfred and William Neale, and the deed was to be in Jackson's name until the loan was repaid.

It was a generous offer. "It appeared to me I ought to run the risk for him," Jackson told Laura. But the risk was a bad one. Wirt immediately broke the agreement by paying not seven but eight dollars per acre and by purchasing the land without the approval of the Neales. Still, the loan was not withdrawn.

Wirt was far from settled. When he had had enough of farming, he did not scruple to beg for a second loan to buy cattle, which he proposed to drive to California, a venture Jackson wisely refused to finance. He feared Wirt would run wild so far from home and relatives. On 16 February 1857 he told his aunt Clem (Anna Neale) that "to assist him in going to California would in my opinion be cursing rather than blessing him."

It was not long after he had returned to Lexington that Jackson, in a letter to Laura explaining his plans for Wirt, made his first known statement about the political unrest in the country and the possibility of future conflict: "I do not want him [Wirt] to go into a free state if it can be avoided, for he would probably become an abolitionist; and then in the event of trouble between North and South he would stand on one side and we on the opposite."

The purchase of land for speculation was very much on Jackson's mind in 1856, and more than once he consulted Laura's husband, Jonathan, whose views he respected. At one time he considered buying "about two thousand acres of land warrant"[2] in Illinois or Kansas. He wanted land in a free state, which he thought Kansas would become, for "this will give the advantage of a free State in selling should I years hence wish to dispose of them."

A few months later, on 6 June 1856, he asked Laura to tell her husband: "I design following out his idea of locating some land in a

2. Land warrants were transferable certificates issued by the United States government that entitled holders to specific tracts of government land.

Northern State, but I am a little afraid to put much there for fear that in the event of a dissolution of the Union that the property of Southerners may be confiscated. I want to locate about three thousand acres, maybe a little more; and if I can please myself, will probably put about one-half of it in a Northern state."

That summer he planned to go first to Washington for more information about land warrants and then to Illinois, Iowa, Missouri, and perhaps Arkansas to look for land. However, he suddenly changed his mind, and Laura unexpectedly received a note from him from New York written on 9 July 1856: "I sail in the steamship *Asia* for Europe at twelve o'clock today for Liverpool. The reasons for doing so I will give you in my next." With the letter he enclosed thirty dollars and suggested that she apply it toward care of their father's and sister's graves.

On 4 July, after commencement exercises, the VMI records show that: "A leave of absence to go beyond the limits of the U. States, was unanimously granted to Major Thos J. Jackson." Jackson then had to scramble to catch the mail packet boat that went by the North River Canal and the James River to Richmond, a forty-four-hour trip that cost four dollars. In Richmond he caught the train for Washington. There he was issued a passport[3] and immediately entrained for New York City, arriving just in time to catch the ship.[4]

In a letter written at sea he tried to explain to Laura why he was not going west and why he chose the cities of Europe over Beverly, Virginia:

> You have doubtless been surprised at my sudden leaving for Europe instead of going west to purchase or locate land. . . . This year, as the time for going West drew near, I became more and more discouraged in regard to investing money in such distant lands, and a gentleman with whom I conversed, and who has had much experience, told me that he did not think it a safe and profitable investment. Another friend told me that he had come very near losing a part of his in consequence of his being so far off. . . . I have rather concluded to keep my money invested in stocks of

3. A description of Jackson is included on his passport application: age thirty-four, stature five feet nine and three-quarters inches, forehead full, eyes gray, nose aquiline, mouth small, chin oval, hair dark brown, complexion dark, face oval.

4. Winifred Hadsel of Lexington, who has thoroughly researched Jackson's European trip and to whom I am indebted for much of the information regarding it, learned that a last-minute passenger would have had no difficulty obtaining a ticket as the *Asia* at this period was never completely booked.

different kinds, and thus get my dividends regularly, and to trust to the blessings of Providence for gradually increasing my worldly goods.[5] . . . You are a very kind and affectionate sister, yet even with you I would be reminded of the loss of that happiness which I once enjoyed with dear *Ellie*. So I have to some extent torn myself away from that state of mind which I feared, should my summer have been passed at home, or in the United States.

The *Asia*, a Cunard Royal Mail paddle steamship built in 1850 of British oak, was 280 feet long, the largest ship ever built in the Clyde up to that time and certainly one of the best ships sailing the North Atlantic.[6] On Monday, 21 July, she docked at Liverpool. Not waiting to get his land legs, Jackson caught the train to Chester that same day. After checking into a hotel, he hurried out to visit the medieval red sandstone cathedral, which he found "quite interesting." Jackson, who frequently fell asleep in church, was particularly impressed by the handsomely carved misericords, so constructed that if monks became drowsy, "their seat suddenly dropped them on the floor." Not yet sated, he walked around the old city wall and "saw the tower on which King Charles I stood and saw the defeat of his army at Rowton Moor." It was an energetic first day ashore, but the active Jackson had no complaints about his health.

On his second day in England he hired a carriage to take him to Eaton Hall, then the great Gothic-style country home of the Marquess of Westminster. This was the only great house Jackson saw in England, but he could not have selected a more splendid one.[7]

From Chester he took a train to Scotland, and with John Menzies's *Scottish Tourist Pocket Guide to Scotland* in hand, he industriously toured the country, going from Glasgow to Stirling to Edinburgh. Next on his itinerary was York, where he found his most memorable sight:

5. The nature of the stocks Jackson held and the sources of his money for purchasing them remain a mystery, but he had accumulated in only five years at VMI nearly four thousand dollars, the equivalent of more than three years' salary. A ledger found in the basement of the Rockbridge County Courthouse reveals that Jackson placed some money with a private banker who lent it for mortgages.

6. The ship mounted twenty coal-burning boilers that produced the steam for turning the huge paddle wheels. Steam engines could be supplemented by sails. It had two decks for passengers and could carry 140 first-class and 30 second-class passengers.

7. This vast "magnificent palace covered with pinnacles," as Jackson described it, has now disappeared and has been replaced by a contemporary house.

the five thirteenth-century lancet windows of gray (grisaille) glass at the end of the north transept of York Minster.[8] There are brilliantly colored stained glass windows elsewhere in the church, but to Jackson's Presbyterian taste, these great gray windows were the most beautiful.

From York Jackson traveled to Ely, where Cromwell had once lived, then to Cambridge and finally to London, where he bought a two-volume illustrated history of the city for Dr. Junkin and a ceramic figure of Little Red Riding Hood for Laura.

Having sailed to Antwerp (where he paused to admire a Rubens painting), Jackson then began a classic tour of the Continent. He visited Brussels and journeyed out to the Waterloo battlefield, the only battlefield he toured. He did not take time to make a detailed study of the battle, but looking over the field, he quickly decided that Napoleon ought to have launched his main attack on the village of Mont St. Jean instead of the Château of Hougoumont. He was in Europe not to study military history but to absorb European culture, and he went about his task as conscientiously as he had attacked his West Point textbooks. Traveling up the valley of the Rhine, he saw Cologne, Bonn, Frankfurt am Main, Heidelberg, Baden-Baden, and Strasbourg with its "wonderful clock," then crossed into Switzerland, where he found the landscape "very grand." He visited Basle, Thun, Bern, Freiburg (containing, he believed, "one of the best organs in the world"), and Geneva. He crossed the Alps into Italy by way of the Simplon Pass—Napoleon's route, he noted—and visited Lake Como and Lake Maggiore, Milan, Venice, Mantua, Verona with "the most perfect amphitheatre in the world," Modena, Florence, Pisa, Leghorn, and Naples, a whirlwind tour. By the time he reached Naples he had been in Europe only six weeks. Florence was one of his favorite cities, and his copy of H. C. Wilson's *A New Guide of Florence* is heavily underlined. He particularly admired the sculptures "in the room called the Tribune."[9] While at Naples he ventured out to Vesuvius and, he told Laura, "went about half-way down one of the active craters. The scene was truly grand."

8. In the autumn of 1862, when Colonel (later Field Marshal and Viscount) Garnet Wolseley visited the by then famous "Stonewall" Jackson near Winchester, Virginia, he was disappointed to find the American general reluctant to discuss his own campaigns but eager to talk about his experiences in Britain. Asked what he considered the most remarkable sight, Jackson said, "The seven [*sic*] lancet windows in York Minster."

9. The room in the Uffizi Gallery in the Piazza della Signoria is an octagonal room now called Room XVIII, where some of the most important sculptures are preserved, including the *Venus of the Medici*, a third-century B.C. Greek masterpiece.

Europe could hardly have held a more energetic and conscientious sightseer—and en route he tried to teach himself French.

In the month remaining, he visited Rome, Leghorn again, Genoa ("probably the most beautiful of all cities"), Marseilles, Lyons, Paris, and finally back, via Calais and London, to Liverpool. He probably recrossed the Atlantic on the *Washington*. He arrived in Lexington in mid-October.

The academic year at VMI began on 3 September. Jackson had not intended to arrive until early in October, but the ship had been slow, and he arrived later than intended. His punctuality being near legendary, he was chaffed about his tardiness, but he was not to be upset. "I did all I could to be here at the appointed time," he said, "but when the steamer was delayed by Providence, my responsibility was at an end."

He came back to Lexington revitalized. He had thoroughly enjoyed himself. As he told his Aunt Clem, "It appeared to me that Providence had opened the way for my long-contemplated visit, and I am much gratified at having gone." It had been two years since Ellie had died. The nearly four-month trip to Europe, strenuous as it must have been, seemed to have enabled him to put his grief behind him. He resumed his teaching, delivered a talk on his trip to the Franklin Society,[10] and again plunged into church activities.

On the day after Christmas 1857 he was gratified to be elected a deacon. It was an office he performed so conscientiously that Dr. White came to consider him the best in the church. He appears to have been exceptionally good at collecting money for church needs, levying indiscriminately rich and poor. Every Sunday he attended two services and taught two Sunday schools, one for slaves and free blacks.

Early biographers and Jackson admirers have made much of Jackson's "black Sunday school," as though it were a unique establishment. Such was not the case. There were many such schools throughout the South. The Synod of Texas summarized the attitude of the vast majority of Presbyterians in the South when it declared: "We recognize the hand of God in placing this benighted race in our midst, and heartily

---

10. Cadet Thomas H. Boyd heard the lecture and twenty-five years later wrote about it. Jackson's talk, he said, "was full of thought and facts, showing that he was a close observer and careful thinker. There was no effort at display. He lectured as I had often heard him lecture in the class room. His audience was deeply interested. . . ." (from a typescript of an unpublished manuscript in the West Virginia University Library).

accept the duty of pointing them to Christ." And the Presbyterian was not the only church to hold such a view. Colonel Francis Smith was not only the superintendent of VMI but also the superintendent of an Episcopalian Sunday school for slaves established before Jackson came to Lexington.

In 1845 Dr. Henry Ruffner, then president of Washington College and known for his antislavery views, and the Reverend Tucker Lacy had established a Presbyterian Sabbath School for Slaves that was attended by about a hundred pupils. With the departure from Lexington of both Ruffner and Lacy the school languished until it was revived by Jackson. With his usual energy he canvassed slaveowners in the area and prodded free blacks influential in the black community to attend themselves or to send their children. Although attendance was not compulsory, Jackson kept careful records and regularly paid visits to the owners of backsliders.

School began promptly at three o'clock each Sunday, and there were no latecomers. Jackson locked the doors. Service began with a hymn, invariably "Amazing Grace," for this was the only song he could manage to make recognizably tuneful. (Dr. White, speaking of Jackson's ignorance of "the science of music," declared that he had "neither ear nor voice for singing.") Jackson then led the school in prayer, which was followed by relating a story or reading a passage from the Bible, after which pupils were turned over to teachers for lessons drawn from the *Shorter Catechism* or perhaps Charles Colcock Jones's *A Catechism for Colored Persons* (Charleston, 1834). When called together again, they sang, said a prayer, and were dismissed. Under Jackson's supervision, the entire session lasted exactly forty-five minutes.

Although most whites approved of such schools, Jackson's evangelical efforts did not meet with universal approval. It was at this time in Virginia not only illegal to teach slaves to read but, with memories of Nat Turner's slave insurrection in 1831 fresh in mind,[11] also forbidden

---

11. Nat Turner (1800–1831), a slave in Southampton County, Virginia, became a religious fanatic, convinced other slaves of his divine mission, and with their help murdered sixty-one whites, including his master's family. He was captured, tried, convicted, and, on 11 November 1831, hanged. This was the bloodiest slave insurrection ever in the Southern states.

There was a scare in Rockbridge County during the Christmas holiday in 1856, when a letter was discovered on a road outside Lexington containing plans for three hundred slaves to attack the VMI arsenal and kill all the whites. Colonel Smith wrote to General William Richardson: "I do not presume to say whether or not it was a hoax—it may not be—but my confidence is not excessive in the colored population

for groups of slaves to assemble or to be assembled. Late one afternoon in front of the courthouse Jackson was bearded by Colonel Samuel McDowell Reid and William McLaughlin. "I have examined the statute and conferred with the commonwealth's attorney," Colonel Reid informed Jackson. "Your Sunday school is an 'unlawful assembly.' "

McLaughlin added his bit. He, too, had examined the statute and was forced to agree that the school was certainly against the letter of the law. J. D. Davidson, another lawyer, joined the knot of men and chimed in: "Major, I lament that we have such a statute in our books, but I am satisfied that your Sunday school is an 'unlawful assembly,' and probably the grand jury will take it up and test it."

Jackson, cornered, turned on Davidson with some heat: "Sir, if you were, as you should be, a Christian man, you would not think or say so."

When Davidson retorted angrily, Jackson turned on his heel and stalked off.

Almost immediately Davidson regretted his behavior, and after his supper he returned to his office to write an apology. He was sitting at his desk, pen in hand, when there was a tap at his door and Jackson entered, saying, "Mr. Davidson, I am afraid I wounded your feelings this evening. I have called to apologize to you."

Davidson hastened to apologize in turn, and the two men sat talking amiably for a half hour. As he was leaving, Jackson observed with satisfaction, "Mr. Davidson, these are things that bring men together and make them know each other better."[12]

After his return from Europe Jackson stayed on in his and Ellie's rooms in his father-in-law's house. Julia Junkin's marriage to Junius Fishburne in 1856 left only himself, Dr. Junkin, and Maggie in the once-bustling home. The deaths of her mother and the sister to whom she had been so close had left Maggie a lonely woman. She and Jackson, sharing the same sorrow, drew close to each other. He offered to teach her Spanish, a language she declared herself eager to learn, and

---

here." He issued a "confidential order" in which he outlined precautions to be taken against "insurrectionary designs among the slaves," and live ammunition was issued to the guard.

12. Some twenty years later Davidson found among his papers the unfinished apology: "Dear Sir: As I shall not have an opportunity of meeting you again before Monday, I will not rest content until I shall have tendered you a becoming apology for the hasty, and I fear uncourteous reply made by me to you in conversation this evening—"

she came to his study each night at nine o'clock for lessons. Not surprisingly they strayed from Spanish grammar, and Jackson talked to her of his boyhood, of West Point and of Mexico, and even of "his service among the everglades of Florida," about which he had not told either Ellie or Laura. Just how thoroughly and in what way he presented his quarrel with French, if he talked about it at all, is unknown. He spoke of his delight in dancing in Mexico, a pleasure he had abandoned in Presbyterian Lexington. Maggie thought him only mildly apologetic for such dissipation. "I did not then, nor do I now, reproach myself," he told her. He seldom, in fact, ever reproached himself for anything.

Maggie came to feel at this period that she knew him better than did anyone else. She was probably right, but he remained a very private person. Her affection deepened, perhaps even turned to love for the man who had been her sister's husband, and she may have cherished hopes of an even closer relationship, but Jackson appears never to have felt other than a brotherly affection. When he could again think of love, he hearkened back to the summer of 1853 when he had played the brother to the Morrison sisters. Shortly after their visit to Lexington, Eugenia had married a young lawyer, Rufus Barringer, destined to become a Confederate general. Jackson's thoughts focused on her sister, Mary Anna, whom he had last seen when he had wedded Ellie.

Anna Morrison (she was never called Mary) was the fourth child (of ten) of the Reverend Dr. Robert Hall Morrison, a Presbyterian minister who had been the first president of Davidson College, a Presbyterian school for men founded in 1836. When ill health had forced him to give up his presidency, he had retired with his family to Cottage Home, which Anna fondly described as "a large, old-fashioned house surrounded by an extensive grove of fine forest trees, on a plantation in Lincoln County, North Carolina."

The Morrisons were wealthy people of influence in the county and the state. Anna's maternal grandfather was General Joseph Graham, and her uncle William A. Graham was successively governor of North Carolina, United States senator, and secretary of the navy under President Millard Fillmore. Describing rather ingenuously the life she and her sisters led, Anna later wrote: "We were simple country maidens, knowing little of the world outside of our father's home, where all was purity, peace, and contentment." She had, however, made long visits to Lexington and to her uncle in Washington, D.C., where she had taken tea at the White House and vastly enjoyed the cosmopolitan social life of the capital.

The Spanish lessons had not progressed far before Jackson wrote to Anna, expressing, as she said later, "blissful memories" of the summer they had met in Lexington. Puzzled by the letter's rhapsodic tone, she showed it to Eugenia, who was home at the time. Eugenia read it and, "laughing most heartily," predicted that the stiff-backed major would soon be paying them a visit. And indeed, one cold day near Christmas 1856 Jackson, splendid in a blue uniform with gleaming brass buttons, arrived at Cottage Home and, shown into the library, was warmly welcomed by Dr. and Mrs. Morrison. Dr. Morrison was delighted to find him a "Christian gentleman"—indeed, a Presbyterian—and Mrs. Morrison was charmed by his "extreme politeness."

Anna's account of this first short visit sounds too casual. There had doubtless been a number of letters exchanged, and probably the purpose of the major's visit was clear to all. Jackson and Anna were discreetly left alone in the parlor but were three times routed by a smoking fire. Nevertheless, they somehow had time enough together, for according to family history, they were engaged on the second day of his visit. Jackson had need to act fast, for he was on special leave from VMI and had to hurry back. The couple did not see each other again until the following July.

Although he was now about to take on the responsibilities of marriage, Jackson at this time complained of feeling financially pinched. Perhaps the European trip had been more expensive than he had expected; perhaps some of his investments had turned sour, for there was a "panic" in 1857. He had not received an increase in salary since he came to VMI, and inflation had raised the cost of living. On 16 February 1857 he told his aunt Clem: "I have been more pressed for money in the last month or so than I remember having been for years." Ten days later he told Laura that his aunt Clem had asked him to lend several hundred dollars to the ever-troublesome Wirt. "I did not have the money," he told Laura, "and even if I had, should not have lent it. . . ."

In his letters to Anna during the seven months between his proposal and their marriage, Jackson made no mention of money. There was, perhaps, a dowry, although no record exists, or perhaps Anna had property in her own right, which might well have provided financial relief and also account for Jackson's evident prosperity, his considerable investments in land, slaves, and businesses in the four years following his marriage. Within a year, on 1 July 1858, he had purchased $600 in shares of the Capital Bank of the Commonwealth and made other substantial investments. By 1859 he had $4,322 in a checking account at the Rockbridge Bank—a sum equivalent to about $80,000 in 1992 dollars. When he died four years later, his estate was valued at four times this amount: $8,548 in property, including slaves valued at $5,700, and $8,500 in bonds and stock.

This time Jackson was free to tell Laura of his engagement. Anna had urged him to invite her to the wedding. "I told her I didn't think you would be able to accept," he wrote. Laura did not attend. Although he stayed with the D. H. Hills in Davidson when he came for the marriage, Jackson chose for his groomsmen another member of the Davidson faculty, Clement Daniel Fishburne, whom he had known when Fishburne was a student at Washington College, and Thomas P. Cocke, who substituted for his cousin Thomas Preston, sick with typhoid fever.

Commencement day at Davidson College, Thursday, 16 July 1857, was the date set by Anna for the marriage. In the days preceding it, Jackson met members of the Davidson faculty, attended some of the final examinations, and on Sunday went to church to hear Dr. Drury Lacy, who had succeeded Dr. Morrison as president of the college, preach a long sermon. A young woman behind Jackson was mesmerized by "his perfect immobility" as he stood through an extraordinarily long prayer. He was, she said, "the *stillest* human being I had ever seen." On Thursday morning he sat on the platform at the college during the commencement exercises, again immobile, but this time it was remarked that he was fast asleep.

Fishburne had heard it said that Jackson did not like to use his middle name, and when he wondered aloud to Jackson about the form of the wedding and what the bride and groom would be called, Jackson, who only used the initial he had assumed at West Point, became agitated and took steps to ensure that first names only be used.

The wedding day was sweltering, with a full set of emergencies. Dressing for the wedding, a sweating Jackson had to ask for help with his stiff collar; the trousseau of the bride did not arrive from New York until a few hours before the ceremony; there was some uncertainty about a marriage bond required by the state; but by "early candlelighting" all was ready at Cottage Home. Dr. Lacy, the "favorite old ministerial friend" of Anna's, presided. Perhaps struck by the groom's rigid bearing and moved by his fondness for the bride, he sternly required Jackson to promise to be an "indulgent husband." Jackson's bridal gifts to Anna were a gold watch and a set of seed pearls.

And so, for a second time, Jackson married the daughter of a Presbyterian minister and a college president. A few days later the couple set off on their honeymoon, an itinerary almost identical to that

Jackson had followed with Ellie. There was an alarm when in Richmond Anna developed an enlarged gland in her neck, but she was not too sick to continue the trip and go on to Baltimore, Philadelphia, New York, Saratoga Springs, and Niagara Falls. In New York the couple climbed the spire of Trinity Church, where "the view was indeed grand, embracing the whole city—graceful sparkling rivers; the bay and sound, studded with vessels in motion and at rest; and beautiful rural scenery stretching out as far as the eye could reach."

On 30 July 1857 "T. J. Jackson and Lady" checked in at the Cataract House in Niagara Falls, New York, and were assigned Room 166, just down the hall from Room 158, where "A. Lincoln & family" of Springfield, Illinois, had stayed on 24 July.[13]

They agreed that their favorite places were Niagara and Saratoga. At the latter spot Anna complacently noted that her husband "took not a particle of interest in the gay and fashionable throng." They had planned to go to Beverly to see Laura and her family, but Jackson was eager to get his wife back to Lexington, from which they could visit the Rockbridge Alum Springs, his favorite spa. He had always felt that the mineral waters improved his health, and he was sure they would be good for Anna.

In Lexington the newlyweds took rooms and boarded for a time at the Lexington Hotel and then for a time in private homes, but they were eager to have a house of their own. To a friend Jackson wrote: "I hope in the course of time we will be able to call some house our home. . . . I shall never be content until I am at the head of an establishment in which my friends can feel at home in Lexington. I have taken the first important step by securing a wife capable of making a happy home, and the next thing is to give her an opportunity."

That winter Jackson suffered a variety of illnesses: inflammation of the throat and of the passage leading to the ear, "very painful neuralgia," trouble with his ears and his eyes. On 19 December he wrote Laura: "I never remember having suffered so much as within the last three weeks." He swallowed preparations of ammonia and used chloroform liniment externally; he tried a variety of medicines for his eyes. Nothing seemed to help. Still, he continued his work at the institute.

In January 1858 the Jacksons moved into a comfortable two-story house of stone and brick with an English half basement on Washington

13. The original hotel guest book, containing the signatures of Jackson and Lincoln, is now in the possession of the local history division of the Niagara Falls Public Library.

Street in downtown Lexington. It was the only house Jackson ever owned, and he was destined to enjoy it for less than three years. It was not a new house. His friend, colleague, and business partner John T. L. Preston had been born there in 1811. The deed was signed on 4 November 1858, after Jackson had paid Dr. Archibald Graham about three thousand dollars. (The actual price is not known.) The young couple had already ordered furniture; the first shipment had arrived by canalboat on 1 September.

Before they were properly settled, tragedy struck. On 30 April 1858 Anna gave birth to a daughter, whom they named Mary Graham after Anna's mother. On 22 May Jackson warned Laura that the baby was "very ill of jaundice; and she may at any hour take her place among the redeemed in Paradise." Three days later she died, "a great, a very great sorrow to him," Anna wrote later. Store records indicate that on 26 May Jackson purchased "one fine cloth coffin and box." Only a few weeks after this tragedy Anna suffered another loss, a "crushing stroke," in the death of her adored sister Eugenia. On 20 July Jackson's friend and mentor John B. Lyle died after a lingering illness.

Jackson responded to the repeated blows with a series of illnesses. In a letter to his "Dear Little Niece" on 7 June telling her that his daughter had gone "to enjoy the heavenly happiness of Paradise," he added that "my own health is so delicate." To Laura he complained that his eyes were worse and his throat so inflamed that he was taking glycerine "through the nostrils for the purpose of curing the inflammation at the entrance of the nasal tubes into the mouth. . . ." On 19 June he informed her that he must go north: "My disease is not understood by my physicians here and I have nearly if not entirely lost the hearing in the right ear." In the following month, as soon as the school year ended, Jackson and Anna hurried to New York, where he placed himself in the hands of Dr. John Murray Carnochran, a professor of surgery at New York Medical College, who recommended that his right tonsil, which was inflamed, be removed. The operation was performed on 19 August, and although at first it seemed a success, Richard H. Catlett, quartermaster and treasurer at VMI, wrote to Colonel Smith, then in Europe[14]: "Major Jackson has returned not improved in health,

14. Superintendent Francis Smith sailed from New York for Europe on 6 June 1858, taking three cadets, one his nephew, with him. They did not return until mid-December. Smith was authorized to examine European schools and on his return wrote a report on "Scientific Education in Europe."

but on the contrary worsted by his *new system of treatment.*"

Shortly after the death of Anna's sister Eugenia (Mrs. Rufus Barringer) her three-year-old son was sent to the Jacksons, with whom he lived until war broke up the household,[15] and late in October Laura's son, thirteen-year-old Thomas Jackson Arnold, came to them to attend school in Lexington. He remained until the following July. Jackson had often corresponded with both Thomas and his young sister, Grace, spurring them to work ever harder at their studies. When Grace was twelve, Jackson wrote: "When I was young I committed the blunder of learning to read before I had learned to spell well, and though I am now thirty-six years old, yet still I am mortified at my spelling words wrong." Thomas, he wrote, must "never give up his Latin grammar." Grace, he advised, should stick to English, for he did not "attach much importance to Latin for females."

Jackson was fond of Thomas, who was old enough to be a companion; he oversaw his lessons, took him on long walks, to concerts and to lectures, and together they worked in his prized vegetable garden. Jackson was a solicitous uncle—too solicitous, thought the boy when he refused to permit him to go camping with his teacher and classmates at Peaks of Otter, a primitive resort four thousand feet high in the Blue Ridge Mountains. While the other boys sported in the Otter River and climbed the twin mountain peaks, Thomas stayed home and studied Spanish.

When grown and looking back on those months in Lexington, he dismissed the eccentricities so often attributed to his uncle, declaring, "I do not recall a single circumstance during my residence there, or in fact at any other time, that could be termed eccentric upon his part. I do not think he was so."

The house on Washington Street needed some repairs and improvements, which Jackson threw himself into with a will, pleased, indeed, to have, as he said, "a place for everything and everything in its place." To his aunt in Parkersburg he wrote: "I am living in my own house, I am thankful to say, as, after trying both public and private boarding, I have learned from experience that true comfort is only to be found in a house under your own control."

Anna later wrote: "He luxuriated in the freedom and liberty of his home, and his buoyancy and joyousness of nature often ran into playfulness and *abandon* that would have been incredible to those who saw

15. The child grew up to become Dr. P. B. Barringer, a professor at the University of Virginia.

him only when he put on his official dignity." He seemed, she said, "transformed." His "buoyancy and sportiveness" were, she confessed, "quite a revelation." He liked to hide behind doors and spring out at her with a "startling caress." He called her his *esposa* or his *esposita*, and himself her *esposo*, for Spanish remained for him a language of romance.

During the engagement his letters had been sedate affairs, highly spiritual in tone: "When in prayer for you last Sabbath, the tears came to my eyes and I experienced an unusual degree of emotional tenderness. . . ." Those written after the marriage, during Anna's short absences from home, were filled with lively domestic detail and studded with endearments, and reveal a man joyously, exuberantly in love. Anna was his "little dove," his "darling of darlings," "somebody's sunshine."

He settled into unbridled domesticity. A handsome piano, manufactured by Knabe Gachle & Co. of Baltimore, was ordered for Anna. Although quite tone-deaf, he was eager to have music in his own home. He bought a bay horse, which he prosaically named Bay, and he reveled in the possession of "two splendid milch cows, and a lot of chickens." His attendance at the Franklin Society dwindled.

The young couple owned six slaves. Before the marriage Jackson had bought two: Albert and Amy. Albert, according to Anna (writing long after the war), asked Jackson to purchase him, offering to pay for his freedom by working as a hotel waiter. (An extant ledger from the Rockbridge Alum Springs shows that in the summer of 1859 Jackson was paid fifteen dollars per month for Albert's services.) Again, according to Anna, Amy, a mature woman "about to be sold for debt," had petitioned Jackson to buy her. A fine cook and a good housekeeper, she had worked in "a good Christian family." Hetty, chambermaid and laundress, had been Anna's nurse and had so clamored to join her that Dr. Morrison transferred her ownership to Anna and, not wishing to separate her from her two sons, Cyrus, age twelve, and George, sixteen, transferred their ownership as well.

Two, perhaps three, other slaves, perhaps brought into the marriage by Anna, may have been sold off by the Jacksons, perhaps to buy the house.

The sixth "servant," as household slaves were euphemistically called, was Emma, a four-year-old orphan whom Jackson had taken "under his sheltering roof at the solicitation of an aged lady in town," said Anna. Jackson, who made the acquisition without consulting his wife, optimistically thought that the little girl could be reared to be a "nice little maid" and that Anna would enjoy training her and teaching her to read, but Anna found her "troublesome" from the beginning and "never a treasure."

Made of sterner fiber than Anna, Jackson was a "very strict but kind master" who undertook to train their slaves. As a result, they became, in Anna's words, "as polite and punctual as that race is capable of being, and his system soon showed its good effects." All the slaves in the household attended daily family worship, church on Sunday, and, of course, Jackson's black Sunday school, for there was never a legal challenge to this activity.

Writing after the Civil War, Anna maintained that Jackson "would prefer to see the negroes free, but he believed that the Bible taught that slavery was sanctioned by the Creator himself, who maketh men to differ, and instituted laws for the bond and the free. He therefore accepted slavery, as it existed in the Southern States not as a thing desirable in itself, but as allowed by Providence for ends which it was not his business to determine." The attitude of most Rockbridge citizens was probably close to that expressed in the *Lexington Gazette* on 26 September 1860: "[S]lavery is the highest state of happiness that a negro can reach."

With domesticity came the fancy to own a small farm. When in 1859 Jacob Fuller, a schoolmaster and businessman, offered to sell for five hundred dollars an irregularly shaped plot on elevated land on the edge of town only 1 mile from Jackson's house, he bought it and became the happy owner of 18 acres and 20 poles (110 square yards).[16] Here, with the help of his slaves, he raised wheat, corn, and vegetables and planted an orchard.

Jackson's daily routine was, according to Anna, "perfectly regular and systematic." He was up at six o'clock each morning, knelt in prayer, then took a cold bath, "never omitted even in the coldest days of winter." After dressing, he went out for a brisk walk, rain or shine, returning "the picture of freshness and animation." Prayers attended by the entire family were at seven o'clock sharp, and he waited for no one, not even his wife. Breakfast followed prayers, and then he was off to the institute.

Teaching occupied only three hours, and he was home by eleven. Only during the last few weeks of the school session was he required to

---

16. Anna mistakenly said the farm "embraced twenty acres." The land is now the site of quarry operations, and when Winifred Hadsel, who successfully located it, took me to see it in 1989, it was covered with large piles of gravel and rocks.

return for artillery instruction. As he stood in front of a high made-to-order desk, his Bible and textbooks occupied him until dinner at one o'clock. During these two hours he permitted no interruptions. After dinner he spent a half hour or so in "leisure and conversation." (He considered it unhealthy to work immediately after eating.) Then came gardening, supervising his slaves, or handling business. Weather permitting, he and Anna took an evening walk or drive, sometimes in summer driving by moonlight. After supper and the obligatory relaxation he reviewed his lesson for the next day. As he never read in artificial light, he used no books but sat motionless facing a wall, concentrating "dumb as the sphinx," said Anna. When finished, he would look up with a smile, a sign that he was ready to enjoy himself. Anna then often read to him.

With ample spare time Jackson became a man of affairs. In 1857 the Rockbridge Bank was founded in Lexington with Colonel Smith as president and Jackson as a member of the board of directors. In 1858 he was elected to the board of the Lexington Savings Institution, and he was involved with a group called the Lexington Building Fund Association. (When the building fund was dissolved in 1863, he realized a profit of $1,644.)

In April 1860 Jackson, together with Jacob Fuller, from whom he had bought his farm, and VMI professors John T. L. Preston and William Gilham, purchased a tannery, for which the principals paid $4,889.86, including all finished stock. Fuller was the financial agent and in charge of operations.

Jackson purchased, again with Gilham and Preston as partners, a lot 100 by 131 feet on Randolph Street for $1,050. The same three later purchased 320 acres in the Blue Ridge some 8 miles from Lexington for $1,280.

Jackson was now a businessman, a respected citizen of the town, a deacon in Lexington's largest church, a married householder and slaveowner as well as a professor at the institute. But this happy life of domestic comfort and increasing prosperity was soon to come to an end, and evidence of its coming demise accumulated rapidly.

10

War

J ohn Brown (1800–1859) was a nervous, highly strung man; there was insanity in his mother's family. Life had not been kind to him. He was a bankrupt, frequently in the courts, often accused of dishonesty, and his only success had been in siring twenty children by two wives. A religious fanatic, he came to believe that God had given him a mission to abolish slavery by violent means. In Kansas in 1856 he headed a gang of seven who murdered five defenseless settlers by splitting their skulls with broadswords (the Pottawatomie Massacre); he fled the territory after a small but bloody, inconclusive battle with pro-slavery men. Shooting at men who shot back was not Brown's style.

He next appeared in Canada, where he hatched a plot to liberate American slaves and to found a new nation with them in the mountains of western Virginia with himself as commander-in-chief. His first step to this end was to be an attack upon the United States arsenal at Harper's Ferry, Virginia (today West Virginia), followed by a distribution of the arms he would capture there to the slaves he was certain would flock to join him. Tensions between the North and South had been steadily worsening in the 1850s, and the halls of Congress rang with the agitated voices of Daniel Webster, Henry Clay, Stephen A. Douglas, William H. Seward, and John Calhoun. The Methodists and Baptists separated into Southern and Northern churches. The institution of slavery became a social and political powder keg. Brown intended to light the fuse that would explode it.

On the night of 16 October 1859, with twenty-one men, including four of his sons, four free blacks, and one escaped slave, Brown launched his attack and successfully captured the arsenal, not a difficult task, for it was defended by a single watchman. Only one man was killed by Brown's gang in the action: an unarmed free black railroad employee.

He then seized sixty leading citizens as hostages, including a wealthy descendant of George Washington's; cut telegraph wires; blocked the railroad tracks; and tried to rouse the slaves. Although he had confidently predicted that five hundred would join him, only ten were hustled in, and none volunteered for his "army."

Within hours the local militia and every townsman with a weapon had assembled, and in the fire fight that followed, Brown with a handful of his faithful was forced to take refuge in the small brick firehouse. Two of his dead, left outside, were used for target practice by the enraged militia and townsmen; a third corpse was chewed on by hogs.

Word of Brown's attack quickly reached Washington by telegraph, and the next day a small force of marines led by army Lieutenant Colonel Robert E. Lee, was hastily dispatched. On arrival Lee sent First Lieutenant J. E. B. Stuart, serving as a volunteer aide, to the firehouse to demand Brown's surrender. The moment he refused, marines launched an assault, broke down a door, and within three minutes killed or captured all inside.

Of those who participated in the raid, including those left to guard their rendezvous in Maryland on the night of the raid, ten were killed or mortally wounded, including two of Brown's sons; seven were taken prisoner, including Brown, who was wounded; and five escaped. Brown and his men killed five, one of whom was the black railway worker, and wounded nine others.

Justice was swift. Although Brown insisted that he ought to be treated not as a criminal but as a prisoner of war, federal authorities turned him over to the Commonwealth of Virginia, and he was taken to Charles Town, six miles away, where the circuit court of Jefferson County was about to begin its session. There on 27 October 1859 his trial began. Four days later a jury, after deliberating forty-five minutes, convicted him of treason, conspiring with slaves to commit treason, and murder. On 2 November he was sentenced to be hanged one month hence.

Brown's raid and his trial electrified both the North and the

South. The raid appalled Southerners and conjured up their worst fears; many Northerners saw it as a daring stroke by a brave man in a just cause. When sentenced, Brown was permitted to make a self-serving statement which Ralph Waldo Emerson, an ardent abolitionnist, later misguidedly compared with Lincoln's Gettysburg Address.

Fearing that there might indeed be a slave insurrection or that Northern abolitionists would attempt to rescue Brown, Governor Henry A. Wise requested federal troops and called out the cadets of VMI as well as units of the Virginia Militia under the command of Brigadier General William B. Taliaferro, who was commander of the 4th Brigade of Virginia Militia and a former member of the VMI Board of Visitors.

Colonel Smith had anticipated Governor Wise's action. On 19 November he had issued Order No. 237, detailing Major Gilham to the command of the cadets who would act as infantry and Major Jackson to "be prepared specially for the use of howitzers." Smith wanted no nonsense:

> He implicitly confides in the cadets that they will promptly discharge every duty and obey every command, that they will abstain from all thoughtless levity and from all forms of indiscretion and immorality and that they will remember that called into service as men they will acquit themselves like men. . . . Let no boisterous noise be heard at any time. . . . The recitations will be regularly kept up, but lessons will be so regulated as to impose light burdens upon the student.

On 23 November Smith received orders to have his unit in Charles Town by 1 December; Brown was scheduled to be hanged the following day. Smith, ordered to proceed there at once, left with Majors Preston, Colston, and two other professors as staff officers. Departure date for the cadets was advanced, and at eight o'clock on the evening of 25 November Gilham received orders to march at once. Two hours later the VMI detachment set out. Eighty-five cadets, most from the two upper classes, had been selected: a sixty-four-cadet unit armed as infantry directly under Major Gilham and three lieutenants; a twenty-one-cadet battery of two howitzers under Major Jackson and Lieutenant Daniel Truehart.

Harman and Company, brothers who operated the largest stage-coach line in the upper Shenandoah Valley, placed, free of charge, their entire stock based in Lexington and Staunton at the disposal of the institute to transport the cadets to Staunton. There they boarded a train to Richmond, Washington, and finally Charles Town. Jackson and his howitzers arrived on the evening of 27 November. The next day he wrote to Anna that "seven of us slept in one room," and he estimated there were about a thousand troops in and around the town. Two days later Lieutenant Colonel Robert E. Lee arrived with four companies of regulars from Fortress Monroe.

Regulars, cadets, and the many militia units presented a colorful sight and an almost festive air. An eyewitness described the scene:

> Among the gay and animated groups which continually filled the streets of Charles Town, representatives of all classes and from all parts of the State might have been seen. Each company disported the uniform of its fancy, and all the colors of the rainbow shone out resplendent in the various costumes which met the eye. . . . In many corps, each gentleman selected his own uniform. . . . Some wore slouched hats, some military caps, and some stovepipe beavers of the latest style. It was a merry gathering, and everyone was gay and happy as a lark. They talked of war as a pastime, and seemed to think it was a glorious thing.

The cadets were issued muskets, sabers, and ammunition from the Harper's Ferry arsenal, improvements over their usual arms, and on 1 December, the day before the execution, special orders were issued: "Every cadet will have his musket in perfect working order, for inspection this evening at 3½ o'clock and 12 rounds of ball cartridges in good order in his cartridge box. The cadets will lie down in their clothes and accoutrements, with their arms loaded by their sides, to be ready at a moments [*sic*] warning for any emergency tonight."

Shortly after eight o'clock the following morning the cadets, wearing long gray overcoats over red flannel shirts, were paraded and marched silently to the high ground southeast of town where the gallows had been erected. Most of the assembled troops were infantry, but the dashing thirty-one-year-old Turner Ashby from Fauquier County was present with a militia cavalry troop mounted on black horses. Smith, in charge of military arrangements on the field, formed the various units into a hollow square surrounding the gallows. The VMI infantry detachment under Gilham was prudently posted between the two best militia infantry units in Virginia, the Richmond Grays and

Company F, also from Richmond. In the ranks of the former, although he was not a member, was John Wilkes Booth.[1] He was not the only ringer: sixty-six-year-old Edmund Ruffin, an advocate of scientific agriculture, a friend of Major Gilham's, and a chauvinistic Southern fire-eater, managed to borrow a uniform and marched with the cadets; less than two years later, as a member of the Palmetto Guards, he laid claim to having fired the first gun at Fort Sumter. Jackson's guns were posted on either side of the cadets. The howitzer on the left was commanded by Lieutenant Truehart, and Jackson himself commanded the gun on the right.

Civilians had been advised to stay home, but provision was made for them to attend, and some men did, although no blacks, free or slave, were permitted to watch the execution.

That evening Jackson wrote Anna a detailed account of the hanging:

> John Brown was hung to-day at about half-past eleven A.M. He behaved with unflinching firmness. . . . Brown rode on the head of his coffin from his prison to his place of execution. The coffin was of black walnut, enclosed in a box of poplar of the same shape as the coffin. He was dressed in a black frock-coat, black pantaloons, black vest, black slouch hat, white socks, and slippers of predominately [*sic*] red. There was nothing around his neck but his shirt collar. The open wagon in which he rode was strongly guarded on all sides. Captain [Lewis B.] Williams [formerly assistant professor at the institute] marched immediately in front of the wagon. The jailor, high-sheriff, and several others rode in the same wagon with the prisoner. Brown had his arms tied behind him, and ascended the scaffold with apparent cheerfulness. After reaching the top of the platform, he shook hands with several who were standing around him. The sheriff placed the rope around his neck, then threw a white cap over his head, and asked him if he wished a signal when all should be ready. He replied that it made no difference, provided he was not kept waiting too long. In this condition he stood for about ten minutes on the trap door, which was supported on one side by hinges and on the other (the south side) by a rope. Colonel Smith then announced to the sheriff "all ready"— which apparently was not comprehended by him, and the colonel

---

1. Carl Sandburg *(The War Years),* among others, described Booth as a lieutenant in the Richmond Grays, but he was not, in fact, a member of any military unit. He had simply talked his way into accompanying the Richmond Grays in order to witness the hanging.

had to repeat the order, when the rope was cut by a single blow, and Brown fell through about five inches, his knees falling on a level with the position occupied by his feet before the rope was cut. With the fall his arms, below the elbows, flew up horizontally, his hands clenched; and his arms gradually fell, but by spasmodic motions. There was very little motion of his person for several moments, and soon the wind blew his lifeless body to and fro. . . . [I]t was an imposing but very solemn scene. I was much impressed with the thought that before me stood a man in the full vigor of health, who must in a few moments enter eternity. I sent up the petition that he might be saved. Awful was the thought that he might in a few minutes receive the sentence, "depart, ye wicked, into everlasting fire!" I hope that he was prepared to die, but I am doubtful. He refused to have a minister with him. His wife visited him last evening. His body was taken back to the jail, and at six o'clock P.M. was sent to his wife at Harper's Ferry. When it arrived, the coffin was opened, and his wife saw the remains, after which it was again opened at the depot before leaving for Baltimore. . . . We leave for home via Richmond to-morrow.

As John Brown was hanged on a Friday, Jackson's letter probably traveled on a Sunday, as did he himself, but he made no comment on this departure from his religious scruples. Although as a civilian he scrupulously kept the Sabbath free of worldly concerns, he was never to allow his religious sentiments to override military necessities.

On their way home Jackson paused in Richmond to drill the cadets before an admiring audience in the town square, and he took the opportunity to make hurried calls upon political friends, such as William L. Jackson, his cousin and soon to be a judge, and Jonathan M. Bennett, the state auditor and a prominent politician from Lewis County. He would soon have need of his political friends and relations.

In January 1860, seven weeks after Brown's hanging, Jackson wrote to his aunt in Parkersburg: "Viewing things in Washington from human appearances, I think we have great reason for alarm, but my trust is in God; and I cannot think that he will permit the madness of man to interfere so materially with the Christian labors of this country at home and abroad."

On 2 February he wrote in much the same vein to Laura telling her, "I am much gratified to see a strong union feeling in this portion of the state, but it may be a little further than I think it ought. . . . I intend to vote for the Union candidate for the convention. . . . But if after we have done all we can . . . there shall be a determination on the part of the Free States to deprive us of our rights . . . I am in favor of secession." He added that he thought Colonel Smith was "throwing his influence in favor of secession." Indeed, this was so, and there were complaints when Smith made a secessionist speech at a picnic; some declared they would no longer contribute to a state institution at which "treason was taught."

When the Virginia General Assembly met after John Brown's raid, it passed a new militia act which, among other items, formally recognized the VMI officers as a part of the state's military establishment and placed the cadets in "the service of the state, under the military command of those appointed to govern [the institute]." Jackson and the other senior professors were appointed majors in the Corps of Engineers[2] and received a welcome 50 percent pay increase (their first) to $1,800 per year, with a promise of a raise of $100 every five years. Even this was scarcely enough, for American army pay had done more to keep up with inflation, and even a second lieutenant in 1860 made $1,242 per annum. Army colonels made $2,616, which was on a par with the salary of a Harvard professor.

The legislature also appropriated five hundred thousand dollars, an enormous sum, to pay for the purchase and manufacture of arms and ammunition; Colonel Smith was appointed one of the three administrators of this ambitious program. John Letcher (1813–1884), a Lexington lawyer and pro-Unionist, took office as governor of the state in January 1860, and in April he with the three commissioners went north on a ten-day tour of munition plants to buy arms and military equipment and stores. It was certainly a curious mission: the governor of Virginia with three commissioners buying arms and military equipment from Northern states which, it was presumed, would soon be their enemy and against whose citizens the weapons would probably be directed.

At Cold Spring, New York, a village on the Hudson twenty miles south of Poughkeepsie, Colonel Smith encountered a friend, Robert Parker Parrott (1804–1877), who had been graduated number three from West Point in 1824, the same year in which Dennis Mahan had been number one. Parrott, after service in the artillery and the ordnance department, had served since 1836 as superintendent of the West Point Iron and Cannon Foundry. Parrott knew a great deal about ordnance, and he was particularly interested in rifled cannon. He had developed a rifled gun with a wrought-iron hoop welded into a ring and

2. The commissions still conferred no rank in the active militia.

cooled onto the breech for the greater strength needed there in rifled artillery. Smith and the other commission members were interested and asked him to send a gun and a hundred shells to VMI for testing.

On 18 July the gun arrived at Lexington. Jackson was then taking a hydrotherapeutic cure at Brattleboro, Vermont, and two weeks later, still feverish and bilious, he moved on to try another water cure at Northampton, Massachusetts, and so did not return until 3 September. Smith had fired a few shots from the gun during the summer but reported that his powder was "very indifferent" and his results unreliable. Jackson on his return, with Gilham and Colston assisting him, conducted more extensive tests, firing at white tent flies across the North River. The three were greatly impressed by the gun's range and accuracy. Primarily upon the basis of Jackson's enthusiastic report, it would seem, the state ordered twelve Parrott guns and a supply of the special shells with a brass ring around the base that they required.

In the presidential election of 1860 Jackson did not vote for John Bell of Tennessee, the candidate of the old-line Whigs of the Constitutional Union party, who carried Virginia by a scant plurality of 358 votes, or for Stephen A. Douglas, the choice of the Northern Democrats. He cast his vote for John C. Breckinridge of Kentucky, the Southern Democratic party candidate who favored slavery in the territories and had walked out of the Democratic convention in Charleston in April, splitting the party.

With the election of Lincoln as a "minority president"[3] and the adoption of the ordinance of secession by South Carolina on 20 December 1860, secession was debated hotly throughout the South, and a few days after South Carolina's dramatic move Jackson wrote to Laura asking about the political feeling in Beverly. Like most of western Virginia, Beverly was, in fact, strongly pro-Union, as was Jackson, who told his sister: "I am strong for the Union at present and if things become no worse I hope to continue so. I think that the majority of the county are for the Union, but in counties bordering on us there is a strong secession feeling."

A month later, after Mississippi, Florida, Alabama, and Georgia had seceded and on the day Louisiana left the Union (26 January

3. Although Abraham Lincoln did not receive a majority of the popular votes, he would have won the election even had all three of his opponents combined, for his electoral college votes were so strategically distributed that he would still have carried every state that he won except California and Oregon, which between them had only seven electoral college votes. Lincoln received one vote in Rockbridge County.

1861), Jackson wrote at some length to his nephew, Thomas Arnold, who had just turned fifteen:

> In this county there is a strong Union feeling. . . . I am in favor of making a thorough trial for peace, and if we fail in this, and the state is invaded, to defend it with a terrific resistance. . . . I desire to see the state use every influence she possesses in order to procure an honorable adjustment of our troubles, but if after having done so the free states, instead of permitting us to enjoy the rights guaranteed to us by the Constitution of our country, should endeavor to subjugate us, and thus excite our slaves to servile insurrection in which our families will be murdered without quarter or mercy, it becomes us to wage such a war as will bring hostilities to a speedy close. People who are anxious to bring on war don't know what they are bargaining for; they don't see all the horrors that must accompany such an event. For myself I have never as yet been induced to believe that Virginia will even have to leave the Union. I feel pretty well satisfied that the Northern people love the Union more than they do their peculiar notions of slavery, and that they will prove it to us when satisfied that we are in earnest about leaving the . . . [Union] unless they do us justice.[4]

Texas left the Union on 1 February, and a week later deputies from seven Southern states, meeting in Montgomery, Alabama, adopted a provisional constitution for the government of the Confederate States of America.[5] On 18 February Jefferson Davis, who had been graduated number twenty-three out of thirty-three in the West Point class of 1824, was elected president of the Confederate States of America, with Alexander Hamilton Stevens, a Georgia lawyer and until the last minute a strong Unionist, as vice president of the new government.

On 4 March 1861 Abraham Lincoln was inaugurated president of the United States. He gave an emotional, eloquent speech, begging Americans not to destroy "our national fabric, with all its benefits, its memories, and its hopes," and he closed by saying: "We are not enemies, but friends. We must not be enemies." But it was too late. The national fabric was shredding fast. Southerners were no longer the

4. *Early Life and Letters of General Thomas J. Jackson* by Thomas Jackson Arnold, p. 23f.

5. Interestingly, the Confederate Constitution, although declaring each state sovereign, imposed the same restrictions upon the powers of the states as did the U.S. Constitution, and it made no provision for a right to secede.

friends of Mr. Lincoln and his Northerners. Still, Virginia, the most populous Southern state, had not yet committed itself. Jackson was not alone in agonizing over the question of secession, but like most, he was convinced of the right of the people in a state to secede.

Lexington, like every other city, town, and hamlet in Virginia, was caught up in the political excitement that swept through the state as Virginians worried and debated the desirability of following the other Southern states in secession. In Rockbridge County the *Valley Star* changed its masthead slogan from "The Union and the Constitution" to "The Union must be preserved." The *Lexington Gazette* carried on its masthead: "Let us cling to the Constitution as the mariner clings to the last plank when the night and the tempest close around him." The difficulty, of course, was that not everyone read the same meaning into the Constitution, and on 25 April the *Gazette* quoted a letter from New York published in the *Richmond Dispatch:* "There is hope that this insane besotted and blood-thirsty passion of the North has had time to cool a little and reaction set in. . . . But what are we to expect? Madness and villainy rule the hour." A month later, on 30 May 1861, the *Gazette* had progressed to lambasting "treacherous Yankee tyrants" and "tyranni-cal Northern rule."

Throughout the county there were meetings, demonstrations, and debates. In Lexington many of those in favor of secession flew the palmetto flag of South Carolina, while strong Unionists, the majority of citizens, showed the Stars and Stripes.

Most of the VMI cadets and the Washington College students were strongly for secession, and there had been incidents. At six-thirty on the morning of 22 February 1861, when Jackson arrived at the institute to fire a thirteen-gun salute in honor of Washington's birthday, he found a secession flag flying from a flagpole on top of the barracks. Made from a sheet, it carried the device on the state shield—the god-dess of liberty—and the state motto, *Sic Semper Tyrannis.* Over this the cadets had written "Hurrah for South Carolina." At Jackson's order, the guard hauled down the flag, and the affair ended, but this was only the first of a series of provocative flag raisings.

On 13 April (the day Fort Sumter surrendered) a second flag raising in Lexington threatened to become serious. There are numer-ous accounts of the incident, none of which agrees in detail with any other. Apparently secessionists raised a flag in front of the courthouse; Unionists in turn tried to raise the Stars and Stripes, but cadets had broken their flagpole. Because it was a Saturday, many cadets were in town; discussions quickly turned into arguments, and arguments into fights. Rumors flew, and one excited cadet, A. J. Summers of Gap Mill, Virginia, raced into the barracks, shouting that a cadet had been murdered. In short order the barracks were emptied as cadets snatched up their muskets and poured down the hill into the town, loading as they ran. Colonel Smith, in bed with pneumonia, heard the uproar, saw from his window the running cadets, and, weak as he was, dressed and hastened after them.

The bewildered mayor unwisely called on the Rockbridge militia, which was drilling that afternoon, to face the cadets. Civilians joined the militia ranks, and battle lines were forming when one of the junior professors, twenty-five-year-old Captain John McCausland, gained enough control over the cadets to hold them in check until Smith came panting upon the scene. Reminding them of their duty to obey orders, he marched them back to their barracks, where a group of professors, including Jackson, waited.

There Smith made a speech, appealing for reason and calm, that brought a degree of order, but no more, to the restless cadets. Turning to Jackson, he said, "I have driven in the nail, but it needs clinching. Speak with them."

Major Jackson, the tedious professor and the awkward debater, stepped forward and spoke. Accounts of his words vary, but all agree on his closing words:

> Military men, when they make speeches, should say but few words and speak them to the point. I admire, young gentlemen, the spirit you have shown in rushing to the defense of your comrades, but I must commend you particularly for your readiness with which you have listened to the counsel and obeyed the orders of your superior officer. The time may be near when the state needs your services, but it has not come yet. If that time comes, then draw your swords and throw away the scabbard.[6]

The words and manner struck home. The hero of Contreras and Chapultepec had spoken, and he had indeed clinched Smith's nail. The cadets could safely be dismissed. One, James H. Wood, in later years

6. There exist eleven descriptions (at least) of this march on the town by the cadets and of Jackson's talk to them. All differ considerably in their details, and Jackson is placed at different places during the affair, but all agree that he spoke to them, and there is remarkable agreement on his last sentence, which obviously made a deep impression. The version followed here is that used by Colonel William Couper in *One Hundred Years at V.M.I.*, vol. 2, p. 86.

remarked: "How strange it was that that this quiet professor who had performed his every duty, monotonous in its regularity, should with a bound leap into view and establish in the minds of his audience that he possessed the qualifications of a brilliant and dashing leader."

The following day, 14 April, Lincoln issued his fateful call to the states for seventy-five thousand volunteers "to execute the laws of the Union; and suppress insurrections." Governor Letcher thundered in reply that "militia of Virginia will not be furnished to the powers at Washington for any such use or purpose as they have in view." On 17 April the Virginia Convention, in secret session, adopted an ordinance of secession. Secrecy was imposed to enable the arsenal at Harper's Ferry, Fortress Monroe, and the navy yard at Portsmouth—the three most important military and naval installations in Virginia—to be seized, but of course, such dramatic news could not be suppressed for even twenty-four hours.

With few exceptions, those Virginians who had been in favor of preserving the Union now cheered the Confederacy, and throughout the state men prepared to fight. In Lexington James J. White, son of the Reverend Dr. White and professor of Greek at Washington College, organized a company of college students calling themselves the Liberty Hall Volunteers (Liberty Hall Academy was the forerunner of the college). Often called simply "the college company," it was completely outfitted by the patriotic ladies of Lexington, even to red flannel waistbands to be worn next to the skin to ward off diarrhea. The Reverend William Nelson Pendleton, fifty-two, the West Pointer who was rector of the Episcopal church, drilled the college company until he organized and commanded the Rockbridge Artillery, a unit which came to contain "seven Masters of Arts of the University of Virginia, twenty-eight college graduates, twenty-five theological seminary students, and among the others many of the most accomplished young men of the South, including R. E. Lee, Jr., son of the great commander." (Pendleton was to become a general and Lee's chief of artillery.)

Colonel Smith quickly offered the services of the institute to the state, "a company of 250 well armed and well disciplined men," and promised Governor Letcher that he could "raise a command of 1,200 chosen troops in 15 days." On 18 April he was ordered to Richmond to be a member of a three-man executive council. That same day two companies of the Rockbridge Rifles and a company of the Rockbridge Dragoons (mounted and eager to fight, although unarmed), along with various other Virginia militia and volunteer units, set off down the Shenandoah Valley for Harper's Ferry.

Feelings ran high, and in Lexington there was intense excitement. It was no longer possible to sit astride the political fence. At Washington College Dr. Junkin, who had once shouted in church, "God Almighty can't do without this United States government in His work of evangelizing the world, and he won't let you break it up!" and had angrily torn down and burned the secessionist flags raised by his students, found his faculty had united against him and joined the students in protecting their flag. When secession became a fact, he loaded his carriage and taking his daughter Julia and a niece with him, fled north to Philadelphia, leaving behind his college, his daughter Margaret (now Mrs. Preston), his two sons (both Presbyterian ministers; one of whom, William, was to raise a company of Confederate infantry and be its captain), and his former son-in-law, Thomas Jackson, whom he had called "My dear son." There is a story, perhaps apocryphal, that when he reached the state border, he stopped to wipe the dust of Virginia from his horses' feet.

If Jackson had any qualms about where his duty lay, he did not express them. Indeed, he seemed quite certain in his mind that his first loyalty was to Virginia. At the institute lessons were forgotten as the corps of cadets prepared to move to wherever they would be needed by the state. The Presbytery of Lexington was holding its semiannual meeting at this time of crisis, and many of the invited ministers were in town, some staying with the Jacksons, but for once Jackson had no time to talk theology. He had hoped that on Sunday, 21 April, he would be able to attend their meetings, but at dawn a messenger appeared at his door with marching orders, and Jackson did not hesitate.

Major Preston, who had been left in charge of the institute, had received orders to send the corps of cadets to Richmond together with "all the ordnance and ordnance stores and with full supply of ammunition." Preston had already prepared orders: "In the march the Corps will be under the command of Major Jackson. Major Colston is assigned to duty as Acting Commandant of Cadets, and will report to Major Jackson. . . . The 'Kits' will be prepared . . . and be ready to be inspected at 10 o'clock. At 12½ o'clock they will be formed to march. Dinner at 12 o'clock."

After giving Anna hurried directions for packing his necessities, Jackson made all haste to the institute, where he busied himself with arrangements for the move, including a request to Dr. White to come to the barracks at twelve-thirty to pray over the departing officers and cadets. Departure would be at one o'clock. About eleven o'clock, remembering that he had had no breakfast, he rode home for a final meal, a reading of the Bible (fifth chapter of Second Corinthians), and a prayer with Anna before mounting his horse and riding off to war.

The 47 cadets told off to stay behind to guard the arsenal were objects of pity to all the others. "They were in tears," wrote Preston, "that they cannot share danger and glory." The remaining 176 cadets and 8 officers (not quite the 250 Smith had promised Governor Letcher) were lined up in front of the barracks.

Dinner was over, the silver-haired Reverend William White— who had been a stout Unionist but now declared that he had "become a rebel, but never a secessionist"—had offered up a prayer, and the assembled cadets stood in front of the barracks, crying impatiently, "Let's go! Let's go!" Unperturbed, Jackson dismounted, seated himself upon a small mess stool,[7] and announced calmly, "When the clock strikes the hour we will march, and not until then."

When the clock at last struck, he remounted, gave the welcome command, "Right face! By file left. March!," and the eager cadets moved off over the bridge across the North Branch of the James River, leaving behind them the castellated barracks of the Virginia Military Institute. Many, including Major Jackson, were never to return alive.[8]

They did not march far and soon mounted the stagecoaches of the Harman brothers and were taken to Staunton, thirty-eight miles away, arriving about 10:00 P.M. At 10:15 the next morning they "took the cars" of the Virginia Central Railroad for Richmond. On the way Jackson had time to write to Anna: "We are stopping for a short time on the eastern slope of the Blue Ridge. . . . The war spirit here, as well as at other points on the line, is intense. The cars had scarcely stopped before a request was made that I would leave a cadet to drill a company."

Arriving in Richmond the evening of 22 April, Jackson marched his cadets to the Hermitage Fair Grounds a mile and a half from the city. Converted into a camp of instruction, it was soon jammed with thousands of volunteers. The Virginia Militia had long been a ram-

---

7. Jackson seemed to be attached to this small stool; he is said to have carried it about with him throughout his service in the war. After his death it came into the possession of the family of William N. Pendleton, whose granddaughters presented it to the VMI Museum.

8. In addition to the services of the cadets, the Virginia Military Institute's faculty and alumni contributed to the Confederate army 1 lieutenant general (Jackson), 3 major generals, 18 brigadier generals, 160 colonels, 110 majors, 306 captains, and 221 lieutenants.

shackle institution, its muster rolls a farce; men were only required to drill four times a year, and often even these were neglected or turned into picnics. Senior officers in the militia were usually prominent citizens with good political connections but little military experience. Even at this late date none of its cavalry regiments was armed, and few artillery units possessed cannon. There was even a dearth of infantry weapons, and units were armed, if at all, with old muskets, bowie knives, and squirrel rifles.

The cadets were immediately pressed into service as drill instructors. John B. Jones, a clerk in the Richmond War Department, wrote in his diary: "The cadets of the Military Institute are rendering good service now, and Professor Jackson is truly a benefactor." Many recruits had no conception of a soldier's life and were accustomed to obeying no one; army life came as a rude shock. One such was thirty-three-year-old George Bagby of Lynchburg, who later wrote:

> To get up at dawn to the sound of fife and drum, to wash my face in a hurry in a tin basin, wipe on a wet towel, and go forth with a suffocated skin, and a sense of uncleanliness to be drilled by a fat little cadet, young enough to be my son, of the Virginia Military Institute, that, indeed, was misery. How I hated that little cadet! He was always so wide-awake, so clean, so interested in the drill; his coat-tails were short and sharp, and his hands looked so big in white gloves. He made me sick.

All the old volunteer groups which had retained their organization were quickly filled, and new ones formed, and as religion and politics were closely related in the minds of most Southerners, many volunteer and militia units were accompanied by a local minister, although the status of chaplains had not yet been made clear. Even some of the guiding lights of the leading churches—Presbyterian dignitaries such as Robert Dabney, Moses Hoge, and James Woodrow—passed out religious tracts and preached at the camps of instruction around Richmond, admonishing young men: "It is your homes and firesides you go to protect. Wives, mothers and sisters are now looking to you to defend them against a merciless enemy." Beset by preachers and drillmasters, the recruits were whipped into shape to fight the "damned Yankees."

Just a few hours ahead of Jackson, Colonel Robert E. Lee, having resigned from the American army, arrived in Richmond dressed in civilian clothes and wearing a tall silk hat. The following day he was commissioned a major general and placed in command of Virginia's military and naval forces. Jackson, delighted, told Anna that Lee was "a better officer than General Scott."

Jackson had no important duties at the fairgrounds. He fretted to Anna that the "Governor and others holding responsible offices have not enough time for their duties, they are so enormous at this date." Frustrated and bored, he was eager to share the burden. On 25 April he was commissioned a major of engineers in the Virginia Militia, but this must have been disappointing.

Fortunately, throughout his ten years at the institute he had been careful to keep his political fences mended, visiting political friends whenever he could, writing to them, and writing letters on their behalf when they campaigned. They were to stand him in good stead throughout the next two years. Jonathan M. Bennett now pleaded with Governor Letcher for a more appropriate assignment and rank for Jackson. Letcher, who was from Lexington, knew Jackson and agreed. Consequently his name was put before the Constitutional Convention to be confirmed in the rank of colonel and to be assigned to Harper's Ferry.

On the convention floor someone asked, "Who is this Major Jackson that we are asked to commit him to so responsible a post?" Another political friend, Samuel McDowell Moore of Rockbridge County, answered grandly: "He is one who, if you order him to hold a post, will never leave it alive to be occupied by the enemy." With that ringing endorsement, Jackson's rank and assignment were confirmed, his rank dating from 27 April 1861. He set off at once for Harper's Ferry. This was, he gleefully told Anna, "the post I prefer above all others, and has given me an independent command."

THE SEAT
OF THE WAR

0   10   20   30   40   50
miles

Potomac R.

South Branch Potomac R.

Romney

Moorefield

Faubis

Strasb

Columbia
Furness

North F

Beverly

Rude's
Hill

Massanutten
Gap

Franklin

New
Market

Le

Luray Valley

Harrisonburg

Conrad's
Store
(Elkton)

Monterey

Cross Keys

McDowell

North R.

Elk Run
Valley

Swift Ru
Gap

Lebanon
Springs

Mt. Solon

Port
Republic

Semon's Gap

South R.

Brown's Gap

Staunton

Jaman's Gap

Waynesboro

Rockfish
Gap

Meachum's
River Station

Charlott

Rockbridge Bath

VIRGINIA CENTRAL R.R.

Irish Cr. Gap

Lexington

White's
Gap

Robertson's Gap

ORANGE & ALEXANDRIA R.R.

Ja

Petit's Gap

Peak Gap

VIRGINIA & TENNESSEE R.R.

PETERSBURG & LYNCHBURG R

Appomattox

Allegheny Mtns

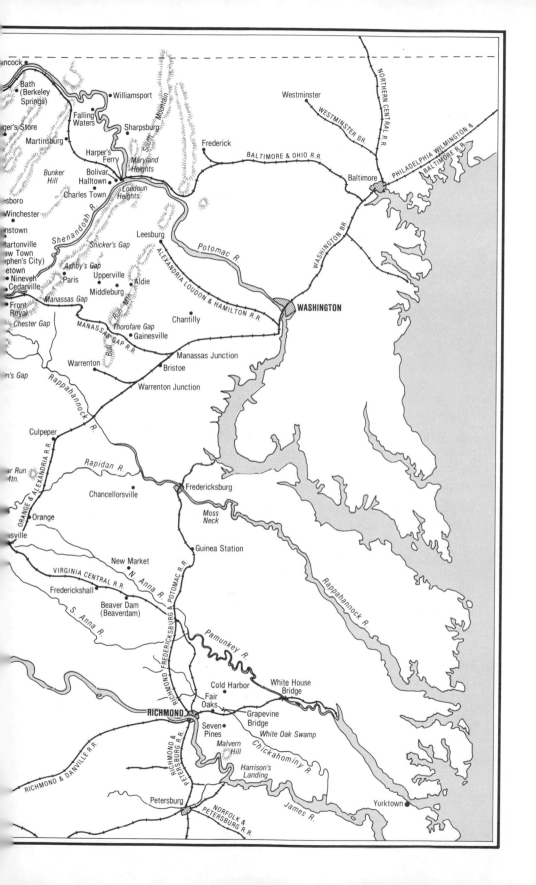

11

☆ ☆ ☆ ☆ ☆ ☆ ☆ ☆ ☆ ☆ ☆ ☆ ☆ ☆

Harper's Ferry and Falling Waters

On 27 April 1861 Major General Robert E. Lee ordered Colonel Jackson to "proceed, without delay, to Harper's Ferry, Va. . . . and assume command of that post." Jackson was charged with two important tasks: Volunteer companies reporting there were to be mustered into the service of the state and organized into battalions or regiments, and all of the arms, machinery, and raw materials at the arsenal were to be hustled back to Richmond as soon as possible.

At this moment there were few posts as important to the Confederacy as Harper's Ferry. Not only was the arsenal there, but the town was also a communications center on the border of as yet uncommitted Maryland. The Baltimore & Ohio Railroad, the principal line connecting Washington, D.C., with the West, passed through it, and the busy Chesapeake & Ohio Canal lay just across the Potomac on the Maryland shore. A small branch railway ran some thirty miles south to Winchester, and telegraph lines followed the railways.

The town sits on a triangle of land formed by the confluence of the Shenandoah and Potomac rivers. Maryland Heights looms over it to the north; to the east, across the Shenandoah, it is dominated by Loudoun Heights; and it is overlooked to a lesser extent by Bolivar Heights to the southwest. From a military point of view the town and its arsenal, which was not designed as a fortress, could not be more awkwardly placed for defense.

The configuration of the land at Harper's Ferry presented Jackson with what he regarded as his principal problem in defending the place, for unless that massive height across the Potomac in Maryland could be held, the town was indefensible, but Lee was to warn him of a related problem which in terms of the larger strategy might be of greater importance. To cross the Potomac was to invade Maryland, a neutral state the Confederacy was wooing and did not wish to alienate. Jackson, however, was to pay scant attention to this complication. Wholly concerned with the defenses of the town, he largely ignored Lee's admonition.

In early April 1861 the town had been defended by only forty-five Union soldiers commanded by First Lieutenant Roger Jones, Jr., a native of Washington, D.C., and a 1851 West Point graduate. Alert to the dangers of his vulnerable position and fully aware of the value of the arsenal should it fall into hostile hands, Jones, with commendable energy and foresight, had mined the arsenal, and on 18 April, just before its capture by Virginia militia, he set fire to the stored muskets, destroying thousands. He tried as well to fire the factories and destroy the machinery but was largely prevented from doing so by workmen at the arsenal.[1] He had fled with his men just ahead of the Virginia militia who streamed in from all directions in time to help the workmen and townspeople put out the fires.

Harper's Ferry instantly became the Confederate focal point for the assembly of militia for miles around. Within a week some thirteen hundred were assembled there, many outfitted in fantastic costumes. One volunteer, Charles Grattan, later described them: "I do not suppose that at any time before or since was there ever such a collection of variegated uniform, so much tinsel, so many nodding plumes, so long or so many sashes, cocked hats, jingling spurs and swords, or such resplendent dress parades of the first week or two at Harper's Ferry."

Militia Major General Kenton Harper, sixty, a former newspaper publisher and mayor of Staunton, took charge with the aid of three militia brigadier generals, each with a large, glittering staff who, innocent of military duties, scurried aimlessly through the day. Although a

1. Roger Jones was given the thanks of the government and promoted to captain for his services at Harper's Ferry, but although he became a brigadier general in 1888, he never rose above the rank of major during the war.

parade was held almost every evening, not much drilling was done. The troops remained largely unorganized in any unit above a company. Horses and limbers for the artillery were scarce. There was no hospital and little ammunition. Ordnance, stores, and accoutrements of all sorts were acutely needed.

The trains of the Baltimore & Ohio, loaded with coal and other strategic materials, continued to pass east and west unhindered through the town.[2] Governor Letcher had forbidden the passage of Federal soldiers through Virginia, and one train, believed to be carrying troops, was stopped, but it contained only Brigadier General William Selby Harney (1800–1889), commanding the Department of the West. He was treated with every courtesy; his parole was accepted, and he proceeded to Richmond, where he was released and sent on his way to Washington.

Many men, even privates, had brought along slaves to look after them. Henry Kyd Douglas, twenty-three, who was later commissioned and joined Jackson's staff, but was then a private in the 2nd Virginia, described the jolly atmosphere: "Society was plentiful, for the ranks were filled with the best blood of Virginia; all its classes were there. Mothers and sisters and other dear girls came constantly to Harper's Ferry and there was little difficulty in seeing them. Nothing was serious yet; everything much like a joke."

Such was the situation when Jackson arrived on 29 April, only a few hours before the first combat death of the war. (Captain John Quincy, thirty-six, a VMI graduate, was killed at Fairfax Court House by troopers of the 2nd U.S. Cavalry on patrol.) Few at Harper's Ferry were impressed with the new commander. One Southern newspaper correspondent noted that he lacked the "pride, pomp, and circumstance of glorious war." Unperturbed, Jackson quickly assembled a small staff composed mostly of VMI men: Colonel James Wood Massie, a VMI graduate (1849) and VMI professor, served as his inspector general; Major John T. L. Preston, his VMI colleague and business partner, became his adjutant; and two captains who had been VMI instructors served as assistants.

---

2. Three-quarters of the Baltimore & Ohio Railroad lay in Virginia. Not long after the John Brown raid, John W. Garrett, speaking in Baltimore, said of the B&O: "It is a Southern Line. And if necessity should require—which heaven forbid!—it will prove the great bulwark of the border, and a sure agency for home defense." However, when war came, the railroad's board of directors, unconvinced that the South could successfully break away from the Union, gave its support to the federal government.

On the same day that Jackson arrived, an order was received depriving all militia officers above the rank of captain of their commissions. Ex-General Harper and all of the former generals and field grade officers lost no time in filing off to Richmond to protest their demotions. Within a week some quietly returned with less exalted ranks. Harper came back to serve as colonel of the 5th Virginia with William H. Harman, former commonwealth's attorney for Augusta County and former militia brigadier general, as his lieutenant colonel.

By this time Jackson had already begun remolding the mob of amateur soldiers. Captain John Imboden, an intimate friend of the governor's who had been in Richmond delivering requisitions, was astonished when he returned. He found Jackson and his adjutant working at a small pine table dressed in "dingy, well-worn uniforms of professors of the Virginia Military Institute." Gone were the gold braid and the glitter. "What a revolution three or four days have wrought! I could scarcely believe the change," he exclaimed. There was no more playing at war. Second Lieutenant G. W. Booth of the 1st Maryland later recalled that "it was drill, drill from morn to night."

Another young officer, John G. Gittings, a VMI graduate who had known Jackson in other days, arrived at Harper's Ferry on a morning in early May and marveled at the metamorphosis of his former professor:

> [Jackson] would dispatch business in a very prompt and energetic way. He knew exactly what ought to be done and how it should be done. There was no wavering of opinion, no doubts and misgivings; his orders were clear and decisive. It occurred to us at the time that Jackson was much more in his element here, as an army officer, than when in the professor's chair at Lexington. It seemed that the sounds and sights of war had aroused his energies; his manner had become brusque and imperative; his face was bronzed from exposure, his beard was now of no formal style, but was worn unshorn.

Jackson was indeed in his element. He wrote to Anna: "I am very much gratified with my command, and would rather have this post than any other in the State." Although he had warned his "little one" that she would not hear from him often as "I expect to have more work than I have ever had in the same length of time before," he found time to send her frequent notes. "I haven't time now to do more than to tell you how much I love you," he wrote, assuring her that her "precious letters . . . gladden your husband's heart." His only physical complaint was of a lack of sleep, a commodity of which he always had a deep need.

When Anna suggested joining him, Jackson, convinced that Virginia would soon be involved in a large-scale war, wrote that "whilst I should be delighted to see you, yet if you have not started, do not think of coming." Resigned, Anna closed their house, disposed of their horse and rockaway, found homes for their slaves, and, escorted by a brother, returned to Cottage Home in North Carolina. Jackson wrote admiringly, "I just love my business little woman."

An often repeated story of this period describes how Jackson tricked the Baltimore & Ohio Railroad into bunching up its trains at Harper's Ferry, enabling him to capture fifty-six locomotives and more than three hundred cars. A wonderful tale, it illustrates Jackson's aggressiveness. But it almost certainly never happened.[3]

It was at Harper's Ferry that Jackson acquired the horse which has ever been associated with his fame. When the Federals stopped a supply train traveling from Baltimore to Virginia, Jackson retaliated by seizing five carloads of cattle and one of horses, which he turned over to his quartermaster. One small horse, less than fourteen hands, took Jackson's fancy, and he bought him, thinking he might be a good horse for Anna after the war. Although he named the new horse Fancy, the soldiers always called him Little Sorrel or Old Sorrel or simply Sorrel. It was, said Henry Kyd Douglas, "a plebeian-looking little beast, not a chestnut; he was stocky and well-made, round-barreled, close coupled, good shoulder, excellent legs and feet . . . heavy head and neck, a natural pacer with little action and no style." He had a peculiar habit of lying down like a dog to rest. He had an easy gait—"as easy as the rocking of a cradle," said Jackson—and like a good soldier, he possessed great endurance. Jackson rode Little Sorrel in most of his battles.[4]

3. The story of the captured locomotives was told by John Imboden, who said that he himself took part in the operation, but there are disturbing elements to his story. Such a dramatic event ought to have stimulated many accounts, as did the later transfer of the locomotives from Martinsburg to Strasburg. If it occurred, Jackson did not report it to Lee, and that would have been most odd. It would also have been a direct violation of Jackson's orders not to disturb commerce and not to cross into Maryland unless it was absolutely necessary. The story is, however, reported as gospel in every other biography.

4. After Jackson's death Little Sorrel led a pampered life. He was often taken to fairs, where he was revered as a hero. Anna Jackson gave him to VMI, where, as

Among the human raw material at Harper's Ferry Jackson found some good or potentially good officers. Perhaps the greatest acquisition to his staff was John A. Harman, one of the owners of the stagecoach line in the Shenandoah Valley which had more than once carried the VMI cadets. He first came to Jackson's attention by his energetic impressment of horses belonging to Quakers in neighboring Loudoun County. He became Jackson's efficient, indispensable quartermaster. A civilian, Herman was reluctant to join the army until Jackson procured a major's commission for him. Another fortunate find was Wells J. Hawks, a former mayor of Charles Town and a builder of stagecoaches, who became chief commissary officer.

Hunter McGuire from Winchester, tall, thin, and boyish-looking, was a private in the 2nd Virginia; he was also an excellent doctor. On orders from Richmond he reported to Jackson, who mutely stared at him for some moments and then ordered him back to his quarters, where he waited without a word for several days before orders were published appointing him a surgeon. Later, when the two men were better acquainted, the doctor asked why his appointment had been delayed, and Jackson told him: "You looked so young, I sent to Richmond to see if there was some mistake."

McGuire, twenty-five, was older than he looked, but most of the volunteers were indeed young, and a sizable percentage were under twenty.[5] An effort was made to get them to sign up for the duration of the war, but most, at Harper's Ferry and elsewhere, would agree to serve for only twelve months, thus creating a future problem for Jackson and other commanders. No physical examinations were required until the autumn of 1862, and even then the loss of an eye or a few fingers, partial deafness, and other such disabilities were not considered disqualifying. It is ironic that Jackson himself, with his poor eyesight

---

a living treasure, he did no work and was allowed to graze on the parade ground. He died on 17 March 1886 at the age of thirty-five or thirty-six, and his stuffed body was kept in a glass case at the Confederate Soldiers' Home in Richmond until the demise of that institution. It may now be seen at the Virginia Military Institute Museum.

5. In the course of the war, 296,016 white males between the ages of fifteen and twenty served in the Confederate army, and of these, 56,601 were from Virginia— more than from any other state. The ages of the men at Harper's Ferry are unknown, but a study of the records of 11,000 Confederates who enlisted in 1861 and 1862 showed that 1,572 (14.3 percent) were under the age of nineteen, and some of these were officers.

and partial deafness, would today be found unfit to hold a commission in the American army.

Although Lee was in frequent touch with Jackson—giving him orders to call for volunteers from seven surrounding counties in Virginia, setting the number of men for each company at eighty-two, warning of a possible attack from Pennsylvania, and giving instructions for moving the machinery from the arsenal south to Winchester, to Strasburg, and thence to Richmond—Jackson, who was inclined to ignore advice from Richmond, did not give Lee a progress report until 6 May. Then he reported his strength and advised him that all volunteers and militia had been mustered into Confederate service but that he suffered from a shortage of instructors to drill them, although he had drafted instructors wherever he found them. (Ten VMI cadets who had been detailed to escort five wagonloads of powder to him were retained as drill instructors.)

In the same report Jackson asked that more small arms, cannon, caissons, powder, artillery ammunition, harnesses, and other equipment be sent to him. He reported that two-thirds of the machinery had been removed from the arsenal and that he was confiscating wagons to transport it. He had also confiscated flour which was being shipped from the Shenandoah Valley to New York.

As for his dispositions, Jackson told Lee: "I have occupied the Virginia and Maryland Heights, and I am about fortifying the former [Loudoun Heights] with blockhouses of sufficient strength to resist an attempt to carry them by storm. Whenever the emergency calls for it, I shall construct similar works on the Maryland Heights. Thus far I have been deterred from doing so by a desire to avoid giving offense to the latter State." The following day, 7 May, before he received an answer from Lee, he reported that he had "finished reconnoitering the Maryland Heights" and that he was "determined to fortify them" at once. "I am of the opinion," he wrote, "that this place should be defended with the spirit which actuated the defenders of Thermopylae, and if left to myself, such is my determination."

On 9 May he reported: "I have occupied the Maryland Heights with the Kentuckians and one company of infantry from Augusta County, making about 500 in all."

Jackson's letter of 7 May made Lee uneasy. He replied: "Your intention to fortify the heights of Maryland may interrupt our friendly relations with that State, and we have no right to intrude on her soil, unless, under pressing necessity, for defense. . . . At all events, do not move until actually necessary and under stern necessity."

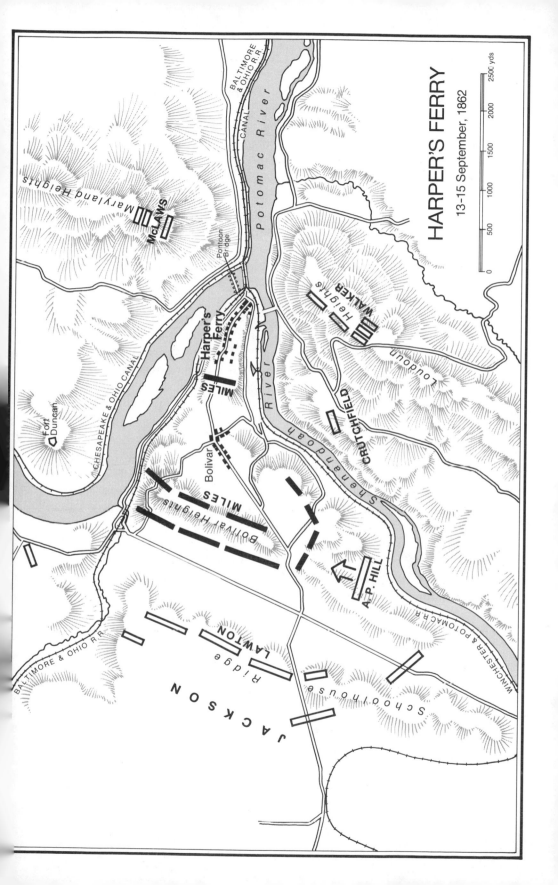

HARPER'S FERRY

13-15 September, 1862

On 10 May Lee wrote again. He praised Jackson for his zeal and the progress he had made and told him of the help he was able to supply, but he warned that "in your preparation for the defense of your position it is considered advisable not to intrude upon the soil of Maryland unless compelled by necessities of war. The aid of the citizens might be obtained in that quarter. . . ." He also cautioned Jackson that confiscations should not "embarrass the legitimate commerce of our citizens."

In a second letter written that day he wrote: "Your letter of May 9 has just been received. . . . I fear you may have been premature in occupying the heights of Maryland. . . . The true policy is to act on the defensive, and not invite an attack. If not too late, you might withdraw until the proper time."

On 11 May Jackson replied in a letter personally delivered to Lee by Jonathan M. Bennett, one of Jackson's political friends who had visited Harper's Ferry. Describing his deployment of troops—he had distributed men along the Potomac from Shepherdstown to Point of Rocks, just north of Leesburg—he pleaded for more men and supplies, warning that "Marylanders, with artillery, are opposite Shepherdstown, and have threatened us."

Jackson's vigor was beginning to disturb Lee. He replied sternly the next day: "I am concerned at the feeling evinced in Maryland . . . and fear it may extend to other points besides Shepherdstown. It will be necessary, in order to allay it, that you confine yourself to a strictly defensive course. . . . You know our limited resources, and must abstain from all provocation for attack as long as possible."

Among the many visitors to Jackson's headquarters was James Murray Mason (1798–1871), who had been a Winchester lawyer before he launched his political career. He had served first in the state legislature and then in both houses of Congress in Washington. For ten years he served as chairman of the Senate Committee on Foreign Affairs before giving up his seat only a few weeks earlier. When he returned to Richmond after two days with Jackson, he wrote a long letter to Lee arguing strongly the legal and moral rights as well as the absolute necessity of occupying Maryland Heights, concluding with: "But Maryland is not *suo jure;* she remains one of the United States, a power now foreign to Virginia, and in open and avowed hostility to us. Occupying her territory, therefore, is only occupying territory of the enemy; nor is it invasion in the proper sense of that term, because the occupation is defensive and precautionary only, and not for aggression, and will cease as soon as the enemy withdraw from Maryland." Assuring

Lee, "Of course I did not inquire of Colonel Jackson," although he obviously had, he went on to report that "things appear to be fast assuming the aspect of good military organization, and officers and men cheerful and buoyant." Although Jackson was often called stiff in social situations, he knew how to charm and persuade politicians.

On 21 May Lee answered Mason's letter, telling him:

> I had hoped that the Maryland people would relieve us of the necessity of occupying the Maryland Heights. Colonel Jackson was directed to give their occupation the appearance of being done by the people of that State, and not to take possession himself till necessary; but the time has been left to his discretion which I am sure will be wisely exercised. There is no doubt, under the circumstances, of our right to occupy these heights.

In need of an unbiased report, Lee sent to Harper's Ferry Lieutenant Colonel George Deas, inspector general of the Confederate army. On 23 May, the day the Ordinance of Secession was submitted to the people of Virginia, Deas wrote his report. The infantry, he said, had been formed into eight regiments—five from Virginia, two from Mississippi, and one from Alabama—and two battalions—one each from Maryland and Kentucky. There were also eight companies of Virginia cavalry, five batteries of artillery, and a naval battery. The cavalry under Captain Turner Ashby, whom Deas considered an "excellent officer," was praised for its reconnaissance work; the cavalry companies under Lieutenant Colonel J. E. B. Stuart were also praised. Jackson was not mentioned, but it was obvious that he had ignored Lee's advice to withdraw from Maryland. Although he did not climb Maryland Heights, Deas had met with the officers in charge and reported it well fortified with no necessity for improvement.

In all, there were about eight thousand men at Harper's Ferry, of whom seventy-three hundred were armed and available for active service. It was a large command indeed for a colonel. Deas reported that the Mississippi regiments were unhappy with their arms: obsolete flintlocks altered into percussion pieces. The Virginia regiments were well armed but lacked cartridge boxes, belts, and other accoutrements. In general, there was plenty of food, except for bacon (Harper's Ferry possessed one of the largest and best flour mills in the area), but there was a serious shortage of clothing.

Deas found the 2nd Mississippi deficient in everything and its officers "entirely without military knowledge of any description." Although he praised the VMI cadets, he found in all other units "a lamentable want of knowledge of the first principles of formation into line and the change of front and breaking into column. There are no regular parades established, upon which to form quickly, in case of alarm. The Virginia regiments are only partially equipped with tents, and the main body of them are quartered in houses in the towns of Harper's Ferry and Bolivar. Crowded together as they necessarily are, I fear that utter confusion must be the consequence of any sudden movement." He pronounced the hospital "very deficient in every respect. There are a few beds in the general hospital, but there is no provision whatever made for the care of wounded men, in the event of an engagement taking place." Should Harper's Ferry be threatened by a large Federal force, he recommended that it be abandoned.

On the following day, 24 May, Jackson was relieved of his command.

On 15 May, unknown to Jackson and, it would appear, also unknown to Lee, the new Confederate War Department had issued orders for Brigadier General Joseph E. Johnston to take command of the forces in and around Harper's Ferry. It came as a surprise, and doubtless a shock and a great disappointment, to Jackson when Johnston with his own staff officers appeared. Certainly Jackson knew Johnston, at least by reputation. Johnston, fifty-four years old, had served in the Black Hawk expedition, in the Seminole War, and with great distinction in the Mexican War, where he was five times wounded, had led the forlorn hope at Chapultepec, and won three brevets; since then he had served on the Kansas border during the disturbances there and had taken part in the Utah expedition against the Mormons. A brigadier general when the war broke out, he was the highest-ranking United States Army officer to throw in his lot with the Confederacy. Nevertheless, the punctilious Jackson, courteously but stiffly, at first refused to hand over his command until he received "further instructions from Governor Letcher or General Lee." Johnston, although reputed to be petulant and autocratic, seems to have taken no offense; he rummaged about among his papers until he found a document which appeared to prove the validity of his claim. Satisfied, Jackson yielded.

Three days later, fearing that Anna might be mortified by his loss of command, Jackson wrote to her: "My precious darling, I suppose you have heard that General Joseph E. Johnston, of the Confederate army, has been placed in command here. You must not concern yourself about the change. Colonel [John T. L.] Preston will explain it all to you. I hope to have more time, as I am not in command of a post, to write longer letters to my darling pet."

Jackson had organized the disparate volunteers and militia companies into battalions and regiments; Johnston now organized the regiments into brigades and gave the 1st Brigade to Jackson. It consisted at the time of four and soon of five regiments of Virginia infantry (two of them commanded by VMI graduates) and a battery—the Rockbridge Artillery under the former pastor of Lexington's Episcopal church, the Reverend Dr. Captain William N. Pendleton, who baptized his four guns Matthew, Mark, Luke, and John. Virtually all of the rank and file were from the Shenandoah Valley.

On 4 June Jackson wrote to Anna, telling her of his new command and chiding her fondly: "You say that your husband never writes you any news. I suppose you meant military news, for I have written a great deal about your *esposo* and how much he loves you. What do you want with military news? Don't you know that it is unmilitary and unlike an officer to write news respecting one's post? You wouldn't wish your husband to do an unofficer-like thing, would you?" His secrecy was to become proverbial, and Anna soon understood that even she must never inquire too closely into military affairs.

Johnston was dismayed by the difficulties of defending Harper's Ferry with the raw, untrained troops under his command. Unlike Jackson, he did not see himself as a latter-day Leonidas or Harper's Ferry as Thermopylae. Two days after his arrival he reported to Richmond: "I regard Harper's Ferry as untenable by us at present against a strong enemy." On 31 May, in a memorandum for Lee, he stated flatly: "The place cannot be held against an enemy who would venture to attack it."

Although Lee replied that he was sending additional troops, ammunition, and supplies and urged Johnston to hold out as long as he could, Johnston began to collect wagons, to mine buildings and bridges, and to make preparations for getting out.

On 14 June Jackson wrote to Anna: "We are about leaving this place. General Johnston has withdrawn his troops from the Heights (Maryland and Virginia), has blown up and burnt the railroad bridge across the Potomac, and is doing the same with respect to the public buildings. Yesterday morning I was directed to get ready to evacuate the place. . . ."

Two days later Johnston's entire force was on the road south, toward Charles Town. On this same day Federal troops of Major General George Cadwalader, operating under the command of sixty-nine-year-old Major General Robert Patterson, moved to the banks of the Potomac. In response, Johnston moved his force westward toward him on the Martinsburg turnpike in order to be between Cadwalader and Winchester.

On 18 June, three miles north of Winchester, Jackson found time to write to Anna again: "Yesterday morning we were to have marched at sunrise, and I hoped that in the evening, or this morning, we should have engaged the enemy; but instead of doing so, General Johnston made some disposition for receiving the enemy if they should attack us. . . . I trust that through the blessing of God we shall soon be given an opportunity of driving the invaders from this region."

On the following day, given orders to destroy all the property he could not take with him that belonged to the Baltimore & Ohio Railroad in and around the main depot and roundhouse at Martinsburg, Jackson put the buildings to the torch and burned or otherwise destroyed 42 locomotives and 305 cars, mostly loaded with coal. Most of the citizens of Berkeley County, of which Martinsburg was the seat, had voted against secession, and Jackson's destruction of the railroad, which had provided many with their livelihood, did not endear the Confederates to them.

To Anna, Jackson confessed: "It was your husband who did so much mischief at Martinsburg. To destroy so many fine locomotives, cars and railroad property was a sad work, but I had my orders, and my duty was to obey. If the cost of the property could only have been expended in disseminating the gospel of the Prince of Peace, how much good might have been expected! . . . One of the most trying things here is the loss of sleep."

It was not simply a distaste for vandalism that made Jackson regret his work of destruction. After a furious decade of railroad building, the United States had by 1860 a larger rail network than the rest of the world combined, but most of the track and rolling stock was in the North. The South needed railroad equipment, particularly locomotives, and a bold plan was concocted to salvage at least some of those captured around Martinsburg and not yet destroyed.

Locomotives, cars, and supplies were to be hauled thirty-eight miles overland to the Confederate railhead at Strasburg. Although Jackson is usually credited as the originator of the idea, this seems doubtful. Captain Thomas R. Sharp was sent up from Richmond to take over the salvage project, and in his diary he mentioned going to Jackson's headquarters to ask him to stop the work of destruction. In a remarkably short time Sharp was able to assemble a crew of teamsters, mechanics, and laborers—and a large herd of horses.

Tenders were taken off, and every bit of weight that could be removed was stripped from the engines: bells, sandboxes, whistles, even side rods and piston rods. Forward wheels were replaced by thick iron-shod wooden wheels. Pulled by forty stout horses, four abreast, at times augmented by straining crews of men, each rescued locomotive began its slow journey south.

Through June and into July the big engines crawled through the Virginia countryside. The last to go was B&O locomotive No. 199, a Ross Winans camelback with the cab in front of the boiler. Because it could not make the Manassas Gap Line before the Federals closed it, it was decided to haul it farther south on the turnpike to the railhead at Staunton. All went well until it reached the outskirts of Staunton. There it broke loose on a hill and careened wildly through the town until it collapsed ignominiously into a bog.

The number of locomotives carried off is uncertain, but on 7 September a newspaper reported from Strasburg: "Fourteen locomotives, a large number of railroad cars, nine miles of track, telegraph wires and about $40,000 worth of machinist's tools and materials, all belonging to the Baltimore and Ohio Railroad, have successfully been hauled overland by the Confederates. . . ."

Although often credited with doing so, Jackson played no active part in the endeavor. Bivouacked with his troops, he was waiting impatiently for his first fight of the war. On the night of the 27–28 June, hearing rumors that the enemy was preparing to march, he worked late arranging an early-warning screen of pickets. When the Federalists failed to advance, he complained to Anna: "I had my rest disturbed, and am feeling the effects of it today." Although he was now sleeping "out of doors without any cover except my bedding," his health was splendid. "I find that sleeping in the open air, with no covering but my blankets and the blue sky for a canopy, is more refreshing than sleeping in a room," he wrote.

On 2 July Patterson, now reinforced, sent the brigades of George Cadwalader and Virginia-born George H. Thomas (the future "Rock of Chickamauga") to Williamsport. There four infantry regiments and part of a fifth waded across the Potomac (then about four feet deep) into Virginia. Patterson soon followed with the remainder of his army of nearly fifteen thousand men. His instructions were vague: He was to press Johnston and, if possible, take Winchester; otherwise, he might swing east and take Leesburg. In the event, he did neither.

The Federal crossing was unopposed, but "Jeb" Stuart's reconnoitering cavalry spotted their advance, and by seven-thirty that morning (2 July) Jackson was informed that Northern troops were only four and a half miles away. After alerting two regiments to stand by as a ready reserve and pointing out to McGuire a sheltered spot for his field hospital, Jackson moved with the 5th Virginia and one gun from the Rockbridge Artillery, fewer than five hundred men. His orders were to fall back on the main body around Winchester if the Federals were seen to be advancing in force. He was not to bring on a general engagement.

On rolling ground of woods and wheat fields rimmed with rail fences near Hoke's Creek, at the site of a church called Falling Waters, Jackson's Valley boys collided with farm boys from Wisconsin and Pennsylvania under Colonel John Joseph Abercrombie, a professional soldier who had won brevets for gallantry fighting in Florida and Mexico. (He was also Patterson's son-in-law.) Colonel Kenton Harper, the former militia general, seized a farmhouse near the church and made it a strongpoint while he threw out skirmishers.

Many excited young Confederate soldiers believed the Northerns must be a different breed from themselves. Some broke ranks and scrambled up trees or mounted fences to catch sight of them. Private John Opie of the 5th Virginia was impressed with what he saw:

> On they came in battle array, the first army we had ever beheld; and a grand sight it was—infantry, artillery, and mounted men; their arms and accoutrements glittering in the sunlight, their colors unfurled to the breeze, their bands playing and drums beating, the officers shouting commands, as regiments, battalions, and companies marched up and wheeled into position. Then a battery took position and commenced firing at us. . . .

The Federals Private Opie watched were probably the 11th Pennsylvania and 1st Wisconsin infantry; two guns of Company F, 4th U.S. Artillery; and the artillery's escort, the Philadelphia City Troop.

Jackson's Virginians drove back the Federal skirmishers, but Abercrombie's two regiments were quickly reinforced by two Pennsylvania regiments under Colonel Thomas, and several guns were hurried forward. In the rush and press of the movement, the Federal cavalry was crowded on the road, and Jackson, seizing his opportunity, ordered the Reverend Pendleton to bring his gun into action. Crying, "May the Lord have mercy on their wicked souls! Fire!" Pendleton cleared the road with his first shot.

Corporal William M. Brown, the section chief of Pendleton's gun, never forgot his sight of Jackson that day:

> Jackson had been in the road within a few steps of our gun. While there a courier from Joe Johnston galloped up and handed him a dispatch. Seating himself on a large, loose, round stone on the north side of the road, he commenced to write an answer, the courier waiting on foot, bridle in hand. A shot from a Federal battery struck centrally, ten feet from the ground, a large white oak that stood in the fence corner close to Jackson and knocked a mass of bark, splinters and trash all over him and the paper on which he was writing. He brushed away the trash with the back of his hand, finished the dispatch without a sign that he knew anything unusual was going on, folded it, handed it to the courier and dismissed him courteously, but with quick decisive utterance. . . .

Confirming that the force opposing him was at least four times greater than his own, Jackson, as ordered, pulled back. Although it is difficult to maintain order in a slow retreat under fire, particularly with raw troops, such as Jackson commanded, in this small battle, his first as a battlefield commander, he skillfully disengaged and retreated in good order for three miles. Stuart's cavalry was active. Sweeping around the Federals' right flank, they scooped up two officers and forty-seven enlisted men of the 15th Pennsylvania.

The fight was page one news in the *New York Times*. General Patterson had reported that "the force we scattered yesterday was 3,500 strong, and their loss about 60 killed." Southern newspapers claimed 360 Federal casualties, and the *Charleston Courier* editorialized: "With such material to fight our battles, victory must perch upon our banners."

It was all nonsense. The "affair at Falling Waters," as Johnston rightly called it, was little more than a skirmish. Looking back later, Private Opie said, "[W]e were all novices in the art of killing each other." Confederate losses were two men dead, twelve wounded (one mortally), six captured, and two missing. Federal losses, in addition to the forty-nine prisoners of war, were three killed and seventeen wounded, one mortally.

Had Patterson attacked with his entire force of nearly fifteen thousand, he might well have overwhelmed Johnson's force of about twelve thousand. But each general believed the other to be superior in numbers. Thus was a major battle avoided, leaving Johnston free to take his place at Manassas, where his would be the decisive force that would turn the tide of battle.

That night Jackson's men slept in the open under a canopy of stars. Lieutenant John Newton Lyle of the 4th Virginia watched in fascination a comet which, he said, "for size, brilliance and beauty . . . excelled any that have come our way. Its head was near the zenith and its magnificent tail, spreading like a curtain, swept a broad expanse of the sky nearly to the horizon." Remembering his Homer, he wondered uneasily what this one might portend.

General Johnston praised both Stuart and Jackson for their roles at Falling Waters (or Hoke's Run, as it was often called), and in the strongest terms he recommended that Stuart be promoted to colonel and Jackson to brigadier general.

Promotion had long been on Jackson's mind. Since June he had been nudging his political friends in Richmond. He knew that Jonathan Bennett, who had been largely responsible for his colonelcy in the army of Virginia, wanted to see him a brigadier general and sent to take charge of northwestern Virginia, their mutual birthplace, which on 26 June had been invaded by Jackson's old classmate George McClellan. On 5 June Jackson wrote Bennett: "The sooner it is done the better. Have me ordered at once. That country is now bleeding at every pore. I feel a deep interest in it and have never appealed to its people in vain." Indeed, all his life Jackson retained a partiality for the area of his birth and boyhood.

Bennett answered: "I presume all commissions will issue from the Confederate government [rather than the state government]; if so, I have no pledge for any commission, but I shall never cease until I get it. You will hear from me soon again."

Jackson continued to fret and on 24 June impatiently wrote Bennett again:

> Knowing your success in carrying your measures, the energy with which you press them, and not having heard from you, the thought struck me that there might be some obstacle in the way, which, if made known to me, I might be able to remove. I am in command of a promising brigade, and I would be greatly gratified if you could secure me a brigadier-generalcy, and if it cannot be ordered to Northwestern Virginia, of course I would be continued in my present command, and as I am so far west, an opportunity might soon offer of having me with my command ordered to that region.

I feel deeply for my own section of the state, and would, as a brigadier-general, willingly serve under General [Richard Brook] Garnett in its defense.[6] I know him well.

Jackson greatly feared that a brigadier general would be sent from Richmond to take over the command of his brigade. He need not have worried.

On 3 July Lee wrote Jackson: "My dear general, I have the pleasure of sending you a commission of brigadier-general in the Provisional Army, and to feel that you merit it. May your advancement increase your usefulness to the State."

There were at this time three classes of Confederate officers: those in the state militia, those serving with volunteers, and officers in what was called the Provisional Confederate Army, which it was assumed would someday be the Confederacy's regular army. Jackson's promotion to brigadier general, along with the promotions of Barnard E. Bee, Edmund Kirby-Smith, and his former battery commander in Mexico, John Bankhead Magruder, to the same rank, was approved to date from 17 June. Jackson passed the good news on to Anna, writing jubilantly that "my promotion was beyond what I anticipated, as I only expected it to be in the volunteer forces of the State.[7] One of my greatest desires for advancement is the gratification it will give my darling, and of serving my country more efficiently. I have had all that I ought to desire in the line of promotion. I should be very ungrateful if I were not contented, and exceedingly thankful to our kind Heavenly Father."

Confederate insignia of rank had not yet been established, so Jackson had a star sewn on the shoulders of his old blue army jacket, making him indistinguishable from a Federal brigadier general.

The newly created brigadier general in the worn blue jacket was now about to acquire his *nom de guerre*.

6. Brigadier General Robert Selden Garnett (1819–1861), who was graduated from West Point in 1841, had won two brevets in the Mexican War and was generally regarded as one of the most accomplished officers in the American army. He was at this time in command of the area west of Beverley. He was destined to be the first general officer on either side to die of wounds sustained in battle.

7. Officers commissioned in the Provisional Confederate Army took precedence over all officers of equal rank in the volunteer forces.

12

☆ ☆ ☆ ☆ ☆ ☆ ☆ ☆ ☆ ☆ ☆ ☆ ☆ ☆

The Battle of
First Manassas

T he two armies now facing each other fewer than twenty miles apart at the lower end of the Valley of Virginia, Johnston's at Winchester and Patterson's at Martinsburg, were on the sidelines of the main event which in mid-June 1861 was shaping up in Washington and north-central Virginia.

Although the most experienced senior officers in the Union army protested that their men were too green, too untrained to be used for offensive operations, Lincoln and the leading Northern politicians argued that the Southern soldiers were equally raw and inexperienced and, moreover, that the Northern field armies were filled with militia and volunteers who, having signed up for only three months' service, had little time left. It seemed to them that a decisive battle must be fought now or never.

Irvin McDowell, who had been promoted brigadier general only a month before, was commanded to move south and engage the forces under Confederate Brigadier General Pierre Gustave Toutant Beauregard, a former classmate at West Point (class of 1838), a Louisianan now known as the Hero of Fort Sumter, who was protecting the vital railroad junction at Manassas, Virginia. On the afternoon of 16 July McDowell's formal order to move was issued. By the following day his army had merely managed to cross the Potomac and reach Fairfax

Court House. There some of his troops encountered Confederate pickets and exchanged fire.

The *New York Times* (18 July) assured its readers that the Union army "now advancing on Richmond" would soon "reduce [the South's] obdurate temper to the peaceful and prosperous rule of the Republic." This would be done, it predicted, "without much bloodshed" because the Confederates were "weak, disheartened and demoralized." Nothing could have been further from the truth.

On the afternoon of 18 July McDowell, still moving cautiously, reached Centreville, and there, about six miles from Manassas Junction, he halted. Most students of the ensuing battle agree that had McDowell, who by now commanded 30,700 men, launched a determined attack upon Beauregard's 20,000 Confederates, he would have carried the day and the course of the war would have been altered. But McDowell, aware that most of his officers were inexperienced and his troops untrained, hesitated.

Nevertheless, on this date Brigadier General Daniel Tyler, commanding a Federal division, made a reconnaissance in force southward. At Mitchell's Ford and at Blackburn's Ford on the banks of a small stream called Bull Run, he fought short, sharp engagements and was repulsed. Tyler suffered eighty-three casualties; the Confederates sixty-eight. In Confederate histories this became the First Battle of Bull's Run; in Union histories it was called merely the Affair at Blackburn's Ford.

When the authorities in Richmond were informed of the Federal advance, they at once ordered Brigadier General Theophilus Hunter Holmes, a West Point classmate of Jefferson Davis's, to bring up his brigade of three thousand men from Aquia Landing southeast of Manassas and called on Johnston to bring up his troops from Winchester.

Johnston no longer had twelve thousand effectives. Some seventeen hundred of his young men, sick with measles, mumps, and other diseases, had to be left behind. However, he was much aided in his delicate disengagement from Patterson by a complete communications failure among the Federals. Mutually irritated and frustrated, neither General Scott in Washington nor Patterson, now in Charles Town, seemed capable of understanding the other. Patterson's main purpose ought to have been to prevent Johnston at all cost from reinforcing Beauregard at Manassas. In this he signally failed.

On the morning of 18 July Jackson's men prepared three days' rations, folded their tents, left them on the ground to be collected by others, and began their march to Manassas. The fifteen hundred men were delighted to move from a camp where, the "college boys" from Lexington complained, "the location was unsightly, the water was bad and the rations abominable." As they marched through Winchester, their bands played merrily while citizens lined the streets to cheer. Morale was high. In fine fettle the marchers called out boastful assurances to the young women who watched them go. Miss Julia Chase remarked that "if their actions are as great as their words, I fear the Federal troops chances are rather against them."

Bee's 2nd Brigade, then E. Kirby-Smith's 4the Brigade, each with its quota of artillery, followed Jackson. Jeb Stuart's 1st Virginia Cavalry would come away last after doing everything possible to convince Patterson that he still faced Johnston's entire army.

Not until Jackson's brigade was an hour and a half southeast of town did Jackson call a halt and read to his troops the order he had received from Johnston: "Our gallant army under General Beauregard is now attacked by overwhelming numbers. The commanding general hopes that his troops will step out like men, and make a forced march to save the country." Thirty years later D. B. Conrad, a veteran of the 2nd Virginia, wrote: "There is no man living of all that army today who can ever forget the thrill of 'Beerseeker rage' which took possession of all of us when the news was understood. . . . We footed it fast and furious."

This was the first and last time Jackson's troops were told where they were going. Revealing their destination was certainly not the idea of the taciturn Jackson, but he was impressed by the effect of Johnston's rhetoric. In his next letter to Anna he wrote: "At this stirring appeal the soldiers rent the air with shouts of joy, and all was eagerness and animation where before there had been lagging and uninterested obedience."

The troops crossed the Blue Ridge at Ashby's Gap, and at dusk leading elements of Jackson's brigade reached Berry's Ford on the Shenandoah River, where they waded through waist-deep water, holding their muskets or rifles over their heads, and marched on, gaining the village of Paris about two o'clock in the morning after a march of some twenty miles. Here they caught a few hours' sleep. "I mean the troops slept," Jackson told Anna, "as my men were so exhausted that I let them sleep while I kept watch myself."[1] This was not true, as even

1. Jackson standing guard while his men slept inspired stories, poems, and paintings and became firmly embedded in the Jackson legend after his death. It also inspired disbelief in those, such as D. H. Hill, who knew Jackson's dependence upon

Anna later admitted. Yielding to the entreaties of a staff officer, he threw himself down on some leaves in a fence corner and slept soundly.

At first light on the morning of 19 July the brigade was under way again, marching almost straight south for ten miles to Piedmont (today Delaplane), a station on the Manassas Gap Railroad where trains waited. The head of the column reached the station about six o'clock in the morning. "After getting our breakfast, the brigade commenced going aboard the cars, and the same day all that could be carried arrived at Manassas about four o'clock in the afternoon, without much suffering to my men or to myself," Jackson informed his wife. "The next day we rested, and the following day was the memorable 21st of July."

This movement of Johnston's army about thirty miles by railroad marked the first time in history that a railroad had been used to achieve strategic mobility. The troops thoroughly enjoyed this novel way of going to battle, and rattling through the Virginia countryside, they cheered and sang.

The last of Jackson's regiments did not leave until midafternoon, and some did not arrive at Manassas until the following morning. Lounging about, waiting to board the cars, the soldiers were well fed by the people of the countryside, who flocked to see them. "We had a regular picnic," remembered Private John Casler of the Potomac Guards (soon to be Company A, 33rd Virginia), "plenty to eat, lemonade to drink, and beautiful young ladies to chat with."

Jackson was the first of Johnston's brigade commanders to reach Manassas, and he immediately reported to an astonished Beauregard, who was at that moment explaining to his brigade commanders that he expected Johnston to continue marching east from Paris, through Upperville and Aldie, to fall on McDowell's right flank. Wasn't Johnston "on the direct road, so as to get on the enemy's flank?" he demanded.

Jackson, always cautious in the presence of officers he did not know and secretive by nature, balked at being quizzed. Answering curtly that he thought all would arrive by train, he asked where he was to position his brigade and immediately left to lead his men into a pine coppice near Mitchell's Ford. One officer present recorded that he answered in "rather a stolid manner" and had made an unfavorable

---

sleep. Hill called the story "monstrously absurd" and pointed out that in any case it takes more than one man to guard a brigade. A similar unlikely story was told of Napoleon finding a sentry asleep and taking his place while he slept.

impression. After he had left, Beauregard assured his officers that Jackson was probably mistaken.

Although Jackson's brigade had arrived at Manassas safely, Johnston was uneasy, for his troops were scattered along the road from Winchester, and some had to wait two days at Piedmont to "take the cars." Some of his men, who arrived on the twenty-first as the battle was taking place, marched directly from the train to the battle. The last did not arrive until the battle was ended. Johnston himself came in about noon on Saturday, 20 June. He was senior to Beauregard, but being unfamiliar with the rolling terrain (Beauregard had been at Manassas for two weeks) and of the dispositions of troops, he was reluctant to assume command. He appealed to President Davis for direction, and Davis replied: "You are a general in the Confederate Army, possessed of the power attaching to that rank. You will know how to make the exact knowledge of Brigadier-General Beauregard, as well of the ground as of the troops and preparation, avail for the success of the object in which you co-operate. The zeal of both assures me of harmonious action."

Fearing that Patterson, when he discovered that Johnston's army was on its way to Manassas, would himself swing east and reinforce McDowell, the Confederate commanders determined that rather than wait and allow McDowell to be reinforced, they would attack first. Their forces were at this time in generally good defensive positions strung along the banks of Bull Run[2] facing east or northeast. It was settled that Beauregard would remain the battlefield commander, and he sat up most of the night of the twentieth drawing up a plan for Johnston's approval in which a heavy attack would be made upon the Federal left flank. It was a plan based upon two assumptions: that all of Johnston's army was or would be at Manassas and that McDowell would not move. Both proved to be wrong. Many of the brigade commanders, presented with Beauregard's orders, which were less than crystal clear, were perplexed. Some could not puzzle out exactly what was expected of them. In the event it scarcely mattered. McDowell struck first.

McDowell's plan was a counterpart of Beauregard's: He moved to strike the Confederate left flank with his main force, which he sent off

2. Bull Run is a small stream twenty miles long that forms the boundary between Prince William and Fairfax counties in northern Virginia. The stream runs generally southeasterly and falls into the Occoquan, a tributary of the Potomac, about twenty-five miles from Washington.

on a wide swing northward, while a diversionary attack was launched at a stone bridge where the Warrenton Turnpike crossed Bull Run. It was, in general, a good plan, but McDowell was unaware of the arrival of Johnston with a large portion of his army, and the maneuver proved to be too complicated for his slow-moving green troops.

On 21 July 1861, at eight forty-five in the morning of what was to be a scorching day, Beauregard's signal officer, Captain Edward Porter Alexander (West Point class of 1857), caught the glint of Federal cannon and bayonets to the north and, employing a wigwag device he had helped develop, promptly signaled to Colonel Nathan Evans, who commanded a brigade guarding the stone bridge which arched over Bull Run on the far left of the Confederate line: "Look out for your left. You are turned."[3]

Without waiting for orders and on his own initiative, Evans moved most of his brigade to meet the threat. In nearly an hour of bitter fighting he delayed the Federals long enough for the Confederates to hustle reinforcements to their vulnerable flank.

When the opening shots of the battle were fired at about ten o'clock in the morning, Jackson's 1st Brigade was on the right of the Confederate line in support of the brigade commanded by James Longstreet. Johnston and Beauregard were slow to react to the Federal initiative, but by noon the brigades of Jackson, Bee, and that part of Colonel Francis Stebbins Bartow's brigade which had reached Manassas had swung to the left flank to support Evans. Beauregard took personal command while Johnston hurried reinforcements to him. The Federal attack was initially successful. Evans and Bee were pushed back to the Warrenton Turnpike. More units were moved from the Confederate right to the threatened left to stop the hemorrhaging in the line.

Captain John Imboden, commanding a battery of artillery in Bee's brigade, felt that Bee's infantry had failed to provide sufficient protection for his guns. He was swearing profusely when he encountered Jackson bringing up his sweating brigade through the thick dust at the double-quick to form a defensive position on the edge of a low plateau just above the house owned by the Henry family. The Henry house, in which lay the aged and bedridden Judith Henry (she was soon mortally wounded by an exploding shell, becoming the first civilian casualty of the war), sat just south of the soon-to-be-famous Stone House that became a landmark on the field of both the battles fought on this ground. Jackson listened with disapproval to Imboden's report,

3. This was the first use in battle of this method of signaling.

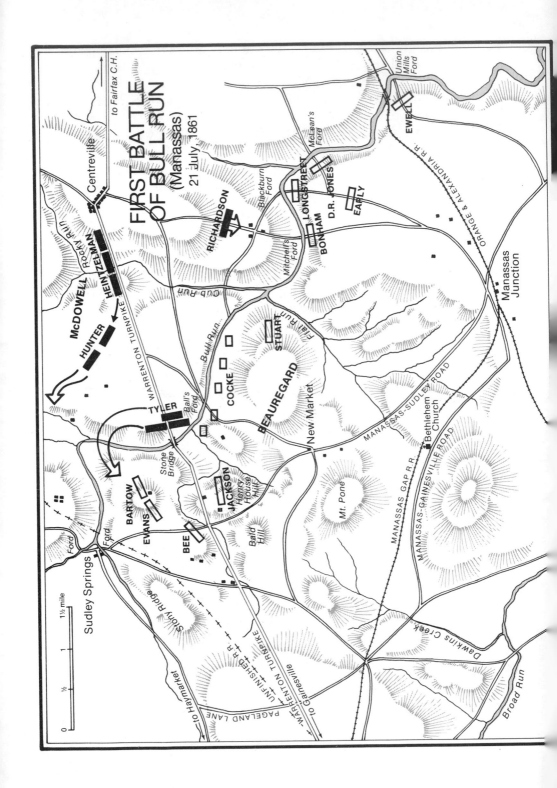

FIRST BATTLE
OF BULL RUN
(Manassas)
21 July 1861

to Fairfax C.H.

Centreville

McDOWELL

HEINTZELMAN

Rocky Run

HUNTER

TYLER

Ball's Ford

Stone Bridge

BARTOW

EVANS

BEE

JACKSON

Henry House Hill

Bald Hill

Sudley Springs

Ford

Stony Ridge

to Haymarket

to Gainesville

WARRENTON TURNPIKE

PAGELAND LANE

UNFINISHED R.R.

Bull Run

COCKE

STUART

BEAUREGARD

New Market

Mt. Pone

Cub Run

RICHARDSON

Blackburn Ford

Mitchell's Ford

LONGSTREET

BONHAM

D.R. JONES

EARLY

McLean's Ford

Union Mills Ford

EWELL

ORANGE & ALEXANDRIA R.R.

Manassas Junction

MANASSAS-SUDLEY ROAD

MANASSAS GAP R.R.

MANASSAS-GAINESVILLE ROAD

Bethlehem Church

Dawkins Creek

Broad Run

Flat Run

0   ½   1   1½ mile

"expressed with some profanity," and then said stiffly, "I'll support your battery. Unlimber right here."

When two fresh batteries arrived—the Leesburg Artillery and the Rockbridge Artillery (no longer under the Reverend Pendleton, who had been promoted colonel and was now Johnston's chief of artillery)—Jackson placed his guns in front and two regiments, the 4th and 27th Virginia, each in two lines, behind them, making a formidable strongpoint. The 5th Virginia, still under Colonel Harper, he placed somewhat at an angle on the right among some pines. On his left he assigned the 2nd Virginia, and still farther left, also in some pine trees, the 33rd Virginia. (Sergeant Major Randolph Barton of the 33rd, a recent VMI cadet who was severely wounded here, remembered all his life how the odors of the battlefield—sweat, blood, and burning powder—mixed with the smell of pine.)

The brigade faced northwest, and while Jackson was forming his line of battle, the cowards, the walking wounded, and the survivors of crushed regiments streamed past and through his position, an unnerving sight to young soldiers. Throughout the exodus Jackson walked his horse slowly back and forth in front of his brigade, "his chin cocked up as if he was expecting a rain and was not averse to having a drop of it on his face." His calm doubtless did much to reassure his men and keep them steady.

Nothing is more trying, particularly for untrained troops, than to lie immobile in the open under artillery fire. The two regiments supporting the guns suffered heavily from being in this position, and Lieutenant John Newton Lyle of the 4th Virginia later confessed: "I was scared. I said all the prayers I knew, even to 'Now I lay me down to sleep,' and threw in some shorter catechism and scripture for good measure." He admired Jackson, who "rode about in that shower of death as calmly as a farmer about his farm when the seasons are good." Along the lines of infantry he rode and "mingled with the uproar could be heard his: 'All's well, all's well,' distinct and in tones as soothing as those of a mother to a frightened child. The repose of his face was of itself reassuring."

From his position Jackson could see some of the action taking place ahead and particularly on his right front. It was from that quarter that about noon (it was said) Brigadier General Bee came galloping up to say that his men were falling back and the enemy would soon be upon him. "Then, sir, we will give them the bayonet," Jackson replied—or words to that effect. Bee dashed back and attempted to rally his men by crying out, "Look! There stands Jackson like a stone wall. Rally behind the Virginians!"

Such is the legend, and it is firmly embedded in Civil War mythology. A correspondent of the *Charleston Mercury,* whose brief account of the battle published on 25 July, is generally credited with being the first to quote Bee. His report was reprinted in other newspapers, notably in Richmond: "General Bee . . . rallied the remnant of his brigade, and his last words were: 'There is Jackson standing like a stone-wall. Let us determine to die here and we will conquer. Follow me!' "

D. H. Hill labeled this entire episode "sheer fabrication." Whether Bee actually said these words or something like them and, if he said them, where and when are all in dispute. John Cheves Haskell, adjutant of the 1st South Carolina (Bee's old regiment), believed that his words were a reproach, accusing Jackson of standing fast instead of coming to Bee's support. Haskell's authority was Major Thomas Rhett, Johnston's assistant adjutant general, who was with Bee almost from the time he was shot until his death.

It was also noticed by more than one member of Jackson's brigade that in fact, at that time (about noon), except for a few artillerymen, not a Virginian was standing. Jackson himself was sitting on his horse, and his infantry were lying prone on the ground.

From eyewitness accounts it would appear that Bee's men were actually behind the line Jackson had established on the ridge. Bee seemed bewildered when he came upon the 4th Alabama about five hundred yards on Jackson's right rear and asked the remains of the regiment, now commanded by a captain, to follow him back to the spot where Jackson's brigade was now heavily engaged. Thus it would appear that it was Bee who went to the aid of Jackson rather than the reverse. In a letter to his political friend James Bennett in Richmond, Jackson gave confirmation of this, for he said that when he was coming forward, he met Bee's brigade falling back: "I passed on, with the understanding that he would try to rally his troops in my rear."

Lieutenant William Robbins of the 4th Alabama was present and claimed to have heard Bee say, "Yonder stands Jackson like a stone wall, let's go to his assistance." This took place about three o'clock, not the "noon" of legend, and Jackson's men were by then on their feet and heavily engaged.

Bee was killed before the battle ended, so the truth will never be known, but it little matters. In such cases legend becomes more important than truth and Jackson became in the public mind "Stonewall" and the 1st Virginia Brigade—containing the 2nd, 4th, 5th, 27th, and

33rd Virginia regiments from the eighteen counties of the Valley of Virginia—became the Stonewall Brigade.[4]

If one can for a moment set aside the moss and gloss which has since become attached to the name of Stonewall, it will be seen that the name was singularly inappropriate for Jackson, particularly as applied to the remainder of his military career, for it implies stolidness and steadfastness in defense. While it was indeed his defensive line at this first battle at Manassas which gave him the sobriquet, it was not through his defensive positions that his towering military reputation was founded but, on the contrary, through his energetic offensive maneuvers, his mobility, dash, and daring.

The Federals launched several gallant charges, but Beauregard managed to line up an estimated sixty-five hundred men to oppose some twenty thousand of McDowell's Federals. Jackson himself was wounded, a musket ball breaking the middle finger of his left hand between the palm and the knuckle and carrying away some of the bone. He hastily bound the wound with a handkerchief. (Later he discovered a bullet hole through his coat near the hip.) Little Sorrel was also hit but was still functioning.

Two o'clock in the afternoon was the time of crisis for the Confederates. Although outgunned, they generally maintained their cohesion. Beauregard ordered a charge, and Jackson's calm vanished as the "flame of battle lighted his face" (Lyle), and he called, "Charge, men, and yell like furies!" The 4th and 27th Virginians, whooping, ran forward, somewhat to the left, and were quickly joined by the 5th Virginia under Harper, who, although a bad militia general, proved himself a fine regimental commander in battle. The Federal line was pierced at the center, and the momentum of the Virginians carried them to the far edge of the plateau. Elements of the 2nd Virginia captured a number of Federal guns in their front, and James Glenn of the 27th Virginia triumphantly carried back the flag of the 1st Michigan.

4. It was not until several months after the battle that "Stonewall" came to be applied to Jackson personally. He himself always maintained that the honorific, for such it was, applied not to him but only to the brigade. His men never called him that; to them, he was Old Jack. On 30 May 1863, a few days after Jackson's death, the Confederate War Department officially approved of the name Stonewall Brigade, and thus it became the only unit of any size to have its nickname so honored. In spite of severe attrition, this unit remained a coherent fighting force to the end of the war. Of the six commanders who succeeded Jackson, three were killed while leading it.

For the account of Bee's true location and the sorting out of the eyewitnesses, the author is indebted to John Hennessy's scholarly article in *Civil War*, vol. XXII.

Jackson's brigade, said Beauregard later, was driven forward by "the determination of veterans and the spirit of men who fight for a sacred cause." He added: "But it suffered severely."

The Federals, although taken aback, did not break. They rallied behind a protective slope, were reinforced by a fresh brigade, and again charged. The fighting was particularly ferocious in front of Jackson's brigade, around the Federal batteries of Captains James Brewerton Ricketts and Charles Griffin, which were defended by the colorfully dressed Fire Zouaves (11th New York), recruited from New York City firemen.

A soldier in the 2nd Virginia later described the action: "Charging, capturing, retreating, and retaking this battery, resisting charges of each fresh regiment as it came forward at quickstep up the slope of the hill, across the tableland, on its top and into the pine thickets where we were, until we were as completely broken up into fragments and as hard pressed as men ever were. . . ."

In most cases the cohesion of the units engaged disappeared during the confused action and often hand-to-hand fighting. A newspaper correspondent aptly described the scene below the hill as "a boiling crater of dust and smoke."

In the stew of battle it was often difficult to tell friend from foe, for the wide variety of cuts and colors of the uniforms made both sides resemble circuses rather than armies. Some combatants even wore civilian clothes. Major William Nelson, fifty-three, of the 33rd Virginia wore a somber dark suit and a "very high old black hat," and as he slowly rode among the troops in the piney woods, a sepulchral voice from the ranks cried out: "Good Lord, what have I done that the devil should come after me?"

Adding to the difficulty of identification was the similarity of the Confederate Stars and Bars and the Union's Stars and Stripes. It was this confusion that led Beauregard after the battle to suggest a Confederate battle flag. The War Department approved a design, and a few months later the first three flags were sewn by Miss Constance Cary and her two cousins Hettie and Jennie Cary.

The battle raged on through the afternoon. By three o'clock McDowell had the impression that he was winning, but Beauregard did not consider himself beaten. He put Jackson in charge of the troops on Henry Hill (the ridge on which stood the Henry house), and he sent forward the reinforcements Johnston fed him: the 6th North Carolina, 49th Virginia, and 2nd Mississippi. He again ordered an all-out charge. Once more the Federals were thrown back, but at great cost. Brigadier

Generals Bee and Bartow were mortally wounded. Many regimental commanders fell, and surviving junior officers valiantly struggled to organize the tired, confused, and disorganized troops.

Two North Carolina regiments and a battery came up at an opportune moment and were thrown against a threatening Federal enveloping movement, checking it until about three-thirty, when Brigadier General E. Kirby-Smith's brigade, the last seventeen hundred men from Johnston's Valley Army, arrived on the far left of the Confederate line. The men were tired, hungry, thirsty and, of course, knew nothing of the importance of their arrival on the field, but they were eager to engage in their first battle. Kirby-Smith himself was almost immediately felled by a serious wound. His place was ably taken by Colonel Arnold Elzey.

Sergeant McHenry Howard, twenty-two, of the 1st Maryland, one of the regiments composed of Marylanders sympathetic to the Confederate cause now under Elzey, wrote later:

> The order was now given to charge bayonets . . . and we pressed forward with a cheer, not in a very regular line but each one striving to be foremost. But in passing over the stubble or pasture field we discovered it bore an abundant crop of blackberries, and being famished with hunger and our throats parched with thirst, the temptation was too strong to be resisted, the men stopped with one accord and the charging line of battle resolved itself into a crowd of blackberry pickers. Officers swore or exhorted, according to their different principles, and presently succeeded in getting the line to move on. Still, whenever an unusually attractive bush was passed over, we reached down without stopping and stripped off berries, leaves and briars, which we crammed into our mouths; for days afterwards I was occupied extracting the thorns from the palms of my hands.

It was not this charge by Elzey's men but another by Brigadier General Jubal Early's brigade which proved to be decisive. The Federal line broke, beginning on the right, which had now been subjected to three Confederate charges. Initially there seemed to be no panic. Captain James Fry, an officer on McDowell's staff, said that "the men seemed to be seized simultaneously by the conviction that it was no use to do anything more and they might as well go home." Then the Federal center melted. Minutes before the end McDowell threw a brigade at Jackson's flank, but Jackson had anticipated this, and his guns stopped the attack in its tracks.

An attempt at an orderly retreat failed. Panic seized the Union army, and the retreat became a rout. "Such a rout I never saw before," said Brigadier General Samuel Peter Heintzelman, fifty-six, an Indian fighter and Mexican War veteran who was wounded at Manassas. William Howard Russell, the famous correspondent of *The Times* (London), wrote that the road to Centreville, on which all Federal forces were converging, "presented such a sight as can only be witnessed in the track of runaways of an utterly demoralized army."

McDowell made energetic efforts to re-form his army at Centreville, but his defeated men were not to be stopped. Rain added to their misery. At dawn the next day Walt Whitman watched them pour into Washington: ". . . all the men with this coating of muk and sweat and rain, now recoiling back, pouring over the Long Bridge—a horrible march of twenty miles, returning to Washington baffled, humiliated, panic struck. . . ."

So great was the Federal panic that ambulance drivers threw out the wounded or unhitched their horses and fled on them. The Sanitary Commission was later unable to find a single wounded soldier who had been carried to Washington by an ambulance.

The battlefield was strewn with the broken bodies of the dead and wounded, the latter parched and moaning for water as they lay bleeding in the dust on this sweltering day. Some pitiably begged to be killed to end their agony. Those carried off to makeshift hospitals fared little better than their comrades lying on the field. Edwin Barrett, a Massachusetts officer taken to Sudley Church, now converted to a hospital, watched blood trickling from ambulances "like water from an ice cart." In front of the church door lay "a large puddle of blood."

The Federal wounded suffered horribly. Deserted by their comrades, they were passed over by most Confederate doctors, who told them, "We have not lint enough for our own wounded, and they must be served first," or, in at least one case, "Tell your master, Lincoln, to raise the blockade, and we will attend to you."

Now, with the Federal ranks shattered and its soldiers fleeing, was the time for Johnston, Beauregard, and the other Confederate generals to pursue their beaten foe and garner the choicest fruits of their victory. But little was done. McDowell's entire army was ripe for capture, Washington lay open to Confederate arms, the possibility of the war's end was palpable, and all the slaughter that in fact did follow might have been avoided. Now, as never again, did the Confederates enjoy military superiority over the North. Present before the generals—and Jefferson Davis, too, for he appeared on the field at battle's end—was

Elinor Junkin Jackson, General Jackson's first wife
*(Courtesy of Stonewall Jackson House,
Historic Lexington Foundation, Lexington, Virginia)*

General Jackson's house, Lexington, Virginia
*(Courtesy of Stonewall Jackson House,
Historic Lexington Foundation, Lexington, Virginia)*

The Virginia Military Institute, 1857
*(Courtesy of the Preston Library,
Virginia Military Institute·Archives, Lexington, Virginia)*

Mary Anna Morrison Jackson, General Jackson's second wife
*(Courtesy of Stonewall Jackson House,
Historic Lexington Foundation, Lexington, Virginia)*

Lt. General Thomas J. Jackson and staff
*(Courtesy of Stonewall Jackson House,
Historic Lexington Foundation, Lexington, Virginia)*

Behind the stone wall on Marye's Heights
after the Battle of Fredericksburg, 1862
(Matthew Brady Collection, courtesy of Josephine Berti)

Confederate dead at Antietam
(Matthew Brady Collection, courtesy of Josephine Berti)

The destruction caused by a shell at the Battle of Fredericksburg
(Matthew Brady Collection, courtesy of Josephine Berti)

The "Winchester" photograph of General Thomas Jackson,
taken by Routzahn
(Eleanor A. Brockenbrough Library,
The Museum of the Confederacy, Richmond, Virginia. Photo by Katherine Wetzel)

one of those rare moments when the history of the Western world could have been radically changed, but it was a moment lost, and it would never occur again. The disheartened Federals were allowed to stream back to their capital unhindered.

The Confederate troops were indeed exhausted, hungry, thirsty, and emotionally drained. Many, too, suffered from untreated wounds. Still, there were troops on hand who had not been committed to the fray, who would have been capable of vigorous pursuit had they been so ordered. But the Confederate commanders seemed as stunned by their victory as the Federals were by their defeat.

President Jefferson Davis had arrived from Richmond late in the afternoon as the flight of the Federals was beginning, but not until eleven o'clock that night, when he sat down with his senior officers, did he inquire about pursuit. When he learned that no plans whatever had been made, he personally drafted an order for the brigade of Milledge Luke Bonham (soon to be governor of South Carolina), which consisted of reasonably fresh troops, to lead the pursuit, but his officers raised objections. The rain which had contributed to the misery of the retreating Federals discouraged pursuit; roads were mired, streams were rising, the men were exhausted; there were a dozen reasons for inertia, so it was decided to postpone a decision until morning. It was still raining in the morning, and the orders were never issued. The Confederacy's golden opportunity to end the war and dictate its terms in the enemy's capital was washed away with the rain. Failure of the victor to pursue a beaten foe was to be a characteristic of almost all Civil War battles, and in this, the Battle of First Manassas (or First Bull Run) was typical.

Historians have written that the Federals retreated into the defenses of Washington, but there were no defenses. Five days after the battle General George B. McClellan, who had been hastily summoned from northwestern Virginia, rode around the capital. He was appalled:

I found no preparations whatever for defense, not even to the extent of putting troops in military positions. Not a regiment was properly encamped. . . . All was chaos . . . a perfect pandemonium. . . . There was really nothing to prevent a small cavalry force from riding into the city. . . . If the secessionists attached any value to the possession of Washington, they committed their greatest error in not following up the victory of Bull Run.

That same day Secretary of War Edwin Stanton wrote: "The capture of Washington seems now to be inevitable. . . . The rout, overthrow, and demoralization of the whole army were complete."

Soon after the battle Jackson made his way to the field hospital Dr. McGuire had set up near a small stream (Young's Branch). When McGuire saw him, he left the patient he was tending and asked if he was seriously hurt. "No," Jackson said, "not half as badly as many here, and I will wait." Sitting on the bank of the stream, he settled himself to wait until "his turn came," but when McGuire finished working on the man whose wound he had been dressing, he insisted on treating him.

Upon examination, McGuire decided that the finger could be saved. He later recorded that while he was engaged in splinting and bandaging it, President Davis rode up:

> He stopped his horse in the middle of the little stream, stood up in his stirrups (the palest, sternest face I ever saw) and cried to the crowd of soldiers, "I am President Davis—follow me back to the field." General Jackson did not hear distinctly. I told him who it was and what he said. He stood up, took off his cap and cried, "We have whipped them—they ran like sheep [in other versions by McGuire, dogs]. Give me 10,000 men and I will take Washington City tomorrow."

President Davis either did not hear Jackson or was not aware that this was one of his generals—or the incident did not occur, at least in this way.[5]

The next day, when Jackson wrote to Anna, he made no mention of an encounter with President Davis:

> My Precious Pet—Yesterday we fought a great battle and gained a great victory, for which all the glory is due to *God alone.* . . . My preservation was entirely due, as was the glorious victory, to our God, to whom be all the honor, praise and glory. . . . While great credit is due to other parts of our gallant army, God made my brigade more instrumental than any other in repulsing the main

5. This dramatic scene and the shouted remarks to President Davis are suspect. McGuire was generally a reliable witness, and certainly it was he who dressed Jackson's wound, but the story did not appear in print until more than twenty years after the war. The version used here, which does not differ substantially from the earlier account, was included in an address delivered by Dr. McGuire at the Virginia Military Institute on 23 June 1897, at the inauguration of the Stonewall Jackson Memorial Building.

attack. This is for your information only—say nothing about it. Let others speak praise, not myself.

A week later, in a long letter to his political friend Jonathan M. Bennett, he cast such reticence to the wind: "I am more than satisfied with the part performed by my brigade during the action. . . . You will find, when my report shall be published, that the First Brigade was to our army what the Imperial Guard was to the First Napoleon—that through the blessing of God, it met the thus far victorious enemy and turned the fortunes of the day."

Jackson, although praised in after-action reports by Beauregard and Johnston, was not acclaimed the hero of the hour, and neither was he the most lauded brigade commander.[6] Beauregard was, quite rightly, given the lion's share of the credit for the victory, and Davis promoted him to general on the field. Generous in his praise of others, Beauregard wrote of Jackson:

> The conduct of General Jackson also requires mention as eminently that of an able, fearless soldier and sagacious commander, one fit to lead his efficient brigade. His prompt, timely arrival before the plateau of the Henry House, and his judicious disposition of his troops contributed much to the success of the day. Although painfully wounded in the hand, he remained on the field to the end of the battle, rendering invaluable assistance.

General Johnston praised Jackson for his "high soldierly qualities" and "admirable conduct," adding that "the firmness of Jackson's brigade" had greatly contributed to the restoration of order on Henry Hill. When Anna staunchly declared that the newspapers ought to have given her husband more credit than they did, Jackson assured her: "My brigade is not a brigade of newspaper correspondents. . . . I am well satisfied with what I did, and so are my generals, Beauregard and Johnston."

He had again fought a battle on a Sunday, but neither he nor Anna mentioned this. Not only was 21 July a Sunday, but it was also

---

6. The number of Confederate generals who have been credited with "saving the day" at Manassas, besides Jackson and, of course, Beauregard and Johnston, includes Nathan Evans, Edmund Kirby-Smith, and Arnold Elzey. The battle was, perhaps more than most, a conglomerate of separate engagements, and it was, of course, the combined efforts of all those gallant men that won the victory on the banks of Bull Run.

Anna's birthday, a coincidence for which he was thankful, he told her playfully, for "you can never tell me any more that I forget your birthday."

On the field and in combat that day about 18,000 men on each side had been actually engaged. Union casualties were between 2,600 and 3,000, of whom 460 to 480 were killed. Confederate losses were nearly 2,000, of whom 360 to 390 were killed. Jackson's brigade suffered by far the heaviest losses: 119 killed and 442 wounded. Most were in the Valley regiments: the 4th, 27th, and 33rd Virginians. The cost of the battle was felt keenly in Rockbridge County, which suffered the loss of 12 killed and 35 wounded.

Among the choicest booty captured by the Confederates were twenty-eight pieces of artillery, most with rifled tubes. The South was in need of more and heavier artillery. Most of the forty-seven Confederate guns at First Manassas were small 6-pounder smoothbores.

All through the South news of the battle was avidly read. The *Winchester Republican* singled out Jackson's brigade, filled as it was with men and boys from the Valley, for special praise: "If Virginia does nothing more than was done by this Brigade on the field at Manassas, she has repelled the imputation of degeneracy, and proved that she is equal to her best days."

But newspaper accounts were sketchy and unreliable. Everywhere people were hungry for news from participants, and nowhere more so than in Lexington, where crowds gathered at the post office waiting for news that letters might bear. When the Reverend Dr. White was handed an envelope addressed in Jackson's familiar handwriting, he exclaimed triumphantly: "Now we shall know all the facts." Eagerly tearing it open, he read: "My dear pastor, in my tent last night, after a fatiguing day's service, I remembered that I had failed to send you my contribution for our colored Sunday school. Enclosed you will find my check for that object, which please acknowledge at your earliest convenience and oblige yours faithfully, T. J. Jackson."

CHAPTER

13

Dam No. 5
and Bath

Instead of boldly marching on Washington, Johnston was content to move his army cautiously only as far north as Centreville. Jackson's brigade made camp about five miles east of the Manassas battlefield. It was not far enough away. The stench of the corpses and carcasses rotting in the July heat was overpowering. A cannoneer with Joseph Carpenter's battery later wrote: "Those who have never witnessed the horrifying effect of the burning sun upon the corpse of a human being . . . have been spared a most pitiable and lamentable sight . . . and the odor emanating from it is the most intolerable stench that could possibly burden the olfactories." To make matters worse, the water was foul. With grisly humor, the men dubbed the place Camp Maggot.

On 1 August the brigade moved about eight miles north of Manassas Junction to a field a mile east of Centreville. Jackson wrote jubilantly to Anna that it was "the best encampment we have had. We are blessed with excellent water and a good drill-ground." Here the brigade remained throughout the month, the peace disturbed only by three advances to Fairfax Court House in response to false alarms. Each time the twelve-mile ride inflamed Jackson's wounded finger. Dr. McGuire instructed him to bathe it, advice he carefully followed. As McGuire said:

I think he had a kind of fancy for this kind of hydropathic treatment and I have frequently seen him occupied for several hours pouring cup after cup of water over his hand with that patience and perseverance for which he was so remarkable. Passive motion was instituted about the twentieth day and carefully continued. The motion of the joint improved for several months after the wound had healed, and in the end the deformity was very trifling.

Among the visitors to General Beauregard's nearby headquarters in this quiet time was Prince Napoleon (nicknamed Plon-Plon), a nephew of Napoleon I's. Beauregard organized a three-regiment parade in his honor, and Jackson was gratified to have one of his regiments selected. Although the three were handpicked on the basis of appearing the least ragged and most presentable, it was noted that "the Richmond boys were a bit out at the seat," an observation Major Frederick Skinner of the 1st Virginia responded to by cheerily assuring the prince that "the enemy won't see that part of them."

Much to Jackson's pleasure, doctors of divinity flocked to his camp, including Dr. Robert Dabney, a teacher of theology from the Union Theological Seminary. From Lexington came Dr. Francis McFarland and Jackson's own Presbyterian pastor, Dr. William White, who preached to the troops twice daily for five days. On one memorable occasion White once again asked Jackson to lead in prayer. "Never while life lasts can I forget that prayer," White declared. Jackson prayed for everyone. Beginning with Dr. White and his church in Lexington, he progressed to the deacons, other church members, a list of other preachers, every member of his family, and the Confederate army. When he had at last finished, he turned to White and said earnestly: "Doctor, I would be glad to learn more fully than I have yet done what your views are of the prayer of faith."

To Anna, Jackson wrote with enthusiasm about his flock of divines. Dr. Dabney so impressed him that he reported some of his sermons in detail. In a lighter vein he sent lists of presents he had received from friends and unknown well-wishers: bread, a half barrel of tomatoes, a box of "beautifully packed and delicately flavored plums," and a bottle of blackberry vinegar.

During this lull in the war Anna asked in a letter if her husband could not get a furlough. Replying on 17 August, he pointed out that it would not be fair for him to take leave when he would not give it to others. To stay with his command had become such a firm principle that he was never a day absent from duty, and he demanded the same devotion from all of his officers. Not even the pleas of one who received word that his young wife was dying could shake him. "Man, man, do you love your wife more than your country?" he asked.

Still, he longed for Anna. On 22 August he wrote: "Don't you wish your *esposo* would get sick, and have to take a sick leave and go home. . . ?" But there was no prospect of such a leave, for camp life agreed with Jackson and battle seemed to banish all of his former ailments. If he was ever seriously ill, no one ever knew of it.

In the same letter he wrote: "I wish my darling could be with me now and enjoy the sweet music of the brass band of the Fifth Regiment. It is an excellent band." The 5th Virginia band was becoming famous. Organized as the Mountain Sax-Horn Band in Staunton in 1845, it was equipped with fine instruments made in Belgium.[1] Although Jackson, whose deafness had increased his difficulties with music, was not able to recognize its skill, often not even the tunes it played, he at least reveled in the sound. Years later Anna fondly recalled his struggles with "Dixie":

> When he learned that the tune of "Dixie" had been adopted by the Confederates as a national air, he felt that he ought to be able to know it when he heard it, so during the first visit I paid him in camp he requested me to sing the air to him until he could impress it upon his memory, so as to be able to recognize it. It was a tedious service, and became so perfectly ridiculous from his oft-repeated command of "again" and "again." . . .

He never did learn the tune. At one time a young woman who had just finished a stirring rendition of the song inquired if he had a request. "Yes," he said in his courtly manner. "Sing 'Dixie.' "

On 16 September Jackson's brigade moved up to within a mile of Fairfax Court House, and the 33rd Virginia went on picket duty near

---

1. The saxhorn was invented by a Belgian, Adolphe Sax (1814–1894), in 1840s. There was an entire family of brasses in eight sizes from sopranino saxhorn to double bass saxhorn. He also invented the saxtromba and the saxophone. Related to flügelhorns, the instruments had wide conical bores and cup mouthpieces and were played with valves.

The band of the 5th Virginia played its sweet music throughout the war and was present at Appomattox. It continued its existence long after hostilities ceased, playing in 1885 at U. S. Grant's funeral, in 1897 at a private reception for President McKinley, in 1904 at the St. Louis World Fair, and in the inauguration parade of William Howard Taft. In May 1942 it led the first war bond parade. Women were admitted in the 1950s, and it is still in existence.

the Potomac, within sight of Washington. Here on 30 September President Davis arrived, and Jackson with other officers called on him. Jackson was not impressed. As he told Anna:

> His voice and manners were very mild. I saw no exhibition of that fire which I had supposed him to possess. The President introduced the subject of the condition of my section of the State, but did not even so much as intimate that he designed sending me there. I told him, when he spoke of my native region, that I felt a very deep interest in it. He spoke hopefully of that section, and highly of General Lee.

After seven weeks in Fairfax Jackson's brigade was pulled back to Centreville and went into winter quarters. At last Anna was able to join her husband, a joyous reunion for both. Jackson rented a room from a family named Utterbach, in whose yard his tent had been pitched, and Anna took her meals with her husband and his staff at a mess table set under the trees. She found "every moment . . . full of content and enjoyment." There was time for Jackson and the Reverend Pendleton, now a colonel of artillery, to drive her by ambulance over the battlefield at Manassas, explaining the positions to her and talking the battle over in what she dutifully reported to be a "very interesting way." Some of the horse carcasses, a few human bones, and much of the debris of battle remained. They pointed out the Henry house "riddled with shot and shell," and she was surprised to find the famous Bull Run "a small insignificant stream."

It was at this time that Captain Imboden came to inquire about Jackson's wound and found him bathing his hand with springwater. Over breakfast he asked: "General, how is it that you can keep so cool, and appear so utterly insensible to danger in such a storm of shells and bullets as rained about you when your hand was hit?"

In a low, earnest voice Jackson answered: "Captain, my religious belief teaches me to feel as safe in battle as in bed. God has fixed the time for my death. I do not concern myself about *that*, but always to be ready, no matter when it may overtake me." He paused, and then, looking Imboden full in the face, he added sternly: "Captain, that is the way all men should live, and then all would be equally brave." Imboden got the point: Jackson had not forgotten his profanity on Henry Hill. He made haste to apologize. Jackson listened and then said simply: "Nothing can justify profanity."

Anna's visit was short. "The army was ordered to change its location in less than a fortnight," she wrote, "and I was sent back sorrow-fully to North Carolina."

On 14 October Jackson wrote to his "sunshine," his "sweetest little woman," a letter brimming with good humor and good news. His finger had healed, and its use was restored. He thought it likely he would go into winter quarters and asked playfully, "Will little ex-Anna Morrison come and keep house for me and stay until the spring of the campaign of 1862?" The best news he saved for the end: "I am very thankful to that God who withholds no good thing from me (though I am so utterly unworthy and ungrateful) for making me a major-general in the provisional Army of the Confederate States. The commission dates from the 7th of October. . . ." In less than six months he had moved from VMI major to major general. James Longstreet was pro-moted to the same rank on the same day.

There were at this time only three general officer ranks in the Confederate army, the rank of lieutenant general did not exist and the rank of major general was new. No insignia of rank differentiated the generals. All wore three stars in a wreath. Jackson was uncertain as to his pay but thought it would be more than the $301 per month paid to a brigadier general. He was pleased to discover that he would receive an additional $100 for being commander of an army.

By this time Federal troops firmly controlled all of the territory north of the Great Kanawha River and west of the Alleghenies. To Anna back at Cottage Home he wrote: "If General Lee remains in the Northwest, I would like to go there and give my feeble aid . . . in retrieving the downtrodden loyalty of that part of my native State." To his friend Jonathan Bennett he wrote: "Should you have any occasion to ask for a brigade from this army for the Northwest, I hope mine will be the one selected. This of course is confidential, as it is my duty to serve wherever I may be placed. . . . But it is natural for one's affections to turn to the home of his boyhood and family."

On 21 October Secretary Judah Benjamin, Confederate secretary of war, wrote to Jackson:

> The exposed condition of the Virginia frontier between the Blue Ridge and Alleghany mountains has excited the deepest solicitude of the Government, and the constant appeals of the inhabitants that we should send a perfectly reliable officer for their protection have induced the Department to form a new military district, which is the Valley District of the Department of Northern Virginia. In selecting an officer for this command the choice of the

Government has fallen on you. This choice has been dictated not only by a just appreciation of your qualities as a commander, but by other weighty considerations. Your intimate knowledge of the country, of its population and resources rendered you peculiarly fitted to assume this command. Nor is this all. The people of that district, with one voice, have made constant and urgent appeals that to you, in whom they have confidence, should their defense be assigned.

It was not the assignment he had agitated for, but it was a highly gratifying one. Only one restriction dampened his pleasure: He would have to leave behind the Stonewall Brigade. He confided to Dr. White that had the assignment not come as an order, he would have declined it to stay with his brigade. On 4 November he ordered his brigade drawn up in column of regiments and rode out to give his only known personal address to his troops. After praising the endurance and courage of the men who had followed him from Harper's Ferry through Manassas, he ended by rising in his stirrups, reaching out toward them his gauntlet-covered right hand, and in ringing tones declaimed: "In the army of the Shenandoah you were the First Brigade; in the army of the Potomac you were the First Brigade; in the Second Corps of this army you are the First Brigade; you are the First Brigade in the affections of your general; and I hope by your deeds and bearing you will be handed down to posterity as the First Brigade in our Second War of Independence."[2]

The speech was moving and long remembered by those who heard it, but in the event Jackson was not long to be separated from his beloved brigade. On that very day, over the strong objections of General Johnston, Secretary Benjamin ordered that it and the Rockbridge Artillery, now under Captain William McLaughlin, be sent to the Valley District "with the least practicable delay."

Jackson left by the first train and reached Winchester the following morning, 5 November. Within twenty-four hours he rushed Colonel Preston off to Richmond to complain of the "defenseless condition of this place" and to beg for more men, more guns, a senior artillery officer, and an engineer. This was to become a familiar refrain; Rich-

2. There are several versions of this speech, but they do not significantly differ. The most accurate is probably that put together by Lieutenant Henry Kyd Douglas and Sergeant T. Harris Towner, who immediately after the speech wrote down their recollections and compared their versions. Their combined effort was published in the *Richmond Dispatch* on 8 November 1861.

mond was to be bombarded with messages from Jackson arguing the need for more of everything and clamoring to be given the command of all the forces he knew of in the mountains to the west: a brigade of about twenty-five hundred men under Colonel (soon to be Brigadier General) Edward Johnson and a larger force of three brigades (six thousand men) 150 miles southwest under one-armed Brigadier General William Wing Loring.

On 9 November he wrote to Anna: "I am making up my staff slowly in consequence of desiring to secure a good one." In the same letter he enclosed a check for one thousand dollars, advising her to invest it in Confederate bonds. "You had better not sell your coupons from the bonds," he added, "as I understood they are paid in gold, but let the Confederacy keep the gold. Citizens should not receive a cent of gold from the government when it is so scarce. . . . [I]t will be taking just so much out of the Treasury, when it needs all it has."

Before the welcome arrival of the Stonewall Brigade on 10 November, Jackson had available to him only 1,651 men, of whom 442 were in Winchester while the remainder were scattered in small groups over the Valley. Of these, only 190, under Lieutenant Colonel Turner Ashby, were cavalry. The Federals had about 1,200 men at Williamsport, 800 opposite Shepherdstown, and 4,000 in a force under Brigadier General Benjamin Franklin Kelley that had captured and occupied Romney. Jackson wanted not only to hold Winchester but to repel "the invaders from this district before they secure a firm lodgment."

On 20 November, two weeks after his arrival, still pressing for more troops, he proposed to Secretary Benjamin through General Johnston that he be given Loring's brigades to commence a winter campaign to recapture Romney. Johnston's endorsement was encouraging, for he observed "that the troops under General Loring might render valuable services by taking the field with General Jackson, instead of going into winter quarters, as now proposed." The next day Johnston followed this up with a letter to Adjutant General Samuel Cooper stating that although it was "inexpedient" to transfer all the additional men to Jackson, whose proposal was "more than can well be accomplished in that high, mountainous country at this season," still, "if the means of driving the enemy from Romney (preventing the reconstruction of the Baltimore and Ohio Railroad and incursions by marauders . . .) can be supplied to General Jackson, and with them these objects accomplished, we shall have reason to be satisfied, so far as the Valley District is concerned."

On 24 November Secretary Benjamin wrote a curious letter to

General Loring. He enclosed a copy of Jackson's proposal and gave Loring the option of cooperating in the scheme or not. Loring replied on 29 November that he considered a winter campaign practicable if transportation could be found, but he wanted to move his army all at once, including his stores, his ammunition reserve, and his many sick. It would take more time than Jackson had anticipated, but Loring assured Benjamin that he would enter into the campaign "with a spirit to succeed" and that he would be "seconded by a command as ardent in the cause as any in the country, men who will cheerfully endure all the hardships incident to a winter campaign."

Loring, now about to come under Jackson's command, was an experienced soldier who on 4 December would be forty-three years old. When not yet twenty, he had taken part in operations against the Seminoles in Florida. He had then studied law and had been elected to the Florida legislature. In 1846, the year Jackson was graduated from West Point, Loring received a direct commission as a captain in the regular army, serving in the newly instituted Regiment of Mounted Riflemen. During the Mexican War he had won brevets to major and lieutenant colonel and had lost an arm at Chapultepec. He remained in the army after the war, serving mostly in the West, and on 30 December 1856 he became the youngest colonel in the regular army. In May 1861 he resigned his commission in the United States Army and was made a brigadier general in the Confederate army.

Jackson, eager to begin his winter campaign, was irate that Loring's men were taking so long to arrive. On 9 December he wrote Benjamin:

> As the Federal forces may move on this place any day, I would respectfully recommend that General Loring be directed not to postpone the marching of his troops in consequence of a desire to save a large supply of subsistence stores. . . . It does appear to me that the capture of General Kelley's army, including his munitions of war, would be of far more value to our Republic than General Loring's subsistence stores.

Meanwhile, there were other anxieties. As the first Christmas of the war drew near, homesickness inspired desertions of epidemic proportion. When the 33rd Virginia arrived at Winchester, its Company E, composed of unmanageable Irishmen, was without officers. Its commander, a first lieutenant, had "absented himself without leave," and

Colonel Arthur Cummings, the regimental commander, had refused to march with them because they all were drunk after draining the contents of a barrel of stolen whiskey. Acting promptly, Jackson put thirty-three-year-old Second Lieutenant Wilfred Emory Cutshaw, a VMI graduate, in charge, converted the company into a section of artillery with a 4-pounder rifle and a 4-pounder smoothbore, and packed off the lot to join the picket of militia at Hanging Rock, only fifteen miles from Romney.

Supplies were a problem and would continue to be throughout the war. Jackson complained that government commissary officers were offering competing bids for food, and he begged Richmond for more axes, picks, shovels, and hatchets. In the meantime, he sent a brigade foraging into Morgan County. It returned loaded with one thousand pounds of lead pipe and other valuable property impressed from a railroad depot.

In the midst of it all, Jackson's thoughts returned often to Lexington, and he found time to inquire about local and church affairs. On 5 December he asked: "Is there anything due from me for the Building fund at the end of the month . . . ?"

Many citizens of Winchester patriotically offered their homes to officers, but Jackson insisted that regimental officers remain with their men, who were camped four and a half miles north of town. When he went so far as to issue orders requiring all but general officers to obtain passes from headquarters before going into Winchester and posted pickets to ensure compliance, he raised a storm. His colonels were particularly offended, and all five regimental commanders in the Stonewall Brigade signed a letter accusing him of "an unwarranted assumption of authority" and "an improper inquiry into their private matters."

Jackson's assistant adjutant general replied, advising the protesters that the commanding general "claims the right to give his pickets such instructions as in his opinion the interests of the service require." Furthermore, their protest was "in violation of the Army Regulations and subversive of military discipline." Two of the colonels were rebuked for incompetency and neglect of duty, and all were admonished: "If officers desire to have control of their commands, they must remain habitually with them, and industriously attend to their instruction and comfort, and in battle lead them well, and in such manner as to command their respect."

It was not a letter calculated to soothe the egos of senior officers, but it was Jackson's way, and it was to be the beginning of a long series of problems of the kind not readily solved by an imperious attitude and the citation of Army Regulations.

Not until 8 December did the first of Loring's brigades arrive. It consisted of four regiments of infantry under Colonel William Taliaferro, the Tidewater aristocrat and former militia general who had been head of the VMI Board of Visitors and who had commanded the troops at the hanging of John Brown. The trek of his brigade over the Alleghenies had been arduous. According to Lieutenant Lavender Ray of the 1st Georgia, "The wagoneers were forced to throw out tents, blankets, etc., all of which were burnt; they also abandoned broken wagons and horses. . . ." Many of the men, assuming they were headed for comfortable winter quarters at Winchester, jettisoned their arms. They were to be rudely disappointed.

While waiting for the remainder of Loring's troops, Jackson attempted to cut the Chesapeake & Ohio Canal, which was carrying strategic material eastward for the Federals. If he could break Dam No. 5 on the Potomac about seven miles above Williamsport, which supplied the canal with water, he could successfully intercept a vital Federal artery.

He dispatched a small force of infantry and cavalry, which reached the dam on 6 December, skirmished with Federal troops there under Colonel Samuel H. Leonard, and the following night tried without success to break the dam. On the sixteenth Jackson himself mounted a larger effort. Taking the Stonewall Brigade, some militia, artillery, and cavalry, he made a feint at Williamsport, deployed troops to protect his flanks, and sent Captain Raleigh Thomas Colston of the 2nd Virginia and a demolition party to the dam. The Federals were not deceived by his maneuver. They laid down a heavy curtain of fire and drove Colston and his men back.

At last, on the night of 19 December, two brave men, Captain Henry Robinson of the 27th Virginia and Captain Frederick Holliday of the 33rd Virginia,[3] waded into the icy waters of the Potomac at night and under the fire of Federal musketry managed to make a small break

3. Frederick William Mackey Holliday (1828–1899) was a graduate of Yale and of the University of Virginia Law School. He was serving as commonwealth's attorney in Frederick County when the war broke out. Elected captain of Company D, 33rd Virginia, he rose to become colonel of the regiment and lost his right arm at Cedar Mountain. He then served briefly in the Confederate Congress and, continuing his political career after the war, became governor of Virginia in 1877.

in the dam. The damage was so slight that Colonel Leonard reported traffic restored both ways on the canal before Jackson returned to Winchester. Only one man was killed in the effort, but even so, it had been too costly.

Jackson arrived back in Winchester on 23 December, just a few hours ahead of his wife. Anna joined her husband in his quarters on North Braddock Street in the house of a Winchester lawyer, Lieutenant Colonel Lewis Tilghman Moore, now of the 4th Virginia. Moore had been severely wounded in the knee at Manassas and had not yet returned home. The Jacksons took their meals at the nearby house of the Reverend James R. Graham, pastor of the Presbyterian church in Winchester, and, at the urging of the Grahams, later moved in there. The Reverend Graham, who always stoutly denied that Jackson exhibited any eccentricities, later described him as "just a simple gentleman. . . . He was a shy, reserved family man, and a Christian."

Both Anna and her husband loved Winchester, a town, said Anna, "rich in happy homes and pleasant people, in social refinement and elegant hospitality." Jackson was "in such fine health," and Anna found many friends, particularly two "excellent matrons . . . conspicuous for their lovely Christian characters," who "were descended from old Virginia families, true specimens of patrician blood." Now began the happiest three months of her married life. It was, she said, "as happy a winter as ever fall to the lot of mortals on this earth." But for many of Jackson's officers and men it was the most miserable winter they would ever endure. Even Anna had to admit that the Bath/Romney expedition, Jackson's winter campaign, marred her "perfect enjoyment."

On the day after Christmas newly commissioned Lieutenant Colonel Charles James Faulkner, just released from a Federal prison, reported for duty and was appointed an aide-de-camp by Jackson. Faulkner, whose home was in nearby Martinsburg, had been United States minister to France when the war began. When he returned to Washington to give his final report and resign, he had been arrested and thrown in prison. Because he refused to sign an oath of allegiance, he was held for four months before being exchanged for Congressman Alfred Ely of New York, who had been captured by the Confederates at Manassas on 21 July.

On the same day that Faulkner arrived, Loring finally turned up with the remainder of his command: two brigades commanded by Brigadier General Samuel Read Anderson and by Jackson's former VMI colleague, friend, and business partner Colonel William Gilham.

Replacing Jackson as head of the Stonewall Brigade was Brigadier General Richard B. Garnett, a West Pointer (class of 1841) who had seen action in Florida and in the Southwest.

Loring's men were given little time to rest. On New Year's Day 1862 Jackson's command, now amounting to some eighty-five hundred men and five batteries of artillery (twenty-two guns), moved out of its camps around Winchester and headed toward the mountainous land to the northwest. It was an unseasonably warm day, reminding men more of April than of January; many optimistically left their blankets and coats with the wagons. They carried with them no tents. Jackson's ultimate aim was the destruction of Brigadier General Kelley's force at Romney, but his first objective was the small spa town of Bath (today called Berkeley Springs, West Virginia), for he did not want the Federals there to be on his flank and perhaps in his rear, as they might well be if he made a direct attack. Although Loring had been shown Jackson's plan by Benjamin, Jackson gave him no details, nor did he inform his officers or men of their destination.

The army bivouacked the first night just past Pughtown (now Gainesboro, Virginia). During the night storm clouds gathered, and the temperature dropped precipitously. Henry Kyd Douglas, not yet an officer on Jackson's staff, called it the "most dismal and trying night of the terrible expedition." The next day a cold rain fell, and the marching men churned the roads to mud; a biting wind blew, and streams froze. Jackson's hard-swearing, hard-driving, efficient quartermaster, Major John Harman, too ill to travel, was sorely missed. The wagons failed to come up. The hungry men, many without their blankets, tried in vain to sleep. In spite of orders forbidding it, they tore down fences and burned their rails in a futile effort to warm themselves. The men grumbled and complained; morale plunged.

That night Lieutenant Lyle, having failed to locate the wagon containing Jackson's blankets and gear, set out to find the general. After "an all-night flounder through mud and mire," he discovered him about dawn in an abandoned log cabin. With a roof over his head and a fire in the fireplace he had slept in a chair comfortably enough. " 'Old Jack' could sleep as soundly sitting up as he could lying down, and he looked refreshed," Lyle said.

Jackson always liked an early start before dawn, but on 3 January he waited for the laggard wagons bringing up food and blankets to arrive. The delay put him in a foul mood. Coming across his old brigade eating beside the road when he thought they ought to have been marching, he growled at their new commander. When Garnett protested that it was impossible for the men to march without eating, he snapped, "I never found anything impossible with this brigade."

That day, the second of marching in bitter cold weather on muddy roads through mountainous terrain, many men, too weak from exposure and sickness to go on, had to be left with farm families along the way.

Ten miles from Bath, Jackson sent his militia off to the left to approach the town from the other side of the mountain (Warm Spring Ridge). Here, on the evening of 3 January, it encountered a Federal picket and drove it back. On that dark night in a biting sleet storm the leading elements of the main force, still undetected, had marched to within four miles of Bath, where Federal commanders and their troops imagined themselves secure from a Confederate attack in such weather.

The little army suffered through another miserable night, and the following morning, three miles outside Bath, Loring's advance guard ran into a Federal picket of "probably 30 infantry and as many horse." In a brief fight Loring suffered a lieutenant and three privates wounded and captured eight prisoners, but secrecy was lost. Although Loring's troops were disheartened and unnerved, Jackson kept them in the lead. Loring himself infuriated him, for "without sufficient cause," according to Jackson in his scathing after-action report, he "permitted the head of the column repeatedly to halt, and thus lost so much time as to make me apprehensive that unless I threw forward other troops I would have to remain out of Bath another night."

Loring was directed to send a regiment along a mountain ridge on the left, and the 1st Tennessee performed this task with "patriotic enthusiasm." Another column was thrown out on the right flank while the main body moved down the road. On the edge of Bath Lieutenant Colonel William Smith Hanger Baylor, a Washington College graduate and attorney now serving as Jackson's inspector general, took command of the cavalry and led a charge into town. Scattering the Federals, he pursued their cavalry as it fled out of town down the road north toward Hancock, Maryland.

Jackson, dashing into town behind the cavalry, found himself ahead of Loring's skirmishers. "So prematurely and repeatedly had General Loring permitted the head of the column to halt, that even his skirmishers were not kept within continuous sight of the enemy," Jackson wrote scornfully. In fact, by the time Loring arrived it was dark and the fleeing Federals were nowhere in sight. Enraged, Jackson sent infantry flying to hunt them down, and when the victorious cavalry rode back in, having abandoned their pursuit, he ordered them out to resume it. Colonel Armistead Thomson Mason Rust was directed to take his 19th Virginia, the 37th Virginia, and two guns over the mountain to destroy the important Baltimore & Ohio railroad bridge over the Cacapon River, five miles southwest of the town where the Cacapon empties into the Potomac. Colonel Gilham was hurried off to attack the railroad depot at Sir John's Run, across a mountain ridge two and a half miles west of Bath,[4] but on this night when so much went wrong, he, too, went astray, serenely leading his brigade down the wrong road until Jackson found him and set him right.

Colonel Rust had encountered Federals and had vigorously attacked them but was unable to destroy the bridge completely. Colonel Gilham failed to take the depot. He had come up to the retreating Federals at Sir John's Run, where, according to Jackson, "he neither attacked them nor notified me of the cause of not doing so, nor even of his having overtaken the Federal forces, their artillery and infantry were permitted to escape." Indeed, some had simply boarded a waiting train, others fled up the tracks toward Alpine (across the river from Hancock), and still others, infantry and artillery, waded through the icy waters of the Potomac to reach the safety of Maryland.

In Gilham's defense it must be said that Sir John's Run is approached by a long, narrow gully, which favored the Federals, whose rear guard fought stubbornly and effectively, but Jackson was not mollified by explanations. Although by 9 January Jackson's erstwhile friend Gilham had returned to VMI, he preferred charges of "neglect of duty" against him, the first of the many senior officers against whom Jackson would prefer charges in the next twelve months.[5]

When the 1st Tennessee marched into Bath, Private Sam R. Watkins, filthy, freezing, and exhausted, saw a sight he remembered more than twenty years later: "At this place a beautiful lady ran across the street. I have seen many beautiful and pretty women, but she was the prettiest one I ever saw."

The thermal and mineral springs that gave Bath its name had

---

4. Sir John's Run, named after Captain Sir John Sinclair, who had been General Edward Braddock's quartermaster on his Duquesne campaign, is an insignificant stream that empties into the Potomac near the railway station. There is now a small unincorporated community here. There are still railroad tracks and frequent trains pass by, but none stops, and the depot is gone.

5. The charges against Gilham were later dropped.

attracted many who suffered from "Dyspepsia in its various forms, Gout, Nervous Weakness, diseases peculiar to females, and Neuralgia," as well as those who wanted to enjoy the mountain air, the hunting, and the rich social life of a fashionable spa. Between 1845 and 1848 a number of cottages and a large hotel, able to accommodate four hundred guests, had been built there by Colonel John Strother. The spa was deserted in winter, its cottages and hotel tightly closed. A number of troops broke into the hotel and, using furniture as firewood, built a roaring fire in the large banquet hall, enabling some to sleep that night in relative comfort. Other fortunate ones found shelter in the cottages, but most were forced to sleep on the ground, and, said one, the suffering was "awful to witness."

In his after-action report Jackson estimated the Federal force at Bath to have been fifteen hundred infantry and cavalry with two guns. Large amounts of stores were captured in and around Bath, and what could not be carried away was destroyed. At Sir John's Run rails from the track were twisted out of shape by fire, and the depot and the hospital were burned. In Bath the houses of Union sympathizers were sacked. (Colonel Strother, whose son was in the Union army, was so outraged by the destruction of his fine hotel and his home, which was "pillaged from cellar to garret," that he took to his bed and on 16 January died.)

On the next day (5 January) snow fell, but Loring successfully completed the destruction of the railway bridge over the Cacapon River and destroyed several miles of telegraph line and railroad property nearby. Meanwhile, Jackson moved men up to Alpine and sent Turner Ashby to demand the surrender of Hancock, threatening to shell it if his demand was not met. When the Federals refused to surrender, he brought up a battery and "cannonaded the place" for a short time.[6] He justified this by declaring that as the Federals had shelled Shepherdstown when it held no troops, he wanted "to intimate to the enemy that such outrages must not be repeated."

Jackson began the construction of a bridge two miles above the town, but the following day the Federals at Hancock were reinforced, and he abandoned the idea of capturing it. Instead, he sacked the large

6. On the back of the Presbyterian church in Hancock there can still be seen a cannonball lodged in the wall and a plaque which claims it was fired by Jackson when he shelled the town. But as the cannonball is on the outside of the north wall, it was obviously fired by a Union gun trying to return Jackson's fire.

Federal supply depot at Alpine, burning what could not be carried away. Then, in spite of the snow and the bitter weather, he prepared to move on Romney, his main objective. Romney, captured by the Federals the previous October, dominated the valley of the South Branch River, a tributary of the Potomac.

On the seventh Jackson marched to Unger's Store (today Unger). The march through the mountains in yet another ferocious winter storm was a nightmare. The temperature dropped lower still, and the ground froze. Locals declared the winter one of the worst in memory. "The roads were one glare of ice," said Private John Casler of the 33rd Virginia. "Four men were detailed to go with each wagon in order to keep it on the road. . . . In going up a little hill I have seen one horse in each team down nearly all the time. As soon as one would get up, another would be down, and sometimes all four at once." Cuts on the knees and the muzzles of the exhausted horses streamed with blood as they plodded along.

To First Lieutenant John Newton Lyle "the oaths of the teamsters were a revelation as to the variety, point, pith and eloquence that men of that calling can give to their profanity. The peaks and gorges echoed and multiplied the cursing and swearing into a blasphemous roar that must have shocked the vermins that dwelt in the mountains. The domesticated animals hitched to the wagons were used to it."

Private Casler saw Jackson dismount and put his shoulder to a wagon wheel and heard a colonel who had no love for him mumble bitterly: "Yes, that is the business he ought always to be at." John Worsham of the 21st Virginia, twenty-two years old and six feet tall, later recalled seeing Jackson trudging along on foot. Describing the march, he wrote that "at many hills the pioneers had to cut small trenches across the road in order that the men might have a footing. . . . Although the men underwent great exertion in this march, the cold was so intense that their suffering was great."

Another private in the 21st Virginia, Tucker Randolph, who saw two men die in the road of what he thought to be pneumonia, wrote indignantly to his father: "Genl. Jackson has a great load on his shoulders to answer for in *this* Campaign."

But Jackson had other thoughts on his mind. That evening he received the discouraging news that the militia and the "unmanageable Irishmen" (about seven hundred men in all) he had sent to Hanging Rock with two guns had been attacked and overwhelmed, the guns lost. At the same time he was forced to recognize that his forces must halt.

He spent several frustrating days in and around Unger's Store, "resting the men and ice-calking the horses."[7] The men, sleeping in the open without shelter, found little rest. Artilleryman William Poague later wrote: "In all the war I never . . . endured such physical and mental suffering."

Although on 10 January Jackson reported that he had 8,000 infantry and 375 cavalry at Unger's Store, many of his men were not fit to fight, and it is doubtful that he still had that number with him. Hundreds, who could bear no more, made their way without leave back to Winchester, and the town was soon filled with uncontrolled soldiers, who wandered the streets and imposed upon the hospitality of the citizens.

Captain James K. Edmondson, commander of Company H, 27th Virginia, wrote from Unger's Store to his wife, Emma: "My men, many of them are sick and getting sick and being sent away." He had worn through his boots, he told her, and "my feet have been on the ground." James H. Langhorne of the 4th Virginia wrote to his mother, confessing that the romance of war was gone: "I have endured and seen others endure that if a man had told me 12 months ago that men could stand such hardship I would have called him a fool."

In his official report Jackson devoted only a single sentence to the weather, merely noting the difficulty it created for the horses and wagons.

---

7. In ice-calking pointed pieces of iron were added to horses' shoes, usually on the hind feet, to prevent slipping.

14

☆ ☆ ☆ ☆ ☆ ☆ ☆ ☆ ☆ ☆ ☆ ☆ ☆ ☆

Romney and Resignation

Not until 13 January did Jackson resume his march. The Union forces under General Kelly at Romney had not waited to be attacked but retreated in haste on the tenth, abandoning, among other property, a large number of tents. Romney was occupied without a shot fired. Not content with this, Jackson planned to lead Taliaferro's brigade, the first to arrive, on another "important expedition against the enemy": the destruction of the railway bridges across the North Branch of the Potomac, which would cut the Union forces' supply line from the west, but he was forced to abandon this enterprise because, he said, of the "demoralization" of Taliaferro's men.

Confederate losses in the Bath/Romney campaign caused by enemy action were four killed and twenty-eight wounded. According to Dr. Hunter McGuire, "the number of deaths resulting from the expedition amounts to twenty-five or twenty-six." Of the thirteen hundred reported sick, most were from Loring's command. James H. Langhorne wrote to his father: "This army has suffered terribly from exposure and hard duty since we left our camp below Winchester. Not more than ⅓ of each Regiment is now reported for duty." Union losses were unknown, but Jackson was sure they were higher than his. He had captured sixteen prisoners.

Jackson now sent the militia off to guard their own districts. The

Stonewall Brigade was ordered back to Winchester. Loring's three brigades (four thousand men), together with three companies of cavalry and thirteen guns, were to remain as a garrison in Romney. Jackson himself, after ordering this deployment of his forces, hurried back to Winchester. Riding forty miles in a day on Little Sorrel, he reached Anna's welcoming arms on 23 January. He was, she said, "so full of animation and high spirits." Sitting by the cozy fireside in the Reverend Graham's house, he exulted, "Oh, this is the very essence of comfort!"

Although almost all of the Union forces across the Potomac from Jackson were in winter quarters and Jackson was later to maintain that Loring was in no danger at Romney, on the day after his return to Winchester he wrote to Secretary of War Benjamin, declaring that he was "apprehensive that an attempt be made to surprise General Loring at Romney" and begging for more cavalry. He made a similar plea to General Johnston.

Loring, too, was uneasy, but far from requesting more troops, he was bent upon abandoning bleak, cheerless, and frozen Romney. The expedition to capture Bath and occupy Romney in the midst of the devastating winterstorms had seemed to Loring's troops, officers and men alike, an act of madness. Private Worsham, who fought the war from beginning to end, later declared the Romney campaign to have been "the most terrible experience of the war. Many men were frozen to death; others were frozen so badly that they never recovered. The rheumatism contracted by many was never gotten rid of. Many of the men were incapacitated for service, and large numbers, having burned their shoes while trying to warm their feet at the fires, were barefooted."

Indeed, every public building and church and almost every private home from Romney to Winchester were filled with the sick and frostbitten soldiers of Jackson's army. Private Isaac Herman of the 1st Georgia, who came down with pneumonia on the campaign, described the use of Winchester's churches as hospitals: "The men were packed in the pews wrapped in their blankets, others were lying on the nasty humid floor, for it must be remembered that the streets of Winchester were perfect lobbies of dirt and snow tramped over by men, horses and vehicles."

Loring's men bitterly resented being left to freeze in the mountains while the Stonewall Brigade, Jackson's "pet lambs," were luxuriating in Winchester. Indignant letters began to arrive in Richmond. Colonel Samuel Vance Fulkerson of the 37th Virginia in Taliaferro's brigade, a former judge, wrote angrily to two congressmen he knew. He notified Congressman Walter Staples that Romney was "of no importance in a strategical point of view," that there was not enough fuel and the men were in distress. Declaring that "all of the officers of this army take the same view of the case," he urged Staples to "see the Adjutant General, the Secretary of War, and the President if necessary. . . ."

Colonel Taliaferro wrote as well, assuring Staples that "every word and every idea conveyed by Colonel F in his letter to you is strictly and unfortunately true. The best army I ever saw of its strength has been destroyed by the bad marches and bad management. It is ridiculous to hold this place."

On 25 January Fulkerson forwarded to Loring a protest document which Taliaferro and ten other officers had signed. It was obviously designed to be seen by the authorities in Richmond. The signers, beside Fulkerson, included Colonel Jesse S. Burks (now commanding Gilham's brigade) and Colonel John A. Campbell—each of whom in the coming months would, to his chagrin, get to know Jackson much better. A lieutenant colonel, three majors, and three captains added their signatures. However, the eleven signers represented only two of Loring's brigades. No officer in Brigadier General Samuel Anderson's brigade signed the paper, although Anderson, fifty-eight, deciding that arduous campaigning was for younger men, resigned.

Fulkerson's document was explicit. He charged that before being sent to Winchester, Loring's troops were "worn down with unremitting toil and wasted by death and disease"; that the Romney campaign had exposed the troops to "a degree of severity, of hardship, of toil, of exposure and suffering that finds no parallel in the prosecution of the present war, if indeed it is equalled in any war"; that some regiments that had left Winchester six hundred strong could now boast of fewer than two hundred fit for duty; that their position at Romney was "one of the most disagreeable and unfavorable that could well be imagined. We can only get an encampment upon the worst of wet, spouty land, much of which when it rains is naught but one sheet of water and a consequent corresponding depth of mud"; that the closeness of the enemy required "very heavy picket duty"; and that the countryside was exhausted of supplies.[1]

1. Not all the men were unhappy with conditions at Romney, at least initially. Many took up quarters in houses that had been abandoned by their owners and in public buildings. Company F, 21st Virginia, occupied the bank building, and Private

Fulkerson closed with a petition to Loring to "present the condition of your command to the War Department and earnestly ask that it may be ordered to some more favorable position." On 26 January Loring endorsed this remarkable document, which he labeled a "respectful communication" depicting "the true condition of this army" as well as "the united feeling of the army." Not until 4 February did Jackson add his endorsement: "Respectfully forwarded, but disapproved." By this time, however, so much had happened that Jackson's endorsement was irrelevant.

Even before the protest document was written, officers and men had begun canvassing their elected representatives in Richmond, protesting that although Jackson was undoubtedly brave and a good brigade commander, he was incompetent to administer so extensive a district and hold a separate command and that it was his vaulting ambition that had led to the foolhardy Romney campaign. On 26 January Secretary Judah Benjamin wrote to General Johnston at Centreville, informing him that "the accounts that have reached us of the condition of the army in the Valley District fill us with apprehension" and that the president wished Johnston to look into the situation and to recommend ways to "restore the efficiency of that army."

Johnston replied that he was not quite sure why the secretary was apprehensive but that he would send his inspector general to the Valley District.

Earlier, probably before he had seen Benjamin's letter, Johnston had written to Jackson, informing him that he could not have the extra cavalry he had asked for to protect Loring's troops and politely voicing his uneasiness at Jackson's widely scattered command. "It would be imprudent, it seems to me, to keep your troops dispersed as they are now. Do not you think so?"

Meanwhile, Taliaferro was given leave by Loring to carry a copy of the protest with Loring's endorsement to Richmond. Here on 28 January he showed the letter to every congressman he could find and to Vice President Alexander H. Stevens. The following day he met with President Davis and showed it to him. Thus the president probably saw the document before Jackson did. Davis read the letter carefully and,

---

Worsham wrote: "We lived well there. My mess employed an old darky, about two squares off, to cook our rations. She added to them any good thing she could get. There was a hotel that had buckwheat cakes in splendid style, plus fine butter and syrup for breakfast, and it only charged twenty-five cents for meals. It took only three days for us to eat it out."

after being shown on a map the deployment of troops in the district, agreed that Jackson had indeed blundered. In a "Private and Confidential" letter to Loring, Taliaferro reported on his progress and described his meeting with the president: "When I told him of Jackson's having left us at Romney and having withdrawn his forces to Winchester I never saw anyone so surprised. . . . I think from all I can find out that the Presid't is disposed to do us justice. . . . Jackson's prestige is gone, public sentiment is against him. The leading men of the N.W. [northwestern Virginia] have asked me if he is not deficient in mind."

Davis endorsed the protest letter and directed Taliaferro to take it to Secretary of War Benjamin with the following note: "It will be necessary to act promptly. Have you been notified of the return of General Jackson and the withdrawal of the brigade with which he undertook the service from which he is reported to have retired, leaving only those who were sent to re-inforce him? Will confer with you at your pleasure. J. D."

Apparently Davis and Benjamin did confer, but they seem to have consulted no others, neither Samuel Cooper, the adjutant general, nor General Johnston, Jackson's superior, before they acted. A telegram directly from Benjamin reached Jackson on the morning of 31 January. It must have staggered him more than any shot or shell: "Our news indicates that a movement is being made to cut off General Loring's command. Order him back to Winchester immediately."

Jackson fired off a letter to Secretary Benjamin that same day:

> Sir: Your order requiring me to direct General Loring to return with his command to Winchester immediately has been received and promptly complied with.
>
> With such interference in my command I cannot expect to be of much service in the field, and accordingly respectfully request to be ordered to report for duty to the superintendent of the Virginia Military Institute at Lexington, as has been done in the case of other professors. Should this application not be granted, I respectfully request that the President will accept my resignation from the Army.
>
> I am, sir, very respectfully, your obedient servant,
>
> T. J. Jackson
> Major-General, P.A.C.S.

As was proper, the letter was sent through Johnston, who himself had reason to be nettled with his civilian superior for deploying his troops and giving direct orders to one of his subordinate generals. Johnston delayed endorsement until 5 February and then wrote: "[R]espectfully forwarded, with great regret. I don't know how the loss of this officer can be supplied. General officers are much wanted in this department."

Jackson had been slow to recognize his danger, but he now swung quickly into action, bringing his own political big guns to bear. On the day that he received the telegram from Secretary Benjamin, he wrote directly to fellow Lexingtonian Governor John Letcher:

> This morning I received an order from the Secretary of War to order General Loring and his command to fall back from Romney to this place immediately. The order was promptly complied with, but as the order was given without consulting me, and is abandoning to the enemy what has cost much preparation, expense and exposure to secure, and is in direct conflict with my military plans, and implies a want of confidence in my capacity to judge when General Loring's troops should fall back, and is an attempt to control military operations in detail from the Secretary's desk at a distance, I have . . . requested to be ordered back to the Institute, and if this is denied me, then to have my resignation accepted. I ask as a special favor that you will have me ordered back to the Institute. . . . A sense of duty brought me into the field, and thus far has kept me. It now appears to be my duty to return to the Institute. . . . I regard the recent expedition as a great success. . . . I desire to say nothing against the Secretary of War. I take it for granted that he has done what he believed to be best, but I regard such a policy as ruinous.

The next day Jackson wrote to Johnston's headquarters, and, referring to Benjamin's surmise that Loring might be cut off, said: "Such danger I am well satisfied does not exist, nor did it, in my opinion, exist at the time the order was given." Loring, he proposed, should be sent back without delay to Romney. Johnston passed this on to Benjamin with the endorsement: "Respectfully referred to the Secretary for War, whose orders I cannot countermand."

Loring, too, was busy. He forwarded to Richmond a report by his chief engineer, Captain Seth M. Barton, determining that Romney could not be defended by a small force such as his. But whether or not Romney could be defended and whether or not Jackson had skillfully deployed his troops were by this time irrelevant.

Davis and Benjamin had clearly not anticipated such a violent

reaction from Jackson. They were now faced with the political consequences of the resignation of a major general, one of the Manassas
heroes, who had just completed a successful winter campaign. Moreover, this particular major general had political friends. On receipt of
Jackson's letter Letcher had at once seen Benjamin and made clear his
disapproval. Then, calling in Jackson's allies, he mounted a campaign
to persuade him to withdraw his resignation.

In the meantime, Johnston had written to Davis and gently reminded him that a general could not be held responsible for troops if he
did not have control of them and that disaster was inevitable if such a
system as Benjamin's was to prevail. To Benjamin he wrote: "I regret
very much that you did not refer this matter to me before ordering
General Loring to Winchester. . . ." To the impetuous and outraged
Jackson he dispatched a warm and gentlemanly letter:

> Let me beg of you to reconsider this matter. Under ordinary cir-
> cumstances a due sense of one's dignity, as well as a care for profes-
> sional character and official rights, would demand such a course as
> yours, but the character of this war, the great energy exhibited by
> the Government of the United States, the danger in which our very
> existence as an independent people lies, requires sacrifices from us
> all who have been educated as soldiers. . . .
>
> Let us dispassionately reason with the Government on this
> subject of command, and if we fail to influence its practice, then ask
> to be relieved. . . .

Jackson would have none of this. His dander was up. He had been
humiliated. His rights had been violated. As for sacrifices, he had made
them. He was beyond reasoning.

However, from friends and strangers, soldiers, politicians, and
clergymen came powerful arguments pressuring him to withdraw his
resignation. One T. Basset French wrote that all Richmond was in
despair and that his resignation had "blanched the cheek of many a
brave heart and thousands have united in their expressions of grief."
Congressman Boteler paid him a personal visit. On 6 February Jackson
relented and gave Letcher permission to withdraw his letter unless
Benjamin desired his resignation. Then he filed court-martial charges
against Loring.

He listed two charges. The first was "Neglect of duty," in that
Loring had failed to see that his men had been properly encamped on 1
January, that he had failed to "attack and press forward" when he

encountered the Federal picket on 3 January, that he had been too slow on the following day, that he had permitted his troops to become demoralized while in Romney, and that he had permitted his officers to "unite in a petition" against Jackson's orders. The second charge, "Conduct subversive of good order and military discipline," carried two specifications, particularly that Loring had on 3 January near Unger's Store in the presence of one of Jackson's staff officers said, "By God, sir, this is the damnedest outrage ever perpetrated in the annals of history, keeping my men out here in the cold without food," and that he had endorsed and forwarded the protest of his officers to the War Department.

Johnston, who received Jackson's charges on 7 February, forwarded them to General Cooper with the endorsement that he thought a court-martial should be held but that he lacked sufficient officers of rank to form a court.[2] Loring, in turn, forwarded a heated denial of the charges, but by this time Davis and Benjamin wanted nothing more than to forget the entire incident. There would be no court-martial.

Naturally, officers and men in the Valley District chose sides in the Jackson-Loring brouhaha. Major John Harman wrote scornfully, "Loring is like a scared turkey and so is his command." On 6 February he recorded that "Loring's command has been dropping in [to Winchester] all day, a terribly disorganized band."

On 9 January Benjamin ordered Johnston to break up Loring's command, and most of his troops were sent to Tennessee; Loring was reassigned to Georgia. Although Davis and Benjamin had recommended that all of Loring's troops be removed from Jackson's district, Johnston permitted Jackson to retain the Virginia regiments and two batteries.

By the end of the month Jackson was again firmly in control. To a militia colonel who complained that he could not get his men to obey his orders, Jackson wrote firmly on 11 February: "If your cavalry will not obey your orders, you must *make them* do it. . . . I desire you to go out and post your cavalry where you want them to stay, and arrest any man who leaves his post and prefer charges and specifications against him, that he may be court-martialed. It will not do to say that your men cannot be induced to perform their duty. *They must be made to do it.*"

Notified that a Winchester merchant was refusing to accept Confederate currency for his goods, he acted with his usual promptitude

2. Then, as now, officers were not tried by officers of lower rank than themselves.

and arrested the man. From that time on Confederate money was always at par, at least when Jackson was in town.

The Loring incident still rankled, and to Boteler he wrote on 12 February that Federal forces had occupied Moorefield, a town in the mountains seventy miles west of Winchester. "Such is the fruit of evacuating Romney," he said bitterly. "Loring should be cashiered for his course." Two days after the seizure of Moorefield, Union forces attacked a small brigade of Jackson's militia and took a number of prisoners, among them seventeen officers.

Unknown to Jackson, his West Point classmate, now Major General George B. McClellan, in command of the Army of the Potomac, paid him a handsome compliment. When he authorized the advance of Federal forces back to Romney, McClellan cautioned: "If you gain Romney look out for the return of Jackson, whom I know to be a man of vigor & nerve, as well as a good soldier."

Indeed, Jackson was coming to the attention of an ever-wider circle. George Bagby, a reporter for the *New Orleans Daily Crescent* who was in Winchester, sent a lyrical report to his paper (15 February): "He is as brave and cool as a human being can be; a Presbyterian who carries the doctrine of predestination to the borders of positive fatalism—the very man to storm the infernal regions in case of necessity. Silent and uncommunicative, exceedingly polite, yet short and prompt in his speech, he has but little to do with the commanders under him, but is devoted in his attentions to his men, especially to those who are sick."

Admirers wrote and sent presents. From two women in Jefferson County came the tribute of several bottles of homemade wine and a basket of food with a note declaring that with Jackson present they had the "utmost confidence in the safety of themselves, and the sanctity of their homes from the invasion of a ruthless and mercenary foe." As soon became apparent, they were much too sanguine.

On 28 February Jackson offered the post of assistant adjutant general with the rank of major to his political friend Jonathan Bennett in Richmond. "The position of Adjutant-General," he warned, "is one of great labor and requires much study and the entire ignoring of personal ease. As it is the chief staff position, its head should be an example of military adherence to regulations." Bennett turned down the position, and Jackson offered it to Faulkner, who accepted.

In late February Jackson renewed his pleas for more men and more guns. He now had good reason for doing so. A strong Union army under Major General Nathaniel P. Banks was moving on him.

Although entirely without military experience, Banks was one of the most senior officers in the Union army and commanded the forces across the Potomac from Jackson's Valley District. He had had little formal education but at age twenty-three had been admitted to the bar. A persistent man, he tried eight times before he was elected a member of the Massachusetts legislature, where in time he became Speaker of the House. In 1853 he was elected to Congress for the first of ten terms under five different political affiliations. In 1856 he became Speaker of the House after 133 ballots, and in 1858 he was elected governor of Massachusetts, a post he held until Lincoln commissioned him a major general of volunteers. Jackson was fortunate indeed to have such an inexperienced and, in the event, inept antagonist.

Banks crossed the Potomac, and by 4 March he had occupied Harper's Ferry, Martinsburg, and Charles Town with a force estimated to be thirty-five thousand. Jackson at this time had fewer than five thousand effectives. He begged for more, but they were not to be had. On 8 February legislation was passed requiring all males aged eighteen to forty-five to enter the army or join the militia. Two days later Letcher was authorized to draft militia into the army. As a result, a few recruits came in, but there were never enough.

With the approach of spring, the normal campaigning season for nineteenth-century armies, civilians in Winchester and elsewhere at the foot of the Valley began to ask anxious questions.[3] The Union buildup just north of Winchester was known, and soldiers from private to colonel were constantly asked, "Will Jackson evacuate?"

3. Few could imagine that Winchester would change hands seventy-five times in the course of the war, once changing hands four times in one day.

CHAPTER

15

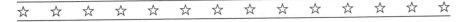

The Battle
of Kernstown

As Jackson sat down with the Graham family for the midday meal on 11 March 1862, he appeared to be his stiffly courteous self; he gave no hint of his future plans, but the Grahams knew that his little army had packed up and was at that moment leaving Winchester. A few days before, Anna had been sent off south on a train with the Confederate sick and wounded, an experience she found "harrowing": "Many of the poor soldiers looked as if they were almost at the point of death. Some were so helpless they had to be carried on the backs of their comrades—their pale, emaciated, and despairing faces and moans of suffering being pitiful and heart-moving beyond description. . . . I was never so impressed with the horrors of war." Jackson was not to see her again for thirteen months.

All the army's stores and baggage were on their way up the Valley. Four days earlier Major John Harman had written to his brother, Colonel Asher Harman, who was in charge of Jackson's main supply base at Staunton: "I have just had an order from Gen'l Jackson to send his wagon to headquarters; this looks like we are about to be off. . . . What is to become of us God only knows."

Federal troops had advanced to within four miles of Winchester only the day before, and Jackson had drawn his troops up in line of battle, daring Banks to attack, but he drew back a dozen miles east to Berryville to concentrate his forces.

The Confederate rank and file were eager to fight, though many had not been issued weapons and would have to wait to pick up the muskets or rifles of those who fell. (The 4th Virginia, reduced by sickness and desertions to scarcely more than three hundred men, had only 203 muskets.) Three thousand muskets had been requested, but Richmond had been unable to supply them. Jackson, who always thought the bayonet a superb weapon, then asked for pikes: "Make them 6 or more inches longer than the musket with the bayonet on, so that when we teach our troops to rely upon the . . . [pike] they may feel that they have the superiority of arm resulting from its length." Lee approved the request, and some were made, but they were never issued. Throughout the Valley Army, in spite of the shortage of weapons and accoutrements, morale (the state of which often depends upon the degree of ignorance prevailing) was high. Private Jonathan Green of the 21st Virginia wrote jubilantly to a friend: "I was never in a better mood to fight."[1]

With the Federals concentrating in such overwhelming numbers, all knew that now the Confederates must retreat. The Grahams did not expect to see Jackson again when he left after lunch, but to their surprise he returned for supper. At his host's courteous request he conducted the evening worship. Prayers over, he sat and chatted amiably with the family for a while.

When at last he rose to leave, one of the Grahams must have said an emphatic good-bye, for he turned and uncharacteristically remarked, "Oh, I'll see you again. I don't expect to leave." Indeed, he returned only an hour later, an agitated and shaken man. The Reverend Graham, summoned to his office, later described the scene: "I found him walking the floor under more excitement than I had ever seen him exhibit before. He had undergone in the brief space of time a surprising change. His countenance betrayed deep dejection." Jackson, in a mood rare for him, needed to talk, and as he paced, he revealed the reason for his distress.

He had, or so he thought, ordered that his wagon train be parked just south of town and that his men withdraw from their positions north of Winchester, pass through the town, and eat their evening meal by the wagons. He had planned not to continue the retreat but to whirl around and launch a night attack on an unsuspecting portion of Banks's army. It was a bold and daring—probably rash—scheme con-

---

1. Most of Jackson's troops were young men from the Valley of Virginia, and of his ten regiments of infantry, six were commanded by VMI graduates.

sidering the insignificant size of the Valley Army. Although the Federal forces were not yet concentrated, Banks could count on about twenty-five thousand effectives; Jackson had only thirty-one hundred infantry, six hundred cavalry and six batteries with twenty-seven guns, and no major Confederate force was near enough to support or reinforce him.

Night attacks were almost never undertaken during the Civil War, and with good reason. Unit cohesion could not be maintained, and units became lost and disoriented, even firing into their own troops. Nevertheless, this was Jackson's plan, and the full moon that night might have enabled him to succeed. He had summoned his senior officers to his headquarters up the street from the Grahams to reveal the maneuver and to give them their orders. There he had been staggered to learn from them that his wagon train had not halted just south of town but had lumbered on some five or six miles farther and that his troops had followed. His orders, it seems, had not been clear.

For his plan to succeed now, his men, already weary from a day's march, would have to turn around immediately and march the long way back to the town and through it, find the enemy, form a line of battle, and attack. The whole maneuver had become impossible, but Jackson, pacing up and down, "his face fairly blazing with the fire that was burning his soul," according to Graham, announced: "I may execute my purpose still; I have ordered my officers to return at half past nine." However, by that hour he seems to have cooled and to have accepted defeat. The nine-thirty meeting with his officers was canceled. Instead, he packed hurriedly, said good-bye to the Grahams, and, picking up Dr. Hunter McGuire at his home, rode off.

On a hillock just south of Winchester Jackson and McGuire reined in their horses and in the moonlight sat looking back at the town. McGuire was, he said, "utterly overcome by the fact that I was leaving all that I hold dear." Beside him, Jackson was sunk in silence, bitterly reviewing his dashed hopes. Rousing himself, he cried out "in a tone almost savage," according to McGuire: "That is the last council of war I will ever hold!" And so it was. Although the meeting with his officers had not been a true "council of war," Jackson never again put himself in a position where he might be humiliated by having his subordinates, in effect, point out how ambiguous had been his orders and how unworkable his plans.

That night Jackson slept in a fence corner, and early the next morning, the twelfth, he prepared to lead his men toward Strasburg, eighteen miles south of Winchester. About the same time Brigadier General Charles Smith Hamilton, a West Point classmate of U. S.

Grant's, clattering into Winchester with his brigade, found the streets deserted except for a handful of Ashby's cavalry, who exchanged parting shots before they rode off. Jackson was well away.

The retreat up the Shenandoah Valley was conducted in good order. The Confederate commissary general of subsistence later notified Secretary Benjamin with satisfaction that "no stores whatever were lost." On 15 March Jackson moved out of Strasburg to Woodstock (twelve miles) and on the nineteenth to Mount Jackson (twenty-four miles from Strasburg), choosing the macadamized Valley Turnpike,[2] which passed up the Shenandoah Valley to the west of the Massanutten range, rather than the east side with its dirt roads in the Luray (or Page) Valley.

To pursue him, Banks belatedly sent Brigadier General James Shields with a division—three brigades of infantry from Indiana, Ohio, and western Virginia, plus some cavalry and artillery. Shields, almost fifty-two years old, was to play a significant role in Jackson's military career. Born in County Tyrone, Ireland, he had come to the United States when he was sixteen, surviving a shipwreck en route. Unlike most Irish immigrants of this era, Shields was a well-educated man, the master of four languages. For a time he had taught French and read the law in Illinois, where he settled. He fought in the Black Hawk War, involved himself in Democratic politics, became known as a powerful orator—some called him a demagogue—and at the age of twenty-six was elected to the state legislature. Seven years later he was appointed to the Illinois Supreme Court. When he was attacked in several scurrilous newspaper articles, published anonymously, but commonly believed to have been the work of Miss Mary Todd and another young woman, perhaps aided by Miss Todd's friend Abraham Lincoln, he wasted no time in challenging Lincoln to a duel. Happily the affair was settled peacefully, and the two men eventually became friends.

In the Mexican War Shields served as a brigadier general of volunteers and, as noted, was severely wounded at Cerro Gordo and was breveted major general. After the war he was appointed governor of Oregon Territory but immediately gave up this post to become a

2. In 1834 the Virginia legislature authorized the Valley Turnpike Company to make a macadamized road from Staunton to Winchester. The road was bedded with cement and buttressed on both sides with limestone shoulders, and its smooth surface was supported by layers of compacted gravel piled on top of the cement bed. It was thought a wonder that travelers on the turnpike sometimes had a clear view ahead for two or three miles.

United States senator.[3] On 19 August 1861, soon after the outbreak of war, Lincoln appointed him a brigadier general of volunteers.

He has been described as "[m]artial in carriage, scrupulously neat, urbane and courteous of manner, graceful and humorous in debate. . . . In temper he was sharp and somewhat arrogantly independent."

It was the division of this impressive, intelligent Irish-American that Jackson was soon to face in his first major battle as an independent commander, but in mid-March there was nothing for Jackson to do but keep his little army ahead of the superior forces Shields was pressing on him. On 19 March Shields entered Strasburg, but he was too slow. On the following day Jackson had found an excellent defensive position at Rude's Hill, two miles south of Mount Jackson. This was a rugged piece of mountain jutting out from the Massanutten range around the western side of which the North Fork of the Shenandoah River curls like a moat. Into this natural fortress Jackson withdrew his army. A single bridge, which he kept open for the mobility of his cavalry, crossed the North Fork here. It would have been difficult, perhaps impossible, for Shields, even if strongly reinforced by Banks, to have attacked him successfully without unacceptable losses as long as the Confederates controlled the bridge.

The Valley campaign, now about to begin, found Jackson operating on interior lines in a sympathetic environment. A significant number of the people in the lower Valley had been strongly for the Union before the war, but the behavior of Banks, who chose to consider all as rebels, had converted many to the Confederacy, and Jackson now moved among friends, people who for the most part shared Confederate aspirations. Eager to help, they readily supplied him with any information they possessed about the local topography or the movements of Federal troops. Although Jackson never revealed details of his intelligence system, he told Ewell on 3 May: "I have been relying on spies for my information from the enemy." Banks, on the other hand, was operating in enemy territory, surrounded by a tight-lipped population whose information, if given, was likely to be false. Guerrilla bands and bushwhackers harassed him, pouncing upon his outposts, looting supply wagons, and stealing his horses. Chaplain Horace Winslow of the 5th Connecticut wrote home: "The people are thoroughly hostile, they would cut our throats the instant they thought they could do it safely.

---

3. Shields in his lifetime earned the distinction of being the only man ever to have represented three different states in the United States Senate.

This whole Southern race is a miserable set. There is nothing about them or in them to admire."

Banks was so deceived by the reports he received that he had no idea where Jackson might be, and he came to believe that he had, in fact, left the Valley and was probably on his way to help in the defense of Richmond. He was, therefore, not troubled when ordered to send a division to McDowell, and when, on 20 March, Shields was ordered to pull his division back to Winchester, Banks himself calmly prepared to go to Washington.

Although Jackson's intelligence far surpassed that of the Federals, his sources were not infallible, as he was soon to learn. On 21 March a spy he believed to be reliable informed him that Strasburg was being evacuated. When, later that afternoon, Turner Ashby, his able cavalry commander, who kept in close touch with friendly locals, confirmed that Banks had, indeed, abandoned Strasburg and was falling back on Winchester, Jackson determined to act.

Early the next morning, the dawn of a raw, blustery day, the Valley Army, with the Stonewall Brigade in the van, turned itself around and set out on a twenty-six-mile march north to Cedar Creek, near Strasburg. Later that same day Ashby informed Jackson that all but four Federal infantry regiments and a few guns had left the Winchester area and that even this small rear guard was scheduled to leave for Harper's Ferry the next morning.

Jackson immediately changed his route, hurrying his whole force toward Winchester. His advance guard reached an area south of Kernstown (now a suburb of Winchester) at ten o'clock on Sunday morning, 23 March. At one o'clock in the afternoon the remainder arrived. Reluctant to fight on the Lord's day, he decided to rest his exhausted men. One eyewitness declared that "the men were utterly broken down when they reached the battlefield, and so footsore and weary, that if they trod on a rock or any irregularity, they would stagger." The army was well below strength because of furloughs and, above all, straggling. (Straggling was to remain the curse of all of Jackson's hard-marching armies.)

Shields's division, falling back as ordered, had not yet reached Winchester. His three infantry brigades were still stretched along the turnpike within a few miles of one another.

About two or three o'clock in the afternoon of 22 March Colonel Thornton F. Brodhead of the 1st Michigan Cavalry had advised Shields that Confederates were in force close by. Shields could not believe that Jackson would seek to fight so far from his supports, but when the information was repeated a few hours later, he was sufficiently roused to ride with his staff south of Winchester to join Brodhead and see for himself. Ashby, with about three hundred troopers and Chew's battery of "flying artillery,"[4] was in the low hills south of the village of Kernstown.

Riding up to Brodhead "with an air of incredulity," Shields asked where the enemy had been seen. The colonel pointed toward the hills about three-quarters of a mile away, and Shields, still skeptical, trotted toward them with his staff. They had ridden no more than a few yards when a Confederate shell, undoubtedly from young Captain Chew's battery, burst a few feet from them, its fragments wounding Shields in the chest and shoulder. In great pain he was carried off to Winchester. Command of his division in the field now passed to thirty-nine-year-old Colonel Nathan Kimball, a doctor who had seen service in the Mexican War and had been elected to command the 14th Indiana when the war began; he was commanding a brigade when Shields was wounded.

At eight o'clock on the morning of 23 March, Shields, confined to bed, dispatched Colonel John S. Mason of the 4th Ohio to reconnoiter. Unaware that Jackson was only hours away, Mason reported back that only Ashby's men were nearby. Banks, who was to leave for Washington at midday, was still in Winchester and, when consulted, agreed with Shields that Jackson would not be tempted to risk battle so far from his main support.

Jackson, however, trusting Ashby's assessment of Federal strength, determined to attack the next day. Then, apparently worried that the Federals might be reinforced or escape during the night, he impulsively changed his mind and, in spite of the weary state of his men, the lateness of the hour (it was between three and four o'clock), and the fact that it was a Sunday, decided to attack at once.

Placing one infantry brigade plus the 5th Virginia (the largest regiment in the Stonewall Brigade) under Jesse Burks, an 1844 VMI graduate who had served in the Virginia legislature and had been a successful farmer, across the turnpike, Jackson sent Ashby with half of his cavalry to cover his right flank, east of the turnpike. He dispatched

4. This was horse artillery; all gunners were mounted, so the battery could keep up with cavalry. Chew's battery, the first in the Confederate army, was commanded by Captain Roger Preston Chew, a former VMI cadet who, although not yet nineteen years old, was destined to be one of the best artilleryman in the Army of Northern Virginia. All in the battery were young. The first lieutenant was seventeen, and the second lieutenant eighteen.

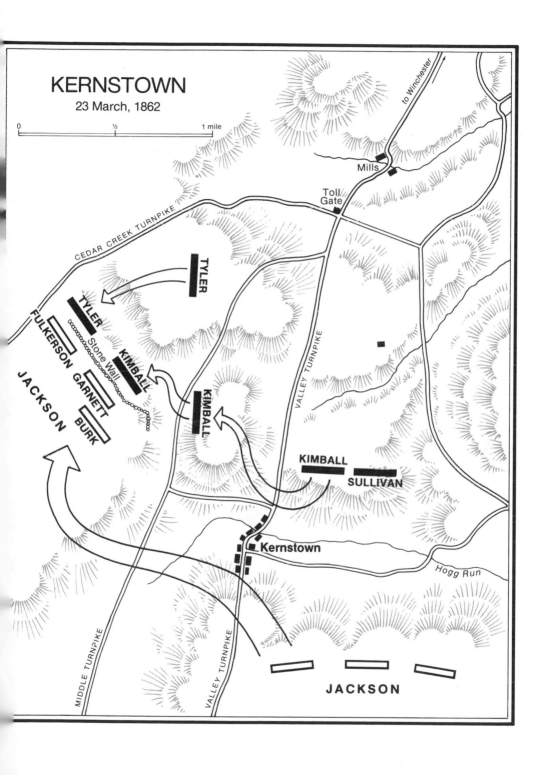

KERNSTOWN
23 March, 1862

0   ½   1 mile

to Winchester

Mills

Toll Gate

CEDAR CREEK TURNPIKE

TYLER

TYLER

FULKERSON

Stone Wall

KIMBALL

GARNETT

JACKSON

BURK

KIMBALL

VALLEY TURNPIKE

KIMBALL

SULLIVAN

Kernstown

Hogg Run

MIDDLE TURNPIKE

VALLEY TURNPIKE

JACKSON

Colonel Samuel Vance Fulkerson's brigade (consisting of only two regiments, all that was left of Loring's division in the Valley) with part of Carpenter's battery, followed soon after by Charles S. Winder's Stonewall Brigade with the rest of Carpenter's battery and McLaughlin's battery, to occupy the ground on his left flank where a ridge ran about two miles to the west and parallel to the turnpike. The other half of Ashby's cavalry, under Major Oliver R. Funston, was to cover the left flank of the Confederates' line. "My objective," said Jackson later, "being thus to turn the enemy's right flank, to get in his rear."

Directly facing the Confederates on a height called Pritchard's Hill were, indeed, only some cavalry and four regiments of infantry, Shields's 2nd Brigade under thirty-one-year-old Colonel Jeremiah Sullivan, a former naval officer and lawyer. But behind Sullivan lay Kimball's 1st Brigade, and behind Kimball was forty-year-old Colonel Erastus Tyler's 3rd Brigade with four regiments of stalwart Ohio infantry. Tyler was a tough man, and as Jackson was to learn, his men were rough fighters. Before the war he had been a hunter and a dealer in furs and skins; although without previous military experience, he helped raise the 7th Ohio, whose members elected him their colonel in preference to future President James A. Garfield. This was the first but not the last time he and his Ohioans would face Jackson and his Valley Army.

The exact strength of the Federal division at this time is not known, but to George Neese, a cannoneer in Chew's battery, it seemed that "the hills west of Kernstown were blue with Yankee infantry." Shields reported that he had 6,000 infantry, 750 cavalry, and 24 guns—something over 7,000 men—and this was probably close. Though Shields in his hasty after-action report claimed that his men faced "the combined forces of Jackson, Smith [Gustavus W. Smith?], and Longstreet . . . about 15,000," the Confederate force was only about a third of that number. Jackson's after-action report more accurately estimated the size of the Union force to be "probably 8,000."

As the Confederates marched into battle, many an apprehensive young soldier reviewed his short life of profanity and sin and essayed an eleventh-hour appeal for salvation. Clement D. Fishburne of Captain William McLaughlin's Rockbridge Artillery later recorded: "Several well known packs of cards were thrown away, and men who had not been credited with a scrupulous knowledge of *meum* and *tuum*, where cooking utensils, etc., were involved, were seen to draw out of their pocket 'Testaments' and go to reading diligently." Second Lieutenant Samuel Harrison Lyle, twenty-two, of the 4th Virginia thought "it was time to look pale and anxious."Private Edward Moore, nineteen, who had joined the Rockbridge battery only the day before, recorded his sensation: "We began to feel that we were 'going in,' and a most weakening effect it had on the stomach."

The ground over which the battle was fought was undulating and generally open, although patches of oak and birch, thick bushes, rail fences and stone walls, and some ravines made maneuver difficult. In moving toward the ridge on the left, Fulkerson's men were forced to dash across an open space where they were exposed to artillery fire so intense that, in the words of their commander, "it might have made veterans quail," but the raw troops plunged ahead, gained the timber on the ridge, and formed line of battle behind a convenient stone wall. Skirmishers were thrown out at once and soon ran into Federal fire, for an alert Kimball, now the Union battlefield commander, had ordered Sullivan's brigade to shift to the right, and Tyler had been ordered to take position on Sullivan's right. Seeing this, Jackson ordered Garnett's brigade to support Fulkerson.

Jackson, hurrying his men along, paused to applaud and cry, "Good! Good!" as a gun from Carpenter's battery[5] threw a well-aimed 6-pounder shell into a barn sheltering a nest of Federal sharpshooters. His elation was short lived. Alexander ("Sandie") Pendleton, one of his young staff officers, who had been told to reconnoiter, had found a piece of high ground and had seen, stretched out in the distance, Shields's entire division. Awed by the sight, he dashed back and breathlessly informed Jackson that the enemy must number at least ten thousand; they had fallen into a trap.

"Say nothing about it," warned Jackson. "We are in for it."

They were indeed, and the tumult of the battle that followed was compounded by the confusing, unclear orders Jackson hurled in all directions. Ignoring the chain of command—as he was often to do in subsequent battles—he sent aides and couriers flying with orders. He even delivered some himself; only occasionally did his orders pass through the hands of Garnett, his second-in-command, who knew nothing of his plans or what he was doing, even with his, Garnett's, own brigade.

Garnett, ordered (or so he thought) to aid Fulkerson with one of

---

5. Carpenter's battery, originally a volunteer infantry company calling itself Allegheny Roughs, became Company A, 27th Virginia, and performed well as infantry in Jackson's brigade at First Manassas. They had just been converted to artillery, and this was their first time in action as a battery.

his regiments, pushed forward with the 33rd Virginia, only to receive a second order to advance his entire brigade, an impossibility since Jackson, who had found his remaining regiment sitting idle, was at the moment personally leading them forward.

Confusion bred confusion. Someone, Garnett or Andrew Jackson Grigsby, another regimental commander, gave such conflicting orders to the 1st Virginia (Irish) Battalion, sent by Jackson to protect Carpenter's battery, that it split into two groups, each of which marched away.

The battle soon turned into a hard slugging match with little maneuvering on either side. Men raced for any cover they could find or, when they found none, simply stood and fired at each other. Private Moore saw a Union shell plow through the two rear horses of his team, tear the leg off the driver, and go on to maim another man.

When a gun of the Rockbridge Artillery was knocked askew and all its cannoneers killed or wounded, a young officer dashed up, corralled some nearby infantrymen, and with them put the gun back into action. When the color-bearer of the 2nd Virginia fell, a lieutenant caught up the staff. When he, too, fell wounded, Private R. H. Lee held it until he in turn was struck down. In all, seven men carried the 2nd Virginia colors. All were hit.

Bullets did not spare rank. Colonel John Echols of the 27th Virginia, a huge man standing six feet four inches tall, was a prime target and was severely wounded. Colonel Jesse Burks had his horse shot from under him, as did Lieutenant Colonel Charles Ronald of the 4th Virginia, who reported, "The firing was so heavy that my horse became ungovernable and ran away with me, hurting me very much." Major Raleigh Colston of the 2nd Virginia, a VMI graduate who only a few months earlier had been a farmer near Hedgesville, saw his brother, William, fall mortally wounded. In the melee he was powerless to reach him.

For more than two hours the battle raged, the Federals as well as the Confederates taking heavy losses. Both sides soon drew upon their reserves, which were thrown helter-skelter into the smoking vortex of the fight. A cannoneer in Chew's battery, fighting his first battle and awed by the roar of musketry and artillery fire, predicted, "There will be no more fighting between these two armies after today, for they will all be killed by evening." Private John Casler of the 33rd Virginia claimed to have seen Federal formations so dense that "a bullet could hardly miss them if aimed low enough." Soldiers of the 5th Ohio rushed forward crying, "Remember Cincinnati." Five times their colors were shot down. The colors of the 7th Ohio were pierced by twenty-eight balls.

On the edge of a clearing the men of the 37th Virginia in Fulkerson's brigade spotted a Federal regiment opposite them. A stone wall stood in the middle of the clearing, and the advantage of possessing it was instantly obvious to all. There was a race for it. The Virginians won, and from its protection they fired into the faces of the Federals.

In such a battle, with both sides containing men equal in stamina and valor, it is the weight of numbers and resources which determines the outcome. Twice the Federals were thrown back, but their pressure and a shortage of ammunition made the Confederate position desperate. Men borrowed ammunition from each other and snatched it from the dead. As long as they could fire, the line held. Private John Worsham of the 21st Virginia believed that his regiment "would have held the line indefinitely if it had been supplied with ammunition." Only when no more could be found did men of the Stonewall Brigade begin, at first by ones and twos, to make their way to the rear. It was about six o'clock, and the sun was almost down; there would be about another hour of evening nautical twilight,[6] but Garnett, seeing his line crumble, felt compelled to order a retreat. It was a painful and, for him, a fateful decision.

Later, justifying his order, he wrote: "Had I not done so, we would have run imminent risk of being routed by superiority of numbers, which would have resulted probably in the loss of part of our artillery and also endangered our transportation."

His regimental commanders concurred with his decision. Lieutenant Colonel Andrew Jackson Grigsby, 27th Virginia, a tough and valiant warrior, wrote: "The position was held until the regiment was ordered to retire, which order was received after the men had fired their last round of cartridges."

In such close action it was not always easy to retreat. Sergeant Charles Arnall of Captain James H. Waters's battery was limbering up to get away when one of his horses was killed. He worked feverishly to cut the traces of the dead animal as the Federals advanced. They were only fifty yards away when he at last succeeded and fled with the remaining three horses, leaving the gun behind—one of two captured

---

6. Nautical twilight is that period after the sun has set or before it has risen when objects on the ground can be seen at four hundred yards. During evening and morning nautical twilight most Civil War soldiers could see well enough to fight.

by the Federals that day. Garnett's retreat exposed Fulkerson's flank, and he, too, was forced to retire.

Jackson, ignorant of Garnett's order, was hurrying forward the last of his reserves, including the large and well-disciplined 5th Virginia. He was enraged to see men hastening to the rear. Collaring one soldier, he demanded to know why he was leaving. He had shot away all his ammunition and could find no more, the young man explained, secure in the soundness of his reason, but he reckoned without Jackson, who listened to him with mounting fury. "Go back and fight with the bayonet," he thundered. Sighting a drummer boy, he ordered him to "Beat the rally!" The frightened boy halted and obediently drummed the call, but the men streamed past him unheeding.

When Garnett appeared, leaving the field, Jackson exploded. On the head of this fine soldier fell his full wrath. Galloping up to him, he cried out, "Why have you not rallied your men? Halt and rally!" It was too late. Garnett did his best to stem the tide, shouting until he was hoarse to no purpose.

Jackson later maintained that Garnett "did not manifest any concern" and failed to use any effort to rally his men. "Could the troops have held their position five minutes longer before falling back we would not have been forced from that part of the hill," he declared. "My great desire was to hold the position on the hill till after dark." He remained certain that the tide of battle could have been reversed by his reinforcements, but he alone of all the officers on the field held this view.

Using his reserves, Jackson managed to establish a line and to give the pursuing Federals some discouraging volleys. It must have been about this time that the color-bearer of the 5th Virginia leaped over a stone wall and, waving his flag, dared the advancing Federals to shoot. Word went down the astonished Federal line to spare him, and for a few moments, while he stood defiantly, a hush fell over the battlefield. Only when he at last obeyed a frantic order to take cover did the battle rage on.

The reserves' delaying tactics gave valuable time to Jackson's discouraged, exhausted, and beaten men, who now streamed down from the ridge and made their way to the turnpike. The retreat did not become a rout. Colonel E. H. C. Cavins of the 14th Indiana spoke admiringly of the Confederate withdrawal: "Yet many of the brave Virginians . . . laagered [sic] in rear of their retreating comrades, loading as they slowly retired, and rallying in squads in every ravine and behind every hill—or hiding singly among the trees. They continued to make it hot for our men."

Ashby's cavalry, with Chew's battery, had performed splendidly, keeping the Federals from falling on Jackson's right flank, and now at battle's end they ably covered the retreat of the infantry.

Chew's battery at this time consisted of only two guns: a 6-pounder made at the Tredegar Iron Works in Richmond and a British 12-pounder Blakely. Until it grew too dark to fight, young Chew's guns let fly when the Federal pursuers drew too close. Private George Neese, twenty-one, a blue-eyed farm boy turned painter now serving in Chew's battery, rammed a final shot home and later wrote: "Mother, Home and Heaven are all sweet words, but the grandest sentence I ever heard from mortal lips was uttered this evening by Captain Chew when he said, 'Boys, the battle is over.'"

Private Casler wrote:

> We all scattered back as far as Newtown [today's Stephens City] that night, about five miles from the battlefield, and lay along the road, every fellow for himself, building fires out of fence rails, and making ourselves as comfortable as we could after the fatigues of the day. I did not see but one regiment in any kind of order, and that was the Fifth Virginia. . . . There was no attempt to rally us that night, but next morning we were all at our posts in our respective regiments.

But not all were able to answer the morning roll call. Confederate losses were severe. Jackson had suffered 455 wounded, at least 80 were dead, and 263 were missing, most captured. Among the latter were First Lieutenant George G. Junkin, Jr., thirty-five, a brother of Jackson's first wife who since February had served as an acting assistant adjutant general, and Joseph Graham Morrison, twenty, Anna's brother, an aide-de-camp.[7] The total casualties, 798, were nearly a

---

7. General Shields asked in his after-action report for permission to parole these two officers "for special reasons, which will benefit the service." Lincoln himself made the decision to grant a discharge to Junkin but only if he would sign an oath of allegiance. Junkin later claimed that he was persuaded by his father to take the oath because his refusal was causing his mother to lose her mind, an assertion he found to be untrue. He violated his parole, returned to the South, and sent Jackson an account of his father's deception with his offer to resign. Jackson accepted his resignation, effective 4 April 1862. Lincoln refused to parole Morrison at this time, but he was later exchanged and rejoined as one of Jackson's aides-de-camp on 23 July 1862.

third of those engaged. In terms of percentages, the losses nearly equaled those the Confederates later suffered at Gettysburg. The Federals lost 568, of whom 103 were dead.

Jackson slept little. With some of his staff, he wandered about in the rear of his defeated army. When he paused at a fire of fence rails, a young soldier made bold to speak to him: "The Yankees don't seem willing to quit Winchester, General."

Jackson, perhaps thinking of the pleasant days he and Anna had spent at the Grahams', replied: "Winchester is a very pleasant place to stay in, sir."

The young soldier was not to be deflected. "It was reported that they were retreating," he said brashly, "but I guess they're retreating after us."

"I think I may say I am satisfied, sir," snapped Jackson.

There must certainly have been little about which any other Confederate in the Valley Army could feel satisfied. Dr. McGuire and his surgeons worked through the night. Although every wagon in the army was pressed into service as an ambulance, there were still not enough to transport the wounded. The next morning, when McGuire reported that some would have to be left behind, Jackson ordered him to commandeer wagons and buggies from the neighborhood. It could not be done quickly, McGuire warned. According to the Reverend Robert L. Dabney, an admiring biographer who was not present, Jackson answered firmly: "Make yourself easy about that. This army stays here until the last wounded man is removed. Before I will leave them to the enemy, I will lose many more men."[8] These bold words have been taken to mean that all his wounded were carried away, but in fact, at least seventy were left on the ground. The Confederate dead were buried, and the abandoned wounded tended by the women, boys, and old men who came onto the field from Winchester the next morning.

First Sergeant John Wade of Company G, 4th Virginia, told his wife, "It was a terrible fight." He had escaped unhurt, but like all the survivors, he was exhausted. "The boys that are here are tolerably well but much broken in spirit," he said.

In his first major battle as an independent commander, Jackson had been soundly beaten. General Shields tended to exaggerate in his

8. It is uncertain who told Dr. Dabney of this incident. It would appear to have been Dr. McGuire, but although he told many stories about Jackson after the war, he never told this one. The thought expressed is uncharacteristic of Jackson. Although he was always willing to bury the dead and remove the wounded if there was time, he never allowed corpses or wounded to interfere with military operations.

official reports, but he was not far off when he reported: "The enemy's sufferings have been terrible, and such as they have nowhere else endured since the beginning of the war." Had the Federals vigorously pursued, the entire Valley Army might well have been scuppered. But Jackson was lucky, for the results of the battle were astounding. It was the Federals themselves who turned their tactical victory into a strategic defeat.

Federal intelligence was so poor that neither Shields nor any other Federal general knew who or what lay behind Jackson up the Valley of Virginia. It seemed so incredible to them that Jackson would have launched his small force against Shields's division without strong supports close by that they assumed their presence. As Shields himself said, "I could not have believed that Jackson would have hazarded a decisive engagement, so far from the main body, without expecting re-enforcements; so to be prepared for such a contingency, I set to work during the night to bring together all the troops within reach." Instead of boldly advancing to reap the fruits of the victory Kimball had won for him, Shields drew himself into a defensive position.

General Banks, who had left Winchester about noon on the day of battle on his way to Washington, was at Harper's Ferry when he heard of the fighting. He at once turned back. The division of Alpheus S. Williams (seven thousand men), which had just been detached from Banks and sent to McDowell at Manassas, was ordered to return at once and in haste. John Sedgwick's division, then at Harper's Ferry, was put on the alert. McDowell with thirty-seven thousand men was instructed by Secretary Stanton on 11 April: "For the present, and until further orders from this Department, you will consider the national capital as especially under your protection, and make no movement throwing your force out of position for the discharge of this primary duty." Thus was McClellan deprived of more than sixty thousand men whom he needed, or believed he needed, to capture Richmond while a massive buildup of Federal forces began in the lower end of the Valley.

Jackson's rash attack, based upon faulty information, resulted in his drooping, defeated, miserable little army's becoming a force the Federals so feared that they siphoned off strength from their main thrust toward Richmond. Jackson had sown deep apprehensions and considerable puzzlement among the Union's leadership.

Had Jackson won the Battle of Kernstown, he could scarcely have achieved a more favorable strategic result. History can provide few examples of a defeat that so favored the defeated. Jackson's lucky star had begun its ascendancy.

Retreat and Reorganization

There were many repercussions from the Battle of Kernstown, the most telling of which, for Jackson, came from Anna, who demanded to know why he had chosen to fight on the Sabbath. Although at Manassas he had fought on a Sunday, she understood that the battle there had not been of his making, but he had initiated the battle at Kernstown. He delayed his answer for nearly two weeks.

In the meantime, still seething over Garnett's conduct, he wrote an official complaint: "I regret that General Garnett should have given the order to fall back, as otherwise the enemy's advance would have at least been retarded, and the remaining part of my infantry reserve would have had a better opportunity for coming up and taking part in the engagement if the enemy continued to press forward."

Not content with official criticism, on 1 April he relieved Garnett of his command, filed court-martial papers, and placed him under arrest, charging that he had ordered a withdrawal when he should have rallied his men to hold their position. Jackson threw into the papers a stew of other charges and specifications, some demonstrably untrue.

Later he wrote bitterly to the adjutant general: "I regard Gen. Garnett as so incompetent a brigade commander that, instead of building up a Brigade, a good one, if turned over to him, would actually deteriorate under his command."

Not many of Jackson's officers concurred with his opinion; most believed that Garnett had only done what he had to do under difficult circumstances. Officers and men alike grumbled, resentful of the harshness of his treatment. Stony silence instead of cheers now greeted Jackson when he rode by. The War Department disagreed with him as well and tried, unsuccessfully, to persuade him to drop his charges. Only Jackson regretted that the stirring events of the months ahead delayed a trial until August. Eventually, to the general relief, the charges were simply dropped.[1]

By 2 April Jackson had drawn back to Rude's Hill and established his headquarters there. On the tenth a staff officer wrote: "We have had three days of uninterrupted storm, terrible for soldiers and our men have suffered much. . . ." It was still raining the next day when Jackson sat down, probably at Locust Grove, the home of the Reverend A. R. Rude, a retired Lutheran pastor of Danish extraction, to write a long letter to his "precious pet."

By this time some of the more important strategic results of the battle were becoming apparent, the Confederate Congress had given Jackson a vote of thanks, and General Joseph Johnston had, Jackson was happy to tell his wife, "issued a very gratifying order upon the subject." He was, therefore, writing from the high ground. Still, the man who refused to mail a letter or read one on a Sunday, who would not, if he could avoid it, even speak of mundane affairs on the Sabbath, had to struggle manfully to explain why choosing to fight a battle on Sunday was somehow different:

> You appear much concerned at my attacking *on Sunday.* I was greatly concerned, too; but I felt it my duty to do it, in consideration of the ruinous effects that might result from postponing the battle until the morning. So far as I can see, my course was a wise one; the best that I could do under the circumstances, though very distasteful to my feelings; and I hope and pray to our Heavenly Father that I may never again be circumstanced as on that day. I believe that so far as our troops were concerned, necessity and mercy both called for the battle. . . . Arms is a profession that, if its principles are adhered to for success, requires an officer do what he fears may be wrong, and yet, according to military experience, must be done, if success is to be attained. And this fact of its being

1. Garnett was returned to duty and reassigned to Pickett's division of Longstreet's corps. He was killed at the head of his brigade in the famous charge of that division at Gettysburg.

necessary to success, and being accompanied with success, and that
a departure from it is accompanied with disaster, suggests that it
must be right. Had I fought the battle on Monday instead of Sunday, I fear our cause would have suffered; whereas, as things
turned out, I consider our cause gained much from the engagement.

Certainly the most important gain was the battle's effect upon the
Union leadership in Washington, for Kernstown changed the course of
events in southeastern Virginia, where McClellan was preparing to
attack Richmond from the Peninsula (Virginia's South Neck). When
Lincoln had given approval for the Peninsular campaign, he had done
so only after extracting a promise from McClellan that Washington
would be fully protected, but in adding up the numbers of troops available for this task, McClellan had included some units, such as Nathaniel Banks's division, which were in reality quite distant from the
capital.

Instead of the promised thirty thousand men for the Washington
garrison, Lincoln discovered that there were actually fewer than twenty
thousand, many of whom were untrained recruits, and Secretary Stanton reported that McClellan had left little artillery. Not a single battery
of serviceable field artillery was available, and all the heavy guns were
manned by partially trained infantrymen.

Convinced that in this crucial time Washington was poorly protected and that McClellan could not possibly control all of the Army of
the Potomac from the Peninsula, Lincoln took it upon himself to make
some radical changes in the command structure. He first withdrew
from McClellan the division commanded by Brigadier General Ludwig
(or Louis) Blenker, which had been attached to Edwin Vose Sumner's
II Corps, and ordered it to report to John Charles Frémont. Frémont,
called the Pathfinder because of his exploration in the Far West, now
commanded a separate department in the Alleghenies known as the
Mountain Department and reported directly to Secretary of War Stanton and President Lincoln.

The fate of this unfortunate division, known as the German Division and filled with recent immigrants from Central Europe, was to be
closely tied to the career of General Thomas Jackson. But before
Blenker joined Frémont, he was temporarily placed under Banks, who,
after Kernstown, was told by Lincoln: "Keep him until you are sure
what you have in front. . . . The most important thing at present is to
throw Jackson well back and then to assume such a position as to

enable you to prevent his return." Lincoln had planned to move Banks closer to Washington, but Kernstown convinced him that this could not be done until Jackson was pushed well back up the Valley.

By mid-April Lincoln had established three separate commands independent of McClellan: McDowell in the Manassas area, Banks in the Valley of Virginia (which included the Shenandoah Valley west of the Massanutten range and the Luray, or Page, Valley east of it), and Frémont in the Allegheny Mountains west of the Shenandoah Valley. No senior general was placed in charge of these three "departments"; all three commanders reported directly to Washington, where Lincoln, aided by Stanton, took his title of commander-in-chief literally. The defense of Washington now in his own hands, Lincoln ordered McDowell, who had been scheduled to join McClellan, to stay put, and Banks to take care of Jackson before moving his forces eastward.

Jackson, meanwhile, lingered at Rude's Hill. On Sunday, 13 April, he attended religious services with one of his brigades and after the ceremony handed out religious tracts. That same day he acquired an unwelcome addition to his command when Brigadier General William Taliaferro reported for duty. Taliaferro, as Jackson well knew, had been one of the principal supporters of Loring in his protest against the order to winter at Romney and, indeed, had carried the petition to Richmond. Saddled with such an undesirable as one of his senior generals, Jackson protested vigorously. To the adjutant general in Richmond he wrote:

> Through God's blessing my command, though small, is efficient, and I respectfully request its efficiency may not be injured by assigning to it inefficient Officers. Last winter Gen. Taliaferro had charge of a Brigade and he permitted it to become so demoralized that I had to abandon an important enterprise in consequence of the inefficient condition in which he reported his Brigade. Notwithstanding the demoralized condition of his Brigade he left and visited Richmond, thus making a second visit there within two months. His Brigade since he has left it, has, under other hands become efficient, and it, as well as others bids fair to render good service if not placed under incompetent Officers. I attach so much importance to this matter as to induce me to send this communication direct.

Although Jackson sent a copy to Johnston, he had done exactly what Loring had done: In appealing to Richmond, he had gone over the head of his superior. This time Richmond ignored the protest. Taliaferro took command of the 3rd Brigade, the smallest, which Fulkerson of the 37th Virginia had ably commanded at Kernstown, and set about proving himself a capable brigadier.

With Garnett under arrest, the Stonewall Brigade was taken over by thirty-three-year-old Brigadier General Charles Sidney Winder, a Marylander and a graduate of the West Point class of 1850. He had missed the Mexican War but had fought Indians in the Northwest. Always immaculately dressed, he rode splendid chargers. Some thought that with his curling beard and his fine, waving hair combed carefully back to show his broad forehead, he looked more like an intellectual than a fighting soldier.

Because Garnett had been a popular commander and his arrest created so much resentment, the regimental commanders refused to call upon Winder, as was customary. One regiment hissed him as he rode past. Although to the angry soldiers he appeared oblivious, he immediately called their regimental commander on the carpet, informed him that such conduct was a reflection of bad discipline, and warned him that he would be held responsible for any future occurrence.

Private John Casler said of Winder: "As he was kind of a fancy General and seemed to put on a good many airs, and was a very strict disciplinarian, the boys all took a dislike to him from the start, and never did like him afterwards." Winder and Jackson began with a cool relationship, which soon warmed, for appearances aside, Winder was Jackson's kind of commander: brave, smart, obedient, and strict.

Four additions to his staff at this time pleased Jackson. Perhaps the most important of these was Jedediah Hotchkiss, a schoolmaster with a talent for mapping. It was a rare talent, for maps, even of a long-settled state such as Virginia, were rare. Most Americans had never seen one. Even natives of an area usually knew little of the geography fifty miles from their homes and to the Union generals the Valley of Virginia was almost as unfamiliar as the African interior. Jackson, who had lived in the Valley for ten years, still had only a hazy idea of its topography, but he quickly recognized the need to know it intimately, and he understood the value of maps.

Three days after the Battle of Kernstown Jackson summoned Hotchkiss. Impressed with the maps he had made the previous year of northwestern Virginia, he told him, "I want you to make me a map of the Valley, from Harper's Ferry to Lexington, showing all the points of offense and defense in those places. Mr. Pendleton will give orders for whatever outfit you need."[2]

Thus began a long and valuable association between the two. On 4 April Hotchkiss wrote to his wife, Sara, giving her his first impression of Jackson: "General Jackson does not say much. He is quite deaf; spends much of his time in his room, by himself, except when in the saddle; but he is very pleasant and I like him much." Eventually Hotchkiss was given the rank of major, but throughout most of his time on Jackson's staff during the Valley campaign, although often assigned officers' tasks that were unrelated to mapmaking, he served as a civilian.

Acquiring Jed Hotchkiss was a stroke of good fortune. The acquisition of the Reverend Robert L. Dabney as his assistant adjutant general (AAG), a post corresponding to chief of staff, required a deliberate campaign on Jackson's part and seemed quixotic to many of his officers. The Reverend Dabney, forty-two years old, a friend of the Morrisons, was a nationally known Presbyterian minister famed for his theological scholarship and his powerful sermons. A professor of theology at Union Theological Seminary at Hampden-Sydney College in south-central Virginia when the war began, he went off to war as chaplain of the 18th Virginia and saw action at First Manassas. After this initiation to battle and a bout of "camp disease," he returned to the more congenial pursuits at the seminary.

As early as January 1862 Jackson had written to him, saying he would like to have him as a chaplain, although regrettably there was no vacancy. Six days after Kernstown he wrote again, suggesting that Dabney come as an aide-de-camp. Then, on 8 April, he wrote offering him the AAG post with the rank of major, warning him, however, in a footnote that he would be able to preach only on Sundays and that "Your duties will require early rising and industry."

Dabney, who was accustomed to working late and sleeping late, was puzzled by the offer. He knew nothing of military administration and considered himself incapable of filling such a position, but Anna, who was staying with the Dabneys at the time, urged him to accept, and the friends and associates whose advice he sought were almost unanimously encouraging. Still uncertain, in late April he journeyed to see Jackson to explain in person his reservations. He began by pleading

2. Hotchkiss's valuable maps were often beautiful creations, but he did not use contour lines. Ground was delineated only by the use of hachures and color.

his unfitness to cope with the rigors of camp life. Jackson countered with "But Providence will preserve your health if he designs to use you."

When Dabney changed his ground, protesting that he knew nothing of military science and was ignorant of staff work, Jackson said simply: "You can learn."

He had "neither outfit, nor arms, nor horse, for immediate service," Dabney submitted. Jackson assured him that Major Harman would supply his immediate needs.

"When do I start?" Dabney sighed.

"Rest today and study the Articles of War, and begin tomorrow," Jackson said.

Dabney was at first an object of fun for the troops as he rode about in his Prince Albert coat and a tall beaver hat, sheltering under an umbrella. Irreverent young men would call out: "Come out from that umbrella! We know yer thar! We can see yer feet a-shakin'. "

If the rank and file were amused by his appointment, Jackson's senior officers were astonished. The indomitable forty-three-year-old Colonel Andrew Jackson Grigsby of the 27th Virginia, "a bluff soldier much given to swearing," announced that "Old Jack must be a fatalist sure enough when he put an Ironside Presbyterian parson as his chief of staff" and, with the field soldier's disdain for staff, proclaimed that he at last had "bright hopes of headquarters seeing they are no longer omniscient."

Dabney worked hard at his new job, and he preached, too; he even relinquished his beaver hat and umbrella after Jackson roughed him up by leading him through some rugged woods. Jackson was well satisfied with him as his AAG, and although the young officers on the staff never warmed toward him, he earned the respect of many others. Grigsby, a fair man, later recorded: "Our parson is not afraid of Yankee bullets, and I tell you he preaches like hell." Dabney soldiered for nearly a year before resigning, overwhelmed by exhaustion and illness.

The third addition to Jackson's staff was Lieutenant James Keith Boswell, a young man who fitted in well with such gay blades as Dr. McGuire, Sandie Pendleton, and later James Smith, Joseph Morrison, and handsome twenty-one-year-old Henry Kyd Douglas. Pendleton, Smith, Morrison, and Douglas all were sons of preachers. If Jackson could not have a staff of parsons, he could appoint divinity students or sons of preachers.

Douglas earned his place on the staff after making a wild, arduous ride in the rain over the Blue Ridge to deliver a message to General

Ewell, a trek of 105 miles which he accomplished in twenty hours, a feat of which he was justly proud. When he reported back to Jackson, he found the general asleep on the floor of a building at Conrad's Store (Elkton). Jackson, never at his best when awakened and always slow to praise, simply asked if he had reached Ewell on time, mumbled a "very good" and a "good night," and went back to sleep, leaving young Douglas thoroughly deflated. Nevertheless, he was overjoyed when soon after Jackson appointed him to his staff.

On 5 May Colonel Stapleton Crutchfield, twenty-eight, joined the staff as chief of artillery. A VMI graduate (1855) with first honors, he had served first as a major in the 9th Virginia, then as a major and colonel of the 58th Virginia, where he failed of reelection. At the beginning of the war volunteers in both the Union and Confederate armies elected their regimental officers, sometimes for a fixed period. Crutchfield was later elected colonel of the 16th Virginia, but he declined the appointment. Although never a very effective officer, he was a Jackson favorite, and Jackson even tried to have him promoted to brigadier general.

Along with the new officers came a fresh influx of men. On 16 April Jefferson Davis approved a Conscription Act.[3] The Confederates had finally realized that patriotic zeal alone would not fill the ranks of their field armies. Applying originally to men between eighteen and thirty-five, the act raised the age limit to forty-five on 27 September, and on 17 February 1863 it was widened to include those from seventeen to fifty-six. Still, Jackson's army remained young. Although this first act provided for substitutions and exemptions—overseers of twenty or more slaves were exempt—it made no provision for pacifists or conscientious objectors.[4] Jackson was delighted with it and exclaimed to Major Harman, "Now, Major, we'll have war in earnest. Old Virginia has waken up!"

3. At the same time the Confederate Congress passed another act legalizing the conscription of free blacks and slaves for noncombatant services. The North passed the Enrollment Act on 3 March. This was the first conscription act in North America.

4. Substitutes were usually found among foreigners, fit men who were overage, and others who were exempt from the draft. Substitution was much resented and was abolished at the end of 1863. The Confederates' second Conscription Act did make provision for the exemption of religious objectors and a wide variety of occupations, including civil servants, millers, doctors, nurses, railroad employees, tanners, telegraphers, clergymen, sailors, printers, druggists, shoemakers, miners, and employees of river and canal companies—as well as certain slaveowners.

Not all Virginians were content to be conscripted. The settlers in the Blue Ridge area of Rockingham County—mostly members of an offshoot of the Mennonites who called themselves the German Baptist Brethren but were generally known as Dunkards—refused to serve. Pacifists, they also opposed secession. In their zeal they even attempted to dissuade young men of other persuasions from enlisting. Jackson dispatched four companies of infantry, a half company of cavalry, and two or three guns under the command of Lieutenant Colonel John R. Jones of the 33rd Virginia to bring them to heel. On 14 April Jedediah Hotchkiss wrote in his diary: "We caged and ironed today the leader of the militia rebellion in Rockingham. He is a tigrous [*sic*] looking man."

But Jackson, ever practical, saw clearly that though the Dunkards could be forced to fight, they could also "very easily take bad aim." Because they had a reputation for being good teamsters, "faithful laborers and careful of property," Jackson wisely organized them into companies of one hundred, gave them wagons, and assigned them to the quartermaster, the commissary, and other noncombatant departments. By way of precaution, he saw that they were drilled as well, so that "in case circumstances should justify it, arms may be given them."

Dunkards were not the only ones to object to the war. Already martial enthusiasm had ebbed considerably. Many of Jackson's veterans had had enough. Many felt like Private E. D. Cottrell of the 4th Virginia, who, marching in the rain toward Swift Run Gap, swore that neither Congress nor draft law would keep him in the army when his one year's enlistment expired. Private Joseph Boyd wrote (12 April 1862) to his brother: "I advise you, and as strongly as ever to not come to war. I tell you you will repent it if you do I do believe. You have no idea of what it is to be a soldier. . . . If I had your chance to stay out of it I would do [so]."

More than 28 percent of the 33rd Virginia deserted and never returned. It was hard for free and independent mountaineers and Valley boys to realize the heinousness of leaving the army to go home, particularly as it was almost planting time, but Jackson took a stern view of those who did so. He ordered Major Harman to "arrest every man you possibly can find from this District, unless he produces proper permission to be absent[,] and send all such delinquents to their posts in irons as deserters."

With conscription came a great reorganization of the Confederate army. In theory, every able-bodied male served in the militia, but many lacked arms and accoutrements; many militia units had never drilled. It was now decided that the militia would be disbanded and its members amalgamated with the volunteers. A new election of regimental officers was held. Company officers (lieutenants and captains), elected by the rank and file, in turn elected their regiment's field officers (major, lieutenant colonel, and colonel). This was the last time officers were elected in this fashion in the Confederate army.

Not all of the best-qualified candidates were elected. Some good officers refused to participate. Colonel James W. Allen, thirty-three, of the 2nd Virginia, once an associate of Jackson's at VMI, was so embittered by Jackson's treatment of his officers, particularly Garnett, that it was with difficulty that he was persuaded to stand for reelection. Among those who refused was Colonel Arthur Cummings, who had commanded the 33rd Virginia and had performed brilliantly at Manassas. Disgusted by Jackson's command style, he resigned and was succeeded by the regiment's adjutant, twenty-eight-year-old John Francis Neff, the son of a Dunkard preacher.[5] Promoted to major in the regiment was Frederick W. M. Holliday, thirty-four, the hero of Dam No. 5.

Jackson had been some weeks at Rude's Hill when General Lee, still serving only as President Davis's military adviser, wrote to draw his attention to the disorganized state of his cavalry, a problem of which Jackson was well aware. He admired Colonel Turner Ashby, who had proved himself to be a bold, brave, and charismatic cavalry leader, but the cavalry had expanded rapidly without a corresponding change in organization and leadership; it now included about twelve hundred men in twenty-two separate companies, most of whom were undisciplined and undrilled. Colonel Ashby and Major Funston were the only field officers and by themselves could neither control nor properly train their men. The troopers generally performed admirably when Ashby was present, not so well when he was not, and he could not be everywhere. When assigned duty as couriers, they often failed to deliver messages. One careless company of fifty or sixty men, having failed to post pickets or send out patrols, had been captured almost in its entirety at Columbia Furnace, seven miles west of Woodstock and thirteen miles north of Rude's Hill.

For Jackson to organize, discipline, and train his cavalry without giving offense to Ashby and Funston required tact, a quality in which he was deficient. There were some exceptional difficulties arising from

---

5. John Francis Neff was born near Rude's Hill. Over his parents' objection, he attended VMI. After graduation he became a lawyer and was practicing in New Orleans when the war began. He hurried home to enlist in the 33rd Virginia.

the special orders initially issued to Ashby by Secretary of War Benjamin, which, in effect, gave him a separate command and even authorized him to raise units of infantry and artillery. Although Jackson officially commanded only his own division, he tried, without consulting Ashby, to solve the problem by assigning Funston with ten companies of his cavalry to Taliaferro's brigade and Ashby with the remaining dozen companies to Winder's. Ashby and Funston, outraged, cited Ashby's special authority and sent in their resignations. Major Harman wrote to his brother: "A great calamity has befallen us; there is a rupture between Ashby and Jackson. . . . Ashby will not submit, and we are in great danger from our crack-brained Genl."

It appears to have been Winder who poured oil on the troubled cavalry waters, making several trips back and forth between Jackson and Ashby. According to Major Harman, Jackson backed "square down," but Jackson saw the confrontation in practical terms, for he was, after all, in the presence of the enemy and he could ill afford to lose these valuable officers. Ashby was so popular and influential within the cavalry, said Jackson, that "I became well satisfied that if I persisted in my attempt to increase the efficiency of the cavalry it would produce the contrary effect, as Colonel Ashby's influence . . . would be thrown against me." Wisely he reversed himself.

When Banks received Lincoln's order to push Jackson well up the Valley, he sent Shields south, where his troops skirmished with Ashby without disturbing Jackson, who was safe at Rude's Hill as long as he controlled the sole bridge over the North Fork of the Shenandoah. Ashby, who had been ordered to burn it should it be in danger of falling into Federal hands, found that that time had come on 17 April, when his cavalry pounded across the bridge just ahead of pursuing Federals. Captain John Winfield and a dozen men, dropped behind to fire it, succeeded in setting the prepared kindling ablaze, and sent several shots into the oncoming Federal cavalry before they were swept aside. Ashby himself narrowly escaped capture when his pursuers galloped across the unharmed bridge while Federal troopers doused the flames.

The Valley Army was forced to begin a retreat south toward Harrisonburg. Jackson rode in a brooding, heavy silence. Private J. Samuel Harnsberger, who was assigned to act as a courier, rode beside him for two days before Jackson spoke to him. On the evening of the second day Jackson roused himself to ask if the troops had wood and water. "Yes, General," said Harnsberger. Those were the only words they exchanged.

Banks assumed that Jackson would continue south. Instead, he turned east, passing around the southern end of Massanutten Mountain range to Conrad's Store, where he tucked his little army safely into a position at Elk Run Valley at the foot of Swift Run Gap, a position which enabled him to protect his main base of supply at Staunton.

The site of the Valley Army was cleverly chosen by Jackson. If necessary, he could retreat over the Blue Ridge and fall back upon the main Confederate forces under Johnston, or he could be reinforced by the forces under Major General Richard S. Ewell which were stationed in and around Culpeper and Brandy Station, not far east of the Blue Ridge. Should Banks venture to continue his line of operation south of Harrisonburg, Jackson was in an excellent position to cut his line of communication or attack his flank. Indeed, when Banks reached Harrisonburg, Lincoln worried about his line of communication, and on 26 April Stanton instructed Banks: "In the present state of things it is not the desire of the President that you should prosecute a further advance south. You are requested to consider whether you are not already making too wide a separation between the body of troops under your immediate command and your supporting force."

Ashby kept in touch with the enemy, and over a one-month period he and his troopers engaged in no less than twenty-eight skirmishes. Although Jackson was able to keep track of the movement of the Federals, Banks at this time had little knowledge of Jackson's movements.

Lee, with what authority is unknown,[6] placed General Richard Ewell's forces at Jackson's disposal should he need them, and in a series of communications, beginning on 19 April, Jackson directed Ewell to move closer to him, first to Gordonsville, close to the east side of the Blue Ridge, where Jackson told him, "You are in the position I desired," but then to Stanardsville, even closer to the Blue Ridge by Swift Run Gap, only a day's march away from Jackson.

Everyone on the Union side misread Confederate intentions. The official record clearly reveals that the Federal commanders at this time had no idea where Jackson was or what his intentions were. On 20 April Shields was convinced that when Jackson gave up Rude's Hill, "the strongest position in the Valley," he was "flying from this department." He even concluded, and so reported, that "there are no troops needed in the Shenandoah Valley but those who are necessary to garri-

6. Jackson at this time assumed that Lee would be appointed secretary of war. (See letter from Jackson to A. R. Boteler in the collection of the New-York Historical Society.)

son the different posts." By 28 April he thought that Jackson had crossed the Blue Ridge and that probably two or three regiments stationed at Strasburg would be all that was necessary to hold the Valley. Two days later he reported to Stanton that Jackson and his army were on their way to Richmond. "This is the fact, I have no doubt," he said.

McDowell, too, was deceived. He informed Banks that "Jackson has pushed through Gordonsville and is on his way to Hanover Junction, on the line to Richmond. . . ." Reassured, Secretary Stanton on 29 April judged it safe to order Banks back to Strasburg and to send Shields with his strong, eleven-thousand-man division to reinforce McDowell.

One wonders from whom these Union generals received such a quantity of false intelligence. It is not inconceivable that Jackson himself deliberately supplied some—it would have been in character—but evidence is lacking, and Jackson had no intelligence officer on his staff. However, the Union generals' surmises that Jackson was bound for Richmond were not nonsensical. McClellan was ponderously moving his huge army of some hundred thousand men through the mud on the Peninsula ever closer to Richmond, and the Confederates there, commanded by Joseph E. Johnston with about half McClellan's strength, certainly did need every man they could get to protect their capital.

Jackson, more than a hundred miles from Hanover Junction, was indeed on the move, and had Shields, Banks, McDowell, and Stanton seen his movements, they would have been fortified in their belief that he was quitting the Valley, but in the next few days Banks was to smarten up considerably.

Plans to strike at Banks or Frémont so as to prevent reinforcement of McDowell or McClellan were discussed at length by Jackson and Lee through letters. Initially Jackson, as usual, had asked for another five thousand men with whom to strike Banks directly, but no such force could be spared. Lee told him (29 April) that "unless a sufficient force can be obtained by a union of the command of Genls Johnson, Ewell and your own, there is no other way of obtaining one." In his polite way, he added that if Jackson could not make do with his force, it should be broken up and its elements sent elsewhere. Faced with this possible diminution of his command, Jackson put forward three plans for Lee's consideration. Lee responded (1 May) by telling him to use his own judgment, adding only that if he could "strike an effective blow against the enemy west of Staunton," it would be "very advantageous." Following this advice, Jackson did just that.

17

The Battle of McDowell

Shortly before midnight on 30 April a courier from Jackson pounded up to the door of General Smith's quarters at the Virginia Military Institute with a dispatch that began: "Please march the cadets at once to Staunton . . . to cooperate in an important movement which I will explain to you when we meet." The cadets, it continued, "will be absent from the Institute for a few days."

A few hours later Smith issued stirring general orders: "The enemy are hovering upon our borders, and are threatening to drive us from our home. The army of General T. J. Jackson is preparing to meet and repel their invasion. . . ." The corps of cadets—except those who thought their parents would object—under the command of Major Scott Shipp began their trek to Staunton that very day, marching under a cold rain, each cadet carrying his own blankets, tin cup and plate, haversack, and canteen. Accompanying them were a couple of wagons, but they brought no ambulance. Only eleven cadets were left behind.

They found the march in the rain hard going, but they were not the only ones suffering from the weather. It was shortly after midnight on the morning of 30 April when, as Private Joe Kaufman of the 10th Virginia remembered, he and some six thousand of his comrades were awakened by shrilling fifes and pounding drums echoing through the camps of the Valley Army. By four o'clock Jackson's army was in motion, marching southwest through heavy rain toward Port Republic.

Their stay at Elk Run Valley at the foot of Swift Run Gap had been a miserable experience. The spring was unseasonably cold. They had suffered from chilling rains and from sleet, and on 24 April it had even snowed. Most of the young men appeared pleased to be on the move, but on that first day they were able to cover only five miles, for the entire Valley was drenched in the downpour. Bogged down, they spent a miserable night in the cold mud. Jackson, who had ridden ahead, passed the night just two miles from Port Republic at Lewiston, the comfortable plantation of John F. Lewis, a retired militia general.

The following day, while the cadets struggled on toward Staunton, Jackson's men endured another trying march. Guns, limbers, and supply wagons sank to their axles in a road that had become a quagmire. Jackson, who had rejoined his marching column, having dismounted at one point to lend a hand, admonished one of the many grunting, swearing soldiers who were cursing him that day. "It is for your own good, sir," he said sternly. That evening, as his men prepared for another miserable night in the mud, Jackson washed away the day's grime and ate his supper at Madison Hall, the elegant home of Dr. George W. Kemper, Sr., on the western edge of Port Republic.

It took two and a half weary days for the Valley Army to struggle through the sixteen miles from Elk Run Valley to Port Republic, and the grumbling increased. Private John P. Charlton wrote to his brother, Oliver: "It has been raining for five days and it is nothing but mud everywhere and we are without tents, too." On 3 May the sun came out at last, but long before it appeared, the army was on the march, not on the road to Staunton, as all had assumed, but, to the astonishment of officers and men alike, eastward over the Blue Ridge at Brown's Gap.[1]

Even gaps in the Blue Ridge are high, and the approaches steep, but the road was firmer, and the men bent forward to their task. The march must have been enlivened by considerable speculation about their destination, but many Valley boys were sorry to turn their backs on their homes, unprotected now it seemed from Banks's Union army.

The Valley was, in fact, better protected than it had been, for on Jackson's orders, his old campsite had been occupied by the eight thousand men under General Richard Ewell, though Ewell was as much in the dark as any Valley Army private as to Jackson's plans and movements. He had been told only, "I am leaving for the west in great haste."

1. There is no longer a passable road over the Blue Ridge at Brown's Gap.

James A. Walker, the cadet who had challenged Jackson to a duel, was now colonel of the 13th Virginia in Ewell's division. One day at this time he found Ewell in a towering rage. "Colonel Walker," he exploded, "did it ever occur to you that General Jackson is crazy?"

"I don't know," Walker answered. "We used to call him 'Tom Fool Jackson' at the Institute, but I don't suppose he's really crazy."

"I tell you, sir, he is as crazy as a March hare," Ewell insisted. "He has gone away, I don't know where, and left me here with instructions to stay until he returns, but Banks' whole army is advancing on me and I haven't the remotest idea where to communicate with General Jackson."

Major General Richard Stoddert Ewell, forty-four, was a hard-swearing man who spoke in a high-pitched voice with a noticeable lisp. Often regarded as an eccentric, he was a brave and able soldier, popular with officers and men alike. His young soldiers called him affectionately Old Baldy or Old Baldhead. Because he believed he had an ulcer, he ate largely frumenty, a porridge of hulled wheat boiled in milk, with egg yolk, sugar, and raisins added when they could be found. He was a bachelor, and many of his troops were sure he cared only for his servant, an Apache named Friday whom he had brought from the West.

Ewell came from an educated northern Virginia family.[2] He was graduated from West Point in 1840, ranking thirteenth out of a class of forty-two. William Tecumseh Sherman and George Thomas were classmates, and P. G. T. Beauregard, Jubal Early, Henry Halleck, James Longstreet, and Ulysses S. Grant were at West Point at the same time. When Ewell was about to be graduated, he wrote to his brother: "I have no particular wish to stay in the army but a positive antipathy to starving or to do anything for a living that requires any exertion of mind or body." A superb horseman, Ewell was assigned to dragoons and sent to fight Indians on the plains. A modest man, he often said that he had learned everything there was to know about leading fifty dragoons and had forgotten everything else.

In the Mexican War he won a brevet for his bravery. When the Civil War broke out, he was a captain. In May 1861 he resigned his commission in the United States Army and the following month was commissioned a lieutenant colonel in the Confederate army; two months later he was a brigadier general, and on 24 January 1862 he

2. His father was a doctor and a graduate of the University of Pennsylvania; his mother was the daughter of Benjamin Stoddert, first secretary of the navy.

was appointed a major general. A tough and canny soldier was Ewell, and he could be counted on to pose the same threat at Swift Run Gap to Banks's flank should he advance as had Jackson.

In the afternoon of 3 May the first units of Jackson's little army, having crossed the Blue Ridge, came streaming down from the mountains into the beautiful, rolling countryside of northwestern Albemarle County. People there had not seen many soldiers, and they turned out to watch them march by; smiling women and girls in bright colored dresses passed food to them, though some taunted them for deserting the Valley. When they marched into Mechum's River Station, they found trains waiting for them on the Virginia Central Railroad, but—again surprise—the locomotives were facing west.

Although Jackson had ordered every piece of rolling stock in the region to be collected, only a half dozen trains could be assembled, so the artillery and wagons kept to the road and wearily recrossed the Blue Ridge at Rock Fish Gap, while the infantry, packed as tightly as humanly possible, entrained and rode back across the mountains to Staunton. There, as they detrained, they saw, rehabilitated and back on the tracks, soon to be ready to resume service on a new line, the now-famous B&O Locomotive No. 199, which had been hauled all the way from Martinsburg only to topple into a bog just short of the railyard.

On 2 May Banks had learned that Jackson's army, which he characterized as "reduced, demoralized, on half rations," was on its way to Port Republic. This led him to make an accurate surmise. Jackson must be on his way either to Staunton or, fifteen miles east, to Waynesboro, and if the former, then perhaps he planned to attack Brigadier General Robert Milroy, who was spearheading Frémont's drive south through the Allegheny Mountains toward Knoxville, Tennessee. Opposing Milroy was the bravely named Army of the Northwest, a brigade-size force of about twenty-eight hundred men under Brigadier General Edward ("Allegheny") Johnson. This "army" was scarcely a threat, but Banks saw clearly that if Jackson joined forces with Johnson, Milroy was in danger.

On 4 May Banks telegraphed two important messages. One to Secretary Stanton correctly placed both Jackson and Ewell where they had been only the day before: "Our officers all confident that Jackson is near Port Republic and Ewell's division at Elk Run, near Miller's Bridge on the Shenandoah River, Jackson's old position." The second was a warning to Frémont, who at once alerted General Milroy: "General Banks informs me that he occupies Harrisonburg. He adds that

Jackson has been seen moving towards Port Republic and suggests that his intention may possibly be to join Johnson and attack you." This was, indeed, exactly Jackson's intention. In spite of his secrecy, Banks had not been deceived. However, as Frémont failed to inform Milroy that Ewell had replaced Jackson at Elk Run, Milroy thought he was safe, for he reasoned that Jackson "cannot move from Port Republic without leaving Banks in his rear."

That it had been Jackson's intention to march directly to Staunton is revealed in a letter he wrote to General Smith at VMI on 3 May saying, "[T]he heavy roads have prevented my reaching Staunton, as I hoped by marching across the country by Port Republic." What has since been regarded as a clever stratagem—crossing the Blue Ridge on foot and then recrossing by rail—was simply a practical attempt to get his infantry out of the mud.

On 4 May, about five o'clock in the afternoon, Jackson and members of his staff rode into Staunton on horseback. Jedediah Hotchkiss, who had dropped off to take a bath "in the clear cold water of a stream on the western side of the Blue Ridge," noted that in the Valley it was "a fine spring day and the farmers are planting corn."

After establishing his headquarters at the Virginia Hotel, Jackson sent out Ashby's cavalry to seal off the town; no one was to be allowed in or out. He then had his hair cut and, for the first time, donned a Confederate uniform with the insignia of a Confederate general officer. (Thriftily he kept his comfortable old blue coat from VMI and wore it often.)

The next day he wrote to Anna to tell her of his march from Swift Run Gap to Staunton. As usual, he said nothing of his plans, but he explained that while he had hoped to observe Sunday, 4 May, with "a very agreeable family named Pace," a dispatch "stating that part of the enemy's force had arrived within one day's march of Brigadier-General Edward Johnson's camp" had forced him to press on to Staunton.

The VMI cadets, about two hundred strong, had marched into Staunton that Sunday. General Smith had been quick to answer the summons of his former professor of natural and experimental philosophy—too quick, said the institute's Board of Visitors, who were "unanimous in their disapprobation of the cadets being in any wise subjected to the risk of battle unless in the immediate defense of the Institution at Lexington." Smith found himself in the midst of a brouhaha of major proportions. Sending the cadets to take the field on active service was, the board warned, "a breach of good faith on the part of the Institution towards parents and guardians." The matter was referred to Governor

John Letcher, who, although he, too, objected strongly to Smith's action, answered with calm common sense: "I do not see how the cadets can be sent back. I think it best to let them go on. The mischief is done and we shall have to let it alone."

A much-embarrassed Smith wrote to ask Jackson how he intended to use his cadets. Jackson gave an evasive reply. Saying only that he intended to post them as a reserve, he added that although he regarded their presence as "of great importance," if Smith thought it was his duty to recall them, he could do so. A compromise was reached by sending back to VMI only those under eighteen who did not have their parents' consent. After reviewing the remaining cadets on the grounds of the Deaf and Dumb Asylum at Staunton, Jackson assigned them to General Winder's Stonewall Brigade.

Not everyone welcomed the addition of the VMI cadet corps to the Valley Army. Some of Jackson's young veterans resented the attention the natty cadets in their smart uniforms received from the Staunton belles, while they in their ragged, muddy, battle-worn clothes looked on. There was, however, to be little time for soldiers or cadets to enjoy the pleasures of Staunton.

On 6 May Jackson took the time to write to his friend and sometime aide Congressman Alexander Robinson Boteler in Richmond.[3] Ashby's name had been put forward for promotion to brigadier general, and Jackson objected: "I would gladly favor it if he were a good disciplinarian, but he has such bad discipline and attaches so little importance to drill, that I would regard it as a calamity to see him promoted. . . . I recommended him for a colonelcy and will always take pleasure in doing all I can for his advancement consistent with the interests of the public service." He went on to complain again about Taliaferro, citing him as an example of a political officer who ought never to have been promoted to brigadier general, and he lashed out against political appointments in general: "The great interests of the country are being sacrificed by appointing incompetent officers. . . . [T]he times demand that we should for the moment make professional merit the basis of promotion."

On 7 May Jackson made contact with Johnson just seven miles west of Staunton, and both armies moved west, led by Johnson's Army of the Northwest. Allegheny Johnson, although born in Virginia in

---

3. Boteler, forty-six, was a member of the Rules and Officers Committee in the Confederate Congress. When the Congress was not in session, he served as an aide on Jackson's staff.

1816, had been reared in Kentucky. He was graduated from West Point in 1838. He had seen service in the Seminole War in Florida, Indian campaigns in the West, and the Mexican War, where, like Jackson, he had won brevets to captain and major for "gallant and meritorious service." He had also been presented by the commonwealth of Virginia with a sword of honor.

A large, rough-looking man with a goatee, Johnson had an oddly shaped head that resembled "a cone or an old-fashioned bee hive." One eye winked continually, the result of a wound suffered in the Mexican War, and because a recent wound in his foot had not yet healed, he carried a large, thick staff, leading some of his men to refer to him as Fence Rail Johnson. He possessed a hot temper, and some considered him uncouth, but Jackson liked and respected him, for he was a good soldier.

On the march westward into the Allegheny Mountains on the Staunton–Parkersburg Turnpike[4] Johnson's little Army of the Northwest was followed after a gap of several miles by Taliaferro's brigade, Colonel John A. Campbell's brigade, and Winder's Stonewall Brigade. This order of march, with Winder's brigade (the largest and best) in the rear and Taliaferro, whom Jackson regarded as incompetent, in the lead, would certainly not have been chosen if Jackson had had an inkling of the nature of the battle ahead.

The VMI cadets were given a good taste of what it meant to march with Jackson. Joining the Stonewall Brigade on 7 May at two o'clock in the morning of what became a warm, balmy day, they arrived at their bivouac twenty-two hours later after a march of thirty-four miles, most of it spent toiling up and down steep mountain roads. One exhausted cadet cadged a ride behind General Winder, without at first realizing who he was; McHenry Howard, an aide of Winder's carried another behind him.

That day Johnson encountered some of Milroy's outposts and drove them back. The 32nd Ohio, posted as an advanced picket, was pounced on so suddenly that it was forced to abandon its tents and most of its baggage. Jackson spent the night of the seventh at Rogers's toll gate, near Ramsey's Draft, twenty-three miles from Staunton. To confuse any spies, he had ridden south out of Staunton, as though going to Lexington, then had cut across northwest to the Staunton–Parkersburg Turnpike. Whether or not Federal spies were puzzled, his own officers

---

4. The Staunton–Parkersburg Pike is today's U.S. Route 250, but locally it is still known by its old name.

were. As he had told no one where he was going, some of his staff rode a considerable distance in the wrong direction looking for him.

The weather remained warm, but the Confederates encountered hard marching on the dusty mountain roads—across Calfpasture River, over the Shenandoah Mountain, over Cowpasture Mountain, across Cowpasture River—until on the eighth Johnson reached a flat-topped ridge on rugged, precipitous Bullpasture Mountain, deep in the Appalachian Mountains. Just beyond the ridge runs Bullpasture River, a small stream on the west side of which lies the village of McDowell. A rugged, lumpish, curved spur of the mountain, 2,250 feet high, called Sitlington's Hill rises south of the Staunton–Parkersburg Turnpike; north of the turnpike lies Hull's Ridge, an almost equally high piece of ground.

It was obvious to Jackson and Johnson when they reconnoitered with Jedediah Hotchkiss about midday that Sitlington's Hill was a commanding position, dominating both the crossroads village of McDowell, where Milroy had his headquarters, and the Union camps in the Bullpasture River valley. Jackson ordered Johnson to occupy Sitlington but, curiously, did not order any of his artillery to be brought up although Hotchkiss had found a practicable route for the guns and a position on top of the steep hill that would have provided effective counter battery fire and protection against Union infantry. After the war Taliaferro, who thought the guns should have been hauled to the top of Sitlington's Hill, wrote that Jackson "was urged [by him? by Johnson?] to send them but declined—why, nobody knows. He rarely gave reasons; he gave orders, that was all—short, sharp, quick, decisive. The tone and manner stopped inquiry."

However, Jackson did not intend to launch a frontal attack upon Milroy from Sitlington; he had sent various staff officers to reconnoiter, and he hoped by the following day to occupy a more favorable position in the Federals' rear. It must have seemed highly improbable to Jackson that Milroy would attack the much larger Confederate force on high ground. Jackson had so little intention of fighting that day that he sent most of his staff three miles back to take their dinner at the comfortable home of Mr. John Wilson on Cowpasture River. But Johnson and Jackson were facing a bold, aggressive fighter in Robert Huston Milroy, one who did not choose to wait to be attacked.

Like Johnson, Milroy was forty-six years old—almost elderly for Civil War generals. He was an Indiana lawyer and a former judge who had seen active service as a volunteer in the Mexican War. Two weeks after the firing on Fort Sumter, he was mustered into service as a

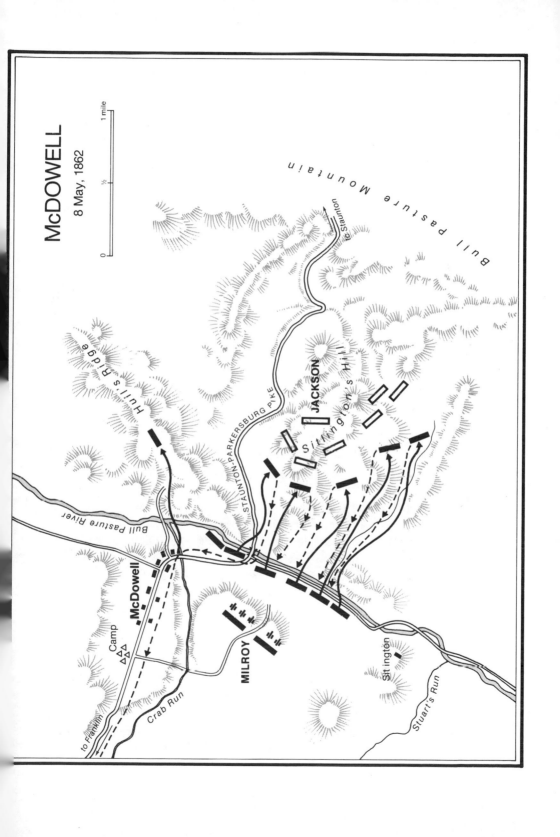

McDOWELL

8 May, 1862

0 ½ 1 mile

Bull pasture Mountain

to Staunton

STAUNTON-PARKERSBURG PIKE

Hull's Ridge

JACKSON

Sitlington's Hill

Bull Pasture River

McDOWELL

Camp

to Franklin

Crab Run

MILROY

Sitington

Stuart's Run

captain in the 9th Indiana and was elected its colonel four days later; the following September he was promoted to brigadier general of volunteers.

On 7 May Milroy learned through "scouts and spies" that Jackson and Johnson had joined forces and were on their way to attack him. He requested reinforcements, and on the morning of the eighth Brigadier General Robert C. Schenck brought forward three regiments of infantry (1,300 men) three companies of cavalry, and a battery of the 1st Ohio Artillery, giving him a total of 3,500 infantry, 250 cavalry, and 4 batteries. Although senior in rank, Schenck deferred to Milroy, who was eager to attack, even though he knew he was throwing his troops against a force twice the size of his own.

Morning and early afternoon saw some skirmishing by the infantry, and Milroy's gunners dug in the trails of their guns to increase the elevation of their tubes and shelled the Confederates on Sitlington's Hill, who, lacking artillery, could not respond. About three o'clock that afternoon Milroy was told (incorrectly) by Captain George Lathan of the 2nd [West] Virginia that the Confederates were trying to put guns on the hill. Immediately he launched a major attack about a mile southeast of McDowell.

From the time Johnson's men first reached Sitlington's Hill until the fighting ended, the battle was controlled, as much as any Civil War battle was ever controlled, by General Milroy. The Confederates initiated no aggressive action; they did little more than react and respond to Federal movements.

Late in the day Johnson received a nasty wound which tore open his ankle and was to keep him out of action for several months. By this time Taliaferro's brigade, leading the Valley Army, had arrived on Sitlington's Hill, and Taliaferro assumed command as Johnson was carried from the field. It was, therefore, the much-maligned Taliaferro who threw back Milroy's final attacks.

When Jackson learned of Johnson's wound, he ordered Hotchkiss: "Go up to General Taliaferro and give him my compliments and tell him I am coming in person with the Stonewall Brigade and he must hold his position until I come." Hotchkiss climbed Sitlington's Hill and later recorded in his diary what he found: "A scene of great confusion. It was between 8 and 9 P.M.; we had repulsed the enemy's attack on our left and our troops were all mingled together in the greatest disorder imaginable, like a swarm of bees, calling out for comrades, commands, etc., no one being able to distinguish another in the darkness. I soon found Gen. Taliaferro and delivered my message."

Jackson himself arrived on the hill sometime later, but not with the Stonewall Brigade; it was dark, and the battle was long over. After conferring with Taliaferro, he and his staff rode back to the Wilson house, reaching it about two o'clock in the morning of the ninth.

That night Milroy and Schenck burned their camps and, carrying their wounded, successfully retreated, first westward to Monterey and then northeast toward Franklin. Jackson did not attempt an immediate pursuit.

Milroy described the battle in a letter to his wife, Mary, five days afterward:

I took 4 of my Regts. and one of Gen Schencks [*sic*] and by the most incredible exertions got two light pieces of artillery [6-pound-ers] up on a Mountain [Hull's Ridge] as high as the ridge on which the rebles [*sic*] were. I sent two of my Regts. around to the right (the 25th and 75th Ohio) to attack the enemy in front and sent around the 3rd Va. [West Virginia] 32nd Ohio and the 82nd Ohio (the latter Gen. Schencks Regt) to attack them in the rear. My two Regts. in front attacked them and most splendidly received and returned the enemy's fire with such spirit that they fell back when my boys charged and drove them over to the first ridge behind them . . . a higher ridge covered with woods. The Regts. I sent around to the left now attacked the rebles with great spirit[,] hav-ing to get at them by clambering down and up tremendous rocky heights. The battle now raged with great fury on both sides. The rebles had a vastly superior force and a strong position and I found after repeated charges that it was impossible to dislodge them . . . night come [*sic*] on in the midst of the fight—the combatants were gradually completely obscured from view by smoke and darkness and all that could be seen was the quick flashing of the small arms and the far flashing of the artillery—finally about 8 ½ oclock [*sic*] the ammunition on both sides give [*sic*] out—it was completely exhausted on my side. My boys were anxious to hang on and send for more, but I deemed it prudent in their exhausted condition to withdraw them down to camp—which was done in good order[,] bringing off all our dead and wounded, amounting to about 240.

Milroy had been in an excellent spot to see the action, for he had found "a position on a high peak or ridge" from which he could "see the whole combat on both sides like a map." He was delighted with the fight and jubilantly told Mary: "It was the most splendid battle I have yet seen." He certainly did not sound like a defeated general.

The casualty figures for the Battle of McDowell are remarkable, for it is rare in any engagement in any war that the losses of successful defenders are greater than those of unsuccessful attackers. At McDowell, Federal casualties amounted to 256, with 28 killed, 225 wounded, and 3 missing. Jackson lost 75 killed and 428 wounded, the 12th Georgia of Johnson's army suffering the severest losses with 175 casualties. Among the dead was Colonel Samuel Gibbons of the 10th Virginia; 4 field officers were seriously wounded.

It was certainly a Pyrrhic victory for the Confederates, and Jackson, who had personally played no direct part in directing the action on the field, understandably found it difficult to compose an after-action report. At Mrs. Phoenix Hull's fine brick house (still extant) in McDowell, where the next day (9 May) he established his headquarters, he paced restlessly up and down, then penned two lengthy versions, both of which he found unsatisfactory. Finally settling on a short note to Adjutant General Samuel Cooper in Richmond, he wrote simply: "God blessed our arms with victory at McDowell yesterday," an announcement that inspired officials and the public alike to assume that it was Jackson who had fought and won the battle.

Jackson's brief announcement of the victory is often cited as an example of his modesty and piety, but it seems far more plausible that he simply found it difficult to explain why, with a force twice the size of Milroy's, he had, while remaining completely on the defensive on high ground, sustained double the Federal casualties and allowed the enemy to slip away undisturbed in the night. Then, too, if he had written a full and honest report, he would have faced the unpalatable necessity of giving most of the credit to Taliaferro, the man whom only forty-eight hours earlier he had damned as completely incompetent, for at McDowell Taliaferro unquestionably displayed generalship of the highest order. Only on 7 March 1863—ten months after the battle— and only after much prodding from Lee did Jackson complete a proper report. Even then, although he stated that Johnson had turned over the command to Taliaferro and that the Federal movement on the right had been "speedily detected and met by Taliaferro's brigade," he omitted Taliaferro's name from the list of those to whom he gave special thanks, and he wrote nothing about his valor or his generalship as the field commander. In contrast with Jackson's meanspirited report, the wounded Johnson in his after-action report generously praised Taliaferro for "having behaved most gallantly."

The battle at McDowell was claimed as a victory by both sides, but historians, if they mention it at all, credit the Confederates as the winners, for they remained in possession of the field and the battle had indeed halted Frémont's reckless drive toward Tennessee. For the South it was a most welcome victory, following as it did the most disastrous month of the war for the Confederacy.

In April 1862 Federal forces had captured New Orleans, and the entire length of the Mississippi River fell into Federal hands. McClellan was moving his enormous army to the Peninsula and had begun the siege of Confederate forces under Joseph Johnston at Yorktown. There was a growing Northern army in Tennessee; Fort Pulaski in Georgia had fallen; Fort Macon had surrendered, and its garrison had been taken prisoner; Confederate forces in Arizona and New Mexico were in retreat. Worst of all, at the Battle of Shiloh the Confederates had lost 1,723 killed, 8,012 wounded, and 959 missing. The little battle at McDowell, Virginia, was not much to crow about, but Southerners grasped eagerly for any scrap of good news. Jackson was credited with the victory, and his star accelerated its already rapid ascent.

Jackson delayed his pursuit the next morning because his wagons had not come up. This was not surprising. Major Harman's task of getting supplies to the right place at the right time was considerably hampered by his general's secrecy. He complained bitterly that "Jackson's mysterious ways are unbearable." Since he was never told where the army was bound, it was little short of miraculous that he was able to do as well as he did. On the approach to McDowell he had appealed to Jackson several times to tell him where they were going, but he was never informed. Instead, annoyed by his persistence, Jackson berated him for prying into military matters which did not concern him and accused him of having lost some of his former zeal. Harman, in his own words, "thanked him for his candor and told him I would resign." Recognizing that he had gone too far and knowing that Harman's talents were indispensable, Jackson, as he had done with Ashby, backed "square down." In Jackson's defense it must be said that his quartermaster was a gossip and often revealed more than he ought in letters and, one presumes, in conversations.

The pursuit of the Federals over the route Jackson and Ellie had taken to visit Laura was short-lived. Mountain fighting usually favors those on the defensive, and Milroy and Schenck, falling back upon Frémont, were able to set innumerable ambushes and to fire the woods behind them, creating a smoke screen that considerably slowed the Confederate pursuit. Jackson, impressed by this technique, wrote that it was "the most adroit expedient to which a retreating army could resort to embarrass pursuit."

The VMI cadets, who, safe in the rear, to their chagrin, had seen nothing of the battle, were to see nothing of the pursuit, for they were left at McDowell to take charge of the prisoners and captured property and to bury the dead. This, of course, was not the task "of great importance" Jackson had had in mind for them, but the fight at McDowell was not the battle he had intended or anticipated.

What seems likely is that Jackson, not suspecting that Milroy would attack his superior force, had planned a flanking attack using Winder's Stonewall Brigade (the largest in his army and reinforced by the cadets) and probably his artillery, which would explain both his order of march that day, putting the despised Taliaferro in the lead, and his failure to put his guns on Sitlington's Hill. However, since Jackson never told anyone what he planned to do, he could never be faulted for failing to accomplish what he had set out to achieve. Not for the last time his secrecy helped preserve his reputation.

Fearing that Frémont might send troops eastward over the mountains to the Shenandoah Valley and come up on his rear or attempt to cut his line of communication, Jackson dispatched Hotchkiss, with a small force of cavalry, to ride along the eastern side of the mountains and block off every road and pass into the Shenandoah Valley. Shaking his index finger in Hotchkiss's face for emphasis, he told him: "Take a squad of couriers . . . and send me back a messenger every hour telling me where you are and what you have done." Hotchkiss did a thorough job, felling trees, rolling down boulders, and burning bridges. Although Frémont had no intention of moving on Jackson's line of communication, Hotchkiss's work was to prove beneficial indeed before the month was out.

On Monday, 12 May, Jackson and his troops were about two miles from Franklin, twenty-five miles northeast up a valley from Monterey. It was another "fine, warm spring day," and he halted to proclaim a half day of rest and prayer:

> Soldiers of the Army of the Valley and North West, I congratulate you on your recent victory at McDowell. I request you to unite with me, this morning, in thanksgiving to Almighty God, for thus having crowned your arms with success; and in praying that He will continue to lead you on from victory to victory, until our independence shall be established; and make us that people whose God is the Lord.
>
> The chaplains will hold divine service at 10 o'clock A.M., this day, in their respective regiments.

Jackson joined a battery of artillery for the service, and Major Dabney preached one of his fine, blistering sermons, thundering that the war was God's punishment for Southerners' sins.

Meanwhile, in Swift Run Gap Ewell was in a rage over a message he had received. Advising him that "through God's assistance" he had captured some of Milroy's wagons, Jackson repeated his earlier order: "Hold your position—don't move." To Colonel Thomas T. Mumford, the former VMI cadet adjutant now Ewell's cavalry commander, Ewell fulminated: "This man Jackson is certainly a crazy fool, an idiot. . . . What has Providence to do with Milroy's wagon train? . . . General Lee at Richmond will have little use for wagons if all these people close in around him and we are left out here in the cold."

After the twelfth Jackson pursued no longer. His own line of communications were overextended, and he could summon no reserves, while Milroy and Schenck were falling back upon supplies and Frémont's reinforcements. Turning his army around, he began a leisurely march back toward the Valley. It seemed a good time to tighten up march discipline, and the next day he issued the following orders:

Canteens must be filled before marching and during halts only. Upon leaving Camp when not in the vicinity of the enemy the troops will march with unfurled colors and music until the command "route step" is given by the Regtl. commander. Upon leaving Camp and after each subsequent rest the men will carry arms and march as though they were on drill, until they have advanced two or three Hundred yards when the command "route step" will be given, when the company commanders will fall to the rear of their companies & the men will carry their arms at will until the command "attention" is given by Brigade commanders which will precede every halt & be repeated by each of the Regimental Commanders. At this command Captains will return to the front of their Companies[,] which will march and carry their arms as they were previous to the command "route step." Every hour the infantry must be halted, arms stacked on one side of the road, ranks broken and men rested for ten minutes.

About 12 or 1 o'clock the halt will be an hour that the men may take their lunch. The sick of each Regt. will be in charge of a Regimental Officer, who will accompany his ambulances immediately in rear of his Regt. If the Regimental Qr.Mr. [quartermaster] has any empty wagons they move with the Ambulances for the purpose of carrying the sick, their arms [,] accutrements [*sic*], & Knapsacks. The men will carry their Knapsacks.

Nothing will be carried in the baggage wagons except entrenching tools, cooking utensils and officers baggage. Officers baggage must be in separate wagons.

No man[,] unless he is too unwell to keep up with his company, will be permitted to leave ranks, except in case of Necessity and then only for a few minutes, and during this time he will not be permitted to take his Musket with him, but it will be carried by another man whom the Company Commander will detail for that purpose. If a man is too unwell to keep up with his Company, his Comp. Commander will see that he is examined by the Regimental Medical Officer in charge of the Ambulances and if excused by him from marching he will be carried with the sick. Rolls will be called immediately before leaving camp & also immediately after arriving in camp and at such other times as Brigade or Regimental Commanders may indicate for the purpose of verifying the presence of their men, and delinquents will be duly punished. During marches men will be required not only to keep in ranks but the proper distance will be preserved as far as practicable, and thus convert a march, as it should be, into an important drill, that of habituating the men to keep in ranks. Each Brigade Commander will see that the foregoing orders are strictly adhered to, and for this purpose will from time to time allow his command to move by him, so as to verify its conditions, he will also designate one of his staff officers to do the same at such times as he may deem necessary.[5]

In this fashion McDowell was reached on the fourteenth, and Lebanon Springs the next day. Here Jackson called a halt to rest his men. The following day the VMI cadets were released with Jackson's thanks; they had suffered no casualties, and only one cadet had come down with a serious illness. The rain, which had begun on the night of the thirteenth, continued through the sixteenth and, as Captain H. W. Wingate wrote in his diary, the weather was "so rainy and disagreeable . . . we are but little rested."

President Jefferson Davis had declared 16 May to be a day of fasting and prayer throughout the Confederacy. Jackson's army observed it while still in the mountains around Lebanon Springs. Probably most young soldiers would have agreed with Hospital Orderly John Apperson, who observed that while a day of prayer was needed, the Valley Army had done enough fasting.

5. Confederate Records, vol. 7, ch. II, pp. 9–11, National Archives.

The day was not as peaceful as planned. Some companies in Colonel Grigsby's 27th Virginia, part of the Stonewall Brigade, required by the Conscription Act to remain in service even though their enlistments had expired, downed arms and demanded their discharges. When the matter was referred to Jackson, he exploded. "What is this but mutiny? Why does Colonel Grigsby refer to me to know what to do with a mutiny? He should shoot them where they stand."

Jackson immediately dictated to Major Dabney an order for Grigsby to parade his men at once, face the disarmed mutineers with loyal soldiers with loaded muskets, and give them a choice of returning to duty or being shot. Not surprisingly, they decided to a man to return to duty.

The next day Jackson's army streamed down from the mountains and back into the "Great Valley of Virginia." The sun was shining; flowers were in bloom; peach and cherry trees were in full blossom; clover for the horses flourished in abundance. Sergeant Ed Moore remembered that "The old Valley looked like Paradise."

Front Royal

hile Jackson was still at Leba-
non Springs, he received an urgent message from Lee in Richmond
dated 16 May, informing him that Shields was marching from New
Market northeast to Front Royal, that Banks had fallen back upon
Strasburg, and that it appeared he planned to move east to assist
McClellan. Lee concluded:

> Whatever may be Banks' intention, it is very desirable to prevent
> him from going either to Fredericksburg or the Peninsula, and also
> to destroy the Manassas road. A successful blow struck at him
> would delay, if it does not prevent, his moving to either place, and
> might also lead to the recall of the re-inforcements sent to Frémont
> from Winchester. . . .
>   But you will not, in any demonstration you may make in that
> direction, lose sight of the fact that it may become necessary for
> you to come to the support of General Johnston, and hold yourself
> in readiness to do so if required. . . . Whatever movements you
> make against Banks do it speedily, and if successful drive him back
> toward the Potomac, and create the impression, as far as practica-
> ble, that you design threatening that line.

Nothing could have suited Jackson better than permission to attack Banks, but to do so, he needed the help of Ewell. Wasting no time,

he at once ordered Ewell to move his division near New Market, adding: "Let us, relying upon God for success, prepare for attacking Banks. I can only give you these general instructions." Ewell, having on the same day received from Johnston orders to cross the Blue Ridge and move east toward Richmond, was in a quandary. A flurry of telegrams and dispatches among Jackson, Ewell, Lee, and Johnston followed. In just two weeks Ewell was showered with twenty-seven, each complicated by information and misinformation about the movements and intentions of Banks, Shields, and Frémont. No other general in the war received such a conglomeration of contradictory orders and conflicting information.

Ewell, far less discreet than Jackson, aired his frustrations in a letter to his niece:

> I have spent two weeks of the most unhappy I ever remember. . . . I have been keeping one eye on Banks, one on Jackson, all the time jogged up by Richmond, until I am sick and worn down. Jackson wants me to watch Banks. At Richmond they want me everywhere and call me off, when, at the same time I am compelled to remain until that enthusiastic fanatic comes to some conclusion. Now I ought to be en route to Gordonsville, at this place [Spring Run Gap], and going to Jackson, all at the same time. The fact is there seems no head here at all, though there is room for one or two. I have a bad headache, what with the bother and folly of things. I never suffered as much from dyspepsia in my life. As an Irishman would say, "I'm kilt entirely."

Generals who wish to keep their commands do not willingly disobey their superiors, but Ewell's quandary was the difficulty of determining who his superior was. The Confederate command structure was murky. Lee had placed him under Jackson without consulting Johnston, but Lee was only the military adviser to the president and was not in the direct chain of command,[1] and Johnston, although his hands were full watching McClellan east of Richmond, did not take kindly to Lee's interference with operations in the Valley of Virginia. Even so, Ewell, whose instincts were for attacking Banks, sided with Jackson, although he thought him mad.

1. Although Lee's position is usually referred to as "military adviser" to President Davis, he was officially "charged with conduct of military operations in the Army of the Confederacy," but he had no command. Lee was unhappy with his post and told his wife: "I do not see either pleasure or advantage in the duties."

On Sunday, 18 May,[2] Ewell rode to Mount Solon, a crossroads in a picturesque area of prosperous farms ten miles southwest of Harrisonburg at the head of Mossy Creek, to confer with Jackson. He attended church services with him and, aptly enough, heard Major Dabney preach what Hotchkiss described as "a soul searching sermon" from the text "Come unto me, all ye who are heavy laden and I will give you rest." The service over, Jackson, in spite of his aversion to talking business on the Sabbath, retired with Ewell to an old mill, and the two concerted their plans for doing what they wanted to do in spite of orders to the contrary.

These were dark days for the Confederacy. In early April the Confederates had lost more than 10,500 men at the Battle of Shiloh, and Union forces under Major General John Pope had captured Strategic Island No. 10 in the Mississippi River. By the end of the month New Orleans had fallen, and Federal forces claimed most of Tennessee. The Confederate ironclad *Virginia* had been scuttled after the fall of the great naval base at Norfolk, and McClellan was moving on Richmond. In the Confederate capital itself there were signs of panic: The government had seized control of telegraph lines, foreigners besieged the passport office, the Richmond & Danville Railroad dismantled its repair shops and prepared to ship them south, almost every store in town was offering trunks and packing cases for sale, and prices of goods soared—a pair of boots could not be had for less than $30, and the price of coffee rose to an unprecedented $1.50 per pound. The Confederacy badly needed a victory—something grander than McDowell, which, when compared with recent greater battles elsewhere, now seemed little more than a skirmish.

Whether either Jackson or Ewell had recently read or remembered the teachings of Henri Jomini or Karl von Clausewitz, they understood the advantages of operating on interior lines. Jackson certainly knew Napoleon's formula for defeating a large army with a smaller one: Concentrate one's forces; induce the enemy to disperse his; then direct a superior force at the weakest point at the most advantageous time. The Union forces in western Virginia were scattered, spread out in an arc: Frémont in the Allegheny Mountains; Banks at Strasburg, where he was entrenching; and Shields marching east to join McDowell at Manassas. The Confederates had only to concentrate

2. Jackson and Ewell conferred on the eighteenth, not the seventeenth, as is sometimes stated.

their forces and strike any one of them. Banks was the obvious and preferred target, but it was first necessary to sort out the vagaries of the Confederate high command.

Jackson, Ewell, and probably Lee had tried to explain to Johnston the military situation west of the Blue Ridge, and Jackson had requested instructions. There had been no response. Yet speed was essential if an effective blow was to be struck. It was Ewell who contrived a solution and drafted a letter to himself, dated 18 May, which Jackson signed:

> Your letter of this date, in which you state that you have received letters from Generals Lee, Johnston and myself requiring somewhat different movements, and desiring my views respecting your position, has been received. In reply I would state that as you are in the Valley District you constitute part of my command. Should you receive orders different from those sent from this headquarters, please advise me of the same at as early a period as practicable.
>
> You will move your command so as to encamp between New Market and Mount Jackson on next Wednesday night, unless you receive orders from a superior officer and that of a date subsequent to the 16th instant.

Ewell and Jackson were walking a thin line. If they failed, Joseph Johnston would certain have their heads—and perhaps Lee's as well. That Sunday Ewell hurried back to his command, and the next morning both forces were in motion. Jackson put his men on the Valley Turnpike and camped that night between Harrisonburg and New Market. Ewell sent two of his three brigades marching up the Luray Valley, between the Massanutten and the Blue Ridge on a parallel course, while his third brigade, consisting of the 6th, 7th, 8th, and 9th Louisiana under Brigadier General Richard Taylor, was sent around the southern end of the Massanutten to join Jackson.

The Valley Army had been composed mostly of Virginians who came from farms and small communities within the Valley. Of Irish, Scottish, English, and German descent, they generally shared a common Protestant heritage. The Louisianans of Taylor's brigade differed from them wildly. Although some of the rank and file were Creoles from Acadian country and a few were the sons of planters, most were foreign-born, representing twenty-four nationalities, principally Irish, the sweepings of the back streets of New Orleans and the scum of the levees. If they owned to a religion, it was Roman Catholic.[3] When Taylor took command of this lawless mob, he sent a strong signal by court-martialing two young Irish troublemakers and having them shot by a firing squad—the first executions in Lee's army.

In Taylor's highly colored version of his first encounter with Jackson, the Louisiana brigade arrived in style. Some three thousand strong, the men sported clean gray clothes, their trousers held up by spotless white suspenders. Each regiment was preceded by its band, and the setting sun shone on brightly polished bayonets. Leading the brigade was the 1st Louisiana Special Battalion, commanded by twenty-six-year-old Major Chatham Roberdeau ("Rob") Wheat, its band playing "The Girl I Left behind Me." Jackson, dressed in gray homespun, watched the performance from a fence rail where, according to Taylor, he sat sucking a lemon.

When he reported to Jackson, Taylor wrote later, Jackson asked him the route he had taken and how far his brigade had marched that day. "Twenty-six miles," boasted Taylor.[4]

"You seem to have no stragglers," Jackson remarked.

"Never allow straggling."

"You must teach my people," said Jackson wearily. "They straggle badly."

As the two generals talked, a regimental band struck up a waltz, and an exuberant troop of Creoles began dancing. Jackson, watching them, remarked pensively, "Thoughtless fellows for serious work."

---

3. According to the 1860 census, more than 10 percent of the population of Louisiana was foreign-born.

4. It was Taylor who provoked the myth about Jackson's always sucking lemons. In a book written after the war, *Destruction and Reconstruction*, he said: "Where Jackson got his lemons 'no fellow could find out,' but he was rarely without one." Although often repeated, it seems to have no basis in fact. Taylor had a talent for exaggeration. There are, in fact, only two mentions of Jackson's sucking lemons, and Taylor's is one of them. Jackson's staff officers were those closest to him during the war and they assiduously studied his habits; many—Smith, Douglas, Dabney, Pendleton, McGuire—wrote accounts of their experiences or spoke often of Jackson in letters. None mentions an addiction to lemons. Anna Jackson also said that such a habit "was entirely unknown to me."

Taylor's entire account of his first meeting with Jackson here described, like much else in his memoirs, must be taken with more than a grain of salt. It takes a considerable stretch of the imagination to believe that a Civil War brigade marched twenty-six miles with no stragglers, arrived with shining weapons in clean clothes, and immediately began dancing.

Taylor rushed to their defense. Their gaiety would not affect their work as soldiers, he insisted. Jackson made no reply. Perhaps he agreed with the views of some of his evangelical soldiers that such caperings in public smacked of sin.

For their part, the Louisiana Tigers, as they called themselves, were not impressed by their new commander. One who "stared at him for a long time" declared that "there must be some mistake about him; if he was an able man, he showed it less than any of us had ever seen."

Taylor, who seemed to find most of his superiors odd, was also puzzled by Jackson. Ewell had told him that he "was certain of his lunacy, and that he never saw one of Jackson's couriers approach without expecting an order to assault the north pole." But Taylor's opinion of Ewell was not high, and his description of him was unflattering: "Bright, prominent eyes, a bomb-shaped bald head, and nose like Francis of Valois, gave him a striking resemblance to a woodcock, and this was increased by a bird-like habit of putting his head to one side to utter his quaint speeches."

Taylor himself was a wealthy Southern aristocrat, the thirty-six-year-old son of former President Zachary Taylor and a brother of Jefferson Davis's first wife. He had studied at the University of Edinburgh as well as at Harvard and Yale, graduating from the latter at the age of nineteen. He had been a Louisiana planter and a state senator. Although he had no military experience other than serving briefly as his father's secretary during the Mexican War, he had been elected colonel of the 9th Louisiana Infantry when the war broke out and had been appointed brigadier general in October 1861. Disappointed that he had arrived at Manassas just at the end of the first battle there, he was now eager to prove himself.

In spite of the good initial impression made by Taylor's brigade (at least according to Taylor), Jackson might well have had his doubts, for he must have known of its reputation. The Louisianan's path to war had been marked at every stop of their train by drunken sprees, looting, robbery, and the terrorizing of civilians. One group had even hijacked their train and left their officers behind. In Richmond they were said to have "roamed about the streets like a pack of untamed wildcats," and records of the provost marshal show men arrested for drunkenness, desertion, robbery, forgery, and embezzlement. A number were shot and killed by their own officers in trying to restore order.

Off their trains and on the march the troops sowed havoc, killing farm animals and robbing farmers. When the 10th Louisiana camped on Jamestown Island, General Lafayette McLaws reported that they "eat up every living thing on the Island but two horses and their own species."

Untrained as soldiers, they were unaccustomed to camp life. One soldier reported that "the general rule in camp is not to wash the dishes as long as you can recollect what was in them last." Not surprisingly, they suffered severely from a variety of diseases. In August 1861, out of 920 men in the 7th Louisiana, 645 were taken sick. Acute diarrhea was the most common complaint, but medical discharges were given for opium addiction, lead poisoning, venereal diseases, epilepsy, and idiocy. Many died from measles, mumps, and typhoid. One wrote that death had become so commonplace that when comrades died, "it seemed to me that it was not noticed no more than if a dog had died."

The toughest, roughest, and most loutish of all the Louisiana troops were, by general consent, those in Wheat's battalion. One soldier from Alabama described them as "adventurers, wharf-rats, cut-throats and bad characters generally." Even the other Louisianans were afraid of them. Only their commanding officer, Rob Wheat, the black sheep son of an Episcopal minister, could exercise any control over them. Wheat was a giant of a man, standing six feet four inches, thick-set and dark-complexioned, who had abandoned the study of law to become a soldier of fortune. He had fought for the United States in the Mexican War; later, under Narciso López in Cuba, where he had been wounded; under José María Carajal and later Juan Álvarez in Mexico; and with the American filibuster William Walker in Central America. He had most recently served with American volunteers under Giuseppe Garibaldi in Italy. At First Manassas, as part of Colonel Nathan ("Shanks") Evans's brigade, he had been shot through both lungs. Defying all doctors' prognosis that he would not survive—"I don't feel like dying yet," he told them—he was now back at the head of his ruffian troops.

On the morning of 20 May Jackson received two disturbing messages. One was from Ewell, who informed him that the brigade of Brigadier General Lawrence O'Bryan Branch, which had just arrived in Virginia from North Carolina and had been assigned to Ewell, had been ordered not to cross the Blue Ridge into the Valley but to turn back to Hanover Court House. The order had come directly from Richmond, and Branch was obeying it. The second message was from Johnston for both Jackson and Ewell. Ewell was ordered to return east; Jackson was forbidden to attack Banks at Strasburg and directed merely to "observe" him. Ewell immediately informed Jackson that he saw no choice but to obey, but Jackson was not deterred. He fired off a telegram to Lee: "I am of opinion that an attempt should be made to defeat Banks, but under instructions just received from General Johnston I do not feel at liberty to make an attack. Please answer by telegraph at once."

This action, much resembling Loring's at Romney, was treading a fine line between initiative and insubordination. Jackson then stuck his neck out completely by countermanding the direct order of Johnston, the commander of the Confederate armies in Virginia. He ordered Ewell: "Suspend the execution of the order for returning until I receive an answer to my telegram."

What happened next is unclear from the records, but Jackson appears to have obtain some approval from Lee or from Johnston, for he wasted no time in moving to the attack. Dawn found his army marching north with Taylor's brigade leading the infantry and Ashby's cavalry screening his movements from the Union forces. Taylor riding beside the taciturn Jackson, who said scarcely a word, had ample time to observe his new commander. He later wrote: "An ungraceful horseman, mounted on a sorry chestnut with a shambling gait, his huge feet with outturned toes thrust into his stirrups, and such parts of his countenance as the low visor of his shocking cap failing to conceal wearing a wooden look, our new commander was not prepossessing."

At New Market the head of the infantry column turned sharply east on the only road that crossed the Massanutten.[5] Speculation about their destination ran through the ranks of the marching troops. Were they going to continue east, over the Blue Ridge at Thornton's Gap, or would they turn northward in the Luray Valley? Taylor, still at Jackson's side, was as uninformed as the least of his men. Although he watched as couriers bearing messages galloped up to Jackson, then wheeled and dashed back in the direction of Luray, not a word about the contents of the dispatches was granted him. Having read each message and answered it or not as required, Jackson simply rode calmly on. Coming down from the Massanutten range into the Luray Valley, the column crossed the South Fork of the Shenandoah at White House Bridge and bivouacked just west of the town of Luray. There Ewell with his remaining two brigades and his cavalry, joined Jackson, giving him an army that now numbered almost seventeen thousand men with forty guns.

The smaller of Ewell's brigades was commanded by Arnold Elzey,

5. The road is now U.S. Route 211, and it is still the only road across the Massanutten range.

forty-six, a Marylander who had been promoted to brigadier general for services at First Manassas. Elzey had been born Arnold Elzey Jones but had dropped his patronymic at West Point before he was graduated in 1837. He had fought the Seminoles in Florida and earned a brevet for gallantry during the Mexican War. Although his brigade consisted of only two regiments—the 13th Virginia and 1st Maryland—instead of the usual four, they were excellent regiments.

Ewell's other infantry brigade was commanded by Isaac Ridgeway Trimble, at sixty years of age one of the oldest brigade commanders in the Confederate army. He had graduated from West Point in 1822, retired after ten years in the artillery, and made a mark for himself as a railroad construction engineer.

Early on the morning of 22 May Jackson's Valley Army set forth; when it turned north down the Luray Valley, generals and privates alike could see that they were on their way to attack Banks. The advance force under Ewell camped that night just ten miles from Front Royal, where Banks had formed a huge supply depot and stationed about a thousand men under Colonel John R. Kenly of the 1st (U.S.) Maryland Regiment, a man whose reputation for bravery had been established at Monterrey during the Mexican War.

Jackson's men had as yet encountered no pickets and had not yet been spotted by a Federal patrol. Between Front Royal and Strasburg lay about eight hundred Union soldiers, and at Strasburg, where Banks had constructed field fortifications, about forty-five hundred infantry, sixteen hundred cavalry, and sixteen guns waited.

It is often said that Jackson's bold attack upon Banks caught the Union general completely by surprise, but Banks, although certainly far from being a great general, was shrewd, and he was well aware of his precarious position. With Shields's division, which had been half his force, now with McDowell at Manassas, his army was no longer formidable. Blenker's division had arrived at Harper's Ferry but was in a condition too wretched to be useful. As Jackson's army was marching down the Luray Valley toward his left flank, Banks wrote a long letter to Secretary Stanton from Strasburg:

> From all the information I can gather—and I do not wish to excite alarm unnecessarily—I am compelled to believe that he [Jackson] meditates attack here.
>
> We are preparing defenses as rapidly as possible, but with the best aid of this character my force is insufficient to meet the enemy

in such strength as he will certainly come . . . our situation certainly invites attack in the strongest manner.

At present our danger is imminent at both the line of the road and the position of Strasburg. Our line is greatly extended; the position and property to be protected of vital importance, and the enemy is in our immediate neighborhood in very great superiority of numbers.

Front Royal, lying between the Blue Ridge and the northern end of the Massanutten, surrounded by high ground on all sides, was indefensible against an army the size of Jackson's. Kenley's force stationed there was intended only to discourage attacks by "guerrilla parties that infested the area."

The two forks of the Shenandoah River join just north of the town, which lay on the east side of the rivers. Capturing the wagon bridge and the railroad bridge west of town before they could be destroyed was vitally important to Jackson if he was to get at Banks. He must also have known that Front Royal was a great supply depot, and he was doubtless eager to capture the supplies stored there. He could not afford to delay getting into the town as quickly as possible.

Ashby, after leaving a small cavalry contingent south of Strasburg, had rejoined Jackson, who now had not only part of Ashby's mob of undisciplined cavalry, but also Ewell's 2nd Virginia Cavalry under Colonel Thomas Mumford and the 6th Virginia Cavalry under Lieutenant Colonel Thomas S. Flournoy.

In concentrating all of his available force east of the Massanutten, leaving only a few cavalrymen south of Strasburg in the Shenandoah and a few more in the Alleghenies, Jackson was, consciously or unconsciously, following a principle laid down by Clausewitz, affirming the necessity "to concentrate our power as much as possible against that section where the chief blows are to be delivered and to incur disadvantages elsewhere, so that our chances of success may increase at the decisive point." Jackson took the risk that Banks would not plunge south and that Frémont would not turn east to plunder his main supply depot at Staunton and concentrate in his rear. It was a risk well worth the taking as the results proved.

On the twenty-third Jackson sent Ashby's and Flournoy's cavalries trotting westward across the South Fork of the Shenandoah with orders to swing north and cut the road, the railroad, and the telegraph lines which connected Manassas and Strasburg. At a crossroads called Asbury Chapel Jackson ordered Ewell to peel off eastward onto Gooney Manor Road, which would bring his division into Front Royal directly from the south and avoid a dangerous defile where Kenly could easily delay them. Ewell's division was led by the 1st (Confederate) Maryland and Wheat's Louisiana battalion, followed by the remainder of Taylor's brigade.

The engagement began at three o'clock in the afternoon about a mile and a half from town. The advance was held up for a time because the 6-pounder smoothbores and 12-pounder Napoleons Colonel Crutchfield had brought forward were not effective against the defenses Colonel Kenly had erected above the river. Jackson was forced to wait for Ewell's rifled guns with longer ranges to be brought forward, and Crutchfield, Jackson's chief of artillery, had no notion of where these guns were.

It was probably during this pause that Lieutenant Douglas called Jackson's attention to a figure darting across the fields toward them. Through field glasses it was seen that the runner was a woman wearing a blue dress and a white apron. When she came within artillery range of the Confederate guns, without breaking stride, she tore off her bonnet and waved it vigorously. Describing her run later, she modestly reported that she had "bounded over fences with the agility of a deer." Jackson sent young Douglas to see who she was and what she wanted.

The runner was Miss Belle Boyd, a wildly romantic eighteen-year-old tomboy whom Lieutenant John Lyle described as "not beautiful but she was attractive and fascinating to a degree that would charm the heart out of a monk and cause him to break his vows of celibacy." Henry Kyd Douglas had known her from "her earliest girlhood," and his account of their meeting is probably the most correct:

> Nearly exhausted and with her hand pressed against her heart, she said in gasps "I knew it must be Stonewall, when I heard the first gun. Go back quick and tell him that the Yankee force is very small—one regiment of Maryland infantry, several pieces of artillery and several companies of cavalry. Tell him I know, for I went through the camps and got it out of an officer. Tell him to charge right down and he will catch them all. I must hurry back. Goodby. My love to all the dear boys—and remember if you meet me in town you haven't seen me today."

According to Douglas, Miss Boyd did not meet Jackson and talked only to him, but Boyd herself later insisted that Jackson rode up and offered her a horse and an escort. General Taylor's account of this incident places himself on the scene:

> Breathless with speed and agitation, some time elapsed before she found her voice. Then, with much volubility, she said we were near Front Royal, beyond the wood; that the town was full of Federals, whose camp was on the west side of the river, where they had guns in position to cover the wagon bridge, but none bearing on the railway bridge below the former; that they believed Jackson to be west of Massanutten, near Harrisonburg; that General Banks, the Federal commander, was at Winchester, twenty miles northwest of Front Royal, where he was slowly concentrating his widely scattered forces to meet Jackson's advance, which was expected some days later. All this she told with the precision of a staff officer making a report, and it was true to the letter.

It is doubtful that Miss Boyd could have told Jackson much that he did not already know, but she may have confirmed previously received information. She was then visiting her aunt, the proprietress of the Strickler Hotel, and Colonel Kenly had made his headquarters in cottages just behind the hotel. According to Boyd's accounts, she supplied copious information to Jackson and Ashby throughout the Valley campaign and once even shot and mortally wounded a Union officer. Because she exaggerated shamelessly and because her accounts contain so many obvious errors, it is difficult now to know how much of her story to believe. She claimed to have received a note from Jackson, thanking her for "the immense service you have rendered your country today," but if so, no one ever saw it, and there is no evidence in any extant Jackson papers that Jackson knew her or ever spoke to her. If she did not aid the Confederate cause, however, it was not for lack of trying, and for her efforts the Federals threw her into prison in Washington.

It was shortly after Boyd's appearance on the battlefield that Taylor led his Louisiana Tigers forward to capture the town. The Federals, working furiously, set fire to the wagon bridge and to as many of the supplies as possible before beating a hurried retreat, north toward Winchester. Jackson, still waiting for his rifled guns, watched this movement through the smoke and cried: "Oh, what an opportunity for artillery! Oh, that my guns were here!"

Bypassing the burning wagon bridge, Taylor, with Jackson's permission, sent his 8th Louisiana tripping across the ties of the railroad bridge. Some men, knocked into the swollen floodwaters below by

Federal musketry, were swept away, but most crossed successfully. Other Louisiana troops rushed to the burning wagon bridge. Some tried stamping on embers, some used their hats to scoop up water, and some simply rushed through the smoke and flames to the other side. Although about half the planking was gone, Flournoy managed to get four companies of the 6th Virginia Cavalry across by moving in single file, and Jackson crossed with them.

Once over the river, Flournoy's troopers dashed down the pike and crashed into Kenly's rear guard near Cedarville, about four or five miles north of Front Royal. Federal musketry emptied a few saddles, but in a rare case of Civil War cavalry performing as cavalry was supposed to perform, Flournoy charged back and forth through the Federals until almost all threw up their hands. Although outnumbered by more than three to one, the Confederate cavalry captured 750 and killed or wounded more than 100 others for a loss of only 36 killed and wounded. Colonel Kenly himself, desperately wounded, was taken prisoner. Even Jackson, so averse to giving praise, was impressed and admitted that he had never seen a cavalry charge carried out with such "efficiency and gallantry."

Ashby's cavalry had also done good work. After crossing the South Fork of the Shenandoah, they attacked with élan a large supply depot at Buckton Station, about eight miles west of Front Royal, and set it afire, but the two companies on guard there, from the 27th Indiana and the 3rd Wisconsin, made a stiff resistance, and among the Confederate dead was the gallant Captain George Sheetz, who had left his grocery store at New Creek Station, raised a company of cavalry, and become, it was said, "the most promising cavalry officer on the continent."

The Battle of Front Royal has been called the Battle of Brothers, for the 1st Confederate Maryland Infantry fought the 1st Federal Maryland Infantry. Friends, even relatives, found themselves pitted against each other. Colonel Kenly, captured by the 6th Virginia Cavalry, found a cousin serving in its ranks, and in at least one instance a Confederate did indeed capture his Federal brother.

The fight between the two Maryland units was one which almost failed to take place. When thirty-three-year-old Colonel Bradley Johnson, in civilian life a lawyer and Baltimore politician and now commanding the 1st (Confederate) Maryland, received an order from Jackson to lead the attack on Front Royal, he was facing a mutiny such as Grigsby had faced earlier at Lebanon Springs: Half his men, their terms of enlistment having expired, had demanded their discharges in order to join the cavalry. Johnson had disarmed them and placed them under guard of their loyal comrades. Faced now with Jackson's peremptory command, Johnson ordered his mutinous men paraded. Standing before them, fingering his waxed handlebar mustache, he read aloud Jackson's order: "Colonel Johnson will move the 1st Maryland to the front with all dispatch. . . ." Putting aside the paper, he thundered: "Go home. . . . Boast of it when you meet your fathers and mothers, brothers, sisters and sweethearts. Tell them it was you who, when brought face to face with the enemy, proved yourselves . . . to be cowards." Young George Booth remembered his words years later as "the most effective eloquence to which it has been my fortune to listen." Effective Johnson certainly was. The mutineers, many boys not yet twenty, now clamored for their arms and, colors unfurled, marched boldly into battle, clearing the main road into Front Royal.

It was as well that the units that took part in the battle behaved so creditably, for some units Jackson had ordered forward failed to receive their orders. One of the couriers Ashby had assigned to Jackson that day, a raw young man facing his first battle, had decamped without delivering his dispatches.

In Front Royal Kenly had not been able to burn everything, and a vast amount of quartermaster, commissary, and ordnance stores fell into Jackson's hand, including five hundred revolvers, two splendid rifled 10-pounder (three-inch) Parrott guns, several hundred beef cattle, and what one soldier described as a "perfect God-send": a wagonload of coffee. A Federal supply train that had chugged into the depot during the battle was promptly captured and looted by Wheat's ruffians. In his after-action report Jackson wrote: "The fruits of this movement were not restricted to the stores and prisoners captured; the enemy's flank was turned and the road was opened to Winchester." It was indeed a fine victory and an important one, gained at a cost of just over one hundred casualties.

Winchester

Although Banks had indeed anticipated an attack, he had not expected Jackson to move north down the Luray Valley. Neither had anyone else. On 22 May the *Lexington Gazette* reported: "We know little of Gen. Jackson's movements, but we are expecting to hear of him creating a *stir* somewhere between Harrisonburg and the Potomac before many days." Even when Banks learned of the attack upon Front Royal, he could not bring himself to believe that Jackson's entire army was on his flank, and for a time he still thought he might hold on to his fortifications at Strasburg, but on the evening of 23 May, sometime between nine and eleven o'clock (accounts differ), he concluded that he must retreat, and he gave orders for the sick and wounded and as many stores as possible to be loaded on wagons and started on the road to Winchester. His orders, he said, were obeyed with "incredible celerity," but he had delayed too many hours in issuing them.

Fortunately for Banks, Jackson was not sure what his next step should be. He did not know the disposition of Banks's army or its size, and he did not know what Banks planned to do. These uncertainties induced him to pause when he ought to have been on the move.

Early on the morning of 24 May Jackson sent Ashby's cavalry to watch Strasburg. Colonel George Steuart was dispatched with Ewell's cavalry to strike the Valley Turnpike about nine miles south of Win-

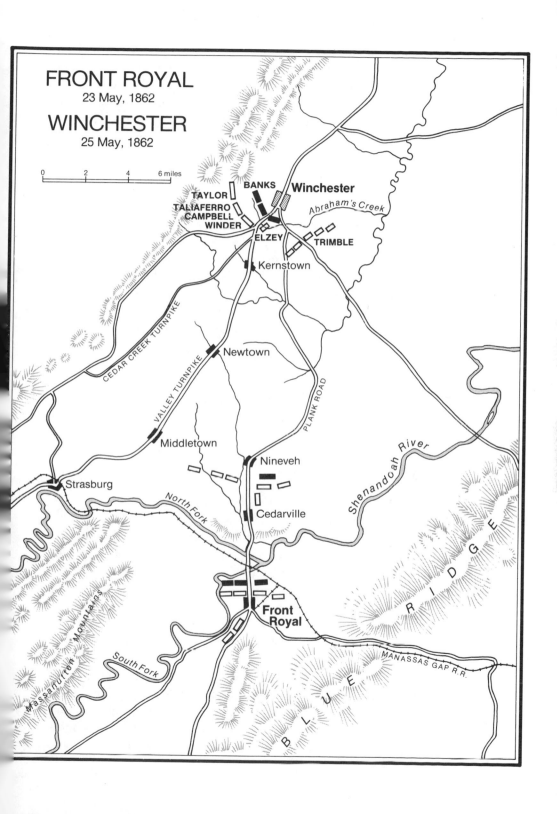

FRONT ROYAL
23 May, 1862

WINCHESTER
25 May, 1862

0   2   4   6 miles

TAYLOR
TALIAFERRO
CAMPBELL
WINDER
ELZEY
TRIMBLE
BANKS
Winchester

Abraham's Creek

Kernstown

CEDAR CREEK TURNPIKE

VALLEY TURNPIKE

PLANK ROAD

Newtown

Middletown

Nineveh

Shenandoah River

Strasburg

North Fork

Cedarville

BLUE   RIDGE

Front
Royal

MANASSAS GAP R.R.

South Fork

Massanutten Mountains

B L U E

chester. Meanwhile, Jackson himself joined Isaac R. Trimble's brigade, leading the infantry on the road directly from Front Royal to Winchester. About 8:00 A.M. he halted Trimble three miles north of Cedarville, near the tiny hamlet of Nineveh. Most of his command was still some way behind; some units were slowly making their way over the two forks of the Shenandoah. Time was needed for Jackson's lagging brigades to come forward.

The halt lasted all morning. Jackson's army was sprawled in ditches along the road, nursing bruised and blistered feet, dozing, exchanging ribald comments, and swatting flies. The men would need all the rest they could get. Ewell joined Jackson at a farmhouse where he was breakfasting, and the two conferred. About 11:00 A.M. a hatless young courier came pounding up to the farm with the news that Steuart had found the Valley Turnpike jammed with Banks's wagons making their way to Winchester. He had cut the turnpike and scattered the wagons, but he needed help. With uncertainty about Banks's movement, if not his strength, now ended, Jackson acted with alacrity.

From Cedarville a rough road ran seven miles northwest to the Valley Turnpike at the village of Middletown. Hotchkiss was sent scurrying along it to scout, for on a map he had made earlier this area was labeled "unexplored." Ewell with two brigades was ordered to stay around Nineveh as a reserve. Jackson himself set forth, Ashby's men with Chew's guns and two rifled long-range guns of the Rockbridge Artillery in the lead, followed by Wheat's battalion, Jackson's own three brigades of infantry, then the rest of the Louisianans. Drums beat and bugles blew and the tired soldiers rose, groaning, to their feet. Still, it all took time. Jackson himself had to ride back three miles to Cedarville to get on the road to Middletown.

It was not an easy march. The terrain was hilly and heavily forested. Rain began to fall, and the rough road turned muddy and slippery. Some Union cavalry skirmished with Ashby, and the poor condition of the road caused delays in spite of the efforts of Jackson and his staff to hurry the regiments along.

It was not until about three-thirty that afternoon that Ashby's troopers arrived on the high ground overlooking Middletown. There they saw the road north and south, for as far as the eye could see, choked with wagons, ambulances, and Union cavalry. The guns of Chew's and Poague's batteries speedily wheeled into battery while Wheat's battalion opened fire from the cover of a stone wall. Corporal George Neese, one of the artillerymen, watched the Federal wagons fleeing toward Winchester "like clouds scudding before a driving storm. At a half mile range we opened on the flying mixture with all four of our guns, and as our shells plowed gap after gap through the serried column it caused consternation confounded, and vastly increased the speed of the mixed fugitive mass."

Jackson wrote:

The turnpike, which had just before teemed with life, presented a most appalling spectacle of carnage and destruction. The road was literally obstructed with the mangled and confused mass of struggling & dying horses and riders. . . . Among the surviving cavalry the wildest confusion ensued, and they scattered in disorder in various directions, leaving, however, some two hundred prisoners with their equipments in our hands. A train of wagons was seen disappearing in the distance towards Winchester, and Ashby, with his cavalry some artillery and a supporting infantry force from Taylor's brigade, was sent in pursuit.

In the colorful prose of the Reverend Dabney, "Ashby swooped down on their right like an eagle, cut through their path, and arrested their escape on that side; while General Taylor, throwing his most forward regiment into line, advanced at a doublequick to the centre of the village, his men cheering, and pouring a terrific volley into the confused mass that filled the street."

Some Union cavalrymen, mad to escape, tried to cut their way to Winchester but were met by Lieutenant Henry Kyd Douglas with a scratch force of Taylor's men, whose volleys dissolved them into a "shrieking, struggling mass of men and horses, crushed, wounded and dying."

Captain Poague came upon a regiment of Federal infantry lying unseen in the grass. Ashby's cavalry, which was supposed to be protecting him, was nowhere to be seen. However, instead of seizing their chance to capture his fine rifled cannon, the Federals started up like startled rabbits and dashed away.

Private Randolf Fairfax of the Rockbridge Artillery wrote: "Such a rout has not been seen since Manassas; arms, knapsacks, blankets and all sorts of accoutrements, were strewn along the route of their flight." Corporal George Neese saw "plenty of knapsacks strewn over the fields and roads," but most had already been ransacked, and he complained: "After a real ragged Rebel rifles a knapsack I would not give a cancelled postage stamp for what he leaves." Neese also saw a "Yankee breastplate" but noted that it did not appear to have been effective because "it had a bullet hole right through the center." Even officers were tempted by some of the abandoned property. First Lieutenant McHenry Howard picked up a handsome red sash, and when he saw a dog lying on "a fine officer's great coat," he "dismounted, routed the dog and secured it."

Jackson had dealt Banks a heavy blow, but many men and wagons of the Federal force had escaped. The long delay around Cedarville had cost the Confederates much. As Banks himself wrote, "Had the enemy vigorously attacked our train while at the head of the column it would have been thrown into such dire confusion as to have made the successful continuation of the march impossible."

Jackson was now astride the Valley Turnpike with Banks's men and wagons fleeing both north and south, but he still did not know how many Federal troops had already passed toward Winchester. He first turned his troops south, but the Federal forces melted away as they sought the many parallel dirt roads to take north. One body of Pennsylvania troops commanded by a captain marched in a huge westward arc that carried them more than 140 miles until they could cross the Potomac at Hancock.

Realizing after several hours that he was on the wrong tack, Jackson reversed his line of operation and headed north. Some of his nearly exhausted men were still able to give elated whoops when they realized they were marching on Winchester.

Although it was now late in the day, Jackson sent a dispatch to Ewell to march north. The untrained courier from one of Ashby's companies failed to find him, but Ewell, who had been fussing at his inactivity, anticipated the order, and nightfall found him camped within two miles of Winchester. Jackson did not halt for the night. He was determined that "if Banks reached Winchester, it would be without a train, if not without an army." Down the pike he went, past the abandoned wagons, a pontoon train, ambulances, the gear and accoutrements abandoned by an army in flight.

Nearing Newton, he heard artillery fire and was enraged when he came upon Poague's two rifled guns firing steadily but without protection. Ashby's cavalry, which ought to have been protecting the guns and closely pursuing the flying Federals, had dissolved in an orgy of looting. They had soon been joined by the Louisiana Tigers, and Taylor found them "looting right merrily, diving in and out of the wagons with the activity of rabbits in a warren." Some Virginians, after capturing a horse or two, simply started home with them. Valuable time was lost waiting for the infantry to be brought forward. In the meantime, the Federals reinforced their fighting rear guard with a brigade of infantry under Colonel George H. Gordon (a classmate of Jackson's at West Point) and fired many of their wagons.

Jackson with members of his staff and the advance guard of fifty cavalrymen—all that could be found of Ashby's scattered cavalry—had brushes with Federal troops more than once during the night. When the Federals fired a volley at the first encounter, Jackson turned to his cavalry and called out: "Charge them! Charge them!" Instead, at a second volley his horsemen fled. To a staff officer at his side Jackson exploded: "Shameful! Did you see anybody struck, sir? Did you see anybody struck? Surely they need not have run, at least until they were hurt!"

The 33rd Virginia came up and cleared the Federals away, and the horsemen were corralled, but near Bartonsville they met an even more formidable force, and again the cavalry whirled about and fled, crashing through the 33rd Virginia and creating, said Colonel Neff, "a scene of most mortifying confusion." His regiment broke.

Jackson, always with the most forward troops, was untouched. Taylor wrote: "I remember thinking at the time that Jackson was invulnerable." It was Winder, throwing forward the remainder of the Stonewall Brigade, who brought order out of the chaos, but near Kernstown another roadblock delayed the march.

All along the turnpike utterly exhausted men were dropping by the roadside, unable to go on. Private Edward Moore of the Rockbridge Artillery wrote: "A long weary night it was, the most trying I ever passed in war, or out of it. . . . About ten o'clock we passed by a house rather below the roadside, on the porch of which lay several dead Yankees, a light shining on their ghastly faces." Another artilleryman wrote that moving and halting, moving and halting, "falling asleep at the halts and being suddenly wakened up when motion was resumed, we fairly staggered on, worn almost to exhaustion by the weariness of such a march." Colonel Fulkerson pleaded with Jackson to let his men rest, arguing that even if they did reach Winchester, they would be in no condition to fight. Jackson told him: "Colonel, I do not believe you can feel more for your men than I do. This is very hard on them, but by this night march I hope to save many valuable lives. I want to get possession of the hills of Winchester before daylight." The 5th Virginia under Colonel W. S. H. Baylor in the advance was not allowed to lie down even briefly; some other units managed to catch an hour's rest. It was marches such as these that earned Jackson's infantry the title of foot cavalry. Colonel Crutchfield, however, was heard to mutter, "This is uncivilized."

Major Harman came up to report that he was having difficulty bringing up the wagons. Jackson asked about those carrying ammunition. "All right, sir," Harman replied. "They were in advance and I doubled teams on them and brought them through."

Jackson gave a satisfied "ah."

Taylor, who heard this exchange, tried to make a joke about breakfasting in Winchester, but Jackson was in no mood for levity. Taylor had long ago decided that he was a man who cared nothing for his own comfort or for that of others. "But woe to the man who failed to bring up ammunition! In advance, his trains were left far behind. In retreat he would fight for a wheelbarrow."

Jackson, familiar with the topography of Winchester and its environs, was able to predict where the Federals would take a stand, and he was right. Some three to four thousand Union soldiers with several batteries were in place on hills on both sides of the Valley Turnpike. Banks's total force at Winchester was probably about sixty-five hundred; Jackson had at least fifteen thousand, although many of them were now stragglers.

With the dawn came a heavy mist, and southeast of town, where Ewell was advancing, fog was thick. Leaving Elzey as a reserve on the pike, Jackson deployed his troops west and southwest of the town with Taylor and the 10th and 23rd Virginia on the far left, Winder nearest the turnpike, and Taliaferro and Campbell in the center of his line. As soon as the mist began to rise, the Federal artillery opened fire, and Jackson brought forward his guns to reply.

The Battle of Winchester was a splendid example of the havoc to be wrought by bringing a superior force to bear at the right place at the right time. East, west, and north were large Federal forces, but all were too far away to aid Banks on this day. Here at Winchester on Sunday, 25 May 1862, Jackson had brought a Confederate army that outnumbered Federals on the ground by more than two to one.

As his troops were deploying, Jackson rode to the crest of a ridge where the firing was heaviest. With him was Colonel Campbell, commanding the 2nd Brigade, and Colonels Grigsby of the 27th Virginia and John M. Patton of the 21st Virginia. Shot and shell and musket balls hummed thick around them. Campbell was wounded; Grigsby cursed as a ball passed through his sleeve. Jackson, calm and untouched, ignored his profanity as he studied the ground over which his men must move. Noting a stone wall behind which Federal sharpshooters were firing, he ordered up two more batteries to add to the fire of Poague's guns and watched as the wall with those it was protecting disintegrated.

Coming off the ridge, he rode to young Colonel Neff, and ignoring the chain of command, which would have been through Winder, he pointed to a hill forward and said: "I expect the enemy to bring artillery to this hill, and they must not do it! Do you understand me, sir? *They must not do it!* Keep a good lookout, and your men well in hand, and if they attempt to come, charge them with the bayonet, and seize their guns. *Clamp them, sir,* on this spot!"

"Very well," Neff replied, "but my regiment is rather small."

Jackson merely pointed again and barked, "Take it!"

Seeing that the Federals, commanded here by Colonel Gordon, were shifting to a low ridge on the Federal right, he ordered Taylor to take position on the extreme left of the Confederate line, extend his line of battle, and then attack. He sent the 10th Virginia to extend the Confederate line farther to the left, overlapping the Union right, and the 23rd Virginia to strengthen the right of Taylor's line. He then joined Taylor, who tried in vain to persuade him that this was no place for the head of the army to be. When Taylor in his fervor began to swear at his men—"What the hell are you dodging for? If there is any more of it, you will be halted under this fire for an hour!"—Jackson gave him a reproving look and, leaning over, touched him on the arm and said: "I am afraid you are a wicked fellow." He then trotted over to the Rockbridge Artillery to watch the Louisianans form their line of battle.

When all the units of Taylor's brigade were in line, with three thousand bayonets bared and the Confederate and the Louisiana pelican colors unfurled, Taylor rode to the front, drew his sword, and ordered his lines forward. Across open fields and up a steep bank they marched as though on parade. On their right the men of the Stonewall Brigade and Jackson himself watched. At the top of a rise the Confederates encountered a stone wall shielding a line of riflemen. Many of the attackers fell dead or tumbled, screaming from wounds, but the line moved inexorably forward. When they were halfway up the ridge, Taylor turned in his saddle, raised his naked sword, and bellowed, "Forward, double quick, charge!" and his men sprang forward, whooping the "rebel yell."[1] Gordon's Federals, badly outnumbered, broke

---

1. An Irishman in Trimble's brigade, watching Taylor's charge and listening to the rebel yell, called out: "Ah, me boys, that's the 'jinewine' Irish yell!"

and ran across the broad top of the ridge and spilled into Winchester. Private John Worsham of the 21st Virginia had a good view of the Louisianans and was impressed: "That charge of Taylor's was the grandest I saw during the war . . . every man was in his proper place. There was all the pomp and circumstance of war about it that was lacking in our charges. . . ." Taylor later said that his most vivid recollection of the charge was of a bluebird, a worm in its mouth, flying through the gunfire.

Seeing Taylor's charge successful, Jackson, "in that sharp and crisp way of his," as one soldier put it, barked, "After the enemy, men!" and the brigades of Winder, Taliaferro, and Campbell charged up the heights and over them into Winchester. To the east of the turnpike, Ewell's men, too, after encountering an initial stiff resistance, came charging into the town.

"Now let's holler!" shouted Jackson as he directed the pursuit. "Order forward the whole army to the Potomac!" he cried. As Gordon, fleeing with his beaten men, later remembered, "The yells of a victorious and merciless enemy were [heard] above the din of battle."

As the Federals fled through the streets of Winchester, civilians fired into their backs and women threw scalding water on them. Horror stories were told by Federal commanders, who reported the shelling of a hospital and the bayoneting of Federal sick and wounded, but Banks, to his credit, declared that such reports were "greatly exaggerated or entirely untrue." What is certain, however, is that most citizens of Winchester were wildly happy to see the backs of the Federals and the return of the Confederates.

Those in Jackson's army who had stayed the pace and had not straggled on the long, arduous march from Front Royal now found themselves heroes. The next day Captain James K. Edmondson of the 27th Virginia described the scene to his wife, Emma:

> We entered Winchester about 10 o'clock yesterday at a double quick in hot pursuit of the Yankees and I never saw such a demonstration as was made by the citizens, the ladies especially as we passed through—every window was crowded and every door was filled with them and all enthusiastically preparing for our Generals and soldiers, waving handkerchiefs and flags and others were engaged in supplying the soldiers as they passed with food and water. I have never seen such an exhibition before.

In his official report Jackson said his troops "were received with the most enthusiastic demonstrations of joy by the loyal people who

. . . had been suffering under the hateful surveillance and rigours of Military despotism."

Private John Robson of the 52nd Virginia never forgot the food that was pressed upon him "by the warm-hearted people of that famous old town" and later wrote: "Allow me to say from personal experience, that it was perfectly safe, under any circumstances, to force nice roast beef, ham, biscuits, pies, cakes, pickles and the like upon any marching column of Confederate soldiers. . . ."

Some of the civilians joined in the looting of Federal wagons. Kate Sperry, a young Winchester woman, took a new Federal knapsack and filled it with a jacket, a bayonet, and some ginger cakes she picked up. A Mr. Pitman found the beautifully made red and white silk flag of the 1st Vermont and gave it to her.

Private Robson spoke of the "frantic delight" of the citizens but added that "they with one breath blessed us for coming, and the next blamed us for letting so many Yankees get away."

One buxom young woman, "with bright eyes and tight ankles, and conscious of these advantages," distressed that so many Federals were escaping, ran out crying, "Oh! You are too late! Too late!" But a lanky Creole from the Bayou Teche left the ranks of the 8th Louisiana and swept her into his arms. Planting a resounding kiss on her lips, he exclaimed: *"Madame! Je n'arrive jamais trop tard!"*

As the Rockbridge Artillery passed down the street, a woman called from her porch: "All of you run here and kiss me!" And still another in her enthusiasm cried: "Oh, you brave, noble, ragged darlings, you! I'm so glad to see you!"

The next day Jackson wrote to his *"esposita"*: "I do not remember having ever seen such rejoicing as was manifested by the people of Winchester as our army yesterday passed through the town in pursuit of the enemy. The people seemed nearly frantic with joy; indeed, it would be almost impossible to describe their manifestations of rejoicing and gratitude. Our entrance into Winchester was one of the most stirring scenes of my life."

David Barton of the 33rd Virginia broke ranks to run down Cameron Street to embrace his mother on her front porch; a few moments later he encountered his black "mammy," and to her he confided that his brother had been killed that day, begging her not to tell his mother until she had savored the victory.

The elation of the Confederate citizens of Winchester was short-lived. This was but the first of three major battles fought within the town limits, and by the end of the war the town had the dubious distinction of having changed hands seventy-five times, more often than any other town North or South. This time it would stay under the Stars and Bars for only a week.

While most Winchester citizens favored the Confederates, the feeling was not universal. Miss Julie Chase, a Unionist, wrote of the "Confederates rushing down pell mell with their horrid yells (which I will never forget). . . . Oh, the horror of those moments. . . . We beheld the troops wild with excitement, firing in every direction up and down the street. We expected every moment to be shot down." She watched civilians shooting Union soldiers. "The citizens of the town have become demons," she wrote." Although strongly pro-Union, Miss Chase wrote bitterly in her diary that "Banks thought more of getting the negroes off than to save the poor soldiers, or save the country."

The Federals fled headlong in spite of all efforts to stop them. "Another Bull Run panic," grumbled a Federal staff officer. Banks himself pleaded with them to stand. To one group he called out, "My God, don't you love your country?"

"Yes," answered one man, "and I'm trying to get to it as fast as I can."

The first batches of Federals gained Martinsburg about midday; many had within forty-eight hours fought two battles and marched more than fifty miles. That evening the troops began to cross the Potomac. The stream of men, horses, and wagons continued through most of the next day before all had reached the safety of the Maryland shore. "How sweet was Maryland, our Maryland," wrote one.

A somewhat different picture of this retreat was painted by Banks when he came to write his after-action report:

> The scene at the river when the rear guard arrived was of the most animated and exciting description. . . .
>
> There were never more grateful hearts in the same number of men than when at midday of the 26th we stood on the opposite shore. My command had not suffered an attack and rout, but had accomplished a premeditated march of nearly 60 miles in the face of the enemy, defeating his plans and giving him battle wherever he was found. . . .
>
> Our wagon train consisted of nearly 500 wagons. Of this number 55 were lost. They were not with but few exceptions, abandoned to the enemy, but were burned upon the road. Nearly all our supplies were thus saved.

Thus can a general with a pen turn defeat and retreat into victory.

The tumultuous reception of Jackson's army at Winchester had slowed the pursuit, but more crucial was the lack of cavalry. "Never," wrote Jackson later, "have I seen an opportunity when it was in the power of cavalry to reap a richer harvest of the fruits of victory." Ashby's undisciplined horsemen were nowhere to be found. Ashby himself had become involved in a subsidiary action and could not be located. Only Ewell's 2nd and 6th Virginia Cavalry under the command of George Steuart were intact. Jackson sent Sandie Pendleton galloping to him with orders "to move as rapidly as possible and join me on the Martinsburg turnpike, and carry on the pursuit of the enemy with vigor."

Pendleton found Steuart three miles east of Winchester, resting with his men by the roadside as they had been all morning, their horses grazing in a clover field. Pendleton passed on Jackson's order, but Steuart, a thirty-four-year-old West Pointer newly promoted to be a brigadier general, refused to obey, claiming that all orders to him must come through Ewell.[2] When he was at last persuaded to move, he "pushed forward in a highly creditable manner," Jackson later reported, "but the main body of Banks' army was now beyond the reach of successful pursuit. . . . There is good reason to believe that, had the cavalry played its part in this pursuit as well as the four companies had done under Colonel Flournoy two days before in the pursuit from Front Royal, but a small portion of Banks' army would have made its escape to the Potomac."

Jackson's weary infantry and artillery bivouacked a few miles north of Winchester, but Jackson remained in town and made his headquarters at the Taylor Hotel.[3] He found the time to pay a quick visit to the Grahams before he collapsed facedown in bed, still booted and spurred, and slept, as Dabney reported, "with the healthy quietude of infancy."

Jackson had again fought a battle on a Sunday, but the next day he ordered religious services to be held at four o'clock in the afternoon,

---

2. "Maryland" Steuart had been a captain in the United States cavalry before the war and had fought Indians in the West. He was a tough fighter but a nasty martinet whose favorite punishment was to tie men by their thumbs to a cross pole.

3. The Taylor Hotel, named after Bushrod Taylor, promoter and first president of the Valley Turnpike Company, was the latest in Valley luxury. The building, its front now defaced by modern commercial architectural adornments, still stands.

and he himself attended those at the bivouac of the 37th Virginia. That same day he issued a general order:

> Within four weeks this army has made long and rapid marches, fought six combats and two battles, signally defeating the enemy at each one, capturing several stands of colors, and pieces of artillery, with numerous prisoners, and vast medical, ordnance, and army stores; and finally driven the boastful host which was ravaging our beautiful country, into utter rout. The General commanding would warmly express to the officers and men under his command, his joy in their achievements, and his thanks for their brilliant gallantry in action and their patient obedience under the hardship of forced marches; often more painful to the brave soldier than the dangers of battle. The explanation of the severe exertions to which the Commanding General called the army, which were endured by them with such cheerful confidence, is now given, in the victory of yesterday.

The next day, too, was declared a day of rest, although Jackson insisted that it include four hours of drill, and discipline was tightened. Many of his ragged troops had acquired Union uniforms to replace their worn-out clothes. Although Jackson himself often wore parts of his old blue VMI uniforms, he warned the troops now that anyone caught in a Federal uniform would be treated as a prisoner of war, and he instructed Major Dabney to issue orders compelling them to give up all loot, reminding them that "all captured property belongs to the Government, and for individuals to appropriate it is theft." This same order announced:

> The shameless pillaging practiced by numbers of cavalry and infantry, who were intrusted [sic] with the advance in pursuing the enemy through Newtown on the 24th instant, under the gallant Ashby, so reduced his command as to render it necessary to discontinue the pursuit until re-enforced by other forces. Such troops cannot be depended upon to secure brilliant results, and hence they shall not be placed in the advance of this army until satisfactory evidence shall be given that their disgraceful conduct will not be repeated.

Although the failure of Jackson's cavalry was costly, the booty reaped by the Confederates was immense: 2 rifled guns, 9,354 small arms, an estimated $425,000 worth of commissary and quartermaster stores, including 100 head of cattle and 34,000 pounds of salt, sugar, bacon, bread, cheese, coffee, and, most valuable of all, a vast array of medical supplies, including anesthetics, of which the South was in great need. According to Dr. Hunter McGuire, the Valley Army had "captured more medical stores than those in the whole Confederacy." In his formal report McGuire wrote: "One of the largest storehouses in the town had been appropriated by the United States Medical Service purveyor and was well filled with medicines, instruments and hospital stores. The supply was very large and intended for the armies under the command of General Shields and Frémont, as well as that of Banks. . . ." Major Harman's teamsters worked for a week hauling as much south as they could in their groaning wagons.

Jackson lost about 450 killed and wounded in the three days' fighting from Front Royal to Winchester, but he had captured more than 3,000 Federal troops. All prisoners able to march were sent south guarded by a regiment of the Stonewall Brigade. In Winchester's hospitals were found many sick and wounded Federals tended by 8 surgeons and assistant surgeons. Jackson allowed them to continue their work, and he assigned to them 64 captured Federals to serve as attendants.

Before leaving Winchester, Jackson paroled those left in the hospital, and at Dr. McGuire's urging, he devised a new and, at the time, a radical form of parole which was in effect an unconditional release of all medical officers taken prisoner of war.

Retreat
up the Valley

There is no doubt that the battles of Front Royal and Winchester were clear Confederate victories for which Jackson deserved full credit. Banks had been driven out of the Valley and across the Potomac, vast quantities of valuable stores had been taken, and thousands of prisoners captured, but as important as the battles themselves was their timing. McDowell was on the verge of joining McClellan, which would have increased the size of his army by some 40 percent, and Richmond, the Confederate capital, seemed about to be taken. In Richmond itself there was deep gloom and anxiety. Then, to the utter dismay of McClellan and McDowell, Lincoln, alarmed by reports from the Shenandoah, changed everything in a twinkling.

At 5:00 P.M. on 24 May, while Jackson was clobbering Banks's army on the Valley Turnpike, Lincoln sent the following urgent message to McDowell:

> General Frémont has been ordered by telegraph to move from Franklin on Harrisonburg to relieve Banks, and capture or destroy Jackson's and Ewell's forces.
>
> You are instructed, laying aside for the present the movement on Richmond, to put 20,000 men in motion at once for the Shenandoah, moving on the line or in advance of the line of the Manas-

sas Gap Railroad. Your object will be to capture the forces of Jackson and Ewell, either in cooperation with General Frémont or, in case want of supplies interferes with his movements, it is believed that the force with which you move will be sufficient to accomplish this objective alone. The information thus far received here makes it probable that if the enemy operate actively against Banks you will not be able to count on much assistance from him, but may even have to relieve him.

Reports received this moment are that Banks is fighting Ewell 8 miles from Winchester.

McDowell reluctantly complied and ordered Shields to turn around and go back to the Valley, but he informed Stanton: "This is a crushing blow to us." It was indeed. Thanks to Lincoln, Jackson and Lee had achieved their principal objective: McClellan would receive no reinforcements from the West.

At 6:50 P.M. on the twenty-fourth Stanton wired Major General John A. Dix in Baltimore: "Please send all the force you can spare to re-enforce Banks, as speedily as possible."

On the twenty-fifth, while Jackson's and Ewell's men were chasing Federal troops through the streets of Winchester, Lincoln telegraphed McClellan: "The enemy is moving north in sufficient force to drive Banks before him. . . . I think the movement is a general and concerted one, such as could not be if he was acting upon the purpose of a very desperate defence of Richmond. I think the time is near when you must either attack Richmond or give up the job and come to the defence of Washington."

On the same day Stanton dispatched alarming telegrams to state governors. Thirteen were warned that the enemy was advancing on Washington and were urged to send troops. Messages to the governors of Massachusetts, Rhode Island, and Pennsylvania from Stanton were more specific: "Send all the troops forward that you can immediately. Banks is completely routed. The enemy are in large force advancing on Harper's Ferry."

On 26 May the assistant secretary of war, P. H. Watson, reported from Harper's Ferry that the three thousand men stationed there were "in a great state of demoralization, because of the terrible stories told by the runaways from Banks, who come straggling in." General Rufus Saxton, a thirty-seven-year-old West Pointer, was at once sent with reinforcements to take charge.

Using the authority of the standby powers given him, Stanton seized the railroads. On the thirtieth he requested from seventeen governors a total of fifty thousand three-year enlistees. On that day Jackson's army was bivouacked in and around Halltown, only five miles west of Harper's Ferry, against which he was making threatening demonstrations. The 2d Virginia was even sent across the Shenandoah River to occupy Loudoun Heights.

Jackson himself was far forward. Watching an artillery duel near Bolivar, he was joined by Elzey and Winder. Elzey reported increasing Federal reinforcements and the presence of "heavy guns on the Maryland Heights." Jackson interrupted him with "General Elzey, are you afraid of big guns?"

This may have been simply one of Jackson's heavy-handed attempts at a joke, but Elzey, a West Pointer eight years older than Jackson, a man who had won a brevet for his gallantry in the Mexican War, and who had recently distinguished himself at Manassas, did not deserve such a remark. His face flushed, but he said nothing. There was an awkward silence, broken only when a courier arrived with a dispatch, which Jackson read quickly; then without a word he turned his horse and rode away.

The dispatch may have been the one informing him that Shields was advancing on his line of communication from the east and Frémont from the west, while Federal forces were building up in front at Harper's Ferry. He knew that it was time to retreat—and that it would have to be done fast. He issued the necessary orders, designating the Stonewall Brigade as the rear guard, then lay down under a tree behind a battery and went to sleep. He awoke to find Congressman Alexander Boteler, now serving as an aide, sketching him.

Jackson took the sketch from Boteler and, after commenting that he himself had one year stood fifty-ninth in a drawing class of sixty-two at West Point, said, "Colonel, I have some harder work for you to do. I want you to go to Richmond for me. I must have reinforcements." Boteler was to explain that if Jackson's command could be "gotten up to 40,000 men, a movement may be made beyond the Potomac, which will soon raise the siege of Richmond and transfer this campaign from the banks of the James to those of the Susquehanna."

Obviously Jackson had no real knowledge of the situation in the Peninsula. There was no way in which Johnston, Lee, or Davis could find twenty-five thousand more men to send him. Nevertheless, Boteler set forth at once for Charles Town to board the train. Riding through a thunderstorm, he was surprised to be overtaken by Jackson, who, leaving his staff behind, boarded the train with him—and at once fell asleep. Before they reached Winchester, Boteler woke him to point out a mounted courier pounding along beside the train, trying to attract attention. Jackson ordered the train stopped.

The courier brought bad news. Major Harman had been unable to carry away all the booty captured at Front Royal. Tons of supplies had been left there, guarded by fifty-one-year-old Colonel Zephaniah Turner Conner with elements of the 8th Louisiana and his own 12th Georgia, the regiment which had behaved so creditably at McDowell. Advance forces from Shields's division under Nathan Kimball, Jackson's nemesis at Kernstown and now a brigadier general, had retaken the town in a surprise attack, capturing 6 Confederate officers and 150 men, routing the rest, and releasing 18 Federal prisoners of war. Captain James Cole, the assistant quartermaster of the 37th Virginia, managed to set fire to some of the store buildings, but most of the supplies, along with two locomotives and eleven cars, fell into Federal hands. The railroad bridge over the South Fork was captured intact. The bridges over both forks of the Shenandoah River were to become crucial strategic points in the following two weeks.

Jackson read the dispatch, tore it into pieces, told the conductor, "Go on, sir, if you please," and went back to sleep.

That evening, once again ensconced in Winchester's Taylor Hotel, Jackson sent for Colonel Conner. Ewell thought him "a brave man, but thrown off his balance by responsibility." Jackson had neither time nor inclination for compassion. After hearing Connor's account of the affair, he inquired how many of his men had been killed.

"None, I am glad to say, General," Conner answered.

"How many wounded?"

"Few or none, sir."

"Do you call that fighting, sir?" Jackson lashed out. The unfortunate Conner was at once placed under arrest, and Jackson subsequently saw him cashiered.

Boteler had been told to delay his departure for Richmond until Jackson could prepare additional messages. It was still raining when he arrived at the hotel to collect them. Wet through, he mixed two whiskey toddies and offered one to Jackson. "No, no, Colonel," Jackson protested, "I never drink intoxicating liquors."

Boteler remarked that he might with reason on this wet, miserable night break his rule. Jackson reluctantly accepted the proffered glass, took a few careful sips, and said, "Colonel, do you know why I habitually abstain from intoxicating liquors? Why, sir, because I like the taste of them, and when I discovered that to be the case I made up my mind at once to do without them."[1] Putting the toddy down, he drank no more.

Lincoln, after studying a map, seems to have recovered his composure, and in a long telegram to McClellan he outlined his view of the situation at the north end of the Valley of Virginia:

> A circle whose circumference shall pass through Harper's Ferry, Front Royal, and Strasburg, and whose center shall be a little northeast of Winchester, almost certainly has within it this morning the forces of Jackson, Ewell, and Edward Johnson. . . . Shields, with McDowell's advance, retook Front Royal at 11 A.M. yesterday . . . and saved the bridge. Frémont, from the direction of Moorefield, promises to be at or near Strasburg at 5 P.M. today. Banks at Williamsport with his old force, and his new force at Harpers Ferry, is directed to cooperate.

From the White House the situation looked promising indeed. Jackson appeared to be in a trap whose jaws were about to snap shut. But the best-laid schemes of men do indeed "Gang aft a-gley," leaving them with "grief an' pain/For promis'd joy." Lincoln's circle was not magic, and Jackson was not yet caught.

It is said that whenever a senior officer was proposed for promotion to Napoleon, he asked, "Does he have luck?" It is an attribute always desirable, but perhaps none need it more than generals. Jackson had, throughout his life generally been lucky, but in the next ten days his luck was phenomenal.

A look at a map and a review of the military situation will readily reveal the real danger of annihilation that faced Jackson's army on 30 May 1862. Saxton at Harper's Ferry and Banks north of the Potomac in Maryland were effective blocks to any further advance north. The troops on Loudoun Heights, indeed, the entire Stonewall Brigade, were in a perilous position. Strasburg, fifty miles to the south, was the center of the narrowing gap through which Jackson's army must escape. On the morning of Friday, 30 May, Jackson's most advanced elements were near Harper's Ferry; Frémont's main body was at Moorefield, thirty-eight miles west of Strasburg, with advance elements ten miles farther east; Shields's division, with the remainder of McDowell's army

---

1. Jackson was often offered liquor, and he always responded in the same way, using almost the same words. Similar stories of such conversations at other times and in other places were recorded by staff officers McGuire and Douglas and by Bradley T. Johnson.

behind him, was only about twenty miles east of Strasburg, and his advance forces were in Front Royal, eight miles closer. It was on this day that Lincoln issued his final orders to McDowell and to Frémont: "Do not let the enemy escape."

By pushing his men so far north that his line of communication was vulnerable to attack and the bulk of his army surrounded, Jackson had dangerously overextended himself. Ewell was not the only officer who thought he had taken leave of his senses. Among his anxious staff officers, Colonel Stapleton Crutchfield was heard to mutter: *"Quem Deus vult perdere, prius dementat."*

If Jackson was worried, it did not show. At noon on the thirtieth, before boarding the train with Boteler, he had dined with his chief commissary, Major Wells J. Hawks, who thought him unperturbed; he had slept soundly on the train to Winchester, and he had displayed no sign of uneasiness.

On 24 May, just one hour before Lincoln had dispatched the fateful message to McDowell, Frémont, in his headquarters at Franklin, had received a telegram from Washington: "You are directed by the President to move against Jackson at Harrisonburg and operate against the enemy in such a way as to relieve Banks. This movement must be made immediately." Had Frémont done as Lincoln directed, placing himself athwart the Valley Turnpike at Harrisonburg and cutting Jackson's line of communication, Jackson would certainly have found himself in even more serious trouble, but the reference to Banks seems to have clouded the meaning of the order in Frémont's mind. When he replied that he would "move as ordered, and operate against the enemy in such way to afford prompt relief to General Banks," Lincoln and Stanton naturally assumed that he was about to push his way eastward over the mountains to Harrisonburg. He was not.

The Federal army floundering about in the Allegheny Mountains needed a better general than Frémont. The illegitimate son of a French dancing master and a Richmond housewife, he had, through his wits and grit, made a name for himself in the world: Leading important explorations in the West, he became known as the Pathfinder; marrying without her father's consent the daughter of Senator Thomas Hart Benton, he achieved notoriety; mixing in the muddied waters of California politics, he had been court-martialed and found guilty of mutiny and insubordination. Still, when California was admitted as a state, he had been elected one of its first United States senators, and in 1856 he had been the presidential candidate of the Republican party. In May 1861 Lincoln appointed this mercurial, headstrong, and unreliable man, now forty-nine years old, a major general in the regular army. In Missouri he had already embarrassed the government by brashly releasing slaves without authority, and he was not a success as a general.

Instead of obeying Lincoln's order to march on Harrisonburg, only 15 miles to the east, Frémont, finding the passes blocked as a result of Hotchkiss's work after the Battle of McDowell, made no attempt to clear them but marched his men north to Moorefield before turning east and crossing the mountains to Wardensville on the road to Strasburg. In all, he was to march his men 120 miles before reaching Harrisonburg. Lincoln, stunned to discover that his explicit orders had been disobeyed, telegraphed: "I see that you are in Moorefield. You were expressly ordered to march to Harrisonburg. What does this mean?"

The following day Frémont telegraphed his excuses: His men were tired, there were shortages of food and forage, passes were blocked, etc. He concluded with this extraordinary statement: "In executing any order received I take it for granted that I am to exercise my discretion, according to circumstances. If I am to understand that literal obedience to orders is required, please say so. I have no desire to exercise any power which you do not think belongs of necessity to my position in the field."

This was vintage Frémont. When at 1:00 P.M. on 28 May Lincoln fired off a message directing him to remain at Moorefield and await orders, Frémont was already at Fabius, ten miles east. Testily, being now literal-minded, he telegraphed that he would return to Moorefield. In reply, an exasperated Stanton informed him that Jackson's army was now believed to be in the vicinity of Charles Town and Winchester and "the President directs you to move upon him by the best route you can."

Frémont's army had had a rough time in the sparsely settled mountains, where his line of communication was harassed by Confederate guerrillas and supplies of any description were exiguous. The physical capacities of men and horses deteriorated. The situation was far from improved by the arrival of Blenker's division, whose immigrant soldiers were in wretched condition. The story of their march from McDowell's command near Manassas to Frémont in Moorefield by way of Harper's Ferry would be ludicrous were it not so tragic. Perhaps few, if any, wars in modern history provide an example of more egregious military bungling and ineptness.

Ludwig (or Louis, as he now preferred to be called) Blenker was born in the principality of Hesse Darmstadt in 1812. He had served in the Bavarian Legion but had been forced to flee to Switzerland after taking part in the failed revolution against the monarchy in 1848. The following year he emigrated to the United States, where he became a successful farmer and businessman. When the war broke out, he raised the 8th New York among immigrants from Central Europe, many of whom did not speak English, and was elected its colonel. When further regiments of recent immigrants were formed, they were placed under him, and he was promoted to the rank of brigadier general and put in command of a brigade and then of a division. Practically all the officers in his division were foreign-born, including Hungarian-born Brigadier General Julius Stahel (real surname: Számvald), who had helped him raise the 8th New York; German-born Brigadier General Adolf von Steinwehr; and Polish-born Waldimir Krzyanowski.

Blenker's division had left Warrenton Junction on 5 April, and two days later, near Salem, it was caught without warm or waterproof clothing in a freak snowstorm. This was particularly unfortunate because the division had left behind its tents as well as its medical stores and most of its ambulances. The next day, plowing ahead through cold rain and sleet, the men ate the last of the food in their knapsacks. It was then discovered that no provision had been made to supply them with food, forage, or any other necessities while they were in transit from one military department to another. No one possessed an accurate map, and Blenker, who appears to have had only the vaguest sense of direction, was frequently lost.

The distance between Warrenton Junction and Harper's Ferry was only fifty miles, but twelve days passed, and no one in Washington or Harper's Ferry knew what had happened to them. A division of nearly ten thousand men who were never within fifty miles of the enemy and never more than thirty miles from a railroad appeared to have been lost, wandering about somewhere in north-central Virginia. Finally Secretary Stanton sent Brigadier General William S. Rosecrans to find them. Rosecrans traveled by train to Harper's Ferry, "despatching messengers from two or three points in my route in search of General Blenker's division." He found it at last halted near Berry's Ferry on the Shenandoah River, where a boat carrying two companies of the 75th Pennsylvania had just sunk, drowning two officers and fifty-one enlisted men.

Frémont immediately ordered Rosecrans to send Blenker's troops to him at Moorefield, but with his utmost effort Rosecrans was able to get them no farther than Winchester. From that town he telegraphed to

Frémont: "We are bivouacked five miles out of Winchester, after thirty-eight days without tents or shelter. Troops wanting shoes too badly to move. Wait for shoes, provisions and forage. Horses much jaded and nearly starved." The men had long since resorted to pillaging and foraging wherever they could. A Northern newspaper reporter described them as being "as lawless a set as ever pillages hen-roosts or robbed dairy maids of milk and butter."

The division, which had marched out of Warrenton Junction on 5 April, finally began to straggle into Moorefield, only 170 miles distant, on 4 May, and all did not come up until 11 May. Frémont in his report (not written until 30 December 1865) described the situation as he had seen it:

> The frequent and earnest dispatches of General Rosecrans also showed that the troops ordered to re-enforce my department were even worse off than my own, and difficulties in the way of rapid and efficient operations, at a distance from the main points of supply, were increased instead of diminished. Over forty horses were demanded by General Rosecrans to get the batteries of General Blenker out of Martinsburg. Thirty-six ambulances and teams were also called for. Forage was scarce, and animals already on hand were reported "starving."

Even when the division arrived, the troops remained unruly. Milroy, in a letter to his wife, described them as "the most infernal robbers, plunderers and thieves I have ever seen." He considered them a disgrace to the army:

> They straggle off from their companies and Regts. for miles on each side of the road as we march along and enter every house— smokehouse—milkhouse—chickenhouse—kitchen—barn— corn-crib and stable and clean out everything—frequently open drawers, trunks, bureaus [sic] etc for plunder—leaving women and children crying behind them—but no tears or entreaties stop or affect them. . . . [T]he name of the Blenker's dutch [sic] will be as celebrated in history as the vandals. . . .

With such troops in such a condition, Frémont might be excused for failing to obey Lincoln's orders, although had he cleared one of the blocked but undefended passes, he could have marched quickly into the fertile Shenandoah Valley, where his supply problems would have vanished.

There may have been a reason for Frémont's dawdling: He feared to face a numerically superior foe. He informed Lincoln that he estimated Jackson's force to be thirty thousand, perhaps sixty thousand men. Lincoln tried in vain to disabuse him of this absurd notion, assuring him that Jackson could not possibly have more than twenty thousand and probably not more than fifteen thousand. (The lower figure was closer to the truth.) Attempting to coordinate his movements with that of Shields, Lincoln ordered Frémont to be at Strasburg by noon of the thirtieth. Frémont perversely replied that he could not be there until about 5:00 P.M. on 31 May.

His march was hardly that of a vigorous pursuer of a trapped enemy. On 28 May, at Fabius, about ten miles east of Moorefield, in spite of his orders to move with the utmost speed, he called a halt. He later reported his reasons:

> At this latter point, upon the vigorous protest of my medical director against further marching of the command without one day's rest, a halt was called on the 29th. Hundreds of stragglers and broken down men from Blenker's division had been left along the road in the ascent of the mountain, and it was plain their condition demanded consideration. They were weak and reduced not only from recent fatigue and want of food, but from previous hardship and privation on the route from the Potomac. I could not venture to proceed with them in disorder and with safety undertake the work in prospect.

During the halt Frémont counted noses and found that Blenker's division, which had left Warrenton Junction ten thousand strong, now numbered fewer than six thousand. However necessary he may have considered the delay, it proved fatal to Lincoln's plans to trap Jackson.

Had Frémont pushed eastward vigorously and had McDowell pushed Shields and reinforcements rapidly and aggressively westward to Strasburg, Jackson's army would almost certainly have been crushed. As it was, Jackson escaped by the skin of his teeth.

On 30 May, while Jackson slept on the train, the greater part of the Valley Army marched under the thunderstorm that became torrential from Halltown to Winchester on the solid turnpike. The Valley Army was now stretched out over perhaps twenty miles. Its rear guard, the Stonewall Brigade, was retreating south as fast as it could while skirmishing with Saxton's men. Curiously, Shields, the advance of McDowell's army, although only twelve miles east of Strasburg, did not advance, for he had not received orders to go past Front Royal, and he gave credence to a rumor that Longstreet was coming down the Luray Valley with an army. As James M. McPherson writes in *Battle Cry of Freedom*, "a strange lethargy seemed to paralyze the northern commanders." On the twenty-eighth Lincoln, having heard that Jackson was at Winchester, had wired McDowell: "Assuming this, it is for you a question of legs. Put in all the speed you can. I have told Frémont as much, and directed him to drive at them as fast as possible." Still, no one had stirred.

The main body of Jackson's army was on the move through the still-heavy rain early on the thirty-first, the wagons traveling two abreast, the total force occupying seven miles of road. Pendleton wrote to his mother: "Where we are to go, I do not know. Our force is too small & broken down by constant marching to do much good work against an overwhelming force." For the Confederates it was very much "a question of legs." Jackson and anxious staff officers hurried the tired soldiers on. Ashby was ahead and to the west of the column, skirmishing with some of Frémont's cavalry. By two-thirty in the afternoon all had cleared Winchester except Winder's Stonewall Brigade, which, having the farthest to march and trailing all others, was in a most perilous position.

Winder had recalled the 2nd Virginia from the army's most forward position on Loudoun Heights, and early on the thirty-first it had set out for some hard marching. Neff, the young Dunkard colonel of the 33rd Virginia, rode along the line of march of his regiment, cautioning his men that this must be a forced march and he could not tell them when they would camp. Those who could not keep up must try to catch up later. In spite of his peril, Jackson remained unruffled. That night he chatted with Taylor "in a low, gentle voice," more communicative than Taylor had ever known him to be.

When McDowell arrived at Front Royal on the afternoon of the thirty-first, Frémont was only twenty miles west; their combined strength greatly exceeded Jackson's force strung out along the turnpike between them. The Federals now had the chance to do to Jackson what Jackson had done to Banks—and at almost the same spot—but incredibly, Frémont and McDowell appear not to have been in communication with each other.

The first day of June, was again a critical one. Ewell's division, given the task of holding off Frémont, moved west at 5:00 A.M. Ashby, on the other side of the turnpike, was watching Shields and McDowell. Winder had pushed his troops to their limit, halting them only at Newton, by which time he had fewer with him than were straggling in his wake. Behind him the turnpike was strewn with exhausted men. The 2nd Virginia had marched thirty-six miles in fourteen hours; the rest of the brigade almost as far. And they were still not safe.

Winder did not allow his men to rest for long. He again pushed them up the turnpike. Now, as they marched, they could hear the sound of Ewell's and Frémont's guns to the west. "The men exchanged glances," remembered one private, "but no one spoke a word, though the same thought was in every mind, 'We are cut off now—it is all up with us.' " That afternoon McHenry Howard, riding ahead of Winder's brigade, saw horsemen near Middletown where the road to Front Royal joins the turnpike. To his relief it proved not to be Federal cavalry but Ashby with some staff officers and couriers.

"Is that General Winder coming up?" Ashby asked anxiously.

Howard assured him that it was.

"Thank God for that," Ashby said.

When Winder appeared, Ashby shook his hand earnestly. "General, I was never so relieved in my life," he said. "I thought that you would be cut off and made up my mind to join you and advise you to make your escape over the mountain towards Gordonsville."

There now seemed a chance that Winder and his brigade would make it safely past Strasburg, the choke point. He halted long enough at Cedar Creek for hundreds of his stragglers to come up, then burned the bridge over the creek and marched on. He reached Strasburg about noon.

Frémont had now roused his men and sent forward a small force of cavalry, artillery, and a brigade under Lieutenant Colonel Gustave P. Cluseret, thirty-nine, a former French officer who had fought Russians in the Crimea, Arabs in Algeria, his own countrymen in the insurrection of 1848, and who had been wounded at Capua while commanding a French unit in Garibaldi's army.

Moving through heavy rain and a hailstorm, Cluseret's cavalry came upon elements of the 6th Virginia Cavalry in the rear of Jackson's retreating army two miles south of Strasburg. Challenged, one of the Federals called out, "Ashby's cavalry." Unrecognized, they rode to point-blank range and delivered a deadly volley. The Confederate cavalry wheeled their horses and fled, riding over their sleeping comrades in the 2nd Virginia Cavalry. Some of the 7th Louisiana fired into their backs. There must have been considerable confusion on both sides, for Frémont later reported that his cavalry "broke in a shameful panic to the rear."

Frémont did not press forward; McDowell remained motionless at Front Royal, and the mass of Jackson's army passed safely through the waves of Federals on both sides. Jackson had been exceedingly lucky, but looking ahead, he was apprehensive about McDowell, who, instead of joining forces with Frémont, had sent Shields and his division on a course parallel to his own east of the Massanutten up the Luray Valley. Although Jackson knew that the dirt roads in that valley must now be quagmires and that the heavy rain would hamper the Federals forced to struggle over muddy roads and across swollen creeks, far more than it would his own men marching down the macadamized Valley Turnpike, still, there was the danger that Shields might get behind him by crossing the New Market Gap in the Massanutten or by continuing south and then swinging around the southern end of the mountain. To forestall such an action, he sent a strong detachment of Ashby's cavalry under twenty-four-year-old Captain Samuel B. Coyner across the New Market Gap to burn the bridges across the South Fork of the Shenandoah at White House and Columbia.

Soon after, he ordered the bridge at Conrad's Store (today Elkton) to be destroyed, leaving standing only the bridge across the North River (the principal tributary of the South Fork) at Port Republic, fifteen miles farther south. Apparently as an afterthought, recollecting the unreliability of Ashby's horsemen, he dispatched Crutchfield to make sure the work was properly done. It was. In a letter to his sister Captain Coyner wrote that "never did a poor being work harder for the preservation of [Jackson's] army than I did. Through wind and rain, the darkness and hot sun, through mud and dust, we went and conquered."

These were exceedingly shrewd moves on Jackson's part, for with all the rivers in the Valley in flood, destroying the bridges in the Luray Valley would confine Shields to the east side of the South Fork unless and until he could find some way to cross by boat or build new bridges, and there was scarcely time for that.

The next day Shields's thoughts turned in the same direction, but he believed Jackson would act as he had after the Battle of McDowell and hole up in the Blue Ridge. To prevent him from reaching Swift Run Gap, he dispatched a flying column of cavalry, artillery without caissons, and infantry without baggage all under the command of Colonel Samuel Sprigg Carroll, a West Pointer, class of 1856, to burn the bridge at Conrad's Store. Shields stressed the need for speed, telling Carroll that "Jackson must be overtaken. The burning of the bridge will effect it." And he added, "You will earn your star when you do all this." But Carroll did not here earn his brigadier general's star, for Ashby's men had done his work for him—and more.

From Mount Jackson on 2 June Jackson wrote to Anna to tell her what had happened: "I am again retiring before the enemy. They endeavored to get in my rear by moving on both flanks of my gallant army, but our God has been my guide and saved me from their grasp. You must not expect long letters from me in such busy times as these, but always believe that your husband never forgets his little darling."

That morning McDowell finally sent eight hundred cavalry under Brigadier General George D. Bayard, a battalion of the famous Pennsylvania Bucktails,[2] and four guns to Strasburg. Frémont, too, finally reached the turnpike, and the Federals vigorously marched south, following the trail of detritus that always lies in the wake of a retreating army. Bayard's force was Shields's only contribution to Frémont's army, but it was a well-led, first-rate combat unit, and Bayard, a twenty-six-year-old West Pointer who had seen active service in the West, was a fine cavalry commander.

About ten o'clock in the morning, near Woodstock, the Federal cavalry caught up with Jackson's rear guard and threw some well-directed artillery shells into it, forcing both Ashby and Steuart to pull back. In the ensuing confusion the 42nd Virginia fired into its own horsemen, wounding several and stampeding the horses.

Both Mumford and Flournoy blamed Steuart for this unfortunate affair, and they called on Ewell to ask that all the cavalry be placed under Ashby, who, Jackson's objections notwithstanding, had just been promoted brigadier general. Ewell discussed their request with Jackson, who recognized the necessity for the change. Steuart was given a brigade of infantry in Ewell's division, and Ashby, with Jackson's approval, took command of all the cavalry, which now constituted the bulk of Jackson's rear guard.

Jackson strove mightily to keep order in his retreating army, but his men were tired, nerves were taut, and units became confused. Coming upon one tangled mass of wagons, horses, and men, Jackson, "with clouded brow and closed lips" (according to Douglas), rode up to a

---

2. The Pennsylvania Bucktails (officially the 13th Pennsylvania Reserves) were recruited from lumbermen and woodsmen who were proven sharpshooters. Each prospective recruit had to bring with him the tail of a buck he had shot, and it was worn on the hat of each soldier. With Bayard there were four companies under Lieutenant Colonel Thomas Leiper Kane, an ardent abolitionist who had organized the regiment.

brigade commander, whose command was split into two or three segments. "Colonel, why do you not get your brigade together, and keep it together and move on?" he demanded fiercely.

"It's impossible, General. I can't do it."

"Don't say it's impossible," snapped Jackson. "Turn your command over to the next officer. If he can't do it, I'll find someone who can, if I have to take him from the ranks."

That night Colonel John Mercer Patton, Jr.,[3] commanding the brigade which Campbell had led before he was wounded at Winchester, reported to Jackson, staying at the home of a Mr. Israel Allen, on the hard fighting the rear guard had faced. Not yet understanding his commanding general, Patton mentioned one party of Federals he regretted had been killed. Jackson listened to his entire report and then asked, "Colonel, why do you say that you saw those Federal soldiers fall with regret?"

Patton, taken aback, explained that the officers and men had fought so bravely and with such vigor that he felt a natural sympathy with them, wishing that such brave men might survive the fight. Jackson shook his head. "No, shoot them all," he said. "I do not wish them to be brave." This was not the first nor was it to be the last time that Jackson abjured sentimentality on the battlefield.

At Mount Jackson, where a major tributary adds its water to the North Fork of the Shenandoah, the river was spanned by an important bridge. The following day, 3 June, Jackson's army crossed it after it had been carefully prepared for demolition: Dry, split wood was stuffed in the roof, and kindling was spread on the floor around several kegs of gunpowder. When the last limping Confederate made his weary way across, it went up in flames. Those who had straggled too far behind were left to be captured or make their own way over.

Jackson now at last gave his men a brief rest. Captain Edmondson of the 27th Virginia wrote to his wife from Rude's Hill that "the march was so heavy that I am satisfied that the Brigade has lost at least 1,000 men broken down, left on the way and captured. . . . This trip has broken me down completely and at one time I thought I could go no farther . . . but fortunately I made the trip and am here but in a state of exhaustion, well otherwise however."

The respite was a short one. Frémont, who had a pontoon train,

---

3. John M. Patton, Jr., a thirty-six-year-old VMI graduate and lawyer, was the brother of General George Patton's grandfather. He resigned soon after the Valley campaign (8 August 1862) with "impaired health . . . stomach, bowels & liver."

quickly threw a bridge of boats across the river. He had begun passing his cavalry to the other side when on the night of 4 June a torrential rain caused the river to rise ten feet in a mere four hours, forcing him to cut loose the southern end of his bridge to keep it from being broken up or swept downstream. Jackson's luck held.

The next day (5 June) Jackson dispatched Hotchkiss to establish a signal station on the southernmost peak of the Massanutten, where he could watch both Frémont and Shields. The Valley Army marched to Harrisonburg, where Jackson turned it off the turnpike and marched east. The sick and wounded, his captured Federal loot, and the excess baggage all were sent farther south, crossing the intervening rivers in crude but efficient boats designed by Confederate engineers. Jackson was left with a trimmed-down, tough, unencumbered fighting force.

The question arises: Why did Jackson not turn and mop up Frémont's cavalry, stranded by the failure of the pontoon bridge? Why, for that matter, did he not turn on Frémont and crush him? The Federal troops were in no better physical condition than his own, and there were fewer of them. Union supply lines were overextended, and although Frémont had been able, thanks to Bayard and some select regiments and batteries, to maintain a close pursuit and harass Jackson's rear guard, he was in no condition or position to fight a major engagement, particularly when his army was divided by an unbridgeable river. Curiously, these questions seem not to have been asked, but in light of the events of the next three days, they are questions deserving consideration.

Cross Keys and Port Republic

By 5 June Jackson, like his officers and men, had had an exhausting and tense week, but Jackson handled tension and fatigue with remarkable aplomb. Through sheer strength of will he was able to keep tired muscles moving. Since his days at West Point he had counted on such determination and perseverance to sustain him, whether on the battlefields of Mexico, in the classrooms of VMI, or through the recent long, hard marches in the Valley of Virginia. His will had seen him through, and he had forced his will upon reluctant, partly trained young soldiers. He could, it seemed, go without food, endure any hardship, or suffer any pain. There was, however, one chink in his armor of fortitude: He needed more sleep than most and could not function normally if deprived of it for long. This was not a matter he could in any way control. He could not fight biology.

From 22 May until 30 May he had had little sleep, but apparently just enough. On the thirtieth, on the train with Boteler, he had had an interrupted nap. That evening he had sat up late writing dispatches and talking; at 3:00 A.M. he was conferring with Hotchkiss. He could have had little sleep that night. Later the next day (31 May) he marched to Strasburg and that evening spent "some time" praying and talking to Taylor.

The following day he had spent observing the skirmishing of his rear guard and that night, riding through a heavy storm, had arrived at Woodstock "late," according to Hotchkiss. He had eaten a meal about midnight and set out again soon after. The next day was spent on a march that came under heavy rains in the afternoon. That night (2–3 June) a false alarm had sent him riding six miles more in the rain. He could have had little sleep, for he was again on the march "very early," which for Jackson could mean two or three o'clock in the morning.

On 3 June he had ridden to Rude's Hill, and his staff officers then remarked on his physical condition. Lieutenant Douglas noted that he had "lost much sleep." He must at this point have been almost at the limit of his ability to keep awake, and he retired early, but he got little sleep, for he was washed out of his tent by a rising creek during the night. Hotchkiss wrote in his diary: "The Gen. was almost afloat from the heavy rainfall." Douglas thought he appeared "wet and wearied" in the morning, as indeed, he must have been.

After a day of marching on the fourth, he had sat up until at least 10:00 P.M., studying maps and talking with Hotchkiss. Although on the next day Jackson ought to have turned on Frémont and demolished him, it seems unlikely that he was capable of successfully conducting a battle. His nerves must have been on the ragged edge, and he was probably incapable of determining what he should do other than to continue the retreat.

The day was spent marching through the rain. Jackson appears to have had some sleep that night, although Hotchkiss reported that he conferred with him until "quite late." The following day, 6 June, he turned his army off the macadamized turnpike onto roads Hotchkiss characterized as "very, very muddy" toward Port Republic, whose bridge, the only one over the swollen North River, higher than it had been for twenty years, ought to have been very much in his mind. Nevertheless, having reached it, he took few precautions to protect it, a failure that nearly proved fatal, for both himself and his army. The bridge was certainly on the mind of Shields, who knew that if he could secure it, Jackson would be unable to reach the safety of the Blue Ridge, would be unable to fall back upon supports east of the mountains, and could be crushed between Frémont and himself.

Biographers have credited Jackson with shrewd planning for the battles of 8 and 9 June, but the facts, as reported by participants in letters and diaries and as revealed in the official records, tell a different story. In a dispatch from Port Republic on 6 June to General Joseph Johnston, who a week earlier (31 May) had been wounded at the Battle of Seven Pines, Jackson wrote:

General: My present position is such that if Shields forms a junction with Frémont by moving west he will have to do so by marching within 2 miles of my advanced brigade or else he must return to New Market. Should my command be required at Richmond I can be at Mechum's Depot, on the Central Railroad, the second day's march, and part of the command can reach there the first day, as the distance is 25 miles. At present I do not see that I can do much more than rest my command and devote its time to drilling. My advance brigade is about 7 miles this side of Harrisonburg. If Shields crosses the Blue Ridge shall my entire command, or any part of it, move correspondingly?

While I rejoice at your success, yet I am grieved to hear that you are wounded.

> Very respectfully, yours,
> T. J. Jackson
> Major-General

It is obvious that Jackson did not expect to fight a battle within the next two days. The dispatch reveals a curious view of the military situation. His statement that he could now do nothing more than rest or drill his men seems curious indeed. To do this in safety, he would have had either to take them over the Blue Ridge by way of nearby Brown's Gap or to defeat one or both of the armies pursuing him. His men certainly needed time to rest, but how did Jackson reason that they could afford such time at this juncture? Frémont's cavalry was biting the heels of his rear guard, and Shields had now reached Conrad's Store, only a day's march from Port Republic, facts which were known or available to him. His judgment was indeed badly clouded.

Frémont entered Harrisonburg on the sixth, and on this day eight hundred Federal cavalry fell upon the Confederate rear guard, principally the 2nd and 7th Virginia Cavalry. The attack was repulsed, and sixty-four Federal cavalrymen were captured.

In Port Republic Jackson was interrogating a Federal officer taken prisoner[1] when he was interrupted about nine o'clock by doleful tid-

---

1. The prisoner was the colorful Colonel "Sir" Percy Wyndham, commander of the 1st New Jersey Cavalry. Very little of what he gave out about himself is credible, but what does seem sure is that he fought under Garibaldi in Italy, where Major Rob Wheat knew him, and he was awarded a medal of the Military Order of Savoy, a medal of five classes with the highest ranking as *cavaliere*. Equating this with a British knighthood, he thereafter styled himself "Sir Percy." After the American Civil War he

ings: Turner Ashby had been killed in a skirmish. Stories of how Ashby met his death are inconsistent, but Dr. Hunter McGuire, who carefully examined Ashby's wounds after his death, was convinced "beyond all question" that he was killed by Confederate infantry, an opinion not made known at the time.

Jackson returned to his room to pace the floor. A few hours later, when Ashby's body was carried to the house of a Mr. Frank Kemper, Jackson sat a long time alone beside it. There can be no doubt that Ashby's death profoundly affected him; it was the most personal loss he had sustained, for as yet no other important commander in his army had been killed, and no officer on his staff had even been wounded. In his formal report on the Valley campaign, Jackson, although rarely given to praising subordinates, said of the dead Ashby that "as a partisan officer I never knew his superior; his daring was proverbial; his powers of endurance almost incredible; his tone of character heroic; and his sagacity almost intuitive in divining the purposes and movements of the enemy."

He would indeed be missed. For all his weaknesses in Jackson's eyes as a drillmaster and disciplinarian, Ashby had been invaluable. No cavalry officer was better at scouting in front or commanding a rear guard. His death was a heavy blow to Jackson's army, which was about to fight its last battles in the Valley of Virginia.

It is probable that added to his woes on this day, Jackson received the letter written to him on 4 June by President Davis. Boteler had eloquently pleaded Jackson's need for reinforcements, but Davis, in a personal reply, after congratulating him on his "brilliant campaign," wrote: "Were it practicable to send you re-enforcements it should be done . . . but it is on your skill and daring that reliance is placed. The army under your command encourages us to hope for all that men can

---

is said to have married a wealthy widow in India, where he founded a comic newspaper; became an impresario of an opera company in Calcutta; and was appointed commander-in-chief of the Burmese Army. He died, it is said, in a balloon accident in Rangoon.

Lieutenant Douglas, who escorted him to Jackson's headquarters in Port Republic, said of him: "He was not an attractive-looking warrior and looked like what he was, a soldier of fortune."

There was, incidentally, a real Sir Percy Wyndham, about the same age, who was the third son of Lord Leconfield. A far less flamboyant figure, he served briefly as a subaltern in the Coldstream Guards and from 1860 to 1865 was a Conservative Member of Parliament for West Cumberland and lived quietly at 44 Belgrave Square.

achieve." Considering the threat to the Confederate capital, it is hardly surprising that there was a reluctance in Richmond to provide additional brigades to the Valley Army, but it must have been a blow to Jackson's ambitions.

The land around Port Republic, at the southern end of the Massanutten, was familiar territory to Jackson; it was an area he knew intimately. He also knew, with some degree of accuracy, the location of Shields and Frémont. In view of this, his dispositions on 7 June seem incredible, to be explained only by the fact that they were made by a man whose mind had been numbed out of all reason by lack of sleep.

Port Republic sits on a narrow tongue of land which divides the South River and the North River, both of which flow generally north and northeast. They join at the northeast end of the town to form the beginning of the South Fork of the Shenandoah. The South River was fordable, at least by cavalry, at two places: a lower ford at the northeast end of town and an upper ford about a half mile upstream. The North River could be crossed only by boat or by the one remaining bridge between Waynesboro and Front Royal. North of the town, across the North River, the land is rolling country, almost any fold of which could conceal a brigade or two, and along the northwestern shore of the South Fork just below the town, high banks dominate the flat bottomland, only about two miles wide, lying between the South Fork of the Shenandoah and the spurs of the Blue Ridge Mountains.

Three miles north of Port Republic, near the tiny hamlet of Cross Keys, General Elzey pointed out an excellent defensive position on a ridge overlooking a small stream called Mill Creek. Jackson wisely put Ewell in charge of this position with three brigades and five batteries, about five thousand men in all. Later Jackson increased this force to about eighty-five hundred by adding Taylor's brigade and part of Campbell's old brigade, now under John Patton.[2] "Let the Federals get very close before your infantry fire," Jackson advised Ewell. "They won't stand long." Ewell's dispositions, facing the advancing Frémont, were excellent, and he could be counted on to do what needed doing if attacked.

At Port Republic, however, Jackson's arrangements could scarcely have been worse. All his combatant arms were left on the north side of the bridge over the unfordable North River while he established his

---

2. Colonel John Campbell, wounded at Winchester, did not return to the Valley Army but resigned in a huff on 16 October, when he was not promoted to brigadier general and given command of his old brigade.

headquarters and parked his entire wagon train on the south side. He chose for his headquarters Madison Hall, the home of Dr. George W. Kemper, Sr., located at the west corner of the town, where he had stayed on 25 April, just before the Battle of McDowell. The road beside the house ran southwest to Staunton, and it was along this road, just outside the town proper, that the wagon train was parked, looking trim under new white canvas covers (probably captured at Front Royal or Winchester). It contained the food, ammunition, and all the stores and tools and gear and impedimenta necessary for an army to march. Without such a train, no army could long sustain itself in the field.

Jackson's headquarters and wagon train were separated from Shields's division in the Luray Valley by a mere day's march and the fordable South River, guarded only by a picket of three officers and twenty-seven men of the 2nd Virginia under Captain Samuel J. C. Moore at the upper ford and a company of cavalry under Captain Emanuel Sipes at the lower ford. Another cavalry company was scattered as pickets along the river. This handful of cavalrymen and a small infantry guard provided the only protection for the vital bridge.

A battery of artillery under Captain James M. Carrington had just joined the Valley Army, the men dressed in blue uniforms. On this Sunday morning it was beside the ordnance wagons, stocking its caissons and limbers with ammunition, and was thus the only Confederate artillery south of the North River. Carrington and his men had not yet been blooded, and their first fight was to be significant indeed.

Between Jackson's headquarters and Shields's Union division there were no more than two hundred Confederate soldiers. Had Ashby been alive, he doubtless would have provided a better screen east of the South Fork, but Ashby was dead now, and Jackson was about to receive a sharp lesson on how much he had depended upon his former cavalry commander.

Although it is not known for certain, it would appear that on the night of 7 June Jackson may have had almost a full night's sleep. The time he went to bed is unknown; he was up at seven o'clock, which was late for him. It was a bright and beautiful Sunday; Major Dabney asked if he expected any action that day, and Jackson replied, "No, you know I always try to keep the Sabbath if the enemy will let me," so Dabney prepared to deliver one of his powerful sermons. It was at about this time that Jackson received a message from Captain Sipes that Federal cavalry had been sighted only two miles away, near Lewiston, where Jackson had spent the night in April while his men were struggling through the mud from Swift Run Gap toward Port Republic. Not knowing what Sipes's information might portend, he sent orders to Ewell not to advance his pickets and to defer action until the situation east of the South Fork became clearer.

Jackson and his staff were standing in the Kemper yard in front of the house waiting for their horses to be brought around when an excited trooper galloped up and gasped out that Union cavalry and artillery had crossed the lower ford of South River and were in Port Republic. "Go back and fight them," said Jackson tersely. He and his staff strode to the southwest end of the main street, and there, not two hundred yards away, they plainly saw Federal troopers. Almost simultaneously, firing broke out in the town. The company of cavalry guarding the bridge fled "in disgraceful order," Jackson later reported. When his horse was brought to him, he swung into the saddle and dashed down the main street for the bridge.

Private R. S. Fortson of Company F, 9th Louisiana, had reported sick that morning, and he and others on sick call had been ferried across the North River just upstream of the town. Most of the sick went to the field hospital, which was with the wagon train, but Fortson and another comrade, perhaps not as sick as they had made themselves out to be, turned toward the town. There, to their astonishment, they found themselves looking into the muzzle of a Federal gun less than a hundred yards away. As they turned to flee, they saw General Jackson, wearing his old blue coat, gallop at full speed down the street, dash through the Federal cavalry, and cross the bridge as bullets began to fly around him. It was the most narrow escape from capture Jackson ever experienced. He was doubtless saved by the color of his coat. Some of his staff, including Pendleton and Douglas, who had galloped after him, also escaped, but Colonel Stapleton Crutchfield and Lieutenant Edward Willis, an aide, still abed when the action began, were too slow and were captured.

Crutchfield surrendered his sword to Colonel Samuel Sprigg Carroll, who, although in command of a brigade in Shields's division, was personally leading this raiding party, consisting of only about a hundred dragoons and two guns. Shields later claimed that he had been told that the bridge at Port Republic had already been destroyed and then blamed Carroll for not destroying it when he had a chance, but Shields was conveniently forgetful, for on 4 June, only four days earlier, he had ordered Carroll to "go forward at once with cavalry and guns to save the bridge at Port Republic." Carroll had marched by night, thus eluding the eyes of the lookout Hotchkiss had posted at the southern end of the Massanutten range, and he was now in Port Republic, where thanks to Jackson's injudicious dispositions, he was in a position to wreak havoc.

In command of the bridge he quickly posted a gun to protect it. He did not yet know the full extent of his prize, but Crutchfield, his prisoner, was beside him when a trooper came pounding up, shouting, "Colonel, you have just got Jackson's whole wagon train!"

"Where?" asked Carroll.

"Just up yonder, in full sight of that old farm—hundreds of wagons and no troops."

Carroll turned to Crutchfield. "Is that so, Colonel?"

"You must find that out for yourself," Crutchfield answered, but his words were a confirmation of the truth.

Carroll immediately directed a captain to take a troop of cavalry and capture the wagon train "in short order." Troopers formed up on the main street and set off at a slow trot in the direction of Dr. Kemper's house.

Meanwhile, the Reverend Major Dabney, who had dashed to the wagon train, was bringing up a gun and cannoneers from Carrington's battery. Captain Moore, in charge of the picket at the upper ford, had heard the firing and came running with his men toward the Kemper house. It was Moore's infantrymen who gave the Union cavalry its first shock with a well-directed volley. The cavalry retreated in some confusion but quickly rallied and came on again, but by this time Dabney had arrived at the Kemper house with one of Carrington's guns, and the Federal troopers received its discharge and retreated back to the bridge. Dabney and Moore had saved Jackson's wagon train, which was now beating a hasty retreat on the road to Staunton.

Across the North River, in Winder's brigade, McHenry Howard was unpacking a bag when he heard the first shot. He at once started repacking. Asked by another officer what he was doing, he replied, "Well, it's Sunday and you heard that shot." By this time Jackson's men thought he *preferred* to fight on Sunday.

Captain Henry Clinton Wood of the 37th Virginia, in the village on an errand that morning, spotted Carroll's cavalry entering the town. Crossing the bridge, he dashed to his regiment and breathlessly reported what he had seen to Colonel Fulkerson, who immediately assembled his men and moved on the double toward the town. On the way he encountered Jackson, galloping up from the bridge. Jackson pulled up, turned his horse, and, swinging his cap, ordered Fulkerson: "Charge right through, Colonel! Charge right through!"

Wheeling his horse, Jackson galloped on to call up the brigades of

Winder, Taliaferro, and Taylor, which, together with Poague's battery, drove the Union cavalry out of town. These had been feverish minutes, but Taliaferro later wrote that Jackson "was not excited—he never was, and never, under any circumstances that I am aware of, lost his presence of mind or yielded to panicky influences." Dabney, confirming this, said of him that "excitement roused his powers, danger only invigorated and steadied them."

When supports had been summoned, Jackson turned back toward the bridge. Seeing a Federal gun, he ordered Poague to open fire on it, but Poague, remembering that Carrington's gunners also wore blue, called out that he feared these were Carrington's men. Jackson simply rode forward a few paces and shouted to the cannoneers, "Bring that gun up here!" When there was no reply, he rose in his stirrups and bellowed, "Bring that gun up here, I say!"

In response the Federal artillerymen began to shift the trail of their gun to bring it to bear on Poague's battery. "Let 'em have it!" snapped Jackson. One of Poague's guns "sent a shot right among them," Poague remembered, "so disconcerting them that theirs in reply went far above us."

Fulkerson and his 37th Virginia soon secured the bridge, captured the Federal guns, and freed Crutchfield. (Young Willis escaped later.) Carroll's men were driven back across the South River, falling back on Erastus Tyler's brigade coming up on the eastern side of the South Fork of the Shenandoah. By this time the high ground across the South Fork was dominated by Jackson's artillery. Carroll suffered nine dead and thirty-nine wounded, nearly half of his detachment.

Sam Carroll, twenty-nine years old, had just missed becoming his country's greatest hero of the war. He had been graduated from West Point in 1856, ranking forty-fourth in a class of forty-nine. Although he eventually became a major general, his name never became the household word his missed opportunity held out to him. In spite of his orders, he ought to have burned the bridge the moment he had the opportunity. Even so, he came within an ace of capturing Jackson, along with his staff and his wagon train. Had he done so, Ewell's escape route across the Blue Ridge would have been cut off, and without food or ammunition, he would have found it well-nigh impossible to save the Valley Army. Instead of glory and promotion, the unlucky Carroll was faced with the full wrath of Shields, who lambasted him for his failure.

Meanwhile, near the hamlet of Cross Keys Frémont had stumbled against Ewell's excellent position on the ridge behind Mill Creek and had drawn up his brigades in order of battle with the fine brigades of

Milroy and Schenck on his right and Blenker's wretched division on his left; Cluseret's brigade was placed in the middle astride the road to Port Republic. The Federal cavalry under Bayard, which had done such good work in harassing Jackson's rear guard, was now about worn out, and many of its horses needed shoes, so it had been left at Harrisonburg—just when it was most needed.

Without cavalry scouts, Frémont had been forced to advance cautiously over one low ridge at a time, never knowing what the next might bring. When he made contact with Ewell, he assumed that he was facing the entire Valley Army and that he was outnumbered. In fact, he outnumbered Ewell by about ten to eleven thousand to Ewell's six thousand to eighty-five hundred. The feisty Milroy was ready to fight, and as soon as a line of battle was formed, he moved forward, only to be halted by one of Frémont's European aides with orders to pull back. Disgusted, Milroy later wrote to his wife: "I was never so astonished or thunderstruck in my life. I could not believe what the dutchman [*sic*] said and made him repeat it three times. . . ."

It was true. Frémont, incredibly, for no reason that makes military sense, had decided to attack with Blenker's division. The main thrust was to be given by the brigade of thirty-seven-year-old Brigadier General Julius Stahel upon the Confederate right, held by Isaac R. Trimble, the vigorous and aggressive sixty-year-old brigadier general. Stahel's attack was easily repulsed, and Elzey's brigade, which had worked its way unseen onto the Federal left flank, poured in a withering fire. Trimble then charged and drove the Federals back, returning late in the afternoon to his original position on the ridge.

After the failure of Stahel's attack, Frémont lapsed into an artillery duel which accomplished nothing. Trimble, flushed with victory, was eager to launch a night attack, but Ewell would not agree to it. Undiscouraged, Trimble carried his case to Jackson, who allowed Ewell's decision to stand.

Jackson's exact movements after about ten o'clock that morning are uncertain. Sometime during the day he turned to Dabney and exclaimed, "Major, wouldn't it be a blessed thing if God would give us a glorious victory today?" He took no part in the fighting at Cross Keys, and although Dabney says that he rode to the field "shortly after mid-day . . . and calmly examined the progress of the struggle," he gave no orders respecting the action. It was a battle fought and won by Ewell, although he generously gave full credit for the victory to Trimble, telling Mumford the next day: "They call it mine, but Trimble won the fight, and I believe now if I had followed his views we would have destroyed Frémont's army." Federal casualties were 684, including 114 killed; the Confederates lost 228, of whom 41 were killed.

Ewell had not requested reinforcements, but Jackson sent him the brigades of Taylor and Patton. When a staff officer opined that Shields might bring up his division and attack his weakened rear while the battle was being fought at Cross Keys, Jackson pointed to his guns on the high banks overlooking the bottomland across the South Fork and said, "No sir! No! He cannot do it. I should tear him to pieces!"

At some point during the day or in the early evening Jackson made a remarkable, not to say rash, decision. He had several alternatives. Given the poor quality of half the troops in Frémont's army and Frémont's abominable generalship, Jackson could have concentrated his entire force at Cross Keys with a good chance of destroying him. East of the South Fork, Shields was pushing forward his splendid division as fast as possible over the miserable roads in the Luray Valley, but his main force had only reached Conrad's Store, and he had failed to establish meaningful communication with Frémont; only two advanced brigades under Brigadier General E. B. Tyler were within striking distance. Jackson might have drawn all of his force east of the South Fork, burned the bridge at Port Republic, and demolished Tyler. He might even have carefully withdrawn by way of Brown's Gap into the safety of the Blue Ridge Mountains and fought no more in the Valley. Instead, he tried to defeat both Tyler and Frémont.

It is doubtful that Jackson had more than a few hours' sleep that night. Leaving only Trimble and Patton to face Frémont, he ordered Ewell to feed and resupply his units and then send his wagons to Brown's Gap, after which he was to bring the bulk of his force to Port Republic. Colonel Patton was given precise instructions in person: "I wish you to throw out all your men if necessary as skirmishers, and to make a great show, so as to cause the enemy to think the whole army is behind you. Hold your position as well as you can, then fall back when obliged; take a new position; hold it in the same way; and I will be back to join you in the morning."

It was a risky and formidable assignment, and Patton was understandably nervous. His "brigade" consisted of only about eight hundred men. (The 21st Virginia, normally attached to it, had been sent to escort south the prisoners taken at Front Royal and Winchester.) How long, he asked, was he expected to hold off Frémont's army? "By the blessing of Providence, I hope to be back by ten o'clock," Jackson assured him.

Taliaferro's brigade was ordered to protect the guns on the west bank of the South Fork. Trimble was to retreat slowly to Port Republic and, when, at last, every Confederate had crossed the bridge, to burn it.

Having made these arrangements, Jackson then devoted his attention to the problem of moving the remainder of his army across the South River. Under his supervision, a bridge was hastily constructed by pulling wagons into the water and covering them with planks found at a nearby sawmill. It was wide enough for men to cross four abreast, but it had a fatal flaw, not at first apparent. At the deepest part of the river the boards on the wagons did not properly join. It was necessary for those crossing to jump down about two feet, and the impact began to dislocate the boards.

At three forty-five in the morning Winder received orders to bring his brigade to Port Republic and to cross over the improvised bridge. Taylor was ordered to follow Winder. Just before dawn Jackson returned to Dr. Kemper's house and immediately fell asleep.

Colonel John Imboden, whose 1st Virginia Partisan Rangers had been stationed at Mount Crawford, just south of Harrisonburg, had received orders from Jackson written on the margin of a newspaper, summoning him and his unit to Port Republic, where his cavalry, four howitzers, and 12-pounder Parrott gun would be needed. When Imboden arrived to report, he found Jackson lying facedown on a bed, fully clothed, still wearing boots, sash, and sword. A low candle threw a dim light in the room. Imboden started to back out, but Jackson rolled over, sat up, and told him to come in.

"Were the men all up as you came through the camp?" Jackson asked.

"Yes, General, and cooking."

"That's right. We move at daybreak."

Jackson talked a bit about Ashby and his death, then instructed Imboden where to place his guns.

After Imboden left, Jackson apparently arose and rode with some of his staff to the makeshift bridge, where leading elements of Winder's Stonewall Brigade in crossing had already encountered trouble with the ill-fitting planks and some men had been thrown into the water. About five o'clock Jackson and Winder, on horseback, apparently unaware of the seriousness of the problem, forded the river. Dabney was left to hustle the infantry across.

About a mile and a half north of Port Republic the shots of skirmishers were heard. Federal Brigadier General Erastus Tyler had distributed his infantry along a road facing pancake-flat fields with wheat "chin high," anchoring his right on the South Fork and his left on a wooded spur of the Blue Ridge on which there was a coaling (a place where charcoal was made). Although it was a cleared space only about twenty feet above the flatland, it dominated the entire battlefield. Tyler had concentrated seven guns there with three regiments of infantry to protect them.

The coaling was located near Lewiston, and Jackson must have known of its existence, and he ought to have recognized its military importance. Had he not been in a daze from lack of sleep, he probably would have had this position strongly occupied on the seventh. It was too late now.

Winder at this time had only four of his five regiments, about eleven hundred men. Tyler, joined by Carroll, whose brigade was also present, now had some three thousand men at hand. He knew he would not be able to withstand an attack by Jackson's entire army, but he was admirably placed, and he hoped that the rest, or at least more, of Shields's division would come forward to support him.

Jackson, in foolish haste, did not wait for Taylor to come up with his Tigers; he did not even wait for all of Winder's brigade to appear on the field. Instead, he did the worst thing possible. He committed his regiments piecemeal. Pushing back Tyler's skirmishers, he attacked with inferior numbers across open fields in full view of Tyler's infantry, which was shielded by ditches and fences and was under the protecting guns at the coaling. The Confederates were met by a withering fire, musketry and artillery. The 1st, 7th, and 27th Virginia and Poague's battery were forced to turn tail.

Jackson ordered Winder to attack the coaling, and Winder directed the 2nd Virginia, under thirty-three-year-old James Walkinshaw Allen, a former VMI professor, and Carpenter's battery to swing to the right through the woods at the foot of the hills. Poague's battery was positioned in a wheat field to the left of the road with the 5th Virginia to protect it, and the 4th Virginia was put in the woods. Allen's men advanced in great disorder through thick underbrush and laurel thickets and were easily repulsed. Carpenter's guns were then dragged down the hill and went into battery beside Poague. But the two batteries could not withstand the fire from the coaling. Ned Moore, a gunner in Poague's battery, said: "More accurate shooting I was never subjected to."

Meanwhile, back at the makeshift bridge there was chaos. The men balked and would move across only in single file. Taylor's brigade was still struggling to cross when Jackson, impatient with the slow rate at which his regiments were arriving on the field, sent Crutchfield back to discover the cause. Winder was calling for reinforcements, and when Taylor's units finally did begin to arrive, they were at once thrown into the fray. The 7th Louisiana, the first regiment to appear, was hurried to the support of the hard-pressed 5th Virginia.

When Taylor himself arrived on the field, he found Jackson sitting his horse, his hand raised "as if in prayer."[3] "Delightful excitement!" he reported Jackson as saying, but this uncharacteristic remark, like many of Taylor's postwar recollections, is suspect. What is certain is that Jackson summoned Jed Hotchkiss and said tersely, "Take General Taylor around to take those batteries." Hotchkiss led the Louisianans on a wider sweeping course than Allen had taken.

Jackson by this time realized that he would be unable to finish off Tyler and go on to attack Frémont. Not only was he unable to defeat Tyler in time to do so, but it was now questionable whether he could defeat Tyler at all. So he sent couriers off with orders for Trimble, Patton, and Taliaferro to fall back on Port Republic and cross both rivers, after which Trimble was to burn the bridge over the North River.

The Confederates who had crossed the makeshift bridge and were being hurried forward encountered large numbers of bleeding walking wounded, some of whom called out as they limped along: "Hurry up! They are cutting us all to pieces!" Not every young soldier found such words inspiring. The sights of the battlefield did not help either. Sergeant (later Captain) Samuel D. Buck in the 13th Virginia stumbled across his first dead man, "a Federal with his head shot off by a cannon ball. It was a terrible sight. . . ."

While Hotchkiss led Taylor through the wooded mountain spur, Winder's brigade remained under a withering fire. Although two of Ewell's brigades had now joined the fight, ammunition was running low; Winder's line began to melt away, and there seemed to be no more reinforcements. The Federals, sensing the Confederate weakness and uncertainty, gave a cheer and charged.

3. Jackson's habit of raising his hand was often interpreted as a sign that he was praying, but Dr. McGuire thought not. His explanation (published in the *Richmond Medical Journal* [February 1866] was that after his wounding at Manassas Jackson had for so long kept his hand in a sling that "when the use of this was discarded, and the hand permitted to hang down, there was, of course, gravitation of blood towards it. . . . In consequence . . . the hand was sometimes swollen and painful, and to remedy this, he often held it above his head for some moments. He did this so frequently that it became a habit and was continued, especially when he was abstracted. . . . I don't believe he prayed much while fighting." But as noted, Jackson developed this habit while at West Point, long before he was wounded. (See footnote 3, page 30).

The Confederate line wavered, and men began to fall back; one of Poague's guns was captured. At this point Ewell came up with another brigade under Colonel William C. Scott, which he threw on the Federal flank. This delayed the Union advance, but the brigade took heavy losses and was pushed aside toward the Blue Ridge.

Chew's battery swung into action, and Corporal Neese later wrote: "The musketry from the front raged fearfully. . . . The shell from the battery on the coaling was ripping the ground open all around us, and the air was full of screaming fragments of exploding shell, and I thought I was a goner."

While Winder fought to save some order out of the growing chaos, Jackson rode about the field, shouting, "The Stonewall Brigade never retreats!" Such was the situation when John F. Neff arrived on the field with his 33rd Virginia. The twenty-eight-year-old colonel had been floundering about without instructions, uncertain as to what was expected of him, but "orders now came in abundance," he later said.

Three fresh regiments under Colonel Walker came up as Winder was striving manfully to hold his line together, but Jackson, realizing that the key to victory in this battle depended upon the capture of the Union guns at the coaling, sent Walker to help Taylor, whose men were struggling toward the guns through thick undergrowth.

When at last the Tigers crossed a ravine and sprang suddenly onto the coaling, they drove off the cannoneers and captured their guns, but the Federals, Tyler's rough fighters who had beaten Jackson at Kernstown and were sure they could do it again, quickly counterattacked, and there was fierce hand-to-hand fighting on the edge of the ravine with bayonets, bowie knives, clubbed muskets, and the ramrods of the cannoneers. Even the musicians, whose duties in battle were to carry off the wounded, joined in. Major Wheat, fearing that the Federals would recapture and carry off their guns, slit the throats of the artillery horses with his bowie knife.

Three times the Louisianans attacked before they drove off the Federals with a bayonet charge that piled dead and wounded of both sides around the wheels and trails of the guns. "It was a sickening sight," Sergeant Buck remembered, "with the horses dying and the blood of men and beast flowing almost a stream. Major Wheat was as bloody as a butcher. . . ."

This sanguinary little victory greatly relieved the pressure on Winder in the wheat fields below, but Taylor could see Union regiments forming up to attack him. "With colors advanced," he said, "like a solid wall [they] marched straight upon us. There seemed nothing left but to set our backs to the mountain and die hard."

At that moment Ewell came crashing through the woods with the survivors of the 44th and 55th Virginia. They were few in numbers—the 44th now numbered fewer than eighty men—but they were strong in spirit, and on their heels came Walker. The dead and the wounded were dragged out of the way of the captured guns, and they were turned to play upon their former owners. Ewell himself helped serve one of the guns. The Federals halted, faltered, and fell back. Below them, Taliaferro's brigade had finally cleared Port Republic and had arrived on the field. The tide of battle turned. As Shields was unable or unwilling to support Tyler and Carroll, they were forced to retreat. Jackson sent Mumford's cavalry in pursuit with Taliaferro's and Winder's infantry brigades behind them.

Couriers caught up with Jackson with news from Trimble: Frémont had been successfully deceived, and now all of the Valley Army was east of the South Fork; both the bridge over the North River and the makeshift bridge over the South River had been destroyed. Frémont was still back near Cross Keys.

Port Republic was certainly a hard-fought victory, made harder by poor Confederate generalship. Jackson had again been lucky, and he credited the victory to the Almighty, as well he might. When he encountered Ewell, he exclaimed: "General, he who does not see the hand of God in this is blind, sir, blind!"

Mumford's cavalry followed up the retreating Federals for eight miles. The Confederate infantry harried them for five, and together they raked in about 450 prisoners, 800 rifles, some wagons, and another Union cannon. As the weary men returned from their pursuit, many passed by a farmhouse which had been converted into a field hospital. Corporal Neese saw the surgeons at work, and as he passed a window, a bloody foot was tossed out.

The swollen North River, impassable now with the smoking embers of the Port Republic bridge sinking into its waters, confronted the dilatory Frémont when he finally arrived on the scene of the battle now ended. Nevertheless, he positioned his guns on the high banks west of the South Fork of the Shenandoah where Trimble's artillery had been in battery during the battle. Here he overlooked the battlefield where the dead, the wounded, and the prisoners were being collected by the Confederates. In his after-action report he boasted that "a parting salvo of carefully aimed rifled guns duly charged with shell hastened the departure of the rebels."

This last Federal shelling enraged the Confederates. Jackson declared that Frémont "opened his artillery upon our ambulances and parties engaged in the humane labors of attending our dead and wounded and the dead and wounded of the enemy." According to Dabney, all the Confederate wounded had been removed. Attention had just turned to the Union wounded, he said, when "this treacherous interruption occurred." The wounded Federals were left to lie in the rain, which had now begun to fall. Dabney surmised that "not a few of their dead, with some, perchance, of the mangled living, were devoured by swine before their burial!"

In Jackson's delayed after-action report (not written until 14 April 1863) he recorded the heaviest losses he had ever suffered: 16 officers and 117 enlisted men killed; 67 officers and 82 enlisted men wounded. In this report and elsewhere Jackson spoke of having fought Shields at Port Republic, but Shields was far from the battlefield.[4] Jackson was nearly defeated by a mere two Union brigades under Brigadier General Erastus Barnard Tyler, who was roundly berated by Shields for accepting battle against a known superior Confederate force. Had Shields quickly pushed forward to support Tyler or had Frémont pressed vigorously forward, Jackson's army could have been crushed, in what would have been a serious loss to the Confederacy, for Lee now badly needed it to defend Richmond.

Jackson had performed clumsily. As the great Civil War historian Douglas Southall Freeman said, "this was, on Jackson's part, a poorly managed battle." Even his admiring and loyal aide Henry Kyd Douglas later wrote: "The fact is, Jackson went into the fight impetuously and was disappointed." His men paid in blood the cost of his rashness. Robert G. Tanner, in his brilliant analysis of this campaign, wrote: "Jackson . . . plunged into an attack without insuring that his brigades were up or that he had sufficient batteries on hand to quell the Union artillery. Jackson swung into battle piecemeal, and his units were strewn over the field in jumbled fragments by the struggle's end. Port Republic can be described as an action wherein Stonewall displayed afresh an inability to handle his army as a single weapon."

Perhaps because he realized that he had not performed well, Jackson was in a foul mood. Late that night in a "dreary and chilling rain," he sent an officer to Taliaferro to ask if he had brought off all the captured artillery. Taliaferro reported that he had taken everything

---

4. Shields, on the other hand, always boasted of being the only Union general ever to have defeated Jackson—at Kernstown—but in bed with his wounds, he was not on that field either.

except one unserviceable caisson. Although the roads were wretched and Taliaferro's brigade was by this time ten miles from the battlefield, Jackson irritably ordered the caisson to be brought in before daylight if it took every horse in the command.

Major Harman, who had been ordered to collect the small arms left on the field, made the mistake of remarking in Jackson's hearing that many of them appeared to be Confederate weapons. Jackson flared up. Shields's men had arms similar to theirs; he would hear no more talk of Confederates abandoning their weapons, he said furiously. Swearing that he would not be spoken to in such a fashion, Harman again threatened to resign and stamped out. Once again Jackson was forced to apologize.

Ewell was summoned for a dressing down when Jackson learned that he had called on his men to spare one conspicuously brave Federal mounted on a white horse. "This is no ordinary war," he lectured him. "The brave and gallant Federal officers are the very kind that must be killed. Shoot the brave officers and the cowards will run away and take the men with them."

The Valley Army withdrew to the safety of Brown's Gap, and Jackson sent a telegram to Lee: "Yesterday God crowned our arms with success by repulsing attacks of Frémont and Shields at Port Republic." This was not quite accurate, of course, as Shields had been miles away from the battlefield and unaware that it was taking place.

A disappointed Lincoln called off both Shields and Frémont, and Jackson camped in the hills at the entrance to Brown's Gap until 12 June, when he came down to the area around Weyer's Cave and rested his men. There the gallant Winder asked for a short leave to attend to personal business, a request Jackson curtly, and in Winder's perception rudely, refused. Winder promptly submitted his resignation. Taylor, by his own account, acted as peacemaker because, he said, he liked Winder and "hoped to save him for the army." Bearding Jackson, he appealed to his "magnanimity," dwelling on "the rich harvest of glory he had reaped in his brilliant campaign. Observing him closely, I caught a glimpse of the man's inner nature. It was but a glimpse. The curtain closed, and he was absorbed in prayer. Yet in that moment I saw an ambition boundless as Cromwell's and as merciless. . . . [H]is ambition was vast, all-absorbing. . . . He loathed it, perhaps feared it; but he could not escape it. . . . He fought it with prayer, constant and earnest—Apollyon and Christian in ceaseless combat." Soon after, Jackson brought himself to call on Winder, and the matter was smoothed over.

Certainly Jackson's record in handling his senior subordinates was not good. Within six months he had brought court-martial charges against two brigadiers (Loring and Garnett) and two senior colonels (Conner and his former colleague, business partner, and friend Gilham). Other senior officers, including Ashby, Funston, Winder, and (twice) Harman, had been so provoked that they had threatened to resign. In addition, he had officially abused Taliaferro and insulted Elzey. No other general, North or South, had shown himself so abrasive and so clumsy in his personal relations with subordinates, and he never improved. But Jackson's days as an independent commander were now almost at an end. He himself was to become a direct subordinate of General Robert E. Lee, newly appointed to replace the wounded Johnston.

Seven Days:
From the Valley
to the Swamps

The Valley campaign was over. To most in the Confederacy it appeared to have been roses all the way. The battles of McDowell, Front Royal, Winchester, Cross Keys, Port Republic—all seemed equally brilliant Jackson victories in Southern eyes. Jackson was a hero, even to his own hard-driven men; those who had cursed him in January cheered him in June. Even before the campaign ended, newspapers throughout the South were singing his praises, and his exploits had become staple news items. He was "a true general," said the *Charleston Mercury* (29 May 1862), which predicted that he would shortly be "leading his unconquerable battalions through Maryland and Pennsylvania."

The South certainly needed some cheering news and a hero. The month of May had been almost as bad as April for the Confederacy. The CSS *Merrimack*, the Confederates' only ironclad, had been lost. Confederate troops had been forced to evacuate Norfolk, Virginia, and Pensacola, Florida. At the Battle of Seven Pines (Fair Oaks) the Confederates had been repulsed and General Joseph Johnston severely wounded. Insult was added to defeat when, just two days before the Battle of Port Republic, Union General Benjamin F. Butler hanged a Southern citizen, William B. Mumford, for tearing down the United States flag flying over the New Orleans Mint.

Lee now took command of the Confederate army in Virginia, but for the moment "Stonewall" Jackson looked like the only winner in the Confederacy. Union generals, like Southern editors, expected him to march north. On 12 June Frémont advised Washington that "Jackson is heavily reinforced and is advancing." A week later he telegraphed: "No doubt another immediate movement down the Valley is intended, with a force of 30,000 or more." And on 28 June, when Jackson was with Lee fighting against McClellan's forces before Richmond, Banks still maintained that "Jackson meditates an attack in the valley."

For a time Davis and Lee did indeed contemplate allowing Jackson again to drive his army down the Valley. On 5 June Lee, who on 1 June had replaced the severely wounded Johnston and now commanded the Army of Northern Virginia, wrote President Davis:

> After much reflection I think if it was possible to reinforce Jackson strongly, it would change the character of the war. This can only be done by the troops in Georgia, South Carolina & North Carolina. Jackson could in that event cross Maryland into Pennsylvania. It would call all the enemy from our Southern coast & liberate those states. If these states will give up their troops I think it can be done.

Five days later, after the battles of Cross Keys and Port Republic, he wrote again: "I propose for your consideration sending two good brigades from this army to re-enforce General Jackson. These, with the Georgia regiments now on the way, and [Alexander R.] Lawton's brigade . . . will make him strong enough to wipe out Frémont."

Although on 4 June Davis had informed Jackson that no reinforcements were available, Lee sent to Jackson in the Valley Brigadier General William Henry Chase Whiting (Jackson's brilliant mentor at West Point) with three brigades, about seven thousand men, including the Texas brigade led by Brigadier General John B. Hood as well as Whiting's own, now under Colonel Evander M. Law.

On 11 June Lee abruptly changed his mind about Jackson's mission and issued new orders:

> Your recent successes have been the cause of the liveliest joy in this army as well as in the country. The admiration excited by your skill and boldness has been constantly mingled with solicitude for your situation. . . . Leave your enfeebled troops to watch the country and guard the passes covered by your cavalry and artillery, and with your main body, including Ewell's division and Lawton's and Whiting's commands, move rapidly to Ashland by rail or otherwise . . . and sweep down between the Chickahominy and Pamunkey,

cutting up the enemy's communications, &c., while this army attacks General McClellan in front. He will thus, I think, be forced to come out of his intrenchments, where he is strongly posted on the Chickahominy, and apparently preparing to move by gradual approaches on Richmond. Keep me advised of your movements, and, if practicable, precede your troops, that we may confer and arrange for simultaneous attack.

Jackson did not answer Lee. He was maturing other plans. He wanted an army of forty thousand men with which to sweep down the east side of the Blue Ridge, then pour through a gap onto Banks's rear in the Valley and destroy him. The road north would then be open, and he could cross the Potomac at Williamsport and invade Maryland and Pennsylvania.

Again Jackson tried to bypass Lee by sending Boteler to lay his ideas before the secretary of war, now George Wythe Randolph. On the evening of 14 June Boteler called on Secretary Randolph, who told him to see Lee. It was late at night when Boteler met with Lee, who, although well aware that Jackson had appealed directly to Randolph, appeared to be unruffled. According to Boteler, he listened "with the kindly courtesy which so eminently characterized his intercourse with every one."

Lee listened, but he was now cool to Jackson's plan to invade the North. To President Davis he wrote: "The first object now is to defeat McClellan." Davis agreed.

On the sixteenth Lee informed Jackson that "the sooner you unite with this army the better," and Jackson set his troops in motion. He turned his army about and marched it south to Staunton, then east, over the Blue Ridge, a maneuver which not only confused the enemy but, since he never explained his movements, also confused his own officers. When Whiting arrived with his division in the Valley and reported to Jackson, he was ordered to move his command from Staunton north to Mount Crawford. Once he was there, Jackson immediately ordered him to march them back again. Any lingering amity Whiting may have held for his former protégé crumbled; exasperated, he stormed: "I believe Jackson hasn't any more sense than my horse." Fuming, he marched his men back to Staunton. When he then received orders from Jackson to leave the Valley and recross the Blue Ridge to Gordonsville, he exploded: "Didn't I tell you he was a fool, and doesn't this prove it? Why I just came through Gordonsville day before yesterday."

It has been widely believed by historians that the movement of Whiting's division to the Valley and back was a clever ruse on Lee's part to deceive the enemy. Although the maneuvers were simply the result of a change in Jackson's mission and not an attempt at deception, they so confused the Federals that Washington was convinced that Jackson was being reinforced in the Valley, and McClellan was denied the reinforcements he thought he needed.

The bulk of Jackson's army, now numbering about 18,500, began its movement eastward on the eighteenth toward Brown's Gap and Mechum's River Station, where trains awaited them. As usual, no one was told where they were going or why. Ewell, although second-in-command, was simply ordered to go to Charlottesville. Whiting's orders from Jackson to go to Gordonsville, like the orders to Ewell, simply pointed the direction Jackson wanted them to go; these senior generals, like the rest of the army, could only guess at their ultimate destination.

Jackson with some of his staff left the Valley by way of Rockfish Gap. It was dark when they reached the top of the Blue Ridge and saw all along the slopes the glowing campfires of Whiting's and Lawton's men. Hotchkiss, sent to locate the headquarters wagons, thought it "a very fine sight," although the wagons were nowhere to be found. After his unsuccessful search he reported to Jackson: "General, I fear we will not find our wagons tonight." He long remembered Jackson's earnest answer: "Never take counsel of your fears."

That night Jackson and Hotchkiss shared a room at the home of a Mr. James McCue, on the eastern slope of the mountain, and Hotchkiss was impressed by the length of Jackson's prayers. Before they went to sleep, Hotchkiss recited the speculations he had heard about the army's ultimate destination. Jackson, as close to wit as he ever came, asked, "Do any of them say I am going to Washington?"

The next day Jackson, in fine spirits, rode to Mechum's River Station with his staff. Here he called Dabney into one of the station's rooms, locked the door, and announced that he was off to Richmond to see Lee. After giving explicit instructions for continuing the march, he wrote out a series of precautions to observe and swore Dabney to secrecy. On the station platform he saw his trunk put on board and shook hands with Dabney. Then, turning to the rest of his astonished staff, he bade them farewell "as if he was off to Europe" and boarded the train for Charlottesville.

The young staff officers looked at one another as the train pulled away, and one blurted out, "What the devil is he up to now?" The answer has never been clear.

That night Ewell dined with Dabney and complained bitterly that "the General has gone off on the railroad without entrusting to me, his senior major general, any order, or any hint whither we are going. But Harman, his quartermaster, enjoys his full confidence, I suppose, for I hear that he is telling troops that we are going to Richmond to fight McClellan."

Dabney assured Ewell that Harman "has not heard a word more than others. If he thinks we are going to Richmond, it is only his surmise, which I suppose every intelligent private is making."

The weather was good, and the men waiting to board trains were in fine spirits. Fewer than two hundred railway cars, most of them freight, and only ten locomotives could be mustered on the Virginia Central, so the cavalry, the artillery horses, and the supply wagons marched. There were not enough cars for all of the infantry, but the trains shuttled back and forth day and night—except on Sunday. Jackson specified no trains were to run on that day. The infantry marched and rode by turns as far as Charlottesville, perched on roofs and clinging where they could. One observer thought they resembled a "cluster of bees."

The troops soon learned that they were not going to Richmond, for they were turned north toward Gordonsville. For the young officers on Jackson's staff—Douglas, Boswell, Pendleton, McGuire, and Crutchfield—the march through the central Virginia countryside took on a holiday spirit. "Seeking new Desdemonas at the close of every day," they never failed to find pretty faces, lively music, and plentiful food and drink. They were rather pleased that Dabney was too busy with his duties to be with them, for as Douglas said, "he was too old, and too reverend, and too unelastic to fit in such a crowd."

Also older and busier were Major Wells Hawks, Jackson's able commissary, and Major John Harman, his energetic quartermaster, who were trying to provide food and supplies for an army that did not know its destination. Among other requirements, Jackson asked for eighteen battle flags, and Harman wrote to his brother, in charge of Jackson's main supply depot at Staunton: "I want battle flags very much. Can you have some made? . . . Try and have the battle flags made, as the General wants them."[1]

Jackson rejoined his army at Gordonsville, where he heard a

---

1. Beauregard's idea for a battle flag proved popular. The still-familiar design—a blue cross bearing white stars on a red field— is today often erroneously regard as the national flag of the Confederacy.

rumor that a large Federal force was on the Rapidan River, only sixteen miles away. He delayed the march until a prominent local citizen, familiar with the countryside, scouted the area and reported seeing no Federals. He then resumed the march.

On the evening of 21 June Jackson arrived by train at Fredericks Hall, about fifty miles north northeast of Richmond in Louisa County, and he and Dabney spent the night at the home of Mr. Frederick Harris, where Whiting and Hood were also staying. He had not, it seems, seen Lee after all when he left Mechum's River Station, and in spite of the fact that Lee called a conference of his generals in Richmond for Monday, 23 June, Jackson appeared in no hurry to leave.

The next day was Sunday, and although his army was stretched out over roads and railroads back to the Blue Ridge and there was an urgent need to get it closed up and in a position to fight, Jackson halted it in place. That afternoon he attended a religious service in Hood's brigade. He had not hesitated to fight on Sundays, but he scrupled at traveling on a Sunday. To avoid that, he waited until one hour past midnight before starting out on horseback for a fifty-two-mile ride to Lee's headquarters. Major Dabney was left to get the troops moving a few hours hence, marching east, they knew not where. No instructions or information of any sort were left for Ewell, Whiting, Stuart, or any of his other generals.

Sunday evening Mrs. Harris had asked Jackson if he would take breakfast with the family, and he had told her courteously that he would if he could. When she came down in the morning, she was surprised to find him gone. Jim Lewis, a free black from Lexington who was Jackson's servant, told her jubilantly that he had left at one o'clock in the morning and must be "whippin'" the Yankees in the Valley again by now.

Jackson's movements remain mystifying. On the nineteenth he had left Mechum's River Station by train for Charlottesville. On the following day, instead of traveling on to Richmond to see Lee, as he easily could have and should have, he had gone to Gordonsville and on the twenty-first was at Fredericks Hall. After keeping the Sabbath on the twenty-second, he suddenly left in the first hours of the morning of the twenty-third on a long, wild ride on horseback. Why he chose to go to Lee's headquarters by horse instead of taking trains is also difficult to understand, particularly in view of the consequences.

Harman and one or two other men rode with Jackson, at least part of the way. It was necessary to change horses, the only delay Jackson tolerated. He pushed his companions and the horses relentlessly as they rode through the night and all through the morning. It was three o'clock in the afternoon of the twenty-third when Jackson swung out of the saddle at Lee's headquarters, a small house owned by a widow named Dabb on Nine Mile Road at High Meadows, just inside the eastern Confederate defenses of Richmond. Lee was busy, so Jackson waited. His friend and brother-in-law D. H. Hill arrived and saw him "leaning over the yard-paling, dusty, travel-worn, and apparently very tired," as he certainly must have been. The long ride itself was exhausting, but more than that, Jackson had not slept.

Hill and Jackson entered Lee's headquarters together. Food had been prepared, but Jackson took only a glass of milk. Presently they were joined by A. P. Hill and James Longstreet. All these senior commanders were to be dependent upon one another in the battles that lay ahead, and although they were acquainted, they knew little of one another's strengths and weaknesses in battle. All must have stared at Jackson, the hero of the Confederacy, covered with sweat and dust. Lee was almost an unknown, his great reputation not yet made. Longstreet had just earned laurels for his success at Seven Pines, but he, too, seemed to stand in Jackson's shadow. Even D. H. Hill, who thought he knew Jackson well, must have looked with new eyes at his friend, so recently the VMI professor of natural and experimental philosophy and now the toast of the South.

Lee, preparing for the first time to direct an attack upon McClellan, outlined his plans. A frontal attack against the well-defended Federal forces across the Chickahominy, which flowed southwesterly and bisected the Peninsula, would by itself be difficult. Lee's plan for getting at "these people" (as he always referred to Union forces) called for Jackson, with Stuart's cavalry on his left flank, to come in fast and hard in rear of the corps of thirty thousand men under Union General Fitz-John Porter holding the Union right flank.

On Jackson's right, at a place called Half Sink, would be a brigade from A. P. Hill's division under Brigadier General Lawrence O'Bryan Branch. South of Branch about five miles, west of Meadow Bridge, was to be the remainder of A. P. Hill's division. On the day of battle (not yet determined), when Jackson was to begin his move forward, he was to communicate with Branch, who in turn would notify A. P. Hill. Branch was then to cross the Chickahominy and wheel sharply south, proceeding down the left bank of the river with Jackson on his left. A. P. Hill would then attack at Meadow Bridge, putting Porter's corps under attack from two directions with Jackson and Stuart well in his rear.

After crossing the Chickahominy, A. P. Hill was to swing southeasterly, pass through Mechanicsville, and continue on, parallel to but somewhat east of the Chickahominy, coming in on the flank of the Federal forces opposite D. H. Hill and Longstreet, who would then attack across the Mechanicsville bridges. D. H. Hill, after crossing the river, was to move east, crossing the wake of A. P. Hill's division and going to the support of Jackson.

On the Confederate right flank were the divisions commanded by Major Generals Benjamin Huger and John Bankhead Magruder (Jackson's old battery commander in Mexico), about twenty-seven thousand men. To them Lee assigned merely a holding operation, but they faced McClellan's fifty thousand.

It seemed on the face of it a good plan, but it was complex. President Davis had expressed reservations, for there was a danger that while Lee was attacking the Federal right with the bulk of his forces, McClellan would come pounding in with a left hook and take Richmond. Lee recognized the risk but told Davis that he counted on Huger and Magruder to provide good delaying tactics and that his reading of the character of McClellan was such that he considered a strong attack by him in this area unlikely. Lee was always a risk taker; McClellan never.

The plan had other weaknesses not readily apparent. Timing was all important, and this made close liaison among the widely separated senior commanders vitally necessary, but Civil War staff work was unsophisticated and often uncoordinated. Communications would have to be carried by couriers, who would be forced to make their way over considerable distances in unfamiliar territory to seek men they did not know and whose locations would be shifting and uncertain.

Having outlined his battle plan, Lee left the room, leaving his four key generals to work out detailed procedures. This was a mistake. Jackson needed to know a great deal more than he did about the situation. All that Lee had talked about—the rivers, bridges, towns, swamps, the units, the enemy forces—was new to him, and he had never before commanded so many men or worked in coordination with other large units. After his fifty-two-mile ride and loss of a night's sleep he could not have been in the best physical and mental condition for making important judgments. That he ought to have traveled at least half of the distance on Sunday or taken a train soon became apparent.

The most important thing to be decided was the day of the battle, and only Jackson could determine when he would be ready to launch his attack. There are two versions of how that date was fixed: Longstreet's and D. H. Hill's. In neither version does Jackson exhibit good judgment.

According to Longstreet, when Jackson was asked when he would be ready, he named 24 June, little more than twenty-four hours away, but when Longstreet suggested he take another day, he readily agreed. According to D. H. Hill, when asked for a date, Jackson replied: "Daylight of the 26th." However the question was raised, the answer was clear: Jackson assured the two Hills and Longstreet that he would be in position to attack by the night of the twenty-fifth. A memorandum of understanding was drawn up which stated that he would begin his movement at "precisely 3 o'clock" on the morning of the twenty-sixth.

The conference of the generals broke up "about nightfall," probably shortly after seven o'clock. It is uncertain whether Jackson stayed for supper, but it is known that he did not sleep, for he mounted his horse and in a pouring rain rode all night, a distance of about forty miles, to Beaver Dam Station,[2] which he reached sometime the following morning. Whether Harman or others accompanied him is unknown. His leading troops had arrived here, but Dabney was not to be found. A middle-aged man who had led a sedentary life, Dabney was overwhelmed by the unaccustomed responsibilities Jackson had thrust upon him and was now sick in bed with an intestinal disorder. Jackson, however, was in no condition to pick up the reins of his command. He had passed the limits of his ability to stay awake. At the home of Henry Carter he picked up a book—incredibly, a novel—opened it, and fell asleep. It was there his staff found him. He was not, said Douglas, "a very refreshing or creditable sight. . . . His wet and muddy uniform was being dried by the fire and the appearance of his ponderous boots indicated that he might have been wading all night through mud and mire." It is not known how long he slept with the open book in his hands, but it must have been a short nap, for it did nothing to revive him.

On this morning of the twenty-fourth Jackson had less than forty-eight hours to get his men roughly thirty-five miles, allow them time to cook rations, rest, and get into position to attack. Had the weather cooperated, it might just possibly have been done, but certainly there was no time to be wasted, and energetic measures were needed if his army was to play its part in the coming battle. Unfortunately the troops

2. Beaver Dam Station, between Fredericks Hall and Ashland, was thirty miles from Beaver Dam Creek.

were now stretched out along fifteen miles of road, marching in the rain under deteriorating conditions. Streams were rising, bridges were out, and without accurate maps every crossroads presented leading elements and lagging units with problems.

No preparations had been made to overcome the difficulties the army now faced. Dabney blamed young and inexperienced officers who were unable to keep the units closed up and in order. He perhaps had the fun-loving young staff officers in mind when he spoke of the "indolence and carelessness of julep-drinking officers." The staff officers, notably young Douglas, thought Dabney "not equal to the occasion." Deprived of will and judgment by loss of sleep, Jackson could provide neither guidance nor encouragement to his officers and men.

Late that night Jackson received Lee's formal orders, General Orders No. 75. Although the overall outline was the same as the memorandum of understanding, the orders differed in details. There was a slightly different starting point; the route was somewhat different; the orders did not specify his responsibilities in the battle, nor did they give him a specific objective. They were, in short, too vague. It is not certain whether at this point Jackson was capable of understanding the differences.

By midnight of the twenty-fifth, with only twenty-seven hours to reach his starting point, he was still more than twenty-five miles away. Jackson, who always liked to start a march early ("early dawn" was a favorite time for him), was slow off the mark. Dabney, recovered enough to pick up his duties, found that supply wagons were not where they should have been, breakfasts were slow, and there was a delay while men cooked rations.

By nightfall Jackson's advance had just reached Ashland after a march of about twenty miles, still six miles from the designated starting point. Instead of pushing his men to make the extra effort, as would have been his immediate decision under ordinary conditions, Jackson called a halt, and his tired men stopped to eat and sleep.

It was just at this time and on this day that McClellan wired Secretary Stanton: "I am inclined to think that Jackson will attack my right and rear." McClellan was fearful, for he had been receiving and believing wildly exaggerated reports of Confederate strength. He estimated that he faced two hundred thousand, though Lee's army was less than half that number.

For Jackson, this was another sleepless night. A message arrived from Lee suggesting that he march east from the Virginia Central Railroad by two roads. This possibility had also occurred to Ewell and

Whiting late that night and they had gone to discuss the matter with Jackson, who, instead of making his usual rapid decision, said he wanted to think about it. As they left him, Ewell said to Whiting, "Don't you know why Old Jack would not decide at once? He is going to pray over it." This was indeed so, for when Ewell returned for the sword he had left, he found Jackson on his knees.

Messages, including reports of clashes between Stuart's troopers and Federal cavalry, came in all night. Sometime during the night Jackson wrote to Lee reporting the cavalry affairs and explaining, almost casually, that because of mud and high water, his troops were not where they ought to have been at this hour.

At two-thirty on the morning of the twenty-sixth Jackson's men were already in motion. This was to be a fateful day, but the great Stonewall was in no condition to command in battle. He had probably not had eight hours' sleep in the previous eighty-eight.

Recent studies have shown that it is common for men deprived of sleep for long periods to believe they are still functioning normally when in fact, their judgment is seriously impaired and they have lost the ability to shift focus or consider new ideas.[3] It has been said that Jackson was physically exhausted and under great stress, as was the case, but as he had proven many times, particularly in the recently concluded Valley campaign, he handled stress and fatigue very well indeed. What he ought to have learned, particularly from his experience at Port Republic, but had not, was that he simply could not for long deprive himself of sleep. This lack of self-knowledge was to cost the Confederates dearly.

3. The author is grateful to Dr. Robert J. T. Joy, chairman of the Medical History Department of the F. Edward Hébert School of Medicine of the Uniformed Services University of Health Sciences, for providing the author with the results of the most recent experiments and studies made of sleep deprivation by the United States Army.

23

☆ ☆ ☆ ☆ ☆ ☆ ☆ ☆ ☆ ☆ ☆ ☆ ☆ ☆

Seven Days:
Jackson at Mechanicsville
and Gaines's Mill

Until June 1862 all the battles fought in Virginia had been short, never lasting more than forty-eight hours, but when McClellan moved all but one corps of his army south of the Chickahominy and prepared to attack Richmond, there occurred on 25 June a battle known as Oak Grove (also Henrico, King's School House, or The Orchards) that was the first of a series of seven battles that were fought over seven days and came to be known collectively as simply Seven Days. This first engagement had been an aborted Federal attack that resulted in 626 Federal and 441 Confederate casualties. Mechanicsville, the second of the battles (also called Ellison's Mills or Beaver Dam Creek), was fought the following day, and Jackson was expected to play a role in it.

Just before sunrise on 26 June Stuart located Jackson, and the two friends conferred by the roadside. As they sat their horses, men marching by cheered them. Stuart had not long before achieved hero status by his famous ride with twelve hundred men completely around McClellan's army.

Stuart's engineer officer, Captain William W. Blackford, who was present, later commented on the contrast the two presented. Stuart, who was something of a dandy, was dressed in a fine gray uniform with a yellow sash, and his brown felt hat sported a black plume; he was splendidly mounted, and his cavalry boots were highly polished. Jackson, on the other hand, "was mounted upon a dun cob of rather sorry appearance, although substantial in build, and was dressed in a thread-bare, faded, semi-military suit, with a disreputable old Virginia Military Institute cap drawn over his eyes. . . ."

In spite of their 2:30 A.M. starting time, Jackson's troops had inexplicably advanced only five or six miles. By 9:00 the head of the column had only reached the Virginia Central Railroad. Jackson was now six hours behind schedule, and his troops had many miles ahead of them. He sent off a message to Branch to put his men in motion and inform A. P. Hill. Perhaps Branch did not receive the message. In any case, he failed to inform Hill.

It was shortly after 3:30 P.M. when Jackson reached the point he should have reached at 9:30 A.M. He had adopted the suggestion to take two roads, and Ewell was on the road somewhat to the west. At one point Jackson was close to the advancing troops of Branch, but the two generals made no contact. Lack of communication was to be a major problem.

Jackson had heard nothing from Lee, Longstreet, or the two Hills, and they had heard nothing from him. Except for some skirmishing, there seemed no occasion for Jackson to fight. A battle involving 160,-000 men was developing, a battle which would affect the outcome of the campaign, perhaps the war, but Jackson and his army seemed to be alone on the fringe of the battlefield.

Tardiness aside, Jackson was, in general, accomplishing his mission as best he understood it. By five o'clock he had marched about sixteen miles, Ewell probably a bit more, on the roads designated. He had passed Pole Green Church and was at least near the headwaters of Beaver Dam and had, arguably, turned it. He was keeping well to the left and bearing on (Old) Cold Harbor, as ordered, and the Federals appeared not to have discovered his presence. Puzzled by the absence of Federal forces, he decided to wait for further orders.

Once again a major problem was a lack of accurate maps. D. H. Hill said that "the maps furnished the division commanders were useless." Lee, relying on a bad map, thought that Pole Green Church was just beyond the headwaters of Beaver Dam Creek, but in fact, church and creek were three miles apart.

Added to the confusion was the fact, apparently unknown to the generals, that there was a New Cold Harbor and an Old Cold Harbor. D. H. Hill was properly directed to New Cold Harbor. Jackson, who should have gone there as well, for this would have placed both Hill and himself on the flank and rear of the Federals, was marching on Old

Cold Harbor and was not, as Lee supposed, in a position to turn the Federal right.

About an hour earlier Jackson had begun to hear from the direction of Mechanicsville firing which he later characterized as "the rapid continuous discharge of cannon, announcing the engagement of General A. P. Hill with the extreme right of the enemy." It was indeed A. P. Hill, who now, he said, was "expecting every minute to hear Jackson's guns on my left and in the rear of the enemy." But although only three miles away, Jackson, instead of marching toward the sound of the guns, as he certainly would have done had he been fully alert, went into bivouac to await orders while Hill's men, fighting alone on this hot summer's day, were badly cut up in Boatswain's Swamp.

A. P. Hill, at age thirty-seven the youngest of the division commanders, was slight of build, nervous and excitable. He had been waiting impatiently all day to hear from Jackson through Branch. "It was expected that General Jackson would be in the position assigned to him by early dawn, and all my preparations were made with the view of moving early," he said later. By three o'clock in the afternoon, unable to restrain himself, he decided to cross the Chickahominy at once "rather than hazard the failure of the whole plan by longer deferring it."

His premature action took Lee by surprise, for still hoping Jackson would attack, Lee had that morning sent A. P. Hill a message not to attack until he heard from Jackson. The fog of war thickened when Jefferson Davis arrived on the field and began to issue orders. However, A. P. Hill's division cleared the Mechanicsburg bridges, and D. H. Hill crossed the Chickahominy.

Lee now sent A. P. Hill's right flank brigade and a brigade of D. H. Hill's to turn the Federal left. This was a failure. Federal musketry and artillery threw them back with heavy losses. By nine o'clock that night the sounds of musketry had ceased, but the artillery fire blazed sporadically in the dark. In his first battle with the Army of Northern Virginia Lee had failed. The Confederates lost nearly 2,000 men; the Federals 361.

Lee had fought under the conditions he had feared and had sought to avoid. Of the fifty-five thousand men he had intended to launch at the twenty-five thousand Federals on the right of McClellan's lines, only fourteen thousand had been actively engaged: A. P. Hill's division and one brigade of D. H. Hill. The golden opportunity to roll up McClellan's right flank was gone forever.

There was blame enough for all. Lee's General Orders No. 75 were too vague. A. P. Hill should not have advanced when he did without orders. None of the commanders communicated with one another or even tried to do so. Inadequate maps and a lack of guides added to the general failure. But the major causes of the disaster lay with Jackson.

Because of his failure to march on Sunday, the twenty-second, and the ragged marching of his army on the twenty-third, twenty-fourth, and twenty-fifth, he had not come up in time. Then, instead of marching to A. P. Hill's aid, he had been content to bivouac and await further orders. Jackson had displayed poor judgment and wretched leadership. He has been excused by biographers and historians because he was exhausted, but the loss of sleep that impaired his judgment was largely the result of his own rash behavior.

The next day, 27 June, Jackson's position on the Federal right was no longer a secret, and the Federals countered by falling back to new defensive positions, leaving a thin line of infantry and a few guns behind. This screening force was so effective that when A. P. Hill again tried to advance, his infantry was pinned down; then, after his guns had fired for two hours, it was discovered that only a skeleton force opposed him. Jackson, too, was deceived and took no pains to discover the strength of the force opposing him. He appears to have had little sleep on the night of 26–27 June, and again, uncharacteristically, his army was off to a sluggish start. With Ewell's division in the lead, his force crossed the creek above Beaver Dam. Here Federal forces could be seen to the west. Moving up from the same direction were D. H. Hill's men. When the Federals fell back, Jackson marched on for another three miles to Walnut Grove Church, where he halted to wait for A. P. Hill to come up.

Lee arrived at this point, and the two conferred, Lee sitting on a cedar stump and Jackson with his cap off standing before him. What was said is unknown, but neither appeared ruffled, and as far as is known, Lee expressed no misgivings or laid any blame, then or ever, for Jackson's slowness. Faultfinding was not Lee's way. While they talked, A. P. Hill's men marched by, and Dabney, watching them, thought the troops looked remarkably fit after their rough handling the day before.

It was about noon when A. P. Hill's leading brigade, South Carolinians under Maxcy Gregg, came upon the Federals under Fritz-John Porter and began the Battle of Gaines's Mill (also called First Cold Harbor or Chickahominy). Gregg was an aggressive fighter. He had passed Gaines's Mill near Powhite Creek and driven in the Federal skirmishers in what Hill was to call "the handsomest charge in line I have seen during the war," but when Gregg found the main Federal line, Hill halted him. The Federals were well positioned in earthworks on the rising ground behind the tangled underbrush and young timber that lined a small, sluggish stream with marshy banks called Boatswain's Swamp, a tributary of the Chickahominy. Unknown to Hill, Porter's twenty-five thousand men had been reinforced by an additional ten thousand under Brigadier General Henry W. Slocum.

A. P. Hill, whose Light Division (so called for its rapid marching) was the largest in the Army of Northern Virginia, summoned up five more brigades and threw all he had at Porter and Slocum. It was a brave but futile effort. Once again the Confederates were beaten back with heavy losses and no gain. Again Jackson had been expected to arrive on the Confederate left, and again he had failed to appear. He was, in fact, lost.

Jackson was pushing his men down the wrong road, and it was his fault. He had found two cavalrymen, native to the area, to guide him. Instead of explaining to them exactly where he wanted to go, he had, typically, merely given them a general direction, saying he wanted the road to Cold Harbor. There were two such roads: a direct route through Gaines's Mill and a longer one farther east. The guides naturally chose the shorter route.

They had marched about a mile and a half when Jackson noticed that the artillery firing they had been hearing was growing louder. He called one of the guides to him and asked where the sound came from.

"Over Gaines's Mill way," the guide said.

"Does this road lead to Gaines's Mill?" Jackson asked incredulously.

When the guide assured him that it did, he protested that he wanted to go to Cold Harbor, leaving Gaines's Mill on his right.

"Then the left hand road was the one which should have been taken," said the guide, "and had you let me know . . . I could have directed you aright at first."[1]

Nearly two hours were lost turning the column around and getting it in the right order on the right road. Jackson, never known to admit that he might have erred, remained calm. When someone suggested that the time lost could not possibly be made up, he replied, "No, let us trust that the providence of our God will so over-rule it that no mischief will result."

But mischief did result. When D. H. Hill and one of his batteries

---

1. Ironically, had Jackson continued on this road, he would have ended up beside D. H. Hill, where Lee wanted him to be.

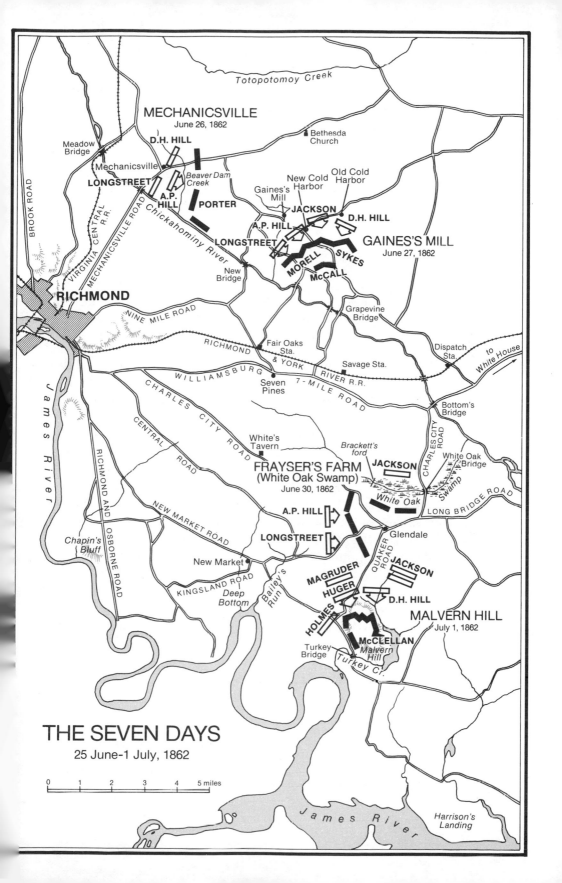

Tototopomoy Creek

MECHANICSVILLE
June 26, 1862

Bethesda
Church

Meadow
Bridge

D.H. HILL

Mechanicsville

LONGSTREET

*Beaver Dam
Creek*

Old Cold
Harbor

New Cold
Harbor

Gaines's
Mill

JACKSON

A.P.
HILL

A.P. HILL

D.H. HILL

PORTER

GAINES'S MILL
June 27, 1862

BROOK ROAD

VIRGINIA CENTRAL R.R.

MECHANICSVILLE ROAD

LONGSTREET

Chickahominy River

New
Bridge

MORELL

SYKES

McCALL

RICHMOND

NINE MILE ROAD

Grapevine
Bridge

RICHMOND

Fair Oaks
Sta.

Dispatch
Sta.

to
White House

& YORK

Savage Sta.

James River

WILLIAMSBURG

RIVER R.R.

Seven
Pines

7 - MILE ROAD

Bottom's
Bridge

CHARLES CITY ROAD

CENTRAL ROAD

White's
Tavern

*Brackett's
ford*

JACKSON

White Oak
Bridge

CHARLES CITY ROAD

FRAYSER'S FARM
(White Oak Swamp)
June 30, 1862

White Oak

Swamp

LONG BRIDGE ROAD

A.P. HILL

RICHMOND AND OSBORNE ROAD

NEW MARKET ROAD

LONGSTREET

Glendale

*Chapin's
Bluff*

New Market

KINGSLAND ROAD

*Deep
Bottom*

Bailey's
Run

QUAKER ROAD

JACKSON

MAGRUDER

HUGER

D.H. HILL

HOLMES

MALVERN HILL
July 1, 1862

Turkey
Bridge

McCLELLAN

*Malvern
Hill*

Turkey Cr.

THE SEVEN DAYS
25 June–1 July, 1862

0   1   2   3   4   5 miles

James River

*Harrison's
Landing*

encountered strong Federal artillery fire, Jackson pulled the entire division back to the shelter of a woods. And there they sat. Eight months later, when Jackson finally submitted his after-action report, he gave a curious explanation for this delay:

> Soon after A. P. Hill became engaged, and being unacquainted with the ground, and apprehensive from what appeared to be the respective positions of the Confederate and Federal forces engaged, that if I then pressed forward our troops would be mistaken for the enemy and be fired into, and hoping that Generals A. P. Hill and Longstreet would soon drive the Federals towards me, I directed General D. H. Hill to move his division to the left of the road so as to leave between him and the wood on the right of the road an open space, across which I hoped the enemy would be driven. Thus arranged, it was within our power to distinguish friend from foe in case the enemy should be driven as expected.

Jackson was alone in taking this stance. He had not known if this suited Lee's plans, and he had not told Lee what he was doing. As is clear from Lee's after-action report, he had expected Jackson to attack.

It was some time before Jackson's clouded mind took in the fact that neither A. P. Hill nor Longstreet, who had now joined in the attack, was going to drive the Federals in front of him for a turkey shoot. He then ordered D. H. Hill, now on the left of the Confederate infantry, to attack and Ewell's division to fall into line on Hill's right.

As the Louisiana Tigers marched past, Major Roberdeau Wheat, the giant soldier of fortune who had survived his grievous wound at First Manassas, left the line of march to approach Jackson. "General, we are about to get into a hot fight and it is likely many of us will be killed," he said earnestly. "I want to ask you for myself and my Louisianans not to expose yourself unnecessarily. . . . What will happen to us, down here in these swamps, if anything happens to you?"

Jackson seemed moved. Taking Wheat's hand, he said: "Major, you will be in greater danger than I, and I hope you will not get hurt. Each of us has his duty to perform, regardless of consequences. We must perform it and trust in Providence."

Rob Wheat was mortally wounded soon after. His last words were: "Bury me on the field, boys."[2]

---

2. Major Wheat was indeed buried on the field, but his family, ignoring his last wish, had his body exhumed and reburied in Hollywood Cemetery, Richmond. After Wheat's death, since no one else could control his unruly Louisiana Tigers, the unit was disbanded.

In midafternoon Major Harman wandered onto the field, and Jackson gave him an order to deliver to Lawton, Winder, and Whiting, whom he wanted to move forward to occupy the area between A. P. Hill and Ewell. Harman was to tell the three brigade commanders, said Jackson, to advance in echelon from the left:

> Each brigade is to follow as a guide the right regiment of the brigade on the left, and to keep within supporting distance. Tell the commanders that if this formation fails at any point, to form line of battle and to move to the front, pressing to the sound of the heaviest firing and attack the enemy vigorously wherever found. As to artillery, each commander must use his discretion. If the ground will at all permit, tell them to take in their field batteries and use them. If not, post them in the rear.

Harman was taken aback. He had never carried an order on a battlefield in his life. It was preposterous for Jackson to assume that his quartermaster could take all this in. It was not, in any case, an order to be delivered verbally. Predictably Harman made a hash of it. Whiting said his instructions were "a farrago of which I could understand nothing." When the unit commanders failed to respond, Jackson took no action. Dabney on his own went back to try to sort matters out, and according to him, "Whiting was in liquor and received my explanations and new instructions very captiously." It was some time before Whiting's two brigades moved into the positions assigned them.

Lee was active on the field. Encountering Jackson, he said mildly, "Ah, General, I am very glad to see you. I had hoped to be with you before."

Jackson bowed. It was the closest thing to a reprimand Lee ever gave him. Asked if he thought his men could stand the heavy fire to which they were being subjected, Jackson listened to it for a moment and then assured Lee that they could. The fighting, which raged for the rest of the day, became ever more confused as the men struggled to fight in the mud and tangled undergrowth. Private Granville Crozier of the 4th Texas later remembered how "the smoke hung thick over the field, and the air was stifling with the smell of gunpowder. Though the sun was shining brightly, the day was nearly as dark as night."

Jackson did not have his brigades in order, and he did not know where they all were; his command arrived on the field in fragments. Some brigade commanders simply went where they thought they could be useful. When Jackson came upon Colonel Bradley Johnson of the

1st Maryland, he had one piece of advice, "Johnson, make your men shoot like they are shooting at a mark, slow and low. Hit them here and here," and he poked his finger at Johnson's waist. Johnson remembered this as the only time he had ever heard Jackson call someone by name alone.

It is impossible to trace Jackson's movements exactly that afternoon. Someone had given him a lemon, which he clutched in his hand for several hours. He began to behave wildly. His face was flushed, and his sleepless eyes burned. He summoned Stuart and ordered a cavalry charge but at once canceled such a foolish order; this was no country for cavalry action. As the sun was setting, about seven o'clock, he called up all his couriers and gave them orders for his commanders: "Tell them this affair must hang in suspense no longer. Sweep the field with the bayonet!"

At about the same time Lee sent out orders for a general advance, which probably reached most commanders before Jackson's fiery command. On the extreme left D. H. Hill's men charged forward and for ten minutes held a key battery of guns, then lost it. Unknown to them, they were attacking the center of a Federal position that was practically impregnable. And they were again fighting alone, expecting in vain to be supported by Jackson. Eventually Ewell came up to the support of A. P. Hill's left, and Lawton's Georgia brigade of thirty-five hundred men made their way through the swamp and came out of a cornfield on Ewell's left.

Whiting's two brigades—twenty-five-year-old Colonel Evander McIvor Law's brigade of four regiments and thirty-year-old Brigadier General John Bell Hood's brigade of three Texas regiments and one from Georgia—wandered lost in the woods and swamps before coming up behind A. P. Hill's men, now exhausted and dispirited.

Lee rode up to Hood and asked if he could break the Union line. Hood answered gallantly that he would try. He and Law positioned themselves in front of their brigades, drawn up in double lines of battle. A Texas private remarked that "Hood always looked grand in battle. Now he looked sublime." Whiting rode along the line and gave the order that arms be carried at the trail without firing. Then began the charge of Hood's Texans, one of the most famous charges of the war.

Through woods and open spaces they moved forward, taking hideous losses, past men retreating from the fight and men cowering behind trees. In his report Whiting wrote: "Men were skulking from the front in a shameful manner. The woods on our left and rear were full of troops in safe cover." Past the dead and the groaning wounded they tramped; across swamp and creek, through thickets, they went forward inexorably. The 11th Virginia streamed past a young Confederate officer, still mounted although his arm had been torn off at the shoulder. "Go on, boys," he shouted. "Do your duty and don't mind me."

Law wrote a vivid description of the charge that finally broke the Federal line:

> Men fell like leaves in an autumn wind, the Federal artillery tore gaps in the ranks at every step, the ground in rear of the advancing column was strewn thickly with the dead and wounded; not a gun was fired in reply; there was no confusion, and not a step faltered as the two gray lines swept silently and swiftly on; the pace became more rapid every moment; when the men were within thirty yards of the ravine, and could see the desperate nature of the work at hand, a wild yell answered the roar of Federal musketry and they rushed for the works. The Confederates were within ten paces of them when Federals in the front line broke cover, and, leaving their log breastworks, swarmed up the hill in their rear, carrying away their second line with them in their rout.

Equally vivid are the words of John W. Daniel of the 11th Virginia, a participant, who said that "it seemed as if the skies above us were made out of sheet iron and the fiends of hell were ripping them up and flinging them around all to pieces."

The charge even evoked the admiration of Jackson. Usually sparing of praise, he reported: "Dashing on with unfaltering step in the face of those murderous discharges of canister and musketry, General Hood and Colonel E. M. Law at the head of their respective brigades rushed to the charge with a yell." The Union line broke. Only then did the Confederates open fire into the backs of Brigadier General George W. Taylor's New Jersey brigade, delivering a fire which, according to a Union staff officer, "was the most withering I ever saw delivered. The New Jersey brigade broke all to pieces."

More than a thousand Confederates fell in the charge. Fourteen guns were captured. In the twilight Porter managed to withdraw his battered units and continue his retreat, burning bridges behind him. Stuart, who even in the dark could have pursued and swept up prisoners, was far out on the left, watching a position which McClellan had abandoned.

Jackson and a few staff officers, riding ahead of his men, blundered into a cluster of fifteen or twenty Federal troops, who surrendered at Jackson's demand. While being marched to the rear, one observant soldier in the group exclaimed with an oath, "Gentlemen, we had the honor of being captured by Stonewall Jackson himself!"

Union losses out of 34,214 engaged were 894 dead, 3,107 wounded, and 2,836 missing. Porter lost a total of 22 guns. Of 54,018 Confederates engaged, 8,751 were killed or wounded—1,914 more than Union losses. The highest proportion of casualties, 25 percent, was suffered by the brigades of Hood and Law. The 4th Texas, composed of older men, many men of substance—ranchers, farmers, merchants, lawyers, et al.—took the heaviest losses: 250 out of about 500. The Confederate artillery was badly used, and the blood of the infantrymen was lavishly expended. As D. H. Hill pointed out after the war, the charging of a battery of artillery or infantry behind earthworks was thought to be grand, but it was "the kind of grandeur which the South could not afford."

Among the Virginian dead, killed by one of the last volleys, was Colonel Samuel Vance Fulkerson, author of the Romney protest. He had proved himself a good regimental commander. Dabney said of him that "his judgment, diligence and talent for command, were equal to his heroic courage."

Longstreet said of the Battle of Gaines's Mill: "There was more individual gallantry displayed upon this field than any I have ever seen." Indeed, there had been valor aplenty displayed in this action, but neither Lee nor any of his senior commanders, including the confused, sleepless Jackson, distinguished themselves by their generalship. Jackson was particularly culpable for setting an unrealistic timetable and for making no attempt to maintain close contact with Lee and the other division commanders. Unit cohesion was lost, and units were badly coordinated. Jackson totally lost control of his. Some units joined D. H. Hill; others moved to support A. P. Hill, while the 2nd and 5th Virginians became lost and ended up behind Longstreet on the right of the Confederate line.

The battle did not demoralize the Federal troops. Most of Porter's men had fallen back in good order, and there was little panic—except in the heart of the commander. McClellan called a meeting of his senior generals that night and announced plans for retreating to the James River and establishing a new base under the protecting guns of Federal warships at the Berkeley plantation.[3] He never referred to this

---

3. Called Harrison's Landing in Federal dispatches, it is the wharf on the three-mile riverfront of the Berkeley plantation.

as a retreat, only as a "change of base," a euphemism that spiced many witticisms.

Shortly after midnight McClellan, who blamed his civilian superiors for not giving him all the troops he demanded, wrote a long and extraordinary telegram to Secretary of War Stanton. "I shall have to contend against vastly superior odds," he asserted. "I will do all that a general can do with the splendid army I have the honor to command, and if it is destroyed by overwhelming numbers at least die with it and share its fate." He closed with "If I save this army now, I tell you plainly that I owe no thanks to you or to any other person in Washington. You have done your best to sacrifice this army."[4] Gone now was any thought of capturing Richmond. McClellan could only ponder how to save the army he had created from what he believed to be a vastly superior Confederate force.

In one week the threatening Federal army had been turned from the gates of Richmond and was in retreat. But the cost was high. While McClellan was writing his telegram to Stanton, Private A. N. Erskin of the 4th Texas persuaded some of his fellows to go out on the battlefield and look for fallen friends. The next day he wrote to his wife:

> On going round on that battlefield with a candle searching for my friends I could hear on all sides the dreadful groans of the wounded and their heart piercing cries for water and assistance. Friends and foes all together. . . . Oh the awful scene witnessed on the battlefield. May I never see any more such in life. . . . I am satisfied not to make another such charge. . . . I assure you I am heartily sick of soldiering.

4. The Washington telegraph operator and the military supervisor of telegraphs deliberately deleted the last two sentences before passing the message on to Stanton.

24

☆ ☆ ☆ ☆ ☆ ☆ ☆ ☆ ☆ ☆ ☆ ☆ ☆ ☆

Seven Days: White Oak Swamp and Malvern Hill

T he movement of the Federal army to the James River was a formidable task, but it was the kind of operation at which McClellan excelled. In a straight line the distance was only about thirty miles from the old Federal supply base at White House[1] on the Pamunkey River to the James, but the roads between were sinuous and largely unmapped, and across the Federals' path were the Chickahominy River and White Oak Swamp, seven miles long and in places nearly four miles wide. To execute McClellan's orders, seventy-five thousand men with all their guns, wagons, and impedimenta would have to cross the Chickahominy and this swamp.

At Lee's headquarters the results of the Battle of Gaines's Mill were not yet known. It was plain that McClellan's army was on the move, but Lee had no idea of its destination, for to his discredit, he had lost contact with his enemy. On Saturday, 28 June, beginning at dawn, Confederate units were reassembled, dead were buried, and wounded brought in. Later in the day Lee ordered Longstreet on the right and Jackson on the left to advance and feel out the enemy. Were the Feder-

---

1. White House was the handsome residence of General Lee's son Colonel W. H. F. Lee, commanding the 9th Virginia Cavalry. General Lee's wife and daughter, both named Mary, were there when McClellan arrived. He treated them with great courtesy and had them escorted to the Confederate lines.

als retreating to White House, or down the center of the Peninsula, or to the James?

Jackson was ordered to send Ewell down the north side of the Chickahominy as far as the Richmond & York River Railroad and to send Stuart toward White House. Both found the ground littered with the debris of a retreating army: burned wagons, broken or abandoned tools, equipment, blankets, and clothing. North of the Chickahominy there remained only a few Federal pickets. There was nothing to fight.

Both Ewell and Stuart were ordered to tear down telegraph wires, tear up railroad track, and capture or destroy supplies as they went. When Stuart arrived at White House, he found McClellan had abandoned his base, and his troops had set fire to supplies and buildings, including the beautiful White House itself, in spite of McClellan's orders to spare it. Still, Stuart's troopers found plenty of food and new accoutrements lying about and jubilantly helped themselves. It was not until evening that Lee learned that McClellan was making for the James River.

The next day, Sunday the twenty-ninth, Jackson was directed by Lee "to pursue the enemy on the road he had taken." This involved rebuilding Grapevine Bridge, destroyed by the Federals, and then marching down the south bank of the Chickahominy. Lee ordered Magruder and Huger to come in on the flank of the retreating Federals before they reached White Oak Swamp, although by this time more than a third of McClellan's men had crossed it. Longstreet and A. P. Hill were to cross behind Magruder and Huger for a dash around the Federal right flank, blocking their further retreat to the James.

It was another complicated plan doomed to failure by the nature of the ground and the generals' ignorance of its topography, their inability to maintain communications among their widely separated units, and an impossible timetable.

No day in Jackson's Civil War career has been more puzzling to historians than this Sunday, which he spent rebuilding Grapevine Bridge. Curiously, although engineers were available, he assigned responsibility for the bridge to the Reverend Major Dabney—according to Dabney. D. H. Hill reported that "my pioneer corps, under Captain [William Proctor] Smith, of the Engineers, repaired Grapevine Bridge on the 29th and we crossed over at 3 o'clock that night." Whoever rebuilt the bridge, it was a long time in the doing. Dabney said that his men were "shillyshally."

Meanwhile, Magruder had made contact with the Federals' covering force near Savage Station, a mile south of Grapevine Bridge, and needed Huger's support on his right and Jackson's on his left. Since Jackson's troops were nowhere in sight, he sent a staff officer, Major Henry Bryan, to investigate the delay. Bryan returned with Lieutenant James Keith Boswell, the young engineer on Jackson's staff, who explained that the bridge would not be finished for another two hours. The time of this report is unknown, but it was obviously later than the time when Magruder needed Jackson's help.

At another unspecified hour of the day Major Walter H. Taylor of Lee's staff, who had carried a message to Magruder, acquired a curious bit of information: Major General David Rumph Jones, in temporary command of Magruder's division, reported that although Jackson was only three miles away, he had sent word that he could not cooperate because he had "other important duty to perform."

When Major Taylor reported this to Lee, Lee added to a communication he was writing to Magruder: "I learn from Major Taylor that you are under the impression that General Jackson has been ordered not to support you. On the contrary, he has been directed to do so and to push the pursuit vigorously."

What this "other important duty" was, other than completing the repair of the bridge, has been much debated. It has been suggested that Jackson deliberately delayed the crossing of the bridge because it was a Sunday, but this is unlikely and unsubstantiated.

At some time during this puzzling day Lee sent a message through his assistant adjutant general directly to Stuart, who was still in the neighborhood of White House:

> The Gen'l Comd'g requests that you will watch the Chickahominy as far as Forge Bridge, ascertain if any attempts will be made in that direction by the enemy, advising Gen'l Jackson, who will resist their passage until reinforced. If you find they have passed down below where they cannot cross, leave a force to watch movements which may be made, & recross yourself to this side for further operations.

Stuart read the order and sent it on to Jackson, who received it at three o'clock in the afternoon. Jackson interpreted it as meaning he should stay in place in case he received word from Stuart that the enemy was trying to cross the Chickahominy. He scribbled in the margin: "3h.5m. P.M. Genl. Ewell will remain near Dispatch Station & myself near my present position. T. J. J." He then returned the message to Stuart.

Jackson may have regarded this watch on the Chickahominy as the "other important duty." In any case, late in the afternoon, to the sound of Magruder's guns, he lay down under an open sky and went to sleep, in the event, probably the best thing he could do.

In the early hours of Monday, the thirtieth, awakened by a rainstorm that drenched him, he rode in the downpour to Magruder's headquarters, reaching it at three-thirty in the morning. Magruder was still awake, and presumably they conferred. Dawn found Jackson sitting his horse where the road to Grapevine Bridge crossed the Williamsburg road. He had ordered Colonel Mumford with his 2nd Virginia Cavalry to meet him, but Mumford was not there.

When the storm hit Mumford's command, his men had scattered to find shelter; later, when he tried to find them in the dark, he could locate only about fifty. Giving up the search for the remainder, he rode with these to his appointment. He found Jackson in a foul mood.

"Colonel, my orders to you were to be here at sunrise," he said.

Mumford launched into a detailed explanation of his difficulties, which Jackson brushed aside with "Yes, sir. But, Colonel, you were to be here at sunrise and I have been waiting for you for a quarter of an hour. Move on with your regiment. If you meet the enemy, drive in his pickets." Mumford grimly set off with his fifty men. When the missing cavalrymen began to ride up, Jackson fired off a message apprising Mumford that his men were straggling badly. The unfortunate Mumford rode back and made a second effort to explain, but Jackson would have none of it. "But I ordered you to be here at sunrise," he snapped.

Robert Stiles, a Yale graduate from New York who had taken sides with the South and was now adjutant of a battery of artillery, was sitting beside the road with his back against a tree that morning when, near Magruder's headquarters, he saw Jackson for the first time:

> Jackson and the little sorrel stopped in the middle of the road, probably not fifty feet off. . . . He sat stark and stiff in the saddle. Horse and rider appeared worn down to the lowest point of flesh consistent with effective service. His hair, skin, eyes, and clothes were all one neutral dust tint, and his badges of rank so dulled and tarnished as to be scarcely perceptible. The "mangy little cadet cap" was pulled so low in front that the visor just cut the glint of his eyeballs.

Nearby were the corpses of men from the 17th and 21st Mississippi, who had been laid in neat rows, hands across their breasts, their eyes open. Soldiers walked slowly down the line, looking in the bleached faces, wet from the rain, seeking comrades. Jackson glanced at the scene, and Stiles noted that "not a muscle quivered." He was waiting for Lee, and he turned to look down the road.

Dressed in a trim uniform, Lee rode up with his staff. He dismounted gracefully, passed the reins to an orderly, removed a gauntlet from his right hand, and warmly greeted Jackson, who climbed stiffly out of his saddle. They immediately fell into serious conversation. Observers could not hear what was said, but they saw Jackson talking earnestly in a "jerky, impetuous way," watched him draw lines in the dirt with the toe of his boot and, when he had formed a triangle, stamp his foot and say loudly, "We've got him."

Jackson's troops, who had been on the march since two-thirty in the morning, tramped through Magruder's headquarters area and over a battlefield uncleared of the Federal dead, the corpses of horses, and the debris of battle. Corporal James E. Hall of the 31st Virginia wrote in his diary: "Passed over part of the battlefield today. Saw a few dead Yankees. Some were as black in the face as the Ace of Spades. Let lie and rot, I expect."

The Confederates were amazed by the riches that had been abandoned by the well-equipped Federal army. Dabney later wrote:

> The whole country was filled with deserted plunder, army wagons and pontoon-trains partially burned or crippled; mounds of grain and rice and hillocks of mess beef smoldering; tens of thousands of axes, picks and shovels; camp kettles gashed with hatchets; medicine chests with their drugs stirred into a foul medley, and all the *apparatus* of a vast and lavish host; while the mire under foot was mixed with blankets lately new, and with overcoats torn from the waist up. For weeks afterwards agents of our army were busy in gathering in the spoils. Great stores of fixed ammunition were saved, while more were destroyed.

Found on the field were also a few steel breastplates and a crude forerunner of a Gatling gun. Many Confederate soldiers took the opportunity to supply themselves with comforts, and one wrote home: "We have had a glorious victory with its rich Booty A many one of our boys now have a pair of Briches a nice Rubber *cloth* a pair or more of Small Tent Cloths."

Not only goods but men, too, were abandoned: Twenty-five hundred sick and wounded were left lying in one white-tented hospital; five hundred more in another. Stuart's cavalry rounded up a thousand prisoners in the woods. Jackson, overhearing an officer remark jocularly about the quantity of food that would be necessary to feed them, interjected, "It is cheaper to feed them than to fight them."

In their official reports neither Jackson nor any of his staff officers mentioned the Federal balloons that floated over Gaines's Mill, but others did. Captain William Poague saw one, and his "first emotion was one of contemptuous indignation for the unfair advantage they thus sought." Joel Cook, who ascended in one, wrote in the *Philadelphia Ledger* of the view: "The white capitol is . . . quite conspicuous and, of course, the Stars and Bars float over the roof. Three church spires . . . are the brightest part of the town. . . . The space between the Chickahominy and fortifications around Richmond is almost filled with rebel camps."

The idea of using balloons for observation was the brainchild of balloonist "Professor" Thaddeus S. C. Lowe, who offered his services to the Union government. So many Confederates fired at his balloon that Lowe was said to be the "most shot-at man" in the war. Not to be outdone, the Confederates sent up their own balloon, stitched together from silk dresses. Anchored to a steamer that had grounded in the James, it was captured with the ship.

At White Oak Swamp, whose waters drain into the Chickahominy, Jackson's men found a partially destroyed bridge of untrimmed poles and crude lumber. Jackson, with Mumford's cavalry, splashed across but soon dashed back under fire from hidden guns. The Federals were in a stronger position than had been thought. Jackson could have forced a crossing; there were fords in the area. But he contented himself with putting Winder's and D. H. Hill's men in the shelter of a pine forest and desultorily shelling the Federals across the swamp. Then he sat beside the road and wrote to Anna:

An ever-kind Providence has greatly blessed our efforts and given us great reason for thankfulness in having defended Richmond. Today the enemy is retreating down the Chickahominy toward the James River. Many prisoners are falling into our hands. General D. H. Hill and I are together. . . . I got up about midnight and haven't seen much rest since. . . . You must give fifty dollars for church purposes, and more should you be disposed. Keep an account of the amount, as we must give at least one tenth of our income. . . .

Late in the afternoon Lee ordered Longstreet and A. P. Hill to launch a major attack in a battle that came to be known as Frayser's Farm or White Oak Swamp. Longstreet dented the Federal line in bitter fighting that in places became hand to hand, but the Federals plugged the gap. The Confederates' only prize was the capture of Union Major General George McCall by the 47th Virginia. (Brigadier General John Fulton Reynolds had been captured two days before.) The battle ended in darkness about nine o'clock. Federal losses totaled 2,853; Confederate losses, 3,615.

For this day, 30 June, Lee had again developed an elaborate battle plan, but again nothing had worked. The main body of Federals slipped from his grasp. Once again the main cause of the failure was Jackson.

Contrary to statements by Jackson's early biographer and admirer G. F. R. Henderson, there is not the slightest evidence that after his initial rebuff at the swamp Jackson made any attempt to assist Longstreet. Mumford found a cow path over the swamp only a quarter of a mile away and reported this to Jackson, but Jackson "made no attempt to cross. . . . Why, I never understood." Only a mile above White Oak Swamp Bridge was Brackett's Ford, a well-known crossing. Either of these could have been used, but Jackson seemed uninterested and lethargic.

Brigadier General Wade Hampton found an area where the swamp was open, "not at all boggy," and the stream "very shallow, with a clear sandy bottom, not more than 10 or 15 feet wide." He crossed easily on horseback and reported his find to Jackson, who asked if he could build a bridge. Hampton thought he could throw one across strong enough for infantry, but not artillery, and a rough bridge was quickly constructed.

When Hampton returned, he found Jackson sitting on a pine log. Hampton sat down beside him and reported the completion of the bridge and the exposed position of the enemy opposite it. He could scarcely believe Jackson's response: "He drew his cap down over his eyes which were closed, and after listening to me for some minutes, he rose without speaking. . . ." That was all.

Jackson was fully informed of Longstreet's position and need for support in his desperate fighting around Frayser's Farm. Longstreet had sent Major John W. Fairfax, a staff officer, to make his position clear, and D. H. Hill, impatient and outspoken, often suffering from a spinal ailment, had sent Captain W. F. Lee, his engineer officer, to ask his brother-in-law if he could not engage the enemy. But lack of sleep had at last completely overwhelmed Jackson. When Winder sent McHenry Howard to see why he was not moving, Jackson's staff pointed out their general asleep under a tree. Howard waited. "At intervals a shell came from across the stream but not falling or passing near us. . . . With the exception of this slow firing everything seemed to be quiet, and it looked to me as if on our side we were waiting for Jackson to wake up. . . ."[2]

When Jackson did awake, he sat as if drugged and seemed in a torpor, indifferent to the war. That evening, while eating supper with his staff, he fell asleep with a half-eaten biscuit in his mouth. When he roused himself, he stood up and said, "Now, gentlemen, let us at once to bed, and rise with the dawn, and see if tomorrow we cannot *do something.*" He was too dazed to realize that tomorrow would be too late.

Brigadier General William Buel Franklin,[3] who commanded the Union corps acting as a strong rear guard on the other side of White Oak Swamp, later said: "It is likely that we would have been defeated . . . had General Jackson done what his great reputation seems to make it imperative that he should have done." Even his greatest admirers have had to admit, as did Dabney, that in this campaign "he came short of that efficiency in action for which he was everywhere else noted."

In his after-action report—filed eight months later—Jackson wrote that he heard the "heavy cannonading" that announced Longstreet's battle and that this made him "eager to press forward; but the marshy character of the soil, the destruction of the bridge over the marsh and creek, and the strong position of the enemy for defending the passage prevented my advancing until the following morning."

After the war Longstreet wrote bitterly: "Jackson should have done more for me than he did. . . . Jackson was a very skillful man against such men as Shields, Banks and Frémont, but when pitted against the best of the Federal commanders he did not appear so well."

2. A modern scholar who has made a close study of the Seven Days Battle, Clifford Dowdey (*The Seven Days: The Emergence of Robert E. Lee,* 1988), says of Jackson: "His performance at White Oak Swamp stood out in dramatic relief because there, in the crisis of Lee's plans, his failure was complete, disastrous and unredeemable."

3. Franklin was promoted to major general four days later. He had been graduated first in his class from West Point in 1843, Grant's class, and so had been in the Corps of Engineers. He was in charge of the construction of the dome of the Capitol when the war began.

Two weeks after the battle Jackson came upon Crutchfield, McGuire, and Pendleton discussing why he had not looked for some way to go to the aid of Longstreet and Hill. He ended the discussion curtly: "If General Lee had wanted me, he would have sent for me."

During the night of 30–31 June McClellan drew his forces into strong positions on Malvern Hill. The following morning White Oak Swamp had no defenders. Jackson could build an adequate bridge and cross his entire force unopposed.

Early that morning a deeply disappointed Lee met with his commanders; his army was all together again, and he directed the advance southward with Jackson in the lead on a road variously called Willis Church Road or Quaker Road. Magruder was to follow him but marched off instead in the wrong direction on the wrong road, one farther east that was also known as Quaker Road.

Again the problem was a lack of maps and guides and the commanders' appalling ignorance of the lay of the land. General Taylor said later: "The Confederate commanders knew no more about about the topography of the country than they did about Central Africa. Here was a limited district, the whole of it within a day's march of Richmond . . . almost the first spot on the continent occupied by the English people . . . and yet we were profoundly ignorant of the country . . . and nearly as helpless as if we had been suddenly transferred to the banks of the Lualaba." Jackson apparently assumed that the area around Richmond would be well mapped, for he had sent Hotchkiss and his assistants back to the Valley.

It seems extraordinary that neither Lee nor any of his generals could find local people to guide or instruct them or that in an army containing thousands of Virginians some could not be found who had been reared in the area. There is no evidence that they looked for any, and when one volunteered, his information was ignored. The Reverend L. W. Allen, on Magruder's staff, knew Malvern Hill well and described to Hill its mile-long irregular configuration, a half mile in width; its difficult approaches; and its steep slopes of thick, tangled brush rising 150 feet above the plain to a plateaulike top. Hill believed an attack on such a place would be fatal, and he repeated the description to Lee and Longstreet. "If General McClellan is there in force, we had better leave him alone," he suggested. Longstreet laughed. "Don't get scared now that we have him whipped," he said.

But McClellan was not whipped, and Lee and Longstreet should have listened to Hill, for their objective was indeed formidable. There were three farms on the plateau, all with fields and barns and outbuildings, and here the Federals had erected earthworks and constructed a strong defensive position bristling with artillery, tier above tier. In addition to the guns of the brigades and divisions, Colonel Henry J. Hunt, McClellan's able chief of artillery, had positioned one hundred pieces of all calibers from the Federal reserve artillery, including even heavy siege guns brought to central Virginia for the purpose of battering Richmond. Union General Fitz-John Porter, the defender of Malvern Hill (McClellan was on a ship in the James), considered the position "better adapted for a defensive battle than any with which we had been favored."

Toward this virtual fortress marched Jackson, Hill, and Magruder. At the foot of the hill they formed line of battle with Magruder on the right, Jackson on the left, and Longstreet and A. P. Hill a mile northwest in reserve. At Longstreet's suggestion, Lee ordered that guns be placed on a slight elevation on the right and in an open field on the left, but this was more easily ordered than executed, for the guns had to be dragged through dense woods, and once free of the woods, they came under heavy artillery fire. Not even half the division batteries were brought into action.

The Confederates were to suffer from a serious shortage of artillery fire this day. D. H. Hill's guns, all their ammunition shot away, were sent to the rear. Lee had a reserve of one hundred guns under General Pendleton, the former Lexington Episcopal minister, but Pendleton spent all day looking for Lee and for good artillery positions. Finding neither, he concluded that he should simply "await events and orders, in readiness for whatever service might be called for. . . ." It was, he said feebly, "all that I could do. . . . [N]o occasion was presented for bringing up the reserve artillery. . . ."

The Confederate guns that did come into action fired bravely enough, but most were blown away by the massed fire of the Union artillery within an hour of the unequal duel. However, Whiting, on the left of Jackson's line, reported what he took to be a retrograde movement on Malvern Hill. On the right of the line, Brigadier General Lewis Addison Armistead in Magruder's division successfully pushed back Federal skirmishers. Lee, sensing a weakening in the Federal position, ordered Magruder to "press forward with your whole command and follow up Armistead's successes." Although Magruder commanded some fifteen thousand men, his brigades were now scattered and he was able to throw forward only two (about twenty-five hundred men), who took position on Armistead's right.

The Federals had shifted their ground, but they were not retreating. The Confederates charged bravely enough, but they were met by a hailstorm of artillery fire. None came closer than one hundred yards to the Federal positions. "It was not war," said D. H. Hill. "It was murder." His own men were to face the same fire.

At five-thirty in the afternoon, following instructions from Lee through Jackson, Hill sent sixty-five hundred men forward in a mad lunge at Malvern Hill. They, too, encountered the awesome fire of the Union guns and fell back. When they gallantly rallied and came on again, they were swept away by a fire storm of canister and grapeshot that cut wide swaths in their ranks. Malvern Hill was largely a battle between Confederate infantry and Union artillery. Hill later said, "Truly, the courage of the soldiers was sublime."

Jackson made no attempt to support Hill until he asked for reinforcements. Then he sent forward Winder's division and part of Ewell's, but as Lee noted in his report, "owing to the increasing darkness and intricacy of the forest and swamp they did not arrive in time to render the desired assistance."

On the right Magruder collected more of his units and some of Huger's and threw them at deadly Malvern Hill. It was, as D. H. Hill said, "grandly heroic," but it was futile. Some stormed the slopes to within twenty-five yards of the guns, only to be met by withering volleys of musketry from Union infantry posted behind breastworks to protect the guns. The lines of young men crumpled. Unit cohesion, vital in an attack, dissolved. Some men, less brave than others, fled in terror. Darkness found the slopes of Malvern strewn with the dead, and the night air was filled with the cries and groans of the wounded.

John Worsham of the 21st Virginia shared his blanket that night with one of the wounded and awoke in the rain to find that he had been sleeping with a corpse. Four days later in a letter home he described the horror he had witnessed at Malvern Hill and wrote, "Mother, I'm real[l]y sick."

Jackson now seemed somewhat recovered. He had established his headquarters that day at a pair of gateposts near the home of Mr. C. W. Smith. Lee's headquarters were nearby, and they conferred several times, but Jackson had little influence on the battle. He did what he was told to do, and he exercised no initiative. It seems not to have occurred to him to send aid to D. H. Hill. He waited until asked. He occupied himself doing things he had no business doing. For a while he helped to pull a gun of a North Carolina battery through a woods. When he learned that another battery was in difficulty and dashed off under fire to see what he could do, Lee sent a staff officer after him with orders to return. Late in the afternoon fiery old General Trimble was putting his men in line of battle when Jackson encountered him and asked what he intended to do.

"I am going to charge those batteries, sir," he answered.

"I guess you had better not try it," Jackson told him. "General D. H. Hill had just tried it with his whole division and been repulsed. I guess you had better not try, sir." Spurring his horse, he rode away.

All night long the woods rang with the cries of the wounded, many grievously mutilated by the fire from the Union artillery. One of Stuart's officers said: "I have never seen a battlefield where there was such frightful mutilation of bodies as there was at Malvern Hill. . . . Many were cut entirely in two. Some were headless, while fragments of bodies and limbs were strewn about in every direction." Lieutenant William Morris of the 37th North Carolina said: "Hundreds of horses were lying around, some not dead, some with legs shot off, trying to get up, moaning and crying like children." Lieutenant George Wilson Booth of the 1st Maryland spoke of "a night of horror that will never be forgotten. The wounded of both armies lay mingled on the field. . . . Their cries for water and help were most piteous."[4] Jim Lewis made a pallet for his master, and Jackson went to sleep on it.

About one o'clock in the morning D. H. Hill and Ewell, alarmed about the state of the army, came looking for Jackson. It had been a grim day: Units had lost their way; artillery had been badly managed; assaults had been uncoordinated. There was still no communication between units and their headquarters; units had no idea where they were or where anyone else was; the battlefield was strewn with uncollected wounded and unburied dead; medical facilities were wholly inadequate, and the surgeons were overwhelmed. Discipline was deteriorating, and the army was almost a mob.

Jackson was deep in sleep. He was always difficult to awaken, and now it seemed impossible. Ewell and Hill tried in vain to rouse him. Finally Dr. McGuire was summoned, and he later described the scene: "At last some one got him into a sitting posture, and another yelled in his ear something about the condition of our army." When he seemed to be awake, his generals tried to talk to him. Squatting around the pallet in the dark, they looked like frogs to Dabney. Jackson had little idea of what was going on or where his units were. He asked Ewell

---

4. This was the only time in the war that artillery caused more casualties than small arms, which accounted for almost 90 percent of all Civil War casualties. Some of the wounded at Malvern Hill were still on the ground three days later.

vaguely where Taylor's brigade was. "General," said Ewell, "practically it is nowhere." Raising his voice, he said, "If McClellan knows what he is doing, he will take the aggressive in the morning, and I tell you we are in no condition to meet it."

"Oh no," countered Jackson, and with what Dabney remembered as "an inexpressible dryness and nonchalance," he said, "McClellan will clear out in the morning."[5] With that he went back to sleep.

He was right. At dawn a thick mist covered Malvern Hill and its environs. The Federal army, protected only by a weak rear guard, had decamped in the heavy rain, trudging down the back slopes to the James River and under the guns of the Union warships.

Jackson was up early and put himself in charge of a burial detail. Captain William Blackford of Stuart's staff was with him and was astonished by his zeal. Bodies were laid out in rows, muskets were stacked, and accoutrements were collected. Jackson hustled the men on the detail so keenly that they scarcely had time to rifle the pockets of the dead. Resentful, they cursed him, "not loud but deep." Everything was to be picked up, he insisted: "every scrap of clothing and caps, and every scrap of human flesh scattered around, such as legs and arms, etc. etc."

When all had been made tidy and Jackson "had swept his dust in piles, like a good housewife, and the floor looked clean though the piles were still there," Blackford could not resist asking, "Why?"

"I am going to attack here presently, as soon as the fog rises," said Jackson, "and it won't do to march the troops over their own dead, you know. That's what I am doing it for." Perhaps so. Still, it was a strange occupation for a senior major general that morning.

But Jackson did not, in fact, march his men over this or any other ground. Rain fell heavily, and through the downpour the work went on of burying the dead, bringing in the wounded, and finding lost men and units. General Trimble thought the army in the "utmost disorder," with "thousands of straggling men asking every passer-by for their regiments; ambulances, wagons, and artillery obstructing every road, and altogether, in a drenching rain, presenting a scene of the most woful [*sic*] and disheartening confusion."

Later in the day Jackson, Longstreet, and other senior officers met

5. According to Hunter McGuire, Jackson's words were: "McClellan and his army will be gone by daylight." According to Henry Kyd Douglas, his words were: "The enemy will be gone in the morning."

with Lee to determine their next move. President Davis arrived, and Lee, looking to be sure he knew everyone, saw that Davis failed to recognize Jackson. "Why, President, don't you know Stonewall Jackson?" said Lee. "This is our Stonewall Jackson."

Davis advanced to greet him warmly, but Jackson stood stonily at attention and saluted. Davis bowed. Doubtless the order recalling Loring from Romney still rankled, and Jackson always found it hard, if not impossible, to forgive. His president was no exception. Throughout the conference Jackson sat morosely silent in a corner and spoke only when spoken to, but he made it clear that he was for pursuing the enemy at once. After talk of the rain and of the muddy roads Lee decided against pursuit. Rain often seemed to dampen the enthusiasm of Confederate generals.

The next day, 3 July, the sky cleared, and the army moved forward. Stuart had found the Union army on the James River behind an undefended ridge called Evelington Heights. Longstreet led the advance, but the muddy roads had been so cut up by McClellan's force that movement was difficult. After going only three miles, Longstreet turned back to look for a better route. Jackson, reasonably rested now but in a foul mood from the delay, went to bed that night in a farmhouse near Willis Church. He warned his staff to be up early and ordered Lewis to have breakfast ready by dawn. "We must burn no more daylight," he said.

The next morning Douglas, awakened by Lewis and told that the general was waiting, leaped into his clothes and rushed to breakfast. But by this time, he said, "the General's temper was beginning to effervesce." It is uncertain whether Douglas or Dabney appeared first, but Jackson snapped at the reverend: "Major, how is it that this staff never will be punctual?"

"I am on time," said Dabney piously. "I cannot control the others."

Jackson was enraged. Turning to Lewis, he barked, "Put that food back into the chest. Have that chest on the wagon, and that wagon moving in two minutes."[6]

Jim Lewis, said Douglas, "obeyed the General with grotesque

---

6. According to Douglas, his words were: "If my staff will not get up, they must go without their breakfast. Let's ride." Douglas and Dabney, who detested each other, naturally had different versions of this affair, and each claimed to be the first staff officer to appear.

gravity and alacrity." (Lewis had eaten his breakfast.) The steaming coffee was poured on the ground, and the still-warm biscuits packed away.

Dabney mildly suggested that Jackson ought to eat something, but Jackson stomped out, mounted his horse, and with the hungry Douglas rode to Ewell's headquarters. Finding Ewell still asleep, he "visited upon him some of his bad humor" and hustled Douglas off to put Ewell's division in motion while its unfortunate commander hurriedly dressed. Jackson found it intolerable that others slept when he wanted to be moving.

The phantom fears and craven behavior of McClellan were exceeded only by the fatuities of the Confederate generals. Stuart, standing on top of Evelington Heights and looking out over the sodden Union army below him in the valley of the James River, was so exhilarated by the sight that he could not resist hauling up a single small gun and banging away at them. Alerted to their danger, the Federals rushed to fortify the heights. Stuart's senseless bravado had been costly. Had he only waited for Longstreet and Jackson to come up, the Confederates could have occupied the heights, and Lee might yet have achieved a considerable victory.

As the Confederates now lined up to make still another attack upon another formidable Federal position, Jackson had second thoughts. Even he did not relish the prospect of storming Evelington Heights. When Lee came up and surveyed the terrain, he agreed that there seemed no good way to attack "these people." He drew back his army. On 8 July it encamped in the vicinity of Richmond. So ended the Seven Days Battles. A month later the Federals packed up and sailed back to Washington.

Confederate dead numbered 3,286; wounded were 16,909, and 946 were missing. Of the 20,141 casualties, 15,590 fell in the assault on Malvern Hill. McClellan suffered only half as many dead and wounded, 1,734 and 8,062 respectively, but his missing, mostly prisoners, numbered 6,053.[7] Union losses in arms, stores, and supplies were considerable. The Confederates acquired from them 52 pieces of artillery and 35,000 small arms, many of the latter being new Enfield and Springfield rifles.

Richmond had been saved, but Lee was bitterly disappointed in the results of Seven Days, and although in a congratulatory order to the

7. More men were killed and wounded in the Seven Days Battle than in all of the Western theater, including bloody Shiloh.

army he spoke of the campaign as a "signal success" which produced "brilliant results," he confided to his wife that "our success has not been as great or complete as I could have desired," and in his formal report he wrote: "Under ordinary circumstances the Federal Army should have been destroyed." Jackson, who almost never regretted anything, expressed different sentiments: "Undying gratitude is due to God for this great victory by which despondency increased in the North, hope brightened in the South, and the capital of Virginia and of the Confederacy was saved." He found no fault in his own performance.

In a letter to Anna (date unknown but shortly after Malvern Hill) Jackson, writing from "about three miles north of the James River and twenty-five miles below Richmond," briefly described the campaign and praised D. H. Hill's performance at Malvern Hill, saying that he "accomplished more than any other part of the army." He then wrote: "During the past week I have not been well, have suffered from fever and debility, but through the blessing of an ever-kind Providence I am much better today." It would appear that he made no connection between his sustained loss of sleep and his "fever and debility," symptoms that all suffer under such circumstances.

From the end of the Mexican War until the beginning of the Civil War Jackson had in virtually every letter to Laura, Ellie, Anna, and friends written about his health, but this was the first time since leaving Lexington that he had mentioned feeling ill. And it was the last time until, ten months hence, he fell at Chancellorsville.

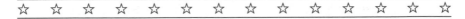

Cedar Mountain

Thomas he Confederates, particularly those from the Valley, were glad to leave what Private John Robson called "this dreary, dismal country" and to escape the mosquitoes and the "ticks and chiggers that camped on us and entrenched themselves in our flesh." He doubtless spoke for most when he said: "This Chickahominy country is not much like the royal Valley of Virginia, and we always felt lost in it."

Jackson, too, disliked the swamp. A week after the Battle of Malvern Hill, Lee's army pulled back into Richmond's defenses. On the march back Jackson halted his corps by a clear, flowing stream and ordered his men to bathe. They undoubtedly stank. He himself slept, in part by dozing in his saddle, watched carefully by solicitous staff officers as he swayed drunkenly. He was once roused by a local sitting on a fence who called out, "I say, old fellow, where the devil did you get your liquor?"

Jackson made his headquarters on the Mechanicsville Road a few miles northeast of Richmond. The Confederate capital was jammed with the twenty-one thousand wounded from the battles of Seven Pines and Seven Days. Citizens from Richmond and Petersburg rode to the battlefields in omnibuses and private carriages to collect the wounded. Churches, barns, warehouses, stores, tobacco factories, hotels, private homes, and even boxcars on the railroad track all housed the sick and wounded. "We lived in one immense hospital, and breathed the vapors of the charnel house," wrote one Richmond woman.

Jackson, reasonably rested at last, his judgment and will restored, became his old aggressive self. He wanted the army to move forward promptly. The error of Manassas was being repeated, he said, by "allowing the enemy leisure to recover from his defeat and ourselves to suffer from inaction." He tried once again to go over Lee's head by sending Boteler to speak to President Davis, but Boteler was reluctant and protested that the president would only refer him, as before, to Lee. "So why don't you speak to General Lee upon the subject?" he asked.

Jackson replied that he had done so and that Lee's had been an unsatisfactory answer. "So great is my confidence in General Lee that I am willing to follow him blindfolded," he said. "But I fear he is unable to give me a definite answer because of influence at Richmond. . . . I therefore want you to see the President and urge the importance of prompt action."

So for the third time Boteler, acting on Jackson's behalf, tried to circumvent Lee, and as he had predicted, he again failed.

Changes were made in the Confederate army following Seven Days. Lee reorganized the Army of Northern Virginia. Magruder and T. H. Holmes were sent to the Trans-Mississippi Department; Huger was made inspector of artillery and ordnance, his place as a commander being taken by D. H. Hill, who then ceased to be under Jackson. Whiting's division was also made a part of this command. The army was divided into two corps (although not yet officially so designated) under Jackson and Longstreet. The latter, who had commanded only six brigades at Seven Days, now had twenty-eight, and Jackson, who had commanded fourteen brigades, was left with seven. Clearly Lee had more faith in Longstreet's abilities than in Jackson's, which, considering the latter's poor performance at Seven Days, is understandable.

Jackson retained Ewell, whose respect for Jackson's generalship in the Valley campaign had altered his opinion so that he now wanted to remain under his command. Major Dabney, sick and exhausted by the Seven Days campaign, was sent home to rest. He never returned. "It was with tearful eyes that I consented to our separation," Jackson told Anna. His remaining staff officers were less regretful. His place as assistant adjutant general was taken by Sandie Pendleton, who proved to be both popular and efficient.

There were also important changes in the Union army in the month following Seven Days. Major General Henry Wager Halleck had been appointed general-in-chief, and Lincoln had issued a call for three hundred thousand additional volunteers. Major General John Pope had been placed in command of what was now called the Army of Virginia, which combined the Shenandoah Department under Banks, the Rappahannock Department under McDowell, and the Mountain Department under Frémont, who promptly resigned in a huff at being put under Pope; Franz Sigel, an equally incompetent general, succeeded Frémont.

Pope had about fifty-six thousand men in his new command, but they were widely scattered. John Pope was a fire-eater who had experienced some success commanding the Army of the Mississippi; on taking over his new command, he boasted: "I come to you from the West where we have always seen the backs of our enemies. . . ."[1] Eager to fight, he moved rapidly southward into central Virginia. Someone remarked to Jackson: "This new general claims your attention."

"And, please God, he shall have it," replied Jackson.

Pope proceeded to incense all Southerners with a series of outrageous orders. His troops were directed to live off the country—an order too often taken as permission to loot—and supplies, if purchased, were paid for by vouchers payable at the war's end if the holders could prove they had been loyal citizens; civilians who lived near railroads damaged by Confederates were required to repair all damage at their own expense; any house from which a Union soldier had been fired upon was to be razed and its occupants taken prisoner; finally, every Southerner living within the Union lines was required to take an oath of allegiance to the United States. Such orders were in striking contrast with those of McClellan, who had taken pains to preserve private property and protect noncombatants.

Sometime in July Jackson summoned to his headquarters Captain (later Brigadier General) Rufus Barringer, 1st North Carolina Cavalry, who had married Anna's sister Eugenia, and the two brothers-in-law spent an evening together. According to Barringer, Jackson was so incensed by Pope's dicta that he declared the Confederates should "raise the black flag"—that is, give no quarter. Examples in the Bible

---

1. A knee-slapping joke among Southerners claimed that Pope had announced that his "headquarters would be in the saddle," thus placing his head was where his buttocks ought to be—or variations on this. Although Pope has been properly credited with having made other ridiculous statements, he never made this one, but it is still often repeated. In his denial Pope declared that he first heard the joke applied to General W. J. Worth during the Mexican War, and he presumed "it could be traced back to the Crusades and beyond."

fully justified the policy, he maintained, and to follow it would bring the North "to its senses."[2] That evening, too, according to Barringer, he spoke of his desire to invade the North with movable columns of cavalry and artillery.

On Sunday, 13 July, Jackson rode into the capital to hear the Reverend Dr. Moses Drury Hoge preach. Hoge was one of the leading lights of the Southern Presbyterian Church and was famed as an orator. According to Dabney, Jackson went to church unattended and after the service visited the mother of a son who had been killed. According to Douglas (whose version is substantiated by McGuire), he, McGuire, and Pendleton accompanied Jackson to the church, where, said McGuire, Jackson promptly went to sleep.

The next day Jackson wrote to Anna: "It is a great comfort to have the privilege of spending a quiet Sabbath within the walls of a house dedicated to the service of God. . . . People are very kind to me. How God, our God, does shower blessings upon me, an unworthy sinner!"

Although he did not, of course, mention it to Anna, he had already received his orders to move north. Lee, who had learned that Pope had occupied Culpeper, had ordered Jackson and Ewell to move to Louisa, about eighty miles northwest of Richmond, and, if possible, another thirty miles northeast to the Central Railroad at Gordonsville.

Jackson marched his corps into Richmond, where it entrained on the cars of the Richmond, Fredericksburg & Potomac Railroad (RF&P) and then near Beaver Dam switched to the Virginia Central bound for Louisa. The entire operation took several days. Jackson was at Beaver Dam on 17 July and at Fredericks Hall, ten miles east of Louisa, on the following day. Learning that Pope had not occupied Gordonsville, he pushed on, arriving there on the nineteenth. As he had fewer than twelve thousand men with him, he made his usual plea for reinforcements. But with McClellan still on the James, reinforcements, Lee told him, were a "difficult question." However, he promised a Louisiana

2. Jackson admirers have felt uneasy about this reference to raising the black flag, but the statement is consistent with sentiments he expressed to his nephew just before the war and of his expressed desire to kill the bravest of the enemy. He also discussed a black flag policy "several times" with Dr. McGuire, who said that he "wondered if in the end it would not result in less suffering and loss of life." Although McGuire maintained that Jackson "never advocated it," he clearly favored a no-holds-barred war. In Anna Jackson's first edition of memoirs of her husband, Barringer's account is quoted at length, but on Hotchkiss's advice, "the Barringer stuff" was omitted from later editions. Henderson deliberately omitted Barringer's remembrances, as did Dabney, Davis, Vandiver, and other admiring biographers.

brigade with a battery and finally A. P. Hill's division, the largest in the Confederate army, for a total of eighteen thousand men.

Because A. P. Hill was ever a prickly subordinate, Lee made some wise and tactful suggestions to the closemouthed and quick-tempered Jackson: "A. P. Hill you will, I think, find a good officer, with whom you can consult, and by advising with your division commanders as to your movements much trouble will be saved you in arranging details, as they can act more intelligently." It was good advice, but Jackson ignored it.

There was much speculation among all ranks about their destination. One officer mused: "It seems strange to see a large body of men moving in one direction and only one man in all the thousands knowing where they are going." Furthermore: "They will go until ordered to stop." Colonel William Dorsey Pender, the twenty-eight-year-old West Pointer who commanded the 3rd North Carolina Cavalry, wrote to his wife from a "Camp near Gordonsville" on 4 August: "I have but little doubt but that this is the commencement of a move into Md. or Penna. If we should ever get there what nice things I will buy you and cram Confederate money down their throats for them. You shall have the cloak, corsets, shoes, baby shoes, etc. so send me your no. [size]." Maryland and Pennsylvania were indeed soon to be invaded by Lee's army, but not just yet. The pompous Pope had first to be dealt with.

At Gordonsville Jackson stayed at first at the home of the Reverend D. B. Ewing and pitched his headquarters tent in the yard. From it he could see through his open tent flaps the Blue Ridge in the distance. He liked the Ewings, particularly the children, whose affections he won. One of the young girls was audacious enough to ask for a brass button from his coat, and he was pleased to give it to her. He stayed with the Ewings or with Mrs. Ewing's mother, for nineteen days, an increasingly busy time.

"I am just overburdened with work," he told Anna, "and I hope you will not think hard at receiving only very short letters from your loving husband . . . people keep coming to my tent."

One of these was John S. Mosby, a young cavalry officer with a note and a present from Stuart: Napoleon's *Maxims of War*—a book which Jackson seems never to have found time to read.

Another was twenty-eight-year-old Captain Charles M. Blackford, a cavalry officer who was summoned to report in person on scouting he had been carrying out west of Fredericksburg. Blackford had scarcely launched into his report when it became apparent that Jackson "was fast asleep." Uncertain whether to go or stay, he sat in an uneasy silence until Jackson opened his eyes and said simply, "Proceed." Blackford gamely began again only to watch Jackson again doze off. This time his wait was longer. When Jackson finally roused himself, his only words were: "You may proceed to your quarters."

Blackford had another encounter with his general's somnolence. He was inspecting roads with Jackson and some of his staff one day when Jackson "suddenly stopped, dismounted at the foot of a tree, unbuckled his sword and stood it by the tree, then laid [*sic*] down with his head on the root of the tree and was asleep in a second. . . . I was much amazed and glanced at the other gentlemen, who I thought were not so much surprised. The General had said not a word. . . . He laid with his eyes shut for five or six minutes, got up, buckled on his sword, mounted and rode on without any explanation or comment."

The doctors of divinity had again flocked to preach to the army, and one, a Virginia minister, unfamiliar with the habits of the corps commander, was "very much amused" to see that on several occasions Jackson was "fast asleep at preaching." Ewell once quipped: "What is the use of General Jackson's going to church? He sleeps all of the time."

On 3 August Jackson rode to Lawton's brigade to hear Dr. Joseph C. Stiles, a famous Georgia minister. Hotchkiss, now back with the army, thought his voice "thrilled like a trumpet" as the perspiration ran down his face and he "prayed that there might be no more straggling when we again went forth to battle." If Jackson was awake, he must have said a deeply felt "amen."

One of Jackson's persistent problems was his cavalry, which had lived a loose and undisciplined life under Ashby and had never taken the bit of discipline in its mouth. Only the 2nd and 6th Virginia Cavalry had been with Jackson on the Chickahominy; the units that had remained in the Valley now rejoined him, and all were consolidated into what was called the Laurel Brigade. Over Jackson's objections, command was given to Brigadier General Beverly H. Robertson, thirty-five. Although Robertson, a West Pointer, was a strict disciplinarian and would seem to have been exactly what the cavalry needed and Jackson ordered, he had his faults as a cavalry commander. Jackson, perhaps taking his cue from Stuart, who thought him "troublesome" and unreliable, disliked him as much as his troopers, who resented his attempts to discipline them. Jackson had asked that he be replaced by Colonel William E. ("Grumble") Jones, commanding the 7th Virginia Cavalry, but Robertson stayed.

One hot day in early August, shortly after Robertson's appointment, he appeared at Jackson's headquarters. There had been numerous cavalry skirmishes, and Jackson asked, as he always asked cavalry commanders, "Where is the enemy?"

"I really do not know," Robertson replied coolly. Jackson's face turned black, and he walked away to send for Stuart.

Now seemed as good a time as any for proceeding with the courts-martial of Brigadier General Richard Garnett, whom Jackson had accused of unnecessarily ordering a retreat at Kernstown, and of Colonel Zephaniah Conner for his failure vigorously to defend Front Royal. The trial of Garnett began on 6 August at Ewell's headquarters, but the next day the court was suspended, never to be resumed. Jackson's corps was again in motion.

Pope had unwisely divided his force, leaving only a portion of his army at Culpeper under Jackson's old adversary Nathaniel Banks. Jackson, eager for a real battle, saw this as a great opportunity, as indeed, it was.

It was a hot August in central Virginia in 1862, the notorious Virginia "dog days." In the first week of the month an average temperature of eighty-eight degrees at two o'clock in the afternoon was recorded at the Lewinsville weather station a few miles north. On 7 August, as Jackson's troops moved toward Culpeper, the temperature soared to ninety-two, and by eight o'clock in the evening it had cooled only to eighty-three degrees. Lieutenant John Summers of the 52nd Virginia wrote in his diary: "The weather so hot men faint and die on the march."

General Winder was too sick to mount his horse, but he did not want to be left behind if the army was going to fight. He sent an aide, McHenry Howard, to ask Jackson if there was to be a battle and, if so, where and when. Knowing Jackson's usual response to such questions, Howard went on his errand with "a good deal of uneasiness." He found Jackson at the home of Dr. John T. Jones, on his knees packing a carpetbag.

Howard blurted out his message, expecting to receive the full force of Jackson's wrath, but Jackson merely smiled "one of his diffident smiles" and said, "Say to General Winder that I am truly sorry he is sick." He then paused for a moment and went on: "There will be a battle, but not tomorrow, and I hope he will be up. Tell him the army will march to Barnett's Ford—and he can learn its further direction from there."

The marching orders issued for the next day, Friday, the eighth, directed Ewell's division to lead the way with A. P. Hill's division next and then Winder's. However, at the last minute Jackson made a change and directed Ewell to take his division higher up the Rapidan River, but he neglected to tell Hill.

Speed was essential if Jackson was to catch the Federals off-balance, but by failing to inform Hill of the change in Ewell's route, he created chaos. At dawn Hill had, as he reported, "my leading brigade resting near the street down which I understood Ewell was to pass" and "ready to take my place in the column of march." When he saw a column of men trudging by, he assumed they were Ewell's troops. It was some time before he learned to his surprise that they were Winder's. Jackson rode up and accosted Hill, furious that his men were not moving. Exactly what the two said is unknown, but in A. P. Hill Jackson had a subordinate as prickly as himself, perhaps more so.

At Barnett's Ford, where the corps was to cross, a traffic jam of monumental proportion clogged the roads with men, horses, and wagons. Hill, who had grown up in Culpeper, knew of a smaller ford, and he suggested to Jackson that his division use it to ease the bottleneck. It seemed a good idea, but Jackson told him in effect to do as he was ordered and keep to the main road.

The eighth was another fiery hot day, the temperature reached ninety-six degrees at two o'clock, and the red dust of the roads was suffocating. The men straggled badly. Hotchkiss noted that the animals also "suffered fearfully." Leading elements managed to make about eight miles, but Hill's division, now in the rear, marched fewer than two. Hill described Jackson's plans for this day as "utter chaos," but Jackson placed the entire blame for the muddle upon Hill.

It was on this day or the next that Jackson spied Private George H. Moffett of the 11th Virginia Cavalry, a former teacher in his black Sunday school. Eager for news of Lexington, he called him to come ride with him. "It was a great gratification to him," said Moffett, "that the school was being kept up in his absence."

Jackson and his staff spent the night of the eighth at the farm of James Garnett (no relation to General Richard Garnett or Colonel Thomas S. Garnett), Jackson sleeping on the porch and his staff on the grass. Two false alarms in the course of the night disturbed the rest of all.

"I am not making much progress," Jackson confessed to Lee early the next morning, but on this day, 9 August, the march went better. Ewell led the way north on the road to Culpeper, the long column with its wagons and guns stretching out for seven miles over rolling, heavily wooded country.

Shortly after noon elements of Elzey's brigade, now commanded by Brigadier General Jubal Early,[3] reached a point about eight miles from Culpeper, where they could see, a mile and a half on the right of the road, a steep hill known as Cedar Mountain or Slaughter's Mountain. (The Reverend Philip Slaughter with his wife and two daughters, both in their twenties, lived on its slope.) Around the base of the hill ran a forked stream called Cedar Run. Here lay a farm owned by the Crittenden family, one of whose sons was Captain Charles Thomas Crittenden of the 13th Virginia.[4] Immediately to the right of the road were a small uneven field planted in wheat and larger fields of corn. On the left ran extensive woods, and on a ridge ahead, perpendicular to the road, the Federals were waiting.

Jackson assumed that his old adversary Banks had concentrated his strength in the cleared land on the right, but the main body of Banks's force was, in fact, to the left of the road.

Less than an hour after Ewell spotted the Federals, Sandie Pendleton, carrying a message to Early, found him near a schoolhouse and reported: "General Jackson sends his compliments to General Early and says advance on the enemy and you will be supported by General Winder."

"My compliments to General Jackson, and tell him I will do it," drawled Early.

Charles Blackford saw this day what he had never seen before: "men pinning strips of paper with their names, company and regiment to their coats so they could be identified if killed."

Early formed his men in line of battle and about three o'clock moved forward without waiting for Hill's division—the largest in the corps—still strung out for nearly seven miles along the dusty road. Early's first move was an attempt to outflank the Federal guns directly in his front. He pushed back the cavalry and skirmishers, but when he crested a hill, heavy fire from Union artillery halted him.

Lawton was the senior brigadier general on the field, but Jackson

3. Brigadier General Arnold Elzey was severely wounded in the fighting on the Chickahominy and was never able to take the field again. Jubal Anderson Early had just returned to duty after having suffered a severe wound at Williamsburg on 5 May. According to Ewell, he "was still so enfeebled . . . as to be unable to mount his horse without assistance." There were an unusual number of physically unfit senior Confederate officers commanding units at Cedar Mountain.

4. There were many young soldiers from the Culpeper area in the 13th Virginia, which was commanded by Colonel James A. Walker, the former cadet who had threatened to kill Jackson.

did not entertain a good opinion of his fighting abilities. He disposed of him by sending him to the rear to guard Confederate wagons from Union cavalry. This enabled Jackson to give the division to Winder, still sick and suffering from the heat but prepared to lead all three brigades. Winder's place as commander of the Stonewall Brigade was taken by Colonel Charles A. Ronald, a thirty-five-year-old lawyer from Blacksburg, Virginia, who on this day was to prove himself an ineffectual brigade commander.

During the first two hours of the battle Ewell's two dozen guns were clustered at four key artillery positions: in a cedar grove on the crest of a small ridge on Early's right; around the Crittenden farm; on a ledge of Cedar Mountain, where Ewell had established his headquarters; and to the left of Early's position. The widely separated batteries were able to deliver a converging fire onto the principal Federal artillery base. Commanding the battery whose guns had been manhandled onto the mountain into what Ewell called "a commanding position" was a former VMI cadet, Captain Joseph White Latimer. He was eighteen years old.

In seizing Cedar Mountain, the Confederates certainly had the advantage of a strong defensive position on the right flank and a splendid platform for their artillery. The guns on both sides opened fire with an exchange of shells which a Georgian soldier described as "the prettiest artillery duel ever witnessed in the war."

Although Federal gunners were active, firing 3,213 shells in the course of the day, only about 2 percent caused casualties, but one struck the gallant Charles Winder. Caught up in the excitement of the artillery duel, he had thrown off his coat and, standing beside the left gun of Poague's battery by the Crittenden farm gate, was directing the battery's fire. He was calling out an order when he was hit in the left arm and chest. According to one of the cannoneers, "He fell straight back at full length, and lay quivering on the ground." His wound was mortal.

Winder's place as division commander was taken by Brigadier General William B. Taliaferro, whom Jackson had been unable to shed from his command. Taliaferro's brigade was taken over by his fifty-three-year-old uncle, Colonel Alexander Galt Taliaferro.

Although Jackson had twice as many guns to hand as did Banks, most were small 6-pounders or weak howitzers; the Federals had the heavier metal: long-range rifles and 12-pounder Napoleons. Many historians have declared the Federals to be the victors in the artillery duel, which lasted from about four o'clock until a quarter to six, but the superior positions of the Confederate guns certainly gave them the upper hand.

Jackson had established his headquarters just south of the Critten-den gate in one of the farm's tenant houses, but he did not stay there. During the artillery duel he moved about a great deal, spending most of his time on the right of the line. He was once seen writing an order while shells crashed around him. A nervous officer suggested that he move because the Federals "have a good range," but Jackson, unper-turbed, wrote on. When a shell hit a nearby pine tree and spewed bark and wood splinters over him, a soldier of the 10th Virginia watched him brush the debris from his paper and unhurriedly finish his order.

John Blue, a trooper assigned to Jackson this day, never forgot the danger to which Jackson exposed himself, his staff, and his couriers. Watching the effect of the artillery fire through field glasses, Jackson sat his horse, his right leg thrown across the pommel, "as immovable ap-parently as a statue." When his aides once protested his exposure, he ordered his entourage back and out of sight. "They will hardly aim at a single horseman," he said.

Soon after, he was informed that Winder had fallen. This was followed by a message from Early, who thought he saw an opportunity to move around Banks's right flank. Jackson ordered Colonel Thomas S. Garnett (again, no relation to Richard Garnett), who commanded a brigade, to "look well" to his left flank and to turn to Taliaferro if he needed reinforcements. At about five-thirty he saw that A. P. Hill's infantry was beginning to arrive on the field.

The Confederates had patched together a line of battle with strong artillery positions, but their infantry was not well placed. Gar-nett's brigade on the left of the line was in the air; the 10th Virginia, struggling toward it, was stumbling uncertainly through the woods; and the Stonewall Brigade, temporarily under the incompetent Colonel Ronald, was too far behind.

Although Pope later claimed that he had instructed Banks to stay on the defensive, Banks swore that he had been ordered to attack as soon as the enemy approached. Certainly he behaved aggressively, even rashly. As the sound of artillery fire slackened, a three-brigade division of Union infantry under Brigadier General Christopher C. Augur, which had been concealed behind tall corn opposite Taliaferro and Early in the middle of the Confederate line, began their advance. Colonel Taliaferro's brigade, reported General Taliaferro, "advanced in fine style and the enemy gave way before the severity of its fire."

Jackson, sitting his horse, watched the entire action.

To Lieutenant Blue it sounded as if "the rattle of musketry was continuous along the whole line." He noticed that Jackson "became a different person altogether." It seemed that only "the greatest exertion" kept him from joining the fight.

After scribbling an ambiguous note to Hill, which he sent off by a courier, Jackson wheeled and dashed off, couriers and staff in his wake, to the spot where Taliaferro's and Early's brigades joined. There he rode along the Crittenden Lane ridge until he was opposite the guns. "The musket balls were flying over and around us pretty thick," said Blue. The air buzzed with "that sizzing, hissing sound peculiar to the Minnie [*sic*] ball, a music which any old soldier will tell you is not pleasant at any time, more especially when compelled to sit quietly and listen to their singing with nothing to do except break one's neck by jerking his head from one side to the other whenever one of those little messengers fanned his cheek or brushed his nose."

Jackson ignored the bullets but looked anxiously over his shoulder for Hill to come up. Soon he summoned an aide and sent him to Early with a message to stand firm as "General Hill will be with him in a few moments."

It was nearly six o'clock when two Federal brigades moved forward to the attack and the brigades of Taliaferro and Early advanced a short distance to meet them. Behind their right was the Georgia brigade of Colonel Edward Loyd Thomas, who, like Early, had just returned to duty after wounds. Thomas's brigade came up after a ten-mile march under "the hottest sun you ever saw."

In this pitched battle Lieutenant Colonel Alfred Henry Jackson, a second cousin of the corps commander's, fell with a wound that killed him fifty-one weeks later. Sam Buck of the 13th Virginia entered the fight without a weapon, but he was soon able to pick up "any number of guns" from fallen comrades. Taking them up one after another, he fired them. If any held a ramrod, he shot that off as well.

A Maryland battery near the Crittenden house fought its guns valiantly, and Jackson cheered on the gunners, calling out for them to "give the Yankees a little more grape," an impossibility, for they had shot away all their canister and shell and had only round shot left.

Jackson personally positioned Thomas's Georgia brigade in the edge of a woods near Crittenden Lane, and the Georgians cheered and "yelled as only Johnnies could yell," as they charged forward into the fray "with nothing to protect them," said a captain in the 45th Georgia, "save the hand of God." Jackson sat on his horse nearby as they burst from the woods. The regiment carried 156 officers and men into battle and suffered 7 killed and 41 wounded—a casualty rate of more than 30 percent.

From their perch on Cedar Mountain, Ewell's infantry and artillery enjoyed a splendid panoramic view of the battle below. Robert H. Miller of the 14th Louisiana later wrote: "Of all the grand sights and sounds this excelled, of all sublimity this was the most sublime sight I have ever seen or imagined. It was worth all the dangers we had passed and more."

Suddenly the entire Confederate line received a severe jolt and was almost routed by a charge of Augur's infantry out of a woods near the wheat field. The Confederate left appeared on the verge of collapsing. The Federals had charged at an auspicious moment: The 10th Virginia had not yet arrived on the field, and the Stonewall Brigade under Ronald's inept management was still stumbling about in the rear. As Colonel Garnett wrote in his after-action report: "Had re-enforcements . . . arrived ten minutes sooner no disaster would have happened." Jackson wrote: "While the attack upon Early was in progress the main body of Federal infantry moved down from the wood . . . and fell with great vigor upon our extreme left."

In the wheat field much of the grain had been cut and stood in shocks. Here Confederates and Federals met in the bloodiest hour of the day, and the Confederates were pushed to the brink of disaster. Garnett's brigade "fell back in disorder," Jackson later reported. The Irish Battalion broke ranks and fled. The brave 42nd Virginia, in the most ferocious hand-to-hand fighting of the war, did all that it could to save the day and was devastated, losing fifty-three killed, fifty-eight wounded, and eight taken prisoner. By its gallant stand it halted and disorganized a part of the Federal advance. Just in time the 10th Virginia now arrived on the field to add weight to the Confederate defense. Major Frederick Holliday, 33rd Virginia, the hero of Dam No. 5 and the future governor of Virginia, was carried from the field with a shattered arm, soon amputated.[5]

5. Captain David Coffman Grayson, who commanded Company K of the 10th Virginia, was shot through the right lung, and the surgeons told him he would surely die, as indeed, he did—more than seventy years later, in June 1933. Major R. Snowden Andrews, an artilleryman, was almost disemboweled by a shell, and his abdominal viscera were covered with dust. McGuire and every other surgeon who saw him pronounced his wound mortal, but a Georgia doctor sewed him up, and he lived to fight again—and again to be wounded. After the war he became an architect and lived until 6 January 1903.

The Stonewall Brigade finally arrived in time to throw back the 3rd Wisconsin. Although the 27th Virginia melted away, its men slinking to the rear, the remaining regiments in the brigade held fast. Nevertheless, the left of the Confederate line was in a chaotic state, and the Federals seemed on the verge of dragging the famed Stonewall Jackson down in a major defeat.

Jackson, watching the fight from a position behind the left of Early's brigade, from time to time looked down the road through his field glasses. Sometimes he cocked his head in a familiar movement, trying to determine the direction of fire, difficult for him with his deaf ear. An officer noticed that he "seemed to be getting a little nervous." Someone pointed out the Federal attack through the wheat field, and he said, "That firing is very heavy." Indeed, this was so.

A courier rode up with a message about the trouble on the left, and Jackson dashed off in that direction, staff officers and couriers scurrying after him. Galloping about four hundred yards, he leaped a fence, gave some orders to a battery, and dashed on. Plunging into the woods, he encountered Garnett's men "falling back in considerable disorder." For a time he sat his horse stonily as frightened Confederate soldiers streamed past him; then he turned and rode to the rear in search of A. P. Hill. Finding him, he told him sharply that he was late and ordered him to deploy his men in order of battle. But this was exactly what Hill had been doing. He had also with bared sword been cajoling and threatening the retreating mob, turning many of them around to face the enemy.

With reinforcements on the way, Jackson turned his horse back to the area where the fighting was the most intense, the flying projectiles thickest, the Confederates in the greatest danger. Lieutenant Blue described the scene:

> The rattle of musketry, the shouting, cheering and yelling was [*sic*] deafening. The smoke of battle and the thick foliage on the timber overhead made it impossible to see but a short distance. The leaves and small limbs were falling thick and the bark . . . [flew] in every direction, often striking a person in the face. . . .
>
> It appeared for a few moments as though we had struck a full-grown tornado, loaded with thunder and lightning. This was the most hair-raising fix I had ever struck.

It was here that Jackson performed his most dramatic feat of the war.

Popular histories recount it as the first time Jackson ever drew his sword in battle. The fact is that he tried to draw his sword but could not free it from its scabbard. After the war Jedediah Hotchkiss described the moment to British Lieutenant Colonel G. F. R. Henderson: "I recollect well his attempt to draw his long cavalry sabre to help him stop the rout, when he found it so rusted in from non use, that he could not withdraw it . . . he deliberately unsnapped it from his belt holdings and used it scabbard and all on the heads of the fleeing panic stricken troops."[6] A courier, William M. Taliaferro of the 2nd Virginia Cavalry (unrelated to the other two Taliaferros on the field), described Jackson's using his sheathed sword to "gesticulate with" and "to arrest the tide of men rolling backward, by threatening them." Although other officers, notably his young aide and brother-in-law Joseph Graham Morrison, fresh from VMI, also were hard at work turning the men back to the fight, according to Hotchkiss, it was Jackson's presence that "restored his lines and snatched victory from threatened defeat."

Jackson did more than belabor the backs of shirkers. Dropping his reins, he seized a Confederate battle flag, and sword in one hand and flag in the other, he stemmed the rout and rallied his men.

No man who saw him in action that day ever forgot the sight. Men told how "the eye flashed, the cheek flushed hot." The "light of battle" seemed to shed a "radiance over him," and "his whole person was changed." His voice "rose to loud and strident tones, as it called like a clarion" and "pealed higher than the roar of battle." Even Little Sorrel "seemed endowed with the style and form of an Arabian." William B. Taliaferro, who was present, thought that "the escape of Jackson from death was miraculous."

Jackson, according to his wife, considered the Battle of Cedar Mountain "the most successful of his exploits." Although he issued few orders this day, his energy and courage had played an important role in holding his position. Once again he had also been incredibly lucky.

By sundown the Stonewall Brigade—except for the 27th Virginia, which had bolted—had scuppered the Federals in front of them (5th Connecticut, 28th New York, and 46th Pennsylvania), killing or wounding every field officer and adjutant in all three regiments and

---

6. As Keith Gibson, director of the VMI Museum, pointed out to the author, it is most unlikely that his sword was rusted in its scabbard. The style of Jackson's scabbard is unknown, but many were of leather, and even the metal ones were lined with thin lathes of wood to protect the edge and prevent rust. Some officers deliberately dented their scabbards, reducing the clatter and rattle but making it difficult to unsheathe.

capturing their flags. Once the Federal attacks had been beaten back, the tide of battle ebbed for the Union side. Night was falling when there was a brave but futile charge by some two hundred Federal cavalry down the road. Jackson praised their "impetuous valor," but the charge collapsed in a bloody tangle of dead and wounded men and horses. A final attack by the Federals against Early's left flank on the right of the Confederate line lacked staying power and was beaten back. A counterattack was led by the 14th Georgia, and soon the entire Confederate line moved forward in what Jackson described as a "general charge" that left the enemy "strewing the narrow valley with their dead."

It was almost dark, but Jackson ordered his troops to pursue the retreating Federals. The Confederate units were badly disorganized, but A. P. Hill attempted a pursuit down the Culpeper Road. Hill came upon Early, who complained that he was out of ammunition and his men were "much fatigued and in some confusion." Knowing well that Jackson would accept no excuse for not obeying his orders, Hill advised Early to join the pursuit anyway. So, dragging with fatigue and with empty cartridge boxes, Early's troops advanced in confused knots through the darkness, dust, and heat.

About an hour after sunset Union Brigadier General Henry Prince was, by his own account, walking his horse "in the dense corn, where the ground was heavy," when his bridle was seized by Private John M. Booker of Company I, 23rd Virginia, and/or seventeen-year-old Private George Pike of Company A, 37th Virginia. Prince quickly found himself a prisoner. For him it was the end of what had been a long and trying day. He was taken to William B. Taliaferro, to whom he surrendered his sword and, resentfully, his horse.

When a bright moon lit the scene, advancing Confederates picked up more weary, sweating prisoners. The temperature was eighty-six degrees. When the 1st Tennessee came across Jackson, they cheered him wildly in the moonlight, and he doffed his cap to them. Men were proud indeed to have "fought under Jackson," and survivors would remain so all their lives.

Jackson wandered all over the field that evening and at one point encountered eighteen-year-old William C. ("Willie") Preston of the 4th Virginia, son of Colonel J. T. L. Preston, his colleague at VMI. Jackson knew him well and said he had "loved him since he was a boy." Willie had just fought his first battle and had found it so exhilarating that he begged to scout forward during the night.

Two brigades in Jackson's corps—Colonel Leroy A. Stafford's

and Brigadier General Charles William Field's—had not taken part in the battle. These Jackson ordered forward to be the spearhead of his advance on Culpeper. He detailed Captain Crittenden, on whose family's farm the battle had largely been fought and who knew the area, to select other locals to serve as guides. While waiting for the relatively fresh troops to arrive, he received a message from General Taliaferro protesting that his brigade was used up. Reluctantly Jackson ordered them to bivouac. Sandie Pendleton and Charles M. Blackford were sent to ask the other brigade commanders if their men were "in a condition to advance after a short rest." The unanimous response was that they were short of ammunition and their men were too exhausted to continue. Launcelot Blackford of the Rockbridge Artillery (no relation to Charles Blackford, the cavalryman) later wrote: "I do not believe anything short of the enemy could have revived them to action." Jackson prepared to pursue with his two fresh infantry brigades, some artillery, and newly arrived cavalry.

Cedar Run had to be crossed by a ford on the road, an obstacle to the artillery, but they successfully splashed across and at Jackson's direction "vigorously" shelled the woods around Cedar Run Church. Many of the Confederate soldiers enjoyed the spectacle. One man at Ewell's headquarters remarked, "If there is anything in war that can be called splendidly beautiful, it is a night cannonade. . . ." The cannonade was, however, merely prophylactic; there were few Federals among the trees. When the brigades of Field and Stafford arrived, Jackson pushed them forward. On the far edge of the woods he ordered the artillery to open another prophylactic fire "with shell and canister" on what appeared to be a Union artillery position. Only the battery of the energetic and combative young William Johnson ("Willie") Pegram was at hand and prepared to unlimber. "Pitch in, men!" Pegram cried. "General Jackson's looking at you!"

Pegram went into battery on a small knoll, laying down what Jackson described as "well-directed and unexpected fire" which "produced much disorder and confusion among that portion of the Federal troops." But Pegram brought down upon himself and upon Field's Virginia infantry the fire from three Federal batteries, and he soon found himself, as he confessed, in "a very hot place." The unequal exchange lasted for perhaps an hour; then the Confederate battery fell silent, and as Hill said succinctly, "No further attempt was made to advance." The battle was over.

General Beverly Robertson's cavalry had not been much in evidence on this day, but during the night "Grumble" Jones, on his own initiative, had taken his cavalry on a wide sweep into the Union lines, almost capturing or killing Pope himself. He returned with fifteen prisoners, including three lieutenants and a black who provided the valuable intelligence that General Sigel was arriving from Sperryville to reinforce Banks and Pope, information that was quickly passed on to Jackson, who had already been warned by Benjamin E. Stringfellow, a Confederate scout who had captured one of Sigel's men.

It was time for Jackson to back off, and he was ready to do so, for like his men, he was "utterly worn out" and badly in need of sleep. He made his way back through the battlefield, now loud with the cries and moans of more than two thousand suffering and thirsting wounded, and sought a place to sleep. Someone found some food for him, but he sank down on the grass and said: "No, I want *rest,* nothing but *rest."* Throwing himself facedown under a tree, he was instantly asleep.

John Blue had not closed his eyes for two nights, and he ached for rest, but he could not sleep. He sat in the wheat field and "stuck a finger in each ear to drown the moans, prayers and cries of the wounded and dying." George Neese wrote in his diary: "I hope that I will never be compelled to bivouac on another fresh battlefield."

Some men moved among the wounded to do what they could for them. Louis-Hippolyte Gache, Catholic chaplain of the 10th Louisiana, wandered about the field in "profound sadness." In spite of a prolonged search, he could find no one to shrive, for, he said, all those he encountered were either Protestants or Federals, and "one poor fellow was a Protestant Yankee."

Some prowled the field not to help the wounded but to rob them. "Their number was greater than you might suppose," said one Confederate who watched two men fighting over a dead man's canteen.

Dawn of 10 August was ushered in by a rattle of musketry, but there was no serious fighting. Jeb Stuart had arrived during the night, and he took charge of the underemployed cavalry. At Jackson's request, he made a reconnaissance, traveling, said Hotchkiss, "out on our right and nearly around the enemy's left." Acting with his usual energy and élan, Stuart not only obtained information on the enemy's whereabouts from prisoners and scouts but captured the Federal signal station on Mount Pony, well in rear of the Union lines. From Stuart, "as well as other sources of information," said Jackson, "I was confirmed in my opinion that the heavy forces concentrated in front rendered it unwise on my part to renew the action." He therefore gave orders for the wounded to be brought in, the dead to be buried, and arms collected from the battlefield.

Both friend and foe were brought into the temporary hospitals, marked by distinctive yellow flags. Nearly all were in by midday, the wounded Federals brought in last. Hotchkiss wrote in his diary: "I rode over the battlefield and heard the most agonizing shrieks and groans from the many wounded Yankees that were lying exposed to the full blaze of the sun . . . but we had our own men to attend to first." On the Northern side Clara Barton was at work, tending to the wounded after her first battle. The dead, Confederate and Federal, were buried, often in graves with multiple corpses, "without ceremony or coffin."

Jackson's casualties were 1,418, including 314 killed, 1,062 wounded, and 42 prisoners or missing.[7] The heaviest losses were in the brigades of Taliaferro and Garnett, who between them suffered about 46 percent of the casualties. In his report Jackson noted "the loss of some of our best officers and men." The death of Charles Winder was a particularly heavy blow for Jackson. "I can hardly think of the fall of Brigadier General C. S. Winder without tearful eyes," he wrote. Union losses totaled 2,403, including 320 killed, 1,466 wounded, and 617 taken prisoner or missing.

Although Jackson was understandably concerned that the strongly reinforced Federal forces might attack him, he had little cause to worry. The Federals had pulled back farther toward Culpeper. His greatest tribulation that day came from disruptions on his line of communication.

The "Comanches," a unit of Loudoun County, Virginia, cavalrymen under Elijah V. White, were lounging about on the grass when they were attacked by a Federal cavalry patrol, which came charging at them, "firing, yelling, and making everything look blue." The Comanches quickly mounted and drove them off, but a few Confederates fled to the rear, spreading fear and disorder. There was soon a panic in the rear area which grew exponentially. "For awhile there was a wild stampede," wrote Jedediah Hotchkiss, "the wagoneers thinking the enemy had flanked us." Even a couple of batteries limbered up and fled. Jackson himself had to go back to quell the uproar, his most challenging action of the day.

The Confederates certainly appear to have been skittish. Jackson gave permission for Federal burial parties and stretcher-bearers to come onto the field, but when they appeared, the Confederates at work

---

7. Casualty figures for this battle are those used by Robert K. Krick, who made a careful study of the casualties, unit by unit. His excellent *Stonewall Jackson at Cedar Mountain* (1990) is the most detailed and complete account of the battle.

there, thinking they were being attacked, panicked. Once the confusion was cleared up and the men were assured of their safety, Confederates and Federals fraternally exchanged newspapers, tobacco, food, and rumors.

At Cedar Mountain Jackson had been again the energetic Jackson of the Valley; he would never again be the Jackson of the Chickahominy. Cedar Mountain[8] added another leaf to his laurels and made more widespread his fame. Even in the North the name of Stonewall Jackson was now a household word. Although he always maintained that the sobriquet belonged only to his brigade and not to him, he could not escape the name which seemed to be the American equivalent of the Roman "Augustus."

On the day after the battle (10 August 1862) a prisoner brought in by the cavalry was taken to Jackson's headquarters for interrogation. While waiting outside, he occupied himself by pulling hairs from the tail of Little Sorrel until Jackson came out and demanded to know what he was doing. Doffing his hat, the culprit said, "Ah, General, each one of these hairs is worth a dollar in New York." According to Captain Charles Blackford, Jackson was "both pleased and amused" and for the moment was so disconcerted that he sent the man away without questioning him. The military fame which the young Jackson had so lusted for was now his, and although he has left no record of his feelings and credited all good to God's personal interest in his career, his fame must have tasted sweet in his mouth.

Cedar Mountain was Jackson's last battle as a completely independent commander. In future battles he acted under Lee as part of the Army of Northern Virginia.

8. Jackson always referred to the battle as Cedar Run; other contemporaries called it the Battle of Slaughter's Mountain. Cedar Mountain eventually became the accepted name, particularly after the Battle of Cedar Creek in October 1864. Today (1992) the battlefield looks much the same as it did in 1862, but it is entirely in private hands and is threatened by real estate development.

26

☆ ☆ ☆ ☆ ☆ ☆ ☆ ☆ ☆ ☆ ☆ ☆ ☆ ☆

The Second Manassas
Campaign

J ackson's star again shone brightly in the Confederate firmament. Lee wrote: "The country owes you and your brave officers and soldiers a deep debt of gratitude. I hope your victory is but the precursor of others over our foe in that quarter, which will entirely break up and scatter his army." At the same time, in the North, Pope and Banks basked in felicitations on what was perceived as a Union victory. General-in-Chief Halleck announced that Banks had won a "hard earned but brilliant success against vastly superior numbers." Each side asserted that it had halted the advance of the other, and this was indeed so. The two forces had collided, fought, and pulled back.

Curiously, even after the battle the Union generals failed to realize the impact their forces had made on the Confederate left or that they had come within an inch of rolling up the Confederate line of battle and winning a decisive victory.

On the night of 11 August Jackson's corps pulled back to Gordonsville. On the thirteenth Lee ordered Longstreet to march there with ten brigades, and Stuart was instructed to learn whether forces under Major General Ambrose Burnside had reinforced Pope. Hood's division was ordered to Hanover Junction, and the next day Hood, too, was told to proceed to Gordonsville.

Lee, his army again concentrated, now planned to capitalize on

Jackson's victory. On 15 August he arrived by train at Gordonsville, and Jackson met him at the station. Typically Jackson said nothing about the meeting when he returned to his headquarters, but that evening at dinner the young aide who had accompanied him mentioned Lee's arrival and drew upon his head a reprimand by Jackson. Staff officers should keep all special information to themselves, Jackson told him. It was not necessary that couriers, servants, and enlisted men should know about such things.

Quick to reprove and chary of praise, Jackson could win the esteem of those who worked for him, but seldom their affection. Captain Charles Blackford contrasted his manner with that of Lee, who always had a kind and encouraging word to young officers delivering messages to him. "This is not the case with General Jackson," he said.

> He is ever monosyllabic and receives and delivers a message as if the bearer was a conduit pipe from one ear to another. There is a magnetism in Jackson, but it is not personal. All admire his genius and great deeds; no one could love the man for himself. He seems to be cut off from fellow men and to commune with his own spirit only, or with spirits of which we know not. Yet the men are almost as enthusiastic about him as over Lee, and when he moves about . . . most men shout with enthusiasm. He rides on rapidly without making any sign of recognition, and no one knows whether he is pleased or not.

Most of the behavior deplored by Blackford and others will be readily recognized by those who have difficulty hearing or who live intimately with those who do. Jackson's deafness had grown more pronounced. He appears to have lost all hearing in one ear and perhaps suffered a partial loss in the other. Such partial deafness is not infrequently found among former artillerymen, and there existed, of course, no effective hearing aids.

At Gordonsville Lee met with Longstreet, Stuart, and Jackson to explain his plan for a campaign in which he proposed to strike Pope's front with both Jackson's and Longstreet's corps while Stuart swept behind him, tearing up his lines of communication. It was a good plan and might well have proved disastrous for the Federals, but (not for the only time) it was doomed to failure by the careless handling of secret orders. Stuart sent out a party under his assistant adjutant general, Major Norman Fitzhugh, to reconnoiter, and Fitzhugh foolishly carried with him copies of Lee's plans. He was captured—Stuart himself was nearly caught—by the 1st Michigan Cavalry, and Pope was soon in possession of Lee's intentions. When, on 19 August, Lee and Longstreet climbed a mountain overlooking the Federal position, they were astonished and dismayed to see nothing but empty campsites and clouds of dust rising along the roads leading north as the Federals drew back. Pope had flown the coop.

Jackson was not with Lee on the mountain that day, for he was busy overseeing the execution of some of his own men. Eight Confederates from Taliaferro's (formerly Jackson's) division had deserted. Three had been caught, tried, convicted, and sentenced to die. Although he possessed the authority to do so, Jackson did not commute the sentence. He never did commute a sentence. The entire division paraded to watch the execution, units marching in slow time preceded by bands playing the "Dead March" from Saul. In an open field the deserters knelt blindfolded in front of their open graves. A firing squad, half with loaded rifles, stood waiting. When the division was assembled, the orders were barked, the rifles cracked, and the deserters fell dead. The entire division was then marched past for an instructive look at the corpses.[1] There is no evidence that Jackson felt any pity or expressed any regret for the day's work.

The following day all of Lee's army was in motion, not to attack, as he had planned, but to pursue. Jackson's corps had started at three o'clock in the morning, but again A. P. Hill was not where Jackson thought he should have been, and his dissatisfaction with Hill's march discipline grew. However, the corps crossed the Rapidan by way of Somerville's Ford without opposition and marched twenty miles north.

The following day, 21 August, Lee found Pope waiting for him in strong positions behind the Rappahannock River in Fauquier County. As a frontal attack across the river seemed unlikely to succeed, Lee decided to swing his army around Pope's right flank and moved up-

---

1. The "Dead March in (or from) Saul" is the popular name for the funeral march in Handel's oratorio *Saul,* composed in 1739.

There are discrepancies in the accounts of the executions in Orange County. Some say the number executed was four or five and the date 18 August. There may have been executions on both days.

In spite of the dire and dramatic punishments, the Confederates suffered an increasing rate of desertions. In a desperate measure to get men the Confederate government on 1 August 1863 granted an amnesty to all deserters who returned within twenty days and pardoned all under arrest for being absent without leave. General Lee complained of such leniency and said that sterner punishments, not amnesties, were needed.

stream while his cavalry looked for undefended fords. Pope easily detected the movement and moved with him. The march upstream, the opposing armies moving parallel with the river between them, continued the next day, Jackson's corps in the lead, Ewell's division the leading infantry. At one point a Federal force crossed the river and attacked the column's right flank but was driven back by Trimble and Hood after some hard fighting.

While this small battle was in progress, Jackson's main force reached a point opposite a spa known as Fauquier White Sulphur Springs (today Fauquier Springs), and although the bridge there had been destroyed, Jackson contrived to throw a Georgia regiment and two batteries across. A mile downstream was a milldam where Early's entire brigade managed to cross. However, rain began to fall, and by late afternoon the Rappahannock was seen to be rising. By morning it was in flood. Early's brigade, the Georgians, and the two batteries were cut off.

Jackson was able to provide artillery support from his side of the river, and Early on the left bank assumed a defensive position while the Confederates worked frantically the next day to construct a bridge. Jackson, in a foul mood, waded his horse into the stream and sat there for an hour brooding. Hill walked his horse out and tried to talk with him, but Jackson was "so abstracted and rude" that he rode back to his division. Early succeeded in repulsing the several attacks the Federals launched against him, and by late afternoon the river had dropped, enabling all to scramble back to the right bank.

Jackson was angry with Taliaferro for not moving up during the night and joining the rest of his corps. But unknown to Jackson, Lee had ordered him to stay where he was. When Jackson encountered Taliaferro, he demanded caustically to know why he had not come up but did not allow him to explain. Captain Blackford, who had given Lee's order to Taliaferro the day before, was a witness to the scene: "Taliaferro behaved with much dignity and, as he was not allowed to explain, made no explanation."

Jackson's headquarters during this anxious time was directly across the river from the spa in a neat yellow farmhouse surrounded by a "very nice paling fence." Jackson gave orders that it was not to be touched, but the South Carolina brigade of Brigadier General Maxcy Gregg camped in the area that night, and in spite of the rain, they managed to build good fires by using the palings for firewood. The next morning, when Jackson discovered their depredation, he placed all of Gregg's regimental commanders under arrest. One of these, Colonel

Edward McCrady, 1st (Provisional) South Carolina, wrote indignantly: "We were released upon arrangement with the owners of the farm to pay for the damage done. Five regimental commanders . . . all arrested for a few palings of an ornamental fence taken under such circumstances! And then to be told that there was no discipline in our army!"

On 24 August Lee met again with Jackson, Longstreet, and Stuart to outline an extraordinarily bold plan. Although his army was numerically inferior and in contact with Pope, Lee proposed to divide his force, sending Jackson's entire corps—including the divisions of Ewell, A. P. Hill, and Taliaferro—with some of Stuart's cavalry on a fifty-mile-wide flanking movement around Pope's right flank and squarely across his lines of communication. Meanwhile, Longstreet and Stuart were ordered to make vigorous demonstrations in Pope's front until Jackson was clear. Then they were to follow him.

On the recommendation of his young engineer James Keith Boswell, who knew the area, Jackson planned to march in a great arc by way of Amissville, Orlean, Salem (today Marshall), White Plains (today The Plains), through Thoroughfare Gap and on to Haymarket, Gainesville, and finally Manassas Junction. Boswell was to lead the way with a company of the 6th Virginia Cavalry.

Orders were issued for three days' rations to be cooked and for all wagons and baggage—except a few ambulances, ammunition carts, and a herd of cattle—to be left behind. The men were to march light, and many marched light indeed, for the commissary arrangements bogged down and there was not time for all to cook their rations before they left.

At dawn on 25 August the complex movements involved in pulling back from the river line were executed, and the long, hard march of Jackson's corps began; Ewell's division, being the farthermost west, took the lead, following Boswell's directions. Only Jackson and Boswell knew their route and destination.

In a note to Anna that morning Jackson wrote: "The enemy has taken a position, or rather several positions, on the Fauquier side of the Rappahannock." He made no mention of his own movements. "I have only time to tell you," he wrote, "how much I love my little pet dove."

Boswell and some cavalry reached Salem without encountering Federals. Boswell had not always kept to the roads but had led the corps by a more direct route through fields and down forest paths. The weather this day had been pleasant enough when the infantry started, and one man said later: "The fine weather, magnificent country, the mysterious march, through fields and byways, the unknown destination, the possible collision at any moment with the enemy . . . all served to keep us intensely interested and all the time on the qui vive." But by noon the heat was blistering, and straggling began. Jackson moved along the line of marching men, a VMI cadet kepi pulled low over his eyes, repeating ceaselessly, "Close up, men! Close up!" Private Allen C. Redwood in the 55th Virginia recalled the look of the men, "gaunt-cheeked and hollow-eyed, hair, beard, clothing and accoutrement covered with dust,—only faces and hands, where mingled soil and perspiration streaked and crusted the skin, showed any departure from the whitey-gray uniformity."

The main body reached Orlean about midday, hot, thirsty, and footsore, wondering where their taciturn general was leading them. At the end of the day Jackson, as dusty as they were, stood beside the road as they filed by. Recognizing him, the men, though weary from their twenty-five-mile march, raised a cheer, as they always did now when he appeared, but he quickly checked this, and the word passed down the line: "No cheering!"

Jackson, affected by their endurance and spirit, turned to a staff officer and exclaimed, "Who would not conquer with such troops as these!"

Lieutenant John Chamberlayne told of this long march "across open fields, by strange country paths and comfortable homesteads, by a little town . . . called Orleans [*sic*], and on and on, as if we would never cease—to Salem, on the Manassas Gap Railroad. . . ."

Although Jackson and Lee had hoped that his movement would be undetected, the Federals were, in fact, able to follow it closely, but Jackson's intentions were unknown, and Pope believed that he was on his way to Front Royal, back to the Valley of Virginia. At noon of the following day, 26 August, Pope wired Halleck that twenty thousand Confederates were on the march and that he had alerted McDowell's corps near Manassas. He did not yet know that on this day Jackson had turned eastward. He, like McClellan, vastly overestimated the size of Lee's army and naïvely assumed that Lee could detach a corps of that size and still maintain a viable fighting force on the Rappahannock, a notion Longstreet and Stuart did their able best to reinforce by vigorous and aggressive maneuvering.

In Jackson's path east of White Plains lay the low Bull Run range of mountains broken by Thoroughfare Gap. Jackson pushed his men forward as fast as possible through the gap, not even stopping for the usual rest every hour or even taking time to eat. Charles Blackford was impressed by "the spirit of the men, their unbounded confidence in their leader, and their perfect faith in the success of the expedition." There continued to be stragglers, men whose shoes, legs, or spirits had given out, but every man knew now that they were marching in the rear of Pope's army, and most strove valiantly to keep up.

Four miles east of Thoroughfare Gap the column reached the small town of Haymarket, and after another two miles Gainesville, surprising and capturing Federal cavalry pickets. Jackson was now astride the main Alexandria–Warrenton Turnpike. Stuart's cavalry, including the brigades of Robertson and Fitzhugh Lee, joined him now, having disengaged from the Confederate line on the Rappahannock and followed rapidly in his wake.

The road forked at Gainesville, one leading to Manassas and the other toward Bristoe (today's Bristow), about four miles south-south-west of Manassas. Jackson took the right fork, leading to Bristoe, but stopped short to allow his army to close up and stragglers to rejoin their units. While waiting at a farmhouse, he slumped into a cane-bottomed armchair and promptly went to sleep. His staff slept around him on the floor; Sandie Pendleton, now his AAG, slept in the hallway, where dispatch riders would easily find him.

Instead of posting a man to stay at each road intersection, Jackson had ordered each brigade to drop off a man to direct the brigade behind. Pendleton was awakened by a courier with the news that one brigade had failed to leave a guide and that those behind had taken the wrong road. Pendleton went immediately to waken Jackson, who listened to this news without moving. "Put him under arrest and prefer charges," he said, and went back to sleep.

It was about sunset when Ewell's division came in sight of Bristoe. Mumford with a troop of cavalry walked their horses to within a hundred yards of the unsuspecting company of infantry and troop of cavalry guarding the railroad station and then charged, whooping, into the village. The Union cavalry fled; the infantry holed up briefly in the hotel but surrendered to the 5th Louisiana Infantry under Colonel Henry Forno, a former New Orleans police chief.

The Confederates had no sooner occupied the station than they heard a train approaching from the south. It was Train No. 6, pulled by a locomotive named Secretary. Ties were hurriedly thrown on the tracks to stop it, but the engineer plowed through the barricade. A storm of bullets followed him as he fled north, carrying the first news of Confederates in the rear of Pope's army.

Forno set his men to tearing up track and erecting a more substantial barricade. A locomotive named President, sporting a likeness of

Lincoln on its dome, came chugging in, pulling twenty empty cars, and crashed into it. Two later trains crashed into the wreckage before a suspicious engineer, sensing trouble, perhaps seeing the fires, stopped his engine and backed up at full speed. The Federals were now aware of the break in their railroad both north and south of Bristoe.

When Jackson arrived on the scene, a civilian from one of the trains who had broken his leg begged for help so that he could see the famous man. Private William Oates, an Alabama soldier, obligingly raised him up and later described his reaction: "He surveyed the great Confederate general in his dingy gray uniform, with his cap pulled down on his nose, for half a minute, and then in a tone of disappointment and disgust exclaimed, 'O my God! Lay me down!' "

It appears that only after reaching Bristoe did Jackson learn that Manassas Junction had been transformed into Pope's major supply depot south of Alexandria. Night had fallen, and his troops were spent, but he was determined to capture it. Old General Trimble, who had once said he would end the war "a major general or a corpse," volunteered for the task and set off into the night with the 21st Georgia and the 21st North Carolina. Later Jackson had second thoughts and, without informing Trimble, sent Stuart to take charge.[2]

It was about midnight when Stuart and Trimble arrived at Manassas, apparently from different directions. The garrison there was alert but inadequate, and the weary Confederates with great élan charged through the defenses and captured eight guns, scores of horses, and three hundred prisoners for a loss of fifteen wounded. Manassas was considered a "city of refuge" for fleeing slaves, and two hundred blacks of all ages and of both sexes were recovered. This was one of the very few night attacks of the Civil War, and considering the confusion as to who was in charge, it is surprising that Trimble's infantry did not battle Stuart's cavalry on this dark night.

Leaving most of Ewell's division at Bristoe, Jackson shifted Hill's and Taliaferro's divisions to Manassas, where the Confederates found waiting for them a cornucopia of military stores of all kinds, for the great depot, covering more than a square mile of ground was designed to supply not only Pope but also McClellan's army when it came up. It held pyramids of ammunition; dozens of guns, including newly de-

---

2. Stuart was indeed the senior officer, but this error on Jackson's part later resulted in an acrimonious dispute between Trimble and Stuart as to who had done what and who should receive credit for the enterprise. Each claimed to have made the capture unaided by the other.

signed three-inch rifled cannon; every description of clothing and accoutrement; hundreds of spanking new tents; an immense quantity of
food, including two thousand barrels of salt pork, two thousand barrels
of flour, a thousand barrels of corned beef, and twenty-five tons of
bacon. In a siding sat two freight trains, said to be a half mile long,
jammed with more goods.

The Confederate generals initially tried to protect these stores, but
their hungry, ragged men would not be held back. There was an orgy
of looting and feasting. As Jackson solemnly stated in his after-action
report, he allowed his men to take "rations and other articles which
they could properly make subservient to their use." J. F. J. Caldwell, a
South Carolina officer, reported that "linen handkerchiefs were applied to noses hitherto blown by the thumb and forefinger, and sumptuous underclothing was fitted over limbs sunburnt, sore and vermin-
splotched."

Although blankets, shoes, and underwear were permitted to be
taken, Jackson forbade the wearing of the new blue uniforms. Cigars,
soap, candy, nuts, fruit, lobster, potted hams, and pickles were to be
had for the taking. Private Robson remembered: "It was more than
funny to see the ragged, rough, dirty fellows, who had been living on
roasted corn and green apples for days, now drinking Rhine wine,
eating lobster salad, potted tongue, cream biscuit, pound cake, canned
fruits, and the like; and filling pockets and haversacks with ground
coffee, tooth-brushes, condensed milk, silk handkerchiefs."

Private John Casler and some pals rifled the medical stores packed
in a railroad car, searching for brandy. Surgeons begged them not to
destroy the medicine and surgical equipment and to save the precious
morphine and chloroform, but as Casler later confessed, "We paid no
heed to their entreaties, telling them that we had no use for medicine."

In an effort to prevent his army from dissolving into a mob of
tosspots, Jackson ordered whiskey barrels broken open and brandy
bottles smashed. "I fear that liquor more than Pope's army," he said.
Major W. Roy Mason later remembered the scene: "Streams of spirits
ran like water through the sands of Manassas, and the soldiers on hands
and knees drank it greedily from the ground as it ran." A Union major
pointed out to Brigadier General Taliaferro a small cask of cognac that
was "much too good to be staved." Taliaferro saved it for himself.

Many men were in a quandary, unable to decide what to take,
picking up one thing and then discarding it for something else, for the
number of items they could carry was limited. One man, wiser than
most, took only French mustard, which for the next ten days provided

him with currency to trade for other food. Infantrymen grumbled because cavalrymen and artillerymen could carry more than they could.

Cavalry and artillery units took the opportunity to replace worn weapons and horse furniture. Sergeant C. A. Fornerden of Carpenter's battery rejoiced that his company was able to replace its worn-out guns with "two new and spanking 12-pounder Napoleons and two English steel 10-pounder Parrotts, replacing as well our old for new limber chests and caissons, while we caparisoned proudly our dear, brave horses with bespangled harness and all needed accoutrements." All that could be neither eaten nor carried away was burned.

The Federals, now stirred by Jackson's foray, were as active as a hive of angry bees, but the Union generals could not comprehend the size of the probe and assumed that only a large raiding party had penetrated their rear, calling for no major response. So on the morning of 27 August only four New Jersey regiments, brought down by train from Washington under the command of Brigadier General George William Taylor, advanced on Manassas Junction.

Poague's battery opened fire on them first, followed by Carpenter's newly captured guns. When most of Hill's division came up, Taylor's men had no chance. Torn apart by the Confederate guns, they were in a hopeless position when Jackson did an uncharacteristic thing: He halted the firing and, waving a handkerchief, rode forward and called for their surrender. He was fired upon. The Confederates then showed no mercy; the New Jersey regiments suffered 335 casualties, and Taylor was mortally wounded before his shattered force was withdrawn. It had fought, in Jackson's words, "with great spirit and determination and under a leader worthy of a better cause."

On this same day Lee and Longstreet were following in Jackson's footsteps while Pope on the Rappahannock was attempting an abrupt about-face. Ewell, attacked by a reinforced division (some fifty-five hundred men) under Major General Joseph Hooker, fell back upon Jackson's main force at Manassas. By the evening of the twenty-seventh Jackson knew that his position was too precarious to be held. Federal forces were converging on him from all directions. Particularly dangerous were the corps of McDowell and Sigel, plus an added division—about forty thousand men in all—who were trying to position their forces between those of Lee-Longstreet and Jackson. If all Federal forces in the area are considered, Pope could call upon nearly seventy-five thousand men to oppose Jackson's twenty-four thousand and Longstreet's thirty thousand.

The twenty-eighth was an anxious day for Jackson. He gave orders that would concentrate his force at Sudley Mountain (a hill, actually, but the highest point around), the position held by the Federals on the right of their line at First Manassas. By midafternoon of the twenty-eighth these movements were completed. At three o'clock Longstreet's leading units reached Thoroughfare Gap. A courier was sent off to inform Jackson, who had been restless and uneasy all day, "an explosive missile," thought one officer. The news that Lee and Longstreet were at Thoroughfare Gap was reassuring, and for the first time that day Jackson relaxed.

The cavalry had been active. One troop captured a courier carrying a dispatch from McDowell to Sigel and Reynolds that disclosed Federal intentions. When it was brought to Jackson, he was found sleeping in a fence corner. Brigadier General Taliaferro described his reaction:

> The captured dispatch aroused Jackson like an electric shock. He was essentially a man of action; he rarely, if ever, hesitated; he never asked advice; he did not seem to reflect, or reason out a purpose; but he leapt by instinct and not by the slower process of ordinary ratiocination to a conclusion, and then as rapidly undertook its execution. He called no council to discuss the situation disclosed by this communication, although his ranking officers were almost at his side; he asked no conference, no expression of opinion; he made no suggestion, but simply, without a word except to repeat the language of the dispatch, turned to me and said, "Move your division and attack the enemy"; and to Ewell, "Support the attack."

However, the enemy was not readily found, and Jackson disposed his forces near the hamlet of Groveton (no longer in existence), about five miles from Manassas in woods parallel to the Warrenton Pike, where they were difficult to detect. They were not allowed fires, but they lounged about, resting, playing cards, talking, "all the careless merriment of troops confident in themselves, their cause, and their leader," thought Blackford. Just at sunset Federal troops—four brigades of Rufus King's division of McDowell's corps—were spotted marching down the turnpike toward Centreville, where Pope supposed Jackson was located. John Porter Hatch in King's leading brigade had sent scouts to look over the area Jackson now occupied, but they were not thorough. They had sighted only a few Confederates, not enough to disturb them.

Jackson was probably reluctant to disclose his position, but on the other hand, this was an opportunity for a surprise attack too good to resist. He trotted toward the pike, within easy musket shot, and rode back and forth, thoughtfully examining the marching columns. Confederates in the woods about two hundred yards away watched uneasily, but not a shot was fired, and the unsuspecting Federals marched on. Suddenly Jackson made up his mind. Pivoting on his horse, he galloped into the woods. "Bring out your men, gentlemen," he called to the waiting commanders. "From the woods arose a hoarse roar like that from cages of wild beasts at the scent of blood," said Blackford.

In his after-action report Jackson stated simply that as King's column "appeared to be moving by, with his flank exposed, I determined to attack at once."

Commands rang out, battle flags were unfurled, and Confederate batteries sprang out of the woods. Three batteries positioned near Groveton, according to Jackson, "poured a heavy fire of shot and shell upon the enemy. This was responded to by a very heavy fire from the enemy, forcing our batteries to seek another position. By this time Taliaferro's command . . . was advanced from the woods to the open field, and was now moving in gallant style until it reached an orchard on the right of our line. . . . The conflict here was fierce and sanguinary."

The lines of opposing infantry were too close in some cases to allow the guns free play. Taliaferro provided a description of the action in his area:

> Twice our lines were advanced until we had reached a farm-house and orchard on the right of our lines and were within about 80 yards of a greatly superior force of the enemy. Here one of the most terrific conflicts that can be conceived of occurred. Our troops held the farm-house and one edge of the orchard, while the enemy held the orchard and inclosure next to the turnpike. To our left there was no cover, and our men stood in the field without shelter of any kind. The enemy, although reenforced, never once attempted to advance upon our position, but withstood with great determination the terrible fire which our lines poured upon them. For two hours and a half, without an instant's cessation of the most deadly discharges of musketry, round shot, and shell, both lines stood unmoved, neither advancing and neither broken nor yielding, until at last, about 9 o'clock at night, the enemy slowly and sullenly fell back and yielded the field to our victorious troops.

The picture of the troops on both sides simply standing closely face-to-face for more than two hours killing each other is a chilling one. It was a scene Taliaferro could never forget: "It was a stand-up combat, dogged and unflinching, in a field almost bare. There were no wounds from spent balls; the confronting lines looked into each other's faces at deadly range . . . and they stood as immovable as the painted heroes in a battle-piece. . . . In this fight there was no manoeuvring, and very little tactics—it was a question of endurance, and both endured."

The casualties on each side at the Battle of Groveton are difficult to assess. Some units suffered fearfully. The 2nd Wisconsin, which carried 500 men into battle, left 298 behind. The 5th New York Zouaves' losses were among the highest percentage suffered by any Federal regiment in a single engagement during the war; of the 490 men it carried into battle, 117 were killed. Union Brigadier General John Gibbon's total losses in his "Iron Brigade" were 751 men or 33 percent. There were perhaps as many as 1,000 casualties on each side, although Union losses may have been somewhat higher than those of the Confederates.

Jackson had gained little by forcing this battle, and he had lost a great deal. Among the fallen were some of his best officers. A soldier in the Rockbridge Artillery wrote home: "The Old Stonewall Brigade suffered on Thursday. . . . Oh, how we suffered in the loss of noble, valuable men and officers."[3] Ewell, Jackson's most valuable subordinate, was shot in the left knee, and Dr. McGuire amputated his leg.[4] Tall, aristocratic Taliaferro received wounds in the neck, arm, and foot. Colonel Lawson Botts of the 2nd Virginia was killed, as was twenty-nine-year-old Colonel John Neff, the Dunkard's son, who was picked off by a noted Pennsylvania marksman, Captain William

3. Reprinted in the *Lexington* (Virginia) *Gazette,* 11 September 1862.

4. Dr. McGuire left an account of Ewell's wound: "He was kneeling on the ground and looking under some pine bushes to get a better view of the field, when he was hit upon the left patella, nearly in the center of it, and his left leg flexed, the ball passing downward, striking the head of the tibia and splitting it into several fragments. The bullet finally lodged in the muscles of the calf of the left leg. . . . I amputated the thigh just above the knee. . . . About ten days after the amputation, to escape capture, he was carried on a litter by some soldiers near fifty miles. The motion of the litter caused the bone to protrude, and in consequence of this and his bad health, the wound sloughed. After much suffering and the loss of an inch of bone, he got well enough to go about, when one day he . . . let his crutches slip from under him, and falling upon the icy pavement, he reopened the wound and knocked off another piece of bone." It was ten months before he was able to return to the field. During his convalescence he married his widowed cousin Lizinka Campbell Brown.

Briner. Also among the mortally wounded was Captain Hugh White, a son of Jackson's Lexington minister, who had been a candidate for the ministry.

William Edwin Starke, forty-eight, newly promoted to brigadier general, was appointed to take over Taliaferro's division, and Brigadier General Alexander Robert Lawton, a forty-four-year-old graduate of both West Point and Harvard Law School, took command of Ewell's division. Both of these badly depleted divisions now joined with Hill's division, first on Sudley Mountain and then in the cuttings and behind the fills made for an unfinished railroad, to fight the defensive battle Jackson knew was in store now that he had revealed his position.

Hill's division was deployed on the left of the Confederate line, its left flank refused; two of Lawson's brigades were in left center with two others on the far right and Starke's division between them. Stuart's cavalry protected both flanks.

Pope, his headquarters near Centreville, learned of the Battle of Groveton at about ten o'clock on the night of the battle. He now knew where Jackson was and, as he later admitted, "felt sure then, and so stated, that there was no escape for Jackson." However, he did not know where all his own units were. Only the next morning (29 August) did he discover to his "great disappointment and surprise" that "King's division had fallen back toward Manassas Junction, and that neither [Franz] Sigel nor [John Fulton] Reynolds had been engaged or had gone to the support of King. The route toward Thoroughfare Gap had been left open by the wholly unexpected retreat of King's division. . . ." At Groveton Jackson's luck held; he had again been saved by Union mismanagement.

The Second Battle of Manassas (or Bull Run) took place on 29–30 August 1862. Pope brought into battle approximately sixty-two thousand men. Lee could muster barely fifty thousand, even after Longstreet forced Thoroughfare Gap and came into line at an angle on Jackson's right at about eleven o'clock on the morning of the twenty-ninth. Longstreet's arrival sent a ripple of cheers down Jackson's battle line, but its significance was lost on the Federal commanders. Before Longstreet's arrival the Federals had had their chance to destroy Jackson, but the attacks launched by Sigel's division were uncoordinated, piecemeal, frontal assaults which accomplished nothing.

Pope himself arrived on the field shortly after noon and established his headquarters on Buck Hill, just north of the Stone House at the corner of the turnpike and Sudley Road, which had been a landmark at First Manassas. He at once organized an attack by Major

General Joseph Hooker's division upon A. P. Hill. Hooker's charge opened the way to the railway cutting, where there was hand-to-hand fighting, most of the killing being done with clubbed muskets and bayonets. A Union brigade under Brigadier General Cuvier Grover made a gallant charge that broke through Hill's defenses. The triumphant Federals stood panting beyond them, but Hill's line was quickly re-formed, and Grover's men were hit hard by Henry Forno's Louisiana brigade and a Georgia regiment. In about twenty minutes Grover left 486 men dead or wounded on the field.

About noon there was a lull broken only by an occasional artillery shell. Jackson walked along a cutting in the open to observe the Federal line. When a staff officer suggested he be more careful, he said mildly, "I believe we have been together in hotter places before."

Among the Confederates ammunition began to run low. After each attack men leaped out of the cuttings and over the fills to strip the Federal dead of their ammunition. Some, finding no dead to strip, gathered stones to throw. Hill sent a courier to Maxcy Gregg on the extreme left of his line, to ask if he could hold. "Tell General Hill," Gregg replied, "that my ammunition is exhausted, but that I will hold my position with the bayonet."

Hill sent a message to Jackson admitting that he was not sure he could withstand another attack. These were not words Jackson liked to hear. "Tell him that if they are attacked again he must beat them back!" he told the courier, and he rode forward to see for himself and brace Hill. "General, your men have done nobly," he said. "If you are attacked again you will beat the enemy back."

As he spoke, a ripple of musketry ran along Hill's front. "Here it comes," said Hill as he galloped off. "I'll expect you to beat them!" Jackson called after him.

Hill did. An adjutant in W. Dorsey Pender's brigade said: "We slaughtered them like hogs. I never saw the like of dead men in all my life." The ground in front of Hill's position in some places was "so thickly carpeted with the fallen that it looked like one vast blue carpet," one soldier noted. But the ordeal was taking its toll on muscles and nerves. A South Carolina soldier later recalled: "Our feet were worn and weary and our arms were nerveless. Our ears were deadened with the continuous roar of battle, and our eyes were dimmed with the smoke."

About three o'clock in the afternoon Pope determined on twin attacks upon both sides of Jackson's line, using for his attack on the Confederate left three relatively fresh brigades from Major General

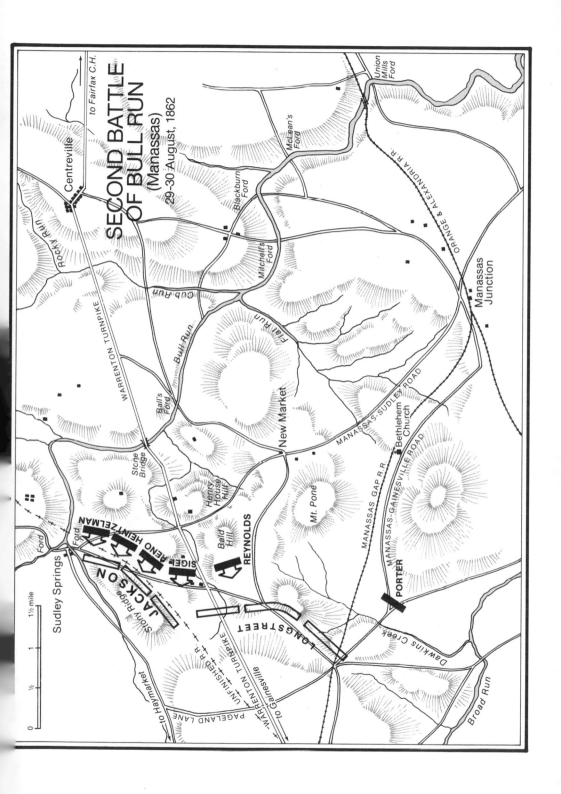

SECOND BATTLE
OF BULL RUN
(Manassas)
29-30 August, 1862

to Fairfax C.H.

Centreville

Rocky Run

WARRENTON TURNPIKE

Cub Run

Bull Run

Flat Run

Blackburn
Ford

Mitchell's
Ford

McLean's
Ford

Union
Mills
Ford

ORANGE & ALEXANDRIA R.R.

Manassas
Junction

Ball's
Ford

Stone
Bridge

New Market

Manassas-Sudley Road

Bethlehem
Church

MANASSAS GAP R.R.

Henry
House Hill

Mt. Pone

Bald Hill

MANASSAS-GAINESVILLE ROAD

REYNOLDS

PORTER

Dawkins Creek

Sudley Springs

Ford

Ford

HEINTZELMAN
RENO
SIGEL

JACKSON

Stony Ridge

LONGSTREET

UNFINISHED R.R.

to Haymarket

WARRENTON TURNPIKE

to Gainesville

PAGELAND LANE

Broad Run

0   ½   1   1½ mile

Philip Kearny's division and two from Major General Jesse L. Reno's division, and McDowell plus ten thousand as yet unused men under Fitz-John Porter to roll up Jackson's right.

Again and again the Federals charged. When they fell back, one-armed General Kearny, his bridle reins in his teeth and his sword in his hand, dropped his reins to shout: "Come on and go in again, you sons of bitches, and I'll make brigadier generals of every one of you!"

The blow that fell upon Hill was the heaviest and most dangerous of the day. Colonel Bradley Johnson saw a Confederate lieutenant fell a Federal soldier with a stone and watched "a Federal flag hold its position for half an hour within ten yards of a flag of one of the regiments in the cut and go down six or eight times." Lieutenant Colonel Edward McCrady, Jr., of the 1st South Carolina described the bitter action:

> It was now about 4 o'clock, and although wearied, we knew the struggle was yet to be renewed. They soon came, now in still greater force. . . . Our men fell fast around us. . . . [The Federals] pressed on, crossed the cut, and slowly compelled us, step by step, to yield the long-coveted position. Here again our men fought the enemy at a few yards. . . . This was a most critical moment. . . . The enemy had by this time driven us back some 300 yards from the railroad cut and were in possession of most of the long-contested field. . . . At this time, when all seemed lost, General [Charles W.] Field, with a portion of his brigade, came up, and charging the enemy, they again broke and fled from the field. . . .
>
> It was now about 5 o'clock in the afternoon. Our regiment had lost half of its officers carried into action and nearly half of the men; our ammunition, too, was exhausted . . . we were thoroughly worn out. . . . [T]he enemy were finally repulsed, but we were not allowed to rest in safety. The enemy . . . commenced vigorously to shell our position. . . .
>
> Night closed upon the scene, and amid the dead of the enemy and our own we rested until morning.

It had been a cruel day for Federals and Confederates alike. Generals Trimble and Field were wounded, and there had been heavy losses among the field and company officers, including Colonel Forno. Among the mortally wounded was eighteen-year-old Willie Preston, the son of Jackson's VMI colleague, who had been so enthusiastic about battle at Cedar Mountain. Jackson had kept him for a time at headquarters, where his cheerful good manners and bearing had won the affection of the staff officers, but just before the heavy fighting this day he had joined his company of "college boys" from Lexington, the Liberty Hall Volunteers.

The death of young Preston was hard to bear. Dr. McGuire broke the news to Jackson. "The General's face was a study. The muscles were twisting convulsively and his eyes were all aglow. He gripped me by the shoulder till it hurt me," said McGuire, "and in a savage, threatening manner asked why I had left the boy. In a few seconds he recovered himself and turned and walked off into the woods alone."

When he returned, McGuire gave him the names of others who had fallen and added: "We have won this battle by the hardest kind of fighting."

Jackson, his voice full of emotion, replied, "No sir, we have won this day by the blessing of Almighty God."

When night fell and there was only some desultory artillery fire, Jackson pulled his men back into some woods for safety and concealment. Early the next morning (30 August), when Federal skirmishers found yesterday's battlefield deserted, Pope, still unaware that Longstreet had arrived on the field and was in a position to enfilade any attack upon Jackson's right,[5] concluded that Lee was retreating and ordered McDowell to pursue.

That morning, when Jackson conferred with Lee and Stuart, there was no talk of retreat. Throughout the morning, except for some skirmishing and exchanges of artillery fire, there was no real action. Jackson rode to the rear and went to sleep in a fence corner. He was there asleep when in the early afternoon nine Federal batteries suddenly opened fire and thirty-seven Federal regiments of infantry, twelve thousand men, surged across the fields toward his center and right on a front more than a mile long. Jackson's men at once rushed from the woods to their fighting positions of the day before.

Longstreet said that Pope's "whole army seemed to surge up against Jackson as if to crush him with an overwhelming mass." It was, he said, a "well-organized attack, thoroughly concentrated and operating cleverly." In his after-action report Jackson described the battle on that hot afternoon in colorful and dramatic language:

5. Porter's failure to carry out Pope's order led to his court-martial on charges by Pope of disloyalty, disobedience, and misconduct in the face of the enemy. The fact that Porter was a loyal supporter of McClellan, who was in bad odor with Secretary of War Edwin Stanton, and that he detested Pope, whom he once called an ass, ensured his conviction and dismissal from the army. Not until sixteen years later was he vindicated. He was eventually restored to his former rank.

In a few moments our entire line was engaged in a fierce and sanguinary struggle with the enemy. As one line was repulsed another took its place and pressed forward as if determined by force of numbers and fury of assault to drive us from our positions. So impetuous and well sustained were these onsets as to induce me to send to the commanding general for re-enforcements; but the timely and gallant advance of General Longstreet on the right relieved my troops from the pressure of overwhelming numbers. . . . As Longstreet pressed upon the right the Federal advance was checked, and soon a general advance of my whole line was ordered. . . . [The troops] exhibiting in parts of the field scenes of close encounter and murderous strife not witnessed often in the turmoil of battle. The Federals gave way before our troops, fell back in disorder and fled precipitately, leaving their dead and wounded on the field. During their retreat the artillery opened with destructive power upon the fugitive masses. The infantry followed until darkness put an end to the pursuit.

It was indeed Longstreet who saved the day, particularly by skillful use of massed artillery, whose enfilading fire into the Federal infantry was followed by a charge in which his men sprang forward "with exultant yells." He was later criticized—although not by Lee or Jackson—for not engaging the enemy as soon as his corps came into line. However, the timing of his attack could not have been better, and it put an end to Pope's hopes for victory.

A regimental commander in General Philip Kearny's division commented later: "We were sent forward to pursue the enemy, who were said to be retreating. We found the enemy, but did not see them retreat."

The Federals, fleeing, left behind them a battlefield even more gruesome than most. Grass on the field, browned by the August sun, had in many places caught fire from bursting shells. Clothes had been burned off the dead, and the flames had charred many of the wounded. "Such spectacles," said one battle-hardened soldier, "made little or no impression at the time, and we moved to and fro over the field, scarcely heeding them." As after First Manassas, Sudley Church became a hospital. One surgeon reported "large numbers of wounded lying on the ground as thick as a drove of hogs."

The grass fires were extinguished as rain began to fall. The Union rear guard was dogged and valiant. Among its fallen was Colonel Fletcher Webster, commanding the 12th Massachusetts, the eldest son of Daniel Webster. The Confederate pursuit flagged in the dark and the rain. Pope's army retreated back to its old lines around Centreville. McDowell and Porter were the last to leave; abandoning their positions on and around Henry Hill about midnight, they marched north over the now-famous Stone Bridge arching over Bull Run. The rain fell steadily through the night and into the next day. It seemed, as Henry Kyd Douglas said, that "the heavens weep over every bloody battlefield."

A. P. Hill's Light Division had borne the brunt of the Federal attacks, and even Jackson was forced to give Hill credit—indirectly: "Assault after assault was made on the left, exhibiting on the part of the enemy great pertinacity and determination, but every advance was met most successfully and gallantly driven back." Hill reported: "The battle being gloriously won, my men slept among the dead and dying enemy."

The next morning, Sunday, 31 August, Hotchkiss walked over the battlefield. "Never have I seen such horrors," he told his wife. So thick were the dead that one soldier claimed that he "could have walked a quarter of a mile in almost a straight line without putting a foot on the ground."

While Lee and Stuart were making a reconnaissance north of Bull Run that morning, Jackson found time to visit several field hospitals. It seemed to Douglas, watching the wounded strain to catch a glimpse of him, that "the sight was a kind of souvenir they wanted to take home." This is the only recorded instance of Jackson visiting his wounded in a field hospital.

Inferiority in numbers never dampened Lee's aggressive tendencies. He now wanted Jackson to pry Pope out of his nearly impregnable Centreville positions and, about noon, started him with his wet and weary soldiers, A. P. Hill's division in the lead, on another wide enveloping movement. Jackson moved north in the rain over roads of thick and sticky red mud about eight miles to the Little River Turnpike,[6] which connected Fairfax and Winchester. About eight o'clock that night the main body of his troops bivouacked in and around the village of Pleasant Valley on Pope's right flank.

The following day Jackson moved eastward to Ox Hill and made his headquarters at nearby Chantilly plantation in the elegant house

6. Little River Turnpike, now U.S. Route 50, ran between Alexandria and Winchester. It was the first toll road in Virginia and one of the first in the United States. By the standards of the time, it was an excellent road. Today, near Chantilly, it runs just south of Dulles International Airport.

owned by the Stewart family.[7] The wagons had bogged down in the mud, and the famished soldiers were "very bad, stealing everything eatable they could lay hands on," according to Hotchkiss, who that morning had rejoined Jackson's headquarters.

Thanks to another foolish bit of bravado on the part of Stuart, who, during a reconnaissance around Ox Hill, could not resist firing on a convoy of Federal wagons, Pope discovered Jackson's presence and ordered brigade-sized reconnaissances. One of these clashed briefly with Jackson's forward units. Pope sent the IX Corps, commanded by one of Jackson's West Point classmates, Jesse Lee Reno, to block further advances, and Jackson deployed his men south of the turnpike with Lawton in the center, Hill on his right, and Starke with most of his artillery on his left. Late in the afternoon in the midst of a torrential downpour the two forces met again to fight another bloody battle. There were attacks and counterattacks over the dark, sodden fields and woodland. Jackson sat "doubled up on his horse, so that his rubber cape would shed the rain over the top of his boots." The battle "raged with great fury," he later wrote, "the enemy obstinately and desperately contesting the ground." When one of Jackson's commanders sent word that he would have to withdraw because his ammunition was soaked, Jackson curtly informed him that the Federal's ammunition was equally wet and that he must stay and fight.

One Federal unit came in on Jackson's flank, and there was much confused fighting in the rain and growing darkness. An officer in the 6th Wisconsin wrote: "The noise of the artillery and musketry intermingling with the roll of very sharp thunder produced a very striking effect. The darkness incident to a sky overcast with heavy, rolling clouds, lighted up alternately by flashes of lightning and the flames of artillery, made a scene long to be remembered."

Jackson lashed out at those who tried to flee, striking at least one man with his doubled bridle rein. When Longstreet arrived, he observed: "General, your men don't appear to work well today."

"No," Jackson said grimly, "but I hope it will prove a victory in the morning."

---

7. Present-day Chantilly, an area of housing developments and shopping malls, stands where Sander's Toll Gate used to be. The Chantilly plantation of 1862 is now generally called Greenbriar. The ground in the entire area of the battlefield has been so much disturbed by real estate development that it is difficult to find the battlefield and its monuments. Even Confederate graves were bulldozed to construct town houses. The May 1987 issue of *Blue & Gray Magazine* provided the best guide to the battle and what little remains of the field.

The battle lasted until after nightfall, when Union forces drew back. That night Jackson wrote to Anna to tell her of the victory God had given him, though, as usual, he provided no details:

> May He ever be with us, and we ever be His devoted people is my earnest prayer. It greatly encourages me to feel that so many of God's people are praying for that part of our forces under my command. The Lord has answered their prayers; He has again placed us across Bull Run; and I pray that He will make our arms entirely successful, and that all the glory will be given to His holy name, and none of it to man. God has blessed and preserved me through His great mercy.

The battle of Chantilly (Ox Hill) had been expensive for the Federals. The Confederates lost about five hundred, the Federals perhaps twice as many. Among the Union dead were Major General Philip Kearny and Brigadier General (posthumously promoted Major General) Isaac Ingalls Stevens, two of the most promising senior officers in the Union army.[8] When Hill, who had known Kearny before the war, saw his bloody, mud-stained body, he said, "Poor Kearny, he deserved a better death than that." Lee returned his corpse and personal effects to Pope under flag of truce in the morning.[9]

Although the Confederates had made a start toward organizing an ambulance service, medical conditions remained primitive. That night, waiting at the Chantilly manor house for the medical wagon of the 13th South Carolina to arrive, Surgeon Spencer Glasgow Welch did what he could: "We filled the carriage house, barn and stable with our wounded, but I could do but little for them."

Although reinforcements were close at hand, Pope withdrew his entire army to safety within the defenses of Washington. The Battle of Chantilly ended Pope's career in Virginia—he was relieved of his com-

8. Stevens was killed by a bullet in his brain while leading his men by carrying the colors of his old regiment, the 79th New York. His son, Captain Hazard Stevens, was wounded in the same engagement. He recovered, however, and was later awarded the Medal of Honor for his bravery at Fort Huger, Virginia, on 19 April 1863.

9. It was Lee, not Jackson, as is often said, who arranged the truce and the return of Kearny's body. A month later, at the request of Kearny's wife, Lee returned, through McClellan, Kearny's sword, saddle, and horse. As these items were considered the property of the Confederate government, Lee had them appraised and paid for them himself.

mand the next day and sent to fight the Sioux in Minnesota—and it marked the end of the Second Manassas campaign. The estimates of the casualties made by Thomas L. Livermore, although not always accurate, are perhaps as good as any for the Second Manassas campaign, including Cedar Mountain:

	Union	*Confederate*
Engaged	75,696	48,527
Killed	1,724	1,481
Wounded	8,372	7,627
Missing	5,958	89
TOTAL	16,054	9,197

Casualty figures, like most statistics, may be viewed in different ways. Although total Confederate losses were 19 percent of those engaged, as compared with Union losses of 21 percent, in terms of killed and wounded, the Confederates lost 19 percent, compared with 13 percent of the Federals.

Both sides claimed a victory at Chantilly, but it was Jackson's men who remained on the field, and Jackson's star continued to rise. Sandie Pendleton wrote soon after the campaign that "Jackson has added new laurels to his brow—not that I like to be under Jackson, for he forgets that one ever gets tired, hungry, or sleepy." Edward A. Pollard, editor of the *Richmond Examiner,* wrote that "no project was thought too extravagant, or enterprise too daring, for the troops of Lee and Jackson." Even in Europe, Jackson's name began to be heard. Francis Lawley, a special correspondent of the *Times* of London, wrote of the "universal wonder and admiration" Jackson's feats inspired, and he told his British readers that "they who have seen and heard him uplift his voice in prayer, and then have witnessed his vigor and prompt energy in the strife, say that once again Cromwell is walking the earth and leading his trusting and enraptured hosts to assured victory."

The Invasion of Maryland

It was obvious that Lee could not attack the strong defenses of Washington, which would hold some 120,000 men when all of McClellan's forces returned, so he turned to that scheme which had long been advocated by the aggressive Jackson: an invasion of Maryland. There were many advantages to be gained if the movement was successful. There was a confident belief that Marylanders were Confederates at heart and that many of the state's young men would enlist in the Southern army. Politically there was the hope that by demonstrating their ability to invade the Union, the Southerners would prove to the world that the Confederacy was a going concern, a true government with a strong army, and fit to be recognized as such by the major European powers, particularly Britain and France. The need for victories had been emphasized by the Confederate commissioners in Europe. "We are still hard and fast aground here," John Slidell wrote from London. "Nothing will float us off but a strong and continued current of important successes in the field." Lee told President Davis: "I do not consider success impossible."

Strategically the move into Maryland, with the threat to Washington that was its concomitant, would keep Union forces out of Virginia, and Maryland fields and orchards could yield food for men and forage for animals in a land as yet little touched by war.

There were, of course, difficulties. Union commanders might not rise to the bait; they might ignore Lee's ragtag army and make another drive on Richmond. And Maryland could not provide Lee with all that he needed. Ammunition, shoes, clothing, even some of the army's food would still need to be brought to it by a line of communications that would grow ever longer as the line of operation extended northward. Also to be reckoned with was the feeling among a significant number of Southerners that the Confederacy ought not to become an aggressor; some who had enlisted to defend their state or the Confederacy from Northern aggression were unwilling to take on the odious role of invader.

Nevertheless, Lee determined to carry the war into the North by crossing the Potomac at the fords near Leesburg.[1] The weather was fine, with warm and sunny days and cool nights. Lee ordered his cavalry well out on the flanks, eastward to Vienna and westward as far as Winchester. Jackson's corps, led by A. P. Hill's division, marched north and west, bivouacking on the night of 3 September near Dranesville, about twelve miles east of Leesburg.

Orders were issued for the start down the Leesburg and Alexandria Turnpike to begin at four o'clock the following morning. Division commanders carefully set their watches by Jackson's, but at the appointed time Hill's men were missing. Seething, Jackson collared Brigadier General Maxcy Gregg and demanded to know the cause of the delay. His wrath was not appeased when he was told that the men were still filling their canteens. When Hill rode up, Jackson lashed out with a public rebuke. According to Hotchkiss, who was there, "Hill took this reprimand rather sullenly, his face flushing up, but he said nothing."

Jackson kept a critical eye on Hill's marching column, and the sight of its stragglers did not soothe him. When the column failed to halt at the end of an hour, as was his standing order, he angrily halted the leading brigade, commanded by Colonel Edward Lloyd Thomas. Hill, seeing his division immobile, galloped up to Thomas and demanded to know why he had halted without permission. "I halted because General Jackson ordered me to do so," Thomas answered.

Hill charged up to Jackson, drew his sword, and presented its hilt. "If you take command of my troops in my presence, take my sword also," he said savagely.

"Put up your sword," snapped Jackson, "and consider yourself under arrest."

1. Leesburg was named after Robert E. Lee's father, Henry ("Lighthorse Harry") Lee (1756–1818), of Revolutionary War fame.

Hill's division was placed under the temporary command of Brigadier General Lawrence O'Bryan Branch, and Hill was now forced to march on foot at the rear of his division. A North Carolina lieutenant recorded: "General Hill marched on foot with the rear guard all the day through Maryland, an old white hat slouched down over his eyes, his coat off and wearing an old flannel shirt, looking as mad as a bull."

Jackson's corps bivouacked that night just north of Leesburg at a place called Big Spring. Hill promptly requested a copy of the charges against him, as he had every right to do, but Jackson made no haste to reply. He had other concerns on his mind. The army was about to march into unknown territory, and he was anxious to learn about it.

He summoned Colonel Bradley Tyler Johnson, who had been born in Frederick, Maryland, and pumped him for information ranging from the topography of the state to the political sentiments of the inhabitants. Johnson had a warning: Many Marylanders, he said, particularly those in western Maryland, were Unionists, and even those who might sympathize with the Confederate cause would be reluctant to show their support without assurances that the Southerners were there to stay. Jackson, impressed by Johnson's acumen, took him that night to see Lee. It was several hours before Lee finished his questioning. By this time, Johnson noted, Jackson was sitting bolt upright and sound asleep.

The condition of Lee's army at the time of the invasion was best described by Private Alexander Hunter:

> For six days not a morsel of bread or meat had gone into our stomachs. Our menue [*sic*] consisted of apples and corn. . . . there was not a man whose form had not caved in, and who had not had a bad attack of diarrhoea. Our underclothes were foul and hanging in strips, our socks were worn out, half the men were barefoot, and many were lame. . . . Many became ill from exposure and starvation, and were left on the road. The ambulances were full, and the whole route was marked with a sick, lame, limping lot, that straggled to farmhouses that lined the way and who, in all cases, succored and cared for them.

Lee's army was hemorrhaging badly. "My army is ruined by straggling," he groaned. *Desertion* would be perhaps the more accurate term. Although some men refused to invade the North through principle, most losses in the Maryland campaign before the Battle of Antietam were caused by the desertion of men who were unshod, plagued by lice, sick, and suffering from malnutrition. The hardships endured by the soldiers in the Army of Northern Virginia could not be endured indefinitely. The Maryland campaign suffered the heaviest defections in the army's history. Of the fifty-five thousand infantry Lee carried across the Potomac, fewer than forty thousand were actually available for battle at Sharpsburg, a loss of more than a quarter of the army.[2]

Those able and willing to keep up looked to Maryland as the promised land, confident that they would fare better there than in the marched-over and eaten-out counties of central and northern Virginia. Lieutenant Robert Healy of the 55th Virginia said, "We heard with delight of the 'plenty' to be had in Maryland," and former VMI cadet Mercer Otey of McLaughton's battery reported that all were filled with "visions of the beautiful and bountiful things we were told awaited our entry in Frederick City."

The following morning, 5 September, the sun again shone brightly, making another delightfully warm day. Preceded by a band, the 10th Virginia led the way, marching smartly in column of fours. In Leesburg, filthy as they were, they were greeted as heroes. Felix G. de Fontaine, the correspondent for the *Charleston Daily Courier,* reported from Leesburg: "Everything that wears a crinoline or a pretty face is out, and such shouts and waving of handkerchief and hurrahs by the overjoyed gender never emanated from human lips. . . . 'Hurrah for you! Hurrah! Kill all the yankees!' screamed a bevy of girls."

As the 55th Virginia marched through the town, an old woman standing at the side of the road raised her hands and cried, "The Lord bless your dirty ragged souls!" Lieutenant Healy commented that he didn't think his regiment was "any dirtier than the rest, but it was our luck to get the blessing."

At White's Ford late wild flowers bloomed along the Potomac's banks. The marchers halted to strip off their trousers, then, yelling and singing, they splashed across to the Maryland shore. Sorrel was unaccountably missing, but Jackson, mounted on a cream-colored horse, waded in to watch the historic crossing. He doffed his hat as the band

2. At this point in the war the size of infantry regiments both North and South were considerably reduced from their full strength of near 1,000. It has been estimated that by 17 September 1862 the average Union regiment mustered only 346 men and a Confederate regiment but 166, little more than company strength. Some Southern regiments had far fewer. The 56th Virginia had 80; the 8th South Carolina 45; and the poor "Bloody 8th Virginia," recruited mostly from Loudoun County, numbered only 34.

struck up "Maryland, My Maryland!" and the men sang the popular new song and cheered him lustily.[3]

Lee was unable to cut such a noble figure. Five days earlier, as he was standing dismounted in the rain, his horse, Traveler, had shied. Reaching for the reins, Lee tripped and fell, badly spraining his left wrist and breaking a bone in his right hand. Unable to ride, he was carried unceremoniously across the Potomac in an ambulance.

Paralleling the river on the Maryland side was the Chesapeake and Ohio Canal, and there the ever-hungry soldiers found a barge loaded with melons, which, said Hotchkiss unconvincingly, "our men bought."

It took two days for all of Lee's army to cross the river. A Maryland farmer, watching the crossing, exclaimed to a reporter for the *Charleston Daily Courier:* "I've been to shows and circuses and theaters and all them things, but I never seen such a sight'n all my life."

There were delays as wagons, guns, limbers, and caissons stalled in the water, but when hard-swearing Major Harman waded in, "the effect was electric." According to one witness, he startled drivers and mules alike. The drivers' curses were "far below the Major's standard," noted Colonel John Imboden. Jackson heard it all but wisely said nothing. When the last wagons had crossed, Harman rode up to him, touched his hat, and said, "The ford is clear, General. There's only one language that will make mules understand on a hot day that they must get out of the water." He expected a lecture, but Jackson only smiled thinly and said, "Thank you, Major."

One of Jackson's first moves in Maryland was to purchase a large field of corn on the line of march. The ears were distributed to the men, the remainder to the horses and mules. Prudently he also bought fence rails for fires before his men could steal them. The corps bivouacked that night near Three Springs, just south of Frederick.

Some friendly Marylanders appeared, and staff officers received cordial invitations to dinner. One admirer presented Jackson with "a gigantic gray mare," which was "strong sinewed, powerful." Jackson

---

3. The lyrics for the immensely popular "Maryland, My Maryland" were written in 1861 by twenty-two-year-old James Ryder Randall and were sung to a modified tune of "Tannenbaum, O Tannenbaum." The "despot's heel" on "Maryland's shore" was presumably Lincoln's. In dealing with Southern sympathizers in that state, Lincoln rode roughshod over the United States Constitution and ignored the decisions of the Supreme Court.

described it as "a fine looking animal, possessed of great muscle and fine powers of endurance." The donor had warned him that the horse "was not gentle." Early the next morning Jackson self-confidently mounted the splendid creature, which immediately, as he later told Anna, "reared up and fell back with me, hurting me considerably." Stunned and unable to move, he was carried to an ambulance. Longstreet was also incapacitated, limping around in carpet slippers, a bad blister on his heel. With all three of the senior generals *hors de combat*, and the commander of the largest division under arrest, the invasion of Maryland did not have an auspicious beginning.

Later that day, 6 September, a part of Jackson's corps marched through Frederick, where Barbara Frietchie, an aged, bedridden woman, lived. Contrary to the famous verses by John Greenleaf Whittier, she did not see Jackson or his army march past, and she was quite incapable of hanging a flag from her window. Jackson, of course, did not, as in the poem, ride mounted through the streets; he rode in an ambulance.[4]

Frederick, a prosperous town of eight thousand, lay between two of those mountain ridges that bisect the Maryland panhandle. It was a pretty town with many high-spired churches. In the farms that dotted the fertile countryside in the valleys around, hardworking farmers, many of German descent and few of whom owned slaves, viewed the approach of the Army of Northern Virginia with apprehension.

The bloodless occupation of Frederick took the Federal forces by surprise. Government stores had been hurriedly set alight, and there had been an attempt, only partially successful, to evacuate two military hospitals, containing several hundred men, along with a considerable store of food and medicines. Catherine Markell watched from the roof of her house and wrote in her diary: "Saw the sick from the Barrick [*sic*] hospital straggling, with bandaged heads, etc., towards Pa."

The reaction of most Marylanders was best expressed by one who

---

4. Because of the immense popularity of John Greenleaf Whittier's poem, the facts have been extensively investigated, beginning almost immediately after the poem's publication in the *Atlantic Monthly* of October 1863. Barbara Frietchie was ninety-six or ninety-seven years old, bedridden, unable to move without assistance. She lived on Patrick Street, which was never traversed by Jackson, and died three months after the supposed incident. Whittier believed his poem to be factual; he learned of the story from newspaper clippings sent him by a friend, E. D. E. N. Southworth, a woman novelist whose main residence was in Georgetown in the District of Columbia but whose summer home was what is now part of the residence of the author in Hillsboro, Virginia, less than a dozen miles from Harper's Ferry.

wrote: "I have never seen a mass of such filthy, strong-smelling men. Three of them in a room would make it unbearable, and when marching in column along the street the smell was most offensive. . . . They are the roughest set of creatures I ever saw . . . and the scratching they kept up gave warrant of vermin in abundance." (Confederates called the body lice with which they were usually infested graybacks.)

A Unionist woman in Frederick wrote to a friend:

> I wish, my dear Minnie you could have witnessed the transit of the Rebel army through our streets. . . . I could scarcely believe my eyes; was this body of men moving so smoothly along, with no order, their guns carried in every fashion, no two dressed alike, their officers hardly distinguishable from the privates—were these, I asked in amazement, were these dirty, lank, ugly specimens of humanity, with shocks of hair sticking through holes in their hats, and thick dust on their dirty faces, the men that had coped and countered successfully, and driven back again and again our splendid legions with their fine discipline . . . ?
>
> And then, too, I wish you could see how they behaved—a crowd of schoolboys on a holiday don't seem happier. They are on the broad grin all the time. Oh! They are so dirty! . . .
>
> They were very polite, I must confess. . . . Many of them were bare-footed. Indeed, I felt sorry for the poor misguided wretches, for some were limping along so painfully, trying to keep up with their comrades.

As for the soldiers, they were disappointed by their reception, which was, said one, "decidedly cool." One infantryman wrote: "This wasn't what we expected. . . . There was positively no enthusiasm, no cheers, no waving handkerchiefs and flags—instead a death-like silence—some houses were closed tight, as if some public calamity had taken place."

On 7 September, three days after his altercation with Jackson and his request for a copy of the charges against him, Hill received a high-handed reply. Written by Jackson's recently appointed acting assistant adjutant general, Major Elisha Franklin ("Bull") Paxton,[5] a lawyer friend from Lexington, it informed him that "should the interests of the service require your case to be brought before a court-martial a copy of

---

5. Major Alexander S. Pendleton, Jackson's young, competent assistant adjutant general, was absent, sick, since before the Second Manassas battles. He rejoined in September, just before the attack on Harper's Ferry.

the charges and specifications will be furnished in accordance with army regulation. In the meantime you will remain with your division."

The Jackson-Hill feud came at a particularly inopportune time, at the very beginning of the South's most adventurous military expedition to date. Since their first meeting twenty years earlier, on the day Jackson reported at West Point, the two had harbored a strong mutual antipathy. Although each could admire the other's professional skills and valor, their personalities were irreconcilably antagonistic, and the hostility of these two brave, capable, and prickly men festered like a cancer in the body of Lee's army. While Hill was not blameless, the greatest troublemaker among Lee's generals was Jackson, whose propensity to arrest every officer who annoyed him regardless of his rank or worth could not be curbed. It should perhaps be noted here that Lee never found occasion to arrest any officer in the entire course of the war.

Within a few days of Hill's arrest Jackson clashed with Brigadier General William Starke. Many of Frederick's merchants refused to sell their goods to the ragged, dirty soldiers who flocked to their stores eager to trade their Confederate dollars for sorely needed supplies or small luxuries. One complained to Jackson that ladies in his shop had been treated discourteously by some of his "foreigners." Jumping to the conclusion that the culprits must have been Cajuns from the Louisiana brigade, Jackson ordered General Starke to parade those regiments in town so that the miscreants might be identified. Starke protested that this was unfair; other troops had also been there. When Jackson brushed his objections aside, he rebelled and refused to obey. Predictably Jackson placed him under arrest. This left Brigadier General Alexander Lawton, commanding Ewell's former division, as the only division commander in Jackson's corps not under arrest. Starke was held until it was discovered that the culprits were from the Stonewall Brigade. A week later he was killed in battle.

On Sunday evening, 7 September, with Henry Kyd Douglas and Anna's brother Lieutenant Joseph G. Morrison, Jackson, who had established his headquarters in a stand of oak trees about two miles south of town, rode into Frederick for church services. Lee had ordered that anyone leaving camp must have a pass, and Jackson, ever punctilious, sent Douglas to obtain one. "Pass Maj. Genl. T. J. Jackson and two staff officers and attendants to Frederick to church, to return tonight. By command of Major Genl. Jackson," it read.

The Presbyterian church was not holding services that evening, so they rode to the German Reformed church, where Jackson listened to Dr. Daniel Zacharias preach—until he fell asleep. "His head sunk upon his breast, his cap dropped from his hands to the floor, and the prayers of the congregation did not disturb him," said Douglas, "and only the choir and the deep-toned organ awakened him." Jackson confessed as much to Anna, blaming his deafness. Sitting in the back pew, he said, "I was not quite near enough to hear all the sermon, and I regret to say fell asleep; but had I been near enough to hear would probably not have been so unfortunate." He was peacefully sleeping when Dr. Zacharias prayed for the health of President Abraham Lincoln.

The following day Lee issued a proclamation to the people of Maryland, promising them help in "regaining the rights of which you have been despoiled." He pledged that there would be no intimidation and that his army would "protect all, of every opinion." No rush of young men eager to enlist ensued. Even those whose sentiments were with the South hesitated to ally themselves with the dirty, smelling, vermin-infested, tattered, barefoot soldiers of the Army of Northern Virginia.

Although quartermasters had been able to purchase some seventeen hundred pairs of shoes, this was only a fraction of the number required. (A Georgia soldier confessed, "I had no shoes. I tried it barefoot, but somehow my feet wouldn't callous. They just kept bleeding.") Not all Maryland farmers, merchants, and manufacturers were eager to do business with the Confederates, and Lee was reluctant to force them.

Lee's attention now focused on Harper's Ferry, still strongly held by the Federals. He needed a secure line of communication, and the best supply route was west of the Blue Ridge up the Shenandoah Valley. The only major obstacle on this line was Harper's Ferry, at the confluence of the Shenandoah and the Potomac. He was surprised that in view of his own position between the town and Washington, the Federals had not abandoned it. McClellan had, in fact, advocated just that but had been overruled by Halleck.

Lee first discussed the capture of Harper's Ferry with Longstreet, but Longstreet thought the troops needed rest, and he pointed out the danger of dividing the army while in enemy territory. On 9 September Lee sent for Jackson to ask his view. General James A. Walker was present while they talked, and when Longstreet arrived at Lee's tent, he, too, took part in the discussion. Longstreet did not press his objections but urged once more that the effort be made with the entire army. Lee listened courteously but overruled him. Jackson, he decided, should move at once upon Harper's Ferry.

Jackson was delighted. In high spirits he mentioned to Lee that he felt he had neglected his friends there. Lee, aware that Union sentiment was strong in the area, remarked jocularly that perhaps "some friends" would not be glad to see him.

Unknowingly Lee may have touched upon a sensitive nerve. Although the war had put an end to Jackson's long, faithful correspondence with Laura, he must have been aware of her strong Union sympathies, and he must have felt keenly the breach with his closest blood relative. Although he was never to know it, Laura was to divorce her husband, citing his Southern sympathies as sufficient cause. She was later said to have taken up with a Union officer and to have moved to Ohio.[6]

Lee decided on a three-pronged attack to secure those positions whose occupation would make Harper's Ferry indefensible: Maryland Heights (1,460 feet); Loudoun Heights (940 feet); and Bolivar Heights, only about 300 feet high but rising sharply from the village in the triangle made by the two rivers. To do this, he had to divide his army into four parts. With McClellan preparing to descend upon him from the east, it was a daring, if not, indeed, a rash, move. Lee was depending heavily upon McClellan's overcautious approach.

All the intricate movements and changes of command necessary for the operation against Harper's Ferry were spelled out in Lee's Special Orders No. 191, destined to become the most famous special orders in American history. John G. Walker's division was assigned to capture Loudoun Heights by 12 September; Major General Lafayette McLaws, with his own division plus that of Richard Heron Anderson—a total of about eight thousand men—was to occupy Maryland Heights by the same date and "endeavor to capture the enemy at Harper's Ferry and the vicinity"; Jackson by the morning of the twelfth was to have captured Martinsburg and was to "intercept such as may attempt to escape from Harper's Ferry." Walker and McLaws were to come under Jackson's command when they all reached Harper's Ferry.

6. Beverly was in Union hands throughout the war, but there was some exchange of letters between Anna and Laura. The last received by Anna was written on 28 November 1862. Anna replied but never learned if her letter had been received. A copy of the Arnold divorce papers can be found in the Roy Bird Cook Collection in the archives of the library of West Virginia University, Morgantown, West Virginia.

Stuart was to provide cavalry for McLaws, Walker, and Jackson. Long-street, with the divisions of D. H. Hill, David Rumph ("Neighbor") Jones, and Nathan George ("Shanks") Evans, the victor of Ball's Bluff, was originally to form a rear guard and reserve, but Lee, hearing that a Union force was being assembled in Pennsylvania, sent Longstreet north to Hagerstown—a fool's errand, for no such force was in being.

At three o'clock on the morning of 10 September Jackson started his men on their way. Accompanied by the Black Horse Troop, a proud cavalry unit from Loudoun County, he rode into Frederick. Stopping briefly at the parsonage of the Presbyterian church, he left a note for Dr. John B. Ross, a minister whom he had known in Lexington, and then galloped off to the head of his infantry.

The day before leaving, in an effort to deceive, Jackson had made ostentatious inquiries among Frederick's citizens about maps and directions for Chambersburg and other places in Pennsylvania. As Douglas said, "his questions only illustrated his well-known motto, 'Mystery, mystery is the secret of success.' "

As the Confederates left Frederick, most inhabitants were glad to see their backs. Dr. Lewis H. Steiner wrote in his journal: "Their friends were anxious to get rid of them and of the penetrating ammoniacal smell they brought with them."

Jackson's column crossed South Mountain at Turner's Gap and dropped down to Boonsboro, marching fourteen miles that day, a bit longer for those who had camped east of Frederick. The soldiers bedded down in the fields; Jackson put up at the home of Mr. John Murdock, about a mile from the village, and his headquarters tents were erected in the field opposite. Henry Kyd Douglas was riding leisurely down Main Street to the United States Hotel when suddenly a squad of Federal cavalrymen appeared. Douglas bolted, pursued by Federals, who put a bullet through his hat, knocking it off his head into the dust.

Topping a rise, Douglas bore down on Jackson, alone and on foot, leading his horse and swinging his hat. Sensing the danger, Jackson leaped into his saddle and fled. Lieutenant A. D. Payne of the Black Horse Troop, who had heard the firing, dashed up with some of his men. Douglas reversed direction, and calling loudly for nonexistent reserves, the two officers charged. The Federals fled.

Jackson had again had a narrow escape, his closest since Port Republic. Douglas later retrieved his hat and picked up the gloves Jackson had dropped when he hurriedly mounted.

On 11 September Jackson decided that instead of taking the direct route to Martinsburg, he would go a bit farther northwest and move on

Williamsport. He moved rapidly, captured a Federal picket and put his column across the Potomac at Light's Ford, just below Williamsport, where the water was only knee-deep and clear enough for the footsore men to see the rocks as they waded across, the bands playing "Carry Me Back to Old Virginny." They pressed on, past the Falling Waters battlefield and over the rolling countryside to Hammond's Mill, about seven miles from Martinsburg, a hard twenty-mile march.

Jackson's men often took pride in being called Jackson's foot cavalry, but the marches of twenty miles and more took their toll and inspired a wry maxim, probably already a chestnut when Lieutenant John Stone of the 2nd Maryland repeated it in a letter home: "Man that is born of woman and enlists in Jackson's Army, has but few days to live, short rations and much hard tack, sleeps but little and marches many miles."

Mary Bedinger Mitchell, who lived in the path of both armies and witnessed the stragglers in the wake of Jackson, wrote: "I know something of the appearance of a marching army, both Union and Southern. There are always stragglers, of course, but never before or after did I see anything comparable to the demoralized state of the Confederates at this time. Never were want and exhaustion more visibly put before my eyes, and that they could march or fight at all seemed incredible."

The same woman spoke of the hunger of the men:

> When I say that they were hungry, I convey no impression of the gaunt starvation that looked from their cavernous eyes. All day they crowded to the doors of our houses, and always with the same drawling complaint: "I've been a-marchin' an' a-fightin' for six weeks stidy, and I ain't had n-a-r-thin' to eat 'cept green apples an' green cawn, an' I wish you'd please to gimme a bite to eat."
>
> Their looks bore out their statements. . . . They could be seen afterward asleep in every fence corner, and under every tree, but after a night's rest they "pulled themselves together" somehow and disappeared as suddenly as they had come.

A. P. Hill, sensing a coming battle, requested through a staff officer to be returned to his command for its duration. He had been riding in an ambulance for the past few days, suffering from an attack of prostatitis caused by his recurring gonorrhea, but he was now recovering, and Jackson, who, whatever his antipathy for Hill, was well aware of his generalship and fighting qualities, at once agreed.

On the night of 11 September Union Brigadier General Julius

White, commanding two thousand men at Martinsburg, decided not to await Jackson's attack. He decamped and marched his men to the tenuous security of Harper's Ferry.

The next day, the twelfth, all the elements in Lee's plans, as outlined in Special Orders No. 191, were to click into place. None was ready. A day late Jackson's troops, divided into three parts to attack Martinsburg, entered the town without a fight and received an ecstatic welcome. General Jackson, hailed as the Valley's own, was the hero of the hour.

He established his headquarters at Everett House and locked himself in the parlor to write a dispatch to Lee and to escape the admiring crowds, but they would not be denied. They called to him through the windows and rattled the shutters and doors. They pulled hairs from his horse's tail until a staff officer drove them away. (Not Sorrel's tail, for Sorrel was still missing.) After a shutter was broken and the windows were endangered, Jackson gave up and admitted the mob, mostly women and children, who swarmed over him, throwing red and white roses, clutching at his hands, and calling out, "Dear, dear, General!" Douglas described the scene: "Blushing, bowing, almost speechless, he stood in the midst of this remarkable scene, saying, 'Thank you, thank you, you're very kind.' "

When a rosy-cheeked little girl begged for a button from his coat, he gave it to her, and in a trice half his coat buttons disappeared. A woman with an autograph album begged for his signature. He signed her album and then was besieged by all until he sat down and wrote "T. J. Jackson" on sheets of foolscap. "Really, ladies," he protested, "this is the first time I was ever surrounded by the enemy." Only when a woman demanded a lock of his hair did he draw the line and escape.

By the end of the day Hill's division was six miles beyond Martinsburg in the direction of Harper's Ferry. Walker had crossed the Potomac farther downstream and bivouacked his column at Hillsborough (today spelled Hillsboro), Virginia, about ten miles from Loudoun Heights. McLaws moved his two divisions into Pleasant Valley, in Maryland, between South Mountain and the Catoctin Mountains, but sent the South Carolina brigade of Joseph Kershaw, backed by the Mississippi brigade of William Barksdale, up a ridge at Soloman's Gap, four miles north of Maryland Heights. Lee, with Longstreet's column, was at Hagerstown, where he learned that McClellan with eighty-seven thousand men was moving on Frederick.

The vise on Harper's Ferry that was supposed to have been in position on the twelfth moved nicely into place on the thirteenth, at least most of the pieces did, and no one involved in the operation appeared concerned that it was all a day late. On the afternoon of the thirteenth Jackson bivouacked near Halltown, about two miles from the Federals on Bolivar Heights. Walker reached Loudoun Heights without difficulty and by two o'clock in the afternoon had five rifled pieces on the crest. Jackson sent Hotchkiss and two officers to establish a signal station and assist him in laying his artillery. Kershaw and Barksdale had some hard fighting but by four-thirty in the afternoon had cleared Maryland Heights. McLaws then had three 10-pounders and a 3-inch ordnance rifle manhandled up its steep slopes.

Lee worried, with good reason, that Major General William B. Franklin's corps would come down on McLaws's rear and crush him. Stuart reported that Union forces had nearly reached Turner's Gap in Maryland. Lee therefore ordered D. H. Hill at Boonsboro to hold Turner's Gap and Longstreet at Hagerstown to go to his support. Longstreet demurred, arguing that to march his men thirteen miles and throw them into a desperate defense of the gaps was asking too much and that it would be better to withdraw to Sharpsburg, but Lee insisted.

In the Peninsula Lee had outgeneraled McClellan in large part through his understanding of the personality and cautious nature of the Federal commander. But now he was puzzled by the unaccustomed vigor and decisiveness McClellan exhibited. It must have seemed to him that McClellan anticipated his every move. Indeed, this was so, and it was not guesswork on McClellan's part. He had obtained a copy of Special Orders No. 191.[7]

On the morning of 13 September the 27th Indiana had marched westward through Frederick, Maryland, and had halted for a rest by an open field of clover. Private Barton Warren Mitchell of Company F, perhaps looking for firewood, found an envelope which, to his delight,

---

7. How Special Orders No. 191 came to be wrapped around cigars in a Maryland field is one of the war's great unsolved mysteries, but it has been much investigated, and there has been much conjecture. Both Hill and his AAG swore that the copy sent out by Lee's headquarters never reached them. Jackson made a hurried copy and sent it to Hill, as Hill's division had been assigned to his command but was by these orders detached from it. Jackson's copy, in his worst handwriting, did reach Hill and is still extant. The natural inference, therefore, would be that it was the copy from Lee's headquarters that was found by Private Mitchell. But the copy made by Jackson omitted the first two paragraphs—they concerned restrictions on entering "Fredericktown" and the route to be taken by sick and wounded back to Winchester—and those two paragraphs were also omitted from the copy seen by McClellan. The order in its original envelope is now in the Library of Congress. It was donated, along with other McClellan papers, by G. B. McClellan, Jr.

contained three cigars. He at once showed his find to First Sergeant John McKnight Bloss (who years later claimed that it was he who had found the envelope), and they were astonished to see that it also held Confederate orders. Headed "Headquarters, Army of Northern Virginia," the orders were addressed to D. H. Hill and were signed by Colonel R. H. Chilton, Lee's AAG.

With astonishing rapidity the orders were passed up the chain of command, from company commander Captain Peter Kopp, to regimental commander Colonel Silas Colgrove, to the division headquarters of Brigadier General Alpheus Starkey Williams, whose AAG, recognizing Robert Hall Chilton's signature as authentic, sent it by galloper to McClellan. Special Orders No. 191 traveled from Private Mitchell to Major General McClellan in less than an hour. No general had ever been offered such a golden opportunity. McClellan now knew not only that Lee's forces were divided but where the pieces were to be found. "I think Lee has made a gross mistake," McClellan wired Lincoln. "I have all the plans of the rebels, and will catch them in their own trap. . . ."

"Here is a paper with which, if I cannot whip Bobbie Lee, I will be willing to go home," he chortled that afternoon to Brigadier General John Gibbon. "Tomorrow we will pitch into his center, and if you people will only do two good, hard days' marching, I will put Lee in a position he will find it hard to get out of."

His words, if accurately reported by Gibbon, reflect McClellan's greatest weakness. A more aggressive general would have had his divisions moving within the hour and would not have waited until "tomorrow." Not until six-twenty that evening did McClellan order Major General William B. Franklin, commanding VI Corps, to move the next morning to "cut off, destroy, or capture McLaws' command and relieve Colonel Miles." If Harper's Ferry held and Franklin was able to interpose his force between McLaws and Lee, McLaws would be doomed. Each hour was now crucial. Eleven precious hours that cost the Union dearly were lost. Fresh intelligence fades quickly. "Tomorrow" was too late.

Speed was essential, but McClellan was not speedy. There was no general in the Union army who could organize, train, and inspire an army better than Major General George B. McClellan, but as he was soon to demonstrate along the banks of a small stream called Antietam, he lacked the genius successfully to fight that army.

Although Special Orders No. 191 told McClellan much, he still could not count upon a complete victory because the orders did not give him the numbers of Confederates in Lee's army. He would have been astonished had he learned that his own army was vastly superior in numbers to the Army of Northern Virginia. Still relying upon the unreliable Allan Pinkerton, McClellan believed that Lee had "not less than 120,000 men," and he spoke of "the gigantic rebel army before us." In fact, McClellan commanded about eighty-seven thousand men, almost exactly twice as many as Lee.

Already news of the discovery of Special Orders No. 191 was being bruited about. A Marylander in Frederick sympathetic to the Southern cause heard of it and galloped at top speed to Stuart's headquarters; Stuart quickly passed the information on to Lee, who probably received the discomfiting message early in the evening of the thirteenth. That the orders had fallen into McClellan's hands was, as Lee said, "a great calamity." Although it was important for him to know that this had happened, there was little Lee could do about it other than to send a message to McLaws to speed up his operations as much as possible. D. H. Hill and Longstreet had been sent to guard the passes over South Mountain; the rest of his fighting forces were involved in the operation to capture Harper's Ferry, about which he was anxious but had heard nothing.

Although McLaws was to have captured Harper's Ferry, Jackson as the senior general took charge of the operation. The fourteenth was a Sunday, but by this time Jackson was reconciled to doing the work of Mars on the Sabbath. He was up early and already in touch with Walker on Loudoun Heights by signals and with McLaws by courier. His own troops were strung out along Schoolhouse Ridge facing the Federals on Bolivar Heights; the ridge, about a mile and a half west of Harper's Ferry, runs from the Potomac almost to the Shenandoah. At seven-twenty he sent McLaws a message, telling him of his and Walker's dispositions and ordering him to "get possession of Maryland Heights," as, of course, McLaws was already striving his mightiest to do. He also told him:

> So soon as you get your batteries all planted, let me know, as I desire, after yourself, Walker and myself have our batteries ready to open, to send in a flag of truce, for the purpose of getting out the non-combatants, should the commanding officer refuse to surrender. Should we have to attack, let the work be done thoroughly; fire on the houses when necessary. The citizens can keep out of harm's way from your artillery. Demolish the place if it is occupied by the enemy, and does not surrender.

In the event, no flag of truce was sent in, and no efforts were made to remove noncombatants to safety. How the citizens were to "keep out of harm's way" with Confederate artillery pounding them is not apparent.[8] Jackson rarely showed concern for what is now euphemistically called collateral damage, and he did not, as far as is known, take the time to ask the Federals to surrender.

When Brigadier General Julius White arrived from Martinsburg on the twelfth, he became the senior Union officer at Harper's Ferry, but as only a few months earlier he had been the collector of customs in Chicago and was without prior military experience, he relinquished command to Colonel Dixon Stansbury Miles, a regular who had been in charge there. Miles, a fifty-eight-year-old Marylander, was the oldest colonel in the Union army. He had been graduated from West Point in 1824, the year Jackson was born, and had served twenty-three years as a company officer. Although he had distinguished himself in the Mexican War and in expeditions against the Coyotero Apaches and the Navajos, no one ever considered him brilliant.

There were now some twelve thousand troops in Harper's Ferry, and on 5 September Miles had been given specific orders by Major General John E. Wool, his superior in Baltimore: "You will not abandon Harper's Ferry without defending it to the last extremity." Apparently thinking this message not forceful enough, Wool later that same day sent Miles another, including the order that "There must be no abandoning of a post, and shoot the first man that thinks of it. Two days later Miles assured Wool: "I am ready for them."

Miles's command was a remarkably large one for a colonel. It was even more remarkable that of all people, he was put in charge of it, for in August 1861 a court of inquiry had found him guilty of being drunk during the Battle of First Manassas. He was spared a court-martial, for the court of inquiry decided that a trial would be inconvenient and would not be "for the interests of the service." This experience and the spectacle of politicians and younger, inexperienced men promoted to general officer rank over his head seem to have embittered him. His defense of Harper's Ferry was certainly inept. It has been suggested that he was a traitor, secretly arranging with Jackson for the surrender.[9] A military commission later found him guilty of "criminal neglect" and

8. There were, however, few civilians remaining in the town, which was but a ghost of its former self, the great arsenal being now blackened ruins. Most of the town's prewar population of three thousand had long since moved elsewhere.

9. The case against Colonel Dixon S. Miles is strongly argued by Paul R. Teetor, an attorney and retired administrative law judge, in *A Matter of Hours*. The historian of

of an "incapacity amounting almost to imbecility." Jackson was again fortunate in contending with an incompetent Federal commander.

By far the greatest number of troops Miles commanded were untrained volunteer infantry who had been employed in guarding the bridges and track of the Baltimore & Ohio Railroad. Six of the twelve regiments consisted of men of insignificant experience and of those who had enlisted for only three months. The 126th New York, which faced McLaws's tough Confederates on Maryland Heights, had been in existence less than three weeks; its soldiers scarcely knew how to load their rifles.[10] Sergeant Nicholas J. DeGraff, who, like his comrades in the 115th New York, had been in uniform less than a week, wrote: "Of course we were greatly supprised [*sic*] at finding ourselves in the face of the enemy so soon."

On the afternoon of the fourteenth Jackson sent A. P. Hill's division along the left bank of the Shenandoah, and it successfully turned the Federal left on Bolivar Heights. Jackson had proceeded methodically to draw a noose around Harper's Ferry, exhibiting an uncharacteristic caution. He was, of course, well aware that if he held the three heights, victory was eventually assured. Although he must have heard the firing from the guns north of the Potomac, where McLaws was heavily engaged with Franklin, and perhaps even the heavy fighting at the passes through South Mountain, he seemed unperturbed. But Lee was under considerable pressure, for although Jackson's operations were drawing to a successful conclusion, his own position was far from comfortable.

McClellan's army, which had reached Frederick on 12 September, forced the passes over South Mountain in spite of a stout defense by D. H. Hill, and Lee considered McLaws's force to be in such grave danger that he ordered him to retreat at once to Sharpsburg. At eight o'clock the night of the fourteenth he wrote McLaws: "The day has gone against us. . . . It is necessary for you to abandon your position tonight." Fortunately for the Confederate cause, the message appears

---

the 115th New York, one of the Federal regiments captured at Harper's Ferry, called Miles the Benedict Arnold of the Civil War.

10. The inexperienced 126th New York, which had been mustered into the army only twenty-one days earlier, after fighting bravely for several hours against the veterans in Kershaw's and Barksdale's brigades and suffering fifty-five casualties, was ordered to retreat. Their retreat became a rout, earning them the name of the Harper's Ferry Cowards. It was a stain the regiment later erased with its blood by its gallantry at Gettysburg and in many another hard-fought battle.

either not to have reached McLaws or to have been ignored. Perhaps McLaws considered it impossible or unwise to execute. Franklin was indeed pressing his rear, and he was able to maintain only a small force on Maryland Heights, but it was enough.

While Lee was writing his despairing dispatch to McLaws, Jackson was writing optimistically of Hill's success on Bolivar Heights. It was, he said, a success he had achieved "through God's blessing," and he now looked "to Him for complete success tomorrow." It is not known when his dispatch reached Lee, but early on Monday morning, 15 September, Lee still despaired even as Jackson's eager gunners laid their tubes on a doomed Harper's Ferry.

It must have been early that morning that Colonel A. L. Long, Lee's military secretary, wrote a panicky dispatch to McLaws from Keedysville, eleven miles south of Hagerstown:

> General Lee desires me to say that he sent several dispatches to you last night; he is in doubt that they have been received. We have fallen back to this place to enable you more readily to join us. You are desired to withdraw immediately from your position on Maryland Heights, and join us here. If you can't get off any other way, you must cross the mountain. The utmost dispatch is required. Should you be able to cross over to Harper's Ferry, do so and report immediately.

An early-morning mist covered the arena of battle, but when it lifted like a curtain on a drama, A. P. Hill's men charged the Federal earthworks on Bolivar Heights, and some fifty Confederate guns opened fire. "It was terrific," said Colonel William Trimble of the 60th Ohio, "there was not a place where you could lay the palm of your hand and say it was safe." Lieutenant Edward Hastings Ripley of the 9th Vermont described the effect: "In an instant . . . artillery, infantry, and cavalry were mixed in an absurd and laughable melee, as the panic increased."

The hour and a half cannonade was impressive, but hardly any shells landed in the village, and it accounted for few casualties. Nevertheless, it not only frightened the inexperienced Federal volunteers but shook their commanders as well. Colonel Miles called a council of war. There seems to have been no understanding on the part of the senior Union officers that every hour they held out was of immense importance to McClellan; Wool's orders were forgotten or ignored. All agreed that they must surrender. A strip of white canvas was cut from a tent and hoisted; others followed.

It took time for all the Confederate batteries to be sure that the Federals were in earnest. Colonel Andrew Grigsby, temporarily in command of the Stonewall Brigade, did not see, or pretended not to see, the white flag, and, although other guns fell silent, he commanded Captain Poague to keep firing: "Damn their eyes, give it to them!" When Jackson's order to cease fire was received, Poague, who had his guns loaded, sent a gunner to ask Grigsby what he should do. "Tell him to fire off the way he is pointed," said Grigsby. "He won't kill more of the damn Yankees than he ought to!" One of the final shots tore off the leg of Colonel Miles, who, after more than twenty-four hours of excruciating pain, died in the Harper's Ferry hospital.

Jackson wasted no time in informing Lee of his victory. At "near 8 A.M." he wrote:

> Through God's blessing, Harper's Ferry and its garrison are to be surrendered. As Hill's troops have borne the heaviest part in the engagement, he will be left in command until the prisoners and public property are disposed of, unless you direct otherwise. The other forces can move off this evening, so soon as they get their rations. To what point should they move? . . . You may expect to hear from me again today, after I get more information respecting the number of prisoners, etc.

Jackson sent Douglas to lead the Union surrender party to him. General White, now in command, rode forward on a splendid black horse. His boots shone, his saber glistened, his uniform was immaculate, as with white-gloved hand he saluted Jackson, described by Douglas as the "dingiest, worst-dressed and worst-mounted general that a warrior who cared for good looks and style would wish to surrender to."

Jackson informed White that the surrender must be unconditional and then turned him over to Hill, telling him to make the conditions liberal. Hill saw that they were. All were paroled.[11] Officers retained their side arms and private baggage; enlisted men kept their blankets, overcoats, and two days' rations. They were even lent a number of

11. Some of the Harper's Ferry parolees, instead of being furloughed, were sent to Camp Douglas, three miles south of Chicago, for training and refitting to fight the Sioux Indians. Camp Douglas, located on part of the estate of Stephen A. Douglas, had been a notoriously unhealthy prisoner of war camp; it was filthy and vermin-infested. Discipline deteriorated in the regiments sent there, and disgruntled soldiers tore down the perimeter fence and burned barracks.

wagons, which, Jackson and Hill later complained, they were slow to return.

The Union soldiers in their neat new uniforms were astonished to see the ragged Confederates. One called out, "Why don't you wear better clothes?" A quick-witted South Carolina boy shouted back, "These are good enough to kill hogs in!"

About eleven o'clock in the morning Jackson rode down from Bolivar Heights into Harper's Ferry. It was no longer the proud and prosperous town it had been before the war. Lieutenant Colonel David Hunter Strother, a Union staff officer who visited the town not long after, noted in his diary that "charred ruins were all that remained of the splendid public works, arsenals, workshops and railroads, stores, hotels and dwelling houses all mingled in one common destruction."

As Jackson rode through the ruined town in which he had served his first command in the war, throngs of Federal troops, curious to see the famous "Stonewall," lined the streets. "Boys," cried one, "he's not much for looks, but if we'd had him we wouldn't have been caught in this trap."

Perhaps because so little blood was shed in comparison with the numbers engaged, the scope and importance of Jackson's capture of Harper's Ferry are frequently underestimated. By Federal count, 435 officers and 12,085 enlisted men surrendered. It was the most complete Confederate victory of the war; it was the largest surrender of American forces in history at that time and remained so until the fall of Bataan and Corregidor in 1942, when almost an equal number surrendered to the Japanese. The only Federals to escape were 1,300 cavalrymen of the 8th New York and 12th Illinois, all under Colonel Arno Voss, who between eight-thirty and ten-thirty on the night of the fourteenth crossed the Potomac by a pontoon bridge and, taking the only route McLaws had left unguarded, traveled sixty miles to Union-held Greencastle, Pennsylvania, capturing forty of Longstreet's reserve ammunition wagons on their way.

Jackson captured 47 guns (not the 73 he reported), 7 of which were spiked. Also captured were much-needed ammunition, food, and an immense amount of stores and accoutrements. Jackson erred when he told Lee that A. P. Hill's division had seen the most fighting. Of the 1,263 Confederate casualties, all but 74 were suffered by McLaws's division. On Bolivar Heights only 3 were killed and 71 wounded. Federal losses in Harper's Ferry included only 21 killed and 73 wounded. The capture of 12,500 men and the failure of Franklin to defeat or capture McLaws shifted the balance of power for the coming battle near Sharpsburg, but the decision to fight there was the worst Lee ever made.

When Major Heros von Borcke, a huge Prussian volunteer serving on Stuart's staff, warmly congratulated Jackson on his victory, Jackson replied, "Ah, this is all very well, Major, but we have yet much hard work before us."

Indeed, this was so.

Antietam

When the formalities of the sur-
render were completed, McLaws's men came down from their aerie on
Maryland Heights and Walker's men came down from Loudoun
Heights and waded across the Shenandoah. There was some hurried
harvesting of the riches to be found in the Federal supply depots, and
an attempt was made to acquire needed essentials from the Federal
stores, but Jackson was eager to rejoin Lee, now at Sharpsburg, Maryland, and Lee was eager to have him. By midafternoon of 15 September
all the troops with Jackson except A. P. Hill's men were back in their
camp west of Bolivar Heights and cooking two days' rations. A Louisiana colonel took the opportunity to write home: "I am completely
tired out with our constant marching. . . . It is too much as the state of
our ranks show, and if Jackson keeps on at it, there will be no army for
him to command." But there was still more hard marching ahead.

Shortly after midnight Jackson's brigades were in motion, moving
north on a seventeen-mile march which even Jackson classed as "a
severe night's march." They crossed into Maryland at Boteler's Ford
(also known as Blackford's or Shepherdstown or Pack Horse Ford), a
mile east of Shepherdstown. The river here was at this time about three
hundred yards across and three feet deep; the current was swift, and
the sharp rocks were painful to the barefooted. The banks on the Maryland shore stood more than twenty feet high, precipitous and slippery,

but the brigades crossed without incident and marched on, crossing a small creek called Antietam to the village of Sharpsburg (named after Horatio Sharpe, a colonial governor of Maryland).

Sharpsburg was a farming community of about thirteen hundred people sited where six roads intersect. It sat surrounded by cultivated fields, patches of woods, and prosperous farms. Passing through the village, the tired troops marched about a mile north, where they stacked arms and fell out on some high ground near a white Dunkard church. Lawton's and Jones's divisions were with Jackson; McLaws's division was following some miles behind.

A. P. Hill and his men were still at Harper's Ferry, hurriedly working out the parole arrangements. They had begun by making an attempt to get the signature of every man, but after a few hours they abandoned the effort and paroled whole companies, the men raising their hands to swear, their company commanders signing for them.

When Jackson found Lee in Sharpsburg, Lee congratulated him on his victory and briefed him on the situation in Maryland. Although he was well aware that his men were in miserable condition and that he was badly outnumbered and outgunned, with his back to an unbridged river, Lee, according to one of his officers, "could not have appeared more composed and confident."

Longstreet and Stuart, who were staying at the house of a Mr. Jacob Grove on the square, invited Jackson to stay for breakfast. He refused, but Miss Julia Grove, "a daughter of the house," sent him his breakfast by way of one of Longstreet's slaves. Jackson asked which young lady had sent it and was told: "I dunno, General, but it was the fair one."

"Well, as she has sent me my breakfast to the field, I will call her Miss Fairfield." Taking up a pencil, he wrote:

Sharpsburg Sept 16. 1862

Miss Fairfield:

I have received the nice breakfast, for which I am indebted to your kindness. Please accept my grateful appreciation of your hospitality.

Very Sincerely Yours
T. J. Jackson[1]

1. This note was often reproduced. Henry Kyd Douglas, writing after the war, said: "I have often seen it spread upon satin and nicely framed, doing duty at bazaars and fairs for 'Confederate Homes,' since the war. During the war it was lithographed

Jackson, who now commanded about seventy-seven hundred men, was assigned the left of the Confederate line, Longstreet commanded the right with D. H. Hill in the center, the line extending north and south about four miles along a ridge that generally paralleled the Hagerstown Pike, a good road of "stiff, red clay" that ran almost in a straight line between Hagerstown, Pennsylvania, and the Potomac. Jackson allowed his men several hours' rest and then, late in the afternoon, moved them about half a mile north on the Hagerstown Pike, just south of Joseph Poffenberger's farm. Here he prepared for battle. Already a Federal battery was beginning to annoy, some of its shells falling close by.

The ground, which at a distance appeared open and fairly level north of Sharpsburg, was in fact quite broken with outcroppings of rocks and folds. Lee's army, facing generally east, occupied a ridge with Antietam Creek in front of it. On the left (west) of the pike, Jones's division (Virginians all) formed line of battle partly in a wood soon to become famous as the West Woods, with Grigsby's Stonewall Brigade on the right, resting on the road, and Bradley Johnson's brigade on Grigsby's left. Each brigade threw forward a company as skirmishers. Early's brigade, with a strong concentration of guns, was positioned to support Jones's left flank. Two other brigades formed a second line some two or three hundred yards behind Grigsby and Johnson; Lawton's division remained near the Dunkard church. Poague's three guns went into battery on a small rise in the front and in twenty minutes silenced the annoying Federal battery. Stuart and Fitzhugh Lee's cavalry brigade linked the left of the line with the sinuous Potomac, and on a small ridge known as Nicodemus Hill, the highest ground on the left flank, were posted three regular batteries and the horse artillery, fourteen guns in all under the redoubtable young Major John Pelham.

East of the Hagerstown Pike were Hood's two brigades, mostly Texans, detached by Lee from Longstreet's corps. As a result of a silly quarrel between Evans and Hood over captured wagons, Longstreet had put under arrest Brigadier General Hood (to be made a major general one month thence). Knowing he would need all the good generals he could find, Lee ordered him released.

East of the Hagerstown Pike, where Hood's division was deployed, lay a pasture and a thirty-acre field of standing corn about head

---

in Baltimore, and five hundred dollars were realized from the sale of those lithographs for the use of Confederate hospitals."

high, both owned by David R. Miller. Some of the most desperate fighting of the war was to take place here. The corn was soon to be harvested by shellfire, and the pasture to be stained red by musketry. To the east of the cornfield stood another woods, the East Woods it would be called. To the north, farther up the pike, was the North Woods, behind which Federal troops of I Corps under Major General Joseph Hooker (about eighty-six hundred men), backed by XII Corps (eight thousand men, McClellan's smallest corps) under fifty-eight-year-old Brigadier General Joseph King Fenno Mansfield, were assembling on Joseph Poffenberger's farm for an attack on the Confederate left.

Although Jackson and Hood faced generally north, the Confederate line curved south-southeast along the low ridge west of Antietam Creek. Lee's army, badly outnumbered and outgunned, with most of its soldiers in wretched physical condition, standing with its back to the Potomac, was in great peril. Lee had more to lose in this battle than he could possibly gain, even if by a miracle he scored a victory. Although he planned to fight a defensive battle, as he knew he must, no field fortifications were erected. There were probably few tools for creating any; still, the idea of trying to throw up some defensive works appears to have occurred to none of the Confederate generals.

McClellan's caution and his firm belief (supported by extravagant numbers given him by Allan Pinkerton's "operatives") that he was outnumbered continued to be Lee's best hope. Indeed, McClellan had punched through a gap in South Mountain on the fifteenth with three corps, and had he pushed forward vigorously, he would certainly have overwhelmed Lee and Longstreet before Jackson could come onto the field. Instead, he had restrained his generals and spent the afternoon of the fifteenth and the morning of the sixteenth with a large contingent of officers inspecting the Confederate line. Not until the afternoon of the sixteenth did the Federals decide to launch an attack upon Lee's left, by which time Jackson's men were in place to receive them.

It was late in the afternoon when units in Hooker's I Corps moved cautiously south and collided with Hood's skirmishers east of the road, producing a sharp but indecisive engagement that ended at nightfall. Hood then asked Lee if he could pull his men back and feed them, for they had been on exceptionally short rations. Lee sent him to Jackson, who agreed to relieve him, on condition that he would return when needed. So at about ten o'clock that night Lawton and Walker replaced Hood, Walker on the right of the line. There was some random firing

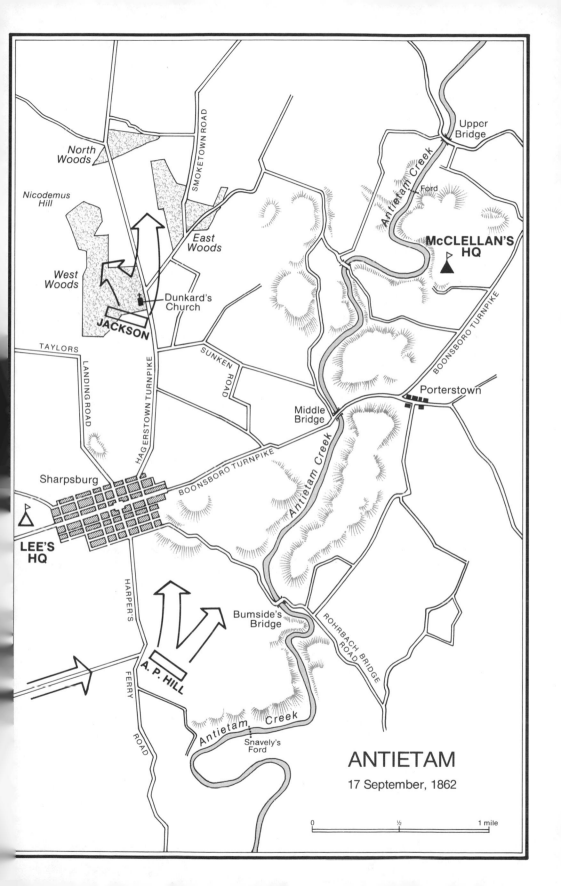

North Woods

SMOKETOWN ROAD

Upper Bridge

Antietam Creek

Nicodemus Hill

East Woods

Ford

McCLELLAN'S HQ

West Woods

Dunkard's Church

JACKSON

TAYLORS

SUNKEN ROAD

BOONSBORO TURNPIKE

LANDING ROAD

HAGERSTOWN TURNPIKE

Porterstown

Middle Bridge

Sharpsburg

BOONSBORO TURNPIKE

Antietam Creek

LEE'S HQ

HARPER'S

Burnside's Bridge

ROHRBACH BRIDGE ROAD

A. P. HILL

FERRY

ROAD

Antietam Creek

Snavely's Ford

ANTIETAM

17 September, 1862

0   ½   1 mile

during the night, but a light rain seemed to put a damper upon way-ward enthusiasms.

Even after McLaws and Anderson reached the field, Lee's army numbered only thirty thousand, so heavy had been the loss from strag-glers, deserters, and casualties on South Mountain. McClellan had eighty-seven thousand men to hand and fourteen thousand more a half day's march away. Yet Lee felt he must fight north of the Potomac. "I went into Maryland to give battle," he said later.

At about five o'clock on the morning of 17 September 1862 the sky was briefly overcast and there were patches of ground fog, but McClellan's twenty long-range, 20-pounder Parrott guns, posted on high ground east of Antietam Creek opened up at two thousand yards, enfilading Jackson's lines and causing casualties. The Confederates had but six such guns with which to reply, but when Hooker sent three divisions pounding out of the North Woods, Stuart's and Lee's guns on the left enfiladed the Federal line of battle with devastating effect. Still, the blue lines continued to advance.

Lieutenant E. A. Stickley, on the staff of the Stonewall Brigade, described the sight: "In apparent double line of battle the Federals were moving toward us at charge bayonets, common time, and the sun-beams falling on their well-polished guns and bayonets gave a glamour and show at once fearful and entrancing." (Lieutenant Stickley lost an arm before the end of the day.)

Out of the North Woods the Federal brigades of Abner Double-day and James B. Ricketts stormed across the open ground of David Miller's farm toward the thirty-acre cornfield where Confederates were waiting. Union General Joseph ("Fighting Joe") Hooker, watching the charge, caught the gleam of bayonets just above the cornstalks. His after-action report included a vivid description of what happened next:

> Instructions were immediately given for the assemblage of all of my spare batteries, near at hand, of which I think there were five or six, to spring into battery on the right of this field and to open with canister at once. In the time I am writing every stalk of corn in the northern and greater part of the field was cut as closely as could have been done with a knife, and the slain lay in rows precisely as they had stood in their ranks a few moments before. It was never my fortune to witness a more bloody, dismal battle-field.

Although soldiers on both sides exhibited exemplary courage, de-termination, and endurance, the Confederates were overwhelmed by numbers and were pushed back through the cornfield and the East Woods. West of the road the Federals fell upon the Confederate lines, pushing the Confederates out of the West Woods, and in turn being pushed back through the woods by the fury of a Confederate counter-charge.

Jones was felled, stunned, it seemed, by the blast of a Federal shell from one of the heavy Parrott guns that burst in the air overhead. Starke personally led the charge out of the West Woods with about 1,150 men and was mortally wounded. Colonel Marcellus Douglass, thirty-one, a small blond Georgian with blue eyes, fell mortally wounded, struck by eight bullets. Out of the 6 regimental commanders in his brigade, 5 also fell. Lawton was wounded, and Early took command of his division (formerly Ewell's). Walker lost 3 of his 4 regimental commanders. The brigade of Louisianans commanded by Brigadier General Harry Thompson Hays, who had recently returned to duty after recovering from a severe wound received at Port Republic, lost 323 out of 550 officers and men, including every regimental commander. Its opponents had included the 12th Massachusetts, which had carried 334 men into battle but returned with only 110 unscathed, giving it the dubious honor of suffering the highest casualty rate of any Federal regiment on this bloody day.

Jackson called on Lee for reinforcements and summoned Hood's two brigades; the hungry men were still cooking their rations, but they responded. Ravenous and angry, they hit the advancing Federals just as they were losing their momentum. Early's brigade crashed into one flank, and D. H. Hill into the other. The Federals were forced back, through the woods and cornfield and across David Miller's farm. Hooker was wounded in the heel and forced to leave the field, but some of the Federal batteries in the Miller pasture were still firing double rounds of canister with deadly effect.[2] Then Mansfield's XII Corps came up, and his two divisions under Alpheus S. Williams and sixty-one-year-old George S. Greene hit the Confederate line at the point where D. H. Hill's troops touched Hood's. Mansfield fell mortally wounded with a bullet in his chest before the attack got under way. Williams took charge and pressed the attack, throwing back Jackson's and Hill's men but failing to break the line until Greene's men fought their way through the West Woods and there followed confused, some-

---

2. Canister consisted of metal cans filled with lead pellets, usually packed in sawdust. When it was fired from a gun, the effect was that of an enormous shotgun. A gun firing double canisters at short range doubled its destructive power.

times hand-to-hand, fighting around the Dunkard church.

Then, as though the men on both sides had simultaneously reached the end of their endurance, all fell back, and there was a lull in the fighting. David Miller's cornfield and pasture were covered with the dead and wounded of both sides. Along the Hagerstown Pike sprawled Confederate and Federal dead, and fences were festooned with the bodies of those who had failed to climb them.

Jackson's exact movements for most of this day cannot be precisely determined, but certainly he was not idle that morning. Lee was rushing all possible aid to him, even pulling men from Longstreet's position on the right and sending them into the action on the northern end of his line. When McLaws arrived on the field, he and Jackson conferred in the midst of a bombardment, both seated on their horses. One shell hit a courier ten feet away and landed between them without exploding. Jackson looked at it and said calmly, "The enemy, it seems, are getting our range." He then, much to McLaws's relief, rode off.

One of the units Lee sent was Walker's division, which included the 33rd North Carolina under Colonel M. W. Ransom, who launched his men on an unsuccessful attack to take a Federal battery. Jackson, riding up, demanded another try, but Ransom protested that McClellan's whole army was on the other side of a screening rise in their front. Skeptical, Jackson called for a volunteer to climb a tall hickory tree nearby. Private William S. Hood, a barefooted seventeen-year-old from Mecklenburg, Virginia, stepped forward and was soon among the top branches calling down that he saw "oceans" of Federals.

"Count the flags, sir," called Jackson.

The target of a considerable number of sharpshooters, young Hood had reached thirty-nine before Jackson called him down. Ransom, secure in such a vindication of his word, was astonished when Jackson rounded on him and demanded to know why he had attacked a superior force in the first place. His explanation that he had not realized the strength of the enemy but felt that he had to attack to avoid being attacked was not acknowledged by a reply. Without a word or any recognition of the feat of the young lookout, Jackson rode off.[3]

On the Union side McClellan had established himself two and a half miles east of the Dunkard church and east of Antietam Creek near the crest of a hill behind the center of the Union line at the fine brick

3. Young Hood was killed in the assault on Fort Stedman, 25 March 1865. (*Confederate Veteran*, vol. XXI, p. 121.)

house of Mr. Philip Pry, a prosperous farmer.[4] From the Pry house he could see and hear the fury of the battle on his right flank, but he issued few orders.

Major General Edwin Vose Sumner (at sixty-five, the oldest corps commander to serve in the war) commanded seventeen thousand men, most of them veterans of the Peninsula campaign. His men were ready to fight, but early that morning, when he went to the Pry house to ask for orders, McClellan, who had little confidence in his abilities, refused at first to see him, and he was left to pace up and down the Pry porch. It was 7:20 A.M. before McClellan finally sent him to the aid of the battered I and XII corps, and then he was told nothing of the situation. He knew nothing of the fate of Hooker's and Mansfield's corps except that Hooker and his corps were out of the action, and he had no idea of the exact location of the Confederate lines, their strengths and weaknesses. Ever cautious, McClellan ordered that Sumner leave one of his four divisions east of Antietam Creek. About 9:00 A.M. Sumner personally accompanied an advance by six thousand men under Major General John Sedgwick toward the West Woods.

They encountered little opposition, and not even the customary caution was taken to protect their flanks. Pressing forward on a five-hundred-yard front, the three brigades advanced in parallel lines only thirty yards apart for what appeared to be an easy victory. But D. H. Hill, Early, McLaws, and Stuart were, all unseen, taking position on their flanks and even in their rear. It is not clear whether Jackson, Hill, or anyone was orchestrating these movements, but they were remarkably well suited to the occasion. When the Confederates opened fire on all sides, it was the Federal left and rear that were heaviest hit, and the rearmost division was the first to break. To Brigadier General Oliver O. Howard, commanding one of the brigades, Sumner called out: "My God, Howard, you must get out of here!" It was a debacle. Within a matter of minutes, 2,355 Union soldiers fell dead or wounded. Sedgwick was hit three times and carried from the field; one of his brigade

4. Philip Pry and his wife, Elizabeth, with their five children, ranging in age from one to fourteen, were sent to Keedysville for safety. In the course of the battle, the wounded General Joseph Hooker was brought to the Pry house, as was General Israel B. Richardson, who died of his wounds in a second-floor bedroom on 3 November. A few weeks after the battle Lincoln visited McClellan here. When the Prys were finally allowed to return, they found their fine 125-acre farm in ruins, their animals slaughtered, their crops gone, their fences burned. The Prys never recovered their former prosperity.

commanders, Brigadier General Napoleon Jackson Tecumseh Dana, although hit as well, continued in command. Among the many severely wounded the 20th Massachusetts left for dead on the field was Captain Oliver Wendell Holmes, Jr., the future justice of the Supreme Court.[5]

McLaws signaled the charge and pursued the fleeing Federals until he grew fearful of his own unprotected flanks. By nine-thirty that morning the Confederates had pounded the Federals back to their original lines, but it had been a close call. Only McClellan's failure to concentrate his forces and Lee's willingness to risk pulling units from other portions of his line enabled them to beat back each successive Federal attack.

The main action now drifted south and east, away from Jackson's front; he and his men had done their fighting for this day. About three thousand had fallen. It had been a painful and bloody morning for both sides with no victory for either, although for Lee's army it was something of a victory to stay in existence. Jackson remarked to McLaws: "God has been very kind to us today."

About eleven o'clock Dr. McGuire, who had heard that the battle was going badly, came to Jackson to inquire if the field hospitals should not be moved south across the Potomac. The Confederate surgeons were overwhelmed by the number of wounded. In Shepherdstown they "filled every building and overflowing into the country around, into farm houses, barns, corn-cribs, cabins." A Federal soldier once confided to Mary Bedinger Mitchell, a volunteer nurse who lived nearby, "I was always sorry for your wounded, they never seemed to get any care." She acknowledged that "there was much justice" in his remark. Of Sharpsburg she wrote: "There were six churches, and they were all full; the Odd Fellows' Hall, the Freemasons', the little Town Council room . . . all the private houses . . . the shops and empty buildings, the school-houses,—every inch of space, and yet the cry was for room." Another volunteer nurse spoke of the "men with cloths about their heads, about their feet, men with arms in slings, men without arms, with one leg, with bandaged sides and back; men in ambulances, wagons, carts, wheelbarrows, men on stretchers or leaning on their comrades, men with inflamed wounds, thirsty, bleeding, weak." These, of

---

5. Two future presidents also fought at Antietam: Major (later Brevet Major General) Rutherford B. Hayes and Sergeant (later Major) William McKinley, both serving in the 23rd Ohio. So, too, did Brigadier General William H. French, Jackson's former commanding officer in Florida.

course, were those who had been fortunate enough to limp off or to be carried off the field.

McGuire had brought Jackson some peaches, and "he began to eat them ravenously," he wrote. "So much so, that he apologized and told me he had had nothing to eat that day." McGuire expressed misgivings about the outcome of the battle, but Jackson, pointing to Federal troops in the bloody remains of the cornfield, said, "Dr. McGuire, I think they have done their worst and there is now no danger of the line being broken."

About an hour and a half later General Walker found Jackson sitting his horse beneath an apple tree, one leg thrown over the pommel, munching on an apple. He seemed not to listen to what Walker had to say but asked abruptly, "Can you spare me a regiment and a battery?" He was then thinking of an attack on the Federal right.

On Jackson's right D. H. Hill continued to feel the weight of Northern power. In a sunken farm road, which came to be known as Bloody Lane, Confederate dead were piled thick. After three hours of fighting, when Hill's division was cut to ribbons and Hill himself was leading attacks which made up in ferocity what they lacked in numbers, the Federals fell back. Franklin's corps, twelve thousand strong, had now reached the field, but Sumner, who had been badly shaken by his experiences this day, held them back, and McClellan supported his decision. The battle now shifted to the Confederate center, where, as Lee was well aware, he was weak. Hoping to draw some of the Federal strength away from this portion of his line, he suggested that perhaps Jackson could turn the Federal right. Jackson asked Stuart to reconnoiter. When Stuart returned with the news of the masses of Federal artillery well positioned there, Jackson wisely decided it was "inexpedient to hazard the attempt."

The third phase of the battle centered on a narrow stone bridge that arched over Antietam Creek. Although there were fords where the creek could be crossed, Major General Ambrose Burnside spent nearly three hours trying to force his four divisions over the bridge, defended by only a few hundred Georgians. Once across, he moved to roll up the Confederate right and cut off Lee's only escape route. The most dramatic movement of the battle now occurred. Just at the most crucial moment, when Burnside's troops were within a half mile of cutting Lee's line of communication and retreat, just as the sun started to set upon a Federal breakthrough, A. P. Hill's division arrived from Harper's Ferry and came crashing into Burnside's flank. The Federals reeled and fell back. A part of the confusion and astonishment of the Union troops was caused by the sight of their enemies dressed in blue uniforms taken at Harper's Ferry.

A. P. Hill, wearing the red flannel shirt he always wore in battle, had pressed his men so fast that a third of them were straggling behind when he went into action. Without bothering with rest stops every fifty minutes, as Jackson ordered, he had hustled his men along at a brisk pace. Curiously, however, he had not taken the most direct route, a thirteen-mile march, but a more circuitous seventeen-mile route. As a result, he entered the fight with only two thousand men, but the shock turned the tide and saved the day for the Army of Northern Virginia.

The dramatic fight at sundown just south of Sharpsburg marked the end of the war's bloodiest day. In this final action Colonel Dixon Barnes of the 12th South Carolina, whom Jackson had arrested a week earlier for a minor military sin, was killed. A bullet struck Brigadier General Lawrence Branch in the cheek and came out the back of his head, killing him instantly. At day's end both sides were, for the most part, in the same positions they had held that morning. Soldiers of both sides lay down to sleep with the piteous cries of the wounded in their ears.

That night Lee called a meeting of his senior commanders and heard their reports. It must have been a dismal recitation, but Lee was determined not to retreat. In spite of the terrible losses, he would stay and fight the next day.

Jackson established his headquarters on the front lawn of the home of Captain David Smith at the west end of Sharpsburg on the road to Shepherdstown. McGuire also established his field hospital there. Jackson, without a tent, stretched out on the grass under a tree. Stuart woke him about midnight to tell him he had located a hill that would be dangerous if the enemy occupied it. Jackson ordered Early to send fifty men to take possession and went back to sleep.

Early the next morning, the eighteenth, Jackson was up inspecting the front. Colonel Stephen D. Lee, Longstreet's chief of artillery and one of the ablest artillerymen in Lee's army, found him and told him that Lee was still intrigued by the idea of attacking McClellan's right and had sent him to see what artillery had been massed by the Federals on this flank. Colonel Lee, Jackson, and a courier rode out to the foot of a nearby hill and, leaving their horses, climbed on foot until they could see the Federal line.

When Lee had had a good look, Jackson said: "I wish you to take

50 pieces of artillery and crush that force, which is the Federal right. Can you do it?"

Colonel Lee thought it impossible, but he hesitated to say so. Where would fifty guns be found? Should he try to collect them? He told Jackson he could try. "I can do it if anyone can," he said.

"That is not what I asked you, sir," Jackson said. "If I give you 50 guns, can you crush the Federal right?"

Lee looked again at the formidable Federal batteries and finally blurted out: "General, it cannot be done with 50 guns and the troops you have here."

Without a word Jackson started down the hill. As soon as they reached their horses, he sent the colonel to report his opinion to General Lee. That ended the matter; Lee gave up the foolish idea. By remaining in Maryland, he was irresponsibly putting at hazard his entire army. A number of stragglers had rejoined their units, but no reinforcements were available to him, as they were to McClellan. Proportionately he was weaker now than he had been at the beginning of the battle. Even so, it was not until 2:00 P.M. that he acknowledged he must retreat and the necessary orders for the delicate disengagement were issued.

Casualties in what had been mostly a twelve-hour battle were horrendous. Captain Samuel D. Buck of the 13th Virginia wrote after the war: "I saw more men torn to pieces by shells in that battle than any other during the war." McClellan lost 12,401, of whom 2,108 were killed, 9,540 wounded, and 753 missing. Lee lost, according to the best estimates, 10,316, of whom 1,546 were killed, 7,752 were wounded, and 1,018 were missing. Of these, Jackson's command suffered 4,713 casualties, of whom 763 were killed. The total casualties for both sides reached 22,717; more than twice as many Americans were killed at Antietam as were killed in battle in the War of 1812, the Mexican War, and the Spanish-American War combined, and four times the casualties suffered on 6 June 1944 by American troops on the Normandy beaches.

Lee retreated by way of the difficult Boteler's Ford below Shepherdstown. Through it passed his wounded, his supplies and ammunition, ambulances, guns, wagons, and lastly the infantry. To conceal the sounds of movement, two guns of Parker's battery (sometimes called the Boy Battery because of the youth of its complement) kept up a fire all night, the cannoneers growing so weary that they were finally too weak to return their guns to battery after each discharge.

Most of the movement had to take place in the dark. By 2:00 A.M. Longstreet's entire corps was across the Potomac, and some regiments were lining the high, steep riverbank as protection for the rest. Jackson's corps followed Longstreet's, and two hours after daylight on the nineteenth Lee's entire army was back in Virginia.

John H. Lewis of the 9th Virginia told those at home: "When going over the river the boys were singing 'Maryland, my Maryland.' But all was quiet on that point when we came back. . . . All seemed to be disgusted with that part of Maryland."

It had not been easy to withdraw the entire army back across the Potomac, and although Jackson sat on his horse in the river for hours, Hotchkiss maintained that it was Major Harman who had "cussed it over." Douglas, too, considered Harman "the genius of this retreat," describing him as "big-bodied, big-voiced, untiring, fearless of man or devil, who would have ordered Jackson himself out of the way if necessary to obey Jackson's orders." He was never rewarded, never promoted.

Lee, too, sat his horse in the water. In the early-morning light, when General Walker entered the stream, Lee asked him what was still to come. Walker assured him there were only some wagons with wounded and a battery, all of which were nearby. "Thank God!" exclaimed Lee.

As the army moved away from the river, the banks on the Virginia shore were protected by only the remnants of two brigades of infantry—perhaps seven hundred men—and some thirty-three guns, which General Pendleton, Lee's chief of artillery, had assembled from the reserve artillery, and eleven more near at hand. In the course of the afternoon two divisions of Federal troops appeared on the Maryland shore and opened fire with small arms and artillery. The fighting across the river continued until after dark. Pendleton began to remove his farthermost guns, but in the darkness there was considerable confusion.

In nineteenth-century armies the sight of artillery packing up and making off to the rear usually had a depressing effect upon the infantry. There seemed to creep into the infantrymen's hearts the fear that they were being abandoned. Alerted, the Confederate infantrymen began to leave the riverbank and were soon retreating in some disorder. Pendleton seems to have lost his head. He galloped to Brigadier General Roger A. Pryor and begged for support. But Pryor, a political general whose grasp of strategy and tactics was shaky, thought that he needed permission to move. Pendleton then went looking for Hood but failed to find him. He looked for Longstreet but could not locate him either.

He was in a panic when he stumbled into Lee's headquarters. By this time he was sure that the Federals had stormed across the Potomac and captured all the reserve artillery.

Lee's staff was in shock; only Lee remained at least outwardly calm. He told Pendleton to lie down, and he sent orders for Jackson to take care of the matter. But news of the possible loss of forty-four guns had already reached Jackson and propelled him into action. According to Anna Jackson, "the news of this appalling disaster caused Jackson more anxiety than he had ever shown before during the war." Douglas said that Jackson was disgusted "beyond words" by Pendleton's bungling. He sent A. P. Hill's division back to the Potomac and ordered Early to follow in support. Lee's couriers found him already on his way back to the river.

When Hill's men arrived on the plateau above the high riverbank, they charged impetuously in the face of what Hill later described as "the most tremendous fire of artillery I ever saw" on the opposite shore. They were met by the Federal units which had just crossed to the Virginia shore, notably the 118th Pennsylvania, a new unit of 737 men who had been in service only twenty days. They had been presented with splendid uniforms and accoutrements by the Philadelphia Corn Exchange, but as they now discovered, half had been issued defective rifles. Still, they tried to fight for nearly a half hour before they fled "in an utterly disorganized and demoralized condition" and were driven into the water. "Then commenced the most terrible slaughter this war has yet witnessed," said Hill. "The broad surface of the Potomac was blue with the floating bodies of our foe." Jackson, too, spoke of "an appalling scene of the destruction of human life." Of the 361 Union casualties, the 118th Pennsylvania suffered a loss of 269.

Thanks to Jackson's prompt and resolute action and the bravery of Hill's and Early's men, a potentially dangerous situation had been nipped in the bud. Cavalry took over the guarding of the riverbank. It was found that thanks to the initiative of Confederate battery commanders and one of Pendleton's staff officers, only four guns were lost; the rest had been pulled back and concealed in a woods.[6]

McClellan was content to allow the Army of Northern Virginia to limp away and lick its wounds. He was pleased with himself and the day after the battle wrote to his wife: "The spectacle yesterday was the grandest I could conceive of—nothing could be more sublime. Those in whose judgment I rely tell me that I fought the battle splendidly &

6. One of the guns lost was a howitzer from the Virginia Military Institute.

that it was a masterpiece of art. . . . Our victory was complete. . . . I feel some little pride in having, with a beaten and demoralized army, defeated Lee so utterly and saved the North so completely."[7]

On 21 September Jackson pulled back his corps and went into camp on the south bank of Opequon Creek near Martinsburg; several days later he moved to Bunker Hill (today in West Virginia), a scattering of houses and two churches—Presbyterian and Episcopal—ten miles north of Winchester. There was a respite from marching and fighting, time now for this "emaciated, limping, filthy mass," as one North Carolina soldier put it, to wash off the weeks of grime, try to reduce the horde of vermin, and to eat at last the rations which now reached them in the commissary wagons.

There was no denying that the Confederates had suffered a defeat. Private John Sawyers of the Rockbridge Artillery in a letter to W. M. McAllister (26 September) wrote: "The yankees slitely [*sic*] got the best of the fight in Maryland. You ought to have seen us skeedadling across the Potomac River and yankees close in our rear."

The government in Richmond was appalled by the casualties. It announced that while it was not "deemed advisable" to publish the names of those who had fallen, "persons can obtain information in regard to their relatives in the army by calling at the Army Intelligence office in the Farmer's Bank, opposite the Post Office."

The Maryland campaign, excluding the capture of Harper's Ferry, had been a mistake and a disaster for the Confederates. The Federals had been kept out of northern Virginia, but the price had been too high. The fresh recruits the Confederates had hoped to find in Maryland had not materialized; probably no more than two hundred had thrown in their lot with the South. The European powers, instead of recognizing the Confederate States, now concluded that the South could not win the war.[8] But Lee put a bold face on the situation and told his soldiers: "History records few examples of greater fortitude and endurance than this army has exhibited; and I am commissioned by the

7. Five years later, when Antietam National Cemetery was dedicated, McClellan was not invited to take any part in the ceremonies; in fact, he was not even invited to be present.

8. The question of recognition was taken up by the British cabinet on 28 October and was rejected. Soon after, the cabinet turned down a French proposal for a joint French, Russian, and British plan to ask for a six-month armistice and an end to the blockade. Lincoln's Emancipation Proclamation, issued on 22 September 1862, further eroded sympathy for the South.

President to thank you, in the name of the Confederate States, for the undying fame you have won for their arms." He added: "Much as you have done, much more remains to be accomplished."

It had been Lee's intention to give his men a brief respite, gather in the stragglers, and recross the Potomac for another battle with McClellan's Army of the Potomac, but his army could not so easily be put back together. It was worn out, both physically and in spirit, and many stragglers would not return. As Lee told Davis, these men "have wandered to a distance, feigning sickness, wounds, &c., deceiving the guards and evading the scouts. Many of them will not stop until they reach their distant homes." Even Lee was forced to conclude that he could not renew the offensive. He told President Davis: "I am, therefore, led to pause."

29

☆ ☆ ☆ ☆ ☆ ☆ ☆ ☆ ☆ ☆ ☆ ☆ ☆ ☆

Respite

Manpower problems continued to affect Lee's plans. The army's efficiency, he told Davis on 21 September, "is greatly paralyzed by the loss to its ranks of numerous stragglers. I have taken every means in my power from the beginning to correct this evil, which has increased instead of diminished. A great many men belonging to the army never entered Maryland at all; many returned after getting there, while others who crossed the river remained aloof."

Lee called on Davis for legislative action which would enable him to treat stragglers as deserters in the face of the enemy, and he gave shocking examples of shirking at Antietam:

> To give you an idea of its extent . . . on the morning after the battle of the 17th, General [Nathan] Evans reported to me on the field, where he was holding the front position, that he had but 120 of his brigade present, and that the next brigade to his, that of General Garnett, consisted of but 100 men. General Pendleton reported that the brigades of Generals [Alexander] Lawton and [Lewis] Armistead, left to guard the ford at Shepherdstown, together contained but 600 men. This is a woeful condition of affairs, and I am pained to state it. . . .

Help came from an unexpected source: Lincoln's Emancipation Proclamation. Although it did not free any slave immediately, it created a tidal wave of anger in the South, and it steeled the hearts and resolve of many Southerners. Recruiting picked up.

The Army of Northern Virginia began to rebuild. Brigadier General John R. Jones was sent to Winchester to round up stragglers, and he was remarkably successful: Within two weeks he sent back to the army nearly six thousand men, an "astonishing" number of them officers. Richmond managed to forward several thousand conscripts and volunteers; men returned from hospitals, and Lee's command began to look more like an army.

There was the perennial shortage of blankets and shoes Longstreet reported 6,648 men without shoes—and for a time a shortage of small arms. Jackson reported a need for 3,000. He sent Boteler to Richmond to exert political pressure to secure clothing, weapons, and other much-needed supplies. Boteler succeeded admirably. In letters to Anna, Jackson praised his efforts. On 10 November he wrote that 1,750 blankets had been distributed and a week later that Boteler was "doing much, and has been the means of greatly contributing to the comfort of our men." Appeals were made to those at home, and from Lexington and Rockbridge County 175 blankets, 75 pairs of shoes, leather for 50 more, and $750 in cash were sent to Jackson's corps.

Henry Kyd Douglas declared that this lull in the fighting following the Battle of Antietam "gave the Confederacy a new lease of life." Jackson changed his headquarters eleven times during this two-month respite but remained in the lower end of the Valley. For a time he was in Winchester, staying at a house only a hundred yards from the Graham home, where he and Anna had been so happy the previous winter. Anna could not join him now. On 23 November, at the home of her sister Harriet (Mrs. James P. Irwin) in Charlotte, she had given birth to a girl, "only eight and a half pounds." The baby was named Julia Laura after Jackson's mother and sister. (In spite of Laura's Union sympathies, Jackson's affection for his sister remained undimmed. Five days after the baby's birth Laura wrote to Anna; the contents of her letter are unknown. Anna replied, but there was no further communication for nearly two years.)

Jackson had wanted a boy, said Anna, for he believed that "men have a larger sphere of usefulness than women," but he was delighted nonetheless. His letters to Anna brim over with joy:

> Oh! How thankful I am to our Heavenly Father for having spared my precious wife and given us a little daughter! I cannot tell you how gratified I am, nor how much I wish I could be with you and

see my two darlings. But while this pleasure is denied me, I am thankful it is accorded to you to have the little pet, and I hope it may be a great deal of company and comfort to its mother. Now don't exert yourself to write to me. . . . But you must love your *esposo* in the meantime. . . .

I expect you are just made up now with that baby. Don't you wish your husband wouldn't claim any part of it, but let you have the sole ownership? Don't you regard it as the most precious little creature in the world? Do not spoil it, and don't let anybody tease it. Don't permit it to have a bad temper. Oh I would love to see the darling little thing! Give her many kisses for her father.

Dated 4 December, the letter was sent from quarters near Guiney's (today Guinea) Station, ten miles south of Fredericksburg on the Richmond, Fredericksburg & Potomac Railroad, about a mile from the house in which, less than four months hence, he would die. At the time he had more than one reason to rejoice, for besides becoming a father, he had also become a lieutenant general, a new rank in the Confederate army.

On 2 October Lee had written to Davis recommending promotions for several general officers:

I can confidently recommend Generals Longstreet and Jackson in this army. My opinion of the merits of General Jackson has been greatly enhanced during this expedition. He is true, honest, and brave; has a single eye to the good of the service, and spares no exertion to accomplish his objective. Next to these two officers, I consider General A. P. Hill the best commander with me. He fights his troops well, and takes care of them. . . .

Lee obviously thought that while there was no need to plead Longstreet's case, something should be said for Jackson. Jackson had made his resentment toward Davis clear during Seven Days, and plainly Davis entertained no high opinion of Jackson. Still, on 11 October President Davis appointed and the Senate quickly confirmed seven lieutenant generals, including Jackson. Longstreet was the senior of these with date of rank as of 9 October. Jackson ranked fifth with 10 October as his date of rank.

Although Jackson and Longstreet had in effect commanded army corps, a unit of this size was not officially created until 6 November, when Longstreet was given command of I Army Corps and Jackson of

II Army Corps.[1] Longstreet's I Corps consisted of 34,916 men organized as 5 divisions of 15 brigades with 99 guns in 24 batteries. Jackson's II Corps contained 31,692 men organized as 4 divisions of 18 brigades with 98 guns in 23 batteries. Thus Lee's Army of Northern Virginia was now twice as large as it had been on the field at Antietam. Jackson's division commanders were A. P. Hill, D. H. Hill, Jubal A. Early (commanding Ewell's old division), and William B. Taliaferro (commanding Jackson's former division).[2]

A number of other senior officers were promoted. George E. Pickett, who had been the goat (ranking last) in Jackson's West Point class of 1846, became a major general, as did John B. Hood. Eleven brigadier generals were also appointed, including one of Jackson's favorites, for whom he vigorously plumped: Elisha Franklin ("Bull") Paxton. Although Paxton was a Lexington lawyer and gentleman planter who had little military experience, had never even commanded a regiment, and had not particularly distinguished himself so far as a staff officer, Jackson not only strongly recommended his promotion but gave him command of the Stonewall Brigade. This was an undeserved slap in the face to that fine combat soldier Andrew Jackson Grigsby, a gallant Mexican War veteran who had been wounded at Malvern Hill and had distinguished himself both as a regimental commander and as the commander of the Stonewall Brigade in the invasion of Maryland. Many believed that Grigsby was denied promotion because he was "such an awful swearer."

The choice of Paxton over Grigsby was both unfair and difficult to justify. A. P. Hill wrote a bitter letter to Stuart—who managed to be friends with both Hill and Jackson—about the promotion: "How do you like *Paxton* Brig. Gen.! The Almighty will get tired, helping Jackson after awhile, and then he'll get the damndest thrashing—and the shoe pinches, for I should get my share and probably all the blame, for the people will never blame Stonewall for any disaster."

1. Army corps, composed of two or more divisions, are in modern usage designated by Roman numerals, and it is convenient to use this form of designation here, although in the Confederate army this usage was never adopted. The numbering of corps was consecutive within each Confederate army.

2. This was the division commanded by Brigadier John R. Jones during the Maryland invasion, but Taliaferro, having recovered from the wound he received at Second Manassas, now resumed command. Jones reverted to brigade commander within the division.

In the event, Paxton failed to live up to Jackson's high opinion of him. Grigsby, humiliated by being passed over, resigned, swearing that when the war ended, he would challenge Jackson to a duel. This was not the only unwise personnel decision made by Jackson, whose quixotic preferences often kindled resentment.

There was time now to revive neglected quarrels. Although A. P. Hill and Jackson had worked together, stiffly but effectively, in the fighting at Sharpsburg and at Boteler's Ford, Hill was still fuming over his arrest, and on 22 September he requested, through channels, a court of inquiry. In his endorsement Jackson listed his complaints about the unsatisfactory march discipline in Hill's division on 4 September. Hill's request and Jackson's endorsement were duly forwarded to Lee, who tried his best, but in vain, to cool the passions of both men. He returned the papers on 24 September, tactfully writing that Hill could now see from Jackson's endorsement the cause of his arrest and that Hill's "attention being called to what appeared to be neglect of duty by his commander, but which from an officer of his character could not be intentional and I feel sure will never be repeated, I see no advantage to the service in further investigating this matter nor could it without detriment be done at this time."

Hot-tempered Hill was not to be appeased. On 30 September, asserting that he could prove his case by "any number of honorable men, including members of General Jackson's own staff," he requested that Lee deny "the truth of every allegation made by . . . Jackson," and he again asked for a court of inquiry. At the same time he filed charges against Jackson. Their exact nature is unknown, for the text is now lost.

Jackson, equally provoked, announced that if Hill wanted a court-martial, he should have one. On 3 October he filed charges of neglect of duty, listing eight specifications. Lee arranged a meeting with the two and did his best to persuade them to call off their quarrel, but even Lee, the peacemaker, could not persuade these prickly, hotheaded men to relent. Beset by more serious problems, he laid aside the papers and did nothing. But this was not to be the end of the matter. The quarrel smoldered on. A. P. Hill wrote to Stuart on 14 November: "I suppose I am to vegitate [*sic*] here all the winter under that crazy old Presbyterian fool. I am like the porcupine—all bristles, and all sticking out too, so I know we will have a smash up before long."

In contrast with his thorny relations with so many senior officers was Jackson's friendship with Jeb Stuart. Both men were strongly religious, and both were teetotalers, but there all resemblance ended. Stuart, fun-loving, witty, and flamboyant, took liberties with Jackson that no one else dared emulate. He liked to tease, and it amused him to pretend that Jackson was in reality a gay and lively young sport, raillery Jackson thoroughly enjoyed. Young Douglas wondered at the friendship: "How could Prince Rupert or Murat be on congenial terms with Cromwell?" But he saw that "Jackson was more free and familiar with Stuart than with any other officer in the army," and he was sure that "Stuart loved Jackson more than he did any other living man."

Late one cool night Stuart rode into Jackson's headquarters. Entering his tent, he unbuckled his saber and otherwise fully accoutred, lay down beside the heavily sleeping Jackson. As the night deepened, it grew cooler, and Stuart, fast asleep, struggled mightily for more of the one blanket. He awoke in the early morning in full possession. When he emerged from the tent, Jackson, warming himself at a fire, looked up and said jocosely, "General Stuart, I am always glad to see you here. You might select better hours sometimes, but I'm always glad to have you. But General, you must not get into my bed with your boots and spurs on and ride me around like a cavalry horse all night."

Early in October Stuart sent his aide Major Heros von Borcke to Jackson bearing a gift, a splendid uniform coat which was made specially for him in Richmond and which, in von Borcke's words, was "in gilt button and sheeny facing in gold lace." According to John Esten Cooke, Stuart's ordnance officer, it was "of dark-blue cloth, with an ample cavalry cape." Jackson unpacked it in "modest confusion," then folded it carefully away. He asked von Borcke to thank Stuart. "The coat is much too handsome for me," he said, "but I shall take the best care of it, and shall prize it highly as a souvenir."

Protesting that Stuart would want to know how it fit, von Borcke persuaded Jackson to don it and wear it to dinner. Transformed, he appeared at the mess table just as Jim Lewis was bringing in a turkey. The bird was forgotten as everyone stared in amazement. Word of the coat spread through the camp, and soldiers gathered around to see their general in his finery. Although he appeared embarrassed by the sensation he created, Jackson was, in fact, pleased with the coat; Hotchkiss bought him a new hat—Anna sent him another, heavy with braid, which he loathed but wore for her sake—and in the future he presented a more elegant figure.

Presents also came from others. Jackson wrote to Anna that Mrs. Graham in Winchester had sent him "two excellent sponge cakes last week, and a Mr. Vilwig, of the same place, sent me an excellent armchair for camp use. I wish I could keep it until the end of the war, as I think my *esposa* would enjoy it." An unknown woman sent him a "beautiful scarf, which I wish my darling had. . . . Don't send me any more socks," he added, "as the kind ladies have sent me more than I could probably wear out in two years." Colonel Elijah White sent him a splendid sword and gilded spurs. Colonel Blanton Duncan of Kentucky gave him imported field glasses. A friend in Winchester presented him with "a beautiful bridle and martingale for a general officer." Lieutenant James Power Smith, a new aide (another son of a Presbyterian minister and former divinity student),[3] reported a virtual flood of presents. There seemed, he said, "no end to the socks and gloves, knit by good and loving women, and there was a great roll of gray cloth for suits to come."

In this quiet period there were many visitors, and newspaper correspondents were thick on the ground, not only American but British as well, including Francis Charles Lawley of *The Times* and Frank Vizetelly of the *Illustrated London News*. Three British visitors, including Colonel (later Field Marshal) Garnet Wolseley, paid a visit. Wolseley was eager to discuss the war, but Jackson, to avoid answering military questions, grew loquacious about his prewar visit to Britain, dwelling in particular on the beauty of the stained glass windows at York Minster.

Belle Boyd came and, by her own account, was warmly greeted by Jackson and given his blessings when she departed. Lieutenant Smith's account was different and probably closer to the truth. Boyd presented, he said, "quite a soldierly figure," but Jackson refused to see "the young woman of whose loyalty he was not altogether assured."

Preachers, too, resumed their work, important figures in the great revival movement that swept through the army this winter. Some regiments held daily meetings and, as one regimental chaplain said, the men were "manifesting a deep interest in reference to spiritual things." Jackson was particularly pleased with the preaching of the eloquent seventy-year-old Dr. Joseph Stiles, the Presbyterian who was, said Jackson, "laboring in a revival of General Ewell's Division." To Anna he wrote: "Oh, it is a glorious privilege to be a minister of the gospel of the Prince of Peace! There is no equal position in this world."

One day while at Bunker Hill Jackson rode into Winchester with Dr. McGuire and ate dinner with the doctor's parents, younger sister Betty, and Dr. Graham. When Betty McGuire asked prettily for a picture of Jackson, he replied that he had none. "Well, then, why don't

---

3. After the war James Power Smith became a distinguished Presbyterian clergyman. He lived until 12 August 1923 and was the last surviving member of Jackson's staff.

you have one taken?" she said. Jackson promised that he would, and dinner over, he kept his word by stepping into a nearby studio, where Mr. Routzahn, the sharp-eyed photographer, noticed that the third button from the top on the left breast of the general's coat was missing. Nothing daunted, Jackson called for needle and thread and, taking a button from his pocket, proceeded tidily to sew it on. But he did not quite get it right. The finished photograph shows it slightly out of line.[4]

It was not all rest and recreation for Jackson's troops. On 18 October they moved to Martinsburg and spent four days ripping up some thirty-five miles of the track of the Baltimore & Ohio. Ties were burned, and rails heated in the fire and bent; telegraph lines and poles were added to the flames. The depot, hotel water tanks, bridges, sand houses, and much of the fixed equipment went up in smoke.[5]

As Jackson was leaving Martinsburg, the pretty young wife of a railroad section foreman ran out to him with her eighteen-month-old son and held him up for a blessing. Jackson, astride Sorrel, seemed no more surprised, said Captain Charles Blackford, "than Queen Elizabeth at being asked to touch for the 'King's Evil.' " He took the infant tenderly in his arms "until his graying beard touched the fresh young hair of the child." To bystanders he seemed to be praying. Soldiers standing about removed their caps, and the young woman bowed her head on Sorrel's shoulder. Then he handed the child back without a word and rode off down the road.

Lee sent Walker's division over the Blue Ridge to Upperville, and Stuart's cavalry roamed farther east, keeping an eye upon McClellan's Army of the Potomac. When McClellan began a cautious advance south of Washington in late October, Lee placed Longstreet's I Corps around Culpeper; Jackson remained in the lower Valley of Virginia. By 6 November McClellan had reached the Warrenton area, and on that day Jackson made his headquarters near Nineveh, between Front Royal and Winchester.

The following day was a traumatic one at the headquarters of the

4. This picture, now famous, was Anna Jackson's favorite, but there is debate on when it was taken. The version followed here is that of Dr. McGuire, who claimed he was present, but the photograph is often described as having been taken when Jackson was in Winchester a year earlier.

5. The Baltimore & Ohio Railroad possessed remarkable restorative powers, however, and soon had its trains running again. Henry Kyd Douglas wrote: "After all it was a waste of time and energy, for when we left we were hardly beyond the sound of a steam whistle before the road was filling the air with the noise and smoke of countless trains."

Army of the Potomac. Lincoln, completely disgusted with McClellan's "slows," relieved him. He was replaced by Major General Ambrose E. Burnside, the thirty-eight-year-old West Pointer who had recently conducted a successful campaign in North Carolina in which he had captured seventy-nine guns and taken thirty-six hundred prisoners. Burnside was well liked in the army, but he was a modest man and was not sure that he was the best man for the work at hand. Events proved his assessment correct.

Burnside, who formally took command on 9 November, brought a new strategy to the campaign, and at first he moved vigorously. His plan was to make a feint southward toward Culpeper, then swing abruptly southeast to Fredericksburg, where, because the railway bridge had been destroyed, he would cross the Rappahannock on pontoon bridges brought down from Washington, and then march on Richmond. Although, as Lincoln repeatedly pointed out to his generals, the object of the Army of the Potomac was to defeat Lee's army, soldiers and politicians alike were possessed by the desire to capture the Confederate capital, and Burnside echoed the old cry of "On to Richmond!"

Lee suggested that Jackson move up the Valley, cross the Blue Ridge at Swift Run Gap, and rejoin the Army of Northern Virginia, but Jackson wanted to come in on Burnside's flank. Early in November he pushed A. P. Hill through Snicker's Gap, between Berryville and Round Hill, and directed him to destroy as much as he could of the Manassas Gap Railroad, a movement which, as Lee explained to Davis, "served to embarrass and produce hesitation in a forward movement of the enemy."

Burnside had reorganized the Army of the Potomac into three "grand divisions" of two corps each, commanded by Sumner, Franklin, and Hooker. By dawn on 15 November Sumner's troops were in motion, and two days later Franklin and Hooker followed behind them. By 19 November Burnside had approximately 115,000 troops within an easy march of the Rappahannock; indeed, Sumner had reached the river opposite Fredericksburg on the seventeenth. In addition, Franz Sigel, now with a corps (XI Corps) of 28,000 mostly foreign-born troops, was in reserve. By this date, too, Lee had started Longstreet toward Fredericksburg, but the first units did not arrive until midafternoon of the twenty-first.

Sumner expected a pontoon train ready at hand, but as a result of negligence and incompetence in Washington, the first pontoon did not arrive until 25 November, by which time all the elements of surprise in

Burnside's battle plan were lost. Sumner ought to have found fords and crossed the Rappahannock anyway, as he easily could have, for the water was low, but Burnside, fearful that high water would cut Sumner off from the rest of the army, held him back. It was a bad mistake on Burnside's part; the delay proved fatal to his enterprise.

The last of Longstreet's divisions arrived at Fredericksburg on 23 November. Even then I Corps was no larger than Sumner's grand division, and Lee had no ready reserves. Lee had daringly divided his forces in the face of the enemy before, and he would do it again, but never was the separation so great: More than 130 miles divided Longstreet from Jackson. Lee, however, appeared unafraid and confident. On the eighteenth, when Lee knew that at least a sizable portion of Burnside's army was advancing on him, he advised Jackson that "unless you think it is advantageous for you to continue longer in the Valley, or can accomplish the retention and division of the enemy's forces by so doing, I think it would be advisable to put some of your divisions in motion across the mountains, and advance them at least as far as Sperryville or Madison Court House," and the following day he informed him that he could remain in the Valley as long as his presence there "crippled or embarrassed" the enemy. He appears not to have known that Jackson had already sent A. P. Hill's division over the Blue Ridge to Snickersville.

On 19 November Jackson moved his headquarters to Winchester, and a flood of false reports and rumors as to his intentions began to pour into Washington and into the capitals of Europe. *The Times* correspondent reported "the universal belief that Stonewall Jackson was ready to pounce upon Washington from the Shenandoah, and to capture President, Secretaries, and all." Burnside, to his credit, appeared undisturbed by all the rumors. He moved rapidly to position himself between Lee's two corps and then swung east toward Longstreet on the Rappahannock, intending to destroy the Army of Northern Virginia piecemeal. It was not a bad plan, and had it been pursued with vigor and aided by better support from the bureaucracies in Washington, it would probably have succeeded.

On 23 November Lee sent a message to Jackson informing him that he would like him to move east of the Blue Ridge, but only if he thought he could "see no way of making an impression on the enemy" where he was, but Jackson had anticipated Lee's need for him either on the Rappahannock or, as he would have preferred, on the North Anna River.

On 21 November he took his evening meal with his friends the

Grahams in Winchester, and they prayed together as they had before Kernstown. The following day he set off with his staff up the Valley, pausing to go over the battlefield at Kernstown, and then hurrying to catch up with his infantry.

At Middletown an old woman called out to him as he rode by, "Are you Mr. Jackson?" When Jackson paused and nodded, she came to his horse's side and said urgently: "I want to see my grandson. I've brought him some clothes and victuals. His name is George Martin and he belongs to your company."

She knew nothing of regiments or brigades, not even the name of her grandson's company commander. She knew only that he was with Jackson, and she was astonished to find that the general knew nothing about him. "Why, Mr. Jackson, you certainly know little George Martin," she said reproachfully. "He's been with you in all your battles, and they do say he fit [*sic*] as hard as any of them."

Jackson silenced with a look the half-smothered laughter of his young staff officers. Dismounting, he took the bewildered woman's hand and courteously explained to her where she might find help.[6]

At New Market Jackson's troops turned east, crossed the Massanutten, and descended into Luray. On 25 November they were making their weary way over the Blue Ridge at Fisher's Gap. Winter came early in Virginia in 1862, the first snow falling on 7 November, and the troops suffered severely from the cold. Straggling remained a problem.

Some of the men who lived in the Valley simply went home for a few days. Jubal Early, whose division held some of the roughest customers in the army, had done everything he could think of to prevent his men from wandering off. He had even spread a rumor that there was smallpox in the mountain huts, but this seemed only to arouse their curiosity. At the end of one tiring day he was incensed to receive a message: "General Jackson desires to know why he saw many of your stragglers in rear of your division today?"

Early replied: "In answer to your note I would state that I think it probable that the reason why General Jackson saw so many stragglers on the march to-day is that he rode in rear of my division."

---

6. This version is told by Private John Robson, who indicated that he was present. John Esten Cooke repeats the story in much the same fashion, saying that he received it from an officer who was presumably present. Anna Jackson told a slightly different story of a woman coming to Jackson's headquarters looking for her son, "John," and that when Jackson heard her he ordered that "every company in his corps be searched for 'John.'"

The officer Jackson assigned to command the rear guard on this march later remembered the duty as "one of my most painful experiences of the war." He had orders to hustle along the stragglers; no one was to be left behind. "I gathered up a party of stragglers," he wrote, "a few of whom were stragglers from pure viciousness, but the rest from sheer suffering. The poor fellows were actually barefooted, and their feet were cracked and bleeding on the ice, and these I had to force on, painfully climbing the mountain road."

In some units, though apparently not all, men had been ordered to make moccasins for themselves from "green cowhides," tying them hairy side inward around their feet. Private F. P. Curtis of the 1st North Carolina reported them to be "both comfortable and serviceable." But curiously, this was not a universal practice.

Once over the Blue Ridge, Jackson made his headquarters near Madison Court House on the road to Gordonsville. Dressed in the new blue coat Stuart had given him and the new hat Hotchkiss had bought for him, he assembled his staff and formally announced: "Young gentlemen, this is no longer the headquarters of the Army of the Valley, but of the second corps of the Army of Northern Virginia." He was now directly under Lee's command, and although he could not know it, he had left the beautiful Valley of Virginia forever.

30

☆　☆　☆　☆　☆　☆　☆　☆　☆　☆　☆　☆　☆　☆

Fredericksburg

On 29 November Jackson set forth with young Smith and four or five couriers to find General Lee, forty miles away on Mile Run Road near Fredericksburg. About noon they stopped at the house of the Reverend Melzi Chancellor, near the Wilderness Church, to eat and rest. Snow was falling when they remounted, but by late afternoon they had reached Salem Church, which was jammed with civilian refugees from Fredericksburg. It was dark before they found Lee's headquarters in a pine forest, its tents covered with snow. Lee, in his courteous way, came out to greet them. Later that evening Jackson found food and a bed at the home of a hospitable Mr. Muscoe Garnett.

The following day Jackson and Smith rode into Fredericksburg. A charming old town, about fifty miles equidistant from Washington and Richmond, it had been an important river port since colonial times. Its many substantial houses of stone or brick, some dating from the eighteenth century, testified to an undisturbed prosperity. Although most of the inhabitants had now fled, leaving the town to the sixteen hundred troops in the Mississippi brigade of Brigadier General William Barksdale, Jackson and Smith were able to dine at the house of a Mr. John Scott.

Jackson did not want to fight at Fredericksburg. He saw that even if Burnside were repulsed, the Confederates would be unable to cross the river in the face of the Federal guns and superior numbers. He predicted to D. H. Hill: "We will whip the enemy but gain no fruits of victory." Jackson wanted to fight on the banks of the North Anna River but was overruled by Lee. Although Lee, too, was well aware of the superior ground offered by the North Anna position, he knew that to fight there would mean retreating another twenty-five to thirty miles and giving up much productive territory, a move politically unsound. He would fight at Fredericksburg.

On the bluff across the river from the town the Federals had put in place a formidable array of artillery under the command of General Henry Jackson Hunt, the best artillerest on either side in the war. As at Antietam, the two armies were divided by a stream, but the Rappahannock was broader and deeper than the Antietam, and the ground on both its shores was higher and steeper. Both armies were in strong defensive positions; the attacker would pay dearly for any attempt on the enemy.

Lee placed his forces upon a ridge which ran for seven miles roughly south-southwest in a curved line from just behind Fredericksburg. His position was better than at Antietam; he did not have the unbridged Potomac at his back, and in his front was a nearly flat, open plain to the river. Longstreet was given the northern two-thirds of this line and anchored his left flank on a high point of land known as Marye's Heights, rising some forty or fifty feet above the river plain. At the southern end of the heights a stone wall ran along a sunken road, a strong defensive position. On the heights Edward Porter Alexander, Longstreet's chief of artillery, had so massed his guns to cover the approaches that, he told Longstreet, "We cover that ground now so well that we will comb it as with a fine-tooth comb. A chicken could not live on that field when we open on it." It was not altogether an idle boast.

Jackson occupied the southern end of the ridge along which ran a military road that aided communications. Between the ridge and the river ran the tracks of the Richmond, Fredericksburg & Potomac Railroad and a road known as the Old Richmond Road or River Road; he was at first unable to concentrate his entire corps on the ridge, for it was necessary to keep an eye on Federal forces downstream. Lee was still uncertain of Burnside's intentions. He thought the Federals might attempt a wide turning movement to the south, perhaps near Port Royal, 15 miles downriver from Fredericksburg, where Federal gunboats controlled the river, so Jackson's troops, who had arrived on the scene on 1 December after a 150-mile march completed in twelve days, were stretched southward as far as Port Royal.

On 3 December Lee, who always preferred to suggest and recommend rather than order, wrote to Jackson to suggest "a proper distribution of Napoleons and rifled guns." Jackson had 127 artillery pieces; Longstreet had only 117. D. H. Hill had no Napoleons, those dependable smoothbore, muzzle-loading 12-pounder workhorses of both armies, and he badly wanted some. He was particularly keen to get the 4 his men had captured at the Battle of Seven Pines the previous June. Lee suggested to Jackson that he give D. H. Hill "a fair proportion."

Jackson balked and wrote a testy letter to Lee, declaring in effect that if Lee ordered the transfer, he would comply but that he would not willingly part with guns, not even to his brother-in-law. "General D. H. Hill's artillery wants existed at the time he was assigned to my command," he wrote petulantly, "and it is hoped that artillery which belonged to the Army of the Valley will not be taken to supply his wants." Lee, instead of insisting, requested the War Department in Richmond to supply Hill with four Napoleons.

On 10 December General Burnside called a meeting of his commanders and principal staff officers at which he outlined his plan to throw five pontoon bridges across the Rappahannock and make a two-pronged attack on the Confederate line: Sumner's grand division to attack Longstreet and Franklin's grand division with attached cavalry (fifty-four thousand men in all) to strike Jackson. Many, perhaps most, of his senior officers thought his plan madness. Brigadier General Rush C. Hawkins bluntly told him: "If you make the attack as contemplated, it will be the greatest slaughter of the war." But Burnside stuck to his plan.

Burnside has been criticized for his plan to make a head-on assault upon Lee, but Lincoln had placed him in charge of this great Union army because he wanted action from his generals. He did not feel that he had the time for maneuvers that would outflank Lee's army, and he did not feel that he could wait in his own strong position in the hope that Lee would attack him; a stalemated position was politically not an option. After all, Lincoln had fired his predecessors for their timidity. He could see no other course than to throw his men across the river and attack the Confederates on the heights, of whose defenses he was ignorant.

The night of 10–11 December was cold, thermometers reading twenty-four degrees. The Rappahannock was coated with a skim of ice, but Union engineers moved their pontoon trains to the water's edge, two opposite Fredericksburg and two just below Deep Run about a mile upstream. The latter were built under the protection of Federal guns, which soon dispersed the Confederate infantry guarding the opposite shore. Opposite Fredericksburg, however, Union engineers encountered stiff opposition from Barksdale's Mississippians, who fired from the shelter of buildings in the town and hastily erected barricades. Nine separate sallies were made by the engineers, but each time they were driven back by Confederate musketry. Under Burnside's orders, more than one hundred guns were brought to bear. Firing fifty rounds each, they reduced the old town to rubble. Still, Barksdale's men held fast. Only when the Federals launched an amphibious assault, using their pontoons as assault boats, were they able to drive the Mississippians back and finally build their bridges.

On the morning of the twelfth Jackson roused his staff for breakfast at four o'clock. It was so cold and foggy that little could be seen, but the sound of many men in motion floated up to the heights. Lee arrived, and he and Jackson were taken by Major von Borcke to a position he had found from which the Union positions could be clearly seen. Through field glasses Lee and Jackson watched the Federal infantry and artillery moving to the river and crossing the pontoon bridges. There could now be no doubt in Lee's mind about Burnside's intentions. A. P. Hill and Early, who had been watching the Federals downstream, were called up to the ridge with the rest of II Corps. There additional troops were placed not to extend the line but to thicken it, making a defense in depth that was most unusual in Civil War battles, particularly for the manpower-starved Confederates.

All that day blue columns, about twenty-seven thousand men from Sumner's grand division, marched to the bank of the Rappahannock and broke step to cross the pontoon bridges. The next day twenty-six thousand of Hooker's men crossed. Federal troops filled the town of Fredericksburg and spread to the plain west of the river. When the weather cleared, the Confederates could see the Federal positions on Stafford Heights across the river and, rising from the Union lines, the observation balloons of Professor T. S. C. Lowe.

Jackson's portion of the Confederate line was wooded and the most vulnerable, for it lay on the lowest part of the ridge, and in front of it the flat plain to the river, not, as now, covered with trees and industrial development, it provided ample space for attackers to maneuver. The area occupied by A. P. Hill's division was to be the most crucial part of the line. Two regiments of Colonel John Mercer Brockenbrough's brigade were placed on the right, and on his left was the brigade of Brigadier General James Jay Archer, whose left rested on a boggy wood, separating Archer from Brigadier General James H. Lane's brigade, thus creating a seven-hundred-yard gap—Hill later preferred to call it an interval in his after-action report—in the Confederate line. Although considered impassable, the gap was to a certain extent covered by Brigadier General Maxcy Gregg's brigade posted along the military road behind the boggy wood. Some later historians have claimed that Jackson deliberately left the gap in order to draw the Federals into the depth of his defenses, but this seems highly improbable. Jackson clearly blamed Hill for the gap. In the first draft of his after-action report he wrote of "the interval between the Brigades, left open by Major-General A. P. Hill." But Jackson himself should have seen the danger and must bear at least equal responsibility.

A second line was formed by Taliaferro and Early; D. H. Hill's division was in reserve. In all, Jackson had about thirty-four thousand infantrymen and gunners. The open ground on Jackson's right was covered by two brigades of Stuart's cavalry division and his horse artillery. Their units extended to Massaponax Creek, a tributary of the Rappahannock forward of Jackson's line, and thus were in a position to flank any Federal force attacking the ridge. From Prospect Hill, the highest point in Jackson's line, the Confederates could look across the Rappahannock and see Ferry Farm, where George Washington had spent most of his boyhood. From his headquarters (now known as Lee's Hill) Lee could look across to Chatham, at that time known as the Lacy House, where he had courted his wife, Mary Custis. It was now the headquarters of General Sumner.

As at Antietam, almost no attempt was made to construct earthworks. There were no trenches, rifle pits, or breastworks to protect Jackson's men. John Worsham said later, "The fight in Jackson's front was a regular stand-up one. The only protection we had was such as the woods afforded." The value of the existing stone wall on Marye's Heights was as yet unappreciated, but the Battle of Fredericksburg was to make an impression on all commanders, alerting them to the advantages to be found in the work of shovels and axes.

On the morning of 13 December, concealed by a thick fog, the grand division of Major General William B. Franklin moved into position to attack Jackson; Major General George G. Meade's division prepared to lead the assault. About nine o'clock the fog began to clear, and from their heights the Confederate generals could make out, in Lee's words, "a large force moving in line of battle against Jackson.

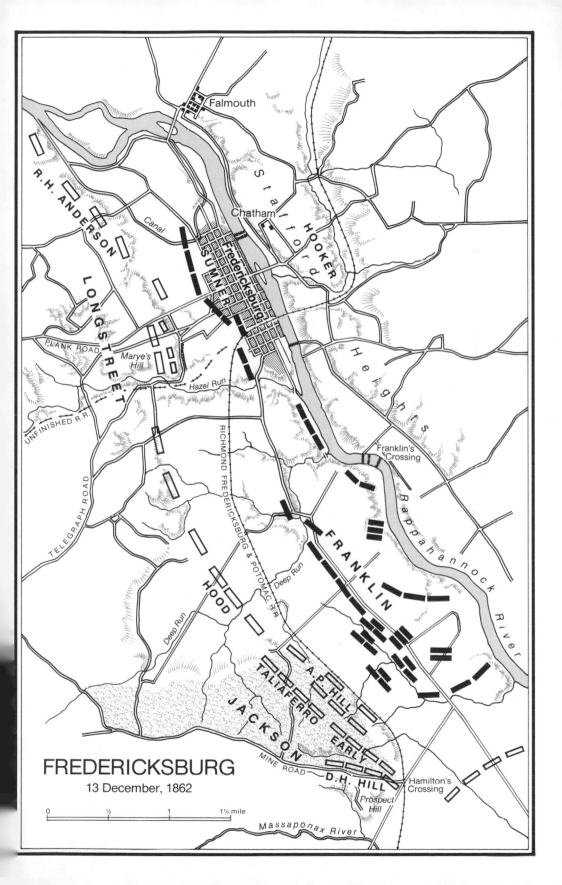

FREDERICKSBURG

13 December, 1862

Falmouth

Chatham

Fredericksburg

SUMNER

R.H. ANDERSON

LONGSTREET

Canal

PLANK ROAD

Marye's Hill

Hazel Run

UNFINISHED R.R.

TELEGRAPH ROAD

RICHMOND FREDERICKSBURG & POTOMAC R.R.

Deep Run

Deep Run

HOOD

HOOD

A.P. HILL

TALIAFERRO

JACKSON

EARLY

D.H. HILL

MINE ROAD

Prospect Hill

Hamilton's Crossing

Stafford HOOKER

Heights

Franklin's Crossing

FRANKLIN

Rappahannock River

Massaponax River

0   ½   1   1½ mile

Dense masses appeared in front of A. P. Hill, stretching far up the river in the direction of Fredericksburg."

By ten o'clock the advancing Federal lines could be clearly seen, the sun glancing from their polished arms. It was an awesome sight. Smith, looking on with other staff officers, thought it "as grand a martial array, perhaps, as has ever been seen in America. The fluttering flags, the long lines of glittering bayonets, the well-dressed officers, the prancing horses, the roll of drums, the notes of the bugles that controlled the skirmish line—it was more like a holiday parade than is often seen on any day of real battle."

Major John Pelham, in charge of Stuart's horse artillery, requested and obtained permission to advance two guns and enfilade the Union lines. Opening with round shot to devastating effect, he drew upon himself the fire of four Union batteries. One of his guns was quickly put out of action, but the other steadily fired, changing its position from time to time, until after a half hour it was withdrawn. Pelham emerged unscathed and with his reputation assured, for Lee, calling him "gallant," said of this performance: "It is glorious to see such courage in one so young!" It is as the "Gallant Pelham" that he now appears in legend and history.[1]

Jackson, dressed in his fine new coat and hat and wearing the splendid sword Colonel Elijah White had given him, joined Lee and Longstreet on Marye's Height. When Heros von Borcke, standing near him, voiced some uneasiness, Jackson informed him testily: "Major, my men have sometimes failed to *take* a position, but to *defend* one, never!"

Longstreet lightheartedly asked Jackson if those "multitudes of Federals" didn't frighten him, but Jackson said grimly: "We shall see very soon whether I shall not frighten them."

For thirty minutes the Federal guns bombarded Jackson's line, but the Confederate guns, following orders, remained silent, their position masked. Then a strong Federal skirmish line drove in the Confederate outposts, and the advancing Federals moved toward the boggy wood. They were only eight hundred yards away from it when they were

---

1. The handsome blue-eyed twenty-four-year-old Major Pelham was the lowest-ranking officer ever to be named in a dispatch by Lee. As a favor to a British Guards officer who was visiting the war, Pelham this day wore around his cap the blue and red striped necktie of the Brigade of Guards; he returned it, slightly blackened, at the end of the day. He has been called "the grandest flirt who ever lived," and when he was killed at Kelly's Ford in March 1863, three young women donned mourning.

blasted by fourteen Confederate guns. Captain Francis Dawson later wrote: "It was thrilling to watch the long line advance, note the gaps in the array, as the wounded fell or else staggered to the rear, and see the gallant remnant melt away like snow before our withering fire." It was perhaps at this time that Lee made his famous remark to Longstreet about war: "It is well that war is so terrible—we would grow too fond of it."

The Federal line wavered, but Union guns opened a deadly counter battery fire, and by noon the Confederate artillery had been silenced. Union infantry plunged into the boggy wood separating Lane's and Archer's brigades and pushed through it, bursting upon the astonished men of Maxcy Gregg's brigade, some of whom had stacked arms, stretched along the military road. Gregg himself was surprised. Somewhat deaf, he did not at first take in what had happened and thought the attackers were retreating Confederates. When he rushed into the fray, calling for his men to cease fire, a Federal bullet crushed his spine and knocked him from his horse.

Both Lane and Archer were losing men as their attacked flanks began to collapse, but they managed to rally, form refused flanks, and stop the hemorrhaging. There was hand-to-hand fighting along portions of the salient made by Meade's men. Not all the shots were fired at the enemy: Some Tennesseans in Archer's brigade deliberately fired into the backs of fleeing Confederates. And in the excitement of battle a few men shot their comrades. A soldier named Nick Watson accidentally shot the cap of his friend George Lemmon, who took off his cap, examined the hole, then slowly turned and drawled reproachfully: "Nick Watson, what did you do that for?"

Meade had made the breakthrough of the Confederate line that Burnside had hoped for, but unaccountably, neither Burnside nor Franklin had made provision to support that breakthrough. The Federal divisions were to hand and available; they were simply not used. Because of the depth of Jackson's defenses, they would probably have made little difference other than to add to the casualties.

Jackson learned of the penetration of his line when an excited courier, dispatched by Gregg before his fall, dashed up with the news. Jackson calmly turned in his saddle, summoned a courier, and sent him off to Early, ordering him to advance. Early was prepared, and his men came forward on the double. Thanks to this reinforcement and skillful maneuvering by Archer and Lane, by early afternoon the Federals had been forced to fall back to the Old Richmond Road. "The contest in the wood was short and decisive," Lee reported later. Impetuous men from two of Early's brigades pursued the Federals almost to the road before being driven back by Federal artillery.

About 2:40 P.M. Franklin received an order from Burnside by wire[2] to "make a vigorous attack with his whole force; our right is hard pressed." Franklin responded that he was unable to comply. Meade had suffered eighteen hundred casualties, some regiments losing as much as 40 percent of their combat strength. The Federals had made their best efforts to succeed on the Confederate right, and they had failed.

On the right of the Union line, Sumner was making vigorous attacks upon Longstreet on Marye's Heights, and he, too, was failing. Standing behind the stone wall, Longstreet's men slaughtered the attacking Federals. In all, the Federals made fourteen separate assaults on the wall. All failed. No Union infantryman came closer than thirty yards. Captain William Blackford, who saw the field the next day, wrote that "from the heights it looked as blue as if it had been covered with a blue cloth. At no one spot during the war were there as many bodies on the same space as here."

Jackson, having beaten back Franklin, gave orders for a counterattack, but unit cohesion was lost in some brigades; some did not get the orders, and those who did and tried to advance were blown away by alert Federal gunners. Stuart's men, eager to join the fight, advanced dismounted, but they, too, were forced back. At last even Jackson was convinced that he could not mount a successful counterattack. The Federal artillery "so completely swept our front," he reported, "as to satisfy me that the proposed movement should be abandoned." Night fell, and the battle ended.

Before leaving the field, Jackson remembered that Maxcy Gregg had been seriously wounded, and he sent Captain Smith to convey his best wishes for his recovery. Smith found Gregg surrounded by surgeons and officers in a large room in the home of a Mr. John Yerby. "He was much affected," Smith reported, "and desired me to thank General Jackson for his thoughtful remembrance."

That night, when Jackson reached his headquarters tent at Darnabus Pond near Curtis Shop, he found his friend Boteler there with several of his Richmond friends. Boteler had brought a bucket of oysters, which Jim Lewis added to the regular fare. Feasting on oysters,

2. This was the first tactical use of a telegraph.

they celebrated a successful Confederate day of battle.

One of the friends Boteler had brought was Adelbert (or perhaps his brother Frederick) Volck, an artist, who asked after dinner if he could sketch his host. Sitting motionless, Jackson was soon fast asleep.

It was little enough sleep he had that night. Boteler, who shared Jackson's tent, recorded that he was busy writing until after midnight. At one point, seeing that the candle was shining in Boteler's eyes, he thoughtfully propped up a book as a shield. About four o'clock he sent for McGuire and asked him to check on Gregg's condition. Then he decided to go himself and roused Smith to accompany him.

Gregg was in intense pain and distressed that he had, a few months before, been so outraged by Jackson's tyrannical and unjust behavior in arresting two of his regimental commanders that he had himself preferred charges against him. Only a month earlier Lee had persuaded him to drop the charges. Now he begged Jackson's forgiveness. Sitting on the edge of the bed, Jackson took Gregg's hand in his. "The doctors tell me that you have not long to live," he said gently. "Let me ask you to dismiss this matter from your mind and turn your thoughts to God and to the world to which you go."

Tears starting to his eyes, Gregg whispered: "I thank you. I thank you very much."

Gregg was not the only senior officer to die on this bitterly cold winter night. Brigadier General Thomas R. R. Cobb, a thirty-nine-year-old Georgian in Longstreet's corps, wounded in the thigh, was carried to a nearby house, where he bled to death. Less notable soldiers, Confederates and Federals, died where they fell. Major General Darius Nash Couch, a classmate of Jackson's at West Point and now a corps commander in Burnside's army, described the night as "a fearful one for the front line hugging the hollows in the ground, and for the wounded who could not be reached. Many died of wounds and exposure, and as fast as men died they stiffened in the wintry air, and on the front line were rolled forward for protection to the living."

McGuire, returning exhausted in the early dawn, asked Jackson wearily how they could contend with the vastly superior numbers of their enemy. Jackson, his manner "savage" and "his voice ringing," according to McGuire, replied: "Kill them, sir! Kill every one."[3]

Lee and Jackson both fully expected the battle to continue the

3. McGuire told of this incident many times, and the words vary somewhat in different versions, but the sense of Jackson's words is the same in all.

next day. Lee ordered ordnance wagons to be replenished with ammunition that very night. A. P. Hill's division, which had borne the brunt
of the fighting, was withdrawn from the line and replaced by the divisions of Taliaferro and Early. In the morning there was indeed much
skirmishing and firing of artillery, particularly on Jackson's front, but
neither side attacked.

In the afternoon the Federals asked for a truce to bring in the
wounded. Jackson refused. The request had not been signed by General Burnside. So the wounded were left on the ground for another two
hours until Burnside's signature was obtained. Late in the afternoon the
truce was finally arranged. Men from both sides seized the chance to
mingle and talk, exchanging tobacco and newspapers. Jackson warned
Smith, one of the officers assigned to oversee the truce: "If you are
asked who is in command of your right, do not tell them I am, and be
guarded in your remarks."

On the field Smith recognized an acquaintance from Lexington,
Dr. John Miller Junkin, an older brother of Jackson's first wife who had
gone north with his father at the start of the war. Junkin asked Smith to
give his regards to Jackson and to deliver a message from his father. "I
will do so with pleasure when I meet General Jackson," Smith replied
guardedly.

Junkin smiled. "It is not worth while for you to try to deceive us.
We know that General Jackson is in front of us."

When Smith reported this meeting, Jackson at once wrote to Margaret Junkin Preston in Lexington, telling her that her brother was still
alive and fit.

When the field was cleared of wounded and the truce ended,
pickets and snipers went back to their work of killing each other. During the night, in the midst of a roaring gale, Burnside, undetected,
withdrew his army. It was a remarkable achievement. When the fog
lifted on the morning of 16 December, the Union army was gone.

Shortly after sunrise John Gittings, adjutant of the 31st Virginia,
saw Jackson:

> As I was walking along the ridge above Hamilton's Crossing, and
> about thirty yards from one of our batteries, I passed within a few
> feet of General Jackson who had taken up his position on this
> vantage ground for the purpose of reconnoitering; but he was not
> doing very much of it just at that time, for he was seated on the
> ground, leaning against a hickory sapling, and fast asleep! He held

his bridle-rein in one hand and his field-glasses in the other, and did not awaken as I walked along the path in touching distance of him, but seemed to be sleeping as calmly as I had seen him sleep years before in the church at Lexington.

Burnside's unsuccessful campaign resulted in 12,527 Union casualties: 1,281 killed, 9,477 wounded, and 1,769 missing, one of the worst Union defeats of the war. Lee's losses totaled 4,837. The heaviest fighting, or at least the most killing, occurred in front of Longstreet's position, at the stone wall on Marye's Heights, where Federal casualties totaled 7,690. Franklin's grand division suffered 4,837 casualties at the hands of Jackson's men. Longstreet sustained fewer casualties than Jackson. A. P. Hill's division alone lost 2,120 men—more than Longstreet's entire corps and two-thirds of Jackson's total loss. Early lost 932 more.

Union soldiers had fought bravely enough,[4] but once again, in another "On to Richmond" campaign, they had been led by a commander whose battle skills did not match their courage. Confederate soldiers had also fought well, and there were more of them in action than might otherwise have been, for Jackson had hit upon the notion of battlefield police. He appointed Major David B. Bridgford, an ordnance officer, as provost marshal of II Corps with orders to "shoot all stragglers who refused to go forward, or if caught a second time, upon the evidence of two witnesses to shoot them."

Bridgford had a better idea. He sent stragglers forward in batches with instructions that they be placed in the forefront of any battle line. Both A. P. Hill and Jubal Early commented on the consequent absence of straggling and skulking. "The number sent in under guard was only 526," Bridgford said.

With the enemy gone and without the strength to follow, the Confederates climbed down from their ridge. Lee, thinking that Burnside might resume the fight by crossing the Rappahannock farther downstream, sent a brigade of Stuart's cavalry to take a look, and on a rumor of Federal activity near Port Royal, Jackson's entire corps was put in motion. When he learned that the Federals were not crossing, Jackson reversed the direction of his columns and rode back along his line of troops. He was cheered now wherever he went, and men, hear-

4. From 11 to 13 December twenty Union heroes of the Battle of Fredericksburg were among the first recipients of the Medal of Honor.

ing cheering, would say, "It's Jackson or a rabbit." Some even threw their hats under his horse's feet so they could say that he had ridden over them.

Night found Jackson and his staff hungry, cold, and wandering about without their headquarters wagons. Moss Neck, a large mansion, could be seen nearby, and staff officers suggested that on this cold, dark night they seek food and warmth there, but Jackson would not hear of it. A fire was made near an old tulip tree, and the unhappy young officers huddled around it until the tree fell over with a crash, scattering them. Someone said that Captain Hugh McGuire, Dr. McGuire's brother, knew this part of the country well, and Jackson sent him to search for some food. He came back with half a ham and some biscuits, which they all ate gratefully, but they still faced a long, cold night. In the face of their misery Jackson relented, and they all trooped to Moss Neck, where Jackson was taken to a bedroom, and his staff made themselves comfortable on the floor. Lieutenant Smith recorded: "I slept before the fire on a costly rug, as comfortable a boy as there was in the army that bitter night."

Jackson made Moss Neck his home for three months, and here and at the nearby Yerby house he found the last bit of tranquil happiness he was ever to know.

31

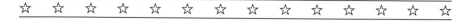

Moss Neck

oss Neck, ten miles south of
Fredericksburg, boasted an impressive manor house. Jackson described
it to Anna as "one of the most beautiful buildings I have seen in this
country. It is said to have cost sixty thousand dollars." It was a new
house built of brick. Its central structure was two-storied with a col-
umned doorway and a second-story porch; a pointed roof supported a
small cupola. Single-storied wings on each side were gabled with a
chimney at each gable roof. The house was lighted by gas and heated
by coal grates. Around it clustered a number of outbuildings: kitchen,
slave quarters, laundry, icehouse, and a small frame building some 140
feet from the left wing that served as the office of the owner.

James Parke Corbin had built the house, and the present owner
was his son, Richard Corbin, now serving as a private in the 9th Virginia Cavalry. Living there were his young wife, Roberta ("Bertie");
their five-year-old daughter, Jane Welford Corbin ("Janie"); and his
attractive twenty-three-year-old younger sister, Kate.

On that cold evening of 16 December, when Jackson accepted the
hospitality offered by Mrs. Corbin, he had a "delightful night's rest."
The next morning he and his officers breakfasted sumptuously on "sau-
sage, pork steaks, waffles, muffins, etc." Roberta Corbin pressed Jackson to stay, offering him all the amenities which Moss Neck could
afford, but he declined. Protesting that the house was "too luxurious for
a soldier, who should sleep in a tent," he camped out under canvas in a

woods about five hundred yards away. However, the winter promised to be a cold one, and cold was bad for his ear; McGuire urged him to sleep under a roof. All the other generals had found quarters indoors (D. H. Hill in an Episcopal church), so Jackson, though still declining a room in the manor house, yielded to the extent of moving into the owner's office.

His new quarters had a small fireplace, some chairs, stools, and a desk; sporting prints hung on the walls. He set up his cot amid the fishing tackle, traps, antlers, and other gear and paraphernalia of a sportsman. In a bookcase were government reports, the *Farmer's Register,* legal, medical, and agricultural books, sporting and fashion magazines. He disturbed nothing.

The troops went into winter quarters, putting together huts for themselves in the absence of tents. Log houses, villages of them, soon sprang up in the woods. The cavalry was active, scouting and making a few raids, but the principal duty of the infantry was to keep watch on the riverbanks and on the enemy's pickets on the opposite shore. Units took turns at this employment. Sometimes there were good-natured shouted exchanges between the opposing pickets; they enjoyed the music of each other's bands. Soon, using small boats, they traded such luxuries as tobacco, newspapers, coffee, sugar.

The fighting at Marye's Heights had awakened the Confederate commanders to the value of breastworks. The belated recognition by generals both North and South of the importance of earthworks and stone walls in a defensive position seems extraordinary, for there was nothing new in the concept of interposing barriers between one's own troops and the enemy's weapons. The practice was centuries old. Yet in no 1861–62 Civil War battle did soldiers fight from behind extensive, deliberately constructed field fortifications. Now, in January and February 1863, Jackson put men to work constructing field fortifications along the Rappahannock. Although the fortifications were to be of no use, the activity helped keep the men busy and warm.

There was work enough for commanders and staff officers. Problems in both the commissary and quartermaster departments persisted. In January there was a diminution of the meat ration. Medical stores were in short supply and the health of men caused concern. Quinine was available for fever, and "blue powders" or "blue mass" were given for intestinal disorders.[1] There was little else. Measles and mumps

---

1. Blue mass was a mercury compound commonly used in the treatment of diarrhea and dysentery.

raged through some regiments. Smallpox broke out in A. P. Hill's division, but prompt quarantine measures checked its spread. Some men took scabs from infected men and tried to vaccinate themselves with pocketknives. Fear of scurvy led in early spring to orders for men to be sent to gather sassafras buds, wild onions, garlic, poke sprouts, and lamb's-quarters. There was little else to give them.

Much thought was given to the sorry condition of the horses. Instructions were issued for them to be taken to browse "as much as possible on the twigs of the poplar, maple, sweet gum, etc." and to be "allowed to graze in the bottoms of the small streams instead of being tied up all day." Even so, the cavalry and artillery lost more than a quarter of their horses.

Jackson had been so busy that he had fallen badly behind in his paper work. After-action reports were long overdue; not even his Valley campaign had been documented. To help him, he summoned his friend and former aide (during the Romney expedition) Lieutenant Colonel Charles J. Faulkner, the former United States minister to France and four-time member of Congress. Faulkner had not taken part in any of the campaigns he was now asked to describe; he had most recently been serving in the office of General Samuel Cooper, the adjutant general, but he was a man clever with a pen, and Jackson had need of him.

Young Sandic Pendleton had proved his worth as Jackson's AAG; he was obviously better than Dabney or any of the other older, more distinguished men whom Jackson had employed, but he was now superseded, at least in title, by Faulkner. Pendleton was promoted to major, but Jackson named him "junior AAG" and Faulkner "senior AAG." These were not appointments recognized by the Confederate or any other army, but Jackson felt they would serve his purpose.

Faulkner's task was not an easy one. Although he had the after-action reports of most of the subordinate commanders, there were, as always in such reports, many discrepancies. According to Faulkner, Jackson insisted that he write with "severe Roman simplicity." His efforts were closely edited by Jackson, who made numerous corrections. He deleted a reference to Winder's being missed after his death lest this be construed as a reflection upon his friend Paxton, the current commander of the Stonewall Brigade, and he allowed scant praise for Taliaferro, who, in spite of his dire predictions, had performed both bravely and capably. Not even bravery and efficiency could make Jackson forgive those, such as A. P. Hill and Taliaferro, who had roused his wrath.

Faulkner was not popular with the staff. Douglas thought that his appointment was "manifestly wrong," that he was "not qualified for the place," and that his versions of past battles were "very unsatisfactory and do both General Jackson and Colonel Faulkner great injustice." He and others believed that the efforts of the staff had been slighted and that the reports ought to have been written by Pendleton. Through it all Faulkner worked on patiently and won the regard of at least one staff officer. Captain Boswell wrote in his diary: "I have always been much prejudiced against him, but find him one of the most interesting men I ever knew." In a later entry he noted admiringly that Faulkner had "one of the clearest minds I have ever come in contact with."

There was so much paper work that Jackson frequently fell asleep with pen in hand. The problem of tens of thousands of men absent without official leave or guilty of outright desertion occupied his mind. He suggested to his friend Boteler in Richmond that rewards be offered for all who would catch and deliver such absent men, the money to be paid by the government, which would be reimbursed by deductions from the pay of those returned.

Jackson himself had never taken leave, and he resented any request from his officers for leave, even compassionate leave. When Brigadier General Alfred Iverson, Jr., an experienced, brave, and capable professional soldier, was denied compassionate leave and threatened to resign, Jackson wrote to D. H. Hill, Inversion's division commander: "No one can tell what day a battle will be fought. Whilst I would regret to see General Iverson resign yet I would rather see him do so than to approve of his furlough under present circumstances."

This was nonsense. There would be no serious fighting this winter, as Jackson was well aware. However, Iverson did not resign. On 20 January Burnside, prodded by Halleck, had crossed the Rappahannock above Fredericksburg and had attempted to come down on Lee's flank, but rain had mired men, wagons, and guns in mud, and this effort, known as the Mud March, ended two days later in dismal failure. On 25 January Burnside was replaced by Joseph Hooker, but "Fighting Joe" was not about to attempt a winter campaign in the Virginia mud.

Enlisted men who had gone over to the enemy and those who deserted in the face of the enemy were, if caught, severely punished. On New Year's Day 1863 troops were assembled to witness the execution of Private Patrick McGee of the 1st Virginia, for perjury, robbery, and desertion. Six captured deserters from the Stonewall Brigade were tried by court-martial. Three were sentenced to be executed, two to be flogged, and one was sentenced to six months' hard labor. Paxton, their brigade commander, shocked by the death sentences, suggested that only one man, drawn by lot, be executed. Jackson, who never granted mercy or reduced a sentence, gave a mild rebuke to his favorite in his endorsement: "With the exception of this application, General Paxton's management of his Brigade has given me great satisfaction. One great difficulty in the army results from over lenient Courts, and it appears to me that when a Court Martial faithfully discharges its duty that its decisions should be sustained. If this is not done, a lax administration of justice and corresponding disregard for law must be the consequence."

Lee, always courteous but ever bloody-minded, agreed entirely. It was President Davis who often spared the lives of deserters, but apparently even he was not able to save all, for Hotchkiss's diary records the execution of one from the Stonewall Brigade on 28 February 1863.

Courts-martial were "in full blast," according to Private John Casler: "Punishments of all kinds were being inflicted on the prisoners, such as shot to death, whipped, heads shaved and drummed out of the service, riding wooden horses, wearing barrel shirts, and all other punishments in the catalogue of military courts-martial."

Colonel Edward Porter Alexander estimated that he spent half of his time on duty participating in courts-martial and the other half in such activities as "seizure & confiscation of Apple Jack."

The case of acting Brigadier General John R. Jones, the only Confederate general ever accused of cowardice in the field, was an embarrassment. Jones was another Jackson favorite, and he had been promoted brigadier general on Jackson's recommendation, though the Confederate Senate never approved the promotion. In February 1863 it became common knowledge that a captain had accused Jones of being "deficient in courage" or "as having misbehaved in the presence of the enemy." It is probable that more than one soldier believed that the shell that stunned Jones at Antietam and prompted him to leave the field had occasioned more fright than injury. To Jackson's annoyance, when pressed to prefer charges or retract his statement, the captain refused to do either. (In his next battle Jones was, to the disgust of his fellow officers, carried from the field "owing to the ulcerated condition of his leg." He was immediately relieved of his command and shipped out of the Army of Northern Virginia.[2])

2. On 4 July 1864 John R. Jones was captured at Smithburg, Tennessee, and spent the remainder of the war in prison. The Confederate government made no

Many changes of senior commanders had to be determined. D. H. Hill was sent to take command of the Department of North Carolina, where the Federals had become active. Longstreet was given an independent command south of the James River with three divisions. Lee's Army of Northern Virginia was thus reduced to about sixty-two thousand men, about half as many as Hooker's army opposite him.

The deaths at Fredericksburg of Cobb and Gregg created two brigadier general vacancies, and there was a need for more major generals. Jackson considered a military education important, but he believed that "something more is required to make a general," and among the qualities necessary, he listed "judgment, nerve and force of character." He felt strongly that all promotion should be by merit, and frequently said so, but his own selections were often colored by his likes and dislikes. He recommended Edward ("Allegheny") Johnson to be a major general, although Johnson had seen no action since receiving his wound at McDowell and had served under Jackson in no other battle, and he adamantly refused to recommend the worthy Taliaferro, who, disappointed, asked to be transferred.[3] Jubal Early and Isaac Trimble were also recommended to be major generals, and their appointments were confirmed.

Historians and biographers have referred often to a "special relationship" between Lee and Jackson without noting that it was fostered and preserved solely by the tact and courtesy of Lee. Jackson could be churlish; Lee simply refused to quarrel. When not all his recommendations for promotions were accepted, Jackson railed against having officers "forced" upon him, and in the exchange of correspondence that ensued he ended his letter of 28 February with these blunt words: "I have had much trouble resulting from incompetent officers having been assigned to duty with me regardless of my wishes. Those who assigned them [including Lee?] have never taken the responsibility of

effort to exchange him. He was released on 24 July 1865. After the war he prospered as a businessman and was appointed commissioner in chancery at Harrisonburg, Virginia. He died on 1 April 1901 at the age of seventy-four.

3. Taliaferro spent the remainder of the war in South Carolina, Georgia, and Florida. Although he was paroled on 2 May 1865 as a major general, no record can be found that he was ever promoted to that rank. After the war he served as a legislator and judge. He died on 27 February 1898 at the age of seventy-six. He was replaced in Jackson's corps by Brigadier General Raleigh E. Colston, a VMI graduate and instructor whom Jackson recommended. Colston was not a success and after Chancellorsville was removed from the Army of Northern Virginia.

incurring the odium which results from such incompetency." Lee sagely left the letter unanswered and ended the exchange.

There was time now during these months in winter quarters for A. P. Hill to resume his feud with Jackson, and it is impossible to read all the charges and countercharges, accusations and demands made by these two most capable but nettlesome generals without admiring the long-suffering patience of General Robert E. Lee.

On 8 January 1863 Hill wrote to Lee, reminding him of the quarrel and again requesting that a court-martial be held soon. Two of his important witnesses (Gregg and Branch) had been killed, and others were being dispersed. He felt so strongly, he wrote, that he was willing to appear before a court composed of officers of lesser rank than his own.

Lee responded on 12 January with a long, tactful letter which ended: "Upon examining the charges in question, I am of opinion that the interests of the service do not require that they should be tried, and have, therefore, returned them to General Jackson with an endorsement to that effect. I hope that you will concur with me that their further prosecution is unnecessary, so far as you are concerned, and will be of no advantage to the service."

This did not, as it ought to have, end the matter. Jackson, his bile rising anew, sent staff officers scurrying to gather information pertinent to the charges. Hill was even approached for testimony that could be used against him.

Two weeks after receiving Lee's letter Hill returned to the attack. Jackson's charges, he said, had caused him to "preserve every scrap of paper received from corps headquarters, to guard myself against this slumbering volcano [Jackson]. I respectfully forward again my charges against Lieutenant-General Jackson, and request that he may be tried on them." Lee simply did not reply.

A new brouhaha erupted. Lee learned that his standing order to keep secret all intercepted Federal messages was being flouted at the headquarters of Brigadier General James Henry Lane. Jackson was ordered to discover who was responsible and relieve him of duty. The culprit was found to be Hill's signal officer, Captain R. H. T. Adams, who informed Jackson that he was responsible only to Hill and that Hill's orders differed from Lee's. Jackson, as ordered, relieved him.

Hill angrily leaped to the defense of his signal officer, and a fresh quarrel was unleashed. Jackson ferreted out a letter Hill had sent five months before stating that an earlier order delivered by Captain Boswell to Captain Adams had been ignored on Hill's orders. With this in hand, Jackson urgently requested that Hill be "relieved from duty in my corps."

Lee again tried benign neglect, but the Jackson-Hill feud simmered on, never to be concluded.

Quarrels and cares were put aside briefly at Christmas, when Jackson invited Generals Robert E. Lee, Jeb Stuart, and William Pendleton with some of their staff officers to join him and his staff for Christmas dinner at his quarters. Lieutenant James Power Smith, who was placed in charge of the arrangements, managed to acquire three turkeys, a bucket of oysters, and other good things. To these were added a fine ham and the wine some "Staunton ladies" had sent Jackson. "Uncle Jim" Lewis produced white biscuits, and some pickles were found. In all, it was a splendid banquet to which they sat down in high good humor.

The recent months had been sad ones for Lee. The war had not gone well, and in October his daughter Annie had died after a short illness. Early in December a grandchild had died, but if he was depressed, he concealed it. He appeared to enjoy himself.

Stuart amused all by pretending to believe that the undisturbed pictures on the wall of the owner's office had been personally selected by Jackson. Smith later related how he "read aloud what was said about each noted race horse and each splendid bull. At the hearth he paused to scan with affected astonishment the horrid picture of a certain terrier that could kill so many rats a minute. . . . [w]ith great solemnity he looked at the picture and then at the General. He paused and stepped back, and in solemn tones said he wished to express his astonishment and grief at the display of General Jackson's low tastes. It would be a sad disappointment to the old ladies of the country, who thought that Jackson was a good man."

Everyone laughed heartily while Jackson beamed and blushed. It was all good fun, but it was not so relaxed that first names were used. Lee always spoke of "General Jackson," and to Jackson as to the other officers Lee was always "General Lee."

When his guests had departed, Jackson took up his pen to thank Anna for sending him a lock of the baby's hair. "How I do want to see that precious baby!" he wrote longingly. He was an anxious father, his letters full of cautions. When Julia was some seven weeks old, he wrote that he was gratified to hear that Anna had "commenced disciplining the baby. . . . She must not be permitted to have that will of her own, of which you speak." He thought it best "not to call her *cherub;* no earthly being is such." He had fears, he confided, that Anna would "make such an idol of that baby that God will take her from us. Are *you* not afraid of it?" he asked.

Winter brought time for the troops to relax. There were games of all sorts, and plays were given by the Soldiers Aid Society. Many of the young men had never seen snow, which fell heavily that winter in central Virginia, and they enjoyed the curiosity. Snowball fights were popular. Tactics were developed, fortifications were built, and some battles became massive affairs of brigade strength with mounted officers and staffs. Private Worsham several times saw "more than 2,500 men engaged in a game of snowball!"

Jackson's staff reveled in the hospitality of the Corbin home, and Sandie Pendleton fell in love with Kate Corbin.[4] They all took advantage of the fine Corbin library, rich in biographies, novels, poetry, and Shakespeare. Jackson found time to read *Moses* by Henry Hunter, finding it "delightful." He confessed to Anna that he felt "more improved in reading it than by an ordinary sermon."

Not every amusement was uplifting. British-born Captain Francis Dawson reported that "the great American game of poker was played nearly every night" and that one of the most successful gamblers, Major Thomas Walton, said to be a kinsman of General Longstreet, at one sitting won two thousand dollars from an unfortunate surgeon. Blackjack, euchre, and keno were popular, and there were raffles, horse races, and an occasional crap game. Near Fredericksburg was a much-frequented gambling house known as Devil's Den.

In January Jackson wistfully wrote Anna that "Mrs. General Longstreet, Mrs. General A. P. Hill, and Mrs. General Rodes have all been to visit their husbands . . . it made me wish I had Mrs. Jackson here too. . . ." But little Julia was only three months old and had come down with chicken pox. Anna could not come.

A frequent and always welcome visitor to his headquarters entranced him. Pretty Janie Corbin, a favorite of all the officers, had taken a fancy to the staid, gray-eyed general. She slipped in almost daily to play contentedly on the floor beside him, and Jackson usually

4. The story of young Pendleton is a sad one. He became a lieutenant colonel and married Kate Corbin on 29 December 1863, but he was mortally wounded at Tom's Brook by a bullet in his abdomen and died on 23 September 1864, just four days short of his twenty-fourth birthday. On 4 November of that year Kate gave birth to a son, Alexander, who died of diphtheria on 1 September of the following year. Kate and the Corbins were impoverished by the war. In 1871 she remarried a VMI professor and was widowed again in 1906. When she died in November 1919, in her eightieth year, she was almost penniless.

found for her a piece of fruit or some little present. One day he took out his penknife and, carefully cutting away the gold braid from the fine cap Anna had sent him, fashioned a crown for her. He had worn the cap at Fredericksburg, but as he explained to Anna, "I became so much ashamed of the broad gold lace . . . as to induce me to take it off."

In March, on the day that Jackson moved his headquarters into tents closer to Hamilton's Crossing, he learned that Janie and two visiting cousins had come down with scarlet fever. Two days later the sorrowful news of her death reached him, and he, who had looked upon the death and dismemberment of thousands of young men without a tear, now wept. James Power Smith was sent back to Moss Neck to express his sympathy and to offer any assistance to the family. Janie's two young cousins were also dead, and carpenters in the Stonewall Brigade made coffins for all three.

The plight of the Fredericksburg civilians cried for attention. In his report of the battle Lee wrote: "History presents no instance of a people exhibiting a purer and more unselfish patriotism or a higher spirit of fortitude and courage than was evinced by the citizens of Fredericksburg." They had indeed suffered catastrophic property losses. A newspaper correspondent from Charleston who saw the town after the Federals had departed wrote: "Had the demons of destruction held an orgy in the town, had all the imps of hell called together and turned loose on the city, it could scarcely have been more blasted, ruined and desecrated than when left by the Yankee army."

The hearts of the Confederate soldiers were touched, and fund-raising campaigns were launched for the townspeople's relief. A. P. Hill's division raised ten thousand dollars; II Corps gave thirty thousand dollars. Jackson himself contributed one hundred dollars, and his staff eight hundred dollars.

The great religious revival that took place throughout the Southern armies and particularly in the Army of Northern Virginia that winter and the early spring of 1863 affected Jackson deeply. "I don't know that I have ever enjoyed Sabbaths as I do this winter," he declared. The Reverend Dabney even thought there was an increase in his "spirituality and Christian activity." He began to hold a prayer meeting at his mess every morning, and although his staff was not required to attend, he was pleased when they did.

President Davis declared 27 March 1863 "a day of humiliation, prayer, and fasting," and the following day Jackson wrote to his father-in-law Dr. Morrison that in the army the president's call had received "a more generous response than I have seen on any similar occasion since the beginning of the war." Many of the units built temporary chapels of logs; the first of these was erected by the Stonewall Brigade. All were filled to overflowing on Sundays, and some units held daily prayer meetings and Bible classes.

There were not enough preachers to go around, and Jackson clamored for more. He wanted preachers of all denominations: "I would like no questions asked in the army as to what denomination a chaplain belongs; but let the question be, does he preach the Gospel?" He organized weekly meetings with his own chaplains. He even offered to pay five hundred dollars of his own money if the famous Reverend Dr. Benjamin Palmer Morgan of New Orleans would come and preach. The unofficial chaplain general, the seventy-year-old Reverend Dr. Joseph C. Stiles, said of Jackson that he "came nearer putting God in God's place than any other human soul I ever met."

The movement had a revival flavor, the ministers preaching simple, emotional sermons, assuring their flocks that the Southern cause was God's cause, their fight a righteous one against the immoral and godless Northerners. Preachers and pamphlets proclaimed the "manifest hand of God in our Revolution."

Many a soldier "got religion," at least temporarily. Even Private Casler, who readily admitted to having "at times" been "wild and reckless," "made a profession and joined the [Methodist] church." Although later he "naturally retrograded considerably," he never forgot "the pleasure I experienced in trying to be good."

Jackson's attitude toward his sister may only be guessed at. He never spoke of her. One evening he and McGuire were reminiscing, and Jackson spoke of his mother and other members of his family, including his half brother, Wirt, whose whereabouts were unknown, but he made no mention of Laura. He knew her sentiments, and she must have been an embarrassment to him, yet he had given his daughter the middle name Laura.

In April, when Jackson moved out of his tent at Hamilton's Crossing and made his quarters at the home of William Yerby, he sent for Anna and the baby. With Hetty, they hurried toward him as fast as his ban on Sunday travel allowed. On Monday, 20 April, in a pouring rain, they arrived by train at Guiney's Station, and Jackson was there to meet them. Water was dripping from him, but "his face was all sunshine and gladness," said Anna, and little Julia gave him "her brightest and sweetest smiles."

Jackson was the proudest of fathers, carrying Julia about in his arms whenever he was free, holding her up in front of a mirror to say playfully, "Now, Miss Jackson, look at yourself!" and demanding of one and all, "Isn't she a little gem?" Three days after her arrival, and five months to the day of her birth, she was baptized by the Reverend Dr. Lacy in the Yerby parlor. Many of Jackson's staff crowded into the room. Later Lee called.

The war made the length of Anna's visit uncertain, but while it lasted, she thought it an even happier time than the idyllic days in Winchester. Everyone was curious about Mrs. Jackson, and when she went to church, all eyes were on her. Hotchkiss described her: "She is slightly built and tolerably good looking, and was somewhat gaily though modestly dressed."

It was at this time that Anna summoned a photographer from the studio of Minnis and Cowell in Richmond to take a picture of her husband. She thought that he had never looked healthier and that he looked so smart in what she called "the handsome suit" Stuart had given him. His hair was unusually long, and she lovingly combed it into large ringlets.

For the photograph Jackson sat on a chair in the Yerby hall; a strong spring breeze came in the open door, causing him to frown slightly, "giving a sternness to his countenance that was not natural"—or so Anna thought, but soldiers who served under him considered that this three-quarter view of their hard-driving general, often reproduced, most resembled the man they knew. Anna always preferred the photograph taken in Winchester, for it had, she thought, "more of the beaming sunlight of his *home-look.*"

Spring was the season for campaigning, and the Federals began to stir menacingly; Federal balloons were up across the Rappahannock, and their cavalry patrols became more active; there was even a raid on Port Royal. Lee advised Jackson not to react to the Port Royal affair, judging correctly that "if a real attempt is made to cross the river it will be above Fredericksburg."

The Jackson's idyll came to an end early on the morning of 29 April, when Jackson was awakened with a message from Major Samuel Hale, Early's AAG: Hooker was crossing the Rappahannock.

Jackson hurriedly dressed and buckled on his sword. There was no time for breakfast, scarcely time to say good-bye. He did not know if he could return to her again, he told Anna. If he could not, he would send his aide (and her brother) Joseph Morrison to see her safely on the train. There was a last embrace, and he was gone.

He was scarcely out the door when Anna heard the crash of guns that marked the end of what had been nine glorious days for them both. As she was packing, the Reverend Lacy appeared with a note from Jackson, telling her that he would not return. Lieutenant Morrison, not wishing to miss a battle, had begged him to send the chaplain rather than himself.

Accompanied by Lacy, Anna rode over the rough, newly made military road to Guiney's Station, where she caught a train for Richmond. Also on board were a pretty young Creole mother and her small boy from New Orleans. As Anna looked at them, it occurred to her that she was not the only lonely woman in the Confederacy. "She came to see her husband as I did," she thought sorrowfully.

32

☆ ☆ ☆ ☆ ☆ ☆ ☆ ☆ ☆ ☆ ☆ ☆ ☆ ☆

Chancellorsville

When Jackson arrived at his headquarters—tents erected about a mile from the Yerby house—he at once dispatched Lieutenant Smith to Lee with the news that Hooker had crossed the Rappahannock.

Two days before, Hooker had put in train an excellent plan for prying Lee from his strong defenses at Fredericksburg. He had divided his 134,000-man army into roughly three parts. One-third, under Major General John Sedgwick, would hold Lee in his entrenchments at Fredericksburg, making a diversionary attack; another third of the army would remain in reserve; and a third segment, to be led by Hooker himself, would make a great turning movement around Lee's left.

Three Federal corps, about forty thousand men, had been marched to Kelly's Ford, twenty-seven miles above Fredericksburg, and on the night of 28 April they had crossed on pontoon bridges against negligible opposition. Now George Meade's V Corps was marching southeast toward Ely's Ford on the Rapidan, and Henry Slocum's XII Corps, followed by O. O. Howard's XI Corps (known as the German Corps, it contained the units which had served under Franz Sigel with Frémont in the Valley campaign), was moving southwest toward Germanna Ford. Lee's army was now threatened in its rear.

The Rapidan, high from the recent rains, proved a difficult obstacle, particularly at Germanna Ford, but the crossing was made in the face of light Confederate opposition. As the Federals swept east, they uncovered other fords on the Rappahannock, notably Banks's Ford and, near the confluence of the Rappahannock and the Rapidan, United States Ford, allowing for the unopposed crossing of other troops, whom Hooker had sited on the north bank ready to move.

Just south of the two rivers lay an area appositely named the Wilderness. Eight to ten miles wide, it was a dense tangle of forest and second growth, interlaced with streams, that stretched approximately fourteen miles east. (Much of the area is still deserving of its name.) Private John Robson thought it a "mournful" looking country, "a good place to die in." Roughly in the middle stood a sizable house and a few outbuildings owned by George E. Chancellor. Not a hamlet or even a settlement, the place was called Chancellorsville. Here five roads converged. Three from fords—Germanna, Ely's, and United States—met there; a fourth—the Old Turnpike (corduroyed and covered with three to four inches of gravel in the swampy sections)—ran from Orange Court House to Fredericksburg; and the fifth was the Plank Road (made of planks two inches thick and sixteen inches long nailed to two parallel logs buried in the ground), which dipped south before joining the Old Turnpike and continuing east. The Federals moved by the roads from the fords toward Chancellorsville on 30 April.

Hooker had maneuvered his army with great skill, and the Army of Northern Virginia was in peril. As soon as Hooker's intentions became clear, Lee began to shift his forces to meet the threat: He sent Richard Anderson's division to Chancellorsville, and Jackson's II Corps was shifted to the west. Jackson moved with his usual energy and decisiveness; those around him seemed to detect a new self-confidence, a surer hand.

When he heard that it had been said they must retreat, he demanded to know who had uttered such a craven thought. "No sir!" he declared. "We shall not fall back! We shall attack them!"

On 30 April, cool, damp, and foggy, Lee and Jackson were together most of the day, making an extensive reconnaissance and then conferring in Lee's tent. They were not looking for a way to escape but determining how they could attack, how they could, in Lee's words, "get at these people."

Anderson, deciding that Chancellorsville was not a good place for a line of defense, pulled his division back about three and a half miles to a more open position that extended across both the Old Turnpike and the Plank Road. Lee sent engineers to lay out a defensive position, and Anderson's men began to dig and to chop down trees.

Meade's V Corps reached Chancellorsville about eleven o'clock on the morning of 30 April, and Slocum's XII Corps arrived two hours later. About four o'clock Howard's XI Corps reached Dowdall's Tavern, some two miles to the west. Officers and men alike were excited by their success. Meade crowed to Slocum, "We are on Lee's flank and he doesn't know it!" They were eager to press forward, but they were halted by orders from Hooker directing them to wait until he came up and until Darius Couch's II Corps and Daniel Sickles's III Corps crossed at United States Ford and Banks's Ford and his forces were concentrated.

General Slocum, the senior Federal officer at Chancellorsville, positioned Meade's corps to the east, Howard's to the west, and his own corps in the center, just southwest of Chancellorsville. An enthusiastic Hooker arrived late that afternoon and issued a proclamation to his troops, assuring them that "our enemy must either ingloriously fly or come out from behind his entrenchments and give us battle on our own ground, where certain destruction awaits him." Lee, however, had different thoughts.

With that boldness taken to the edge of rashness which ever characterized Lee's actions, he divided his forces in the face of a numerically superior enemy. Leaving only ten thousand men under Early to face Sedgwick at Fredericksburg, he took the remainder, about fifty thousand men, and marched on Hooker's corps advancing through the Wilderness. Hooker, astonished by Lee's unexpected aggressiveness, instead of plunging ahead, drew back his advanced elements and entrenched, thus surrendering the initiative to Lee.

By eight o'clock on the morning of 1 May, the beginning of a bright, warm day, Jackson's corps, less Early's division, had reached Anderson. Jackson pulled the men out of their newly built entrenchments and added them to what was to be his striking force. Moving in a two-pronged attack down the Plank Road and the Old Turnpike, he advanced upon the Federals. It was at about this time that Hooker was telling a group at his headquarters that "the rebel army is now the legitimate property of the Army of the Potomac."

Hooker cautiously moved his three corps forward, apparently unaware that Jackson had come up. The two forces advancing on a collision course were approximately equal in size, although Jackson had sixteen more guns. Hooker, unaware that Lee had shifted the bulk of his army westward, belatedly ordered Sedgwick "to threaten an attack in full force at 1 o'clock, and to continue in that attitude until further orders. Let the demonstration be as severe as can be, but not an attack." (Although this order was sent about one o'clock, it did not reach Sedgwick until five o'clock.) Hooker's purpose was to fix Lee in his Fredericksburg position, but the Confederate positions there were now held only by Early, and while a determined attack by Sedgwick would have overwhelmed him, a demonstration would not budge him.

Confederate and Union skirmishers and cavalry on the Plank Road and on the Old Turnpike met just west of the Tabernacle Church, about four miles east of Chancellorsville, where the two roads meet. Rifles cracked, guns were brought into battery and opened fire, and tens of thousands of men began the Battle of Chancellorsville. It was ten-forty in the morning.

Confederate aggressiveness, particularly the energy of their skirmishers on his flanks, led Major General George Sykes, commanding the Federal forces on the Old Turnpike, to believe that he had encountered a superior force, and he confessed to Brigadier General G. K. Warren, Hooker's chief engineer who was riding beside him, that he considered himself in danger of being surrounded. Warren galloped back and passed on this opinion to Hooker, who had just received news from his balloonists that a large force was advancing on him. He therefore ordered both Sykes and Slocum, who was on the Plank Road, to pull back toward Chancellorsville. Even Meade, who was moving east along a road about two miles north known as the River Road, was ordered to pull back. These fateful orders were delivered about one-thirty in the afternoon, and although some of the Federal commanders protested, they obeyed.

As Hooker's divisions fell back, Jackson followed closely. At two-thirty he sent a message to McLaws, informing him that he was "pressing on up the Plank Road" and urging him to "keep your skirmishers and flank parties well out, to guard against ambuscade."

On the far left of the Confederate line was a small clearing at Catherine Furnace.[1] Here the guns of the Confederate cavalry were engaged in an artillery duel with the Federals when Jackson rode up to confer with Stuart. The Federal fire was so fierce that Major R. F. Beckham, Stuart's artillery officer, later said: "I do not think that men

---

1. Catherine Iron Furnace, named after Catherine Wellford, used ore from nearby surface mines to make household and farming items before the war. During the war it manufactured munitions for the Confederates until Union soldiers destroyed it in 1865.

have been often under a hotter fire than that to which we were ex-posed." Jackson, as usual, heedless of danger, was attempting to assess the situation when Stuart said sharply: "General Jackson, we must move from here." Jackson gave way, but not before Major Channing Price, Stuart's AAG, fell mortally wounded beside him.

The Federal forces had now retreated as far as they would go, and Jackson could make no more headway. But why had Hooker retreated? It was a question much debated after the event. Hooker had developed a brilliant strategy, and it was being masterfully executed, but he had recoiled as soon as his army touched the Confederate line, a seeming loss of nerve.

Hooker was, of course, beset by the countless reports, true and false, the rumors, the uncertainties, the doubts and anxieties to which all senior commanders are exposed, and it appears that they over-whelmed him. Jackson, who was presumed to have had, and indeed did have, an inferior force, behaved as if he had a vastly superior army. Hooker was understandably puzzled, and he allowed his puzzlement and his fears to weaken his resolve.

In attacking Hooker as he did, Jackson was exercising his own initiative. His orders from Lee had been only to "make arrangements to repulse the enemy." A lesser general would have interpreted this as an order to strengthen the earthworks Anderson's men had begun to construct. But in Jackson the aggressive spirit was strong, and bolstered by past victories, he was fully confident of his own abilities.

Lee, of course, was faced with the same flow of contradictory reports and the same uncertainties as Hooker. He had scant knowledge of the enemy's strength and did not even know which Federal units he was facing in the Wilderness. But he was not bewildered or hesitant; he looked for a way to attack.

About seven o'clock that evening Lee and Jackson met on the Plank Road near the crossroad to Catherine Furnace. A Federal sharp-shooter spotted them and tried his hand but missed. They prudently drew back, dismounted, and sat down on a log to talk. Staff officers stood respectfully behind them. Both thought Hooker's withdrawal odd. Jackson predicted that the Federal retreat would continue. "By tomorrow morning there will not be any of them on this side of the river," he declared. Lee did not agree; he thought Hooker would make another effort the next day. He sent out Major Thomas M. R. Talcott, an aide, to examine the Federal strength; Jackson sent Captain Boswell with him. While they waited for their report, Stuart rode up with news of vital importance.

Throughout the day Hooker had been handicapped by a lack of cavalry. He had sent the newly formed Federal cavalry corps under Major General George Stoneman (the largest force of cavalry either side had ever put in motion) on a wide end run around Lee's right to create havoc on the Confederate line of communication, but Stoneman had been delayed in starting by the high water in the Rappahannock, and he was able to make no significant contribution to the battle. Hooker had left himself only a small, inadequate cavalry force; Stuart's men had been free to roam unopposed the back roads of the Wilderness and thus discover that the Federal right had no anchor and that instead of being turned back to face westward (a flank refused, in military terms) was instead *en l'air;* the Federal XI Corps, detached from the rest of the Federal line, unprotected, was unsupported and facing south.

Lee and Jackson now concentrated on how best to exploit this significant advantage. Talcott and Boswell reported back that the Federal line in front was strong and well protected by breastworks, trenches, and abatis, but this information no longer seemed important. Poring over an inadequate map, Lee said softly, "How can we get at these people?" The map seemed to indicate a road around the Federal right. Lee pointed this out to Jackson, and Stuart galloped off to verify it. On the assumption that the road would be found, Jackson said: "My troops will move at four o'clock."

Watching them, unseen, was Private Willie Evans of Parker's battery. He could not hear what they said, but he observed Jackson point in various directions and was "forever after proud of the privilege of having seen them."

It was now about midnight, and Jackson was sleepy. He moved away, unbuckled his sword, leaned it against a tree, and lay down beside it. Pendleton offered his coat, which Jackson refused, but at Pendleton's urging, he consented to accept its cape. Rolling himself in it, he slept.

Lee was still awake when the Reverend Beverly Tucker Lacy came up. Lacy had once had a church in the Wilderness and so knew something of the country and its roads. Listening to him, Lee was encouraged to hope that the road they were seeking would be found. After a brief conference they both lay down on some pine needles before a fire and went to sleep. Lacy awoke sometime later to see Jackson sitting on a cracker box by the fire trying to get warm. When he came forward, Jackson invited him to share his seat, and Lacy, with the help of the map, showed Jackson all the roads he knew of that passed around Hooker's right. He was not completely certain of their course, but he was sure that Colonel Charles C. Wellford, owner of Catherine Furnace, would know better than he, and Wellford had a son who would make a good guide. Jackson told him to wake Hotchkiss, sleeping nearby, and go with him to Catherine Furnace, only two miles away.

Jackson turned back to his fire. Colonel Armistead Long, Lee's military secretary, seeing him huddled, shivering and miserable (he began to suffer from a cold), found a mug of coffee and brought it to him. As he did so, he heard a clanking sound; Jackson's sword had fallen to the ground. Long thought this a bad omen, but he said nothing, picked up the sword, and brought it to Jackson. It was not yet dawn when Lee awoke and joined Jackson by the fire to resume the discussion of the day's plans.

An excited Hotchkiss rode up and, quickly spreading out a map, pointed out the available routes. The road he advised made a wide detour around the Federal right; it was wide enough to accommodate guns and wagons, and the way was generally covered. Studying the map, the two generals agreed on a daring plan. Lee would again and further divide his forces in the face of the enemy.

Jackson would take the bulk of the available force, about 28,000 infantry and 112 guns served by 2,240 gunners, over the route suggested by Hotchkiss; Lee would be left with the divisions of Anderson and McLaws, less than 14,000 men, to face Hooker's 50,000. Jackson's men would have to march across the face of a part of the Federal lines for ten to fourteen miles, depending upon their starting position. Stuart with about 1,500 cavalry would cover the movement. Jackson's brigades were scattered; the two divisions left with Lee must be repositioned; there was much to do, and Jackson would no longer be able to make the four o'clock starting time. Staff officers and couriers were sent galloping off with fresh orders.

The only staff officer who seems to have enjoyed a full night's sleep was young Smith, who did not awake until after daybreak, when someone shouted, "Get up, Smith, the General wants you!"

He found Jackson sitting his horse beside the road, watching troops file past him: "His cap was pulled low over his eyes, and, looking up from under the visor, with lips compressed . . . he nodded at me, and in brief and rapid utterance, without a superfluous word, as though all were distinctly formed in his mind and beyond question, he gave me orders for our wagon and ambulance trains."

Corps wagons and ambulances were to take a road farther south so as not to interfere with the marching troops. To prevent straggling, colonels were ordered to ride in the rear of their regiments with a detachment of strong men carrying bared bayonets.

The day dawned clear and cloudless, and the sun soon warmed the marching men. Lee and Jackson met again briefly. Jackson was seen to point down the road to Catherine Furnace, and Lee was seen to nod. Then they parted, never to meet again.[2] Jackson and his staff took position on the march just behind the leading units.

Secrecy was important to the success of Jackson's enterprise, but early in the morning, as his marching column crossed an open space near Catherine Furnace, his men were spotted by Federal troops of Brigadier General David Birney's division of Sickles's III Corps, who were stationed on a patch of high ground known as Hazel Grove, just over a mile southwest of Chancellorsville. Birney was alerted, and he clearly saw the Confederates on the move, but as they were moving away from him at this point, he assumed that they were retreating in the direction of Gordonsville. He sent this news to Hooker and ordered up a battery to open fire, but it did little damage, for the Confederates found a detour around the exposed space. Jackson ordered the 23rd Georgia to be dropped off at Catherine Furnace to deter any Federal attempt to cut the road with infantry.

Hooker's attention being called to the marching Confederate column, he ordered Sickles to advance on it, but to move cautiously. Birney's division struck the 23rd Georgia, and although the Georgians fought bravely, almost all were eventually killed or captured. The firing caused two of Jackson's brigades to turn back to meet the threat, and Lee, fearful that the column would be severed, sent two brigades, but Sickles, instead of moving smartly forward, remembered his orders to proceed cautiously and paused to reconnoiter and wait for reinforcements.

The captured Georgian being herded to the rear exchanged gibes with their captors, and one Georgian blurted out: "You think you've done a big thing just now, but you wait until Jackson gets around on your rear!" But no one paid attention to the boasting of a prisoner.

About three miles south-southwest of Catherine Furnace the head of Jackson's column changed directions to north-northwest onto Brock

2. Much sentiment was later expended on this last meeting of Lee and Jackson. Everett B. D. Julio painted a romantic eight- by six-foot canvas of the scene, and copperplate etchings of it were hung in thousands of Southern homes. The original painting is now owned by Mr. Robert M. Hincklin, Jr.

Road, which led through heavily wooded country to Wilderness Tavern, about five miles west of Chancellorsville on the Old Turnpike. Jackson, his face pale, his lips compressed, leaned forward over the neck of his horse as if he could in this way hurry along his column, repeating over and over to his men: "Press on, press on."

To the front and right flank of his marching column Confederate cavalry were active. It must have been shortly before two o'clock in the afternoon when they found the exact far right of the Federal line. From a hilltop Brigadier General Fitzhugh Lee looked down on the Federal defenses, all facing south:

> What a sight presented itself before me! Below, and but a few hundred yards distant, ran the Federal line of battle. . . . There were the line of defense, with abatis in front, and long lines of stacked arms in the rear. Two cannon were visible in the part of the line seen. The soldiers were in groups in the rear, laughing, smoking, probably engaged, here and there, in games of cards, and other amusements indulged in while feeling safe and comfortable, awaiting orders. In rear of them were other parties driving up and butchering beeves.

Fitzhugh Lee raced back to the column and found Jackson. "General," he said, "if you will ride with me, halting your column here, I will show you the enemy's right."

Jackson, taking only a single courier, followed Lee up Brock Road, across the Plank Road, and then off to the right through trees and undergrowth to a small hill. Dismounting, they climbed the hill and, parting the boughs of trees, looked down on the unsuspecting Federals. Jackson gazed intently at the scene before him, and, said Lee, "his eyes burned with a brilliant glow, lighting up a sad face." He watched motionless for five minutes; then Lee saw his lips moving and said to himself: "Oh, beware of rashness, General Hooker! Stonewall Jackson is praying in full view of your right flank."

Finally Jackson turned to his courier and said, "Tell General [Robert E.] Rodes to move across the Old Plank Road. Halt when he gets to the turnpike, and I will join him there."

Fitzhugh Lee, who did not know Jackson well, expected some thanks for his discovery, but without an acknowledgment of any kind, Jackson simply ordered him to supply cavalry support for Paxton's brigade, which he sent with two batteries a short way down the Plank Road as a flank guard.

When the head of the main column reached the Old Turnpike, Jackson headed them east for another three or four miles. He was now well behind the right of the Federal line.

At about three o'clock Jackson dismounted and sat on a stump to write a note to General Lee: "The enemy has made a stand at Chancellor's[3] which is about 2 miles from Chancellorsville. I hope as soon as practicable to attack. I trust that an ever kind Providence will bless us with success." To this laconic message he added a postscript: "The leading division is up and the other two appear to be well closed." He did not know that the two brigades in Hill's division that had dropped back to help the Georgians at Catherine Furnace had not yet come up. It would be nightfall before they rejoined.

Colonel Thomas Mumford, who had been cadet adjutant on the day Jackson arrived at VMI, was in contact with Jackson frequently that day. Noting the number of VMI graduates and former VMI professors in II Corps, he commented on it to Jackson, who replied: "Yes, the Institute will be heard from today."[4]

It was, of course, impossible for so many Confederates to be where they were without detection, and indeed, Federal outposts, pickets, patrols, officers making personal reconnaissances, and a signal station reported seeing them. Federal cavalry skirmished with Stuart's men, and captured Confederates brashly boasted that they had been a part of a huge army, but when the reports reached the headquarters of Howard and of Hooker, they were largely discounted by their staffs. One officer who did believe them was Lieutenant Colonel C. W. Friend at the headquarters of Brigadier General Charles Devens, Jr., who commanded the westernmost division. When Devens would not listen to him, Friend went to corps headquarters, where he was told to hold his tongue and not start a panic.

Hooker, after personally inspecting his defenses on that morning, arrived back at his headquarters about nine-thirty and found Birney's report of the westward-moving column seen near Catherine Furnace. Turning to a map, he tried to absorb this information. As though

3. Chancellor's (better known as Dowdall's Tavern) was the farm of the Reverend Melzi Chancellor west of Chancellorsville.

4. Sixteen senior officers of II Corps had been professors or were graduates of the Virginia Military Institute, including seven generals, six colonels, and three lieutenant colonels. There were also many company officers who had attended VMI, and probably most had studied artillery tactics and natural and experimental philosophy under Jackson.

talking to himself, he said: "It can't be retreat. Retreat without a fight? That is not Lee. If not retreat, what is it? Lee is trying to flank me."

Hooker had hit upon the truth, and he at once sent a message to Howard:

> The right of your line does not appear to be strong enough. No artificial defenses worth naming have been thrown up, and there appears to be a scarcity of troops at that point, and not . . . as favorably posted as might be. We have good reason to suppose that the enemy is moving to our right. Please advance your pickets for purposes of observation as far as may be safe, in order to obtain timely information of their approach.

Later Hooker maintained that "Howard had culpably disobeyed his orders and neglected his duties," but Howard claimed that the dispatch had never reached him. Nevertheless, he did advance his pickets somewhat. Late in the morning he reported that Brigadier General Devens had also observed Confederates moving west, and he assured Hooker that he was "taking measures to resist an attack from the west." But his measures were halfhearted and insubstantial. Jackson had taken the line of least expectation, and it was difficult for the Federal commanders to realize that the Confederate force on their flank was a grave threat; none could imagine that it consisted of the largest part of Lee's army.

Ironically the Federal sighting of Jackson's moving column at Catherine Furnace had, in fact, worked to the Confederate advantage, for Sickles had tried to pursue; he had called for and received reinforcements that removed Howard's reserve, and by the time Jackson was ready to attack, Sickles had sent twenty-two thousand men marching southwest, away from the action.

Late in the afternoon Jackson began forming a double line of battle, 150 yards between the lines, that stretched north and south on a four-brigade front of seventeen regiments for 2 miles across both the Old Turnpike and the Plank Road. Skirmishers were out. Rodes's division was in the lead. The lines were uneven, and not every regiment correctly got into its assigned position, but they would be advancing through rough, rugged country, and time was of crucial importance, for already the sun was beginning to sink. A third of the infantry had not come up (Hill's two brigades had still not arrived from Catherine Furnace), but Jackson had about 18,500 infantry in line and most of his artillery in position. He could wait no longer.

The troops had had a long march, and they were hungry, but all knew that they had reached an important position on the Federal flank, and morale was high. Jackson's orders to his commanders were simple. They were to charge straight forward through the Federal positions. If there was a stout defense at Chancellorsville, they could wait for the artillery; otherwise they must push forward with all possible speed. If a brigade commander in the first line needed reinforcement, he could call upon the brigade in his rear without reference to divisional commanders.

Shortly after five o'clock the lines were formed as well as they were going to be, extending through forest and clearings and across the roads. Jackson sat his horse, watch in hand. The sun would set about seven o'clock; the end of evening nautical twilight would come a few minutes after eight, but in the Wilderness night would fall much sooner. Turning to Rodes, he asked quietly, "Are you ready, General Rodes?"

"Yes, sir."

"You can go forward then," he said.

The commands rippled along the lines as the men stepped quickly forward. There was a hitch in the beginning, for not all the skirmishers had heard the orders and the battle lines closed in on them, but this was only temporary, and the skirmishers ran ahead.

When the Federal outposts were hit, there was a crash of musketry, and this was a signal to break silence. Bugles sounded the advance, and a roar sprang from the thousands of young throats as they bounded forward. Confederate guns raced down the Old Turnpike, swung into battery, and sent round shot straight down the road.

The first intimation some Federal troops had that something extraordinary was afoot was the spectacle of partridges and quail flying up from the thickets while deer leaped out of the woods to run through their camp, followed by rabbits, squirrels, foxes, and other small creatures. Jackson's battle lines came sweeping down the Northern line, driving game and the panicked Federals before them. Howard's XI Corps collapsed. Brigadier General Carl Schurz, commanding the 3rd Division of XI Corps, said later:

> The officers had hardly time to give a command when almost the whole of General [Nathaniel C.] McLean's brigade, mixed up with a number of Colonel [Leopold] von Gilsa's men, came rushing down the road from General Devens' headquarters in wild confusion, and, worse than that, the battery of the First Division broke in upon the right at a full run. This confused mass of guns, caissons,

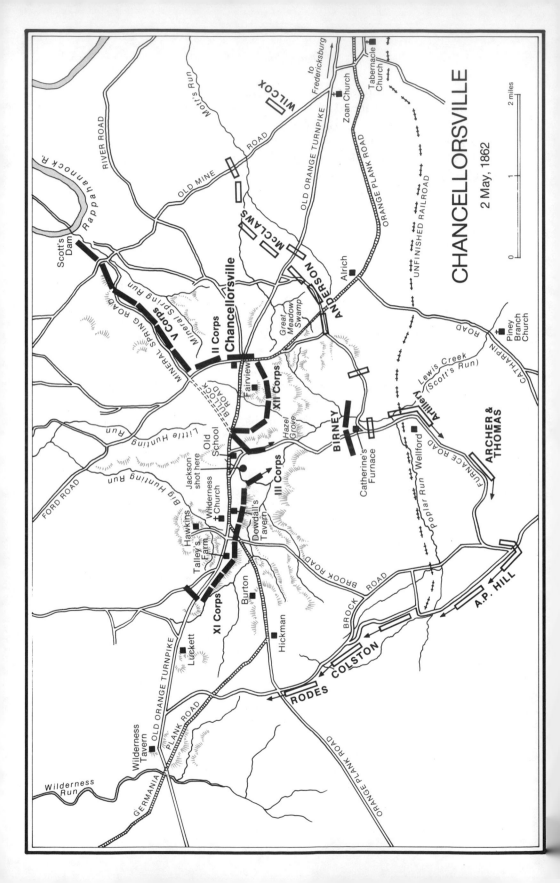

CHANCELLORSVILLE
2 May, 1862

Rappahannock R.

RIVER ROAD

Mott's Run

WILCOX

to Fredericksburg

Tabernacle Church

Zoan Church

OLD ORANGE TURNPIKE

OLD MINE ROAD

ORANGE PLANK ROAD

Scott's Dam

MINERAL SPRING ROAD

Mineral Spring Run

MCLAWS

ANDERSON

Alrich

UNFINISHED RAILROAD

V Corps

II Corps

Chancellorsville

Great Meadow Swamp

Piney Branch Church

CATHARPIN ROAD

ROAD

Fairview

BULOCK ROAD

XII Corps

Hazel Grove

Lewis Creek (Scott's Run)

Artillery

FORD ROAD

Little Hunting Run

Old School

Jackson shot here

Big Hunting Run

Wilderness Church

Hawkins

Talley's Farm

Dowdall's Tavern

III Corps

BIRNEY

Catherine's Furnace

Wellford

Poplar Run

FURNACE ROAD

ARCHER & THOMAS

A.P. HILL

XI Corps

Burton

Luckett

Hickman

BROOK ROAD

BROCK ROAD

COLSTON

RODES

Wilderness Tavern

OLD ORANGE TURNPIKE

PLANK ROAD

GERMANIA PLANK ROAD

ORANGE PLANK ROAD

Wilderness Run

0   1   2 miles

horses, and men broke lengthwise through the ranks of my regiments deployed on the road.

Schurz had tried to get his men in a line facing west, but Jackson's onslaught overpowered him, and his division crumpled. Colonel Edward Porter Alexander reported that the Federals were thrown into "such a wild panic as was never seen in either army before or after; not even after Bull Run in '61."

General Howard rode out from his headquarters at Dowdall's Tavern toward the firing and was soon surrounded by fleeing soldiers. A Pennsylvania cavalryman saw him "in the middle of the road and mounted, his maimed arm embracing a standard of colors that some regiment had deserted, while with his sound arm he was gesticulating to the men to make a stand by their flag. With bared head he was pleading with his soldiers, literally weeping as he entreated the unheeding horde. . . . At last the seething, surging sea of humanity broke over the feeble barrier, and General Howard and his officers were carried away by main force with the tide."

Not far away, at the Federal army's headquarters at Chancellorsville, Hooker and two aides were resting on the porch at the end of the fine spring afternoon. The rumble of cannon they assumed was Sickles pounding on Lee's columns. Thanks to an acoustical effect which sometimes occurred on nineteenth-century battlefields, they were unable to detect the direction of the sounds or its proximity.[5] But when one of the aides, Captain Harry Russell, stepped into the yard and looked toward the west through his field glasses, he exclaimed, "My God, here they come!"

Hooker and his staff mounted posthaste and galloped toward the battle. They encountered, as had Howard, the stream of panic-stricken men from a broken division, no longer soldiers but a mob.

As the hungry Confederates passed through the camps where the fleeing Federals had been cooking their suppers, they sometimes paused to scoop up a cup of coffee or to spear with their bayonets a piece of beef. As the second Confederate line caught up with the first, regiments intermingled, and unit cohesion was lost, but they kept moving.

5. Called an acoustic shadow, it is a phenomenon in which sounds of battle cannot be heard when the fighting is close but can be heard dozens of miles away. The sounds might be blocked by folds in the ground, woods, or air density. The phenomenon was noted in several Civil War battles, including Seven Days, Seven Pines, and Perryville, as well as Chancellorsville.

Once he had launched his men on their wild charge, there was little more that Jackson could do. Captain Charles Randolph, chief of his couriers, saw him at one point praying beside the road, but perhaps he was merely raising his hand to ease his arm. Captain Richard Eggleston Wilbourne, his signal officer, later said, "I have never seen him so well pleased with the progress and results of a fight."

But now that disorder was overtaking his troops, he personally rode out to try to straighten out the tangled commands. Reaching the front, he continued to urge his men forward. Some of his staff gathered around him: Morrison, Boswell, Wilbourne. A courier named David J. Kyle arrived with a message from Stuart, and as he was familiar with the region, Jackson told him: "Keep along with me."

Night fell, but Jackson did not want to stop, and when Hill's division was finally assembled, he pushed it forward. With Kyle and the handful of staff officers, Jackson wandered about, trying to understand the lay of the land, where the roads came from and where they went. He decided to follow one known as the Mountain Road, which made a bow north of the Plank Road and then rejoined it. He and his party passed through the lines of the 18th North Carolina without attracting attention and rode out toward the picket line. When they halted for a moment, they could hear clearly the sound of axes and the commands of Federal officers. Jackson sat his horse without a word. He seemed unusually thoughtful to his staff. Then he turned and rode slowly back the way he had come.

Colonel Thomas J. Purdie of the 18th North Carolina had ridden with his adjutant up the Plank Road to check on his advanced outposts. His unit had been marching and fighting all day; only a short time before, it had repulsed an attack by the 8th Pennsylvania Cavalry, and all were on the qui vive. When Purdie and his adjutant heard bursts of firing ahead, they whirled their horses around and came galloping back into the lines of their own regiment. Their quick return alarmed their men still further, and some fired nervously into the trees.

Later a curious disparity was revealed in descriptions of the visibility at this time. John C. West of the 4th Texas said, "It was a beautiful moonlight night." I. Roseneau of the 4th Georgia remembered it as "the darkest night I ever saw." Lieutenant Smith in his account speaks of "a bright beam of moonlight" about a half hour after the shots were fired. There was indeed a full moon that night, but it was probably just rising as, shortly after eight o'clock, Jackson rode back from his reconnaissance.

A. P. Hill and some of his staff had joined Jackson on the Mountain Road about nine o'clock, swelling the party to about twenty men. Jackson said: "General Hill, as soon as you are ready, push right forward; allow nothing to stop you; press on to the United States Ford." As the group rode slowly back, they approached the right of the line formed by the nervous 18th North Carolina. Its scattered firing startled Sorrel, and Jackson briefly lost control as the horse swerved. Holding his reins in his left hand, he raised his right to protect himself from the overhanging boughs of the scrub oak trees. Hill shouted, "Cease firing! Cease firing!" but the erratic firing continued. Young Morrison pushed ahead and riding directly toward the unseen men of the 18th North Carolina, he called, "Cease firing! You are firing into your own men!"

But twenty-three-year-old Major John Decatur Barry of the 18th yelled: "Who gave that order? It's a lie! Pour it into them, boys!"[6]

As Captain Alfred Tolar of that regiment later recalled, "the tramp of thirty horsemen advancing through a heavy forest at a rapid gait seemed to the average infantryman like a brigade of cavalry."

There was a crash of musketry, and bullets ripped into Jackson's group of horsemen. Jackson was struck in the left arm about three inches below the shoulder joint, "the ball dividing the main artery and fracturing the bone," and by a bullet that struck the outside of his left forearm an inch below the elbow and emerged on the opposite side of the wrist. His right hand was hit in the palm, the bullet penetrating but not completely emerging at the back of his hand.

Sorrel bolted to the rear, and Jackson's head crashed into the limb of an oak tree. Still, he remained in the saddle and with his injured right hand turned Sorrel back. Captain Wilbourne, unscathed, seized Sorrel's reins and braced Jackson in the saddle. Lieutenant Wynn, a signal officer, rode up and supported him on the other side. Jackson, dazed, stared toward the lines of the 18th North Carolina and exclaimed: "Wild fire, that, sir. Wild fire."

"They certainly must be our troops," said Wilbourne. Seeing only the wounded hand, he asked, "How do you feel, General? Can you move your fingers?"

Trying to learn the extent of his wounds, Wilbourne touched Jack-

---

6. No stigma appears to have attached to John Barry for having been responsible for Jackson's wounding. After the Battle of Chancellorsville he was promoted colonel of the 18th North Carolina and on 3 August 1864 was appointed brigadier general. He was wounded shortly thereafter, however, and his appointment was not confirmed. He survived the war and edited a newspaper in Wilmington until he died in 1867 at the age of twenty-seven.

son's left arm. The pain was too intense. "You had better put me down," said Jackson. "My arm is broken."

He was so weak that he could not remove his feet from the stirrups. Wynn and Wilbourne with difficulty lowered him to the ground and propped him against a pine tree. Wilbourne crouched beside him, and Jackson's head fell against his breast. "Captain, I wish you would get me a skilled surgeon," he murmured.

Wilbourne sent Wynn to find Dr. McGuire or any other surgeon, with the caution to tell no one that Jackson had been wounded. Lieutenant Wynn rode off, unsure of his direction. Before him a horse and rider emerged from the darkness and Wynn demanded angrily which regiment had fired. Without a response the horseman disappeared; he has never been identified.[7]

Wilbourne, alone with Jackson, gently removed the general's field glasses and haversack, loosened his clothing, and with a penknife began to cut the sleeve of the rubber coat he was wearing.

The 18th North Carolina musketry had been devastating. At least eleven in the party were killed or wounded by the fusillade. Of those near Jackson, only Wilbourne and Wynn had survived unhurt and still mounted. Boswell and a captain from the 9th Virginia Cavalry were mortally wounded, and a signaler, Sergeant Will Cunliffe, was killed outright. Nineteen-year-old Captain Murray Forbes Taylor on Hill's staff, a VMI cadet whose education had been interrupted by the war, galloped forward to stop the firing, but his horse was shot and fell on him. Lieutenant Morrison on the same errand escaped injury; riding into the ranks of the 18th North Carolina, he quelled the firing and rode back to find Jackson. Hill had been some distance away from Jackson, and he, too, had escaped the fire. Fourteen horses were killed; others had bolted; one carried its rider into the Union lines.

Hill and Captain Benjamin Watkins Leigh found Jackson and Wilbourne under the pine tree. Hill knelt beside the man he had so intensely disliked and asked tenderly if the wound was painful.

"Very painful," Jackson replied. "The arm is broken."

Hill, too, tried to make the suffering man comfortable. Drawing

---

7. Joseph Warren Revere, a grandson of Paul Revere's, claimed to have met Jackson on a steamboat in 1852. He was a brigadier general at Chancellorsville, and he later claimed that he was the unidentified horseman that night. Revere was commanding a division at this time, but because he retreated in the face of Jackson's charge, he was court-martialed and dismissed from the service, though Lincoln later allowed him to resign.

off Jackson's gauntlets, he found them full of blood. James Smith came up. He had not been with the party on the road but had hurried forward when he learned of Jackson's wound.

With Wynn still gone, Hill dispatched Captain Leigh to find a surgeon and an ambulance. Leigh found General W. Dorsey Pender, who sent for Dr. Richard R. Barr, an assistant surgeon in his brigade. Barr could not provide an ambulance; none was available within at least a mile, but he hastened back with Leigh to see what he could do.

Those waiting with Jackson tried futilely to staunch the flow of blood with their handkerchiefs, and they contrived a sling for his fast-swelling arm. Someone produced a flask of brandy, and Jackson drank some and then drank heavily from a canteen of water. Wilbourne was worried about his wounded right hand, but Jackson brushed this care aside. "Never mind that. It is a mere trifle," he said. When Barr arrived, Jackson whispered anxiously to Hill: "Is he a skilled surgeon?" Hill answered that he was and added reassuringly that nothing drastic would be done until Dr. McGuire had seen him. "Very good," said Jackson. Dr. Barr examined the wound but saw that there was nothing that could be done until Jackson reached a field hospital.

Captain R. H. T. Adams, the signal officer who had been embroiled in the Hill-Jackson feud, appeared and joined the group of officers around Jackson. He left the group to investigate when he heard suspicious noises. Adams had gone only about ten yards when he called out, "Halt! Surrender! Fire on them if they don't surrender!" Hill jumped up and drew his pistol. Two Federal soldiers, perhaps skirmishers, quietly surrendered.

At this point Morrison rode up with the news that the Federals were only fifty yards away and advancing. They must move the general, and he proposed that they carry him, but Jackson protested: "No. If you will help me, I can walk."

When they helped him to his feet, his wounds bled so profusely that Captain Leigh's uniform was covered by his blood. They had taken only a few painful steps before a litter arrived, carried by two ambulance men. They helped Jackson lie down on it, and Leigh, Smith, and the two ambulance men carried him, others walking beside and behind, some leading their horses, shielding him as best they could from the Federal artillery that had opened fire. The little entourage of officers excited the curiosity of the soldiers as they passed, but in answer to their questions, Wilbourne said only that they were helping a friend. Jackson whispered, "When asked, just say it is a Confederate officer." Still, the soldiers crowded around, and Sergeant Tom Fogg of the 55th

Virginia, looking closely, exclaimed, "Great God! It is General Jackson!"

Federal artillery fire increased. There was considerable confusion in the Confederate lines, and some panicked. Wilbourne later said that "such was the disorder that I thought that General Jackson and party would certainly fall into the hands of the enemy." In places the Wilderness was set afire, and amid the din of crashing shells could be heard the screams of horses and wounded men dying in the flames. Elsewhere on the field Hill was wounded in the calf by a shell, and Pender, too, was injured. Crutchfield was painfully wounded in the leg.

The miserable little group carrying Jackson pressed on in the dark amid the din. A round of grapeshot ripped both arms of one of the ambulance men (John H. Johnson, 22nd Virginia), and he dropped his end of the litter, but Leigh managed to catch hold before Jackson could fall. Jackson again tried to walk, and they came upon Pender, wounded but still on his feet, who exclaimed, "Oh, General, I am sorry to see you have been wounded!" He had bad news to report: "The lines here are so much broken that I fear we will have to fall back."

At this Jackson, speaking low but firmly, said: "You must hold your ground, General Pender! You must hold your ground, sir!"

Jackson could stand no longer and asked to be lowered to the ground. He was again put on the litter. He asked for spirits, but there was none left. The group pushed slowly through the woods for a half mile, the undergrowth dense and the way difficult. Then one of his bearers caught his foot in a vine, stumbled, and lost his hold. Jackson fell heavily to the ground onto his wounded arm and shoulder. The pain was so intense that he groaned and almost fainted. It seemed to him that his end had come, and for a brief moment, he said later, he had "perfect peace," believing he would momentarily find himself in heaven. But more pain awaited him.

Smith asked stupidly, as people often do in such situations, "General, are you much hurt?"

"No, Mr. Smith," he answered. "Don't trouble yourself about me."

In spite of the increased danger it presented, Jackson was carried out of the woods onto the road, then onto a side road running south. When at last they encountered an ambulance, it was full. Crutchfield lay in it and could not be moved, but a Major Rogers[8] was considered

8. The exact identity of "Major Rogers" has never been determined, but Douglas Southall Freeman has suggested that it was perhaps Captain H. A. Rogers of the

to have a lesser wound, and at the order of Dr. William R. Whitehead,[9] who was in charge, he was taken out and Jackson given his place. They were still four miles from the nearest field hospital.

Morrison climbed into the ambulance and tried to hold his brother-in-law's wounded arm to protect it from the jolts and the lurching of the ambulance over the rutted roads. They drove back onto the Plank Road and then turned west onto the land owned by Melzi Chancellor. Jackson's pain was so intense that he again asked for spirits. When a bottle was found, he drank gratefully.

At last they reached the Melzi Chancellor house, site of McGuire's field hospital, and Dr. McGuire stepped forward and asked, "I hope you are not badly hurt, General."

"I am badly injured, Doctor. I fear I am dying," Jackson answered calmly. He paused and added: "I am glad you have come. I think the wound in my shoulder is still bleeding."

McGuire, shortly after the war, wrote a description of Jackson's condition as he found him:

> His clothes were saturated with blood, and haemorrhage was still going on from the wound. Compression of an artery with the finger arrested it, until lights being procured from the ambulance, the handkerchief which had slipped a little, was readjusted. His calmness amid the dangers which surrounded him, and at the supposed presence of death, and his uniform politeness, which did not forsake him, even under these, the most trying circumstances, were remarkable. His complete control, too, over his mind, enfeebled as it was, by loss of blood, pain, etc., was wonderful.
>
> His suffering at this time was intense; his hands were cold, his skin clammy, his face pale, and his lips compressed and bloodless; not a groan escaped him—not a sign of suffering, except the slight corrugation of his brow, and the fixed rigid face, and the thin lips, so tightly compressed, that the impression of the teeth could be seen through them. Except these, he controlled by his iron will, all evidence of emotion, and more difficult than this even, he controlled that disposition to restlessness, which many of us have observed upon the field of battle, attending great loss of blood.

13th North Carolina in Pender's brigade. The ambulance was probably little better than a wagon with inadequate springs and a covered top; wheels would be of wood with metal rims.

9. Dr. Whitehead was graduated from VMI the year Jackson arrived there as a professor. After obtaining his medical degree at the University of Pennsylvania, he served as a surgeon in the Russian Army at Sebastopol during the Crimean War.

More whiskey and some morphine were given Jackson, and his painful journey continued westward, for the II Corps hospital with Dr. Harvey Black in charge, set up in an open field just north of the Old Turnpike near the intersection of the Germanna Road, was still more than two miles away. (Confederate medical arrangements had improved little since the start of the war.) They were now well back of the lines. Torches could be used to light the way, and the driver of the ambulance could avoid some of the worst of the holes in the road.

McGuire rode in the front of the ambulance with his finger on the artery just above Jackson's wound. Unable to contain himself, Crutchfield groaned aloud, and Jackson pulled McGuire's head down to ask if he was dangerously wounded. "No, only painfully hurt," McGuire assured him.

"I am glad it is no worse," said Jackson.

Soon after, Crutchfield inquired about Jackson's injuries and, when told that the general was seriously wounded, cried out, "Oh, my God!"

Thinking the cry was one of pain, Jackson asked that the ambulance be stopped and that Dr. McGuire see what he could do for the sufferer.

Word of Jackson's coming had reached Dr. Black, and he had a warm tent, blankets, whiskey, and water waiting for him. It was about eleven-thirty when the ambulance arrived, more than two hours since he had been wounded. McGuire waited another two and a half hours for him to recover somewhat from shock, and then, about two o'clock Sunday morning, with Dr. Black, Dr. R. T. Coleman, and a Dr. Walls,[10] he examined Jackson's wounds and told him that amputation would probably be required, asking "if it were found necessary, whether it should be done at once."

"Yes, certainly, Dr. McGuire," Jackson replied. "Do for me whatever you think best."

Dr. Coleman administered the chloroform, and as Jackson felt its effect, he murmured, "What an infinite blessing." He repeated the word *blessing* several times until he lost consciousness.

Lieutenant Smith held the lights for the doctors. A round ball of the sort used in the smoothbore Springfield muskets with which some Confederates were still armed was removed first from the back of his right hand. The bullet had entered the palm, fracturing two bones.

10. This may have been Dr. J. William Walls who had been on the Winchester Medical College faculty before the war.

"The left arm was then amputated," reported McGuire, "about two inches below the shoulder, very rapidly, and with slight loss of blood, the ordinary circular operation having been made."[11]. McGuire made the incision and sawed off the bone. Dr. Black, an internist, monitored Jackson's heart during the operation, and Dr. Walls tied the arteries.[12] The abrasions on his face caused by the tree branch were simply dressed with isinglass plaster.[13]

At some time after he regained consciousness, probably when Lieutenant Smith brought the cup of coffee his doctor had ordered, Jackson inquired if he had said anything while under the influence of the chloroform. Smith assured him that he had not. "I have always thought it wrong," said Jackson, "to administer chloroform in cases where there is a probability of immediate death. . . . I should dislike above all things to enter eternity in such a condition." But it brought, he admitted, "the most delightful physical sensation I ever experienced." He remembered hearing "the most delightful music that ever

---

11. The circular technique was the oldest form of limb amputation, dating back at least to Aulus Cornelius Celsus (first century A.D.), but it is rarely used today. In this procedure the skin only was incised with Lister knives and reflected so as to form the flap. Then the muscle was cut, and the skin and soft tissue, including muscle and muscle covering, were drawn back, either by a retractor or by the hands of an assistant. The bone was sawed, the arteries were tied, and the operation was completed by replacing the cuff of skin and muscle, which acted as a cushion, and by bandaging the wound. According to Dr. Frank Hastings Hamilton (*Treatise of Military Surgery and Hygiene*, 1865), "the bone should be well dissected up before it is severed. The length of the flap is always of less consequence than the depth at which the section of bone is made underneath the mass of flesh."

12. The survival rate for those who had upper-arm amputations was better than those who had leg amputations, but they were still not good. Confederate fatality rates following amputation are unavailable, but they were probably comparable with those in the Union army, where of 6,500 upper-arm amputations, 1,273 died, a fatality rate of 24 percent. Because of the special care taken of Lieutenant General Jackson, his chances of survival were considerably better.

13. Jackson's amputated arm was buried by the Reverend Beverly Tucker Lacy in his family burial plot at Elwood, the plantation then owned by his brother, Major J. Horace Lacy. The marker is still there by a small stand of cedar trees surrounded by a knee-high post-and-rail fence. Elwood, just south of Route 3 and east of Route 20, is now the property of the National Park Service, but for reasons best known to it, the property is not open to the public. In 1921 the Marine Corps held maneuvers in the Wilderness, and Brigadier General (as he then was) Smedley Darlington Butler, curious to know if the arm was still buried, had it dug up and examined. Satisfied that the exhumed arm was genuine, he had it placed in a metal box and reburied. He also had a bronze plaque recording his action placed on the stone, but this has since been removed by the Park Service.

greeted my ears," and he assumed now that this must have been McGuire sawing the bone.

About three o'clock that morning, while Jackson was quietly sleeping, Major Pendleton arrived and asked to speak to him. McGuire was reluctant to permit it, but Pendleton pleaded that A. P. Hill had been wounded, the troops were in disarray, and Stuart, who was now in command, had sent him to see General Jackson. The "safety of the army and the success of the cause" depended upon it. Jackson had, as usual, told no one of his plans, and only he could enlighten Stuart.

McGuire led him into the tent, where Jackson was now awake. "Well, Major, I am glad to see you," he said. "I thought you were killed."

Pendleton explained the command problems which had so suddenly and unexpectedly fallen into the lap of Stuart and delivered his messages. Jackson, alert, asked several questions rapidly. McGuire later described his reaction:

> When they were answered, he remained silent for a moment, evidently trying to think; he contracted his brow, set his mouth, and for some moments was obviously endeavoring to concentrate his thoughts. For a moment it was believed he had succeeded, for his nostrils dilated, and his eye flashed its old fire, but it was only for a moment; his face relaxed again, and presently he said very feebly and sadly: "I don't know—I can't tell; say to General Stuart he must do what he thinks best.

Not even Jackson's remarkable willpower could bring his mind to focus properly on the complex problems facing his command. His fighting days were over. His command and the Confederacy had now to pay for his excessive secrecy. As Winston Churchill was later to say of this episode in history, "Thus on small agate points do the balances of the world turn."

Soon after Pendleton left, Jackson fell asleep, and he slept until nine o'clock that morning, when he woke to the sound of the guns renewing the battle.

33

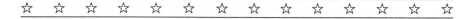

Last Days

Captain Wilbourne, charged with informing Lee of Jackson's fate, arrived at Lee's headquarters about three o'clock in the morning. An aide awakened the general, and Wilbourne poured out his story of the day's events. When he came to Jackson's wounding, Lee moaned and, according to Wilbourne, almost wept and said, "Ah, Captain, any victory is dearly bought which deprives us of the services of General Jackson, even for a short time."

When Wilbourne plunged into an account of Jackson's horrendous journey back to the hospital, Lee stopped him. "Ah, don't talk about it," he said. "Thank God it is no worse."

Wilbourne passed on to the swift changes of command in II Corps from Jackson to Hill, briefly to Rodes, and then to Stuart. Both Stuart and Rodes hoped that Lee himself would come to confer with them, he said, and ventured his opinion that he believed Jackson's intent had been to cut the road leading to United States Ford.

Lee exclaimed, "Those people must be pressed today," and at once wrote a dispatch for Stuart which began: "It is necessary that the glorious victory thus far achieved be prosecuted with the utmost vigor, and the enemy given no time to rally." He stressed the need to unite the two wings of his army in the Wilderness, but he made no mention of cutting off the roads leading to the fords.

Hotchkiss arrived at Lee's headquarters about a half hour later, and he, too, found that Lee did not want to hear the details of Jackson's wounds. "I know all about it and do not wish to hear any more," he said. "It is too painful."

Lee dispatched another note to Stuart, again emphasizing the need to unite Stuart's wing with his. Stuart indeed acted energetically this day. He drove the Federals back and united with the divisions with Lee. There were bitter battles with charging Confederates crying, "Remember Jackson!"

About nine o'clock on this Sunday morning Jackson seemed almost free of pain and was comfortable enough to take some nourishment. His mind was clear, and he sent his young brother-in-law Lieutenant Morrison to Richmond, where Anna was staying, to tell her of his wound and bring her back to him. Smith was told to stay by him; the other staff officers were ordered to return to their duties. He then dictated to Smith a note for Lee.

At about eleven-thirty that morning Lee sat his horse at Chancellorsville, where the main building was still burning, surrounded by his exhausted, dirty, but victorious troops, who greeted him with loud and repeated cheers. He was handed Jackson's note (now lost), which appears simply to have reported the wounding and the changes of command. Lee, turning to Major Charles Marshall, an aide, dictated a reply: "General: I have just received your note, informing me that you were wounded. I cannot express my regret at the occurrence. Could I have directed events, I would have chosen for the good of the country to be disabled in your stead. I congratulate you upon the victory, which is due to your skill and energy."

That afternoon, when this was read to Jackson, he turned his face away and said: "General Lee is very kind, but he should give the praise to God."

About midmorning Jackson complained to McGuire of a pain in his right side; he thought he had struck a stone or a stump when he fell from the litter. McGuire examined him but could find no bruises; that his patient seemed to be breathing easily indicated no damage to his lungs. McGuire recommended "some simple application" and hoped the pain would disappear.

Later that morning the Reverend B. Tucker Lacy visited Jackson and, seeing his stump, could not resist exclaiming, "Oh, General, what a calamity!" But Jackson refused to see his mutilation in such a light. The Heavenly Father had undoubtedly caused him to lose his arm for some good reason, he said, and he was sure that eventually, in this life or in the next, he would learn His purpose. He earnestly assured Lacy that even if he had the power to replace his arm, he would not do it unless he was certain that it met with his maker's approval. "You never saw me more perfectly contented than I am today," he said.

He wanted to talk about the moment of his fall from the litter when he had found peace in the thought that he was dying. "It has been a precious experience to me that I was brought face to face with death, and found all was well," he said.

Later in the day Henry Kyd Douglas came with news of the progress of the battle. When he lauded the fine showing of the Stonewall Brigade, Jackson gave the "peculiar shake from side to side" of his head and said, "Good, good." Turning to McGuire, standing beside him, he said with some of his old vigor that the men of the brigade would "some day be proud to say to their children, 'I was one of the Stonewall Brigade.'"

He wanted more news of the battle, and Smith told him that Paxton had been killed.

"Paxton? Paxton?" he murmured in disbelief.

"Yes, sir," said Smith. "He has fallen."

Jackson turned his face to the wall, closed his eyes, and lay in silence. Smith told him that Paxton had had a premonition of his death and so had given minute instructions and had read devoutly from the New Testament just before leading his brigade forward for the last time.

"That's good. That's good," said Jackson.

About eight o'clock that night he reported that the pain in his side was better.

Unknown to any of the Confederates as yet, a cannonball had struck a porch pillar against which Hooker was leaning. Hooker was knocked unconscious, and for a time neither he nor his surgeons were sure that he could resume his command; the Federal army was for several hours leaderless.

Lee, fearful that some Federal troops at Ely's Ford on the Rapidan might swoop around and capture Jackson, sent orders to McGuire that his patient was to be moved to Guiney's Station as soon as his condition permitted. Jackson protested that he was fine where he was, that he preferred a tent, that Anna would find quarters in a nearby house. "If the enemy does come," he argued, "I am not afraid of them. I have always been kind to their wounded, and I am sure they will be kind to me." He had no objection to Guiney's Station as a resting place. He knew Thomas Coleman Chandler and his family, who had a comfortable house there on a 740-acre plantation called Fairfield, but he had hoped after a few days to go to Richmond and then back to his quiet home and the mountain air of Lexington, where he was certain he would completely recover.

That night Lee sent a second, more urgent message. Sedgwick had stormed Marye's Heights above Fredericksburg and was now advancing on his rear. Jackson must be transferred to Guiney's Station. Preparations were made to move him the following morning.

Jackson, aware of the discontent among the soldiers when surgeons, always in short supply after a battle, left the field to attend to wounded generals, had given orders that if he was moved, McGuire was not to accompany him, but in his second message Lee particularly ordered McGuire to turn over his duties to the next senior surgeon and attend to Jackson. "General Lee has always been very kind to me, and I thank him," Jackson said gratefully.

Early on the morning of 4 May Jackson was placed on a mattress in an ambulance, and again his companion was the wounded Crutchfield. It was twenty-four miles to Guiney's Station, and the road was rough. Hotchkiss had chosen the route and had gone ahead with pioneers to clear obstructions and fill in the worst holes. Nevertheless, the road was crowded with walking wounded, other ambulances, and commissary, quartermaster, and ordnance wagons, plying between the railway station and the front, and teamsters were not noted for civility or courtesy when required to force their mules to wrench their vehicles out of comfortable ruts.

Word spread ahead of them that it was Jackson in the ambulance, and there were cries of "It's Old Jack!" and "Clear the road!" Some cheered; some stood silently with hats off as if the ambulance was a hearse. At Spotsylvania Court House old men and women lined the road.

In the first hours Jackson bore up well under the strain of the move. He was alert and talkative, chatting with McGuire or with Smith and the Reverend Lacy, who were accompanying the ambulance on horseback. Asked what he thought of Hooker's strategy, he replied: "It was, in the main, a good conception, sir, an excellent plan. But he should not have sent away his cavalry; that was his great blunder. It was that which enabled me to turn him, without his being aware of it, and to take him by the rear. Had he kept his cavalry with him, his plan would have been a very good one."

He thought his own operations were a "great success," he said, "the most successful movement of my life. But I have received far more credit for it than I deserve. Most men will think that I had planned it all from the first, but it was not so. I simply took advantage of circumstances as they were presented to me in the providence of God. I feel that His hand led me."

He spoke again of the Stonewall Brigade, members of which had applied for official recognition of the name. He felt they had earned it. The name Stonewall, he said, "ought to be attached wholly to the men of the brigade, and not to me." They were, he declared, "a noble body of patriots."

He was much affected by the deaths of Paxton and Boswell[1] and referred to them as gallant officers of great promise. He spoke of the gallantry of Robert E. Rodes and said he ought to be promoted immediately. He spoke highly of Colston (later much criticized by others and transferred out of the Army of Northern Virginia) and of Colonel Edward Willis of the 12th Georgia.

As the day wore on, hot and dusty, the long, jolting ride began to wear on Jackson. In the afternoon he felt a slight nausea, and he suggested to McGuire that perhaps a damp cloth over his abdomen would be helpful. The doctor agreed, and a stop was made at a spring to wet a towel. This provided welcome relief from the nausea, but the pain in his side returned.

It was about eight o'clock at night, in the midst of a thunderstorm, when the party arrived at the Chandler house at Guiney's Station. Lacy had ridden ahead, and the Chandlers had prepared a parlor for Jackson, but when McGuire learned that there were other wounded officers in the house, he feared that it would not be sufficiently quiet, and when he learned that there was a case of erysipelas in the house, he cast about for other accommodations.

Near the main house stood a small, low frame building similar to the one Jackson had used at Moss Neck. It held four small rooms and a storage area downstairs and two half-story rooms above. In front was a small porch shaded by two oak trees. Dr. Joseph Chandler, one of the owner's three sons (all now in the army), had used this as his office and dispensary before the war. It was now bare except for a few items in store. The Chandlers hurriedly provided a bed, chairs, and a clock to put on the mantelshelf above the fireplace. Jackson was carried through

---

1. Hotchkiss had been a friend of Boswell's and, on learning of his death, went onto the battlefield to find his body. He was dismayed to find that his corpse had been rifled of field glasses, pistol, a daguerreotype, and other personal possessions. He dug a grave and buried his friend in the Lacy family burial ground at Elwood, where Jackson's amputated arm was buried.

the rain from the ambulance.[2] He ate some bread and drank some tea and then fell into a long and peaceful sleep.

He awoke the next morning much refreshed. The thunderstorm had cleared and cooled the air. He was cheerful and "ate heartily for one in his condition," said McGuire, who was pleased with the healing of his wounds. There was no sign of infection in his stump; the wound in his right hand "gave him little pain and the discharge was healthy." A small splint was applied to the palm of his wounded hand "to assist in keeping at rest the fragments of the second and third metacarpal bones." McGuire covered both the stump and his hand with "simple lint and water dressings."

Jackson was pleased when McGuire told him that his wounds were healing satisfactorily, and he wondered how long he would be kept out of action. Speaking of his wounds to Smith, he said: "Many would regard them as a great misfortune; I regard them as one of the blessings of my life."

"All things work together for good to those that love God," Smith, the former divinity student and future minister, replied.

"Yes," said Jackson. "That's it, that's it."

About ten o'clock that morning Jackson sent for the Reverend Lacy and asked him to read aloud from the Bible and to pray by his bedside.

After praying, the two talked. Jackson confided that while he was perfectly willing to die, he believed that his time had not yet come and that God still had work for him to do in defense of his country. He had no doubt, he told Lacy, that prayer and his Christian beliefs made him a better general, calming his perplexities and anxieties, steadying his judgment and preventing him from leaping to rash conclusions. As Lacy prepared to leave, Jackson asked if he would come back every morning.

Later in the day Hotchkiss came to say good-bye; he was returning to II Corps headquarters. Jackson asked him to give his respects to General Lee.

Lee had met Sedgwick's threat at Fredericksburg by sending Early

---

2. The Chandler house caught fire sometime after the Civil War, and its shell was torn down in the early 1900s. However, the outbuilding where Jackson was taken remained and in the 1920s was restored by the Richmond, Fredericksburg & Potomac Railroad Company, whose tracks run past the property. In 1937 it was donated to the National Park Service, which restored it to its original appearance from 1962 to 1964. It is now called the Jackson Shrine and contains about 45 percent of its original materials.

the divisions of McLaws and Anderson, and the Confederates had thrown Sedgwick's force back across the river. Hooker, having given up all thoughts of fighting south of the Rappahannock, had thrown up earthworks in an arc around United States Ford, but Lee, although he could muster no more than thirty-five thousand men, planned to launch an attack upon Hooker's entrenched seventy-five thousand. He was forestalled by Hooker's withdrawal in a heavy rainstorm across the Rappahannock on the night of 5–6 May.

The Chancellorsville campaign had been the bloodiest to date. Hooker suffered 17,278 casualties, and Lee 12,821. It was a Confederate victory, but a costly one, for the Confederates lost nearly 22 percent of those engaged; the Federals about 15 percent.

Dr. McGuire, who had tried to provide his patient with twenty-four-hour care, was nearly exhausted. At his request Lacy rode to see Lee to ask if Dr. Samuel B. Morrison, Early's chief surgeon and a kinsman of Anna's, could be sent to assist. Lee and Early gave their consent, and Lee gave Lacy a message for Jackson: "Give him my affectionate regards, and tell him to make haste and get well, and come back to me as soon as he can. He has lost his left arm, but I have lost my right arm."

On the night of 6–7 May an exhausted McGuire thought it would be safe to sleep on a cot in Jackson's room. Faithful Jim Lewis remained awake and alert. About one o'clock Jackson had an attack of nausea. He did not want to awaken McGuire, so he whispered orders to Lewis, who placed a damp towel on his abdomen.

The towel did not help, and the pain in his right side returned. Still reluctant to rouse McGuire, he held out until dawn. Then, as McGuire later reported:

About daylight I was aroused and found him suffering with great pain. An examination disclosed pleuro-pneumonia [an 1863 medical term] of the right side. I believed, and the consulting physician [Morrison] concurred in the opinion, that it was attributable to the fall from the litter, the night he was wounded. The General, himself, referred it to this accident. I think the disease came on too soon after the application of wet cloths to admit of the supposition, once believed, that it was induced by them. The nausea, for which the cloths were applied that night, may have been the result of inflammation already begun. Contusion of the lung, with extravasation of blood in his chest, was probably produced by the fall referred to, and shock and loss of blood, prevented any ill effects until

reaction had been well established, and then inflammation ensued.[3]

The standard treatment was cupping. Hot glasses were applied to
the afflicted area to draw blood, a process requiring opiates. "Cups
were applied, and mercury, with antimony and opium administered,"
said McGuire. Dr. Morrison had now arrived, and also Dr. David
Tucker from Richmond, who had much experience with pneumonia.
When Jackson saw Dr. Morrison, he said with satisfaction, "There is an
old familiar face."

On 7 May Anna, in mourning for her mother, who had died on 1
April, arrived with five-and-one-half-month-old Julia and Hetty. She
had been staying in Richmond with the wife of the Reverend Moses D.
Hoge, whose husband was in Europe trying to obtain Bibles for distribution to Confederate soldiers. Anna had learned of Jackson's wound
on 3 May but had been unable to leave the city. Stoneman's Federal
cavalry were raiding, the RF&P Railroad had ceased operations, and a
stagecoach was regarded as too dangerous, too likely to be captured.
Her brother had not arrived until the fifth. It had taken him nearly
three days to ride the fifty miles to Richmond. Not until two days later
were they able to leave on an armed train prepared to fight its way
through if necessary.

An aide, probably Smith, met Anna when she arrived at Guiney's
Station. She anxiously asked about her husband, and her heart "sank
like lead" when told that he was doing "pretty well." From his "tone
and manner" she knew at once that "something was wrong."

McGuire was dressing Jackson's wounds when Anna reached the
Chandlers, and she impatiently paced up and down the piazza, watching soldiers exhume a coffin. Her anxieties were not soothed when she
learned that it was the coffin of General Paxton, Jackson's friend and
neighbor, whom she knew well. His corpse was to be returned to Lexington for reburial there. "My own heart stood still under the weight of

---

3. Jackson did not die of his wounds or as a result of the amputation. His
symptoms, as Dr. McGuire described them, are not completely diagnostic in modern
medical terms, and McGuire's daily records were lost after they were captured by
Union troops in 1865. Pneumonia proved fatal for one in six Confederate soldiers who
contracted the disease, and it is generally agreed that Jackson died of pneumonia, but
from McGuire's description of Jackson's complaints, it is possible, according to doctors
who have examined the slender evidence, that he might have suffered some intraab-
dominal injury (below the diaphragm) when his litter was dropped.

horror and apprehension which then oppressed me," she said. "The ghastly spectacle was a most unfitting preparation for my entrance into the presence of my stricken husband."

It had been only eight days since she had said good-bye to him at the Yerby house when he was "in the full flush of vigorous manhood, and . . . I never saw him look so handsome, so happy and so noble." She was shocked when she saw him at the Chandlers: "Now, his fearful wounds, his mutilated arm, the scratches upon his face, and, above all, the desperate pneumonia, which was flushing his cheeks, oppressing his breathing, and benumbing his senses, wrung my soul with such grief and anguish as it had never before experienced."

He was heavily sedated and in a stupor when she entered his room, but when she kissed him, he opened his eyes and smiled. "I am very glad to see you looking so bright," he said. Then he drifted out of consciousness. Once, regaining consciousness, he noted the sadness in her face and said, "My darling, you must cheer up, and not wear a long face. I love cheerfulness and brightness in a sick room." He asked her to speak distinctly, explaining that he wanted to hear each word. Whenever he awakened, he strove to assure her of his love, murmuring, "My darling, you are very much loved," or "You are one of the most precious little wives in the world." Several times Anna suggested that she bring in the baby, but he always demurred. "Not yet. Wait till I feel better."

As Anna watched by his bedside, Jackson was, she said, "too ill to notice or talk much, and he lay most of the time in a semi-conscious state." In delirium he was back with his army giving orders: "Tell Major Hawks to send forward provisions to the men"; "Order A. P. Hill to prepare for action"; or "Pass the infantry to the front."

Someone sent for Mrs. Hoge to come up from Richmond and help care for Anna and Julia, who had not yet been weaned. She was a friend who possessed, said Anna, "a singularly bright, affectionate, and sympathetic nature."

On the evening of the seventh Jackson seemed to rally, and McGuire and Morrison began to entertain some hope. He asked repeatedly when he would be able to go to Richmond. When Dr. Morrison said it would be some time, he directed that Governor Letcher be informed, for he had told Letcher that he would stay with him. Anna protested that it would be better if he stayed with the Hoges as they had a ground-floor room for him, but he said, "No, I told Governor Letcher I was going to his house and I will go there."

The following day, Friday, the eighth, two more surgeons arrived to assist McGuire.[4] The doctors dressed his wounds and found "the process of healing was still going on." Although the pain in his side had temporarily disappeared, McGuire noted that "he breathed with difficulty and complained of a feeling of exhaustion." Anna thought that his fever and restlessness increased and that he seemed to be growing much weaker.

Pendleton, his faithful assistant adjutant general, figured often in his delirium: "Major Pendleton, send in and see if there is higher ground back of Chancellorsville. . . . I must find if there is high ground between Chancellorsville and the river" and "Where is Pendleton? Tell him to push up the columns."

On this day Dr. Morrison mentioned to Jackson his fear that he might not recover, but Jackson disagreed: "I am not afraid to die. I am willing to abide by the will of my Heavenly Father. But I do not believe I shall die at this time. I am persuaded the Almighty has yet a work for me to perform."

The following day his strength was obviously fast fading. In a lucid moment he noticed that the number of doctors attending him had increased, and he said to McGuire: "I see from the number of physicians that you think my condition serious, but I thank God, if it is His will, that I am ready to go."

He asked to see the Reverend Lacy, and when he came, he told him that he must return to the army to preach his regular sermon to the troops the next day. "He suffered no pain today," noted McGuire, "but he was evidently hourly growing weaker." But he was indeed suffering. When Anna suggested that she read some of the psalms to him, he told her that he was in too much pain to pay attention, then said, "Yes, we must never refuse that. Get the Bible and read them."

Late that afternoon he asked her to sing some hymns. Her brother joined her, and they quietly sang a few. In a whisper he asked for Isaac Watts's hymn based upon the Fifty-first Psalm:

> *Show pity, Lord; O Lord forgive;*
> *Let a repenting rebel live;*
> *Are not Thy mercies large and free?*
> *May not a sinner trust in Thee?*

4. The doctors' names were Breckinridge and Smith, but beyond this they have never been identified.

The following morning, Sunday, 10 May 1863, the sun came up warm and pleasant, the beginning of a fine spring day. Dr. Morrison took Anna aside and quietly told her that the doctors had done all that was possible but that her husband was going to die within a few hours. Knowing that he would want time to prepare himself, she went into the little room to tell him.

It was a few minutes before he could be roused. Biographers, quoting Dabney and McGuire, have put words in Anna's and Jackson's mouths, but as only she was present, only her version can be accepted:

> When I told him the doctors thought he would soon be in heaven, he did not seem to comprehend it, and showed no surprise or concern. But upon repeating it, and asking him if he was willing for God to do with him according to His own will, he looked at me calmly and intelligently, and said, "Yes, *I prefer it, I prefer it.*" I then told him that before that day was over he would be with the blessed Saviour in His glory. With perfect distinctness and intelligence, he said, "I will be an infinite gainer to be translated."

Anna then asked if she should return to her father's home, and he said, "Yes, you have a kind, good father; but no one is so kind and good as your Heavenly Father." She asked if he had any messages for his sister, Laura, but he said, "I am too much exhausted." Asked if he wanted to be buried in Lexington, he said: "Yes, Lexington, and in *my own plot.*" (He had bought a family plot when their first child died.)

Mrs. Hoge came in with Julia, Hetty following, and he exclaimed, "Little darling! Sweet one!" Others crowded into the room, and men unaccustomed to tears openly wept, including the faithful Jim Lewis.

About one o'clock Sandie Pendleton arrived, and Jackson asked him who was preaching at headquarters. Pendleton told him that the whole army was praying for him. "Thank God," said Jackson, "they are very kind." Then he seemed to muster his strength and said, "It is the Lord's day. My wish is fulfilled. I have always desired to die on Sunday."

Nineteenth-century doctors watched so many of their patients die that they became adept at predicting the hour of death. At one-thirty McGuire told Jackson he had only two hours to live. He offered him some brandy and water, but he refused, saying, "It will only delay my departure and do no good. I want to preserve my mind, if possible, to the last."

Jackson now sank into unconsciousness, murmuring disconnected words from time to time. At three-thirty that afternoon, quite distinctly and cheerfully, he said: "Let us cross over the river and rest under the shade of the trees." Then his features sank into repose and he died.

Epilogue

☆ ☆ ☆ ☆ ☆ ☆ ☆ ☆ ☆ ☆ ☆ ☆ ☆ ☆

"It becomes my melancholy duty to announce to you the death of General Jackson," Lee telegraphed the secretary of war late on the afternoon of 10 May. "He expired at 3:15 P.M. today. His body will be conveyed to Richmond in the train tomorrow, under charge of Major Pendleton, assistant adjutant-general. Please direct an escort of honor to meet it at the depot, and that suitable arrangements be made for its disposition."

The following day General Orders No. 61 announced to the Army of Northern Virginia the death of "Lieut. Gen. T. J. Jackson." There were numerous official expressions of grief, and soldiers and civilians alike mourned the loss of one of the Confederacy's greatest heroes. Some tried to fathom why God had taken him. One Confederate soldier, Alexander Tedford Barclay, in a letter to his sister expressed the belief of many: "A deep gloom is over the camp over the death of Gen. Jackson. He was taken away from us because we made almost an idol of him."

Jackson's corpse was dressed in civilian trousers and a blue military coat, perhaps the fine blue coat Stuart had given him.[1] His uni-

---

1. The coat Jackson was wearing when he was shot was cut into small pieces by the wife of the plantation owner and given or sold as souvenirs. In June 1891, when Jackson's remains were moved from his family plot to the crypt of a new vault, his

form, cut, and bloodied, was unusable. For a short time the body lay in an open wooden coffin covered with spring flowers in the parlor of the Chandler house; sprays of lily of the valley wreathed Jackson's face. On 16 May a special railway car took the body to Richmond, accompanied by Anna, Julia, Hetty, Mrs. Hoge, Mrs. Chandler, Pendleton, Smith, Morrison, Douglas, Lacy, McGuire, the consulting doctors, Major Hawks, and the provost marshal, Major D. B. Bridgford.

The Stonewall Brigade petitioned to escort the body, but Lee refused to permit it as "those people over the river are again showing signs of movement," adding that Jackson, who had always done his duty, would not rest easy if his old brigade left the fire of the enemy to bury him. Three weeks later, on 30 May, in answer to a resolution submitted to the secretary of war by the officers and men of the brigade, it was honored by being officially designated the Stonewall Brigade, the only unit in the Confederate army ever to have its nickname formally acknowledged.

In Richmond five thousand people waited at the station. At the request of the mayor, all business was suspended, flags flew at half-mast. General Arnold Elzey was in charge of arrangements, and Jackson's coffin was transferred from the train to a hearse surmounted by black plumes and drawn by two white horses. Followed by official mourners, with a guard of honor, and a band playing dirges, it was carried to a large reception room in the executive mansion.

Among those who came to pay their respects was Brigadier General Richard Garnett, who told Pendleton: "I believe he did me a great injustice, but I also believe he acted from the purest motives. He is dead. Who can fill his place?" Pendleton asked him to be a pallbearer, and he accepted.

That night the body was embalmed, Frederick Volck made a death mask, and Jackson's corpse was transferred to a metal coffin.

The official cortege on 12 May, an exceedingly hot day, was as grand as could be managed and included President Davis, the vice president, members of the cabinet, senior officers wearing swords draped in black crepe, Governor Letcher, Jackson's staff officers, and, said the *Richmond Dispatch*, "citizens and good people generally."

On the firing of a signal gun in Capitol Square, a band of the 30th

---

coffin was opened, and those present, unaware that Jackson had been buried in a blue coat, were surprised to find, as the *Rockbridge County News* reported, that "the texture of the cloth was apparently well preserved, but it had turned in color from grey to blue."

Virginia struck up the "Dead March" from *Saul* and the procession began, making a loop through the city and finally bringing the coffin to the black-draped Confederate House of Representatives. Here the body lay in state as long lines of people filed past it. The coffin was draped in the newly adopted Confederate flag, the Stars and Bars, and this was later presented by President Davis to Anna.

Through it all Anna, wearing a "perfectly plain crepe bonnet," which cost her $75, and a "bombazine dress, as plain as could be made," for which she paid "about $180,"[2] sat in a darkened room in Governor Letcher's mansion with her elder brother, Major William Wilberforce Morrison, who had come up from North Carolina.

The following day, again with great ceremony, the coffin was taken to the railroad station and put on board a train. Jackson's route back to Lexington was by way of Gordonsville, where the coffin was switched to another train, taken to Lynchburg, and carried on board a canalboat, the packet boat *Marshall,* which arrived in Lexington on the evening of the fourteenth. There it was taken to VMI and placed in Jackson's old section room.

After a funeral service the next day in the Presbyterian church, Jackson's body, escorted by the VMI corps of cadets, marching with reversed arms to muffled drums, was taken to the Presbyterian Cemetery (today the Stonewall Jackson Memorial Cemetery) and there interred in the presence of a large crowd. It was a sad and solemn occasion, and Cadet John S. Wise recorded that "then I saw that the Presbyterian could weep like other folks."

The wealth of Jackson legends and his near apotheosis began immediately. Arthur James Fremantle, a Coldstream Guards officer traveling in the United States, wrote six weeks after Jackson's death: " 'Stonewall' Jackson is considered a regular demigod in this country." A resolution of mourning passed by the Presbyterian Assembly extolled him as "a warm and zealous Christian, a man that feared God and walked carefully before him." James Ramsey, a Presbyterian preacher in Lynchburg, did not hesitate to compare him in print with Joseph in Egypt, Hezekiah, Daniel, Edward VI, Gustavus Adolphus, and other heroes ancient and modern. For many, even today, he has become a cult figure.

In the interest of lasting renown, Jackson could not have died at a more appropriate time. The Confederacy still had its hopes, he was at

2. These details, with others on the rising cost of living in the Confederacy, were recorded by Margaret Junkin Preston in her journal on 1 June 1863.

the height of his fame, and he had just concluded the most spectacular military maneuver of his career.

As news of his death quickly spread throughout the South, church bells tolled. A plethora of obituaries appeared in newspapers North and South, followed by a flood of highly sentimental poetry. A hymn incorporating his last words was written, and soon numerous adulatory biographies appeared. At the end of the war nearly all his surviving staff officers wrote reminiscences of him; subscriptions were taken for statues, and medals were struck.[3] Even today Jackson stands second only to Lee in the pantheon of Confederate heroes.

Military fame of heroic proportions did not create wealth—not at least in the Confederacy. Jackson left no will, but Anna qualified as his administratrix. When his estate was appraised, his goods and chattels (excluding the house in Lexington) were estimated to be worth $8,548, including two horses valued at $450 and $500, Hetty at $1,100, her two sons at $2,000 each, and Emma at $600. Also left were $8,500 in stocks and bonds and an unspecified interest in a tannery. Since the bonds were Confederate, the slaves were freed, and the tannery, no longer solvent, was sold to pay debts, little was left from the estate for Anna.

Mary Anna Jackson lived on for more than half a century. She never remarried, her widowhood becoming almost her profession as she continued to be honored by veterans and other survivors of the "lost cause." She declined to accept a pension of a hundred dollars per month from the state of North Carolina, but in 1890 as the widow of a veteran of the Mexican War she accepted a pension of twenty dollars per month from the government of the United States.[4] She was then living with her son-in-law (Julia having died the year before) on a small income in Charlotte, North Carolina. She died there on 24 March 1915.

---

3. Among the many statues in the South is that by J. H. Foley, still standing on the grounds of the state capitol in Richmond, which was erected by "ENGLISH GENTLEMEN" in 1875. A two-inch medal bearing Jackson's likeness was struck in England for presentation to members of the Stonewall Brigade, but at war's end these were still in crates at a West Indian port. When brought to America, they languished for nearly thirty years in a Savannah warehouse until finally sold for one dollar each for the benefit of disabled Confederate veterans.

4. Not until 1959 did the United States government provide pensions for Confederate service and to the widows of Confederate veterans. Only three survivors applied. The act was designed to aid the wife of General James Longstreet, who was in want, but she declined to apply for it. Pensions for widows of Mexican War veterans were provided under the Mexican War Pension Act of 1887.

In 1885 Julia Jackson had married William Edmund Christian; they produced two children, Julia and Thomas, many of whose descendants still live.

Jackson did not live to see, less than two months after his death, his birthplace and boyhood home become part of the new state of West Virginia, the thirty-fifth in the Union. Nor did he witness his sister's divorce on 27 August 1870 from Jonathan Arnold, who was required to pay her alimony of four hundred dollars per year. It was not until 12 September 1864 that Anna found an opportunity through "a gentleman in N.Y." to send Laura a letter containing a lock of Jackson's hair and the particulars of his death. It is not known if Laura replied, but Anna seems to have maintained a correspondence with Jonathan Arnold, for in 1877 she wrote of Laura: "She must be an unhappy woman, cut off as she is from part of her family at least, and Mr. Arnold so set against her, but she still goes to Beverly and wants to see his house which is a great annoyance to him and [their son] Tom. . . ."

During the war Laura had nursed Union soldiers and was regarded as "an angel of mercy among the sick." After the war at a meeting of Union Civil War veterans she was greeted as a heroine. Laura lived to be eighty, dying in 1911. She steadfastly refused to call her brother Stonewall and would allow no one else so to refer to him in her presence.

Before the Battle of Chancellorsville, no member of Jackson's staff had been killed or even wounded. But, said Henry Kyd Douglas, "after the protection of his presence and his prayers had been withdrawn, death played havoc with them." Crutchfield, Boswell, and Pendleton were killed; Douglas himself was wounded, but he survived to become a respected lawyer in Maryland. Dabney had a distinguished career at the University of Texas; Dr. McGuire became Lee's medical director and after the war joined the faculty of the Virginia Medical College and became president of the American Medical Association; John Harman returned to his stagecoach line in the Valley; and Hotchkiss, after serving Ewell, Early, and Lee during the war, settled in Staunton.

The reflected glory of Jackson clung to his surviving soldiers. It was the proud boast of many veterans that they had been in the Stonewall Brigade, and many who had served only a day or two in one of Jackson's units were proud to claim that they had "served under Jackson."

In the South one of the immediate results of Jackson's death was an increased bitterness against the North. When Federal prisoners from Chancellorsville were marched through the streets of Richmond, they were jeered at by citizens who lined the streets. Not all were intimidated. When one man in the crowd called out, "What has Hooker got now?" a prisoner snapped back: "Jackson's left arm!"

Many wonder what would have happened had Jackson lived. What if Jackson had replaced Lee? What if Jackson had been at Gettysburg?

It is impossible to answer such questions, but those who believe the outcome of the war might have been different had Jackson survived and been given greater responsibilities can learn much by a study of his battles and his command style. Personally he was incredibly brave. As a commander he was, like Lee, a gambler, daring to the point of rashness. He was also, as soldiers say today, mission-oriented. He refused to allow his personal feelings or his own comfort, the welfare of his men or their danger, to impede the accomplishment of his military objectives. Like Lee, he was exceptionally aggressive.

He had proven himself a most able commander at every level of command up to a corps (the equivalent in size of a modern division), but it seems most doubtful that he would have been equally successful at any higher level, for the commander of a large army must of necessity work through and rely upon his subordinate commanders, and both Jackson's excessive secrecy and his inability to avoid personality clashes with other generals would almost certainly have doomed him to failure. It was by dying when he did, at the height of his career, that he achieved the lasting fame of which as a young lieutenant he had dreamed.

Bibliography

Alexander, Holmes. *The Hidden Years of Stonewall Jackson*. Richwood, W. Va.: West Virginia Press Club, 1981.

Allen, Bernard L. "Lessons" (booklet). Parkersville, W. Va.: Data Day, 1990.

Allen, William. *History of the Campaign of Gen. T. S. (Stonewall) Jackson in the Shenandoah Valley of Virginia from November 4, 1861 to June 17, 1862*. New York: J. B. Lippincott, 1880.

Andrews, J. Cutler. *The South Reports the Civil War*. Pittsburgh: University of Pittsburgh Press, 1970.

Arnold, Thomas Jackson. *Early Life and Letters of General Thomas J. Jackson*. London and Edinburgh: Fleming H. Revell Company, 1916.

Avirett, Rev. James B. *The Memoirs of General Turner Ashby and His Compeers*. Baltimore: Selby & Delany, 1867.

Bauer, K. Jack. *The Mexican War, 1846–1848*. New York: Macmillan, 1974.

Bean, W. G. *Stonewall's Man: Sandie Pendleton*. Washington, D.C.: Broadfoot Publishing Co., 1987.

Beck, Brandon H., and Charles S. Grunder. *Three Battles of Winchester*. Berryville, Va.: Country Publisher, n.d.

Beringer, Richard E., Herman Hattaway, Archer Jones, and William N. Still. *The Elements of Confederate Defeat: Nationalism, War Aims, and Religion*. Athens, Ga., and London: University of Georgia Press, 1988.

Blackford, Charles Minor, compiled by Susan Leigh Blackford, annotated by Charles Minor Blackford, and edited and abridged by Charles Minor Blackford III. London and New York: Charles Scribner's, 1947.

Boatner, Mark M. *Cassell's Biographical Dictionary of the American Civil War, 1861–1865*. London: Cassell, 1973.

Bogue, Major Hardy Z. "Confederate Manpower Mobilization." *Confederate Veteran* (July–August 1989.).

Booth, George Wilson. *Personal Reminiscences of a Maryland Soldier in the War between the States.* Baltimore: privately printed, 1898.

Borcke, Heros von. *Memoirs of the Confederate War for Independence.* Dayton, Ohio: Morningside House, 1895. Reprint, originally published 1866.

Boswell, James Keith. "The Diary of a Confederate Staff Officer." *Civil War Times Illustrated* (April 1976.).

Botkin, B. A. *A Civil War Treasury of Tales, Legends and Folklore.* New York: Promontory Press, 1960.

Boyd, Thomas M. "Thomas M. Boyd's Association with Stonewall Jackson." Typescript of 1880 ms. in West Virginia University Library.

Bradford, Ned, ed. *Battles and Leaders of the Civil War.* New York: Appleton-Century-Croft, 1956. 4 vols.

Brooks, George M., Jr. "The Episcopal Church and VMI in Early Years." *Proceedings of the Rockbridge Historical Society* (vol. X, 1980–89). Lexington, Va.: 1990, pp. 317–32.

Brown, Katherine L. "Stonewall Jackson in Lexington: The Christian Soldier" (booklet). Garland Gray Memorial Research Center, Stonewall Jackson House, Lexington, Va., 1984.

Brundage, Fitzhugh. "Shifting Attitudes towards Slavery in Antebellum Rockbridge County." *Proceedings of the Rockbridge Historical Society* (vol. X, 1980–89). Lexington, Va.: 1990, p. 333ff.

Buck, Captain Samuel D. *With the Old Confeds: Actual Experiences of a Captain of the Line.* Baltimore: H. E. Houck & Co., 1925.

Bushong, Millard K. *General Turner Ashby and Stonewall's Valley Campaign.* Verona, Va.: McClure Printing Co., 1980.

Caldwell, J. F. J. *The History of a Brigade of South Carolinians Known First as "Gregg's" and Subsequently as McGowan's Brigade.* Philadelphia: King & Baird, 1866.

Cannon, Devereaux D., Jr. *The Flags of the Confederacy.* Memphis, Ten.: St. Luke's Press and Broadfoot Publishing, 1988.

Casler, John O. *Four Years in the Stonewall Brigade.* Girard, Kan.: Appeal Publishing Co., 1906.

Catton, Bruce. *Glory Road.* New York: Doubleday, 1952.

Chambers, Lenoir. *Stonewall Jackson.* New York: William Morrow, 1959. 2 vols.

Chase, Julie. "War-Time Diary of Miss Julia Chase." Typescript in Handley Library, Winchester, Va., n.d.

Clopton, J. J. *The True Stonewall Jackson.* Baltimore: Ruth's Sons, Printers, 1913.

Cohn, Captain Douglas A. *Jackson's Valley Campaign.* Washington, D.C.: American Publishing Company, 1986.

Commager, Henry Steele. *The Blue and the Gray.* New York: Fairfax Press: 1982. 2 vols in 1.

Congdon, Don, ed. *Combat: The Civil War.* Secaucus, N.J.: The Blue & Gray Press, 1967.

Connelly, Thomas L. "Lee and Jackson in 1863: The Shift in Historical Opinion." *The Confederate High Command & Related Topics,* ed. R. J. Helerick and Lawrence L. Hewitt. Shippensburg, Pa.: White Mane Publishing Co., 1990.

Cook, John Esten. *Stonewall Jackson and the Old Stonewall Brigade,* ed. Richard Barksdale Harwell. Charlottesville, Va.: University of Virginia, 1954.

Cook, Roy Bird. *The Family and Early Life of Stonewall Jackson,* 4th ed., rev. Charleston, W. Va.: Education Foundation, 1963.

———. *Stonewall Jackson.* New York: G. W. Dillingham, 1893.

Cooper, Everett K. "A Tribute to Stonewall Jackson." *Confederate Veteran* (May–June 1989).

Couper, Colonel William. *One Hundred Years at V.M.I.* Richmond, Va.: Garrett and Masie, 1939. 4 vols.

Crute, Joseph H. *Confederate Staff Officers.* Powhatan, Va.: Derwent Books, 1982.

———. *Units of the Confederate States Army.* Midlothian, Va.: Derwent Books, 1987.

Cullum, Capt. George W. *Register of the officers and Graduates of the U.S. Military Academy at West Point, New York.* New York: J. F. Trow, Printer, 1850.

Cunningham, Horace H. *Field Medical Services at the Battles of Manassas.* Athens, Ga.: University of Georgia, 1968.

Cutright, W. B. *The History of Upshur County, West Virginia.* Buckhannon, W. Va.: privately printed, 1907.

Dabney, Prof. R. L. *Life and Campaigns of Lieut.-Gen. Thomas J. Jackson (Stonewall Jackson).* Harrisonburg, Va.: Sprinkle Publications, 1983. facsimile of 1866 ed.

Davidson, J. D. *A Curiosity in Chancery and Rhyme and Prose.* Printed privately, n.d.

Davis, Dorothy. *John George Jackson.* Parsons, W. Va.: McClain Printing Co., 1976.

Dawson, Capt. Francis W. *Reminiscences of Confederate Service, 1861–1865.* Charleston, S.C.: News and Courier Book Presses, 1882.

DeLaney, Theodore C., Jr. "Aspects of Black Religious and Educational Development in Lexington, Virginia, 1840–1928." *Proceedings of the Rockbridge Historical Society* (vol. X, 1980–89). Lexington, Va.: 1990, pp. 139–43.

Donovan, Timothy H., Jr.; Roy K. Flint; Arthur V. Grant, Jr.; and Gerald P. Stadler. *The American Civil War.* Department of History, United States Military Academy, West Point, N.Y. Wayne, N.J.: Avery Publishing, 1987.

Dooley, Edwin L., Jr. "The American Thomas Arnold: Francis Smith of the Virginia Military Institute." *Proceedings of the Rockbridge Historical Society* (vol. X, 1980–89). Lexington, Va.: 1990, p. 333ff.

———. "Lexington Ledgers: A Source for Social History." *Proceedings of the Rockbridge Historical Society* (vol. X, 1980–89). Lexington, Va.: 1990, pp. 237–43.

Douglas, Henry Kyd. *I Rode with Stonewall.* Chapel Hill: University of North Carolina Press, 1940.

Dowdey, Clifford. *The Seven Days: The Emergence of Robert E. Lee.* Wilmington, N.C.: Broadfoot Publishing Co., 1988.

———, and Louisa H. Manarin, eds. *The Wartime Papers of Robert E. Lee.* Boston: Little, Brown, 1961.

Driver, Robert J., Jr. *The 1st and 2nd Rockbridge Artillery.* Lynchburg, Va.: H. E. Howard, 1987.

———. *Lexington and Rockbridge County in the Civil War.* Lynchburg, Va.: H. E. Howard, 1989.

Dwight, Theodore F., ed. *Papers of the Military Historical Society of Massachusetts,* vols. 1–6. Boston: James R. Osgood and Co., 1881–1907.

Eisenhower, John S. D. *So Far from God: The U.S. War with Mexico, 1846–1848.* New York: Random House, 1989.

Ellzey, Dr. M. "The Cause We Lost and the Land We Love." Unpublished ms. owned by his niece, Mrs. J. A. (Mary Ellzey) McCrary, n.d.

Esposito, Vincent J., ed. *The West Point Atlas of American Wars,* vol. 1, New York, Washington, London: Frederick A. Praeger, 1959.

Fonerden, C. A. *A Brief History of the Career of Carpenter's Battery.* New Market, Va.: Henkel & Co., 1911.

Foote, Shelby. *The Civil War: A Narrative.* New York: Random House, 1953. 3 vols.

Frechette, Fred L. "The Lost Hero of the Lost Dispatch." *Civil War,* vol. VII, no. 3 May–June 1990.

Freeman, Douglas Southall. *Lee's Lieutenant's*. New York: 1944. Charles Scribner's Sons, 3 vols.

Fritz, Jean. *Stonewall*. New York: G. P. Putnam, 1979.

Frye, Dennis E. "The Siege of Harper's Ferry." *The Blue and the Gray* (September 1987).

Gallager, Gary W., ed. *Antietam: Essays on the 1862 Maryland Campaign*. Kent, Ohio: Kent State University Press, 1989, including "The Autumn of 1862: A Season of Opportunity."

————, ed. *Fighting for the Confederacy: The Personal Recollections of General Edward Porter Alexander*. Chapel Hill: University of North Carolina, 1989.

Gavin, William Gilfillan. *Infantryman Pettit: The Civil War Letters of Corporal Frederick Pettit*. Shippensburg, Pa.: White Mane, 1990.

Gittings, John G. *Personal Recollections of Stonewall Jackson*. Cincinnati: Editor Publishing Co., 1899.

Gordon, John B. *Reminiscences of the Civil War*. New York: Scribner's, 1903.

Greene, Will. "Jackson on the Peninsula: Failure or Scapegoat?" *Civil War: The Magazine of the Civil War Society*, vol. XVIII (1989).

Griffith, Paddy. *Battle in the Civil War*. Mansfield, Notinghamshire, England: Fieldbooks, 1986.

Hadsel, Winifred. *The Streets of Lexington*. Lexington, Va.: Rockbridge Historical Society, 1985.

Hagerman, Edward. *The American Civil War and the Origins of Modern Warfare*. Bloomington and Indianapolis: Indiana University Press, 1988.

Hale, Laura Virginia. *Four Valiant Years in the Lower Shenandoah Valley*. Strasburg, Va.: Shenandoah Publishing House, 1973.

Hamilton, Frank Hastings. *Treatise of Military Surgery and Hygiene*. New York: Baillier Brothers, 1865.

Hamlin, Percy Gatling. *"Old Bald Head" (General R. S. Ewell): The Portrait of a Soldier*. Strasburg, Va.: Shenandoah Publishing House, 1940.

————, ed. *The Making of a Soldier: Letters of General R. S. Ewell*. Richmond, Va.: Whittet & Shepperson, 1935.

Hassler, William W., ed. *The General to His Lady: The Civil War Letters of William Dorsey Pender to Fanny Pender*. Columbia, S.C.: University of South Carolina Press, 1988.

Hattaway, Herman, and Archer Jones. *How the North Won: A Military History of the Civil War*. Urbana: University of Illinois Press, 1983.

Heitman, Frances B. *Historical Register and Dictionary of the United States Army from its Organization, September 29, 1789, to March 2, 1903*. Washington, D.C.: Government Printing Office, 1903.

Henderson, Col. G. F. R. *Stonewall Jackson*, 2d ed. London: Longman, Green, 1899. 2 vols.

Hennessy, John. "Stonewall Jackson's Nickname: What Did General Bee Really Say at First Manassas? And What Did He Mean?" *Civil War*, XXII (March–April 1990).

Hermann, I. [Isaac] *Memoirs of a Confederate Veteran, 1861–1865*. Lakemont, Ga.: CSA Press, 1974. Reprint, originally published in 1911.

[Hopley, Catherine Cooper.] *"Stonewall" Jackson, Late General of the Confederate Army, a Biographical Sketch and an Outline of His Virginia Campaigns*. "By the author of 'Life in the South.' " London: Chapman and Hall, 1863.

Horrocks, James. *My Dear Parents: The Civil War as Seen by an English Soldier*, ed. A. S. Lewis San Diego, New York, London: Harcourt Brace Jovanovich, 1986.

Hotchkiss, Jedediah. *Confederate Military History*, vol. 3 *Virginia*. A Library of Confederate State History in Twelve Volumes . . . , ed. Gen. Clement A. Evans of Georgia. Dayton, Ohio: Morningside Bookshop, 1975. Facsimile reprint.

———. *Make Me a Map of the Valley: The Civil War Journal of Stonewall Jackson's Topographer*. Dallas: Southern Methodist University Press, 1973.

Howard, McHenry. *Recollections of a Maryland Confederate Soldier and Staff Officer under Johnston, Jackson and Lee*. Lakemont, Ga.: CSA Press, 1974. Reprint of edition first published in 1911.

Huse, Caleb. "The Supplies for the Confederate Army: How They Were Obtained in Europe and How Paid For." Pamphlet. Boston: T. R. Marvin & Son, 1904.

Jackson, Mary Anna. *Memoirs of "Stonewall" Jackson*. Dayton, Ohio: Morningside Press, 1985. Reprint, originally published in 1895.

Jimerson, Randall C. *The Private Civil War: Popular Thought during the Sectional Conflict*. Baton Rouge and London: Louisiana State University Press, 1988.

Johnson, Bvt.-Col. Geo. K. "The Battle of Kernstown, March 23, 1862." A paper prepared and read before the Michigan Commandery of the Military Order of the Loyal Legion of the U.S. at Grand Rapids, Michigan, December 4, 1890. Detroit: Winn & Hammon, 1890.

Jones, Terry L. *Lee's Tigers: The Louisiana Infantry in the Army of Northern Virginia*. Baton Rouge: Louisiana State University Press, 1987.

Jordon, David M. *Winfield Scott Hancock: A Soldier's Life*. Bloomington and Indianapolis: Indiana University Press, 1988.

Kelley, Harry B. *Port Republic*. Philadelphia: Lippincott, 1886.

Krick, Robert K. *Lee's Colonels*. Dayton, Ohio: Morningside Bookshop, 1979.

———. *Parker's Battery CSA*, 2d ed. rev. Wilmington, N.C.: Broadfoot Publishing Company, 1989.

———. *Stonewall Jackson at Cedar Mountain*. Chapel Hill: University of North Carolina Press, 1990.

Livermore, Thomas L. *Numbers and Losses in the Civil War in America, 1861–65*. Boston: Houghton Mifflin, 1901.

Long, E. B., with Barbara Long. *The Civil War Day by Day*. Garden City: Doubleday, 1971.

Luvaas, Jay, and Harold W. Nelson, eds. *The U.S. Army War College Guide to the Battles of Fredericksburg & Chancellorsville*. Carlisle, Pa.: South Mountain Press, 1988.

———. *The U.S. Army War College Guide to the Battle of Gettysburg*. Carlisle, Pa.: South Mountain Press, 1987.

[McCabe, James Dabney.] *The Life of Lieut. Gen. T. J. Jackson* "By an Ex-Cadet." Richmond: James E. Goode, 1863.

Macon, Emma Cassandra Riely, and Ruben Conway Macon. *Reminiscences of the Civil War*. Cedar Rapids, Iowa: privately printed, Torch Press, 1911.

McGuire, Hunter. "Account of the Wounding and Death of Stonewall Jackson." *Richmond Medical Journal* (May 1866).

———. "Stonewall Jackson." Talk to R. E. Lee Post No. 1, Confederate Veterans, 9 July 1897.

McPherson, James M. *Battle Cry of Freedom*. New York: Oxford University Press, 1988.

Mann, B. David. "VMI Alumni in the Civil War." Booklet. Lexington, Va.: News-Gazette Printing Department, n.d.

Martin, David G. *Carl Bornemann's Regiment, the 41st New York Infantry (De Kalb Regiment) in the Civil War*. Hightstown, N.J.: Longstreet House, 1987.

————. *Jackson's Valley Campaign, November 1861–June 1862*. Bryn Mawr, Pa.: Wieser & Wieser, 1988.

Martin, Robert Hugh. *A Boy of Old Shenandoah*, ed. Carolyn Martin Rutherford. Parsons, W. Va.: McClain Printing Co. 1977.

Mathis, James L. "The Building of the Wall—Thomas Jonathan Jackson." *Military Medicine*, vol. 129, no. 5 (May 1964).

Mitchell, Adele. "Jackson's Engineer." *Civil War Times Illustrated* (June 1968).

Mitchell, Reid. *Civil War Soldiers*. New York: Viking, 1988.

Monroe, Haskell M., Jr. "The Presbyterian Church in the Confederate States of America." Doctoral thesis, Rice University, Houston, May 1961.

Morrison, James L., Jr. *The Best School in the World: West Point, the Civil War Years, 1833–1866*. Kent, Ohio: Kent State University Press, 1986.

Neely, Mark E., Jr., Harold Holzer, and Gabor S. Boritt. *The Confederate Image: Prints of the Lost Cause*. Chapel Hill and London: University of North Carolina Press, 1987.

Neese, George M. *Three Years in the Confederate Horse Artillery*. Dayton, Ohio: Morningside Bookshop, 1983. Reprint, originally published by Neal Publishing, 1911.

Neff, Ray A. *Valley of the Shadow*, 2d ed. Terre Haute, Ind.: Rana Publications, 1989.

Newbraugh, Frederick T. *Warm Springs Echoes*, vol. 2, Morgan *Messenger*, Berkeley Springs, W. Va., 1975.

Patterson, Gerard A. *Rebels from West Point*. New York: Doubleday, 1987.

Pfanz, Harry W. "Special History Report: Troop Movement Maps, 1862, Harpers Ferry National Historical Park, Maryland-W. Virginia." Denver Service Center, Historic Preservation Team, National Park Service, U.S. Department of the Interior, Denver, Colorado, March 1976.

Pierce, John E. "The Civil War Career of Richard Brooke Garnett; A Quest for Vindication." Unpublished Master's thesis. Virginia Polytechnic Institute and State University, Blacksburg, Va., 1969.

————. "Jackson, Garnett and the 'Unfortunate Breach." *Civil War Times Illustrated* (October 1973).

Poague, William Thomas. *Gunner with Stonewall*. Wilmington, N.C.: Broadfoot Publishing Co. 1987. A memoir written for his children in 1903.

Priest, John Michael, ed. *Captain James Wren's Diary: From New Bern to Fredericksburg*. Shippensburg, Pa.: White Mane, 1990.

Quarles, Garland R. *Occupied Winchester, 1861–1865*. Prepared for Farmers and Merchants Bank, Winchester, Va., 1976.

Radley, Kenneth. *Rebel Watchdog: The Confederate States Army Provost Guard*. Baton Rouge and London: Louisiana State University Press, 1989.

Revere, Joseph W. *Keel and Saddle: A Retrospect of Forty Years of Military and Naval Service*. Boston: James R. Osgood and Co., 1872.

Robertson, James I., Jr. *General A. P. Hill*. New York: Random House, 1987.

————. *Soldiers Blue and Gray*. Columbia, S.C.: University of South Carolina Press, 1988.

————. *The Stonewall Brigade*. Baton Rouge: Louisiana State University Press, 1963.

Robson, John S. *How a One-Legged Rebel Lives: The Story of the Campaigns of Stonewall Jackson*. Gaithersburg, Md.: Butternut Press, 1984. Reprint, originally printed in 1898.

Roland, Charles P. *An American Iliad: The Story of the Civil War*. Lexington: University of Kentucky Press, 1990.

Rozier, John, ed. *The Granite Farm Letters: The Civil War Correspondence of Edgeworth & Sallie Bird*. Athens: University of Georgia Press, 1988.

Sears, Stephen. *The Civil War Papers of George B. McClellan: Selected Correspondence, 1860–1865.* New York: Ticknor & Fields, 1989.

———. *Landscape Turned Red: The Battle of Antietam.* New Haven and New York: Ticknor and Fields, 1983.

———. *George B. McClellan: The Young Napoleon.* New York: Ticknor & Fields, 1988.

———. "McClellan vs. Lee: The Seven Day Trial." *Military History Quarterly,* vol. 1, no. 1. (Autumn 1988).

Schildt, John W. *Hunter Holmes McGuire: Doctor in Gray.* Chewsville, Md.: privately printed, 1986.

———. *Stonewall Jackson Day by Day.* Chewsville, Md.: Antietam Publications, 1980.

Scribner, Robert L. "The Stonewall Brigade." *Virginia Cavalcade* (Spring 1956).

Sergeant, Mary Elizabeth. *They Lie Forgotten: The United States Military Academy, 1856–1861.* Middletown, N.Y.: Prior King Press, 1986.

Shapiro, David. *Neurotic Styles.* New York and London: Basic Books, 1965.

Shoop, Michael I., comp. *The Genealogies of the Jackson, Junkin, & Morrison Families.* Garland Gray Memorial Research Center, Stonewall Jackson House, Lexington, Va., 1981.

Sigaud, Louis. *Belle Boyd: Confederate Spy.* Richmond, Va.: Dietz Press, 1944.

Smith, James Power. *With Stonewall Jackson in the Army of Northern Virginia.* Southern Historical Papers, New Series, Richmond, Va., August 1920.

Sorrel, G. Moxley. *Recollections of a Confederate Staff Officer.* Wilmington, N.C.: Broadfoot Publishing, 1987. Reprint.

Sperry, Kate. *Surrender! Never Surrender.* Typescript in Handley Library, Winchester, Va.

Stevens, Capt. Michael W. "Learning from Civil War Battles." *Marine Corps Gazette* (June 1988).

Stevens, Peter F. "Deadly Grapeshot Unleashed." *American Civil War* (May 1989).

Stewart, Guy Harry. "The Pioneer State 4-H Camp: Jackson's Mill." Unpublished Master's thesis, West Virginia University, 1949.

Swinton, William. *Campaigns of the Army of the Potomac: A Critical History of Operations in Virginia, Maryland and Pennsylvania from the Commencement to the Close of the War.* Secaucus, N.J.: Blue and Gray Press, 1988. Facsimile reprint of original published in 1866.

Tanner, Robert G. *Stonewall in the Valley: Thomas J. "Stonewall" Jackson's Shenandoah Valley Campaign, Spring, 1862.* Garden City: Doubleday, 1976.

Teetor, Paul R. *A Matter of Hours: Treason at Harper's Ferry.* London and Toronto: Fairleigh Dickinson University Press, 1982.

Thomas, Emory M. *Bold Dragoon: The Life of J. E. B. Stuart.* New York: Harper & Row, 1986.

Thompson, Benjamin W. "This Hell of Destruction." *Civil War Times Illustrated* (October 1973).

Tucker, Glenn. "John Wilkes Booth at the John Brown Hanging." *Lincoln Herald* (Spring 1976).

Turner, Charles W., ed. "Agricultural Expositions and Fairs in Rockbridge County, 1828–1891." *Proceedings of the Rockbridge Historical Society* (vol. X, 1980–89), Lexington, Va., 1990, p. 387ff.

———, ed. *My Dear Emma: War Letters of Col. James K. Edmundson 1861–1865.* Verona, Va.: McClure Press, 1978.

———. *A Reminiscence of Lieutenant John Newton Lyle of the Liberty Hall Volunteers.* Roanoke, Va.: Virginia Lithograph & Graphics Co., 1987.

Vandiver, Frank E. *Mighty Stonewall.* New York: McGraw-Hill, 1957.

————. *Rebel Brass: The Confederate Command System,* Baton Rouge, Louisiana State University Press, 1956.

Wallace, Lee A. *A Guide to Virginia Military Organizations, 1861–1865,* rev. 2d ed. Lynchburg, Va.: H. E. Howard, 1986.

Warner, Ezra J. *Generals in Blue: Lives of the Union Commanders.* Baton Rouge: Louisiana State University Press, 1964.

————. *Generals in Gray: Lives of the Confederate Commanders.* Baton Rouge: Louisiana State University Press, 1959.

The War of the Rebellion: A Compilation of the Official Records of the Union and Confederate Armies. Washington, D.C.: 1880–1901. 128 vols.

Wayland, John W. *Stonewall Jackson's Way.* 2d ed. rev. Dayton, Ohio: Morningside House, 1984. Facsimile reprint.

————. *The Valley Turnpike, Winchester to Staunton and Other Roads.* vol. VI, Winchester-Frederick County Historical Society, Winchester, Va., 1967.

Wert, Jeffrey. "I Am So Unlike Other Folks." *Civil War Times* (April 1989).

Whan, Vorin E., Jr. *Fiasco at Fredericksburg.* N.P.: Pennsylvania State University Press, 1986.

Wheeler, Richard. *Sword over Richmond.* Harper & Row, New York, 1986.

————. *We Knew Stonewall Jackson: An Eyewitness Biography.* New York: Thomas Y. Crowell, 1977.

Wiley, Bell Irvin. *The Life of Johnny Reb: The Common Soldier of the Confederacy.* Baton Rouge; Louisiana State University Press, 1943.

Williams, Kenneth P. *Lincoln Finds a General: A Military Study of the Civil War.* New York: Macmillan, 1950.

Williams, T. Harry. *Lincoln and His Generals.* New York: Alfred Knopf, 1952.

Wilson, Edmund. *Patriotic Gore: Studies in the Literature of the American Civil War.* London: Hogarth Press, 1987.

Wood, James H. *The War: "Stonewall" Jackson, His Campaigns and Battles: The Regiments as I Saw Them.* Cumberland, Md.: Eddy Press, 1984. Reprint, originally published 1910.

Woodward, C. Vann, and Elisabeth Muhlenfeld, eds. *The Private Life of Mary Chestnut: The Unpublished Civil War Diaries.* New York: Oxford University Press, 1984.

Woodworth, Steven E. *Jefferson Davis and His Generals.* Lawrence: University Press of Kansas, 1990.

Worsham, John H. *One of Jackson's Foot Cavalry.* New York: Neale Co., 1912.

Index

THE SEAT OF THE WAR

```
0     10     20     30     40     50
|——————|——————|——————|——————|——————|
              miles
```

Potomac R.

South Branch Potomac R.

Romney

Moorefield

Faubis

Strasb

Beverly

Columbia
Furness

NORTH

Massa

Rude's
Hill

Massanutten
Gap

New
Market

Luray Valley

L

Franklin

Harrisonburg

Conrad's
Store
(Elkton)

Monterey

Cross Keys

McDowell

North R.

Elk Run
Valley

Swift Run
Gap

Allegheny Mtns.

Lebanon
Springs

Mt. Solon

Port
Republic

R

Semon's Gap

South R.

Brown's Gap

Staunton

Jaman's Gap

Waynesboro

B

Charlotte

Rockfish
Gap

Meachum's
River Station

L

U

E

VIRGINIA CENTRAL R.R.

Rockbridge Bath

R

I

D

G

E

Jam

Irish Cr. Gap

Lexington

White's
Gap

Robertson's Gap

ORANGE & ALEXANDRIA R.R.

Petit's Gap

Peak Gap

VIRGINIA & TENNESSEE R.R.

PETERSBURG & LYNCHBURG R.

Appomattox